praise for

A NEW HISTORY OF BRITAIN SINCE 1688

I've been teaching a British history survey (1688–present) for many years and I have never found the perfect textbook for my students until now. This text truly covers all of the British Isles, not just England, and it incorporates gender analysis throughout, rather than inserting an occasional reference to women, as most textbooks tend to do. The text offers a nice balance of political, social, and cultural history and introduces us to real individuals whose lives are often neglected by scholars. I especially appreciated the Liverpool essays which provide a microhistory of Britain and allow students to trace the impact of "big" events and trends on a particular city and its inhabitants.

—Julie Ann Taddeo, University of Maryland

For decades, scholars have been urging a "four nations" approach to British history. In Susan Kent's ambitious and timely *A New History of Britain*, we finally have a textbook that delivers on that promise. Ranging from 1688 to the present and covering developments in England, Ireland, Scotland and Wales, as well as in the British Empire, this textbook puts "place" front and center in its narrative. The special treatment that Kent accords throughout to Liverpool reflects this priority. Here we see firsthand how the grand themes of modern British history— war, politics, culture, gender, empire, religion, race, class—played out on a smaller and more intimate scale. The result is immensely rewarding.

—Arianne Chernock, Boston University

Through vivid anecdotes and strong thematic threads, *A New History of Britain Since 1688* by Susan Kingsley Kent provides a lively and often gripping account of the ever-changing conflicts that have characterized British history, even in periods when standard accounts have focused more on equanimity and relative consensus. By making histories of Ireland, Wales, Scotland, and the Empire quite central to the story she tells, Kent highlights how gendered and racial discourses have fundamentally shaped the ways in which British power has been expressed, enforced, and contested. Students will appreciate how regularly she explains, in a common-sense way, the connections between the many developments she describes, connections that are not always so clear in other textbook accounts.

—Jennifer Hall-Witt, Smith College

Susan Kent's *A New History of Britain since 1688: Four Nations and an Empire* is a remarkable synthetic overview of modern British history, presented in prose that is accessible and engaging. Kent not only includes the histories of the four "nations" of the British Isles and the vast overseas empire within a single frame, as the book's title suggests; she seamlessly interweaves the thematic concerns of her previous scholarship—gender history, environmental history, and imperial and colonial history—into the history of British politics, society, and imperial culture. As such, it surpasses all other textbooks on the subject.

—Marc Matera, University of California, Santa Cruz

This highly readable survey skillfully integrates the histories of the four kingdoms and their empire. It provides readers with a firm grasp of the causes and consequences of the islands' rise to global preeminence as well as how it arrived at the post-imperial, devolutionary present. This engaging and innovative survey is a significant achievement that deserves a wide readership.

—Michael de Nie, University of West Georgia

A New History of Britain since 1688 is written clearly by an author who is very knowledgeable. The selection of themes, stories, and evidence is clearly based on a lifetime of scholarship, teaching, and thinking about British history. Key themes are developed very well throughout the book. The descriptions, comparisons, and analyses of the histories of England, Scotland, Ireland, and Wales are important for students to think about, especially in light of the possible future break-up of the UK. Most of the British histories available focus largely on England, while Kent's book puts all four nations in constant tension with each other.

—William K. Storey, Millsaps College

A New History of Britain since 1688

A NEW HISTORY OF BRITAIN SINCE 1688

FOUR NATIONS AND AN EMPIRE

Susan Kingsley Kent

New York   Oxford
OXFORD UNIVERSITY PRESS

Oxford University Press is a department of the University of Oxford.
It furthers the University's objective of excellence in research,
scholarship, and education by publishing worldwide.

Oxford   New York
Auckland   Cape Town   Dar es Salaam   Hong Kong   Karachi
Kuala Lumpur   Madrid   Melbourne   Mexico City   Nairobi
New Delhi   Shanghai   Taipei   Toronto

With offices in
Argentina   Austria   Brazil   Chile   Czech Republic   France   Greece
Guatemala   Hungary   Italy   Japan   Poland   Portugal   Singapore
South Korea   Switzerland   Thailand   Turkey   Ukraine   Vietnam

For titles covered by Section 112 of the US Higher Education
Opportunity Act, please visit www.oup.com/us/he for the
latest information about pricing and alternate formats.

Published by Oxford University Press
198 Madison Avenue, New York, New York 10016
http://www.oup.com

Library of Congress Cataloging-in-Publication Data

Kent, Susan Kingsley, 1952 May 9-
  A new history of Britain : since 1688 / Susan Kingsley Kent.
    volumes cm
  Summary: "Based on the most current scholarship concerning gender, race, ethnicity, and empire,
this 15-chapter textbook comprehensively examines the development of and contestations against a
British identity among the constituent parts of the United Kingdom since 1688. It takes seriously the
role of Scotland, Wales, and Ireland in this process, and brings Britain's imperial subjects and lands
into the narrative, showing how integral empire was to the UK's historical development. It examines
the role environmental factors in economic development and their impact on the health and welfare
of British citizens and subjects; and it uses gender, in particular, to illuminate power dynamics across
a variety of settings. All this in a manageable length"--Provided by publisher.
  Includes bibliographical references and index.
  ISBN 978-0-19-984650-4 (acid-free paper) 1. Great Britain--History--Textbooks. 2. Great
Britain--Colonies--History--Textbooks. 3. National characteristics, British--History--Textbooks.
4. Great Britain--Ethnic relations--History--Textbooks. 5. Sex role--Great Britain--History--
Textbooks. 6. Great Britain--Social conditions--Textbooks. I. Title.
  DA16.K44 2017
  941--dc23
                                                                                    2015031359
Printing number: 9 8 7 6 5 4 3 2 1

Printed in the United States of America
on acid-free paper

For Bonnie Smith

CONTENTS

A Place in Time: Identities and Traditions at the
Liverpool Football Club   470

List of
MAPS

ACKNOWLEDGMENTS

I came to this project through the good offices of Bill Spellman, an old friend from undergraduate days who sought me out as a coauthor on a potential British history textbook. Bill was unable to continue with the work, but he got the ball rolling and established the theme of the book. Most important, he introduced me to Charles Cavaliere at Oxford University Press. Charles has been the best kind of editor throughout the development and writing of *A New History of Britain since 1688: Four Nations and an Empire*. Always responsive to my questions, amenable to my suggestions and helpful with his own, flexible about changes to the structure of the book, encouraging and generous in his praise, he also did not flinch from offering a gentle "not your best work, Susan" when it was called for. All authors should be so lucky as to have an editor like Charles. I have enjoyed every minute of our collaboration together.

OUP rounded up a group of external readers who individually and collectively provided invaluable criticism and offered crucial suggestions for improving the textbook. Fred F. Beemon, Arianne Chernock, Jonathan Rose, Tracey Cooper, Geoffrey W. Clark, Christopher Ferguson, Julie Ann Taddeo, Kristen Walton, Moira Egan, and Charles K. Matthews read the original proposal and helped to give it shape and greater coherence. Julie Ann Taddeo, William K. Storey, Patrick McDevitt, Marc Matera, Lydia Murdoch, and an additional anonymous reviewer read the first draft of the manuscript, bringing their expertise to bear on a variety of issues. They identified weaknesses and proposed solutions; they corrected errors and recommended alternative approaches and interpretations. Their comments and criticisms—the sheer amount of time they put into the manuscript!--made this a far better book. Many of the strengths of the book derive from the contributions of this extraordinary group of readers, and I am most grateful to all of them. Antoinette Burton, Arianne Chernock, and Michael De Nie read the final draft of *Four Nations and an Empire* and offered generous comments. Many, many thanks to you all.

The staff at OUP have worked hard to ensure that this textbook sees the light of day. I owe thanks to Lauren Aylward and Michelle Koufopoulos for their early assistance on the project and to Lynn Luecken, who took over from them. Dave Welsh oversaw a challenging production process and Susan Brown copyedited the manuscript with care; they went above and beyond the ordinary copyediting chores to produce a handsome book.

The Center for Humanities and the Arts at the University of Colorado, under the leadership of Helmut Muller- Sievers and the administration of Paula Anderson, and Todd Gleeson and Steve Leigh, former dean and dean of the College of Arts and Sciences, respectively, provided funding and accommodations in London that helped me to complete the book. Their support of the work of our Humanities faculty at CU has been impressive. Lucy McCann, head archivist at the Bodleian Library of Commonwealth and African Studies at Rhodes House, Oxford, introduced me to her valuable collection, from which I was able to use a number of images.

Colleagues and friends have contributed to this book in important ways. I thank Myles Osborne, Paul Hammer, Virginia Anderson, Fred Anderson, Mithi Mukherjee, Antoinette Burton, Aaron Windel, and Patrick Tally for their help with matters large and small. Marc Matera is always a fount of good humor and great conversation about British and global history; he inspires me to think bigger. My graduate students at the University of Colorado have kept me on my toes with their keen questions and insights. Alastair Bellany, the author of the first volume of *A New History of Britain,* came up with terrific ideas about the format of our textbook. Carol Byerly, Lil Fenn, and Peter Wood listened patiently as I went on and on about my most recent finds. In addition to their friendship, I cherish their good natures, sharp minds, and lively enthusiasm for all things historical.

As always, Anne Davidson has been my anchor. She is kind, loving, unflappable, and funny. She brings me tea. I can only do what I do because of her presence in my life.

I dedicate this textbook to Bonnie Smith, in hopes of conveying in some small measure the depth of my appreciation and gratitude for all that she has been and done for me over the course of my career. She has been a generous critic, a stout champion, and an unfailing guide. But above all she has given me the gift of her warm and unstinting friendship, which I count among my treasures.

ABOUT
THE AUTHOR

SUSAN KINGSLEY KENT is Professor of Distinction in the History Department at the University of Colorado, Boulder. Her publications include *Sex and Suffrage in Britain, 1860–1914* (1987); *Making Peace: The Reconstruction of Gender in Interwar Britain* (1993); *Gender and Power in Britain, 1640–1990* (1999); *Aftershocks: Politics and Trauma in Interwar Britain* (2010); *The Global Flu Pandemic of 1918–1919* (2012); *The Women's War of 1929: Gender and Violence in Colonial Nigeria* (2011), with Misty Bastian and Marc Matera; *Gender and History* (2011); *Africans and Britons in the Age of Empires, 1660–1980* (2015), with Myles Osborne; and *Queen Victoria: Gender and Empire* (OUP, 2015). In addition, Professor Kent is the author of an e-text with Great River Technologies entitled *The History of Western Civilization since 1500: An Ecological Approach*. She is currently at work on a history of the global 1930s with Marc Matera and a book on gender in world history.

Yes and No voters square off in Glasgow, 2014.

THE BRITISH ISLES AND THE BRITISH EMPIRE IN 1688

In early September 2014, ten days before Scots were to cast their votes in a referendum that would determine whether they remained in the United Kingdom, polls showed that the decision was too close to call. The results stunned politicians in Westminster, who had cavalierly assumed that the vote for independence would fall decidedly short. Panicked now by the findings of pollsters, the leaders of the three Westminster parties rushed to Scotland, collectively issuing a "vow" that if Scots voted no on the referendum, Parliament would grant them broad and extensive powers to determine their own fates in their own elected assembly. For the next week and a half, David Cameron (1966–), the Conservative prime minister, his coalition partner Nick Clegg (1967–) of the Liberal Democratic Party, and Gordon Brown (1951–), former Labour prime minister and a Scot, lobbied hard for the "Better Together" campaign (sometimes called in the press the "No, Thanks" campaign), while Alex Salmond (1954–), first minister of Scotland and leader of the Scottish Nationalist Party, rallied supporters of independence across the country for the "Yes" campaign. A number of banks issued dire warnings about the fate of the Scottish banking system should "Yes" voters win, and chief executive officers of major companies announced that they would take their businesses south should such an outcome prevail. After church near Balmoral on the Sunday before the referendum, Queen Elizabeth (1926–) walked over to greet well-wishers and, in conversation with them, allowed as how she hoped the Scots would "think very carefully about the future" when they cast their ballots on September 18. The fact that her apparently spontaneous remark had been deeply considered and coordinated with Westminster politicians, as the *Guardian* reported later, demonstrates just how alarmed British officials had become by the real prospect of Scotland leaving the 300-year-old union.

How did this turn of events come to be? The following chapters attempt to address that question, among others, by examining the roles played by each of the four nations in the history of Great Britain since 1688. "British" history is often told from the perspective of English actors, but when the other nations that make up Great Britain are taken into account, the story looks different. England, Scotland, Wales, and Ireland often jostled one another uncomfortably—and sometimes violently—as economic, political, social, and cultural changes unfolded over three centuries. Ethnic and religious antipathies joined those of class and gender to create divisions that disrupted the conventional narrative of a "United Kingdom." The addition of empire to the mix complicates the British story even further.

••

The lands that made up the British Isles in the seventeenth century—England and Wales, Scotland, and Ireland—contained a vast array of peoples who perceived no common tie among themselves beyond that of geography. Differences of language, ethnicity, culture, history, law, customs, and religion divided the kingdoms from each another. Indeed, within each kingdom, many of the inhabitants had little in common with one another. During the reign of Henry VIII (1491–1547), England had brought Wales into the administrative and political structure of England. In the twelfth century, England's Henry II (1133–1189) had conquered Ireland and rendered it a "lordship" of the English crown. "Poynings' Law" of 1494 subordinated the Irish Parliament to the English Parliament and the English crown; in 1541, Henry VIII declared himself king of Ireland and began the process of bringing the country under the administrative control of England. In a bid to secure their power in a now-Protestant state containing a Catholic population, he and Elizabeth I (1533–1603) had established "plantations" of loyal Protestant followers in Ireland, massacring Catholics, confiscating their lands, and granting them to English colonists. On Elizabeth's death in 1603, James VI (1566–1625) of Scotland succeeded her, becoming James I of England, and a Union of the Crowns left England and Scotland as sovereign states that just happened to be ruled by the same king. James continued the Tudor practice of settling colonists in Ireland, ousting Gaelic landowners in five counties in the northern reaches of Ireland and transferring the land to Scottish and English Protestants. More than 10,000 Scots ultimately came to settle there in Ulster Province.

The smallest steps toward empire building were taken during roughly the same period that England established its domination over Ireland, Wales, and Scotland. By the time that Wales became incorporated into English administration, the Venetian explorer John Cabot (c. 1450-c. 1500) had landed in Newfoundland

and claimed it for the English (1497). By 1601, when the English and Scottish crowns became united in the persons of the Stuart monarchs, the English merchant John Hawkins (1532–1595) had begun to trade in enslaved Africans with the New World (1562); Francis Drake (c. 1540–1596) had sailed around the world seeking new trading opportunities for England (1577–1580); would-be English colonists had established a settlement, subsequently abandoned, in Roanoke, Virginia (1585), a land named after their virgin queen; and Queen Elizabeth had chartered the East India Company to engage in trade with the East Indies (1600). By the time our story starts in 1688, English ships were carrying 6,700 enslaved Africans a year across the Atlantic to English colonies in the Caribbean and North America to work on the tobacco, indigo, cotton, and sugar plantations that would secure England's commercial wealth; the East India Company had set itself up in "factories"—trading stations that would become walled fortresses—in Calcutta, Madras, and Bombay; and Charles II (1630–1685) had granted the company the authority to acquire and administer more territory abroad, create and command its own military force, mint coinage, create alliances, engage in war, and make treaties. England had established dominion over its neighbors in the British Isles and was well on its way to building an empire that would make "the United Kingdom of Great Britain," once it came into being, one of the most powerful countries in the world.

Overall, the British Isles held about 9 million souls in 1688. Just under 5 million people lived in England, by far the most densely populated of the four countries. Four hundred thousand people resided in Wales at the time, 1 million in Scotland, and 2 million in Ireland. The Celtic peoples who had emerged originally in the British Isles had left little trace of their culture in England, having been absorbed by the Anglo-Saxons, Scandinavians, and Normans who had invaded the country over a number of centuries, although linguistic holdovers could be found in Cornwall and in Hereford, where Cornish and Welsh, respectively, were still spoken. Celtic culture enjoyed deep sway in the other countries, however: most people in Wales and Ireland spoke no English at all, expressing themselves in Welsh and Irish, whereas a significant portion of those in the Highlands of Scotland used Scottish Gaelic exclusively as well. Lowland Scots spoke a Germanic Scots language till well into the eighteenth century; those who immigrated to the northern areas of Ireland carried it with them to create the "Ulster Scots" dialect. English common law prevailed in England, but only nominally in Ireland and Wales, despite those countries' administrative absorption into England's administrative structures; Scotland based its system of law on the ancient Roman codes.

THE LAND AND ITS PEOPLE

Dramatic environmental differentiations underscored these cultural distinctions. Each country possessed topographies that differed, sometimes markedly, from one another, and within Scotland, the physical attributes of the land varied dramatically between north and south. The lands of Ireland and England tended toward rolling hills, plains, and valleys, with soil and climate conducive to good farming and good grazing. In northern England, a low line of mountains called the Pennines extended in a north–south direction from Northumberland and Yorkshire to the Midlands. The hillsides favored grazing of livestock rather than farming, and eventually these hills would yield significant amounts of coal and iron ore. Mountains comprised a large portion of Wales's geography, especially in the north, leaving much less area for farming. The soil proved poor as well, even in those areas in the south of Wales where it was less mountainous. As a result, Welsh farmers tended to use the land to grow hay rather than food for humans and to pasture their animals on it. Scotland offered the most pronounced topographical variations, with some two-thirds of the country—called the Highlands—made up of rugged, mountainous terrain transected by deep valleys. Cold, wet weather characterizes the Highlands and the rocky islands that sit offshore to the west and northeast. The Lowlands, by contrast, where half of the Scots lived in 1688, enjoys milder weather and more fertile land, even if it is hilly and sometimes boggy.

These divergent ecologies produced different ways and standards of living. The economies of the four countries revolved almost exclusively on agriculture, and the vast majority of people lived on and from the land, but huge disparities of wealth, population, and occupation distribution between and among them existed. The English enjoyed the greatest prosperity by far, having replaced a fair amount of their medieval forms of agriculture—locally based, communal, open field—with new market-oriented, capitalist farming methods and nationwide trade in the goods they produced. The gradual and uneven development of a capitalist economy had differential effects on people. As landowners began to farm their land according to more rational, efficient practices and to produce crops not only for sustenance but also to sell at market, many became prosperous; but those who had depended on common areas and nonarable acreage to grow or raise what they needed to live on could no longer provide food for their families. Many became migrants, seeking waged work where they could find it; others spun woolen thread or wove woolen cloth in their cottages in return for a wage. The enterprising individuals who circumvented guild restrictions on manufacturing and commerce in the towns by setting up these workers in rural cottages to produce cloth and paying them low wages profited nicely from the greater efficiency of domestic industry and from expanding markets. Urban guild masters, faced with competition from domestic industry as well as from increasing numbers of artisans, introduced new impediments to gaining access to their ranks, shutting down the normal avenues by means of which apprentices and journeymen and -women established themselves and made their living. By 1688, a third to a half of the English population could no longer count on the plot of ground that allowed them to establish self-sustaining households or gain entry to a craft that would enable them to become independent adults. They had become employees—men and women who worked for a wage in such areas as agriculture, the silk and linen

Great Britain and Ireland

MAP 1.1
Great Britain and Ireland

A PLACE IN TIME

Liverpool, Second City of Empire

Although London operated as the nerve center of the United Kingdom and stood at the "heart of empire" for three centuries following 1660, a focus on Liverpool's history offers us in many ways a more intriguing, complex, and complete picture of the dynamics that shaped and informed Great Britain between 1688 and 2015. From a sleepy town situated on the eastern bank of the Mersey River about two miles south of where it empties into the Irish Sea, Liverpool grew into one of the most vibrant commercial hubs in England. Its location at the geographical center of the British Isles gave it access to Scotland, Wales, and Ireland by sea and to the rest of England by land transport. In the seventeenth century, trade with Ireland in such commodities as linen dominated Liverpool's economy, but the onset of trade with the American colonies, which began in the 1660s, produced a dramatic upsurge in commercial activity. Starting in 1700, Liverpool merchants began trading in slaves, a venture that brought them and the city enormous wealth and political influence; in the early nineteenth century, Liverpudlian antislavery activists helped to being about the abolition of the slave trade in 1807 and then slavery itself in 1833. Despite what amounted to panic among the city's merchants, commerce did not suffer from abolition; in fact, trade with India increased, as did that with the United States, as newly industrialized regions of Lancashire produced a variety of commodities that held great appeal abroad. Trade with West Africa in the second half of the nineteenth century, particularly in palm oil, used to lubricate the machines of the industrial revolution and then to produce soaps and margarine, kept Liverpool merchants prosperous.

The city became a magnet for Irish, Welsh, and Scottish workers and agricultural laborers seeking a better life. Many of them went on to immigrate to the United States or the white colonies of settlement, but many stayed in the city. In 1851, 47 percent of Liverpool's adult population hailed from other parts of Great Britain. In 1900, more Welsh people lived in Liverpool than in any Welsh city barring Cardiff; more Irish made their homes there than anywhere in Ireland apart from Dublin and Belfast; and more Scots resided in Liverpool than in Scotland with the exception of Glasgow, Edinburgh, and Aberdeen. People of color from the fast-expanding empire who arrived as seamen sometimes stayed to settle and establish families in the city, but their numbers were small until after the First World War, amounting to perhaps 0.04 percent in 1900.

The Second City of Empire thus offers us a rich array of case studies with which to illustrate some of the major themes that will unfold over the following chapters. We begin in 1666, when a small ship named the *Antelope*, laden with a cargo of linen, shoes, nails, and coal, sailed out of Liverpool bound for Barbados. It returned a year later, its hold crammed with sugarcane that sold for twice the amount merchants had paid out for the original voyage. Armed with profits of 100 percent, they outfitted more ships for trade with the West Indies; within ten years, twelve ships were making their way back and forth across the Atlantic to the Caribbean on a regular basis, while other merchants engaged in trade with Virginia. The demand for sugar from Barbados and tobacco from Virginia only increased over the next decades, and merchants and those who helped finance the trade realized handsome returns on their investments. Liverpool began to boom. From a small town of perhaps 1,000 inhabitants living in seven streets in 1660, it grew to about 7,000 people by the end of the century. Building expanded to keep pace with the increased population and the small town became a thriving borough of twenty-eight streets. Its revenues during the same period rose by more than 400 percent, from some £280 in 1662 to £1,200 in 1700.

Liverpool, c. 1680.

The families who benefitted so abundantly from the new trade with Britain's empire in North America established themselves as the political force in Liverpool over the next number of decades, challenging and ultimately wresting power from the landed families who had governed the town and the surrounding countryside. Their wealth attracted the attention of King James II (1633–1701), who in 1684 imposed a new charter on the borough that gave him control over its affairs. This action angered the urban elites, called burgesses, most of them identified with the Whig faction of Parliament; three years later, even those who regarded themselves as Tories, or supporters of the king, joined in the alienation felt by their Whig colleagues when James interceded in a case on behalf of two Roman Catholics. By 1688, Whig and Tory burgesses alike had had enough from their monarch, whose absolutist and pro-Catholic tendencies offended them mightily. Both factions gave their enthusiastic support to James' toppling from the throne by his son-in-law, William of Orange (1650–1702).

industries, the manufacture of soap, glass, paper, and beer, or the mining of coal, lead, tin, and copper.

About 11 percent of the English population lived in London, the thriving capital city. Only two other cities—the port town of Bristol and the manufacturing center of Norwich—could boast populations of 20,000. Another 15 percent of the population lived in market towns that dotted the countryside, but most English people lived in villages of about 300–400 people where their homes were gathered in a cluster surrounded by the fields they worked for their landlords. The 2 percent of the population that comprised the aristocracy and the gentry—some 15,000 to 20,000 families—owned most of the land, but a group of substantial nongentry landholders and farmers had emerged over time. The yeomanry, as this group was called, owned their land and farmed it themselves; they were freeholders. On the strength of their wealth, many of them could be distinguished from the gentry only by their lack of "gentle" birth—that is, they did not descend from knightly or noble families. As was the case with the aristocracy proper (whose titles of nobility were passed down only to the eldest son), the sons and daughters of the yeomanry married into the gentry, replenishing and revitalizing the landed elite.

Husbandmen farmed land they did not own but leased from the yeomanry or gentry. Over the course of the seventeenth century, increasing numbers of these people lost their land to enclosure as landlords fenced in previously available common lands and fell into the ranks of agricultural laborers, who worked other people's land for wages, or cottagers, whose income derived from domestic manufacturing of textiles. Along with paupers, who had no source of income, cottagers made up perhaps a third of England's population. In 1688, the statistician Gregory King (1648–1712) estimated that most people in England could not make ends meet and were judged by their contemporaries to be poor.

In English towns and cities, whose populations were growing faster than the national rate, the expansion of trade and commerce produced a group of wealthy merchants, men quite as rich as gentlemen who did not labor manually themselves but directed those who did. As their numbers grew, so did their significance and sense of importance. Independent artisans and smaller traders occupied the rung below merchants; journeymen and laborers working for wages occupied the next. In terms of civic importance, although perhaps not social status, the great merchants of London in particular joined the group of professionals in the church, the law, medicine, education, the armed forces, and government administration, whose ranks were filled by the younger sons of the aristocracy and gentry who did not inherit their fathers' estates. In time, the sons and daughters of merchant and gentry families came to intermarry, bringing infusions of capital to struggling gentry and "gentle" social status to aspiring merchants. Some historians use the term "gentlemanly capitalism" to describe the economic, social, and political regime produced by this alliance of land and commerce after 1688.

The poor soil and mountainous terrain of Wales, combined with a lack of improvement such as was taking place in England, made for a far less developed agricultural system. The land could not support whole villages of farmers; instead, individual families worked isolated farms with primitive tools, and most agriculture was devoted to growing hay for sheep and cattle. The Welsh could barely feed themselves, let alone produce crops for the market, and most of them lived on the edge of starvation in miserable huts alongside their animals. In good times they ate bread and milk, but few could ever hope to have meat. The cottage industries that helped support English laborers did not exist in Wales, making it difficult to survive in years when crops ran short. Wales did not possess much in the way of an aristocracy, so it was the gentry who owned the land worked by the Welsh people. Often these were absentee English landlords or Welsh men and women who had become increasingly Anglicized over the seventeenth century, turning to London for economic opportunities and a social life that did not exist in Wales. They rarely returned to their ancestral homes and had lost touch with their compatriots, many of them no longer able even to speak Welsh. The assimilation of Wales into English society and politics, involving exclusively the upper ranks of the Welsh, was virtually complete in 1688.

Scotland could well have been taken for two separate countries, so vast were the differences between the lands and the peoples of the Highlands and the Lowlands. Lowland Scots, inhabiting a third of the land, comprised half of the total population of the country. Most of them—tenant farmers, farmers who leased from tenants (called "crofters" and "cottars"), farm laborers, and servants—lived in small, isolated hamlets called "farmtouns," made up usually of a single farm big enough to require a plow to till the land, which produced mostly grain and not a great deal of that, given the unimproved nature of farming. The land was owned exclusively by aristocrats or members of the gentry, called "lairds"; they felt little compulsion to adopt any of the agricultural reforms being tried out in England. Cattle, which made up the bulk of Scottish agriculture and commerce, needed little more than pasturage. Peasants mostly ate oatmeal washed down with milk; cheese and butter made up the rest of their diet. Like the Welsh, they lived in squalid huts.

Scottish urban areas ("burghs") compared poorly with those of England. Some 300 small towns of about 100 people were sprinkled across the countryside. Edinburgh, the capital, contained a sizeable population of 30,000 people, and about 10,000 people lived in the cities of Glasgow, Aberdeen, and Dundee. These commercial centers traded cattle, sheep, and fish products to France and the countries of northern Europe for iron, timber, and manufactured goods. The cattle trade with England in particular provided a good source of income for those merchants who could take advantage of it.

As bad as things were for most Lowland Scots, they were worse in the Highlands. The fertile grain-growing areas of the Lowlands did not exist in the Highlands, which had to import most of its grain from the south. Highlanders raised cattle and lived hand to mouth, most of them, in the deep valleys (called "straths") between the mountain ridges that characterized the area. They organized themselves by clan, groups that claimed kinship with one another, and fought endless pitched battles over cattle, the sign and source of wealth in the Highlands. Bloody feuds, especially those between the families of the Campbells and the Macdonalds, each of which sought to gain dominance over the Highlands, sometimes reached the level of civil war. Lowland Scots regarded the Highlanders with a combination of disdain and terror: the former on account of the "uncivilized" nature of the clans; the latter rising to the fore when Highlander raids on cattle crossed into their territory. The government at Edinburgh tried hard to rein in what they saw as the lawlessness of the clans through "Letters of Fire and Sword," decrees that authorized individuals to take whatever steps necessary to bring the wrongdoers to justice, without having to worry about any criminal ramifications of their actions.

Ireland enjoyed only a bit more prosperity than Scotland in 1688, a surprising fact given the natural gifts of climate and fertility the country possessed. The great majority of the population, living almost entirely in rural areas (Dublin could boast a population of 60,000 in 1675, but Cork, Limerick, Waterford, and Galway had less than 5,000 people each), faced starvation on a regular basis. Their diet consisted of milk, cakes made of oats, and potatoes, which had been introduced in the late 1500s from the Americas by Spanish fishermen who dried their catch on the western coast of the island. The tuber quickly became a mainstay. Irish peasants worked the unimproved fields of their landlords with rudimentary tools, eking out a barely sustainable existence in the good years. In the bad years, which occurred with frequency in the second half of the seventeenth century, peasants died in large numbers.

Blessed with a moderate climate, plenty of rain, and green rolling plains, Ireland should have been able not only to feed its people but also to prosper, much like England. That it did not in 1688 reflects the intense divisions that plagued the country. Seventy-five percent of the Irish people worshiped as Catholics; they lived predominantly in the provinces of Leinster, Munster, and Connacht, where they made up 95 percent of the population. The remaining 25 percent counted themselves Protestant, either Anglican (the established Church of England and of Ireland) or Presbyterian, whose differences we will discuss later in this chapter. Protestants comprised half the population in Ulster Province, and probably half of those were Presbyterian. Presbyterians tended to descend from the Scots who had immigrated to northern Ireland in the earlier part of the seventeenth century and Anglicans from the English who had been planted in Ireland since Henry VIII's time. The Catholics of Ireland came from the original Gaelic population and the descendants of Norman conquerors.

Landholding tended to follow the religious divide. Most landowners were Protestant, having gained their estates through the forcible and violent confiscation of Irish Catholic property. Almost 80 percent of the land was owned by Protestants. In contrast, most of those who worked the land were Catholic, some of whom had once owned the property they now had to lease from their hated landlords. Thus, economic and political power was inextricably entwined with religious divisions, to the benefit of Protestants. Some dispossessed Catholics turned to banditry as a way to express their rage and rebellion against Protestants. Landlords often found themselves isolated in a sea of hostile Catholics who spoke a language they could not understand and harbored long-standing and deep-seated resentments. They had little incentive to try to improve agriculture or better the conditions of their angry tenants.

The province of Ulster proved the exception to this rule. There, Presbyterian landowners worked to bring agriculture into the capitalist system, growing food for market and increasing their output wherever they could. They invigorated the cattle trade and raised sheep and grew flax for woolen and linen manufacture, respectively. Ulster prosperity facilitated the growth of towns there, as did a regular flow of goods, ideas, and people between the northern counties of Ireland and Lowland Scotland, a mere thirteen miles away across the Irish Sea.

OVERSEAS COLONIES

England's considerable wealth advantage owed much to its overseas trade with its colonies in the New World and with countries in the East, especially India. The English overseas empire of the late seventeenth century consisted of holdings in North America and the West Indies, where some 105,000 British Americans lived in the 1660s. The nature of these possessions varied greatly. Most of those in Canada were in the hands of private commercial companies and ranged from a line of fishing ports in Newfoundland to a motley collection of forts in northern Canada operated by the Hudson's Bay Company for the purposes of trading in furs. Colonies south of Canada had been established by religious refugees (Massachusetts, Connecticut, Rhode Island) or individuals granted royal charters by Charles I (1600–1649) and Charles II (New York, New Jersey, Pennsylvania, Maryland, the Carolinas). Only two colonies—New Hampshire and Virginia—actually "belonged" to the monarch. Bermuda and the colonies of the Caribbean (Jamaica, Barbados, the Leeward Islands) fell under direct royal authority, but here, as in North America, the colonies established legislatures through which they governed themselves. The governors appointed by the monarch to rule the colonies enjoyed freedom to govern as they saw fit, since England was some eight weeks away by ship. At the same time, legislatures frequently reminded them of how little power they actually possessed.

In the economic scheme of things, the mainland colonies of seventeenth-century North America contributed little to England's overall wealth. Apart from tobacco and furs (over which the Hudson's Bay Company had a monopoly), there was virtually no demand for products from North America. The Caribbean colonies, on the other hand, turned vast profits in the sugar trade, whose success was powered by a continuous supply of enslaved Africans. Thousands of captives were carried across the Atlantic each year to provide the labor that would undergird the British imperial economy; from 1660 on, they would outnumber white Britons, more dramatically as each year passed.

England protected its economic interests in the New World through a series of Navigation Acts that stipulated that only English ships could trade with its colonies. Scottish and Irish merchants could not themselves trade directly with England's colonies, nor could they gain entry to the two other chartered companies, the East India Company and the Royal African Company, which enjoyed monopolies on trade with South Asia and Africa, respectively, and provided handsome returns for their investors.

A GREAT CHAIN OF BEING

Virtually all Britons, no matter where they resided, understood the world in which they lived to be fundamentally, properly, and irrevocably hierarchical. They imagined their social order to be a "great chain of being," with God the Father and the angels at the top, followed in descending order by monarchs, aristocrats, gentry, and everyone else. Women held their various positions on the chain by virtue of their relationship to men as wives or daughters; as women, they were inferior and subordinate to men, as God had demonstrated in making Eve out of Adam's rib. Moreover, Eve's transgressions had stained all women with her sin. Construed as insatiably lustful, with sexual appetites equal to or greater than men's, women of the seventeenth century were perceived to be potential agents of damnation and destruction, requiring the mastery of men to preserve their propriety and honor and even the stability of the social order itself.

Hierarchies of gender mirrored those of status based on landownership in rural areas and on guild structures in the towns. Just as subjects of the crown knew themselves to be subordinate to their monarch, farmers knew themselves to be fully subordinate to their landlords, and apprentices and journeymen and -women to their guild masters, so too women understood themselves to be subordinate to their fathers and their husbands. Patriarchal rule—whether it be of master to man or man to woman—prevailed.

Patriarchy in state and society as well as in the family rested on the ancient presumption that the male head of household held property not only in his land and his animals, but also in his wife and his children. That property was to be handed down to the eldest son, part of the inheritance system known as primogeniture. Although never legally classified as chattel—property—of men, married English, Welsh, and Scottish women faced restrictions in common law that rendered them, for all intents and purposes, the property of their husbands. At the very least, common law doctrines institutionalized the inferiority and subordination of women to men. Under the law of coverture (unique to England), married women had no legal existence apart from their husbands: they had no legal rights to property, to earnings, to freedom of movement, to conscience, to their bodies, or to their children; all belonged to their husbands. They could not sign contracts, sue or be sued, except under their husbands' names, and if they incurred debt were not legally responsible for it. If a woman was raped, the crime was perceived as a form of theft, not from her, but from her husband or male relatives; cases of adultery were prosecuted only in those instances where the woman involved was married. Women lost their names when they married. All of these circumstances combined to suggest that women were the property of men in fact, if not in law. Certainly they meant that women did not enjoy the autonomy and independence that were vital prerequisites for formal political participation (which, indeed, most men did not possess either, although not because they were excluded by law). Only in rare and exceptional cases did individual women vote for or hold public office. In the Gaelic areas of Ireland where English common law could not overcome traditional medieval legal practices, married women may well have enjoyed a higher legal status and greater property rights. Gaelic women, it appears, could hold property and administer it as they saw fit, independent of their husbands.

In practice, the facts of demography and the need to ensure the survival of all members of the family tended to militate against the inheritance and legal disabilities that English, Welsh, and Scottish women, daughters, and younger sons experienced under common law. First, because death rates were so high and life expectancy so low compared to that in the twenty-first century, the inheritance patterns and legal disabilities enshrined in common law often did not come to pass as expected. Some 40 percent of marriages never produced a son. In the 20 percent of marriages that produced only daughters, they would inherit land jointly from their father. Even when marriages produced a son, more often than not he would not be of age at the time of his father's death; thus, the inheritance would, for some time at least, pass into the hands of his mother to be administered by her until he turned twenty-one. Because married women regained their own legal identity on the death of their husbands, mothers negotiated their children's marriage agreements as often as did fathers.

Perhaps most important, the survival of individuals in the seventeenth century depended on the survival of the entire family; women's material contribution to the family economy made the difference between life and death. New households could not be established until couples had obtained the necessary financial resources to sustain themselves and the children they expected to have— the availability of a plot of land or a cottage, the completion of artisanal training, the inheritance of a marriage portion. Wives were expected to bring to the marriage a dowry, also called a marriage portion, equal to the contribution that their husbands made. Fathers, aware that the most significant component of wealth consisted of an inheritance, tried to ensure that the inheritances they left their children were equal and sufficient for them to marry and set up households; what the eldest son received in land was often matched in value by the moveable household goods left to the other children, although those children had no legal claim on them and were at the mercy of their fathers' goodwill.

A lease to a cottage, a cow, a bed, clothing, utensils, tools—the inheritance of these items made it possible for daughters and younger sons to marry and set up independent households. They were not usually able to do so until relatively late in their life; men of ordinary rank married in their late twenties and women in

their mid- to late twenties. Amongst the aristocracy, for whom marriage constituted a kind of alliance between powerful families, or the gentry, for whom it was
the means by which economic, social, and political interests were furthered,
women and men married earlier, some as early as their mid-teens. They did not
have to wait to amass the resources necessary to establish separate households.

The household was the site of economic activity. Whether it was a farm or an
artisanal workshop, work and family were never separated. The family economy
characteristic of early modern society depended on the labor of all members of
the household; marriage was above all an economic partnership. Within this economic enterprise, clearly demarcated spheres of activity for men and women provided the gender boundaries that ordered everyday life. In rural areas, men
worked in the fields, free to travel fairly long distances from the household to
farm and to labor for long, undisturbed periods of time. Women tended to do
work that was located closer to the house so that the constant interruptions of
small children and the necessities of running a household could be accommodated. They looked after the raising of livestock, dairying, brewing, baking, and
cultivation of vegetable gardens. Women sold the dairy and vegetable products at
market and managed whatever household cash income there might be at their
disposal. This gendered division of labor prevailed at all social levels, although in
the case of the gentry and aristocracy, wives supervised rather than undertook
these activities themselves.

In urban areas and those parts of the countryside where artisanal manufacturing thrived, wives in workshops and small shops proved indispensable to the
family economy. They sold the products of the workshop and provided for the
needs of both family members and apprentices, who lived with the family as part
of their apprenticeship agreement. In those families that depended primarily on
wages to survive, marriage age could be earlier because the material prerequisites
for setting up a household did not require waiting for a plot of land or a position
in a workshop to become available. Among gentry, where neither husband nor
wife worked, both nevertheless had to coordinate their efforts to oversee the
management of the estates and to protect the interests of the family. In law and in
custom, women were certainly the subordinate, inferior sex. In practice, their
contributions to the family enterprise and the management of whatever cash
income came in, without which the family could not survive, provided them with
economic leverage.

But it is also the case that the material and emotional lives of men and women
unfolded within a system of beliefs and values about the natures and roles of their
respective sexes that helped people to make sense of their world and to give it
order. This web of ideas, although it might not correspond to the ways individual
men and women actually behaved or thought, did nonetheless act both to offer
possibilities about and to circumscribe the ways individuals could imagine they
could live. For example, the belief that women were inherently sexual creatures
made it imaginatively possible for women to enjoy sexual intercourse; this belief
also allowed religious thinkers to recognize that the satisfaction of sexual desire

was one of the purposes of marriage, and it also underpinned received medical wisdom that conception—the primary function of marriage—could only occur if both partners experienced orgasm. On the other hand, the sexuality of women could also be construed to cause all sorts of disorder and to render them unfit for any kind of autonomy. The subordination and inferiority of women that was so central to seventeenth-century social, political, economic, and familial organization owed its prevalence in large part to ideas about women's sexual nature. Those ideas prescribed proper and improper behavior for women and thus helped to delimit their activity.

Regardless of social class, women were expected to stay within the confines of the home, the realm of "within," as some ministers put it, as opposed to the world "without." Literature intended to instruct women as to what was proper enjoined them to keep themselves within the private sphere of home and family where they could best cultivate and exhibit the qualities of respectable women. As we have seen, ordinary women did venture out of the private sphere to work their gardens, tend their livestock, and sell their goods at market; the wives of middling artisan households engaged in commercial activity from their front rooms. (They did not, however, join their husbands in the alehouse, where most lower- and middle-ranking men spent their leisure hours.) Upper-class women traveled for business and pleasure and some for education, which they could not obtain from the grammar schools and universities attended by their brothers. These out-of-doors activities violated norms of female behavior, but at the same time women's recognized obligations to contribute to the family economy necessitated these transgressions. This contradiction left women in a potentially precarious state: any misstep outside their prescribed private sphere could incite the disapprobation of society. Few proper women were prepared to risk the displeasure of their communities, and displayed, at least in public, the traditional virtues assigned to them.

Proper women were expected to be modest, humble, obedient, pious, temperate, patient, silent, and above all, chaste. This is not to say that they were all of these things; indeed, the very need to enjoin them to be so may suggest that they were not. Most likely, however, once these norms of femininity became accepted as part of the "natural" order, as was the case by 1600, it would be difficult for women to transgress them with impunity. To do so would be to call down on their heads charges of immorality and unnaturalness, which most people could not have afforded. Observations that women did not enjoy the same legal, educational, or political privileges as men were likely to provoke outrage, culminating in diagnoses of insanity.

Most women accepted and internalized the religious and scientific discourses that proclaimed their inferiority and need for subordination. Educated women, a tiny minority, might be even more likely to subscribe to prevailing doctrines concerning femininity: they would have read the learned treatises that credited the humors with causing the differences between men and women on which women's subordination was based. Ordinary women would not have read the conduct books or scientific treatises that proclaimed their inferiority and subordination.

They would, however, have listened almost every Sunday to sermons that preached the same ideas. They embraced church teachings about their intellectual defects and their exclusion from the masculine domains of politics and learning as part of the religious doctrine that offered them the only source of solace in a harsh and horrific world that carried their children away from them on a regular basis.

THE SECTARIAN DIVIDE

Religion informed the lives of the peoples of England, Wales, Scotland, Ireland, and British colonies in the New World to a degree difficult for us to fathom today. Following the proper religion, as contemporaries saw it, amounted to a matter of life or death, quite literally. From the time of the Protestant Reformation on, worshippers could not agree what that proper religion should be, causing extraordinarily violent upheavals across the British Isles. Ireland provides only the best-known example of religious strife in the Catholic/Protestant divide that would plague the country for the next four centuries. Splits within Protestantism itself also brought about terrible conflicts in all of the kingdoms, as dissenters broke away from the established Church of England and formed themselves into congregations of Presbyterians, Congregationalists, Baptists, Quakers, Unitarians, and other sects. Their contests involved not only—or even especially—theological issues, but also political and economic ones, as we have seen in the case of Ireland.

When Henry VIII broke with the Roman Catholic church in 1543 to divorce his first wife, Catherine of Aragon, and marry Anne Boleyn (1501–1536), he did little to change either the doctrine or the structure of the English church. Instead, he placed himself, rather than the pope, at the head of what was now called the Anglican church, or the Church of England, retaining the ecclesiastical structure of archbishops and bishops presiding over the dioceses of the country. The Anglican church regarded the monarch as its "supreme governor," followed a great deal of the traditional Roman Catholic liturgy, and barely altered the doctrines concerning the sacraments. Like the Roman Catholic church, the Church of England regarded itself as the instrument through which God communicated with individual worshippers.

This kind of reformation did not satisfy many Protestants who embraced the doctrines of continental reformers like John Calvin or Ulrich Zwingli, or the Scottish Calvinist, John Knox (c. 1514–1572). They wished to see a purer church emerge from the Reformation, believing that no intermediary should insert himself between the individual and God. Called Puritans, they sought scriptures that regular men and women could read for themselves instead of relying on priests for their interpretation and championed a simpler liturgy and a more strict moral life. They eschewed the pageantry and grandeur of the Anglican clergy, dressing instead in plain black clothing and foregoing what they regarded as the "idolatry" of decoration and the worship of saints. Within the Puritan fold, two different groups emerged, largely determined by the way they believed the church should

be organized and governed. Presbyterians looked to replace the hierarchical ecclesiastical structure of bishops and archbishops with councils—presbyteries—
made up of ministers and laymen as the means of governance; Independents
went even farther than Presbyterians, placing authority for governance within
the individual congregations themselves. These Independents would come to be
called Congregationalists in the lands of the New World.

England contained only a few Catholics in the seventeenth century, most of
them living in the north and northeast of the country. Most of the aristocracy
and gentry belonged to the Church of England. Puritan strongholds tended to
exist in the cities, especially among merchant and financial families. The Welsh
gentry embraced Anglicanism, whereas the rest of the population of Wales
seemed not to care one way or the other. Elizabeth had made sure to appoint
Welshmen to the bishoprics of the country and to translate the bible and the book
of prayer into Welsh, a circumstance that both preserved the Welsh language in
the long run and kept Wales loyal to Protestantism. In Scotland, the divisions of
the Highlands and the Lowlands tended to include religion, with the Lowland
Scots fervently committing to Presbyterianism and the Highland Scots either
retaining their Catholicism or becoming somewhat lukewarm adherents of the
Anglican church. Ireland, as we have seen, remained overwhelmingly Catholic,
ruled over by a minority Protestant landowning elite.

In the colonies of the New World, "dissenters" enjoyed greater room to maneuver than in England. The New England colonies had been founded by Puritans seeking relief from persecution in England in the early seventeenth century;
the middle colonies of New York and Pennsylvania, initially settled by Anglicans,
received significant in-migration of Scots Irish Protestants from Ulster. The presence of Catholics in New France, north of New England, prompted a good deal
of anti-Catholic sentiment. Catholics had also settled in Maryland, where Lord
Baltimore had established a proprietorial colony during the reign of Charles
I designed to provide religious toleration for Catholics in the New World. The West
Indian planter class tended to embrace Anglicanism, although the Irish indentured servants who came over and worked for them would have been Catholic.

Jews had been banished from the kingdom by King Edward I (1239–1307) in
1290, but some returned in the sixteenth and early seventeenth centuries as converted New Christians. Few in London had any illusions about the sincerity of
their faith, but they did not go out of their way to molest the *conversos*, as they
were called. In the 1650s, after fundamentalist Puritans urged that Jews be read-
mitted to Britain so that they could be converted to Christianity in advance of the
second coming of Christ, an openly professing Jewish community tolerated by
the government emerged in London.

POLITICS

During the first half of the seventeenth century, British politics had been consumed by debates and then armed conflict over the question of the relationship

of the monarchy to Parliament. Royalists believed that the power of the monarch over his or her subjects should always prevail over that of the elites represented in Parliament. Parliamentarians, as their name suggests, argued that their rights to rule should, when push came to shove, predominate. The political fight was informed and exacerbated by religious divisions. Although they did not always break down so neatly, generally speaking, royalists, at least in England, tended to be Anglicans (and sometimes secret Catholics); parliamentarians tended to embrace one of the dissenting sects. In 1660, following twenty tumultuous years of civil war and revolution that involved the beheading of a king, military conquest of Ireland and Scotland, the creation of a republican form of government, and the abolition of the Church of England and of Parliament, English elites asked Charles II to return to the throne. The restoration of the monarchy included, perforce, that of the Church of England as well, an act that had serious repercussions for dissenting and nonconformist congregations. Charles's failed attempts to impose toleration for Catholics and nonconforming Protestants through royal prerogative did little to soften the persecution against those who refused to swear an oath to the Anglican church. Religion continued to play a central role in questions of governance, especially because people suspected that Charles, having spent his formative years in the royal court of France, had come to embrace Catholicism, if only in the privacy of his own quarters. Charles's brother, James, openly practiced Catholicism, creating anxiety and consternation among the political classes of England.

In the late 1670s and early 1680s, Charles's inability to produce an heir and fears of a popish plot to assassinate Charles and place his brother James on the throne provoked debates about the relationship of the king and his subjects. Led by the Earl of Shaftesbury (1621–1683), a coalition of members of Parliament, who came to be called Whigs, organized in 1679 a campaign to exclude the Catholic James from the throne. Charles responded to the so-called exclusion crisis by dissolving Parliament that summer; when he called two others, in 1680 and 1681, he found no way of compromising with the intransigent and increasingly inflammatory Whigs and did not summon another Parliament for the duration of his reign. The violent threats of the Whigs, who arrived armed at the parliamentary session of 1681, provoked a reaction in favor of Charles and James from people who feared another civil war. The king's supporters, called Tories, rallied to his efforts to remove Shaftesbury and other Whigs from local positions of power and gave James their unwavering loyalty.

James ascended the throne in 1685. Because he had no son to succeed him and because both of his daughters by his first wife, Mary (1662–1694) and Anne (1665–1714), were committed Protestants, James was perceived to pose no permanent threat to the Protestant nation. Eager to prevent any recurrence of another civil war, even Whigs swallowed their fears and agreed to let things take their course, confident that a Protestant succession would follow on James's death. But then, in January 1688, the court announced that James's wife of fifteen years, Mary of Modena (1658–1718), was pregnant, shocking all of James's subjects. The potential of a Catholic heir now loomed ominously, compelling a group of Tory and Whig leaders to bury their political differences at the prospect of an unlimited Catholic line of succession if the baby were to be a boy. They began to hatch a plan to invite William, Prince of Orange, the husband of the Protestant Mary, to invade England and secure the line of succession for his wife. At the same time, rumors that the queen's pregnancy was fraudulent began to circulate, claiming that her "great belly" was fake. In what became known as the warming pan scandal of 1688, Queen Mary was accused of having had her newborn son smuggled into her bedchamber in a warming pan rather than having given birth to him herself.

The Prince of Wales's birth provided a powerful justification for William's invasion of England, allowing him to defend the hereditary rights of his wife Mary to succession. As he asserted in his 1688 *Declaration . . . of the Reasons Inducing Him to Appear in Arms in the Kingdom of England*, "the just and visible grounds of suspicion [that] the Pretended Prince of Wales was not born by the Queen" compelled him to act.[1] As we shall see in the next chapter, the Glorious Revolution set off by the birth of a Catholic heir to the throne would have momentous consequences for all of the lands encompassed by the British empire.

Differences of politics, religion, wealth, economy, law, gender, ethnicity, and social structure characterized the four nations that comprised Great Britain in 1688. These were not equal lands or peoples. Rather, England dominated the others to varying degrees and the uneven nature of the relationships among the constituent countries and among and between their peoples provoked a great deal of struggle over the next three centuries. Indeed, Irish Catholics, and to a lesser extent Scottish Highlanders, felt themselves to be in a colonial position vis-à-vis England. In the actual colonies of North America and the Caribbean, English power in the guise of the law, merchants, and settlers prevailed, although over the course of the next two centuries empire would provide one of the only means by which a cohesive "Britishness" can be said to have existed.

NOTE

1. From Robert Beddard, ed., *A Kingdom without a King: The Journal of the Provisional Government in the Revolution of 1688* (Oxford, 1988), pp. 124–28; 145–49.

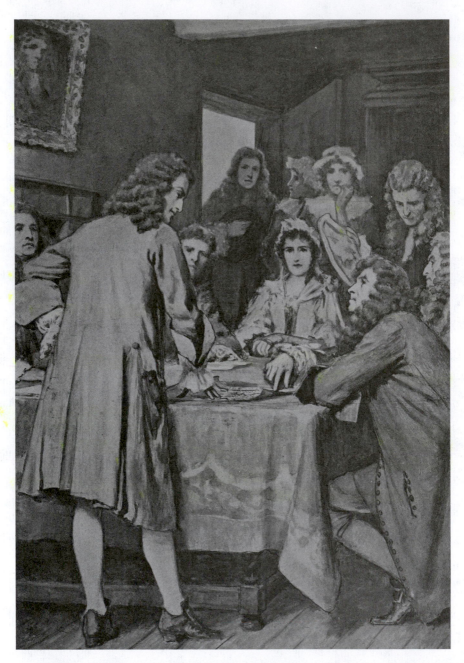

William Paterson explaining the Darien scheme to potential investors, Edinburgh, 1694.

CHAPTER 1

THE GLORIOUS REVOLUTION AND THE CREATION OF "BRITAIN," 1688–1707

In July 1698, 1,200 men and a handful of women and children set sail from the Scottish port of Leith to Darien—on the isthmus of Panama—where they planned to settle a new colony. Supplied with a year's worth of food, drink, and a ridiculously inappropriate array of goods they planned to offer for trade with local Indians, they made their way across the Atlantic Ocean, arriving at the site they would name New Edinburgh in November, having lost 44 of their party to "fever" and the "flux"—dysentery—en route. They planned to establish an entrepôt, or trading center, on the isthmus that would facilitate trade between both the East and the West Indies, thereby positioning Scottish merchants at the center of a lucrative commercial enterprise that would enable Scotland to claim an equal position of power with England.

The Darien venture proved to be a disaster. Not only were the settlers woefully unprepared for the environmental challenges posed by the climate and diseases of the region and incapable of defending themselves against the Spanish troops sent to recover the territory claimed by Spain, but they were also undermined at every turn by an England determined to see the colony fail. By October 1699, the roughly 700 survivors of the colony departed Darien; malnourished, beset by storms, and ravaged by disease, fewer than 300 made it back to Scotland. In the meantime, a second fleet of colonists had set out from Scotland to join what they had been led to believe was a thriving settlement. "Expecting to meet with our friends and countrymen," recalled one member of the second expedition, "we found nothing but a vast howling wilderness, the Colony deserted and gone, their huts all burnt, their fort most part ruined, the ground which they had cleared adjoining to the fort all overgrown with weeds; and we looked for Peace but no good came, and for a time of health and comfort, but beheld Trouble."[1] In April 1700, that group surrendered to the Spanish and abandoned the colony altogether.

From its inception to its ignominious failure, the Darien venture played a crucial role in the events that would lead to the creation of "Great Britain" in 1707 (the union would be augmented by the addition of Ireland in 1801). Its very conception lay in the inequities suffered by the Scots in their relationship with England, whereby they shared a king but nothing else. The circumstances of the Glorious Revolution—by which the Catholic James II lost his throne to the Protestant William and Mary and England entered into war against France—helped turn the dream of a colony in Darien into a concrete effort. Its abysmal failure, which involved the loss of about one-quarter of all the cash in Scotland, compelled powerful factions in both England and Scotland to admit of the necessity of a real union between the two kingdoms. Darien thus stands at the crossroads of the currents that would bind together the individual kingdoms of England and Wales, Scotland, and ultimately Ireland in a union known as the United Kingdom of Great Britain.

The Glorious Revolution of 1688, when William and Mary were invited to England to oust James II, exacerbated the tensions among the various countries that would comprise Great Britain, even as it ultimately created the conditions for formal union among them. These tensions—religious, ethnic, and political—would continue long after union was effected. Great Britain, in other words, far from being a united nation based on a common set of characteristics, was torn by rivalries, conflicts, and divisions. Only when it came to empire do we see any kind of common identity that we might describe as "British." Britishness thus constituted an imperial identity, not a national one; at home, Scottishness, Irishness, Welshness, and Englishness prevailed. And within each country, even these broad categories of belonging were frequent matters of contestation.

••

THE GLORIOUS REVOLUTION

William, Prince of Orange of the Netherlands, landed his troops in Devon in the West Country of England on November 5, 1688, setting off what contemporaries liked to style the Glorious Revolution. The revolution of 1688–1689, ostensibly bloodless, has conventionally marked the establishment in England of constitutional monarchy and the rule of law, dramatically transforming the nature of the English constitution and the relationship of the crown to Parliament. Parliament had, in essence, asserted its authority to remove one king from the throne and replace him with others. In combination with the Bill of Rights of 1689, which restricted the power of the monarchy by placing it under the law and asserted the sovereignty of Parliament, the revolutionary settlement implied that a social contract between crown and subjects existed, one that could be revoked and a monarch removed if he or she failed to fulfill its terms. Hereafter, sovereignty, the source of authority in the state, it might well appear, resided in the nation, marking a constitutional change of immense proportions.

But in Scotland and especially in Ireland, the Glorious Revolution and the revolutionary settlement it spawned had significantly different outcomes. In the short term, Scots found themselves economically disadvantaged vis-à-vis the English kingdom, a situation that brought about financial disaster and ultimately compelled them to give up their independent legislature and join with England in the United Kingdom of Great Britain in 1707. The Irish, riven by sectarian and ethnic divides, fared far worse, their country reduced to the status of a colony, to the surprise and dismay of the Protestant Anglo-Irish elites who had seen in William a champion of their cause. As a prominent Irish Member of Parliament (MP) noted a hundred years later, "glorious it certainly was for England—for Ireland it was disastrous in the extreme, and was attended with the most pernicious effects—the annihilation of her woollen manufacture—the extinction of her commerce, the total loss of her legislative independence."[2] The Bill of Rights that had secured the liberties of English subjects had placed Ireland in a position of subordination to the English monarchy.

William's landing evoked mass popular fervor for revolution across English towns and cities, a demonstration of support that was intensified by widespread rumors of Irish soldiers in James's employ intent on "cutting English Protestants' throats." James II had indeed brought troops from Scotland and Ireland to strengthen his garrison in Portsmouth in September and October, and an incident between some of the Irish troops and local townspeople had resulted in the deaths of 40 citizens. Knowledge of this event helped give credibility to the "Irish Fright" in November, when some of William's supporters warned Londoners that some 8,000 "armed papists" were on their way to carry out a massacre. From London the fright spread along roads and through the mails across the kingdom, leading Englishmen everywhere to take up arms. The Irish Fright convinced many potential supporters of James that armed resistance to William's forces was futile.[3] The Duke of Beaufort had committed himself to raising a force of 10,000 Welsh fighters for James, but was unable to make good on his promise. Many of the gentry of Wales, moreover, who as staunch Tories would have expected to support James, found his use of Irish troops anathema and stayed out of the fray.

As William's troops marched toward London in November and December of 1688, James fled the country for France. His flight provoked a constitutional crisis because now the throne was vacant, and what had started out as a campaign merely to secure the Protestant succession for James's daughter Mary, William's wife, turned into something quite different. William had not been asked to invade England to become king; nor had he intended to take that role in accepting the invitation. With James's abdication, however, there seemed to be little alternative. William summoned a convention in January 1689 to address the crisis, and after two weeks of wrangling, the MPs agreed to settle the crown jointly on William and Mary, which they did formally in April.

The Whigs and Tories who made the revolution of 1688–1689 had profound reservations about what they had done. They did not wish to be seen as revolutionaries, nor could they come to any agreement about what their actions constituted. Crises of conscience compelled contemporaries to devise various stories to justify what was in fact the overthrowing of a legitimate monarch by his rightful subjects. Furthermore, all kinds of questions concerning the relationship of the monarchy to its ministers, to Parliament, to political factions of court and country, and to the public arose, as did those seeking to inquire into the nature of loyalty and virtuous citizenship. Because many of these problems could not be resolved by the law, they were often framed in terms of gender. In other words, the uncertainties about authority and the exercise of power thrown up by the revolutionary settlement found their most satisfying expression in stories about or references to gender and sexuality. In each case, the resolution of issues articulated in gendered terms had profound implications both for women's relationship to power and for the relationships of men and women outside the political arena.

We have seen this already in the case of the warming pan scandal being used to explain William's invasion of England to oust James from the throne. This particular justification for the Glorious Revolution could not be sustained for long, however, because it flew in the face of William's political ambitions. The warming pan story gave rise to the claim that Mary's right to succession had been violated by the introduction of a suppositious son; the logical conclusion would have been for Parliament to crown her as James's legitimate heir, as indeed a number of MPs asserted it must. William, however, would not accept a situation in which he would be but his wife's "gentleman usher," as he put it. Insisting that "he would hold no power dependent upon the will of a woman," he demanded full executive power, which he refused to share with Mary or relinquish in the event of her death.[4] In the face of William's threats to withdraw his troops from England, leaving the door open for James's return, Parliament capitulated to his demands. In early February 1689, it placed the crown jointly in William and Mary's hands and made William the sole executive authority of the kingdom. In doing so, MPs made allusions to women's nature. Their assertions about the nature of women served to uphold a gender ideology that relegated women to private affairs.

The dangerous times, some Williamites claimed, meant that it was not "safe to trust the administration of affairs to a woman" and called for "a vigorous and masculine" administration. "A Man, by nature, education, and experience, is generally rendered more capable to govern than a woman," wrote one of William's supporters in 1689, and thus "the husband ought rather to rule the wife, than the wife the husband." William would protect and defend his wife and her kingdom, removing all of the disturbing aspects of rule and enabling her to "enjoy all the pleasure of being queen without any thing of trouble." Others argued that Mary constituted a security risk to the country, fearing that the guilt that "will perpetually assault her tender breasts" would induce her to let her father James back in. Evoking notions of women as weak-willed, frivolous, emotional, and inconstant, these arguments purportedly drawn from "nature" about femininity enabled the revolutionaries to obscure the contradictions of their actions. Mary, the legitimate heir to the throne, would succeed in name only. The de facto power of the monarchy rested with her husband, who possessed few legal grounds for his claim.[5]

Parliament dealt with William's lack of any constitutional claim to the throne by references to gender hierarchy within and legal strictures that pertained to marriage. Just as it was unthinkable for a woman to rule over her husband in marriage, so too was it unthinkable for William to subject himself to his wife's authority in the kingdom. "Does any think the Prince of Orange will come in to be a subject of his own wife in England?" scoffed one pro-William MP. "This is not possible, nor ought to be in Nature." The argument from marriage proved to be an effective one because it also raised the issue of coverture, under which a wife's property became the possession of her husband. Mary's property, including her estate in the crown, belonged to William. The law of coverture provided a legal coloration to William's claim to power, giving him, he insisted, "such a right as all the world knows to the succession of the crown." As it turned out, Mary herself invoked current thinking about gender to ratify the joint settlement of the crown. It was "unsuitable and ungrateful" and "not to be expected," she maintained, "that so generous and warlike a prince [as William] . . . would suffer his wife . . . to become his sovereign." "My opinion," she wrote later in her *Memoirs*, "has ever been that women should not meddle in government."[6]

In Ireland, news of William's landing in November 1688 sparked a protracted and bloody civil war between factions organized along religious lines. Some 2 million people inhabited the island, a large majority of whom were Catholic. Perhaps 25 percent of the Irish counted themselves as Protestants, and among those were a large number of Presbyterians of Scottish heritage living in the northern counties of Ulster. Protestants of the established Church of Ireland regarded themselves as the English-in-Ireland, or the Anglo-Irish, as historians have come to call them, and it was only the common threat of Catholicism that bound the two sectarian groups together. Protestants had felt themselves under threat in the years of James II's reign because he imposed Catholic administrators and military commanders on the country and instituted land policies that gave Catholics land formerly held by Protestants. The predominance of Catholic power in Ireland in the three years preceding the Glorious Revolution strongly influenced the response of Protestants to William's invasion of England.

Catholic Ireland gave its loyalty to James. In the countryside, poverty-stricken Catholic farmers rose against their Protestant landlords, killing thousands of cattle. Protestants in Derry (which Protestants always called Londonderry) in Ulster closed the city gates against the army led by the Catholic Earl of Tyrconnel (1630–1691) and declared their allegiance to the Prince of Orange. Irish Protestants in London persuaded William that a promise to give land confiscated from the Catholics to Protestants would supply him with an eager military force with which to confront the Catholic rebels, a move that forced the compromise-minded Tyrconnel to turn to France for assistance. By March 1689, when James returned to Ireland from France, Tyrconnel had placed virtually all of Ireland outside Ulster under Catholic administration.

James sought to make his stand against William from Ireland, which he regarded as the jumping-off point from which to secure Scotland. His attitude

A PLACE IN TIME

The Glorious Revolution in Liverpool

When William of Orange arrived in England in 1688 to overthrow James II and place his wife, Mary, on the throne, Liverpool became involved in the conflict almost immediately. One of the local landlords, the Catholic Lord Molyneux, sided with the king, and a force of regular soldiers occupied the town for a brief period. The other great lord in the area, Lord Derby, although a supporter of the king in the past, read the sentiment of the town notables correctly and declared for William, setting up the possibility of significant violence as the two factions squared off against one another. James's flight to Ireland in 1689 altered the situation entirely, eliminating the capacity of Molyneux to effectively oppose the usurper and freeing up the port to provide the ships that would ferry William's soldiers across the Irish Sea to Ulster in pursuit of the erstwhile king.

William's wars with France benefitted Liverpool at the expense of those port towns in the south, especially London. As the French navy and French pirates patrolled the waters of the English Channel, merchants from London and Southampton determined that it would be much safer to transport their American imports by way of Ireland and land them at Liverpool, thence to carry them overland to London rather than risk them being taken in the English Channel. Pirates trolled the Irish Sea, certainly, and posed a threat to English ships, as one report from 1690 attests: it noted "fifteen privateers and two French men-of-war waiting nigh the north channel for the return of the West India ships belonging to Liverpool."[7] The dangers of piracy and sinking by French ships in the channel, however, proved to be far greater than those of the Irish Sea, and the merchants of the south turned increasingly to the Liverpool fleet to conduct their trade with the Americas and the Caribbean, expanding it considerably in the twenty-five-year period during which hostilities with France occurred.

The Glorious Revolution dramatically altered the political landscape of Liverpool, establishing the Whig faction's dominance in power in Liverpool for the next century. Supported by the bulk of the town's residents and especially by its wealthy merchants, Liverpool's Whig politicians in Parliament persuaded the new king and queen to issue a new charter in 1695. This document, which remained in place until 1835, granted the burgesses the right to elect their mayor and created a forty-member town council. Whig merchants took by far the majority of seats on the council and ushered in a new regime that reflected the commercial character of the borough. The merchant interest—which included some Tories as well—proceeded to implement a series of reforms and improvements that led to remarkable changes to the status and the physical layout of Liverpool, positioning it to become in a short amount of time a world-class imperial city.

In 1697 the mayor of Liverpool initiated steps to make the borough its own parish, separate from that of Walton, under which it currently operated. Town councilors petitioned Parliament for an act that would do so, pointing out that because their municipality had "become a place of great trade and commerce, and very populous," the chapel that served them was not sufficient to meet the needs of its residents. Moreover, and indicative of the importance residents had begun to recognize they held in the affairs of the country, the petition noted that Liverpudlians "are desirous to be a parish of themselves."[8] Parliament granted parish status in 1699, at which point the townspeople commenced the building of a new church befitting its new standing, St. Peter's.

More significantly for Liverpool's future, the town councilors in 1708 voted to build a dock. Ships had to drop anchor in the Mersey and load and unload their cargoes onto and from small boats that plied the river from shore. The tidal flow of the Mersey made the transfers difficult at times; a dock would enable ships to tie up and lie without having to worry about the ebb and flow of the tides and facilitate the movement of cargo. Completed in 1715 at great expense, the dock gave Liverpool a pronounced competitive advantage over rival port cities. After seeing the newly built dock when he visited the town, Daniel Defoe declared Liverpool "one of the wonders of Britain."[9] Within a short few years, its role in global commerce and the prosperity it produced would make it one of the most important cities in the world.

Liverpool docks, c. 1830.

toward Irish Catholics, despite his own Catholicism, proved ambivalent because he needed to present a reasonable face to English and Scottish Protestants if he hoped to regain his throne. That and his own interests led him to resist many of the efforts of Irish Catholics in the Irish Parliament of 1689 to restore the Catholic church to a position of supremacy or to separate the country from England. His hopes of reconciliation with Protestants created a great many anxieties for his Catholic supporters. In the meantime, in Derry, 30,000 Protestants determined to withstand a siege by Jacobite forces (so called because *Jacobus* is the Latin term for James). For three months the Derry Protestants held their ground, staving off starvation by consuming the dog, cat, and rat populations of the city, until they were relieved by forces loyal to William.

In August 1689, a Williamite army of some 20,000 arrived in Ireland, causing tensions between Catholics and Protestants in Dublin to intensify. But little military confrontation ensued throughout the fall and winter because weather conditions made it difficult for both the Jacobite and the Williamite armies to successfully position themselves. In the spring of 1690, French troops reinforced James's army; frustrated by the inaction of his general, William himself landed near Belfast in June with 15,000 additional soldiers, intent on defeating his rival once and for all.

The armies met at the Boyne River, northwest of Dublin, on July 1, 1690. After extensive bombardment and fierce hand-to-hand fighting, William's forces prevailed, sending James's troops—and James himself—scurrying south. James's commanders fired on their soldiers to regain control and establish an orderly retreat, although James continued his headlong flight, overnighting in Dublin on his way to Duncannon, whence he embarked to France, never to return to his kingdoms. War continued without him, although the Battle of the Boyne has been seen as the decisive campaign in the Jacobite wars against William. Dublin fell to the new king, as did Athlone a year later, which opened up Galway to English depredations. The final battle between Jacobite and Williamite troops took place in Aughrim in July 1691, resulting in horrific casualties for the Irish army. Retreating to Limerick, where it could still assemble a force of 20,000, the soldiers awaited French aid. When it was not forthcoming, the Jacobites, more demoralized than defeated, sued for peace.

The Treaty of Limerick, signed on October 3, 1691, ended the conflict between Ireland and England, but it served to inflame the passions of the very Anglo-Irish Protestants who supposed themselves to have emerged victorious because William's agents failed to take Anglo-Irish interests into account as they drafted the terms of what they regarded as an instrument merely to end the war, not to establish a postwar civil administration. To that end, the articles of Limerick guaranteed that Catholics should "enjoy such Privileges in the Exercise of their Religion as are consistent with the Laws of Ireland; or as they did enjoy in the Reign of King Charles II," and they gave the privileged group of Jacobite landowners who were in Limerick at the time of the surrender the right to retain their estates, practice as barristers and attorneys, and enjoy exemption from suits for acts of war or debt. Other Catholics enjoyed no such provisions, nor did Anglo-Irish

James II entering Dublin after the Battle of the Boyne, 1690.

Protestants, whose resentment over this slight would color their attitudes toward the English Parliament and the English king in subsequent years. It also set the stage for the draconian legislation aimed at Irish Catholics, known as the penal laws, that would flow from the Irish parliamentary sessions of 1692, 1695, 1697, and 1698–1699, as we shall see below.

If Anglo-Irish approbation for William and for the English Parliament proved inconstant in the years following the defeat of James's forces, the Welsh, whose Tory leanings might have inclined them in the same direction, positively embraced William's Irish policies. William's defeat of Jacobite forces in Ireland had rendered the Welsh coasts secure, an achievement that overrode whatever differences they might have had with him. Welsh elites increasingly turned their eyes toward London, where they would play a significant role in the governance of their own country and that of what would become Great Britain in 1707.

In Scotland, the ancestral home of the Stuart line to which James belonged (when he became king of England as well as Scotland in 1601, the Stewart James I anglicized his name to Stuart), the news of William's landing in Devon did not provoke a rising against the Scottish king. Presbyterians did riot in the capital city of Edinburgh, burning a Catholic monastery, and Covenanters throughout the Lowlands forced Anglican ministers from their livings, but James felt secure enough in the loyalty of the Scots to actually send his Scottish army south to fight William's forces. That turned out to be a mistake, and when James fled to France in December 1688, his supporters did not know what to do. Many of them, eager to be seen on the side of the victor, traveled to London to declare themselves for William. He capitalized on this development to call for a convention parliament in Scotland, just as he had in England. When it met in March 1689, the supporters of James and those of William were about evenly matched.

James, however, squandered his strength. Where William sought to placate convention members, offering conciliatory gestures, James threatened them with treason. His behavior led his former supporters to abandon his cause; in April, the convention proclaimed that James had "Forefaulted the right to the Croune" and offered the crown to William and Mary. In a Claim of Right, the Scottish convention also established parliamentary supremacy over the monarchy, disestablished the Episcopalian church in favor of the Presbyterian church, and declared that no Catholic could ever become king of Scotland. A separate Articles of Grievance sought to cripple the authority of the crown by abolishing the Lords of the Articles, the committee appointed by the monarch that conducted the business of the Scottish Parliament. William chafed against these restrictions, but his dependence on Scotland for military support in his struggles against France's Louis XIV limited his room to maneuver.

The actions of the convention provoked opposition among some of the Scottish Highland clans. Moreover, William had not appreciated the extent to which his appointments in Scotland inflamed an already feuding clan culture. Viscount Dundee (1648–1689) rallied a number of Highland families to his standard and in July 1689 marched them into battle against a larger Williamite army. Vastly outnumbered, they nevertheless soundly defeated the royal forces at the Pass of Killiecrankie. The Glorious Revolution might have turned out differently had Dundee not been killed in the battle; his death left the Jacobite forces without the kind of leadership they would need to emerge victorious. The next two years saw a series of bloody encounters between Jacobites and Williamites; neither side could prevail, and the impasse led William to offer an amnesty to the Highland rebels in return for their oath of allegiance to him.

It was left to William's Scottish secretary of state, Sir John Dalrymple (1648–1707), the Master of Stair, to carry out the arrangements of this truce. Dalrymple despised the Highland clans and hoped that by imposing a strict deadline for the oath-swearing he might catch some of them in violation of it. Most of the clans came in on time, however reluctant they were to capitulate to their enemies. One family, however, the MacIans (part of the Macdonald clan), got caught in a blizzard and missed the deadline by six days. Dalrymple sought his revenge in a despicable act of dishonor.

He sent a company of Campbells—bitter foes of the Macdonalds—to the Glencoe site of the MacIans, where the troops claimed hospitality. To have refused it would have gone against all Highland tradition, so the MacIans allowed the Campbells to ensconce themselves in their homes and enjoy room and board there for two weeks. In the middle of one night in February 1692, the Campbells rose from their beds and murdered all the MacIan men, women, and children they could lay their hands on. Many escaped, but some forty MacIans lay slaughtered in what came to be called the Massacre at Glencoe.

William may or may not have known about the massacre in advance, but whatever his involvement, the incident discredited him in the eyes of Highlanders for the remainder of his reign. The fact that he did nothing to punish the offenders only strengthened the case against him. Glencoe served in the short run to bring the Highlanders to heel, but they never forgot the treachery of William's Master of Stair and would continue to foment instability in Scotland for the next fifty years.

In the colonies of the Americas, the Glorious Revolution produced a wave of political upheaval. Rumors of a variety of plots to institute "popery and slavery" by French Jesuits, Irish servants, and enslaved Africans swept through Barbados in late 1688; in modified form, including Indians now, they reached New England in January 1689 and took hold in the western reaches of Maryland and Virginia in March. By April news of William's invasion, James's abdication, and the creation of a new government under William and Mary had arrived, setting off demonstrations calling for political change, first in Boston and then throughout many of the other colonies. These protests compelled the ouster of a number of colonial governors, leaving political disorder in their wake.

THE REVOLUTIONARY SETTLEMENT AND THE FINANCIAL REVOLUTION

The revolutionary settlement of 1688–1689 marked the establishment in England and Wales of constitutional monarchy and the rule of law, transforming the nature of the English constitution and the relationship of crown to Parliament. Parliament's assertion of its authority to remove one king from the throne and replace him with others, along with its passage of the Bill of Rights of 1689, which restricted the power of the crown by placing it under the law and asserted the sovereignty of Parliament, dramatically altered the nature and practice of government in England and Wales. The revolution concretized the radical notion that a social contract between crown and subjects existed, one that could be revoked and a monarch removed if he failed to fulfill its terms. Indeed, John Locke published his *Two Treatises on Government* in 1689 (although he wrote it in 1679 at the time of the exclusion crisis), a work that explored the conditions under which a monarch might be overthrown by his or her subjects. It came to serve as the theoretical justification for the settlement of 1689 by establishing men's right to resist tyranny and stands as a founding doctrine of liberalism. Hereafter, sovereignty, the source of authority in the state, the revolution suggested, resided in the people of the nation. MPs differed from this interpretation, seeing Parliament and its elite representatives as the "nation" and therefore the source of authority, but the notion of the right of "the people" to determine their government would endure and inform later campaigns to broaden the scope of political participation to include first middle-class men and women and then working-class men and women. For the next seventy-five years or so, however, the Glorious Revolution ensconced in power an oligarchy of Protestant landed and financial elites who ruled by virtue of their domination of Parliament and of the financial institutions that grew out of the deal struck with William to oust James. The alliance of these elites—gentlemen whose wealth derived from land and financiers whose riches came from banking, investment, and the provision of financial services to commercial enterprises—and the political and economic regime over which they presided has been described by two historians as "gentlemanly capitalism."[10] It determined the shape of things to come for the next century and a half.

The Bill of Rights (1689) established the supremacy of Parliament through a series of provisions stipulating that no laws should be made or suspended without the consent of Parliament; that no taxes could be raised without consent of Parliament; that no army could be maintained in peacetime without consent of Parliament; and that Protestants possessed the right to bear arms for their defense. The religious qualification had significant ramifications for Catholics in Ireland and Scotland, in particular, singling them out, among other things, as subjects underserving of the protections and rights afforded their Protestant brethren. Parliament insisted that William and Mary accept the Bill of Rights as a condition of their rule. The two monarchs agreed to the constraints on their power; the opportunity, especially for William, was simply far too great to pass up.

William had agreed to invade England to obtain English resources with which to fight Louis XIV of France. The revolutionary settlement of 1689 obligated England to assist him in that battle, a commitment that had unforeseen consequences in a continued series of continental wars throughout the eighteenth century. To provide the troops and revenue necessary to prosecute King William's War (also known as the War of the League of Augsburg, 1689–1697), the government created a number of institutions of public credit that enabled it to tap the wealth of the country without resorting to taxation or short-term borrowing. Chief among the mechanisms developed by the government to facilitate access to private caches of money and treasures that were literally lying around in safes or buried underground were the creation of the national debt and of the agency charged with administering it, the Bank of England. By 1696, a system of permanent borrowing was in place whereby investors could buy annuities from the bank that would guarantee them an income from the state, thus transforming what had once been short-term loans to the state by individuals or corporate entities into government securities. These investments provided the government with much of the cash necessary to prosecute the wars with France that took place over the next century.

The financial revolution of the 1690s, but most particularly the creation of the Bank of England and the national debt, provoked heated political debate. At issue was the question of personal independence of the sovereign power: the Bank of England, in establishing the means by which government could tap the wealth of the country and of Wales by inducing investors to lend capital and, not incidentally, greater political stability to the state, rendered those investors captive to the state for their material survival. Also, by financing the creation of larger armies and permanent bureaucracies, it enlarged the fund of patronage available to the court. As the volume of investment grew ever greater, the English—and then, after 1707 with the Act of Union with Scotland, the British—government expanded the scope and range of its activities beyond what the investment could cover, guaranteeing creditors that they would be repaid with revenues collected and investments made in the future. Mobile property in the form of government shares based on credit emerged as the engine of capitalist expansion; the financial revolution succeeded in enriching, enlarging, and stabilizing the postrevolutionary regime, making possible the commercial revolution and the pursuit of empire in the eighteenth century.

Scotland had carried on a robust trade with a number of European countries, but neither it nor Ireland could gain a foothold in the commercial ventures that appeared to make England so powerful. English tariffs on such vital Scottish exports as linen, cattle, salt, and coal reduced Scotland's commercial prospects even further. Moreover, William's war with France, lasting from 1688 to 1697, crippled Scotland's trade with the continent. Reduced trade combined with bad harvests to produce terrible economic conditions in Scotland in the 1690s. The years 1696 to 1699 saw outright famine among the poorer classes in certain areas.

A number of Scottish merchants joined with colleagues from London in 1693 to try to create for themselves a monopoly company like the East India or Royal African companies. Led by the Scot William Paterson (1658–1719), who had played a central role in the establishment of the Bank of England, these merchants formed the Company of Scotland Trading to Africa and the Indies. Two years later, while the Scottish Parliament was preoccupied with the report of a commission formed to investigate the massacre at Glencoe by William's secretary of state for Scotland, John Dalrymple, it passed a law authorizing the company. The great outcry caused by the Glencoe commission report, which blamed Dalrymple for the bloody massacre, enabled the supporters of the Company of Scotland to persuade MPs to seek immediate royal assent from the king's beleaguered commissioner to Parliament, the Marquess of Tweeddale (1625–1697). Faced with a Parliament full of men eager to wreak vengeance on the perpetrators of the massacre, Tweeddale capitulated. William returned from his campaign against Louis XIV on the continent to discover that his Scottish Parliament had passed an act deeply harmful to English commercial interests and had done so without his knowledge or his permission. "I have been ill-served in Scotland," he railed, and added, portentously, "I hope some remedies may be found to prevent the inconveniences which may arise from this Act."[11]

The king dared not repeal the act because of his need for Scottish troops and resources with which to fight France, but his displeasure with it emboldened the monopoly companies and their bought men in the English Parliament to forbid English participation in the new company. This and the king's comment enraged the Scots, compelling Andrew Fletcher (1655–1716) of Saltoun to remind his contemporaries that "we voted His Majesty a standing army, though we had more need to have saved the money to have bought bread, for thousands of our people that were starving. . . . Have not the Scots ever since the Union of the Crowns been oppressed and tyrannised over by a faction in England, who will neither admit of an [sic] Union of the Nations, nor leave the Scots in possession of their own privileges, as men and Christians?"[12] Their patriotism aroused, Scots from across the Lowlands paid subscriptions into the company, raising the £400,000 necessary to launch the Scots Company in just more than five months.

Fully capitalized now, the directors of the company had to decide where they would establish their colony. William Paterson, who had spent a number of years in the Caribbean in his younger days and had heard tales of Darien from buccaneers and pirates he associated with, proposed Darien as the ideal place for establishing factories (warehouses) and forts from which goods from the west could be traded for those of the east and vice versa. Straddling the isthmus of Panama, the colony would serve as a trading post between the Atlantic and the Pacific, making it unnecessary for merchants to travel the long route to the east along the coast of Africa to the Indian Ocean. "The time and expense of navigation to China, Japan and the Spice Islands," he insisted, "and the far greatest part of the East Indies will be lessened by more than half, and the consumption of European commodities and manufactories will soon be more than doubled. Trade will increase trade, and money will beget money, and the trading world shall need no more to want work for their hands, but will rather want hands for their work. Thus this door of the seas, and the key of the universe, with anything of a sort of reasonable management, will of course enable its proprietors to give laws to both oceans, without being liable to the fatigues, expenses and dangers, or contracting the guilt and blood of Alexander and Caesar."[13]

Paterson regaled the directors with descriptions of the area provided by a buccaneer and surgeon of his acquaintance, one Lionel Wafer. Wafer offered an enchanting vision of the isthmus, charming the directors with descriptions of a sunlit paradise by a turquoise sea, a land teeming with animals and birdlife, possessed of valuable woodlands, fertile soil, and grassy pastures. The Indians were friendly, he assured them. The directors also read but paid no attention to Wafer's accounts of the rain—endless rains, rains lasting from April till December, rains that swamped the marshes and flooded the rivers, rains that brought scores upon scores upon scores of mosquitos. "Uneasy vermin," he called them. But to men ensconced in their counting houses in squalid, dirty, gray Edinburgh, dreaming of the riches to come, it was easy to overlook the warnings issued by Wafer and to fail to ask themselves why, if Darien possessed such wonderful qualities, the Spanish had not settled there when they had established themselves in the lands to the east, west, and south of it. The directors chalked it up to stupidity and convinced themselves that because Darien was not inhabited by Spaniards, it was open to any country who wished to claim it.

The fantasies of the company directors gained momentum from the desperate economic conditions faced by Scots. The long, cold winters of 1696–1698 decimated the harvests so that food shortages turned into famine for many families. Starvation, malnutrition, and disease carried off untold thousands, and thousands more unemployed—many of them men returning from William's wars with France—crowded the streets and public houses of towns and cities. To them, the Darien scheme, offering each settler fifty acres on which to build a house and plant their fields, seemed an opportunity they could not let pass them by. As Andrew Fletcher put it, the Darien venture appeared to be "the only means to recover us from our miserable and despicable condition."[14] This kind of despair probably led the Scots Company to buy up virtually all the provisions Scotland had to offer, leaving little behind with which to feed a hungry population or to resupply the colonists if it came to that. Along with the stores of grain and wheat carried on board the five ships headed for Darien were inventories of goods the directors intended to trade with local inhabitants: hats, wigs, men's and women's hosiery, combs, 25,000 pairs of shoes, cloth, needles, thread, pewter jugs and basins, and 1,000 glass drinking cups. In London in the meantime, although the Scots did not know it, the directors of the East India, Royal African, and Hamburg companies schemed to thwart the Scots Company by any means they could. Such was their influence that they persuaded the Lords Justices and the Commissioners for Trade to declare the colony antithetical to the interests of the English and their Spanish allies and compelled William's agents to issue a royal proclamation forbidding the governors of any English colonies to offer even the slightest bit of assistance to any ship flying the flag of the Company of Scotland. At a time when Spain's support of William's efforts to oppose Louis XIV's efforts to establish a "universal monarchy" over Europe was crucial, William could not afford to antagonize the Spanish.

The colonists arrived in what they would call New Edinburgh in October 1698 and began to build a fort to defend their entrepôt. The site chosen made good sense militarily, but in other respects it proved entirely wrong-headed. The colonists situated the fort on low-lying marshy ground, the perfect environment for mosquitos. Within seven weeks of landing, thirty-two Scots died, a rate that came to five per week, ten times the rate Europeans experienced back home. And this at the healthiest time of year on the isthmus! As the rainy season began in April 1699, death rates resulting from illness—probably a combination of yellow fever, malaria, dysentery, and dengue fever—doubled to roughly ten persons per day. Food and drink began to run out; old clan rivalries arose; conflicts among the expedition's leaders broke out. When colonists sailed to seek help from other English settlements in the Caribbean, their ship foundered. Worst of all, news of the king's proclamation to all of his subjects in the New World to refuse help to the Scots Company reached the Darien colonists, destroying their morale. Then word that the Spanish planned to attack the colony arrived in early June; four days later, panic stricken, the colonists fled. Their trip home was, if possible, even more lethal than their stay on the isthmus: only 300 survivors returned to Scotland.

A second fleet of colonists left Scotland just days before the first arrived home, landing in New Edinburgh in November 1699. Once again, rains brought mosquito-borne illnesses and rotted food supplies. By late March 1700, 100 Scots per week died from fever; when Spanish troops attacked the outpost, about a third of the remaining colonists could not stand, leaving just 300 men to defend the colony. Facing impossible odds and almost certain death from fever, they surrendered to the Spanish and in April departed the colony entirely. Of the 1,300 who had set out on the second voyage, only 100 made it back. The total losses among the two sets of colonists amounted to 2,000 of 2,500, or some 80 percent. Investors lost all of the £300,000 they had shelled out, a crippling blow to the finances of the kingdom.

Scots reacted to the disasters of Darien with rage. They attacked Englishmen in the streets wherever they could find them; they set on the poor survivors of the expeditions, whom they identified by their sallow yellow complexions and their tattered scarlet uniforms. They excoriated Scots Company directors. Most of all, they blamed the king, whose obstructions of and failure to support the colony of Darien, they believed with all their heart, lay at the core of the catastrophe. When the king dismissed out of hand Scottish MPs demands to call Parliament into session to investigate the events of Darien, riots broke out in Edinburgh. National feeling in favor of the Scots Company and the Scottish Parliament, and against the king and the English Parliament, rose to a fever pitch. When the Scottish Parliament met in the summer of 1700, MPs wished to discuss only two issues: whether to make another claim to Darien despite William's opposition and whether to agree to provide William with the military support he needed to continue his wars with France. These two issues, seemingly independent of one another, soon became fused in the minds of MPs as they deliberated.

The death of the Duke of Gloucester (1689–1700), the last surviving child of Anne, Mary's sister and heir to the throne, in August 1700 and the accession of Philip of Anjou, Louis XIV's candidate, to the Spanish throne three months later, sharpened the debate further. Mary had died childless in 1694; William continued to rule but his lack of heirs meant that Mary's sister, Anne, would ascend to the throne on his death, which occurred in 1702. Anne had tried valiantly to produce an heir, undergoing seventeen pregnancies. Tragically, seven of them ended in miscarriages and five in stillbirths; two infants died within a day of their births and two others before they reached the age of two years. The death of the Duke of Gloucester meant that the succession of the Stuart line now appeared unsettled at best, and the prospect of a universal French monarchy in Europe looked all the more possible. In 1701, the English Parliament passed the Act of Settlement, which placed the succession of the throne in the hands of the German Hanoverians, without consulting the Scots.

THE ACT OF UNION, 1707

In this atmosphere of tension, distrust, and uncertainty, the actions of Scottish MPs vis-à-vis their king took on enormous significance. The Edinburgh Parliament passed the Act of Security in 1703, giving the right to proclaim the Scottish monarch to the Scots themselves in their Parliament. It also declared that the monarch so chosen must hail from the Stuart line, must be a Protestant, and could not be the same monarch who sat on the throne of England unless England recognized the sovereignty of the Scottish Parliament, acknowledged its religious liberties, and allowed for free trade between Scotland and England. These provisions outraged the English, who responded with the Aliens Act of 1705, which threatened that the Scots would be declared aliens unless the Act of Security was rescinded. Such a designation would have stripped Scots of their rights of citizenship in England, enabled Scottish ships trading with France to be captured or destroyed, and blocked all trade goods coming into England. Things could not have been any hotter.

Nor, ironically, could they have been more promising for an act of union between the two kingdoms. William had long sought a formal union between England and Scotland, but could not persuade elites in either country to go along with his plans. Anne, who became queen in 1702 following her brother-in-law's death, continued his war against France and could not afford an unstable Scotland through which the French might mount an attack on England. The Scots had been so financially devastated by the losses of Darien and made so completely aware that their economy could not hope to survive against a hostile England that they were willing to compromise. It helped a great deal that the English were willing to offer, in the form of an "Equivalent," a significant sum of money with which to compensate Scottish elites for the extra taxes they would be required to pay by joining England in formal union, but also to cover their huge losses from the Darien debacle.

The Scots agreed to suspend the Act of Security at the end of 1705, allowing commissioners appointed by Anne to write up an agreement of union in the summer of 1706. By it, both Scotland and England would disappear as sovereign entities and be recreated as northern and southern components of a single, sovereign United Kingdom of Great Britain. Scotland would give up its Parliament, but not its legal system or its Presbyterian church, and it would gain, in the long run, significant economic benefits as an integral part of the British empire.

Forty-five Scottish members would sit in the House of Commons in Westminster, representing the counties and burghs (towns or cities), and sixteen Scottish peers (aristocrats) would sit in the House of Lords.

Act of Union between England and Scotland read before Queen Anne in 1707.

Relative to the English and Welsh Members of Parliament, who numbered 513 in the House of Commons alone, these figures vastly underrepresented Scotland's population, but when seen against the revenues it would contribute to Great Britain's overall tax revenues counted in 1706 pounds, Scottish MPs found it hard to quibble. The English Parliament passed the Act of Union with hardly a word of dissent, but the bill faced significant opposition inside and outside the Scottish Parliament. After much heated debate and extraparliamentary demonstrations that turned riotous, the Equivalent and, it must be said, additional monetary bribes, carried the day, and the Scots agreed to the Act of Union in 1707. With ratification of the bill, the Company of Scotland—and its signature failure, Darien—ceased to exist.

Almost immediately, the Act of Union provoked a resurgence of the Jacobite cause. Supporters of the Stuart line—exemplified after the death of James II in 1701 by his young son, James, styled James III (1688–1766)—regarded the union as perpetuating the Glorious Revolution and ensuring that the Stuart pretender could not regain his rightful crown. Their implacable opposition to the revolutionary settlement and now the union received a powerful shot in the arm by the willingness of France, engaged with Britain in the War of the Spanish Succession (1702–1713), to supply military resources to the Jacobites. With the public commitment of France the credibility of the Jacobites soared, attracting additional followers who in the past would have been wary of joining a losing effort. In March 1708, the French gathered an invasion force of ships and soldiers and sailed with the twenty-year-old James to the Firth of Forth, where a large contingent of Scottish Jacobites awaited them. Bad weather and incompetent piloting thwarted the rendezvous, and then a squadron of the Royal Navy scared off the French, but had they landed and formed up with the Jacobites, a significant force could well have overwhelmed the 1,500 troops available to defend Edinburgh. As it turned out, Scottish authorities took few punitive actions against the Jacobites in the aftermath of the failed rising of 1708; in response, the United Kingdom Parliament extended the English law of treason to Scotland in 1709, despite the efforts of Scottish MPs to block the measure. For now, the supporters of the Stuarts went underground, but their efforts to destabilize the new United Kingdom of Great Britain would continue to cause great concern in London.

The Act of Union between Scotland and England struck Protestant Ireland like a hammer blow, for it contrasted sharply with the position Ireland found itself in after the Treaty of Limerick. Protestants, especially the Episcopal Anglo-Irish, had expected to be treated as partners in the Glorious Revolution; they would have dearly loved to form a union with England. The Treaty of Limerick gave the first sign that such hopes were misplaced. Appointments of Englishmen rather than Anglo-Irishmen to prominent positions in the Irish established church, the legal system, and the armed forces, as well as the granting of Irish peerages to Englishmen who had no relationship with the country, caused deep resentment. England's viceroy to Ireland, Henry Sidney (1641–1704), reported with alarm in 1692 that Irish MPs spoke of "freeing themselves from the yoke of England, of taking away Poynings' Law, of making an address to have a habeas corpus bill, and twenty other extravagant discourses."[15] (Poynings' Law of 1494, as we saw in the Introduction, had subordinated the Irish Parliament to that of Westminster.) Commercial interests in England regarded Ireland as a threat to their trade and were sufficiently well placed to push through legislation in 1696 that prohibited goods of any kind from the American colonies from landing in Ireland. England treated Ireland not as a partner or a sister kingdom, but as a colony. It rankled.

In 1697, two events provoked a showdown between the Irish and English parliaments. In the first instance, MPs representing the woolen manufacturers in the West Country of England introduced a bill that would make it difficult for the Irish wool traders to export their goods to England. In the second, England

MAP 1.1
The United Kingdom, 1707

questioned the right of the Irish House of Lords to act as an appellate body, as it did in England. These provocations led the Bishop of Derry to declare that England had reduced Ireland to a state of slavery; they also compelled MP William Molyneux (1656–1698) to write *The Case of Ireland's Being Bound by*

Acts of Parliament in England Stated, in which he argued that if union with England could not be achieved ("an Happiness we can hardly hope for"[16]), Irish parliamentary rights must be strengthened and protected. Ireland should not be lumped in with those "colonies of outcasts in America," he insisted[17]; rather, it should be recognized as a crucial component within England's empire, an equal to England, with Irish representation in the English Parliament as a means of defending Irish interests. Molyneux's treatise raised the hackles of the English, who pretended to hear in his writings a call for separation from England. They painted him and those many others who thought the same way he did with the brush of "independency" and "Jacobitism," levying charges that the Anglo-Irish could not possibly allow to stand. Although support for Molyneux's position was fairly broad, the Anglo-Irish community backed off from his demands.

The union of England and Scotland in 1707 added insult to injury. Jonathan Swift (1667–1745), the Anglo-Irish satirist, penned *The Story of the Injured Lady, Being a True Picture of Scotch Perfidy, Irish Poverty, and English Partiality* in response to the slap in the face he and others experienced with the Act of Union. For now, in light of the Scottish and English union, Ireland looked more and more like a colony, a position the Anglo-Irish could do little to improve. Conflicts and contests between the two parliaments continued, until in 1720, with the Declaratory Act—"An Act for better securing the dependency of Ireland"—the now-British Parliament explicitly established that it had every power to enact legislation for Ireland. As it turned out, the Declaratory Act was rarely invoked because Westminster knew well that Ireland could not be governed by force; a significant amount of cooperation from the Anglo-Irish was necessary for things to run as smoothly as they did after 1720. Nevertheless, the Anglo-Irish sense of wounded pride, economic deprivation, political oppression, and cultural disrespect remained high throughout the eighteenth century.

A "UNITED" KINGDOM?

Despite the Act of Union of 1707, the lands that made up the British Isles could not be said to constitute a kingdom united by a common culture, religion, political structure, or history. We have seen how the individual kingdoms responded politically to the Glorious Revolution, fomenting rivalries and even hatreds against one another, and will develop this theme in the next chapter. Divisions *within* each component country rendered some individuals less eligible for various "rights" established by the revolutionary settlement than others. Established churches in Scotland and Ireland—Presbyterian and Episcopalian, respectively—discriminated against other sects and religions and held dominant positions in public, political, and social life. Even in England and Wales, where the Glorious Revolution found nearly universal approbation, differences based on religion made some people subject to laws that restricted their ability to participate in public and political affairs.

The revolutionary settlement accepted by William and Mary included a Toleration Act, which allowed dissenters to conduct their religious lives openly and without harassment. Beyond that simple measure, however, toleration encompassed little else. It did not apply to Catholics or Jews. Earlier acts—the Corporation Act of 1662 and the Test Act of 1673—that prohibited dissenters from holding local or national political office remained in force. Anglicans enjoyed preeminence in virtually every secular institution in England and Wales, dominating the political landscape, the universities and public schools, and the offices of the army and navy. To be sure, dissenters found ways to get around the restrictions on their activities, such as taking communion in the Anglican church once a year to qualify for public office, a practice known as occasional conformity. They also built their own institutions of higher learning in London and other cities where their numbers thrived. Jews maintained a relatively low-profile presence, protected by William himself, who had long-standing dealings with Amsterdam Jews as *staatholder* of Holland and who relied on Jewish funds for pay for his armies on the continent. But memories of the momentous events of mid-century, during which a monarch was not only toppled but also killed by Protestants dissenting from the principles and organization of the Anglican church in 1649, and a new monarch and the Anglican church restored in 1660, kept religious tensions, distrust, and outright hostility alive and active for years after the Glorious Revolution. Tories in particular objected to the capacity of dissenters to circumvent restrictions on them and sought continually to undermine toleration. Some of their antipathy to toleration extended to the Glorious Revolution itself and manifested itself in adherence to the Jacobite cause, as we shall see in the next chapter.

In Scotland, religion combined with geography and culture to produce deep divisions among Scots. Unlike in England and Wales, Presbyterians became the masters of the established church, ousting Episcopalians in the course of the Glorious Revolution and imposing their own kirk organization and principles. This involved abolishing the episcopacy of bishops, a course that more than half of them refused to accept. Many Episcopalians also refused to swear an oath of allegiance to William and Mary because it flew in the face of their oath to submit to royal authority and their belief in the hereditary principle of kingship. These nonjurors, as they were called, inhabited a large portion of the Scottish Highlands and, along with their compatriots in the Lowlands, they would contribute significantly to the Jacobite cause following the Glorious Revolution. Catholics, too, although constituting only a tiny proportion of the overall Scottish population, would play a larger role in Jacobite risings than their demographic strength would suggest. Living in parts of the northeastern and western Highlands and discriminated against by penal laws passed in 1689, they brought a commitment to the cause that other Scots did not necessarily possess. They could also appeal to the Catholic powers of Europe, particularly France, for assistance in returning the Stuarts to the throne.

But it was the Presbyterian Lowlands that achieved ascendancy in Scotland. Although they might have been divided over issues of religious purity, Presbyterians dominated in the church, in the law, in politics, and in the extraordinary educational system of the country. Their culture, their attitudes, and their values prevailed, and it was they who benefitted from the union with England. Their relationship with Episcopalians, Catholics, and Highlanders would remain fraught right into the nineteenth century.

The Anglo-Irish who so resented their colonial status vis-à-vis England established their own colonial-style rule over Catholic and, to a lesser extent, Presbyterian Irish men and women. The Anglo-Irish Ascendancy secured both power and wealth in Ireland on the basis of a penal code directed at Catholics, which over time came also to be applied to dissenting Presbyterians. The penal code emerged from a number of laws passed by the Irish and English parliaments between 1695 and 1704: in 1695, the Irish Parliament made it illegal for Catholics to own a horse worth more than £5, to carry firearms, or to attend foreign universities; two years later, it banished Catholic clergy from the country and made intermarriage between a Protestant and a Catholic grounds for disinheriting the Protestant under the law. In 1704, an English Act "to prevent the further growth of popery" extended the English law that forbade Catholics to buy or inherit real estate to Ireland; it abolished the rights of Catholics to inherit from each other; and it prohibited them from taking up a profession or participating in public life. "Test" clauses in the act made it impossible for Catholics—or for dissenters—to hold office. Catholics also lost ownership of their land under laws finalizing the Treaty of Limerick in 1703: although they constituted between 75 and 80 percent of the population, they owned only 14 percent of the land. Fifty years later, that figure would fall to 5 percent.

Three distinct groups had emerged from the maelstrom of late-seventeenth-century politics as they played out in Ireland: a minority Episcopalian elite that looked toward England and established itself as the Anglo-Irish Ascendancy; a minority Presbyterian culture deeply suspicious of the established Episcopal church and the Anglo-Irish Ascendancy that looked to Presbyterian Scotland for inspiration and support; and a Catholic, Gaelic, and Jacobite majority that looked toward France for its redemption. The established and dissenting Protestants had joined forces against Catholicism during the Glorious Revolution, but once William and Mary's victory was secured, fissures among the two groups reappeared, and it would not be long before the dissenting Presbyterians found themselves at a disadvantage relative to Episcopalians under the law and in holding political and administrative offices. In many respects, they were treated not much better than Irish Catholics, who despite the Treaty of Limerick were subjected to harsh penal laws designed to ensure that they would never again threaten Anglo-Irish interests.

The penal code probably sought more to destroy Catholic economic power than to eliminate "popery." The prohibition against priests, for example, was softened by the 1704 act's tacit recognition of them in the clause that required them to be registered, and Irish people of all faiths resisted "priest-catching," although it carried a monetary reward. And one could always find a priest saying mass on any given Sunday in the myriad mass-houses that existed across the country. But whatever the Anglo-Irish motives, the Catholic Irish never ceased to consider themselves a colonized people whose fortunes were governed by a cruel imperial master of alien culture and religion. Nor did the English or the Anglo-Irish conceive of them in anything other than these terms. From the time of the Tudors onward, the English had justified their depredations against the Irish by portraying them as barbarous, primitive, pagan people whose country it was the responsibility of the English to "inhabite and reform." One commentator described Irish society as a collection of people living like "beastes, void of lawe and all good order;" they were, he asserted, "more uncivill, more uncleanly, more barbarous and more brutish in their customs and demeanures, then [sic] in any other part of the world that is known." Just as the Romans had once brought civilization to a backward, uncivil, and uncouth England, declared Sir Thomas Smith, so too would the English persuade the Irish to engage "in vertuous labour and in justice, and . . . teach them our English lawes and civilitie and leave robbyng and stealing and killyng one of another."[18] The Anglo-Irish descendants of the settlers who had conquered Ireland differed little from their forebears in this respect.

Depicting the Irish as by turns savage yet subtle, warlike but lazy, proud and cowardly, primitive yet cunning, English conquerors and observers of Ireland demonstrated a complicated mixture of attraction to and repulsion by Irish people and their mores. The Irish were dirty, violent, dishonest people who lived under inequitable and unjust laws, the English claimed, but they had nonetheless seduced and "degenerated" many an Englishman with their "corrupt customs." The "wild shamrock manners"[19] of women, in particular, both shocked and titillated English travel writers, who saw in their refusal to wear corsets an intentional assertion of sexual invitation. Because Irish women partook of strong drink, presided over public feasts, and greeted strangers with a kiss; because their marriage laws permitted them to retain their names on marriage and to divorce their husbands with relative ease and material support; because Irish custom permitted sexual relations within degrees of kin affinity far closer than those constituted by either English law or the Catholic clergy, English writers concluded that the women of Ireland held positions of authority over men at home and in public. Unmanly men and aggressive, sensualized, licentious women, they insisted, characterized social relations in Ireland, undermining good order and necessitating English intervention if civilization were ever to be established there. English observations of Irish culture and society contained frequent mention of exotic sexual activities and unconventional gender arrangements in languages of sexuality and gender that would later serve to legitimate the English conquest of foreign peoples. Long before Britain acquired an empire of people of different races, religions, and cultures in Africa and Asia in the late eighteenth and nineteenth centuries, Catholic Ireland served as a model of subject peoples in need of British "civilization." The Irish, wrote Philip Luckombe in 1783, echoing decades of Anglo-Irish and English sentiments, "seem to form a different race from the rest of mankind."[20]

In the American colonies, King William's War catapulted colonists into a fight against the French and their allies—Indians in New England and the mid-Atlantic region and Irish servants in places like Barbados. Plantation owners in the American South and the Caribbean believed that enslaved Africans had also been recruited by French agitators against them. The French attacks on local communities on the mainland and in the islands enabled English administrators to cast the struggles as a war to preserve Protestantism; the participation or refusal to assist the English on the part of Irish servants in the West Indies cemented the perception. The English could claim victory in conflicts in the Leeward Islands of the Caribbean and in the northern frontier territories of New England and New York, but failed to take the French stronghold in Quebec. Enemies—whether French, Indian, Irish, or African—still threatened—and terrified—English colonists throughout America, who came to appreciate that their defense against such formidable foes required greater intervention from the imperial center. Royal governors seized on the opportunity to promote not only financial and administrative but also emotional ties to England. They especially drew on anti-Catholic fears to position themselves—and their government at home—as protectors of Protestant freedoms and interests. By and large, they succeeded in establishing a new political culture in the American colonies, transforming the colonies from individual units into more self-identified English participants in a larger empire.

••

The Glorious Revolution and the revolutionary settlement determined the struggle for supremacy between the crown and Parliament in favor of Parliament, ushering in the rudiments of a liberal regime even as they cemented the domination of landed and financial elites over the rest of the country. They culminated in the uniting of England and Wales and Scotland in a single kingdom and the reduction of Ireland to the status of a virtual colony, albeit one with its own legislature. The American colonies, desiring protection from the French, Indians, and enslaved Africans, accepted closer association with the metropole, thus strengthening imperial ties with Britain. The Glorious Revolution and the revolutionary settlement also obligated Britain to involve itself in a series of wars with Europe that played out on a worldwide scale. These wars would have a profound effect on the development of politics, society, and the economy in the new British state and its empire, as we shall see in the following chapters.

NOTES

1. Quoted in John Prebble, *Darien. The Scottish Dream of Empire* (Edinburgh, 2000), p. 238.
2. Quoted in Patrick Kelly, "Ireland and the Glorious Revolution: From Kingdom to Colony," in Robert Beddard, ed., *The Revolutions of 1688. The Andrew Browning Lectures, 1988* (Oxford, 1991) pp. 189–90.
3. See Steven Pincus, *1688, The First Modern Revolution* (New Haven, 2009) pp. 247–49.
4. Quoted in Howard Nenner, "Pretense and Pragmatism: The Response to Uncertainty in the Succession Crisis of 1689," in Lois G. Schwoerer, *The Revolution of 1688–89: Changing Perspectives* (Cambridge, 1992), p. 90.
5. Quoted in Susan Kingsley Kent, *Gender and Power in Britain, 1640–1990* (London, 1999), p. 37.

6. Quoted in Kent, *Gender and Power in Britain*, pp. 37, 38.
7. Quoted in Ramsay Muir, *A History of Liverpool* (London, 1907), p. 123.
8. Quoted in Diana E. Ascott, Fiona Lewis, and Michael Power, *Liverpool, 1660–1750: People, Prosperity and Power* (Liverpool, 2006), p. 171.
9. Quoted in Peter Aughton, *Liverpool, A People's History* (Preston, 1990), p. 59.
10. See P. J. Cain and A. G. Hopkins, *British Imperialism, 1688–2000* (New York, 2001).
11. Quoted in Prebble, *Darien. The Scottish Dream of Empire*, p. 48.
12. Quoted in Prebble, *Darien*, pp. 55–56.
13. Quoted in Prebble, *Darien*, p. 12.
14. Quoted in David Armitage, "The Scottish Vision of Empire: Intellectual Origins of the Darien Venture," in John Robertson, ed., *A Union for Empire: Political Thought and the British Union of 1707* (Cambridge, 1995), p. 107.
15. Quoted in R. F. Foster, *Modern Ireland, 1600–1972* (London, 1988), p. 161.
16. Quoted in Jacqueline Hill, "Ireland without Union: Molyneux and His Legacy," in John Robertson, ed., *A Union for Empire. Political Thought and the British Union of 1707* (Cambridge, 1995), p. 277.
17. Quoted in Thomas Bartlett, "Ireland, Empire, and Union, 1690–1801," in Kevin Kenny, ed., *Ireland and the British Empire* (New York, 2004), p. 70.
18. Quoted in Thomas Metcalf, *The New Cambridge History of India, III: Ideologies of the Raj* (Cambridge, 1994), p. 2.
19. See R. F. Foster, *Modern Ireland, 1600–1972* (London, 1989).
20. Quoted in Richard Ned Lebow, *White Britain and Black Ireland: The Influence of Stereotypes on Colonial Policy* (Philadelphia, 1976), p. 41.

TIMELINE

1688	The Glorious Revolution: William of Orange invades England, King James II flees to France
1688–1697	Nine Years' War
1689	William and Mary crowned king and queen
	Bill of Rights issued
	Supporters (Jacobites) declare for James in Scotland and Ireland
1690	War between forces of William and James
	James defeated in the Battle of the Boyne
1691	Treaty of Limerick ends war between Jacobites and Williamites
1692	Glencoe Massacre in Scotland

FURTHER READING

David Armitage, "The Scottish Vision of Empire: Intellectual Origins of the Darien Venture," in John Robertson, ed., *A Union for Empire: Political Thought and the British Union of 1707.* Cambridge, 1995.

Thomas Bartlett, "Ireland, Empire, and Union, 1690–1801," in Kevin Kenny, ed., *Ireland and the British Empire.* New York, 2004.

Terry Brotherstone, Anna Clark, and Kevin Whelan, eds., *These Fissured Isles: Ireland, Scotland and British History, 1798–1848.* Edinburgh, 2005.

T. M. Devine, *The Scottish Nation, 1700–2007.* London, 2006.

Jacqueline Hill, "Ireland without Union: Molyneux and His Legacy," in John Robertson, ed., *A Union for Empire. Political Thought and the British Union of 1707.* Cambridge, 1995.

J. R. McNeill, *Mosquito Empires. Ecology and War in the Greater Caribbean, 1620–1914.* Cambridge, 2010.

Steven Pincus, *1688, The First Modern Revolution.* New Haven, 2009.

John Prebble, *Darien. The Scottish Dream of Empire.* Edinburgh, 2000.

Lois G. Schwoerer, ed., *The Revolution of 1688–89. Changing Perspectives.* Cambridge, 1992.

Abigail L. Swingen, *Competing Visions of Empire: Labor, Slavery, and the Origins of the British Atlantic Empire.* New Haven, 2015.

Owen Stanwood, *The Empire Reformed. English America and the Age of the Glorious Revolution.* Philadelphia, 2011.

Rachel Weil, *Political Passions: Gender, the Family and Political Argument in England 1680–1714.* Manchester, 2000.

1695–1704	Penal laws against Irish Catholics passed
1696	Establishment of Bank of England
1698	Scots depart for Darien colony in Panama
1699	Scots abandon Darien; 1,200 lost on voyage home
1701	Act of Settlement gives monarchical succession to Hanoverian line
	War of the Spanish Succession breaks out
	James II dies; French King Louis XIV recognizes James's son as James III
1702	William III dies; Anne ascends throne
1707	Act of Union between England and Scotland
1708	Jacobites rise in Scotland

Speculative activity during the South Sea Bubble.

CHAPTER 2

CONSOLIDATING THE KINGDOM AND THE EMPIRE, 1707–1763

I
n the late summer and early fall of 1720, the English stock market crashed in the course of what has come to be called the South Sea Bubble. Thousands of people lost fortunes in the precipitous decline in the price of the stock issued by the South Sea Company, a collapse that spilled over, in the short run, to the general economy. Orders for luxury items like carriages, jewelry, and fine clothing were canceled as investors realized the extent of their losses; houses were left half-built as those who commissioned them ran out of funds; shipbuilders ceased operations on hastily canceled orders. Workers in these industries lost their jobs. Land values, driven up by investors who had bought estates with the spectacular profits they had earned in the months before the bubble burst, dropped dramatically. Advertisements for the sale of furniture and furnishings filled the columns of newspapers as investors tried to recoup their losses.

In the churches and chapels, clergymen blamed the greed and avarice demonstrated by investors for the appearance of plague, which threatened to make its way into Britain from France. "We have abused our plenty by riot and luxury," declared the Church of England, "our liberty by licentiousness, our ease and safety by strive [sic] and envyings." One chaplain pointed out that "the Plague never proceeds from first natural cause, but is sent immediately from God, and that as a punishment of a people for their sins." The Privy Council proclaimed a day of fasting to try to stave off the plague, urging Britons to pray for mercy from "those judgements [sic] which our manifold sins have deserved."[1]

Angry investors rushed the houses of Parliament, determined to punish the parties responsible for their lost fortunes. Authorities responded by reading the Riot Act, legislation enacted in 1715 that punished the refusal of an order to disperse with death. Crowds of people took to the streets in rage, demanding redress and, failing that, accountability from the South Sea Company directors who had duped them, as they saw it. In the coffee houses on Exchange Alley, where stock market transactions took place, disgruntled customers and what we would call stockbrokers talked of replacing King George I (1660–1727), the governor-general of the company, with his son, the Prince of Wales (1683–1760). Members of Parliament from both the Tory and the Whig factions insisted that an inquiry into the calamity be held, a demand the king's ministers could not deflect. Directors of the company and government and court officials found themselves under a microscope as the inquiry proceeded; the cashier of the South Sea Company fled abroad with the records of the company and lists of MPs, ministers, and courtiers who had been bribed to ensure that the share prices of the company continued to rise. Following the parliamentary inquiry, government officials lost their positions and directors of the company forfeited their riches. The man who would become the next prime minister, Robert Walpole (1676–1745), shielded the monarch and most of the government ministers involved in the debacle and then uncovered and foiled another Jacobite plot to return the Stuart king to the throne of Great Britain, thus assuring himself a long tenure in office.

Although seemingly an isolated incident involving the still-evolving financial instruments of the early modern British state, the South Sea Bubble in fact stands at the center of virtually all the crucial developments of the period. As we shall see in this chapter, war, peace, commerce, empire, slave-trading, party politics, Jacobite risings, and governance all intersected at the focal point of the bubble.

••

THE WAR OF THE SPANISH SUCCESSION AND THE ADVENT OF THE HANOVERIAN KINGS

Queen Anne ascended the throne of Great Britain on William III's death in 1702. She inherited from him a conflict begun the year before, called the War of the Spanish Succession, in which England determined not to let France decide who would sit on the Spanish throne when the king died without an heir. William feared for Dutch independence in the face of a potential domination of the continent by France. English notables worried that a more powerful France would try to replace James II on the English throne, a concern validated and enhanced when Louis XIV recognized James's son as James III when his father died in 1701. Together with the Netherlands, the German state of Hanover, and Austria, which put forward its own claimant to the Spanish monarchy, England formed a Grand Alliance to fight the French and the Spanish, both on the continent and in the colonies of the New World. Despite some significant victories won by John Churchill, the Duke of Marlborough (1650–1722), the war proved more costly than many were willing to tolerate. In 1710, the Whig ministry in power lost out to a Tory government committed to peace. The government immediately sent out feelers to gauge the willingness of the French to discuss a settlement, but it would be years before a formal agreement was reached.

The War of the Spanish Succession had followed the Nine Years' War fought by William against France from 1688 to 1697. The need to fund these seemingly endless conflicts consolidated the theoretical powers won by Parliament in the revolution-ary settlement with William and Mary, because without Parliament's agreement to provide resources, the armed forces could not be sustained, let alone fight. Constant warfare required Parliament to meet every year to approve the budgetary requests of the Treasury, a situation MPs took advantage of to further their jurisdiction over other areas of government as well. Thus the power of Parliament increased in the years after 1689, giving greater opportunities for patronage to the political faction in power. Putting an army of 90,000 into the field on the continent and maintaining a naval force of 40,000 at sea cost the government £5.5 million each year, monies that had to be generated either through taxation or through borrowing. The elites who dominated Parliament had seen taxes on their land increase markedly and were loath to accept further obligations; increasing customs duties on goods coming in from outside Britain and excise taxes on domestic products such as alcohol or salt to a level necessary to pay for war would stir popular unrest. That left borrowing.

We saw in the previous chapter that the government, through the Bank of England, borrowed money from the public through the sale of annuities: in return for an initial loan of cash, the Exchequer, backed by Parliament, promised to pay the lender a fixed amount of interest on the loan over a long period of time, thus providing the lender with a regular income. The interest rates on this debt—called irredeemable debt, because the government could not pay off these loans early if it had the money to do so—could be high, as much as 8 percent in 1711, and could not be refinanced at a lower rate when interest rates fell, as they did when the War of the Spanish Succession ended. In the long term, the government could not afford to keep up these payments, so it looked to reorganize its debt obligations through a scheme in which it contracted with the great commercial and joint stock companies—the Bank of England and the East India Company (EIC)—to exchange government debt for equity shares in the companies. The bank and the EIC received commercial and trading privileges—monopolies—in return for loans they made to the government. Interest on those loans was less than that on the annuities the government owed, thus lowering its costs of borrowing. Holders of government debt could trade their debt for shares in the commercial company, exchanging the guaranteed annuity payment from the government for ownership of shares in the company. Such a swap might appeal to government debt holders for a number of reasons. First, no one could be certain that a Jacobite challenge to the monarchy might not be successful, in which case a new regime might default on the former's obligations. Second, equity shares in the bank or in commercial companies could be expected to increase in value as profits grew—earning what we call capital gains. Moreover, shareowners could, if they wished, sell their company shares on what was becoming a stock market for equities, thus ensur-ing the liquidity of their assets. Holders of government debt could attempt to sell their annuities, to be sure, but the process took time and was often cumbersome.

Both the Bank of England and the EIC, as well as most of the other financial interests located in the city of London, Britain's financial center, were dominated by Whigs, a situation the Tory government under Anne found difficult to negotiate. The costs of war continued to mount, driving up the public debt for which the government had no funds to pay the £9 million it owed by February of 1711. In May, in a bid to circumvent the Whig-controlled companies in its search for another debt for equity swap, the Tory government chartered an entirely new company, the South Sea Company, to be run by Tory ministers and their friends. In return for taking on the whole of the £9 million debt (interest on which the government would pay almost £6 million annually), the company received a trading monopoly that encompassed "the kingdoms, lands etc of America, on the east side from the river Aranoca, to the most southern part of the Terra del Fuego, on the west side therof, from the said most southern part through the South Seas to the most northern part of America, and into unto and from all countries in the same limits reputed to belong to the Crown of Spain, or which shall hereafter be discovered."[2] Britons had long sought to gain entry into the trade of the "South Seas," as they called the Caribbean at the time, but Spain, with which Britain was currently at war, had prohibited them from trading with its colonies. That situation was unlikely to change while war between the two countries still raged. Almost immediately, secret peace talks with Paris took on far greater seriousness, and it was understood from the beginning that any settlement with France would have to include privileges for British trade with South America and the Spanish Caribbean. From the start, however, the commercial side of the South Sea Company seemed unlikely to flourish because not a single director of the company had any experience whatsoever with Caribbean trade.

The Treaty of Utrecht brought the War of the Spanish Succession to a close in 1713. In addition to ceding to Britain the territories of Nova Scotia, Newfoundland, St. Kitts, Gibraltar, and Minorca and compelling the French court to expel the Stuart pretender and his followers, it conferred on Queen Anne the *asiento*, the contract that gave Britain the monopoly to sell slaves to Spanish America. Anne turned over the contract to the South Sea Company, significantly boosting its commercial prospects. In collaboration with the Royal African Company and with the protection of the Royal Navy, the South Sea Company entered the slave trade.

Whigs opposed the Treaty of Utrecht, thinking that it failed to give Britain what the country had earned on the battlefield at such a high cost. The heir to the throne, George, the prince-elector of Hanover, saw the treaty as a betrayal of his interests and regarded the Tories who negotiated it with hostility. George had been named heir presumptive to Anne in 1701, after her last surviving son, the eleven-year-old Duke of Gloucester, died. Tories regarded George as a foreigner who had no rights to the crown; they only reluctantly gave their approval to the notion that Parliament, as representatives of "the people," enjoyed the right to name a legitimate king. The Act of Settlement of 1701 bypassed James II and his son, the potential James III, whose Catholicism not even Tories could abide, and tapped instead the closest Protestant members of the Stuart line, Sophia, granddaughter of James I, and her son George, elector of Hanover. Sophia's death early in 1714 left George the sole successor to the throne on Anne's death later that year. In their passion for a legitimate succession, combined with their fears that the Church of England had become subordinated to the state, Tories began to flirt with the idea of returning the pretender, James III, to the throne. Tory leaders such as the Earl of Oxford (1661–1724) and Viscount Bolingbroke (1678–1751) went so far as to suggest that James convert to Anglicanism, an event that would have made restoring him much more palatable to many Britons, but James refused. And without the support of the army, of which he could not be sure, Bolingbroke dared go no further. The installation of the new Hanoverian line would go forward without resistance.

Or so it seemed. Anne died on August 1, 1714. Her Tory government declared the elector King George I, oblivious to the fact that he regarded her ministers as Jacobites. Before the month was out, he embarked on a purge of the entire administration, sacking Tories at every level of government in England, Scotland, Wales, and Ireland and replacing them with Whigs. He also forced Tories out of the army. These actions provoked intense partisan feelings, which spilled over into the streets. On the day of George's coronation in October, anti-Whig riots broke out in some twenty towns in the southern and western portions of England. Although not explicitly Jacobite in nature, these protests often included seditious chants against the Hanoverian king.

The intensity of feeling displayed by Tories and Whigs and their allies in the streets can only partly be attributed to political differences; by far the greatest passions stirred up in 1714 and 1715 derived from the religious divisions, hatreds, and fears inherited from the seventeenth century. Protestant dissenters had been granted toleration in 1689, but in England this seems to have rendered them even more separate from the Anglican majority, who regarded dissenters as heirs to the puritans who had killed their monarch in 1649 and established a military dictatorship under Oliver Cromwell. Dissenters were thought to possess disproportionate power and wealth derived not from land but from commerce and financial manipulation; moreover, their agenda, many Anglicans believed, included the destruction of the Church of England. The Whig faction, Tories maintained, served as the political mouthpiece of dissent, intent on returning Britain to the days of republican tyranny. For their part, Whigs suspected Tories of planning to return the country to a Catholic monarchy, thus undoing the Glorious Revolution entirely. The fact that Tory ministers under Anne had been conspiring with the pretender during the last years of her reign only confirmed the Whigs in their beliefs.

The accession of a new monarch required that parliamentary elections be held, campaigns for which fueled party animosity to even greater heights. With the support and financial backing of the king, the Whigs won the day in a landslide and, immediately on taking their seats in Parliament, proceeded to impeach Anne's Tory ministers. Oxford and Bolingbroke found themselves indicted along with a number of other Tory ministers, including the Duke of Ormonde (1665–1745), who had served as commander in chief of the army. Bolingbroke escaped to France and became chief advisor to James III. These actions led a great many Tories who would ordinarily have had no truck with Jacobitism to join with their colleagues who did seek actively to return the Stuarts to the throne. The actions also led to the outbreak of anti-Hanoverian riots in parts of England in the spring and summer of 1715 so severe as to suggest that civil war might well return to the land. The government responded harshly, sending the army to put down the protesters and passing the Riot Act, which carried the death penalty for anyone who refused a magistrate's order to disband. To those on the outside looking in, Britain appeared ripe for a successful Jacobite rising.

From France, the pretender James interpreted the riots as clear evidence that he would find tremendous popular support were he to invade. Thus encouraged, he plotted with Bolingbroke and others to make his return to the British throne a reality. He hoped to engage the French in his efforts, but France had been seriously weakened by the War of the Spanish Succession and could not muster the resources to support the pretender. More important, the regent for France's new king, a mere boy, opposed any intervention in British politics because he hoped to gain the support of Britain for his regency. There was in France, however, a significant force of Irish soldiers, men who had escaped the oppression of Protestant rule in Ireland and found employment in the French army. Aware that further wars and thus continued employment following the treaty of Utrecht would not be forthcoming, these soldiers, along with civilian members of the Irish diaspora, thrilled at the prospects of a Jacobite rising.

At home, Irish Catholics, who were the most likely supporters of an invasion by Stuart forces, could do little to aid the cause. Catholics could not own firearms under the penal laws of the country; and although huge numbers of them might be keen to see an end to Protestant rule, they lacked the leadership to mobilize their forces. Irish Tories supported the Hanoverian line unconditionally because not to do so threatened the Anglo-Irish Ascendancy. The English and Welsh Tories who counted themselves Jacobites comprised a minority of the party. Scottish Tories almost to a person, by contrast, held strong Jacobite views, and they were far more motivated than their fellow Britons to take action. The Act of Union of 1707 had invigorated the Jacobite cause in Scotland, where probably more than half the population opposed it and looked to reestablish Scottish independence; the financial burden placed on Scots as a result of the War of the Spanish Succession further infuriated them. Moreover, Scottish lords, unlike English or Welsh landowners, could actually call out their tenants to fight on the side of the Stuart king, if it came to that.

THE RISING OF 1715

In early September, the Earl of Mar (1675–1732), who had lost his office the previous year in the purge of Tory ministers, declared from Highland Scotland for James. He had amassed a force of 10,000 infantry and cavalry and proclaimed the end of "the miserie and slaverie of our countrie . . . being under a foreigne yoak."[3] Jacobites in the west of England were arrested at the end of September, making it impossible for them to join the rising, but their fellow conspirators in the north of the country, largely Catholic landowners with a few English Protestants and some

Highland Scots sprinkled in, raised a small army in support of James and in early October proceeded toward Newcastle, on the northeast coast, where they hoped to meet up with French troops accompanying James. James did not show, Newcastle closed its gates to the Jacobite army, and the rebels turned west toward Manchester, where they believed they would find support for their cause. Instead, they encountered a government force at Preston, to whom they surrendered in mid-November after a ferocious battle, much to the disgust of the Highlanders among them, who had determined to fight to the death for their nationalist cause.

That very day, November 14, Mar's forces met a far smaller government army of 3,700 men, led by the loyal Hanoverian the Duke of Argyll (1680–1743), at Sheriffmuir, just north of Stirling. Given his numerical superiority, Mar should have routed the Hanoverian troops. An indecisive general at best, he could not gain the upper hand and the exhausting but inconclusive battle demoralized the Jacobite troops. Refusing Mar's orders to advance, they withdrew north to Perth, allowing Argyll's forces to keep Edinburgh for King George. In late December, James arrived from France, but without the French army he had promised. He met up with Mar and his depleted troops at Perth in January 1716. Argyll, his own forces strengthened by the addition of German and Dutch soldiers, marched toward Perth, forcing the Jacobites to retreat to Dundee on February 1. Three days later, James fled back to France. The rising of '15 had ended ignominiously.

The consequences of the rising varied dramatically for Scotland and England. In England, where rebel activity had been relatively light, the government imposed harsh punishment on those who had taken part. Overall, forty rebels were executed for their treason against George I; thirty-three of them hailed from England. The government transported hundreds of Jacobites to the colonies, all of them from England. Nineteen Scottish peers, to be sure, lost their titles and estates, but the rest of the Scottish aristocracy, related to some degree to the rebels, rallied around them to soften the blow. The common people of Scotland, by contrast, suffered badly from the fighting, in which both government and rebel troops ravaged towns and villages and wrecked local economies. Economically, Scotland would not recover from the '15 for another thirty or more years.

Politically, the failure of the Jacobite rebellion solidified the Whigs in power for the next forty-five years. The Tories had revealed their true colors, as far as George I was concerned; after the rising, he could have no doubts as to whom he could trust at the head of his government. The Whigs further cemented their supremacy with the Septennial Act of 1716, which kept Parliament in session for seven years instead of three, vastly reducing the opportunity for any kind of turnover of MPs. Tories found themselves howling in the wilderness, lacking influence at both the local and the national level, except in Wales, where the lack of Whig landed families made it difficult to replace Tory magistrates. In compensation, George I appointed only English bishops to the Church of England in Wales, much to the dismay of Welsh clergy and intellectuals.

The threat of Jacobite rebellion persisted, however, and continued to haunt the British imagination. In June 1719, English and Scottish Jacobites conspired with

A PLACE IN TIME

Liverpool and the Jacobite Risings of 1715 and 1745

When the Scottish Earl of Mar assembled troops numbering 10,000 in 1715 to advance south into England to place the Catholic Stuart pretender, James III, on the throne, he could count on the enthusiastic support of virtually the entire county of Lancashire. Only Liverpool, dominated by Whig notables, remained loyal to the Hanoverian king, George I. As the Jacobite army made its way toward Manchester, whose inhabitants espoused pronounced pro-Jacobite sentiments, forces from Northumberland and Cumberland marched on and then took the city of Lancaster in the name of the pretender. It appeared that the Jacobite cause would prevail and that its military leadership would soon turn toward Liverpool, where the capture of an abundance of arms, ammunition, and ships would strengthen their position. Ships, in particular, would make it possible to link up with Jacobite interests in Ireland, where the Catholic population could be counted on to provide large numbers of champions of the effort to overthrow the Hanoverian regime.

In preparation for what they expected to be a long siege, the townspeople of Liverpool rallied with everything they could muster. Lacking any kind of fortification, they dug trenches on the eastern side of town and flooded the lower portion to prevent enemy troops from entering. They set up seventy artillery pieces on a piece of high ground to repel invading forces and positioned the ships in the river in such a way as to provide the best possible defense. Sailors formed up in groups while townsmen organized and drilled in anticipation of a showdown with Jacobite troops. However, the troops never arrived. Government forces met them at Preston and, after first suffering a defeat, routed the supporters of James III after fierce fighting. "Heaven had Liverpoole in its particular protection," wrote Daniel Defoe (1660–1731).[4] By early 1716 the rising was over.

Liverpool's loyalty to the Whig regime led government officials to hold the trial of the Jacobite leaders there; they believed they could count on reliable jurors to return the verdicts they sought. The good citizens did not

Spain, then involved in hostilities against Britain, to foment another rising. The Spanish fleet that was to land in western England to signal rebellion there succumbed to stormy seas, scuttling the main thrust of the rising. A smaller fleet landed off the coast of Skye to meet up with Scottish forces, but at the battle of Glenshiel, government troops routed them, closing that particular chapter in Jacobite efforts to restore, as they saw it, their rightful king.

disappoint. Hundreds of rebels were found guilty and sentenced to transportation to colonies in the New World, many of them ending up as slaves on Virginia and Caribbean plantations. (Liverpool ship owners profited nicely from the fees paid to them to carry out the sentence of transportation.) Thirty-four men from Lancashire were hanged, four of them in Liverpool itself at a place called Gallows Field. Afterward, in a gruesome spectacle designed to provide an object lesson to anyone who might entertain further thoughts of rebellion, their intestines were extracted and burned and their bodies cut into four pieces and displayed around the region.

Thirty years later, a second Jacobite rising confronted Liverpudlians. As Bonnie Prince Charlie (1720–1788), the young pretender, led his troops out of Scotland in 1745, the townspeople raised £6,000 to recruit and arm from among themselves a regiment of foot—the Liverpool Blues—to support the king's campaign against him. Seven companies of volunteers also formed to defend the town itself, should it come to that. The Blues embarked on a mission to destroy bridges to slow the rebels' advance; they met and fought successfully against a detachment of Jacobites at Warrington. The Liverpool regiment joined up with the army of the Duke of Cumberland (1721–1765) as he chased the young pretender north back to Scotland; it occupied the town of Carlisle to prevent it from falling into rebel hands. The merchants and tradesmen who made up the Blues acquitted themselves well, earning the respect of at least one officer of Cumberland's army. "No regiment in the campaign made a better appearance than the Liverpool regiment," he declared. "Their officers were a set of soldier-like gentlemen, though they had not been bred in the military way, being mostly gentlemen, tradesmen, etc., yet had a very good discipline, having thrown off their trade and merchandise for a time, and ventured their lives and fortunes and everything dear to them in defence of their king and country."[5]

Back in Liverpool, some townspeople did not behave so well. In the spring of 1746, a number of them in the grip of anti-Jacobite rage attacked and burned the single Roman Catholic chapel in the town and set fire to a house belonging to the widow of a Catholic resident. This kind of anti-Catholic feeling would appear again over the course of the eighteenth and nineteenth centuries.

THE SOUTH SEA BUBBLE

It was in the context of renewed war with Spain and continuous threats to the Hanoverian line that the events leading to the South Sea Bubble took place. In November 1719, George I opened Parliament with an assessment of the country's position. Spain would soon be forced to acknowledge Britain's supremacy in Europe, he declared, although the war had entailed "extraordinary expense." Peace and Britain's prosperity would depend on careful planning; above all, the country's finances had to be put in order. "I must desire you," the king urged, "to turn your thoughts to all proper means of lessening the debts of the nation."[6] His government negotiated with the South Sea Company for another debt-for-equity swap, in which the company took over some three-fifths of the national debt, expecting to make substantial profits by converting government annuities to South Sea Company shares and selling them to investors. Parliament approved the deal in February 1720.

As was true in 1711, people who held government annuities—which provided them a guaranteed fixed income—would have to be convinced that it was worth giving up that income and take shares in the South Sea Company instead. That meant they had to be persuaded that the prices of their shares would continue to increase. A number of factors suggested that earnings would rise, although the South Sea Company had yet to show a profit in the nine years it had been in existence. First, the king himself had become the governor-general of the company, a not-so-subtle sign that the operations of the firm could be trusted. He also made a highly public gesture of investing £100,000 of his funds in the company. Other prominent personages also bought shares and, in the early days of the bubble, made a killing. Success in the market depended on the willingness of investors to continue to purchase and to send up the price of stock, which they did for months of frenzied buying. What people did not know was that the king's mistresses, and most likely the king himself, along with numerous government ministers, had been bribed with offers to purchase large numbers of shares without having to put down any of their own money for them, or at least not much of it.

At the peak of the buying splurge in June 1720, share prices had risen ten times their value in February. Everyone who could, it seemed, jumped into the market, driving up share prices of other companies and creating incentives to start up all kinds of enterprises, frivolous or not. When buying seemed to fall off in mid-summer, the directors of the South Sea Company resorted to all kinds of questionable and dishonest tactics to keep share prices high. They failed, and the stock crashed in September, wreaking havoc on the fortunes of many a prominent family and bringing ruin to thousands of stockholders. Banks saw the price of their stock plummet and could not pay their dividends; businesses dependent on wealthy custom had to lay off their workers. The price of coal declined, although winter was just ahead, an indication of the level of unemployment in the cities. As one observer wrote, "I cannot see how people in London will have money to buy necessaries, what that will produce among all the handicraft people is easy to guess."[7]

At this point, Robert Walpole, who held a minor office in the government, stepped forward to propose a way to save the financial system brought down by the South Sea Company collapse and, not incidentally, the Hanoverian regime. He floated a plan (which, in the event, did not materialize) for the Bank of England and the East India Company to rescue the South Sea Company by lending it substantial amounts of money. When news of what became known as the "Bank Contract" became known, investors took heart that all was not lost, and panic selling and runs on banks came to a halt. Walpole's political stock within the Whig faction and at court rose on this gimmick, a situation he took advantage of to stabilize the position of the king and the government and, in the process, to further his own ambitions.

The South Sea Company's close ties to the state through its charter, its governor-general, its purchase of the national debt, and its bribes to ministerial and court politicians meant that the government could not escape from the scandal unleashed by the bursting of the bubble. Testimony before Parliament's Committee of Secrecy, which had been set up in January 1721 to conduct an investigation of the bubble, revealed that the company had paid out more than £1 million in bribes to members of the court and the government. (An income of £500 a year in 1720 was enormous.) The committee could not get its hands on a crucial piece of evidence, the so-called Green Book in which Robert Knight (1675–1744), the cashier of the South Sea Company, had recorded the amounts that officials of the court and of the government had received in bribes. With the government's assistance, Knight had fled to the Austrian Netherlands, from which he could not by law be extradited. Even without the Green Book, however, it was clear that corruption reached the highest levels, involving the king and his mistresses and the king's chief minister, the Earl of Sunderland (1675–1722), first lord of the Treasury.

Walpole, one of the few government ministers who had clean hands, undertook to shield the king and Sunderland from the charges of corruption being levied against them from every corner. When the Committee of Secrecy offered Robert Knight immunity from prosecution in return for his testimony, Walpole conspired with the Austrian emperor to arrange for Knight's escape from Antwerp, thus screening the king and his top minister from irreparable scandal. Walpole spoke in Parliament on behalf of Treasury Secretary Charles Stanhope (1673–1760), helping to win his acquittal, but knew he had to sacrifice the chancellor of the Exchequer, John Aislabie (1670–1742), if the government was to survive. Parliament found Aislabie guilty of corruption, expelled him from the House of Commons, and threw him in the Tower of London. When the committee turned to impeach Sunderland, a peer of the realm with the support of the Prince of Wales, Walpole had to play a careful game. He knew that the government—and perhaps the country—could not survive Sunderland's conviction, yet he wanted to ensure Sunderland's fall from power. He spoke strongly on the earl's behalf before the House of Commons, obtaining his acquittal. Mortally wounded politically, however, in April 1721, Sunderland resigned his office, ceding it to Walpole, whose actions had won him the gratitude and confidence of the king, along with the label of "Skreen-Master General." As first lord of the Treasury and chancellor of the Exchequer, Walpole gathered into his hands control over the day-to-day operations of governance. He became, in effect, the first prime minister of Great Britain.

But neither the Hanoverian line nor the Whig government had yet been secured because the disaster of the South Sea bubble had so infuriated so many parts of the nation that a Jacobite restoration seemed not only possible but also likely. One Whig MP warned that "our whole multitude will turn Jacobite in a very few months more," a sentiment shared by the speaker of the House of Commons,

Arthur Onslow (1691–1768). "The rage against the Government was such for having as they thought drawn them into this ruin," he declared, "that I am almost persuaded . . . that could the Pretender have then landed at the Tower, he might have rode to St. James's with very few hands held up against him."[8] Jacobite plotters prepared for two options, one constitutional, the other insurrectionary. The personnel involved in each did not necessarily always overlap, but certainly they spoke to and planned with one another, as well as with James's officials in France.

The potential for a constitutional restoration of the pretender received real support from an unlikely quarter, that of the Earl of Sunderland, George I's chief minister. Facing impeachment, as we have seen, Sunderland turned to the Tories for help, implying to them that he might call for an early dissolution of Parliament, not set to complete its session until 1722. Further, he intimated, the elections that would have to be held would be free; that is, the government would not use its influence or resources to ensure that its candidates won. The likelihood of the return of a Tory majority in these circumstances seemed strong, which, in turn, Whigs such as Walpole believed, would "inevitably" result in the restoration of the Stuarts. When the vote for impeachment came before the House of Commons, many Tories voted against it. Saved, Sunderland backed off from his flirtation with them, a move that did not surprise the Jacobites. Then he died suddenly on April 19, completely transforming the situation and limiting the options available to those who wished to see a restoration of the Stuarts, among whom were virtually all the Tories in Parliament. Encouraged by the popular rage expressed against George and his government, they now placed their hopes in armed rebellion in a conspiracy known as the Atterbury Plot, named for Francis Atterbury (1663–1732), the bishop of Rochester and dean of Westminster, the man at the center of the planning. As the bishop wrote to James, "Sir, the time has now come when with very little assistance from your friends abroad, your way to your friends at home is become safe and easy. The present juncture is so favourable and will probably continue for many months to be so, that I cannot think it will pass over without a proper use being made of it."[9] Despite some misgivings, James authorized his supporters to act.

Jacobites, including some of the leading Tories in Parliament, raised approximately £200,000 with which to purchase arms and ships; they recruited soldiers and sailors from the army and navy, watermen along the Thames, disaffected men who had lost their savings in the collapse of the South Sea Company, and smugglers along the coast of England known as the Waltham Blacks. They planned to take London first, capturing the Tower of London, the Bank of England, and the king himself. Bonfires would alert the people of London to rise up and seize Hyde Park, St. James's Park, the Exchange, and Lincoln's Inn. Irish troops from Spain would invade and lead the rebellion across the country.

The Atterbury Plot involved careful, serious, detailed planning and the participation of a large number of Tory elites. It never materialized, however, because Walpole learned of it through spies in France and after a search through Sunderland's papers following his death that revealed the existence of a "horrid conspiracy." In the summer of 1722, he sent agents to arrest the plotters he knew of, throwing them in prison without bail or trial, violating the Habeas Corpus Act (1679), and ensuring that they could not follow through on their intentions. But Walpole had insufficient evidence to try the conspirators, especially Bishop Atterbury, whom he was particularly keen to arrest. He brought Christopher Layer (1683–1723), a lawyer involved in the meticulous planning of the rising, to trial, hoping to persuade him to turn king's evidence and give up Atterbury and other prominent Tories with a sentence of death by drawing and quartering. This method of execution called for being "hang'd by the Neck, but not till you are to be dead, but you are to be cut down alive, and your Bowels be taken out, and burnt before your face; your Head is to be sever'd from your Body, and your Body to be divided into four quarters; and that your Head and quarters be deposed of where His Majesty shall think fit."[10] In an extraordinary display of loyalty to his co-conspirators, Layer refused and went to his gruesome demise at Tyburn in May 1723 without implicating anyone the government did not already know about. Because he was a prelate, Atterbury could not be tried in a court of law, but he was brought before Parliament, where a Bill of Pains and Penalties against him was adopted on the strength of evidence that may well have been forged by Walpole. The act, passed on a party vote, exiled the bishop of Rochester from Britain in June 1723, leaving Walpole the undisputed master of the political scene. Walpole's actions, however illegal and unconstitutional, had finally secured the Hanoverian line after nine years of uncertainty and challenge, ensured George's dependence on the new prime minister for the rest of his reign, and left the Whigs in power for the next thirty-five years.

Although the bursting of the South Sea Bubble had significant short-term financial and economic effects, in the long run it proved negligible. In part, its subdued impact resulted from the willingness of the Bank of England to step in to rescue the South Sea Company by purchasing a great deal of its stock and stabilizing its price. Interestingly, despite the popular depictions of the bubble frenzy as a consequence of the emergence of women and Jewish investors in the sphere of finance, these two groups played a "nontrivial" role, as two economic historians have put it, in Britain's financial recovery. Although Walpole won the acclaim of the political class for his handling of the crisis, the reestablishment of the state's financial security in the aftermath of the bubble occurred because London's wealthy Jews, with their close ties to Amsterdam's financial circles and willingness to put their own funds into play, shored up the confidence in the bank.[11]

Moreover, despite initial slowdowns in domestic manufacturing and commerce, overseas trade remained robust and increased over the next thirty years. British exports grew dramatically, a development we will take up in the next chapter; imports, especially from the East Indies and the New World, grew less fast, to be sure, but no less steadily.

SLAVERY AND THE SLAVE TRADE

Most imperial trade was driven by domestic demand for a small number of agricultural products: coffee, tea, chocolate, sugar, and tobacco. By 1700 or so Britain had become one of the chief consumers of coffee in Europe, but unlike the French and the Dutch, the British turned by 1750 to tea. Between 1650 and 1700 tea imports to Britain from China amounted to about £182,000 annually; by 1750 the British were importing £40 million worth of tea each year, an increase of some 2,000 percent. In part, this shift from coffee to tea drinking was a consequence of the EIC's supremacy in the British market; in part it was a function of cost. Although coffee was cheaper by unit than tea, it took far less tea to produce the desired effect, making tea a more cost-effective, cheaper beverage. As one contemporary text put it, "it makes the body active and alert. It offers relief against violent headaches and vertigo. It vanishes tiredness and cleanses the vital fluids and the liver."[12]

The consumption of sugar tended to follow the patterns established by that of coffee and tea. Although sugar constituted only a small portion of Britons' food budgets, it became an important and then necessary component of people's diets. Sweet tea, substituted for beer throughout much of Britain, reduced the consumption of beer by almost one-half in the course of the eighteenth century. Added to grains that were considered inferior such as oats or rice, sugar rendered them tastier and more palatable and, as employers well knew, provided a vital source of calories to those involved in heavy labor and long working hours. Exports of sugar from the British West Indies increased from 8,000 tons in 1663 to 25,000 tons in 1700. In 1770 sugar exports amounted to 97,000 tons. In 1700, Britons were consuming some four pounds of sugar per person each year; that number had risen to eight pounds a year by 1750 and to eighteen pounds a year by the early nineteenth century.

Markets for sugar could only be supplied, West Indian planters insisted, through the increased utilization of slave labor. "It is as impossible for a Man to make Sugar without the assistance of Negroes," declared a rich West Indian planter, John Pinney, in the 1770s, "as to make Bricks without Straw."[13] The most important sugar producer in the West Indies was British-held Barbados, which exported some 15,000 tons of sugar each year. The growing economy of the West Indies necessitated a larger and larger workforce, which was supplied by the African slave trade. Between 1600 and 1650 some 10,000 enslaved Africans had arrived in the New World from Africa each year. Most of them went to Brazil and to the Spanish colonies of the American mainland. Between 1650 and 1700 that number had doubled to 20,000 captive Africans per year, more than half of whom went to the French, English, and Dutch islands of the Caribbean. In 1800 trade in enslaved Africans had grown to 60,000 per year.

Contemporaries recognized the centrality of slavery and the slave trade to their prosperity. In 1729, a merchant named Joshua Gee observed that "our Trade with *Africa* is very profitable to the Nation in general; it has this Advantage, that it carries no Money out, and not only supplies our Plantations with Servants, but brings in a great Deal of Bullion for those that are sold to the *Spanish* West-Indies. . . . The supplying our Plantations with Negroes is of that extraordinary Advantage to us, that the Planting Sugar and Tobacco, and carrying on Trade there could not be supported without [t]hem; which Plantations . . . are the great Cause of the Increase of the Riches of the Kingdom. . . . All this great Increase of our Treasure proceeds chiefly from the labour of Negroes in the *Plantations*." A mercantilist

16 THE BLACK MAN'S LAMENT.

CUTTING DOWN THE SUGAR-CANE.

But when the crops are ripen'd quite,
  'Tis then begin our saddest pains;
For then we toil both day and night,
  Though fever burns within our veins.

THE BLACK MAN'S LAMENT. 17

THE BRUISING-MILL.

When 18 months complete their growth,
  Then the tall canes rich juices fill;
And we, to bring their liquor forth,
  Convey them to the bruising-mill.

That mill, our labour, every hour,
  Must with fresh loads of canes supply;
And if we faint, the cart-whip's power,
  Gives force which *nature's* powers *deny*.

Enslaved Africans toiling on sugar plantations.

put it more succinctly in 1745: "If we have no *Negroes,* we can have no *Sugars, To-baccoes, Rice, Rum,* etc. . . . consequently, the Publick *Revenue,* arising from the Importation of *Plantation-Produce,* must be annihilated: And will this not turn many hundreds of Thousands of *British Manufacturers* a Begging?" The slave trade, wrote another in 1772, constituted "the first principle and foundation of all the rest; the main spring of the machine, which sets every wheel in motion."[14]

As lucrative as this kind of trading in human beings might be, Britons did not engage in widespread slave trading until the late seventeenth century when Spain, which with Portugal controlled the slave trade, began to lose its hold on the monopoly. In the 1690s, Britons shipped nearly 100,000 enslaved Africans from West Africa to the Caribbean. In 1713, the Treaty of Utrecht, which marked the end of the War of the Spanish Succession, gave to Britain the *asiento,* the right to supply slaves to Spain's colonies in America. In the years between 1700 and 1810, some 6.5 million African men and women were sold as slaves and carried across the Atlantic Ocean in the holds of slave ships. Until about 1750, by which time the natural increase among the slaves in North America could be counted on to meet the demand for their labor, British slavers sold their human wares to colonists in North America and the West Indies. After 1750, the slave trade was largely confined to the Caribbean and to Brazil, but despite the decline of North American markets for newly transported slaves, the trade flourished. Britons managed fully a quarter of the world's slave trade up to 1791 and more than half of it between 1791 and 1806. In the 1780s, more than 880,000 slaves arrived in the Americas, half of them in English ships hailing from the port towns of Bristol, London, and Liverpool.

Life on the plantations was harsh. Slaves worked from dawn to dark, with breaks only for meals. Should they fail to meet production quotas, they were whipped. They could enjoy little in the way of family life, not only because they lacked the time and leisure but also because the level of fertility for both men and women was vitiated by malnutrition and overwork. Death rates sharply outpaced birthrates among enslaved Africans: in the eighteenth century the life expectancy of slave women reached only 25.5 years; African men could expect to live only 23 years. Certainly, living conditions contributed to the heavy mortality of plantation life, but the greatest killer proved to be disease. Dysentery and malaria carried off perhaps one-third of newly arrived slaves. In contrast to North America, natural increase could not sustain slave populations in the Caribbean islands. The great mortality rates of enslaved Africans in the West Indies ensured that the slave trade would only increase.

Enslaved Africans vastly outnumbered white Britons in the West Indies. In 1700, 114,000 blacks worked under the control of 31,000 whites; by 1750, white numbers had increased only by 10,000, whereas African numbers more than doubled to 258,000. British colonists tended not to settle permanently in the islands, unlike those on the North American mainland. They returned to Britain frequently, constituting an absentee class in the Caribbean and establishing themselves in large communities in London, Bristol, and Bath. They used the considerable profits from their sugar plantations to make themselves socially and politically conspicuous; their wealth often elicited disdain among the elites but it also funded a powerful lobby that MPs and ministers could not ignore. Lord North, prime minister from 1770 to 1783, once remarked that the West Indian planters were "the only masters he ever had."[15]

The demographic imbalance of blacks to whites in the Caribbean produced a state of constant terror among white settlers that slave uprisings could take place at any time and that they would be murdered in their beds. In response to even the smallest infraction of rules, planters and their overseers resorted to levels of violence against slaves that exceeded anything in North America. Slave revolts in the islands occurred more frequently than on the mainland, in part because plantations in places like Jamaica and Barbados were far larger than those in the Chesapeake; in part because absentee British planters in the islands left the supervision of their plantations to itinerant overseers; but also because, in contrast to their counterparts in North America, slaves in the West Indies tended to be recent arrivals from Africa. Most of the leaders of slave revolts hailed from the Gold Coast (present-day Ghana), where they had honed their military skills as members of the Asante kingdom. This was especially true in Jamaica, where a fairly large group of runaway slaves called Maroons had established themselves in the mountainous regions of the country. From their remote fortified towns they raided plantations and attacked British troops; during the 1730s their forays became more frequent and more successful, amounting to a state of war against British authorities. In desperation, a British officer suggested that "some remote corner of the Island . . . be allotted [sic] them, and a general amnesty allowed for what is past, upon their submitting to his Majesty's Mercy, acknowledging his Government, delivering up their arms, promising to live peaceably for the future & not to receive any more fugitive Slaves, but to return them to the owners on a reasonable Reward to be agreed on for that Purpose."[16] The governor of Jamaica, with the urging of Lord Newcastle, the secretary of state for the colonies, negotiated just such a treaty with the Maroons in 1739, acknowledging their autonomous communities, ceding them the territory they occupied in the mountains, and exacting from them the obligation to help British authorities capture runaway slaves and return them to their owners. In time, the Maroons came to be regarded as the "King's Negroes," serving as a police force on the island of Jamaica when called on by colonial officials.

Slavery in the colonies of the North American mainland had not yet become the established institution it would become after 1750. The number of white settlers far surpassed that of enslaved blacks, with the natural increase among whites causing a 400 percent increase between 1700 and 1750. The population of slaves certainly grew during that time as well, rising from 18,000 to 247,000, but it proved no match for the 957,000 whites inhabiting the colonies. Large-scale emigration from southern Ireland, Scotland, and Ulster contributed heavily to these figures, with the new immigrants settling disproportionately in the cities of Boston, New York, and Philadelphia. As the white population grew, pressure to be able to move on to lands to the west increased as well, creating confrontations with the native peoples who inhabited them. As we will see later in this chapter, the instability of the situation would lead to a series of wars between Britain and France as they sought to establish their supremacy on the North American continent.

THE ROBINOCRACY

The accession of the Hanoverians to the British throne proved to have significant consequences for the power of the crown. As we have seen, the revolutionary settlement following the Glorious Revolution of 1688 established a constitutional monarchy in England and Wales (and later Scotland and Ireland), checking the power of monarchs and placing significant authority in the hands of the landed elites who sat in Parliament. Monarchs still played an important role in governance. They acted as commanders in chief of the armed forces and could declare or end wars and negotiate peace treaties; they appointed the important ministers of state, governors of British colonies, and the men who sat on the high court; they could ennoble commoners and make them hereditary peers of the realm, thus creating a body of presumably friendly men who sat for life in the House of Lords; they could request that Parliament consider legislation or the appropriation of funds necessary to administer and defend Britain; and, as heads of the Anglican church, they designated the bishops and archbishops who served the Church of England and the Church of Ireland.

The first of the Hanoverian line, King George I, spoke no English, a handicap that may have contributed to the devolution of many of the monarch's powers to the prime minister and his cabinet. Certainly, George and subsequent monarchs expected to be briefed and their opinions solicited before any policies were arrived at or actions taken. And, perhaps most important, monarchs guarded their prerogative to appoint—and dismiss—the prime minister in the first place, although the strength of the majority party in Parliament, and especially in the House of Commons, often dictated the outcome, despite the monarch's wishes.

Robert Walpole's dominance in British politics—reflected in the term "Robinocracy"—rested on his ability to control virtually all of the government at every level. Along with his brother-in-law, Lord Townshend, he used the patronage of the court and of Parliament to remove rivals and Tories from office and replace them with his relatives and friends, men now dependent on him for their wealth and influence. Walpole conducted the king's business effectively, keeping George I happy, and following George's death in 1727, his successor George II as well. By keeping Britain out of war, thus lowering government expenses and taxation on the landed elites, the prime minister maintained a relative calm in the kingdom after years of upheaval.

English and Welsh affairs seemed to go smoothly under the Robinocracy, and even Ireland, under the firm control of the Protestant Ascendancy, raised few concerns. In 1724, for example, Dublin Catholics drew on the occasion of the pretender's birthday to register their support for the Stuart line, but Catholic Ireland possessed so few resources that it could hardly produce any resistance to government control. Scotland, on the other hand, posed more difficult problems of governance. In 1725, Parliament levied a new excise tax on Scotland, in apparent violation of the Act of Union of 1707. Widespread violence bordering on revolt erupted in Glasgow, Stirling, Dundee, Paisley, and a number of other cities. Troops had to be brought in to stem the disorder, which one historian has described as "a movement of national resistance" to the union.[17] Walpole turned to the Earl of Islay and his brother, the Duke of Argyll, to take over Scottish affairs, promising them a monopoly on patronage in Scotland in return for keeping the peace there. So successfully did they administer the northern land that Scotland became largely reconciled to union and was governed almost as a separate polity within the United Kingdom.

This situation changed in 1737, following the Porteous Riot the previous year in Edinburgh. Captain Porteous (c. 1695–1736) had ordered that the town guard fire on a crowd that had gathered to protest the execution of a smuggler; a number of people were killed. Found guilty and sentenced to death, Porteous received a reprieve from George II's wife, Queen Caroline (1683–1737), an action that infuriated many in Edinburgh. A mob of some 4,000 people, possibly with the assistance of Edinburgh authorities, seized Porteous from jail and hanged him. The government in Westminster reacted strongly, issuing proposals for harsh punishment. The Duke of Argyll protested vociferously against such an affront to his authority, persuading Walpole to soften the terms and be content with imposing substantial fines on the city. Not mollified, Argyll went into opposition in 1741, and the Whigs lost a parliamentary election in Scotland for only the first time in the eighteenth century. It bode ill for English/Scottish relations in the near term, as we shall see below.

Walpole paid little heed to the colonies in North America, preferring to let them attend to their own affairs. His hands-off policy led American colonists to think and act as if self-government was simply in the nature of things, an attitude that would persevere and intensify over the next number of decades. In the short run, this posed little problem for Walpole; that cannot be said for his reluctance to pursue a foreign policy against Spain that a sizable group of merchants in Britain and in the American colonies urged on him.

The *asiento* granted to the South Sea Company in 1713 conferred the privilege of selling slaves to Spain's South American colonies. In the immediate short run slave trading had little impact on the British economy, but over the next decades, it would became central to the development of new financial institutions, credit instruments, and stock-jobbing, contributing mightily to the commercial revolution that would make Britain's one of the most powerful economies in the world. The *asiento* also allowed the company to dispatch a ship containing 500 tons of trade goods to the Spanish Caribbean, a concession many hoped would lead to a larger opening of Spanish colonies to British trade. It did not, and British merchants turned to smuggling their goods into Spanish territories instead, invoking the wrath of Spanish authorities who authorized the seizure of British ships on the slightest pretense. The British retaliated with their own confiscations of Spanish ships and cargo, and after many years of this kind of back and forth, British merchant interests finally generated enough popular outrage against Spain to force Walpole to declare war on the country. He did so only reluctantly, fearful that it would embroil Britain in more conflict with France. But for many Britons, war for empire, as hostilities against Spain were represented, topped their political agenda.

Empire served as an important source of Britons' pride in themselves and in the principles that they claimed governed their social, economic, cultural, and political institutions. Although it was palpably not the case for all of the people whose liberty and freedom had been sacrificed to the material interests of their British rulers—native Americans, enslaved Africans, Irish Catholic peasants—supporters of empire depicted their enterprise as one in which notions of liberty and consent were central. Portrayed as commercially prosperous colonies inhabited by free white British citizens, empire was regarded as the source of trade, wealth, military power, and political virtue for the mother country. When colonies flourished, apologists of empire asserted, it was because they reflected the legitimacy and health of domestic political institutions; when they failed to live up to contemporary standards of government and economic viability, it was because Britain's political institutions were in the hands of a corrupt, weak, even effeminate ruling class.

As Walpole had feared, war against Spain turned into a war against France (called the War of the Austrian Succession, 1740–1748) that would last eight years and be prosecuted all over the world. In 1740, the Habsburg emperor, Charles VI, died, leaving his realms to his daughter, Maria Theresa. France and a rising power, Prussia, took this opportunity to try to gain territories for themselves, moves that on the one hand threatened the balance of power on the continent that Britain had fought to maintain since the time of the Glorious Revolution and, on the other, placed the German state of Hanover at risk from Prussian aggression. Ever the reluctant warrior, Walpole acted indecisively, allowing his enemies in Parliament to finally force his ouster from office in 1742. He was followed by a series of ineffective prime ministers until, in 1746, Henry Pelham (1694–1754), Walpole's chief deputy, took office.

In 1743, George II led British, Hanoverian, and Hessian troops against French forces at Dettingen, in Bavaria, handing France a resounding defeat. The French king, Louis XV, responded to the debacle by reviving the policy of supporting a Jacobite invasion of England, which he hoped would require Britain to remove its troops from Europe and perhaps even result in the overthrow of the Hanoverian king, George II. The new Stuart pretender to the British throne, James's son Charles Edward—known in Scotland as Bonnie Prince Charlie—had been recruiting troops for a rising among the Highland clans and believed that the Tory families of Wales would certainly join in the Jacobite effort. In 1744, he rode to Paris to head an invasion force of 10,000 men, who were to be transported across the Channel to the south coast of England, where they would engage George's troops. Before the fleet that was to ship them out could be organized, however, the British navy, acting on information gathered by a British spy, foiled the plot, leading the French to put off the invasion indefinitely.

Impatient and frustrated, Charles decided to act on his own, hoping that a successful invasion would require the French to come to his aid. In July 1745, he landed in western Scotland and marched inland, picking up Highlander loyalists on the way. By the time he reached Edinburgh, which opened its gates to him, he had army of about 2,500; his troops met and handily defeated a government force at Prestonpans, just east of Edinburgh. The whole of Scotland had fallen to the young pretender.

Bonnie Prince Charlie in Manchester, 1745.

Charles pressed on into England in November, marching through Carlisle and then Manchester, reaching Derby, some 130 miles from London, in December. Thoroughly alarmed by the success of Charles's invasion, George II readied himself to flee to Hanover and a financial panic rocked Exchange Alley. The French troops Charles had expected never showed, however, nor did the English and Welsh Jacobites whose support he had counted on. Faced with a refusal of his Highland generals to advance further toward London, he was compelled to order a retreat, realizing that his chances for placing his father on the thrones of England and Scotland had been lost.

An army of 10,000 men led by George's son, the Duke of Cumberland, chased Charles's troops north to Inverness, in the northwest Highlands. Hungry, tired, frozen, and lacking shoes and warm clothing, they met Cumberland's forces at Culloden in April 1746. It was a bloodbath, with the Hanoverian soldiers slaughtering about 2,000 Highlanders in the field and routing Charles's followers entirely. Charles fled the field with his surviving troops and hid out in Scotland for five months as British troops tried to run him down. They failed, and he escaped to France in September 1746.

The end of the rising of 1745.

Now nicknamed "the butcher" for his merciless pursuit of the remnants of Charles's army, Cumberland followed a policy designed to ensure that never again would a Jacobite army be able to take the field. For a year following Culloden, he instituted a reign of terror in the Highlands, destroying villages, burning crops, confiscating cattle, and shooting on sight any rebel found holding a weapon. Some 120 Jacobite officers were executed; regular soldiers were transported to the colonies. In an effort to destroy the Highland culture that had produced such persistent traitors, Parliament passed a law making it illegal for any Highlander to possess arms, to wear the traditional Highland plaid and tartan, or to play the bagpipes. More substantially, the government seized the estates of many clan chiefs and ended the land tenures that had provided so many of them with soldiers. No longer did tenancy carry with it the obligation to perform military service, and changes to the legal system made it impossible for a clan chief to exercise the functions of prosecutor and judge on his estate.

These measures proved effective in vitiating a separate Highlander identity that had existed for so long and had rendered union with England a mere paper proposition. More important to the process of acculturation, however, were the practice of Highlander chiefs sending their sons to be educated in Lowland Scotland, where they imbibed Anglican ways of thinking; the adoption of Lowland- or English-style agricultural practices, which we will address in the next chapter; the employment of Highlanders by the commercial companies trading with the East Indies and the Atlantic colonies; and the recruitment of Highlanders into the British army. In this latter capacity, they turned into forceful agents of imperialism. By the 1770s, the destruction of Highland culture had progressed so far that a visitor to the area could declare that "there was perhaps never any change of national manners so quick, so great, and so general, as that which has operated in the Highlands by the last conquest and subsequent laws. . . . The clans retain little now of their original character: their ferocity of temper is softened, their military ardour is extinguished, their dignity of independence is depressed, their contempt of government subdued, and their reverence for their chiefs abated. Of what they had before the late conquest of their country there remains only their language and their poverty."[18]

For France, the Jacobite rebellion of '45 turned the tide of the War of the Austrian Succession on the continent. With the help of a large contingent of Irish Catholic troops, French forces had defeated the British in the Austrian Netherlands in May 1745, but could not dislodge them from the country. With the '45 in play, however, George had to move troops out of the country, allowing the French to occupy all of the Austrian Netherlands and part of the Dutch Republic. Well ensconced on the continent now, France remained secure, and in India, its Indian troops had defeated those sponsored by the British at Madras. The situation in North America, however, was different: British forces took Louisburg, the fort that secured the St. Lawrence River Valley, and were poised to attack all of French Canada.

This impasse led both belligerents to the peace table in 1748. The Treaty of Aix-la-Chapelle in effect returned everything to the status that had existed before hostilities broke out, at least as far as Britain and France were concerned. Prussia did gain the province of Silesia from Maria Theresa, a huge acquisition, but she held on to all her other territories, including the Austrian Netherlands. Britain returned Louisburg to France; the French gave back Madras. All in all, nothing had been achieved.

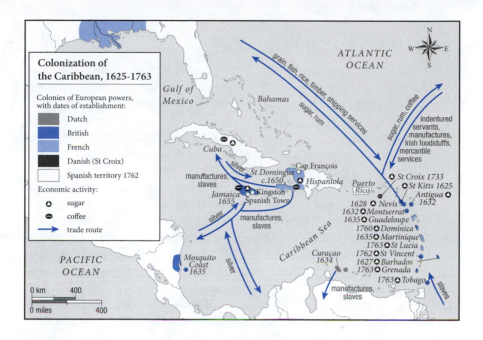

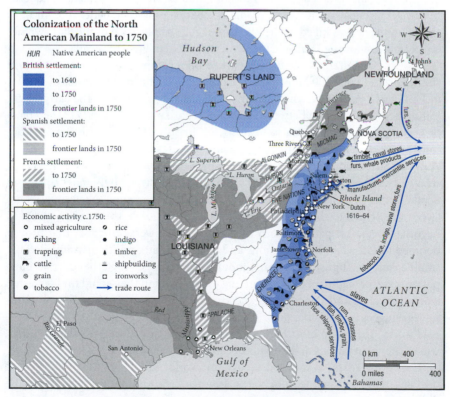

MAP 2.1

The Colonization of the Caribbean and the North American Mainland

WORLD WAR AND EMPIRE

Conflict between the British and the French, given the lucrative spoils of commerce and empire at stake, would reemerge seven years later in a war that had an extraordinary impact on Britain's future. Called the French and Indian War by Americans and the Seven Years' War by Europeans, it broke out first in North America in 1754 and then spread in 1756 to the European continent, the Mediterranean, West Africa, and India. British colonists in America had long feared the spread of French influence on the continent as they and their Indian allies ventured deeper into the interior; now, with the French building forts on the shores of the Great Lakes and along the Ohio River, concern turned into something resembling panic. In 1754, Virginia commissioned a militia troop under the direction of an inexperienced officer named George Washington (1732–1799) to march north to modern-day Pittsburgh, where the French had ensconced themselves in Fort Duquesne. Washington's little force ill-advisedly attacked the entrenched French and Indian army and got itself captured, forcing Britain's hand. It had now to step in and take over what had become a war. In 1755 the newly appointed prime minister, Lord Newcastle (1693–1768), dispatched the navy to the mouth of the St. Lawrence River to block the arrival of additional French troops and ordered General Edward Braddock (1695–1755) to Fort Duquesne to avenge the hapless Americans. Braddock's efforts proved no better than those of the colonists; he was killed in the July battle, and the blockade of the St. Lawrence largely failed, allowing French reinforcements to land in French Canada.

Shortly thereafter, the British embarked on a campaign that would result in the deportation of 7,000 French Canadians from Acadia, on the shores of the Bay of Fundy. The Acadians, who had inhabited their territory since the early 1600s, found themselves caught between a rock and a hard place when in 1713 the Treaty of Utrecht gave Nova Scotia to Britain. The British did little with the territory until 1749, when they established the town of Halifax at the end of the War of the Austrian Succession. Under the governorship of Edward Cornwallis (1713–1776), who had been part of "the butcher's" campaign to destroy Highlander society in Scotland, the British began to harass the French in the region. Now situated between the British to the east and the French to the north, the Acadians tried to negotiate a neutral path between the belligerent powers, an effort that proved doomed to fail when British troops and Massachusetts militiamen invaded the small colony in August 1755. Throughout the next three years, they carried out a policy of terror, capturing and deporting every Acadian they could find. Wrested from their land and their homes and their livelihoods, Acadians found themselves refugees in a number of locations across the French-, Spanish- and British-held world. The group most familiar to Americans landed in Spanish Louisiana, where later generations of Acadians became known as Cajuns.

The Seven Years' War raged across the world, killing soldiers, sailors, and civilians in battles ranging from North America to Europe to the Caribbean to the Philippines and South Asia. The British fared badly for the first few years, suffering defeat at the hands of the French in Quebec, Minorca, Hanover, and India, where native troops under the employ of the East India Company fell to those hired by the French. In 1760, slaves in Jamaica, made even more hungry and distressed by severe shortages of food, took advantage of wartime disruptions to the island to rise up in a series of rebellions against the British. For eighteen months, slaves under the leadership of the charismatic figure Tacky attacked white settlers, killing scores of them, destroying their property, and nearly causing the collapse of the economy of Jamaica. Finally, a combined force of regular British troops, local militia volunteers, and special soldiers of the Maroon communities brought Tacky's Revolt to an end, but not before it had produced losses in capital and property of more than £100,000. The experience frightened the white settlers of Jamaica half to death, and Tacky's Revolt would continue to plague their dreams for decades to come.

The initial disasters of the war led to the rise of William Pitt (1759–1806) to the office of secretary of state in Lord Newcastle's government. Pitt introduced a number of reforms that helped turn the tide of war; one of them entailed recruiting into the army many of the Highland clansmen who had been languishing since the battle of Culloden. Turning disaffected Scots into soldiers of empire turned out to be a brilliant stroke: these battle-hardened men and their former chiefs proved to be excellent fighters for the crown, and their loyalties to their local clans were transferred to Great Britain and the empire. Pitt's reforms helped earn victories in Quebec in 1760 and brought about the British conquest of Guadeloupe, Martinique, and Havana by 1762. The navy ousted the French from slave-trading forts along the West African coast, and a British-led force of Indian sepoys and sailors—called lascars—seized Manila in the Philippines from the Spanish. When the war ended with the Treaty of Paris in 1763, Britain had achieved at least a tentative imperial authority across a good portion of the world. The French ceded all of their holdings in North America to the British except New Orleans, which they gave to the Spanish, along with Louisiana (Louisiana at the time made up almost a third of today's continental United States, so considerable territory remained out of British hands). French colonists in Canada retained the right to their own laws in lower courts and were free to conduct their religious practices without hindrance. The British held on to the West African forts they had won, but gave Manila and Havana back to Spain and returned Guadeloupe, Martinique, and St. Lucia to France. British might had prevailed and seemed incontestable. Appearances could deceive, however, and it is important to note that imperial "control" and imperial boundaries remained unstable and fluid during this period.

Victory over the French enabled Britons to regard their imperial ventures as beneficent, humanitarian endeavors whereby Britain, by taking on the overlordship of the tyrannous French and the cruel Spanish, generously made available to its colonial territories and the native peoples who populated them the fruits of progress, morality, freedom, liberty, and prosperity—all of them a function, pro-imperial Britons believed, of an empire based on trade rather than on conquest. In the 1760s, as we shall see in a later chapter, middling people used this kind of justification for empire in support of their claims to citizenship. At the same time, these justifications glossed over the fact that imperial prosperity rested on the forced labor of hundreds of thousands of Africans sold and born into slavery; the expropriation of land from Native Americans and Irish peasants; and the exploitation of native peoples in parts of India.

One of the battles the British fought against a French-supported army would bring them a prize of incredible significance. On the morning of June 24, 1757, troops under the command of Colonel Robert Clive (1725–1774) came under heavy attack from an army nearly twenty times its size at Plassey, outside of Calcutta in the northeastern state of Bengal in India. The British had been involved with India since the sixteenth century, when the EIC received a royal charter that gave it the right to monopolize trade with India, which it did with great profitability throughout the course of the seventeenth and eighteenth centuries. India was not a colony or possession of the British government in the sense that the American colonies were until 1783 or as Ireland, the West Indies, and Canada continued to be. The British government had no official ties with or jurisdiction over affairs of the various Indian elites who ruled the continent after the disintegration of the Mughal Empire in the first half of the eighteenth century. Rather, local EIC officials, with the military assistance of a private army made up of mercenaries, established the company as an unofficial yet sovereign governing entity in a number of coastal towns of India like Bombay, Madras, and Calcutta.

Clive, leading 3,000 men, 2,100 of them Indian sepoys (from the Persian word *sipahi*, meaning soldier) in the employ of the EIC, had marched his forces north to take on the new French-supported nawab of Bengal, Siraj ud-Daula (1733–1757), who on ascending his throne a year earlier had challenged the EIC and captured its fort in Calcutta. With eight cannons in tow, Clive's army had dug in along a mud bank in a mango grove. Arrayed against them were 35,000 infantry formed up under brightly colored banners, 15,000 cavalry led by commanders on the backs of splendidly clad elephants, and 40 heavy artillery guns. Clive's troops did not stand a chance when the big guns began to pound their position.

But then, two things happened. It began to rain; the seasonal monsoons dumped sheets of water onto the nawab's troops and cannons, destroying gunpowder and fuses and rendering the guns useless. At the same time, the left flank of Siraj ud-Daula's army, a large contingent of cavalry led by a British collaborator, Mir Jafar (1691–1765), turned away from the battle, stranding the nawab's men in what was fast becoming a sea of mud. Daula's forces fled, leaving behind weapons, artillery, food, and supplies that the pursuing EIC troops confiscated for their own use. The next day, after consulting with Clive, Mir Jafar took the nawab's palace and treasury in the nearby town of Murshidabad and was recognized by the company as the new ruler of Bengal. Jafar's men later captured Siraj ud-Daula and killed him.

With their own man in office, the EIC gained a significant territorial hold on the subcontinent of India, marking the moment when the company's interests in trade became inextricably joined with military conquest and, a few years later, the actual administration of lands in India. In 1765, the Mughal emperor of India acknowledged the reality of the EIC's power in his domains when he granted it the *diwani*, or the right to collect taxes in Bengal. Over the next sixty years,

Clive wins dominion over Bengal, 1765.

British armies under the EIC would bring the rest of the subcontinent to heel, expanding the British empire in the east to dimensions that would have been unthinkable in the middle of the eighteenth century. The victory at Plassey aroused little fanfare at home, coming at a time when a new war with France had just commenced, but it serves both as an exemplar of the dynamics informing British politics and economics at the time and as a foreshadowing of a turning point in Britain's relationship with empire.

••

The years following the creation of the United Kingdom of Great Britain in 1707 saw much turmoil and upheaval both in the British Isles and in the empire. Wars with Spain and France; financial collapse; Jacobite risings; insurgencies by enslaved Africans in the Caribbean—all these contributed to a great deal of instability in the decades leading up to 1760. The prime ministership of Robert Walpole helped to alleviate some of the uncertainty and insecurity; the defeat of France in 1763 also mitigated the volatility of the period to some degree. The British empire expanded considerably during these years. In the next thirty years a disparate array of forces thrown up by the economic and intellectual revolutions of the eighteenth century—a prosperous and politically active middle class, an invigorated cadre of Scottish, Welsh, and Irish imperial agents, ongoing clashes with France across the globe, and restive colonial subjects—transformed the peoples and the societies of Britain and its imperial holdings.

NOTES

1. Quoted in Malcolm Balen, *The Secret History of the South Sea Bubble* (London, 2003), pp. 157, 158.
2. Quoted in Richard Dale. *The First Crash: Lessons from the South Sea Bubble* (Princeton, 2004), p. 40.
3. Quoted in Monod, *Imperial Island*, pp. 123–24.
4. Quoted in Peter Aughton, *Liverpool, a People's History* (Preston, 1990), p. 62.
5. Quoted in Ramsey Muir, *A History of Liverpool* (London, 1907), p. 147.
6. Quoted in Balen, *The Secret History of the South Sea Bubble*, p. 69.
7. Quoted in John Carswell, *The South Sea Bubble* (Dover, 1993), p. 164.
8. Quoted in Eveline Cruickshanks and Howard Erskine-Hill, *The Atterbury Plot* (Basingstoke, 2004), p. 61.
9. Quoted in Cruickshanks and Erskine-Hill, *The Atterbury Plot*, p. 112.
10. Quoted in Cruickshanks and Erskine-Hill, *The Atterbury Plot*, p. 181.

TIMELINE

1713	Treaty of Utrecht ends War of the Spanish Succession; Britain obtains *asiento*
1714	Anne dies; George I ascends the throne
1715	Jacobite rising
1720	Creation of South Sea Company
	English stock market crashes
1720	Declaratory Act gives British Parliament right to legislate for Ireland
1721	Horace Walpole becomes first "prime minister"
1722	Atterbury Plot

11. See Ann M. Carlos, Karen Maguire, and Larry Neal, "'A Knavish People. . .': London Jewry and the Stock Market during the South Sea Bubble," *Business History* 50.6 (November 2008): 728–48; and Ann M. Carlos and Larry Neal, "Women Investors in Early Capital Markets, 1720–1725," *Financial History Review* 11.2 (2004): 197–224.
12. Quoted in Sidney W. Mintz, *Sweetness and Power. The Place of Sugar in Modern History* (New York, 1985), p. 115.
13. Quoted in Peter Fryer, *Staying Power: The History of Black People in Britain* (London, 1984), p. 14.
14. Quoted in Fryer, *Staying Power*, pp. 17, 15.
15. Quoted in Andrew Jackson O'Shaughnessy, *An Empire Divided. The American Revolution and the British Caribbean* (Philadelphia, 2000), p. 15.
16. Quoted in Barbara Klamon Kopytoff, "Colonial Treaty as Sacred Charter of the Jamaican Maroons," *Ethnohistory*, 26.1 (Winter 1979), 45–64, p. 47.
17. Rosalind Mitchison, quoted in T. M. Devine, *The Scottish Nation, 1700–2007* (London, 2006), p. 21.
18. Quoted in Thomas William Heyck, *The Peoples of the British Isles: A New History, from 1688 to 1870* (Belmont, 1992), p. 132.

FURTHER READING

Ann M. Carlos, Karen Maguire, and Larry Neal, "'A Knavish People. . .': London Jewry and the Stock Market during the South Sea Bubble," *Business History* 50.6 (November 2008): 728–48.
Eveline Cruickshanks and Howard Erskine-Hill, *The Atterbury Plot*. Basingstoke, 2004.
Richard Dale. *The First Crash: Lessons from the South Sea Bubble*. Princeton, 2004.
Andrew Jackson O'Shaughnessy, *An Empire Divided. The American Revolution and the British Caribbean*. Philadelphia, 2000.
Helen J. Paul, *The South Sea Bubble. An Economic History of Its Origins and Consequences*. London, 2011.
Marcus Rediker, *The Slave Ship. A Human History*. New York, 2007.

1727	George I dies; George II ascends throne
1737	Porteous Riot
1739	Maroons of Jamaica become autonomous of British rule
1740–1748	War of the Austrian Succession
1745	Jacobite rising; Charles the Pretender lands in Scotland
1746	Jacobites defeated at Battle of Culloden
1754	French and Indian War breaks out in North America
1756–1763	Seven Years' War
1757	Robert Clive takes Bengal after battle at Plassey in India
1760	Tacky's Revolt in Jamaica

James Cook and Joseph Banks at Botany Bay, Australia, 1770.

CHAPTER 3

ECONOMIC AND INTELLECTUAL REVOLUTIONS OF THE EIGHTEENTH CENTURY

On April 28, 1770, on the eastern coast of what would be named Australia, Lieutenant James Cook (1728–1779) recorded in his journal that "at day light this morning we discovered a bay." Cook's men would name it "Stingray Bay," after the teeming number they found there, but within a short time it would come to be called Botany Bay, for the extraordinary variety and number of plants collected there by the naturalist Joseph Banks (1743–1820). As the commander of the *Endeavour*, Cook had been charged by the Royal Society of Great Britain to sail to Tahiti so that astronomers aboard might observe the transit of Venus and thereby calculate the distance between the earth and the sun. The admiralty had agreed to commission the voyage for its own reasons: "there is reason to imagine that a Continent or Land of great extent, may be found." Once the calculations were taken in Tahiti, Cook was to sail southward to look for that land; should he find it, honor and dignity for Britain, and the "advancement of Trade and Navigation thereof," were certain to follow.[1]

Cook's directives included instructions "to observe the Genius, Temper, Disposition and Number of the Natives" he encountered and to take possession of any lands that had not been previously mapped or claimed by Europeans. To be sure, the president of the Royal Society had urged on Cook and Banks the need for "the utmost patience and forbearance with respect to the Natives of the several Lands where the Ship may touch." They should avoid shedding blood at all costs because these were God's creatures as much as any Briton, and they were "the natural, and in the strictest sense of the word, the legal possessors of the several Regions they inhabit. No European Nation has a right to occupy any part of their country, or settle among them without their voluntary consent."[2] Cook succeeded in establishing contact with the Maori peoples of New Zealand, but he failed in his efforts to do the same with the aborigines of Australia. And he did lay claim to large portions of Australia and New Zealand, although not, it turns out, with the consent of the people who lived there.

The eighteenth century witnessed a number of transformations in economic, intellectual, and political life, dramatically altering the way Britons ate, drank, dressed, worked, socialized, and thought. As a consequence of revolutions in agriculture, commerce, and industry, significant portions of the populace ate more and more nutritious foods, their health improved, they lived longer, and, in aggregate, they suffered fewer deaths. Trends in intellectual life associated with the movement known as the Enlightenment introduced new concepts about society, politics, government, and economy. All of these transformations interacted with one another to foster the creation of what we can now regard as a global world, a world linked together by the movements of people, most numerous of whom were slaves brought from Africa to the Americas; by the diffusion worldwide of commodities like sugar, tea, tobacco, furs, coffee, and cotton; by vast geographical exploration that produced new bodies of knowledge about distant lands and peoples and flora and fauna; and by the establishment of a British empire across the globe, much of it controlled by multinational trading companies like the Hudson's Bay Company or the East India Company.

Cook and Banks exemplified the new methods of acquiring knowledge thrown up by the Enlightenment. They and others like them observed and collected vast amounts of information pertaining to plants, animals, topographies, and people, bringing back so much data that it could hardly be accommodated by the existing institutions and disciplines devoted to science, learning, and knowledge. Their encounters with peoples across the world, in particular, helped to spur the development of theories about human development that profoundly challenged the universalist assumptions of the Enlightenment about reason and nature.

··

THE DEMOGRAPHIC AND AGRICULTURAL REVOLUTIONS

Early modern population patterns were characterized by high birth rates and high death rates, establishing, over time, a static rate of population growth. That pattern changed in about 1750 when high birth rates were accompanied by lower, although still not low, death rates, enabling the population to take off; from that time on population has grown steadily up to our very day. In England, population grew by around 14 percent between 1701 and 1750; but between 1751 and 1801, when the first national census was taken, it had increased by 50 percent, reaching 8,700,000. The period 1801 to 1851 saw growth amounting to almost 100 percent—that is, the population of England doubled in the space of a half century. Welsh figures are harder to come by, but Wales contained about 500,000 people in

1770 and 1,163,000 in 1851, more than a doubling of its population in the space of two generations or so. Scotland's population growth lagged somewhat: between 1700 or so and 1801, it grew by about 50 percent, from 860,000 to 1,625,000. Ireland saw by far the most spectacular population growth. In 1750, some 2 million Irish inhabited the island; that number had grown to 5 million by 1800. So great was population growth overall in Britain that by the third or fourth quarter of the nineteenth century, when middle-class Britons began to limit their births through contraceptive devices, the population continued to grow. (Working-class families were not able to take advantage of the new forms of birth control, so their birth rates did not start falling until after the First World War. In Ireland, devastated by the great famine of the mid-nineteenth century, Catholic prohibitions against birth control kept the fertility rate high, but continued emigration following the famine kept absolute population numbers low.)

The demographic revolution of the eighteenth century was caused by what historians call the agricultural revolution, which began in the seventeenth century. The land failures and famines characteristic of the late seventeenth century stimulated landowners and farmers to consider ways in which food might be more productively grown, and the warm years of the 1730s may have provided handsome yields that would have encouraged them to continue their efforts. The agricultural revolution consisted of at least four new developments. The first was the introduction of new crops from the New World such as maize (what we in the United States call corn) and potatoes. The second factor had to do with the way fields were farmed, particularly the introduction of what historians call enclosure, or the fencing off of fields to restrict tenants' use of the land. A third factor concerned the organization of the fields themselves with regard to cultivation. Large capitalist farming enterprises, owned by great landowners, introduced a four-field system of cultivation, replacing the three-field system that had prevailed in earlier times. And finally, new fodder crops—that is to say, crops for the feeding of animals—were introduced, which had the added benefit of fixing the nitrogen in the soil so as to increase its fertility. Such crops as turnips enabled cattle to be fed over the winter, allowing farmers to utilize their manure for fertilizer throughout the entire year. Other fodder crops like alfalfa or legumes introduced even more nitrogen into the soil, enabling the soil to yield greater numbers of crops over time.

The potato had a number of attributes that recommended it. Having come from the high plains of the Andes, it was a hardy vegetable and could thrive in soils not conducive to wheat or other grains. Potatoes could be grown in three to four months, instead of the eleven months required by wheat. That shortened growing season enabled potatoes to be harvested roughly three times a year, whereas wheat could be reaped only once a year. Potatoes could also be grown in far smaller plots of land, increasing the yield per acre over that of wheat by about two to three times. Combining these increases meant that the potato increased the food supply by nearly 400 percent: a single acre's yield of potatoes contained a year's worth of energy and protein for ten people. The introduction of the potato into the diets of poor Britons increased their calorie intakes and improved their nutrition levels;

containing vitamins and minerals like vitamin C, it was calculated to improve health, making it possible for formerly vulnerable Britons to withstand scurvy and the everyday diseases such as influenza or conditions like diarrhea that plagued their lives. It may also be that in increasing their calorie intake Britons grew bigger, which may have lowered the age of sexual maturity for men and women. Prior to the agricultural revolution men and women reached the age of sexual maturity at about seventeen or eighteen years of age. With the introduction of the potato, people were able to put on weight, affecting the fat-to-weight ratio that appears to regulate sexual maturity. Although historians seem sure that the demographic revolution was almost exclusively a function of lowered death rates resulting from more- and better-nourished people, it may well be also that a lowered age of sexual maturity increased birth rates at the same time. This was almost certainly the case in Ireland. Indeed, just as population growth was taking off after 1750, rates of illegitimate births also experienced dramatic increases.

Potatoes were regarded by many Britons as the poor man's food, and many were reluctant to embrace it as a staple crop. Over time, however, as famine swept through communities on a fairly regular basis, villagers came to regard it as a welcome source of food when wheat failed. It seems to have played a significant role in people's diets in Ireland early on, where poverty made it difficult for families to access other kinds of food, and it may have spread from Ireland to the rest of the British Isles. As one seventeenth-century observer wrote, "These Roots, although they came at first from the *Indies*, yet thrive and prosper very well in *Ireland*, where there is whole Fields of them; from whence they have been brought into *Wales* and into the North Parts of *England*, where they likewise prosper and increase exceedingly,"[3] although other accounts have it spreading from Ireland to Scotland first. Because its cultivation required only a spade, it could be raised in the small garden plots of landless laborers and workers in the cities, and its ease of cooking in homes that possessed little fuel and few kitchen amenities made it a popular dish for hard-working, tired family members.

The enclosure system, introduced first in England, involved the fencing off of what had been common lands in any given village. The commons were used by villagers to pasture their animals or to grow small vegetable gardens or as places where wood could be gathered to fuel the fires in their cottages. The availability of the commons in a village made the difference between making it or not for many people: the removal of the commons from public use could thus have a devastating effect on the lives of villagers. By fencing off large tracts of land enclosure fostered the development of capitalist farming. Improving landlords could use these large tracts of land and farm them more efficiently than would have been the case when land was organized according to the older strip-farming method. Enclosure certainly produced hardship for cottagers dependent on the common lands for survival, but it had the effect of increasing productivity on the land and increasing crop yields extensively. Capitalist farming was labor intensive as well, providing work for the increasing numbers of peasants who, having lost the commons that once helped to support their families, now relied on waged work to survive.

All of these developments—the introduction of new food crops, the introduction of new fodder crops, the introduction of nitrogen-fixing crops, and the reorganization of the land—improved agricultural productivity by about 1,200 percent. This increase in the amount of food made it possible after 1750 for population growth be sustained rather than fall into the old pattern: high birth rates causing population to grow beyond the capacity of agriculture to maintain it followed by high death rates, reducing population to levels sustainable by existing food supply, leaving stagnant population growth over time. Now those high birth rates could be sustained; populations did not outrun the food supply for the first time in centuries, producing population growth that in turn placed great pressure on the land to increase the food supply.

Scottish landlords in the Lowlands reformed their agricultural practice along the lines of the English model fairly early on in the process; Highlanders, on the other hand, did not do so until after the failure of the '45. From 1750 on, lured by the possibility of higher rents and greater profits and the increased status that such wealth would bring them in Scotland as a whole, many Highland chiefs turned to "improved" farming, consolidating their fields and replacing tenants who formerly offered them military service with those who gave them the highest bid for leasing their land. These practices left thousands of Scots without the ability to sustain themselves and their families, compelling some 20,000 of them, mostly Highlanders, to immigrate to America in the 1760s and 1770s. Other great landlords converted their lands from arable farming to sheep pasturage, eager to capitalize on the growing market for wool (discussed below), evicting many thousands of Scottish peasants. These so-called Highland Clearances often involved terrible violence inflicted on people who had nowhere to go: landlords ordered the burning of cottages, sometimes with the families who inhabited them still inside.

In Wales, improvement occurred at a slower rate than in England and was confined for the most part to the border counties until the 1770s. Landlords did not traditionally interfere with the farming practices of their tenants, but in the last years of the eighteenth century, when wars with France drove up prices, they became far more active in urging new techniques on farmers and began to raise their rents as well. Crop rotation improved corn yields significantly in the areas where arable farming prevailed. For the most part, however, Welsh agriculture centered on livestock, making the growing of fodder crops and the development of better breeding techniques the most important aspects of the agricultural revolution there. An explosion of enclosure acts in the late eighteenth century, designed not so much to consolidate land holdings as to increase the rights of landlords at the expense of their tenants, left thousands of Welsh peasants without the means to support themselves. As was the case in Scotland, many of them immigrated, most to America but a good number to cities in England, especially Liverpool and London.

Irish agriculture remained "unimproved." Irish landlords, predominantly Protestant and absent, interested only in collecting as much rent as possible, did little to introduce new methods of farming. They let out their land to "middlemen," who in turn broke it up into smaller parcels and leased them to tenants. Tenant farmers knew little about the methods of improvement going on in other parts of Britain, and they had no incentive to engage in them if they did because landlords simply raised their rents if their holdings yielded greater productivity and did not recognize the value of the improvements made. An exception to this practice occurred in Ulster, where tenants could recoup the value of any improvements they made to the land. Finally, unlike in England, where tenants were not permitted to subdivide their land, Irish tenants across the island, hampered by penal laws that outlawed primogeniture, continually split their holdings to provide a plot for their sons. With each passing generation, this practice ensured that plots became smaller and smaller in size, barely capable of producing enough food for subsistence, let alone a surplus to sell at market. These conditions made the potato all the more important to the Irish peasantry, till it became virtually the only foodstuff that most of them could depend on. When it failed, as it did a number of times in the eighteenth century, disaster followed.

EARLY INDUSTRIALIZATION

Early industrialization, the application of mechanical power provided by the steam engine to established manufacturing industries such as mining and textiles, took place first in Britain in the 1760s, a consequence in large part of the scarcity of resources caused by the pressure of population growth on the land. Virtually every item consumed by people in the countryside—food, drink, clothing, building materials, fuel, transportation (in the form of horses)—came from the land. As population expanded exponentially, the need to produce more to feed it created a profound shortage of land. As earlier sources of fuel and raw materials such as wood or wool waned in supply, Britons sought substitutes for them; although most of these substitutes were more expensive to produce, requiring more labor and more processing and resulting in a relatively inferior product, the shortages occasioned by population pressure compelled their use.

The most pressing shortage was that of wood. Deforestation went hand in hand with the demographic and agricultural revolutions, as the search for more and more arable land to feed more and more people required the cutting of old growth forests. Another sector of the economy—the fast-growing shipbuilding industry—also put pressure on Britain's forests. The construction of commercial and naval vessels required huge amounts of timber: the great ships of the line, for example, which could carry 2,000 tons, required 4,200 to 5,600 meters of timber, the equivalent of many thousands of full-growth trees. Oak was the favored wood, being strong and resistant to rot. If hit by a cannonball it could not easily be splintered. Oaks of the size necessary to build a ship of the line took a century to grow, and by 1650 they no longer existed in Britain, necessitating their importation from Baltic lands and the far reaches of northern New England, from which fir or white pine for the building of masts had long been harvested. By 1700 those engaged in housing construction or in other industries requiring wood had also to import their materials. The supply of wood for fuel held up longer, but by 1775 the royal forests had been depleted of nearly all their timber and that on private property would not last much longer.

Deforestation caused by shipbuilding and the encroachment on forested lands for the expansion of agriculture compelled an urgent search for a substitute for wood. Increasingly Britons turned to coal to provide fuel for their homes and industries and to new building materials such as brick to increase their housing stock. Deforestation, in other words, played a major role in the process that would lead Britain to industrialize. For the most part, coal was a readily adaptable alternative, despite relatively high transportation costs and the dirtiness of coal smoke, which filled the homes and workshops of its consumers. The demand for coal could not be met by reliance on open coal deposits. As consumers used more and more coal in the course of their daily lives, mine shafts had to be sunk increasingly deeper to reach supplies of coal buried beneath the earth. As mine shafts sought to reach seams below the level of the water table, water poured into them and had to be drained if coal supplies were to be obtained. A variety of attempts were made to drain the mines: simple gravity in the case of mines situated on a hillside, for example, or the use of horse-drawn pumps to get rid of the water. This latter method proved effective, but the number of horses required to carry off so much water was expensive. Horses needed to be fed, and the fodder required to keep them took up a lot of arable land at a time when population growth placed a premium on land used to grow food for human consumption. As it became more expensive to use animals to drive drainage pumps, the search for another means of drainage became more pressing, culminating ultimately in the invention and development of the steam engine. Unlike water-driven machinery, which required that the enterprise be located next to a river or stream, or animal-driven power, which depended on a large food source for horses or oxen, steam power had few constraints on it. Steam engines could be located virtually anywhere; placed at the pithead of mines, they had access to all of the fuel they could possibly need.

Prior to industrialization, manufacturing had taken place in artisan workshops under a guild system. Beginning in the fifteenth and sixteenth centuries, enterprising individuals we call entrepreneurs introduced a new form of manufacturing in textiles as a way to get around guild restrictions in the towns and cities of Britain. In what has been called variously the putting-out system or cottage industry, entrepreneurs would go to farmers in the countryside and set them up as manufacturers of woolens. From the start, this form of manufacturing involved techniques and processes that are the precursors of factory systems of manufacturing. The division or specialization of labor, for instance, characterized cottage industry. The entrepreneur would set up the inhabitants of one cottage, for example, with spinning wheels, beginning the gradual shift away from families owing their own tools to entrepreneurs doing so exclusively, and bring to those cottagers raw wool to be spun into thread.

Early steam engine at a coal mine, c. 1770s.

He would then collect the thread from that cottage and take it to another cottage, where the thread would be woven into cloth. The entrepreneur would come back to retrieve the cloth and take it to another cottage, where it would be cleaned and fulled. In each instance, the entrepreneur would provide the tools and raw materials to the cottagers and would pay them a wage for the labor they performed. We see here the forerunners of the factory system: laborers who do not own what Karl Marx (1818–1883) would call "the means of production"—tools or raw materials—who carry out only one small aspect of the manufacturing of any particular commodity and who are paid a wage for their labor. We also see at work here the principles of capitalist organization. Entrepreneurs paid as low a wage as they could for the work performed, and they sold their products for as high a price as they could, their goal being to maximize their profits.

With the demographic and agricultural revolutions placing great demand on arable land, pastures on which sheep might be grazed grew less available, running up the cost of raw wool and therefore the cost of finished woolen garments. The shortage of wool led entrepreneurs to consider a new source for textiles that would not compete with the demand for arable land. Cotton proved the answer. Certainly, cotton is a land-based product, but it could be imported from either India or America and would not have to compete for land with the food-producing sector of agriculture. Population growth stimulated demand for more and more clothing, which could be met by developing great economies of scale. The protoindustrial form of manufacturing in cottages in the countryside evolved eventually into the establishment of larger places of work. Rather than taking place within individual cottages, cotton manufacturing might be moved into a larger setting involving larger numbers of workers, creating a system of mass production.

A variety of innovations and inventions, first in cotton spinning and then in weaving, increased productivity—output per worker—and dramatically and substantially reduced the cost of goods produced in this way. The spinning jenny, developed in 1764, made it possible for one person to spin six or seven cotton threads at once; subsequent models increased that number to eighty. The spun thread, however, was not tough or durable enough to act on its own; it had to be combined with linen to produce cloth.

114. ACKROYD'S LOOM-SHED AT HALIFAX.—(*Worsted Goods.*)

Weaving shed, early nineteenth century.

Richard Arkwright (1732–1792) responded to this problem with the invention of the water frame, which enabled workers to spin thread strong enough to stand alone without the addition of linen. But this new spinning machine had to be driven by a water wheel, which necessitated that textile operations be situated alongside a stream or river. The steam engine, initially developed as a solution to a problem in mining industries, would later make it possible to move factories or mills away from water sources and closer to population areas or to seaports, where greater access to a labor force and to a means of distributing factory goods made manufacturing much more efficient. In this way, factories could be made large enough to accommodate many machines and the numbers of people required to work them.

More technological breakthroughs quickly appeared. The mule, a combination of the most productive elements of the jenny and the water frame, invented by Samuel Crompton (1753–1827) in 1785, made it possible to spin fine thread at a low cost. These new efficiencies enabled Britain to establish itself as the leading cotton producer in the world; between 1770 and 1790, cotton manufactured goods rose by 1,000 percent. When the cotton gin, credited to Eli Whitney (1765–1825), was developed in 1793, it enabled the United States to grow cotton economically, providing Britain with all the raw cotton it could use.

Although the astronomical growth of textile manufacturing would await the application of steam power in the 1830s, early-stage industrialization provided employment for large numbers of agricultural workers displaced by the techniques of the agricultural revolution and by the growth of population it sustained. New agricultural processes employed greater numbers of workers than ever before, but population growth still outran the numbers that could be absorbed on the land. The availability of jobs in textile mills and factories took that pressure off the land, enabling the increase in food production to continue, providing employment for the excess population, and ensuring a work force for the burgeoning new industry.

Indeed, the massive population growth of the eighteenth century could not have been sustained had not industrialization enabled these new large numbers of people to move off the land and take jobs in booming cities and new factory towns. Ireland and Highland Scotland serve as instructive counterexamples of this phenomenon: domestic industry in Ireland employed a fair amount of people during the second half of the eighteenth century, but once industrialization in England took off after 1815—and England enacted legislation aimed at restricting the importation of Irish goods—Ireland's domestic manufacturing sector could not compete with it, and population pressure on the land increased dramatically, driving down wages in all areas of the economy and further impoverishing much of the Irish peasantry. In the northern parts of Scotland, changes in land tenure and the organization of the land left vast numbers of Highland Scottish peasants without the means to support themselves, destroying traditional farm towns, called *bailteans*, and ushering in the clearances that threw thousands of people of their land. More destructive was the enormous demand for wool generated by industrialization. Industrialization in England, by contrast, absorbed a great deal of the increasing population, which enabled the agricultural revolution to continue and to feed the people in the cities. If each one of these revolutions in demography, agriculture, and industry had not worked in tandem with one another, none of them could have been sustained for long. Population growth provided a workforce for the factories, factories absorbed excess population from the countryside, and the agricultural revolution both produced the excess population and sustained it by providing enough food to keep the increased numbers of people fed. Capitalist agriculture yielded great profits and capitalist farmers sought investment opportunities for their tremendous infusions of cash. They found those opportunities in a variety of commercial ventures, especially investment in mines, factories, and railroads that would enable those industries to power Britain's economic growth in the nineteenth century.

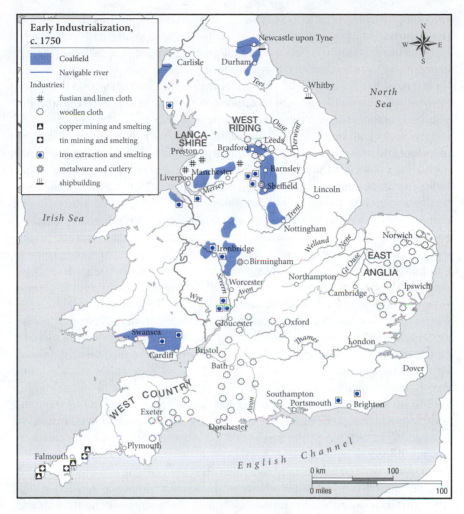

MAP 3.1
Early Industrialization, c. 1750

THE COMMERCIAL REVOLUTION

New and enlarged sources of trade, new means of financial exchange, and new techniques of production generated a commercial revolution in the eighteenth century. Throughout the course of the eighteenth century, many Britons—the English, those Scots living in Edinburgh and the Lowland towns, and the Irish of Ulster—enjoyed a consumer boom. After 1750, it amounted to a revolution in consumption. Individuals delighted in the purchasing of commodities as never before, buying not only necessities but also luxury items. Fashions that once only the rich could afford now made their way into the wardrobes of the middling ranks, enabling those of "meaner condition" to clothe themselves in the garb of the aristocracy.

More people than ever before could afford the new goods appearing on shop counters: spices, sugar, coffee and tea, tobacco, clothing, and metalware. Prosperity displayed itself in embellishments to and new arrangements within the home. Formerly modest dwellings were transformed into elegant homes by the addition of carpeting to wooden flooring, wainscoting to plaster walls, the replacement of stone hearths with marble and of simple oak furniture with more fancy designs in walnut and mahogany. Houses became larger and space within homes increasingly differentiated, so that sleeping quarters were separated from kitchens and living rooms. Privacy became possible and then normative; ultimately, it became seen as a necessary component of middle-class life. The increased availability of domestic consumer goods such as furniture, chamber pots, trinkets and knick-knacks, table and bed linens, mirrors, carpets, wall-hangings, pictures and prints, dry goods, kitchen utensils, and implements rendered homes far more comfortable and gave domestic life an appeal it had not had before. Middling people, who made up at least a quarter of England's population by mid-century, could furnish their homes with items that would not have been found in aristocratic households fifty years earlier. Lower-ranked households benefitted from the commercial revolution as well, although not nearly as fully or as widely as the middling sorts. In fact, many on the lowest rungs, as we shall see below, found themselves displaced by the changes of the economic revolutions, forced into waged work or onto parish relief to maintain their families.

Women produced much of the consumer demand that helped to fuel the commercial revolution of the eighteenth century. Certainly men shopped for clothing and goods, but their forays into the shops of haberdashers or furniture- or carriage-makers tended to be occasional, in contrast to women's consumption patterns, which demonstrated a regularity consistent with the running of a household that required daily purchases of mundane items. Manufacturers and retailers recognized that consumer decisions rested largely with the mistresses of households and pitched their goods accordingly. Novels, themselves a new phenomenon linked to the creation of an expanded market system, testified to the pleasures women experienced in consumption, if only to condemn them, and helped to broadcast the possibilities for pleasure to thousands of readers throughout the country. Newspapers, far more widely consumed than novels, raised awareness even more.

The commercial revolution of the eighteenth century derived as much of its impetus and prosperity from the exchange of human beings as from trade in raw materials and agricultural and manufactured products. The slave trade constituted one crucial leg of the triangular trade between Britain, Africa, and the Atlantic colonies; and the use of slave labor in the West Indian and North American colonies made it possible for small populations of white colonists to exploit the resources—largely sugar and tobacco—of those areas profitably. Slavery stood at the crossroads of foreign trade, colonization, and consumer demand—both domestic and foreign—that stimulated economic growth; in many ways it was the fulcrum on which the development of the British economy of the eighteenth century turned.

As we saw in Chapter 2, British ships carried between a quarter and half of all the African slaves sold in the Americas in the second half of the eighteenth century. Those same ships carried cargoes of spices, tobacco, rum, and molasses, but especially sugar, to the North American colonies and to Britain, where demand for the sweetener had risen dramatically by 1775. Once in England, the ships took on cargoes of manufactured goods such as textiles (especially cotton, much of which had been imported from India), brass pans, copper rods, iron bars and bowls, beads, pots and pans, muskets, gunpowder, and beer and sailed to West Africa, where agents traded them for slaves. African demand for manufactured items was considerable, accounting for about 25 percent of Britain's exports of Indian-made cotton goods in 1792. Exports of wrought-iron goods to Africa were second only to those to the American colonies at mid-century. Demand for these items in Africa played a large part in stimulating English manufacturing, as did the demand of the Caribbean colonists, who consumed some 12 percent of English manufactured goods between 1748 and 1776.

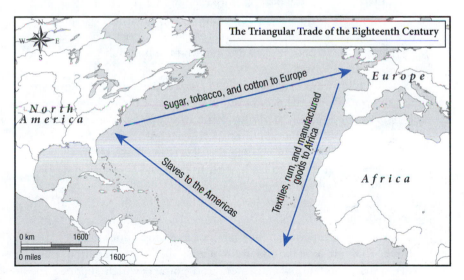

MAP 3.2
The Triangular Trade of the Eighteenth Century

Slavery produced great wealth. West Indian planters used slave labor to generate profits from the sale of sugar; slaves owned by the American colonists produced tobacco and cotton that was sold to manufacturers in England. With their profits, colonists purchased commodities from Manchester, Birmingham, London, Sheffield, Glasgow, and Leeds, enriching the manufacturers of those items. The ships that carried African captives to the Americas and raw materials

A PLACE IN TIME

Liverpool's "African Trade"

Liverpool's involvement in what contemporaries euphemistically called the "African trade" grew dramatically over the course of the eighteenth century, bringing great riches to those who engaged in it and stimulating the development of a variety of industries to support it. A ship from the port had transported slaves to the Caribbean and the Americas as early as 1698, but it was not until the 1720s that commerce in human beings can truly be said to have begun. In that decade, 42 slave ships sailed from Liverpool, followed by 197 the following decade. In the 1740s, war with France and Spain kept slave ships from venturing out of London and other ports along the English Channel, leaving the field free for Liverpool's merchants. In the 1740s, 43 percent of Britain's slave trade was in their hands—more than 200 ships embarked on the voyage that supplied an ever-increasing demand for slaves, and that number nearly doubled in subsequent decades. By the 1790s, almost 80 percent of the slave trade was in the hands of Liverpool merchants, earning the borough the moniker, "the metropolis of slavery."[4]

The slave trade was a crucial element of and depended on the developments associated with the economic revolutions of the eighteenth century. Population growth deriving from the agricultural revolution swelled the numbers of Liverpudlians, creating both a labor force and a source of demand for goods, making possible the commercial revolution that drove both industry and trade with Ireland and Scotland and other parts of the world. From a population of about 7,000 in 1708, the city—and we can begin to call it a city now—grew to 34,000 in 1773 and to more than 77,000 by the end of the century. The inhabitants worked in a great variety of occupations. They labored as sailors, dockworkers, and boatmen; they made sails and built ships; they manufactured glass, metals, guns, soap, cotton and linen, and pottery, which supplied the export trade; they milled salt, brewed beer, and constructed docks, residences, warehouses, offices, stores, pubs, churches, and theaters. They moved textiles produced in the new Lancashire factories down canals others had dug to link the increasingly industrial hinterland with the port. And they consumed the sugar, tobacco, rum, beef, and grains imported both from Ireland and Scotland and from the Caribbean and the American colonies.

Slaving had a powerful impact on Liverpool's population, not least on those who constituted the trade's proletariat, sailors. They worked under harsh conditions, earned little in the way of wages, ate badly aboard ship, and faced dangerous situations while at sea. Accidents occurred, slave revolts broke out, disease ran rampant, and captains often imposed a cruel discipline. Most sailors signed on only because they were broke: "nothing but necessity compels them at the last, especially to Guinea [Africa]," noted one veteran seaman. Anyone with "a Farthing in their pocket" would never willingly join the Guinea trade.[5]

Trade with the rest of the United Kingdom made up the bulk of Liverpool's commercial activity, but by the last quarter of the eighteenth century, the slave trade produced the greatest amount of wealth among its merchants. The "most beneficial trade is to Guinea and the West-Indies," wrote one observer in 1792, "by which many have raised great fortunes."[6] Liverpudlian merchants, the quintessential "gentlemanly capitalists," fared so well in the slave trade—outdoing their rivals in the other port towns such as Bristol—because they cultivated and exploited a number of opportunities that the others did not. They formed deep commercial ties with African slave traders, especially in the Bight of Biafra in West Africa (off the coast of modern-day Nigeria), where entrepreneurs like Antera Duke gave his business exclusively to them. They established social as well as economic ties with their suppliers, urging African partners and chiefs to send their children to school in Liverpool where they could learn the trade and develop contacts in the business. By the end of the 1780s, some fifty to seventy Africans attended schools in the area each year. Liverpool merchants also extended credit to their African dealers, facilitating the exchanges that led to the removal across the Atlantic of millions of African men and women at the prime of their productive and reproductive lives and leading to the depletion of the West African population.

The lucrative trade in human beings made Liverpool merchants not only rich but also politically influential. In disproportionate numbers over the course of the eighteenth century, they sat on the town council; many of them served as mayor of the borough; they held seats in Parliament. Liverpool could boast of being the second largest city in the United Kingdom, the port that served as the entrepôt of empire. But the identification of Liverpool with the slave trade also gave it a reputation among a growing number of influential people in Great Britain as a moral cesspool, a place not to be celebrated but condemned.

to Britain and the manufactures to Africa and the American and West Indian colonies realized generous profits from their carrying trade, as did the insurance companies that protected their cargoes and the banks that financed them.

The interplay between the imperial and domestic economies in the eighteenth century ensured that Britain's economic successes far exceeded those of virtually any other place in the world. Britain's access to sugar grown in the Caribbean and cotton grown in the American South by enslaved Africans meant that the shortages that pushed some aspects of early industrialization did not interfere with its labor needs in factories. Sugar provided much-needed calories to workers who would otherwise have had to obtain their energy sources from potatoes, sugar beets, or grains grown on British soil. Likewise, the cotton that provided workers' clothing did not require British land or labor. In these instances, freed-up wage labor drove down costs for British manufacturers, giving them an advantage over their competitors.

MAP 3.3
Britain's Trading Empire, c. 1770

THE ENLIGHTENMENT: THE PUBLIC SPHERE

Revolutions in demography, agriculture, and industry were joined by a revolution in thinking. During the eighteenth century, in the course of what is known as the Enlightenment, the discoveries and modes of thinking promulgated during the scientific revolution were popularized throughout Europe. Philosophers championed knowledge produced through rational thought and discovery. Enlightenment thinkers believed that human beings were capable of achieving a state of perfection on this earth. Isaac Newton (1643–1727) had developed formulations that seemed to explain all natural phenomena. John Locke (1632–1704) produced a method for reasoning that made sense to educated Britons. His work suggested that the laws discovered by Newton for the universe had their corollaries in laws governing human societies. Together, Newton and Locke provided the two concepts that underpinned much of Enlightenment thinking, nature and reason. Along with other scientists and philosophers such as Francis Bacon (1561–1626) and René Descartes, they put forward new ideas about how knowledge about the natural world, or natural philosophy, could be reliably attained. They promoted an understanding of the natural world as a machine that operated according to knowable laws. Mechanistic theories of the universe, especially those constructed by Newton, came to dominate ideas about how the natural world functioned. Newton provided an elegant, harmonious, single explanation for how the natural world worked. All motion could be described, measured, and explained through mathematical formulas. The universe behaved mechanistically like a clock, originally created and put into motion by God but running smoothly ever since according to laws of motion Newton discovered. Laws of nature existed, and Newton had discovered them; what was to keep human reason from working out the secrets at the heart of every other aspect of life?

This newfound confidence in the capability of humans to understand nature and to control its affairs promoted the sensibility that nature had no intrinsic larger purpose but was made exclusively for the use and well-being of humanity; Bacon declared that "the world is made for man, not man for the world." He, Descartes, Newton, and countless others claimed that it was the proper function of humans to exercise control over nature, to manipulate it, to force it to yield its secrets and its bounty. The new scientific discoveries—gravity, the circulation of the blood, the fact that the earth revolves around the sun, and many, many others—and the methods by which they had been made meant, according to Descartes, that humans were to become "masters and possessors of nature."[7] The language used by thinkers such as Bacon as they set forth their agendas for the domination of the natural word by man became increasingly violent—and often sexually violent—in tone and imagery. Nature was to be "penetrated" by man; her secrets coaxed or coerced from her; her fruits and gifts wrested from her grasp. Such a relationship with the natural world—one in which humans did not belong to it but held dominion over it for their own exclusive benefit—corresponded comfortably to the desires and intentions of Britons involved both in developing new ways to farm, mine, and manufacture and in exploring and colonizing the world.

Botanists, in particular, who were experts in finding, identifying, transporting, and acclimatizing New World plants, furthered the expansionist project considerably: plants discovered in new territories might enable European countries to procure staple supplies of drugs, foods, and luxury items like sugar or chocolate. Substitutes for luxury items that could only be purchased from China or India, which by consequence drained British sterling, might be developed in the New World. Crops such as rhubarb, sugarcane, coffee, and tea could be grown in British colonies and brought to the home country for domestic consumption. One of the most important aspects of the transfer of plants from the New World pertained to their medical uses: not only might Britain become self-sufficient in the production of medicines, thus eliminating the outflow of capital to foreign countries, but also new medicines might allow Britons to live and work in tropical colonies that heretofore sickened and killed frightening numbers of them. Laboratories and botanical gardens sprang up—Kew Gardens being one of the most prominent—bringing the joys of nature to city dwellers, to be sure, but more important serving as arenas within which experimentation and plant acclimatization could take place.

Botanists inventoried and classified their discoveries, following the scientific methods laid down by Bacon, Descartes, and Newton. Europe's naturalists not only collected the stuff of nature, but also laid their own peculiar grid of reason over nature in the form of nomenclatures and taxonomies. Carolus Linnaeus, for example, created a taxonomic system for all living creatures, a table that organized them according to categories of kingdom, phylum, class, order, family, genus, and species on the basis of similarities in structure or origin. These names and categories purported to give each species of plant, animal, or mineral its proper place in the natural world; certainly they imposed a hierarchical ordering that conferred a valuation on the organism, rendering some more important or less desirable than others. This hierarchy and valuation had profound implications for human beings as well.

The scientific revolution developed the concept of laws of nature that pertained to the material world of the universe. Enlightenment thinkers extended that notion to the human world: just as the universe could be shown to be governed by laws of nature, philosophers insisted that society and its political expression or government were also governed by laws of nature. Although seventeenth-century thinkers such as Thomas Hobbes (1588–1679) characterized nature and the humans who inhabited it as violent and brutal, Enlightenment thinkers portrayed it in an almost entirely positive cast. As described by Newton and Locke and popularized by eighteenth-century thinkers, nature was harmonious, orderly, simple, and pure. Moreover, philosophers claimed that it was possible to understand the operations and characteristics of nature through the exercise of reason. If applied to human relations, reason would reveal that political systems and societies based on inequality were unnatural. The use of reason would enable humans to discover natural institutions and relations; once found, people would naturally conform to them and find peace, harmony, and happiness.

One group of Enlightenment thinkers concerned with economic laws of nature believed that in their ignorance of the laws of nature, men promoting mercantilist policies had been acting against nature and constraining the opportunities for progress. They argued that impediments to trade such as tariffs, navigation acts, and regulations governing manufacturing or trade, instead of concentrating wealth in the home country, actually inhibited it. Had they used their reason, these economic philosophers noted, policy makers would understand that restraints on manufacturing and trade reduced productivity and benefited only a few. Understanding correctly the laws of nature, they argued, would lead policy makers to understand that encouraging individuals to pursue their own self-interest—that is, to act naturally—and to buy as cheaply as possible and to sell as high as possible according to the natural flow of supply and demand, would expand the wealth of all. We associate this philosophy, summed up by the French term *laissez-faire*, or let it do as it will, most closely with Adam Smith's (1723–1790) *The Wealth of Nations*, published in 1776. Unlike French philosophers, who saw in agriculture the source of a kingdom's wealth and prosperity, Smith believed that manufacturing was the most important sector of the economy, and his policies of free trade referred as much to labor as to any other aspect of production. His thinking owed much to his observations of the monopolistic practices of the East India Company and of slavery, that ultimate institution of unfree labor. Through unfettered competition, he advised, the invisible hand of the market would ensure that resources would flow to the most efficient and productive of enterprises, maximizing profit and the flow of goods and services to consumers. Society, in Smith's writings, operated in such a way that the exchange of goods and the division of labor by means of which those goods were produced and exchanged worked to transform universal selfishness into universal well-being. The pursuit of self-interest, far from being antisocial, contributed enormously to the welfare of all, he insisted. Smith's theories became enormously influential in the nineteenth century, as we shall see in later chapters, helping to expand Britain's economic might throughout the world, but unfettered competition as a hallmark of western capitalism would also serve to justify and therefore facilitate massive exploitation of people and of the environment, the effects of which are with us today. Smith himself opposed slavery and did not hold with the idea that non-European societies were necessarily inferior to Britain, but his theories were nevertheless used to legitimate regimes of coercion and abuse.

Smith belonged to a group of extraordinarily talented Scottish intellectuals whose collective thinking made up what historians refer to as the Scottish Enlightenment. During the second half of the eighteenth century, Smith, David Hume (1711–1776), and other Scottish philosophers such as William Robertson (1721–1793), Adam Ferguson (1723–1816), Francis Hutcheson (1694–1747), and John Millar (1735–1801) spoke frequently of "the polished nations" of Western Europe, whose increased commercial activity and therefore increased wealth distinguished them from "rude and barbarous" nations characteristic of the ancient, feudal world of farmers and warriors. In an elaborate formulation of the stages in the transition from the agrarian to the commercial society, Smith argued that the increase in wealth from exchange produced a far more just and secure polity than that possible under the reign of feudal lords. Before the advent of commercial activity, great lords had no alternative but to share their surplus agricultural products with their tenants, who owned no property of their own and thus had no security, and with their retainers, who were entirely dependent on their lords and provided them with private armies with which the lords felt emboldened to make war. "The king was . . . incapable of restraining the violence of the great lords," Smith explained. "They [made] war according to their own discretion, almost continually upon one another, and very frequently upon the king; and the open country . . . [was] a scene of violence, rapine, and disorder." With the introduction of commerce and manufacture, goods appeared on which the great lords might expend their surplus wealth: "a pair of diamond buckles, or . . . something as frivolous and useless." The lords found these "trinkets and baubles" so attractive that they chose to spend their wealth not on supporting armed retainers but on commodities. The desire for even greater wealth with which to buy manufactures led them to enter into longer-term leases with their tenants and to engage them in more businesslike relations: "they gradually bartered their whole power and authority" away in return for the possession of luxury objects. "Having sold their birth-right," Smith recounted, "for . . . the playthings of children . . . , they became as insignificant as any substantial burgher or tradesman in a city." The trader, acting on the basis of self-interest, and the now-consuming great lord, motivated by the gratification "of the most childish vanity," produced a political society in which "the great proprietors were no longer capable of interrupting the regular execution of justice, or of disturbing the peace of the country."[8]

In the writings of the Scottish Enlightenment philosophers, then, commerce and capitalism took on the power to "civilize" individuals and whole societies. In introducing the exchange of property in goods between individuals, commerce provided the means by which men learned that they enjoyed things in common, that they shared interests with one another. Commerce acquainted individuals with the arts of social intercourse conducive to smooth social interaction; it helped them to refine their manners and behave "politely." "Commerce tends to wear off those prejudices which maintain distinctions and animosity between nations," insisted the Scottish historian William Robertson in 1769. "It *softens and polishes* the manners of men."[9] This so-called *stadial theory* of the development of societies amounted at least in part to a campaign to vindicate capitalism and to legitimate its practitioners as being engaged in a masculine, virtuous pursuit of wealth. But it is perhaps just as helpful to see their theories of the stages of civilization as an effort on their part to understand and explain the successful merging of Lowland Scotland with England in the United Kingdom and the only fitful accommodation of Highland Scotland to the new entity. Certainly the outlawing of Highland cultural practices after 1745 did not tame the clan chiefs and bring them to give up their warrior ways in favor of those manifested by their southern neighbors; the Highlands remained, for Scottish intellectuals, a site of barbarism where kinship and violence still ruled. The process of "civilizing" the Highland peoples into something resembling "Britishness" came about as a consequence of the Highland lords' gradual and slow involvement in the new agricultural and commercial activities we saw developed in the earlier part of this chapter. It took the better part of half a century and was immeasurably aided by the widespread participation of Scottish soldiers and civilians in the obtaining, keeping, and ruling of empire from the 1760s onward. The Scottish philosophers utilized their stadial theories to supply a history of that process.

THE ENLIGHTENMENT: THE DOMESTIC SPHERE

Although men displayed their virtue in the realm of the public sphere, it was in the domestic sphere, from women, that they learned it in the first place. The family, moralists and philosophers insisted, constituted the site where "the natural affections" and the "habitual sympathy" required of commercial society were taught and experienced. A new emphasis on domesticity developed over the course of the eighteenth century as moralists struggled to find ways to render men and society more virtuous. Private morality imbibed in the home promised an effective safeguard against the corruption of public life. As one Scottish poet attested in his paean to "The Married State" in a 1764 issue of *Scots Magazine*,

> *If you ask from what source my felicity flows,*
> *My answer is short—From a wif,*
> *Who, for chearfulness [sic], sense, and good-nature, I chose*
> *Which are beauties that charm us for life.*

> *To make home the seat of perpetual delight,*
> *Ev'ry moment each studies to seize,*
> *And we find ourselves happy, from morning to night,*
> *By the mutual endeavour to please.*

As the key figure responsible for the creation of domestic bliss in the midst of the vicissitudes of commercial society, women took on a new significance and importance over the course of the century. Because they enjoyed a natural "complacency," Scottish and English moralists believed, by which they meant a capacity for sympathy, women possessed the power to soften men and to encourage in them the development of the sensibility that would preserve morality and virtue in a public world fraught with selfishness, corruption, and dissipation. In the writings of many, such as James Fordyce (1720–1796), Adam Smith, and Adam Ferguson, women appeared to be the single greatest bulwark against moral disintegration, responsible for reforming the manners of men and for maintaining the integrity of the moral community as a whole.

The moral power imputed to women by the latter half of the eighteenth century was considerable, and it produced a far greater appreciation of women than had existed earlier. But women's newly recognized influence with men was effective only insofar as women exercised it through example or through gentle persuasion, moralists insisted, and their behavior should in no way suggest that they were not fully subordinate to their husbands, functioning under their beneficent but watchful gaze within their proper sphere of the home. The new recognition of women's importance to society, in other words, carried with it many prescriptive constraints on women's behavior and would have significant ideological power to contain their activities in later decades. Women should expect "to command by obeying," argued James Fordyce in the wildly popular *Sermons to Young Women*, published in 1765, "and by yielding to conquer."[10] Only in this way could the reformation of male manners be brought about and sensibility inculcated in men.

Historians have assumed, following the prescriptive literature, that the commercial revolution brought about a reduction of middling women's employment; that it moved them out of economic production and/or commerce and into the home where they acted merely as consumers. Although it is certainly the case that women's consumption helped to fuel the commercial boom of the eighteenth century, it is also true that significant numbers of respectable middling women worked throughout the eighteenth century, either in their own trades or in the shops of their husbands. They continued to trade in luxury goods like silks, tea, chocolate, or chinaware; they prepared and sold food and drink; they acted as nurses and midwives; they undertook all manner and kind of needlework; they took paying boarders into their homes. As it became increasingly less respectable for women to work, many status-conscious individuals, especially among the middling ranks, may not have reported the work the women in their families did, but it appears from all the data historians have been able to gather that not much changed in either the kinds of work women performed or the proportion of women working over the course of the eighteenth century. What did change, and with profound consequences, was the *meaning* that was attached to women's work.

While upper- and middle-class women were being transformed, ideologically speaking, into the embodiment of virtue over the course of the eighteenth century, representations of plebeian women were changing too. These were not unrelated phenomena: the very processes of commercialization that compelled the imaginative creation of separate spheres for elite men and women involved the development of new understandings of women's work. From constituting the industrious, productive, invaluable contributors to family and national wealth at the beginning of the eighteenth century, plebeian women came by the end of the eighteenth century to be regarded as coarse, profligate, and degraded; portrayed as shameful, suspect, and even criminal, working women were depicted as posing a serious danger to the nation's moral, physical, and economic health.

Middling and lower-ranked women took responsibility for work located around the cottage while men went off to labor in the fields some distance from home. They spent long hours tending crops, looking for firewood, and gleaning fields, in addition to the never-ending and ubiquitous chore of spinning, labor that earned them the approbation of their neighbors and society as a whole. In towns and cities, women's work in spinning, knitting, weaving, stitching, and lace-making sustained a widespread, lucrative foreign and domestic trade in textiles; women provided the domestic labor force in thousands of homes and small workshops. The early eighteenth-century plebeian women of England, Scotland, and Wales were nothing, contemporaries agreed, if not industrious, and their productive value to the family, the community, and the nation was recognized and acknowledged.

This image of plebeian women as industrious, productive contributors to the commonwealth suffered numerous assaults after mid-century. A combination of increased unemployment, urbanization, and an intensification of conflict between classes acted to produce in the minds of elites a picture of laboring people as immoral and even criminal. Plebeian women served as the object of many of the negative portrayals of the poor drawn by fearful elites. In cities like London, which were growing at a rapid pace, migrant rural women came to be regarded as responsible for the burgeoning ranks of thieves, beggars, and prostitutes. The numbers of poor women did not change appreciably over time—some 86 percent of those classified as poor in 1755 were women, a percentage that had not changed much by 1803—but attitudes toward them did. Now they were regarded with distrust and suspicion as illegitimate burdens on the state. In virtually every area of women's employment, from cottage industry to domestic service to the earliest factories, the valuation placed on the work women performed dropped dramatically.

The middle-class domestic ideal called for women to stay at home to look after the needs of their husbands and children. These new societal attitudes could not prevent women from working because necessity was a harsh taskmaster, but they had enormous consequences nonetheless. If the definition of "worker" no longer included women, if workers were men, then men could easily displace women in areas of work that were traditionally theirs. Women who had to work to feed themselves and their families found it nigh impossible to command employment that paid a wage sufficient for them to do so. "Women's work," by definition, paid poorly and was by its nature intermittent. The negative connotations attached to women's work also placed enormous pressure on men and women to live up to a standard of exclusively male breadwinning that few working families could afford. The psychic stresses resulting from the failure of working-class men to support their families on a single pay packet could be severe, helping to produce alcoholism, domestic violence, or desertion.

The ideology of separate spheres, then, had a powerful, if uneven, impact on the men and women of various ranks. Where it depicted middling and upper-ranked women as nearly divine in character and elevated them to a level of influence they did not have before, it reduced working women to nearly subhuman status. The picture of the virtuous "angel in the house," as the middle-class woman would be called in the nineteenth century, required her mirror image, the degraded, brutish, immoral working woman. The crystallization of these portrayals of femininity would not occur until the time of the French Revolution, as we shall see in Chapter 5, but the process by which they emerged had begun long before with the advent of commercial society. It would continue over the course of the eighteenth century as British society faced the challenges of empire building and loss, dealt with a surge of popular disquiet after 1760, and, after 1789, fended off the threat of republican France.

OVERSEAS SCIENTIFIC DISCOVERIES

In the eighteenth century the broadening of scientific and intellectual horizons and the enterprise of colonial expansion became entwined. Vast expanses of ocean were traversed and new lands "discovered" by adventurers, explorers, and scientists seeking to enlarge the body of knowledge available to Europeans. The islands, lands, and peoples of the Pacific, in particular, fascinated voyagers and the audiences that impatiently awaited their accounts and images of the exotic flora, fauna, and humanity inhabiting seemingly utopian landscapes. These new lands appeared to be a veritable paradise, an Eden even, where, it was said, native peoples—deemed "noble savages"—lived in a pure state of nature in harmony with one another, free of the institutions of government and of social distinctions based on wealth or status. The inhabitants of islands described by Captain James Cook—places like Tahiti and Hawaii, for example—became the model for Enlightenment thinkers in Europe whose theories of politics and government derived from a contrast between a state of nature and a state of civilization.

Contact with other lands and peoples across the globe compelled a great deal of thinking about the nature of human beings, leading philosophers and scientists to conclusions that could not always be squared with some of the most fundamental aspects of Enlightenment thought. Colonization of indigenous peoples and the existence of slavery and the slave trade, in particular, flew in the face of notions of the basic unity of men, of equality of rights of all men, and of the steady progress of humankind, a situation that spawned ambitious efforts to impose the principles and practices of taxonomic classification to bear on the subject of race. Where French naturalist George-Louis Leclerc, Count of Buffon, believed that humankind was of "a unity" and that differences of race could be explained by exposure to the sun, Linnaeus argued in his 1740 *Systema Naturae* (*System of Nature*) that humans did not share a common unity; rather, they could be sorted into four different categories based on race: white Europeans, red American Indians, black Africans, and brown Asians. If we recall that his taxonomic system for plant and animal life placed species on a hierarchical structure that conferred value on them, we will not be surprised to learn that his taxonomies of race, too, could justify ruling over or enslaving large numbers of people of color. Johann Gottfried Herder, an influential critic of the Enlightenment and an early proponent of German nationalism, drew on both Buffon and Linnaeus to argue for a recognition that although there may once have been a common origin for and unity of humankind, differences of climate and geography had intervened to create a variety of separate peoples who looked different, spoke different languages, had different histories, and enjoyed different cultural, social, legal, and political practices.

Enlightenment thinkers drew upon climatic theories to assert that racial differences in social structure, political organization, legal practices, and the status of women in different societies, in particular, corresponded to habitation in one of three climatic zones: torrid, temperate, and frigid. As you might expect, given the use of at least two of these terms to describe the degree of interest one might have in sexual relations, the levels of "civilization" these zones determined were intimately associated with sexuality. Hot climates—those found in the torrid zones immediately adjacent to the equator—stimulated inordinate sexual desire and behavior; the populations residing there displayed few inhibitions and in fact indulged in riotous sexual activity on a regular basis. The further one moved away from the equator, toward Europe, say, in the temperate zone, the degree of sexual passion exhibited by populations diminished or at least was much more readily controlled. Further north, in the frigid zone, men and women were so indifferent to passion as to practically ignore each other. As the Scot Adam Ferguson claimed in his 1767 *Essay on the History of Civil Society*, "The burning ardours, and the torturing jealousies, of the seraglio and the haram, which have reigned so long in Asia and Africa, and which, in the Southern parts of Europe, have scarcely given way to the difference of religion and civil establishments, are found, however, with an abatement of heat in the climate, to be more easily changed, in one latitude, into a temporary passion which ingrosses the mind, without enfeebling it, and which excites to romantic achievements: by a farther progress to the North, it is changed into a spirit of gallantry, which employs the wit and the fancy more than the heart; which prefers intrigue to enjoyment; and substitutes affectation and vanity, where sentiment and desire have failed. As it departs from the sun, the same passion is further composed into a habit of domestic connection or frozen into a state of insensibility, under which the sexes at freedom scarcely chuse to unite their society."[11] These various regimes of sexual desire and activity correlated with the extent to which societies participating in them had developed their social, economic, and political systems.

Civilization and political liberty scarcely existed, according to many Enlightenment thinkers, in the hot climates of the torrid zone, where heat and uninhibited sexual activity sapped the energies of individuals and rendered them lethargic and compliant. In the more temperate zones of Europe, climate and sexual restraint enabled the development of societies that enjoyed the energy, productivity, and discipline necessary to produce political liberty and civic virtue. The commercial society of Britain, for instance, noted theorists such as David Hume, characterized by wealth, industry, political freedom, and polite social relations; and the "backward" societies of Africa, populated by indolent, slavish, lascivious men and women, provided a vivid contrast of the differential effects of climate and geography on progress and civilization. These new, scientifically systematized ideologies of race and of gender, oftentimes intertwined with one another, served as justifications for the rule of Protestant Britons over subject peoples in Ireland, North America, and the West Indies and women at home. And they constituted ambitious efforts to reconcile slavery and the trade in human beings with British tenets of freedom and justice and the Enlightenment project of human progress.

Theorists drew on earlier medieval and Renaissance understandings of race as a contrast of darkness and light, which in turn connoted good and evil. Long before the English laid eyes on people whose skins were dark, they utilized terms of black and white that carried deep and portentous meanings for them. In a literary, religious, and cultural context, "black" signified such negative things as death, mourning, evil, sin, and danger. "White," by contrast, stood for purity, innocence, goodness, and beauty. As England entered into long-distance trading relationships with other states, engaged in military operations with its European rivals, and became involved in overseas colonization, the term black proved to be a ready means of distinguishing English civilization from "barbarism," a quality long associated with Africa. Moreover, blackness could be ascribed to virtually any group of people who fell under English control—Native Americans, Indians, Irish, and even Welsh and Scots might become "black" as the English cast about for ways to justify coercive measures against them by rendering them different, inferior, unruly, and in need of English discipline and tutelage. Racial discourse provided a shorthand for rationalizing English and then British colonizing efforts.

Because purity, innocence, and beauty were qualities often represented by women or, indeed, by women's noticeable lack of them, the use of blackness to characterize subordinated peoples contained a gendered and sexualized component right from the start. In fact, the earliest travel writings about Africa drew on notions of gender, specifically those having to do with sexual chaos or disorder, rather than race, to convey the sense of difference and alienness experienced by European explorers as they came in contact with African societies for the first time in the fifteenth century. Blackness, in these early narratives, appears to be merely a physical curiosity for Europeans, but gradually, as it became increasingly enmeshed with the familiar yet still threatening signs of gender disorder, blackness began to stand in for the idea that difference, strangeness, diversity, or disorder could be construed as destructive to or harmful of the European social and cultural practices that constituted civilization. In 1760, an English observer embedded his description of African sexual practices within a long list of qualities believed to be the antithesis of those characterizing the manly English gentleman and the proper English lady: the African was "proud, lazy, treacherous, thievish, hot and addicted to all kinds of lusts, and most ready to promote them in others, as pimps, panders, incestuous, brutish, and savage, cruel and revengeful, devourers of human flesh, and quaffers of human blood, inconstant, base, treacherous, and cowardly," noted an entry in *The Universal History*; one could no more "be an *African* and not lascivious" than to "be born in *Africa* and not be an African."[12]

Africa, in the minds of the British, came to signify unalterable, fundamental difference from European social and gender roles, European morals, mores, customs, values, and traditions, difference usually expressed by European explorers and writers as a disordered gender system and promiscuous sexuality among its inhabitants, especially women. So overwhelming was the sexuality of African women in the minds of British men that it exceeded all bounds. "If they meet with a [white] Man," William Smith averred in a 1745 account of his experiences in Guinea, "they immediately strip his lower Parts and throw themselves upon him."[13] These descriptions reduced Africans and African societies to the level of primitive savagery, a state of being that excused British involvement in the slave trade on the grounds that Africans could hardly be counted as human and would come to justify later British efforts to subdue and control the peoples of Africa and Asia by an imperial rule that promised to raise them up to "civilized" status.

Enlightenment thinkers often measured the level of progress and civilization of any given society by examining the status of women in that society. John Millar's 1771 *Origin of the Distinction of Ranks* argued that as societies moved through the hunting-gathering, pastoral, and agricultural stages of development to reach the final, optimal commercial stage, the treatment of women in those societies improved markedly. Hunter-gatherer societies, which Millar and others identified with contemporary societies in Africa and Asia, "entertain very gross ideas concerning those female virtues which, in a polished nation, are supposed to constitute the honour and dignity of the sex." These "savage" societies enslaved women, entailed ceaseless work on them, and rendered them helpless before the whims and brutalities of men. During the second and third stages, characterized by pastoralism and agriculture, greater social stability and then settlement increased men's competition for women, which in turn helped to stimulate the development of greater refinement and sentiment than was necessary in a hunter-gatherer society. Respect for virtuous women increased, although those women found wanting in sexual loyalty met with severe disapprobation. In the final stage, commercial societies benefitted even further from the refinement of manners and cultivation of sensibility that women evinced. In return, these latter-stage societies, like Britain, generated "great respect and veneration for the ladies," Millar exulted. Ensconced in the home, where they indulged in the domestic pleasures of family life most suited to them, women in commercial society—the highest stage of civilization—enjoyed the respect, the friendship, and companionship of men.[14] But women's bodies contained a "torrid zone," too, an inconvenient feature that seemingly defied geographic location and threatened to undermine the progress and civilization of European countries by its very existence. Sexual desire among middle-class women could not readily be tolerated, and it had to be displaced on to other women. Identified with "savage" women who inhabited societies of lesser development, sexual desire came to be regarded as the mark of primitive, uncivilized, degraded individuals, who in turn became the foil against whom virtuous British women would define themselves.

This kind of formulation served to persuade many women that British control over large areas of the world was not only legitimate but also moral. With few exceptions—such as Lady Mary Wortley Montagu (1689–1762), whose extensive travels convinced her that European ideas about sexual attitudes and behavior in the Middle East were grossly inaccurate—the upper- and middle-class women of Britain believed that the fortunate position they held relative to "primitive" women of the world obligated them to support efforts to lift up their less fortunate sisters of the seraglio and the harem where they were reduced to sexual slavery.

These racial and sexualized descriptions also worked to reinforce two visions of "womanliness" to distinguish British women of the middle and upper classes from those of the working classes. Just as sexual desire was being displaced from middle-class women onto savage women of Asia and Africa in the course of establishing the cult of domesticity, it was also being displaced onto working-class women at home, who were themselves identified as savage. It was here, in the conflation of female sexuality with racial difference, especially as it pertained to Africa but also, as we shall see, to India and Ireland, that differences among women of the middle classes on the one hand and the working classes on the other could so easily be established through the use of blackness to represent degradation, sexual immorality, and danger. In a formulation that would become far more prevalent in the second half of the nineteenth century as imperial and class tensions became acute, the West Indies planter Edward Long warned in 1772, "the lower class of women in *England* are remarkably fond of the blacks."[15]

..

Commerce and imperial trade swelled the ranks of middling people in Britain over the course of the eighteenth century. Their growing numbers and the wealth they produced and consumed combined to form them into an increasingly significant political force. More and more, as we shall see in the next chapter, men and women of the middling ranks made known their political concerns and demands through the commercial press and voluntary trade, philanthropic, and social associations. Their role in influencing the social, political, economic, and imperial directions Britain would take in the second half of the eighteenth century would be profound.

NOTES

1. Quoted in Maria Nugent, *Captain Cook Was Here* (Cambridge, 2009), p. 3; quoted in Glendwr Williams, "The Pacific: Exploration and Exploitation," in P. J. Marshall, ed., *The Oxford History of the British Empire, Volume II: The Eighteenth Century* (Oxford, 1998), p. 558.
2. Quoted in Williams, "The Pacific: Exploration and Exploitation," pp. 558, 559.
3. Quoted in Cormac Ó Gráda, *Black '47 and Beyond. The Great Irish Famine* (Princeton, 1999), p. 15.
4. Quoted in Kenneth Morgan, "Liverpool's Dominance in the British Slave Trade, 1740–1807," in David Richardson, Suzanne Schwarz, and Anthony Tibbles, eds., *Liverpool and Transatlantic Slavery* (Liverpool, 2007), p. 15.
5. Quoted in Marcus Rediker, *The Slave Ship. A Human History* (London, 2007), p. 225.
6. Quoted in James Walvin, *The Zong. A Massacre, the Law, and the End of Slavery* (New Haven, 2011), p. 21.
7. Quoted in Steven Matthews, *Theology and Science in the Thought of Francis Bacon* (Hampshire, 2008), p. 46; quoted in Darryl M. DeMarzio, "Dealing with Diversity: On the Uses of Common Sense in Descartes and Montaigne," *Studies in Philosophy and Education* 29 (2010):301–13, p. 302.
8. Quoted in Susan Kingsley Kent, *Gender and Power in Britain, 1640–1990* (London, 1999), p. 66.
9. Quoted in Kent, *Gender and Power*, p. 66.
10. Quoted in Kent, *Gender and Power*, p. 69.
11. Quoted in Kent, *Gender and Power*, pp. 88–89.

TIMELINE

1764   Spinning jenny invented

1765   James Fordyce publishes *Sermons to Young Women*

1767   Arkwright and Kay invent water frame

1770   Cook arrives in Botany Bay in Australia

1776   Smith publishes the *Wealth of Nations*

12. Quoted in Anne McClintock, *Imperial Leather: Race, Gender and Sexuality in the Colonial Contest* (New York, 1995), p. 22.
13. Quoted in Kim Hall, *Things of Darkness: Economies of Race and Gender in Early Modern England* (Ithaca, 1995), p. 34; McClintock, p. 23.
14. Quoted in Kent, *Gender and Power*, pp. 89, 90.
15. Quoted in McClintock, *Imperial Leather*, p. 23.

FURTHER READING

Jane Burbank and Frederick Cooper, *Empires in World History. Power and the Politics of Difference*. Princeton, 2010.

Anna Clark, *The Struggle for the Breeches: Gender and the Making of the British Working Class*. Berkeley, 1995.

James S. Donnelly Jr., *The Great Irish Potato Famine*. Gloustershire, 2001.

John Dwyer, *Virtuous Discourse: Sensibility and Community in Late Eighteenth-Century Scotland*. Edinburgh, 1987.

Kim F. Hall, *Things of Darkness: Economies of Race and Gender in Early Modern England*. Ithaca, 1995.

Anne McClintock, *Imperial Leather: Race, Gender and Sexuality in the Colonial Contest*. New York, 1995.

Felicity A. Nussbaum, *Torrid Zones: Maternity, Sexuality, and Empire in Eighteenth-Century Narratives*. Baltimore, 1995.

Cormac Ó Gráda, *Black '47 and Beyond. The Great Irish Famine*. Princeton, 1999.

Jane Rendall, "Virtue and Commerce: Women in the Making of Adam Smith's Political Economy," in Ellen Kennedy and Susan Mendus, eds., *Women in Western Political Philosophy*. New York, 1987.

John F. Richards, *The Unending Frontier. An Environmental History of the Early Modern World*. Berkeley, 2005.

Londa Schiebinger, *Plants and Empire. Colonial Bioprospecting in the Atlantic World*. Cambridge, 2004.

Wolfgang Schivelbusch, *Tastes of Paradise. A Social History of Spices, Stimulants, and Intoxicants*. New York, 1993.

Deborah Valenze, *The First Industrial Woman*. New York, 1995.

Richard G. Wilkinson, "The English Industrial Revolution," in Donald Worster, ed., *The Ends of the Earth. Perspectives on Modern Environmental History*. Cambridge, 1988.

Larry Zuckerman, *The Potato*. New York, 1998.

1781	Watt invents rotary motion steam engine
1784	Power loom invented
1785	Crompton invents spinning mule
c. 1790	Eighty percent of slave trade controlled by Liverpool merchants
1793	Whitney invents cotton gin
1801	Population of England reaches 8,700,000

Punishment of an enslaved African following a revolt in Guiana, 1770s.

CHAPTER 4

POLITICS AND IMPERIAL TURNS, 1760–1789

West Indies

Jamaica

Caribbean Sea

O n July 15, 1776, the overseer on a Jamaican sugar plantation discovered a young slave tampering with his pistols, intent on removing the shot and re-placing it with cotton and oil. A week later, a planter heard that a significant amount of guns and gunpowder had been secreted in a hiding place in the village of Lucea, but when he went to find it, he discovered that it had already been removed from the spot. Shortly after that, authorities learned that two Maroons from Trelawney Town had urged a number of enslaved Africans in the parish of Hanover to "make haste, take the Country to themselves, and drive the white people entirely out of it;" that they, the two Maroons, could "find Guns, Powder, and Shot, for the Ne-groes belonging to the different Estates, and likewise added, that they were angry too much with the white people." Once they sounded a signal, the Africans on these estates were to run into the woods, and while the whites were engaged in pursuing them, the Maroons would set the cane fields on fire. When the whites returned to put out the fires in the fields, the Maroons and the "estate Negroes" were "instantly to repair to the Towns, break open the Stores, and houses, and from thence supply themselves plentifully, with Gun Powder &c."[1]

An insurrection was afoot in the Jamaican parish of Hanover, set off by free blacks and enslaved Africans who suffered harsh treatment at the hands of their owners and who did not have enough food because of a serious drought and the embargo of American products by British ships engaged in hostilities with rebel-ling colonists. In an unusual display of cooperation, both Creole (Africans born in Jamaica) and African-born slaves met together numerous times and appointed captains and other officers to organize their respective parishes. They planned to signal one another with a series of gunshots: "First by discharging a Gun at

Batchelors Hall by Mingo which was to be Answered by Adam at Richmond and after that to be followed by firing at the Baulk Estate by Charles and that they were then to Rise in General Rebellion and Attack the several Estates and put to death all the White people they could."[2] The ringleaders planned their moves to follow the departure of troops from the parish: on July 3, 1776, His Majesty's Fiftieth Regiment had sailed from Fort Lucea to reinforce the troops of General William Howe (1729–1814) against the American colonists who would, the next day, declare their independence from Britain. The rising involved hundreds of slaves in a number of incidents taking place over the course of two months.

The rebellion ultimately proved ineffective in securing its ends—to free the enslaved Africans across the island and drive the whites out—but it instilled terror in the hearts of the planter class and of British colonial administrators for quite some time. This little-known and largely failed revolt on the part of Jamaican blacks embodies a number of the developments of the period following Britain's success in the Seven Years' War: the expansion of an empire dependent on enslaved and suppressed people; the American Revolution and its impact on domestic politics; the role played by the West Indian colonies in the defeat of the British at Yorktown; and the politics of antislavery.

••

POPULAR POLITICS AND THE RISE OF THE MIDDLING CLASSES

Increased prosperity consequent on the commercial revolution changed the character of Britain's social order, expanding the number of those people who comprised the middling ranks—shopkeepers, manufacturers, wealthier independent artisans, civil servants, professionals, and lesser merchants, people whose annual income of £50 to £500 enabled them to live with some degree of "independence." Some 170,000 middling people lived in English cities in 1700; by 1800, those numbers had swelled to 475,000. Many others populated smaller villages and rural towns. Middling people as a whole constituted perhaps 25 to 30 percent of the entire population of England and Wales, compared to the 1 percent of the population who made up the aristocracy and gentry, and the 70 to 75 percent of the population who, if they were fortunate, labored on the land or in the workshops of others in return for wages. Certainly the ranks of the middling enjoyed the fastest growth during the course of the eighteenth century.

The combination of their numbers and of the wealth they produced and consumed over the course of the eighteenth century helped to form the middling classes into an increasingly significant political force. Some men of the middling ranks had direct access to Parliament through the vote, but because representation for cities was so uneven, their influence remained "out-of-doors," as contemporaries would say. Through the commercial press and voluntary trade, philanthropic, and social associations, men and women of the middling ranks made known their political concerns and demands. Patriotic and high minded, these clubs, societies, and associations acted as vehicles through which men of commerce and the professions could contribute to the public good as they defined it. They did so confident in the belief that their possession of property and their status as heads of households entailed on them the requisite independence that undergirded and authorized political activity, according to a set of political principles referred to as "civic humanism." Beginning in the 1760s, middling people, joined by many from the artisan ranks, began to adapt their civic humanism to assert more forcefully a new political idiom of "social contract" and its corollary, "resistance to tyranny," drawn from the writings of John Locke, and to claim their "rights" to representation in Parliament. As we have seen in past chapters, many of their demands, concerns, and causes— and the responses to them—were framed in terms of gender and sexuality, a circumstance that would have serious practical consequences for men and women with regard to their power, their opportunities, and their identities in the nineteenth century.

The accession of George III (1738–1820) in 1760 inaugurated a new era in British politics. At the elite level, it was signaled by a fusion of Tory and Whig politicians into a united ruling class whose political aspirations consisted of obtaining offices and patronage for themselves, their kin, and their friends. The patronage system provided the means through which the state and the church obtained the personnel necessary to operate in the days before professional bureaucrats carried out the administrative functions of government on the basis of their talent, education, and expertise. Through networks of wealthy and well-positioned patrons, clients, and the brokers through whom the latter worked, the patronage system also provided opportunities to gain access to place, power, and preferment as well as avenues for social advancement. What we would regard as old-boy and old-girl networks operating through practices of corruption and bribery and according to the principle of "who you know" in fact constituted, in eighteenth-century terms, a central, if unofficial, political institution.

Included among those who obtained positions in governmental, financial, and commercial offices were Scots who took advantage of the opportunities provided by the union to advance their careers and their wealth. Scots could be found in prominent positions within the East India Company and the Bank of England, for example; they held important offices within the armed forces, in the ministries of government, and in the legal and medical professions. One such Scot, John Stuart, Lord Bute--pronounced "Boot"--(1713–1792), served as King George's most intimate advisor and ultimately reached the highest level of government, becoming prime minister in 1761. Appointed by the king without the support of Parliament, his presence served both to encourage "Scottophobia" among those who believed Scots were rising too far and too fast within the British establishment and to rally popular forces against the "tyranny" of the king. Bute signed the peace treaty with France in 1763, which many people regarded as a gift to the French. Depicted in the press and in the streets as an effeminate "Scotch-Jacobite" who put French interests before those of Britain and who sought to fill the offices of state with his fellow countrymen, Bute was the object of rumors that charged him with sleeping with the king's mother. One cartoon portrayed the princess dowager with her hand under Lord Bute's kilt, saying, "A man of great parts is sure greatly to rise."[3] Crowds marched through the streets displaying a petticoat and a boot, representing the princess and Lord Bute, respectively, to make the symbolic argument that in infiltrating the bedroom of George's mother, an alien and French-loving Stuart aristocrat threatened the very existence of constitutional government as it had been established in the Glorious Revolution. As was true of pornography aimed against the monarchy in the seventeenth century, these vivid tales of Lord Bute's sexual liaisons with the princess dowager expressed acute political anxieties and served pointed political ends.

At the popular level, politics became marked by increasing radicalism among the middling ranks, whose taxes had financed the long and hard-fought wars with France that secured empire for Britain. The commercial and trading classes of the urban centers became increasingly supportive of reform efforts seeking to curb the arbitrary actions of self-interested MPs and ministers and to make them accountable to the people. Many of their extraparliamentary protests focused on the actions taken by the crown against the press; on the suppression of individual liberties in the form of general warrants; on the Townshend Acts that sought to augment royal authority in the American colonies by making governors less reliant on the colonial assemblies for revenues; and, most spectacularly, on Parliament's interference in the election for Middlesex in 1768, when it voided John Wilkes's (1725–1797) victory and gave the seat to his defeated rival, a ministerial candidate by the name of Colonel Lutterell.

By that time, Wilkes had become the centerpiece of a broad-based and deep-seated campaign among the middling ranks against what they saw as the tyranny of the crown and its attacks on liberty.

Proclaiming for "Wilkes and Liberty" and drawing on ideas of social contract, Wilkes and his supporters lambasted the "secret influence" of the king's ministers, claiming that the threats they posed to the constitution and to individual liberty could only be

Popular song in support of "Wilkes and Liberty," 1760s.

countered by the resistance of "the people" to tyrannous actions by the crown. Arguing that a man's patriotism should not be gauged "by the number of his acres"—a reference to franchise restrictions that limited voting to those holding substantial landed property (except in parts of London, where property-holding criteria enfranchised men owning freeholds worth forty shillings)—Wilkes's followers claimed that their love for liberty in fact made them better patriots, better Englishmen, and thus more deserving than landed elites of the right to active citizenship.

GENDER, POLITICS, AND RELIGIOUS CULTURE

Women contributed heavily of their time and money to the Wilkite campaigns: the "patriotic Ladies of Worcester" and the "lady freeholders of Middlesex," to name only two such instances, appeared at demonstrations and balls held in support of Wilkes and his radical cause. Others participated in debates and the dissemination of propaganda on his behalf. But women who did involve themselves in politics had to be careful to present themselves as "auxiliaries" to male citizens if they were to remain unmolested by press or public opinion. They had to conform to the middling ideals of domesticity and sexual virtue that were being consolidated in the second half of the eighteenth century, and if they did not, they faced ridicule and charges of disreputability, as did the objects of their support, which became tarnished and degraded by their association with "the feminine." The presence of women in public at a time when middling and plebeian men claimed for themselves a larger role in the political nation generated acute anxiety. Demands for political participation in the 1760s and 1770s by property-owning and independent but not landed shopkeepers, professionals, and tradesmen, and for universal manhood suffrage in the 1780s, opened up the possibility for single or widowed—and perhaps even married—women to make the same claims. If active citizenship no longer depended on the possession of landed estates but could be extended to those who owned other kinds of property as well, what was to stop property-owning women from claiming citizenship for themselves? And if voting could be extended to all adult males on the basis of their "natural rights" regardless of their property-owning status, how would the exclusion of women be justified?

One solution was to render women utterly unlike men, to disqualify them from political life by highlighting the emotional, physical, and intellectual differences from men already suggested by separate sphere ideology. The very qualities that gave women their moral ascendancy in the domestic sphere made them unfit for political life. They possessed greater tenderness and humanity than men, we saw Adam Smith assert in Chapter 3, but lacked the self-denial and self-command required by public life. Women were emotional, passive, submissive, and dependent, philosophers, theorists, and public moralists proclaimed; these characteristics suited them in their role as moral guardians and inculcators of virtue, but would serve them—and the polity—ill if transferred to public life, which called for men's capacity for reason, action, aggression, and independence. Moreover, women who ignored their weaknesses, who abandoned their children and husbands to step out into the world of politics, demonstrated their unnaturalness and, worse, placed society in danger by their actions.

As if to underscore its intent to remove women from politics altogether, the House of Commons in 1778 banned women from the gallery and the floor of the House, where they had, since the early part of the eighteenth century, gathered to listen to debates. But the increased masculinization of political culture did not prevent women from embracing radical principles or participating in political activities throughout the latter half of the eighteenth century. Indeed, the intensification of separate sphere ideology, designed to shore up the boundaries differentiating men from women, occurred precisely because those boundaries between public and domestic had become so unstable and showed no signs of firming up.

Resistance to the tyranny of absolute government, portrayed in the guise of the king's foreign, effeminate, corrupt ministers who threatened the hard-won liberties of Englishmen, came to be represented as "manly patriotism." Those who risked life and limb to defend the country against illegitimate usurpations of monarchical power, as Wilkes and his supporters would have it, displayed a love of liberty and a "virtuous and manly resistance" to tyranny. American colonists resisting illegal authority, Wilkes often claimed, expressed a "manliness of sentiment" unavailable to their European counterparts. They were "fighting like men—like ENGLISHMEN, for law and liberty supposed to be violated," as one publication in the Midlands put it in 1775. Those who did not resist, by the same token, who complied with and even furthered encroachments on the liberties of the people at home or abroad, demonstrated their "effeminacy."[4]

The protean nature of gender as a signifier becomes amply clear in the representations of the religious developments that took place over the course of the eighteenth century. In 1738, in a reaction against the established Anglican church, a clergyman by the name of John Wesley (1703–1791) began to preach a new series of doctrines that came to be called Methodism. The Anglican church tended to cater to the socially respectable and seemed to care little for either the lives or the souls of the poor. Methodism sought to bring salvation to all God's flock, rich and poor, men and women alike. Against the secular, rationalized, logical doctrine of Anglicanism, it appealed to the emotions of individuals, to "the hearts" of sinners seeking God's forgiveness. Traveling from parish to parish, Wesley and his followers brought their evangelical revival to all parts of England and Wales, conducting open-air meetings where passion and "enthusiasm" took hold of vast crowds of congregants who yearned to be saved. By the 1780s, Methodism constituted a cohesive religious sect with an ecclesiastical structure and coherent doctrine.

Methodism championed workers and the poor and gave women opportunities to play unconventional roles and to understand that they enjoyed spiritual, if not political and social, equality within its activities. To many elites, therefore, it seemed to challenge the social and gender order of eighteenth-century Britain, the order represented by the Anglican church. Critics declaimed against Methodist men by labeling them "feminine," a charge that accrued weight because of the sect's association with the emotions and attitudes ascribed to women. Wesley saw his brand of Christianity as a "heart-religion" and sought to bring it to the masses by appealing to feeling, to "the reasons of the heart," attributes identified as more natural to women than to men. Passion, enthusiasm, deep feeling, expressed through the tears, groans, sighs, and tremblings of mass congregations, could readily be called on to show that "womanliness" rather than "manliness" characterized the men who cast their lot with Methodism. Wesley preached against dueling, cockfighting, bear-baiting, drunkenness, bawdiness, profanity, and public violence. He sought to reform the manners of men to make them more gentlemanly; he urged men to be chaste before marriage. These teachings made it easy to taint his male converts with the charge of "effeminacy." But he also appealed to men and women to work hard, be disciplined in their conduct, and save, messages that attracted thousands of people to his side. Industrial workers, especially those in the coal fields of Wales, found solace and strength in Wesley's message. By mid-century, Welsh Methodists had organized themselves into more than 400 *seiadau*—fellowship meetings—and from this time forward, Nonconformist sects—so called because they did not "conform" to the Anglican church--dominated the Welsh religious and political scene. Nonconformists, which included Baptists, Presbyterians, and Congregationalists as well as Methodists, tended to follow radical politics, despite Wesley's regular denunciation of them.

The efforts by Wesley and his followers to inculcate in the men of Britain a new culture of politeness, manners, and deep feeling took hold. By the 1790s, Methodism and the gentlemanly code it promulgated had become an accepted and respected part of British life. As they became increasingly respectable and established, Methodist ministers purged their ranks of radical elements, especially women who had preached the doctrines of the heart-religion in its earlier days. Women of the Methodist church became "ladies," wholly embracing the ideologies of domesticity and separate spheres that developed among the middle classes. The evangelical initiative that had grown up within the Anglican church, seeking spiritual reform within the church and social reform outside it, also promoted the ideology of domesticity writ large, calling for the extension of the individual and private qualities of discipline, obedience, chastity, propriety, cleanliness, and temperance to society as a whole.

Methodists, Quakers, and evangelical Anglicans fomented a broad-based humanitarian movement during the last decades of the eighteenth century. They sought prison reform, protection for children, education for the poor, and more enlightened care for infants, which included breastfeeding. Above all, they involved themselves heavily in the antislavery campaign that sprang up after mid-century, a story we will take up later in the chapter.

THE REVOLT OF THE AMERICAN COLONIES

The resistance and then revolt of the American colonies played a significant role in the popular politics of England, Scotland, Wales, and Ireland. The Peace of Paris ending the Seven Years' War had, as we have seen, made Britain a powerful imperial nation, a status in which Britons took great pride; for North American colonists, however, it proved a disappointment. They had been asked to contribute men and treasure to the war and had done so expecting to reap rich rewards. Instead they found that the Peace of Paris guaranteed the rights of French Catholics in Canada, which enraged Protestants; worse still, a royal proclamation following the peace treaty barred the colonists from settling lands west of the Appalachian mountains. Little could have infuriated colonists more: in a conflict that they referred to as the French and Indian War, their aim was to obtain more Indian land, not less.

To add insult to injury, as the Americans saw it, Britain expected them to help pay for the expenses of policing the new empire, especially because the colonists themselves often instigated conflicts with Indians over land as they moved westward in violation of the king's orders. In 1765, the prime minister, George Grenville (1712–1770), extended the Stamp Act--a tax on paper that Britons at home already paid--to the American colonies. The tax itself amounted to little, but to the Americans it constituted an attempt to impose the rule of Parliament over that of their own colonial legislatures. They determined to resist it and any other effort to tax them without their consent. "No taxation without representation," they cried, earning the admiration of a number of British reformers who sought to replace their own system of "virtual representation" by one in which all adult men, regardless of their wealth, could vote for their Members of Parliament. As resistance to British efforts to exercise their power over unruly colonists turned into outright revolution against the "tyrannous" King George in the 1770s, a good number of influential Britons at home rallied to the American side. In England, Wilkes and other radicals such as Christopher Wyvill (1740–1822) and John Cartwright (1740–1824) applauded the Americans for fighting to secure the "rights of free-born Englishmen." More established figures like MPs Charles James Fox (1749–1806) and the Irishman Edmund Burke (1729–1797) spoke sympathetically of the American position. In Wales, radicals such as Richard Price (1723–1791) and David Williams (dates unknown) saw in reform of Parliament a solution to the problems that had led the Americans to rise up against the mother country. Even Welsh establishment Whigs sought to abolish patronage and to extend the franchise to larger numbers of voters.

Britons' confidence in their right to rule over colonial territories received a serious blow with the revolt of the American colonies. At home, British opinion divided over the policies that had produced the war and the rightness of the colonists' cause. Radicals seeking greater participation for middling people in the political process believed that the corruption of a government monopolized by landed elites—who, reformers charged, saw in politics the means by which to enrich themselves and their friends and connections—had established policies toward the

American colonies that acted against the interests of the nation as a whole. In their view, the Americans' refusal to buckle under the tyranny of the king and his ministers demonstrated a manliness that Britons would do well to emulate. Apologists for the colonists argued that by resisting illegal authority, Americans were defending liberty, a practice that all manly and patriotic Englishmen should applaud.

Against these claims of a manly resistance to illegitimate authority, supporters of the war against the Americans conjured an image of the colonists as a rebellious, unruly, disordered, insubordinate female and savage power that threatened the very existence of the British nation. One anti-American print published in April 1776 in the *Westminster Review*, titled *The Parricide* (which

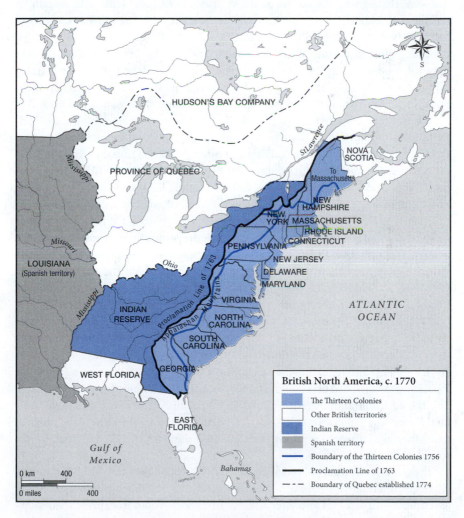

MAP 4.1
British North America, c. 1770

means the killing of the father), depicts America as a dagger-wielding woman in Indian headdress. She is cheered on by a dark-skinned man with snakelike hair, dressed in a loincloth and waving fiery torches in the air. The associations of "unnatural" femininity, distinctive racial characteristics, and "savagery" with the Americans' resistance to legitimate authority marked that legitimate authority as masculine, white, and civilized.

The politically active Irish—almost exclusively the Anglo-Protestant Ascendancy—took advantage of the American Revolution to push their own agenda of obtaining for the Irish Parliament the right to legislate for Ireland. As we saw in Chapter 1, Ireland enjoyed its own Parliament, but executive power rested in the hands of the lord lieutenant, who answered not to the Irish Parliament but to Westminster. Throughout the course of the eighteenth century, Irish MPs sought to change that, although never did they seek separation from Great Britain, knowing full well that their survival in the midst of an overwhelmingly Catholic country depended on British arms. When the American Revolution broke out, Britain embargoed food and supplies to the colonists, a move that harmed Ireland and a number of the West Indian colonies, whose prosperity rested in large part on trade with North America. Irish MPs protested loudly against the provision, to no avail.

When France entered the war in support of the American colonists in 1778, Britain felt compelled to transfer the massive number of troops stationed in Ireland to more pressing locales. Fearing a possible French invasion, Irish Protestants formed themselves into military units of Volunteers drawn from the gentry, merchants, and tenant farmers, sometimes enrolling Presbyterians to their ranks and even, in some places, Catholics as well. Without any connection to the local militias or to the government, the Volunteers were free to act at will. Amounting in some estimates to 40,000 men, they paraded, splendidly uniformed and fully armed, through Dublin in support of such political measures as ending the British embargo of their products, threatening to withhold the payment of tax revenues to Britain until they had achieved their goals. Hamstrung by the need for funds to prosecute the American war, the prime minister, Lord North (1732–1792), had little recourse but to give in to their demands, granting "equality in trading rights" to Ireland in 1779. In 1782, in an even bolder move, the Volunteers in effect blackmailed the British government into changing the centuries-old Poynings' Law and repealing the Declaratory Act of 1720, thus granting the Irish Parliament what it had been calling for for decades—autonomy from Westminster and the concomitant power to rule for Ireland. This victory was, of course, precisely what the American colonists had been seeking in the early days of their resistance, and it would not have been granted the Irish in 1782 had Britain not found itself mired in crisis.

The American revolt proved to be an exclusively continental affair, despite the close commercial ties between the mainland and Caribbean colonists. Some assemblies—in Jamaica and Grenada, for instance—voted to express their sympathies with the rebellious colonies to the north; many colonists in Barbados, Bermuda, and the Bahamas supported the cause. But the British colonists in the

West Indies did not join the rebellion, in part because they depended so heavily on Britain for protection against the French and the Spanish, whose presence in the Caribbean had not been diminished by their defeat in the Seven Years' War. More important, West Indian whites saw in Britain the chief means by which to protect themselves and their interests from enslaved Africans, who fomented rebellion in the Caribbean increasingly over the course of the 1760s and 1770s. Vastly outnumbered, whites looked to British arms for their salvation and had little truck with rebellious colonists to the north.

West Indian planters and merchants did, however, feel the effects of the revolution because the embargo on trade with the North American mainland made it impossible for them to sell their products there. Nor could they import food from America, a situation that, combined with acute conditions of drought in Jamaica, meant that their slaves suffered from severe lack of food. Hunger drove many of them to revolt in 1776, as we saw in the opening of the chapter. According to one of the leaders, Pontack, of the Blue Hose estate in Hanover, "they were angry too much with the white people, because they had taken from them their bread."[5] Coordinating their rising with the departure of the Fiftieth Regiment troops to meet up with General Howe to fight the Americans, enslaved Africans carried out raids for two months, defying the efforts of local authorities and planters to put down their activities. The governor of Jamaica, Sir Basil Keith (governed 1774–1777), finally declared martial law, ordered out the militias from across the island, dispatched a detachment of regular British troops to Hanover, and arranged for armed ships to sail to the rescue of planters, thus further diverting resources from the war against the American colonists, whose insubordination against British authority over the past two years was well known to the leaders of the slave rebellion and may have emboldened them in their actions. As Keith reported to the Colonial Office in August, "there is now an apparent Spirit of insolence among the Slaves, over the whole Island, and in several Parishes there have been executions and Punishments for open Acts of Rebellion, since the commencement of this alarm, so that I may truly say, we are now in the most imminent Danger, and the most pressing Necessity." Once control was finally reasserted, the authorities tried 135 blacks. Of those, 62 were acquitted; 11 received harsh corporal punishment; 45 were transported, and 17 were put to death in a gruesome manner—"some have been burnt alive, some hanged, some gibbeted."[6]

The American Revolution thus had profound effects on the islands of the Caribbean, the defense of which in turn played an important role in the outcome of the revolutionary war itself. France and Spain entered the war in 1778 and 1779, respectively, introducing the need to defend British holdings in the Caribbean. But facing a possible invasion of the home islands from France, the British could not provide sufficient ships to stave off attacks in the West Indies: France took the island of Dominica in September 1778 and then St. Vincent in June 1779. Grenada fell a week later. The situation was dire, made all the more so as the potential for slave insurrections increased across the British West Indies, heightening colonists' fears and inducing panic.

The British navy did finally score a victory in February 1781 when Admiral Sir George Rodney (1718–1792) captured the Dutch island of St. Eustatius, which had been supplying the French and the Americans. Rodney and his officers proceeded to ravage the island, confiscating goods and property indiscriminately and enriching themselves at the expense of the island's inhabitants. So intent were they on looting that Rodney kept his forces there for three months, neglecting to undertake further operations against the French. While they were not looking, the French fleet slipped through to meet up with the American forces at Yorktown in Virginia. It was there, in October 1781, that the British were compelled to surrender to George Washington, effectively ending the American war.

Although the fighting in America had ceased for all intents and purposes, that in the Caribbean had not; naval battles continued to rage as the French gathered up more British islands. Finally, as if to redeem his ignominious actions on St. Eustatius, Admiral Rodney managed to intercept the French in April 1782 in the seas between Dominica and Guadeloupe. At the Battle of the Saintes, as it was called, Rodney captured the French ships en route to laying siege to Jamaica. The war was over. Britain had lost the American colonies, to be sure, but its victory over the French in the West Indies enabled it to garner favorable terms at the peace table in 1783.

With defeat and the loss of the American colonies came an intense round of national soul-searching. Not surprisingly, given the gendered language through which the imperial enterprise was articulated, what was regarded as imperial failure came to be spoken of as a failure of manliness. Many eighteenth-century Scottish moralists, for instance, saw in British losses in the American Revolution the product of effeminacy brought about by too much refinement and luxury; they believed that the English, like the French, had begun the moral decline consequent on luxurious living that accompanied prosperity. The *Caledonian Mercury* prominently displayed a letter from "An Old Fellow and an Englishman," who attributed Britain's military defeat in 1783 to "the loss of our ancient manners. Virtue is always connected with plainness and simplicity; effeminacy always with luxurious refinement. Our ancestors were men; we are, alas!, we are very despicable." Other letters and articles in the Scottish press identified the disgraced General Howe as being "debilitated by luxury and dissipation."[7]

In a short period of time, the drive for empire resumed with even greater intensity. The American colonies might be lost, but new opportunities arose that promised even greater glory for Britons. In what has conventionally been regarded as the "second British empire"—so called to distinguish it from the first British empire of the Atlantic colonies—a whole new world of conquest opened up in British North America (what would come to be called Canada by the middle of the nineteenth century), the Caribbean, South Asia, Australia, New Zealand, and Africa. The manliness of the nation, shaken by the successful challenge of the American colonists, would ultimately be redeemed through Britain's conquest of and control over large tracts in India and later Africa, whose nonwhite, non-Christian inhabitants were represented as in thrall to arbitrary and tyrannous rulers enervated by luxury and sensuality, subjects in dire need of a beneficent imperial master whose rule would expose them to enlightened principles of progress and civilization. As one historian has noted recently, the transition from one empire to another was made possible in large part by those very Americans—former enslaved Africans—who had fought alongside Britain in what they regarded as an American civil war.

When British troops marched out of New York City on Evacuation Day in late November of 1783, marking the official end of the British presence in the United States, thousands of Americans who had remained loyal to the mother country—some 20,000 of them enslaved African Americans who had responded to the British appeal for support in return for their freedom; some of them American Indians who had chosen an alliance with the British over one with the Americans—faced serious difficulties. Should they stay and face the wrath of people who regarded them as traitors and enemies, or should they give up everything they had known and leave their homes for other lands? The violence directed against them before and after the American victory made the decision easy for many of the loyalists: 60,000 left, taking 15,000 slaves with them. Half of them moved north into Quebec, Nova Scotia, and New Brunswick, transforming the latter two of the once largely French Catholic region into a bastion of English speakers. Approximately 6,000 loyalists, drawn largely from the southern states of America, took the majority of the 15,000 enslaved African Americans with them to settle in Jamaica and the Bahamas; some 8,000 whites and 5,000 freed blacks voyaged to Britain, where they found themselves in an alien land of people not necessarily well disposed toward them. About 1,200 freed blacks colonized the land of Sierra Leone on the west coast of Africa.

Some American loyalists joined the army of the East India Company and made their living as officers of the empire in South Asia. A few others found themselves among the first of the convicts transported to Australia in 1787 to serve out their sentences there, after the American victory made it impossible for the British to continue to ship their criminals to the former American colonies. In fact, the plan to colonize Australia had been drawn up by an American loyalist, a New York–born seaman in the Royal Navy by the name of James Matra (1746–1806), who had sailed with Captain James Cook on his 1768–1771 voyages to the Pacific and who believed that the territory of New South Wales could readily accommodate the dislocated Americans. Matra ultimately redesigned his plan to make Australia a penal colony rather than a settlement for loyalist American colonists, although seven freed black loyalists had fallen afoul of the law in Britain and were among those convicts aboard the First Fleet as it sailed into Botany Bay. We will take up this story in the next chapter.

THE ANTISLAVERY MOVEMENT

Given the hardships facing black loyalists who had journeyed to Britain following the end of the American Revolution, it is a wonder that more did not end up in the new penal colony. Many loyalists, black and white, found life in their new home stressful and difficult. Dreary weather, crowded cities, and the fast-paced bustle of urban life among strangers proved disconcerting to many, even those with the

The Zong *Murders: Prelude to Abolition*

In 1781, the slave-ship *Zong*, owned and operated by a Liverpool syndicate headed by William Gregson (d. 1800), sailed from Africa with a cargo of 442 slaves bound for Jamaica. Nearing the end of its voyage in November, it miscalculated its charts and found itself off course and short of drinking water some ten days beyond its destination. A large number of the slaves had fallen ill by this time, suffering badly enough that their sale value, it appeared, had plummeted. The crew of the *Zong* decided to cut their

Sailors Throwing Enslaved Africans Overboard, Early Nineteenth Century.

losses by getting rid of them. On November 29, they pushed 54 women and children through the cabin windows into the sea; two days later they threw 42 men overboard; another 38 Africans went to their deaths sometime later.

In the ordinary scheme of things, the murders of 134 slaves would have passed unnoticed and unremarked. In this instance, however, the subsequent actions of William Gregson and his colleagues ensured that not only would word of the deaths get out, but also it would cause a political earthquake among the people of Britain and dramatically change the course of events when it came to the slave trade. The Gregson syndicate sued their insurers for the loss of their cargo, claiming money damages for the people their employees had themselves destroyed. An initial court ruling found in favor of the merchants, but the insurance company demanded a new trial, setting off a court case in 1783 that publicized the sordid affair far and wide and caused revulsion among a significant portion of the British public.

Testimony by the merchants before the court and comments by the presiding judge, Chief Justice Lord Mansfield (1705–1793), revealed to ordinary Britons details about the slave trade and the culture of slavery that they had been able to avoid knowing about in the past. The characterization of human beings as "things" that could be jettisoned "of necessity" particularly offended people, as when the solicitor for the syndicate asserted that because they were cargo goods, the act of Africans being thrown into the sea could not carry with it "the least imputation of cruelty."[9] Lord Mansfield's equation of slaves with horses inflamed public opinion, although he meant his comparison to hold only in a legal sense. The counsel for the insurance company, by contrast, consistently presented his case in humanitarian terms, referring to the "rights" the slaves on board possessed and the "equality" Africans enjoyed with Britons when it came to apportioning water supplies or protecting life.

Mansfield ultimately ruled that a new trial should be held when he learned that it had rained in the interval between the second and third batch of murders aboard the *Zong*, undermining the argument about the need to eliminate some slaves so that the rest might have sufficient water to survive. It appears that the Gregson group saw the light and chose not to continue in their claim, because no evidence of a subsequent trial exists. (The Gregson fortunes only increased in subsequent years, as the slave trade and their involvement in it grew and produced ever more wealth in the 1790s and 1800s.) In the court of public opinion, however, the murders on the *Zong* continued to disturb the consciences of greater and greater numbers of people. They ultimately led to the formation in 1787 of the Society for Effecting the Abolition of the Slave Trade, a lobbying group whose adoption of popular politics would achieve precisely what its title demanded.

Until the advent of the abolitionist movement, political lobbying had largely been restricted to elite groups. The sensational and heart-breaking revelations of the *Zong* murders helped to change that dynamic, bringing significant numbers of ordinary people into the public sphere of policy and law-making. While William Wilberforce (1759–1833) led the charge in Parliament, Thomas Clarkson (1760–1846) organized people across the United Kingdom, using the instance of the *Zong* and other horrific incidents of cruelty against slaves to recruit people to the abolitionist cause. He also played up the violence of the slave trade for the sailors crewing the ships, having taken their testimonies and descriptions of "different scenes of barbarity" they suffered at the hands of captains and shipowners.[10] The moral case against the slave trade grew exponentially, leading the prime minister, William Pitt (1759–1806), to put the issue before the Privy Council for discussion. The outbreak of the French Revolution, and especially the Haitian Revolution, derailed what might have been a momentous shift regarding the slave trade in the 1790s. As it was, Parliament outlawed the "African trade" in 1807 by an overwhelming majority. Abolitionists had the obtuseness and greed of Liverpool slave merchants to thank for that extraordinary turn of events.

financial means to settle in comfortably. Beginning in 1783, a Loyalist Claims Commission began hearing cases from better-off people whose property and wealth had been confiscated by the American rebels. Ultimately, the commission paid out millions of pounds in restitution, on the grounds that Britain had a moral responsibility to look after those who had aided the war effort. "The honor of the nation" demanded action if the "national character" of Britons was not to fall into "disgrace."[8]

For those without resources, making ends meet was impossible without the assistance of poor relief. But soup kitchens could do little to stem the unemployment and poverty exacerbated by postwar depression. Prominent among the poorest loyalists were the 5,000 ex-slaves who had served as sailors, soldiers, or laborers during the war. Most of them became servants and married white women in the local communities in which they settled. Their highly visible presence on the streets of London excited much adverse comment, some of it verging on racist hatred. But another, more generous, response emerged as well, drawing on the spirit that undergirded the Loyalist Claims Commission and receiving impetus from the newly bourgeoning antislavery movement. How could it be fair to withhold assistance from black loyalists when white loyalists had been handsomely rewarded for their service? How could it be right, advocates demanded, that blacks be enslaved in the first place, carried aboard British ships to British colonies where they labored under the harsh regime of the whip? The Committee for the Relief of the Black Poor, established initially to offer material support at home, soon began to hear appeals from the black poor themselves to help them settle in Africa instead, a proposition taken up and advanced by abolitionists Granville Sharp (1735–1813) and Henry Smeathman (1742–1786). Smeathman especially urged the colonization of Sierra Leone, where a deep harbor promised greater possibilities of success; more pointedly, Bunce Island, one of Britain's largest slaving stations, lay in the harbor at Sierra Leone. What better method of advancing the cause of antislavery could be imagined than planting a colony of freed slaves at that very spot? Smeathman convinced the committee to join in on the plan, and by 1786, under the leadership of Granville Sharp, the committee had persuaded the British government to provide ships and supplies with which to transport and settle 300 blacks in Sierra Leone.

After months of wrangling and delays, during which time fifty colonists died from fever on board ships that sat in harbor as if becalmed, the small fleet of black emigrants set sail in 1787. They landed on the coast of Africa at an inauspicious time—the rainy season was underway, and its torrential downpours destroyed crops, turned the land to mud, and fostered the explosion of disease-bearing insects. By the time the colonists had negotiated a treaty with the local King Naimbana for the land on which they established Granville Town, a quarter of their number had died. Hungry, sick, and lacking adequate shelter, many others abandoned their settlement to join the slavers at Bunce Island, where they could at least find food. The slavers, eager to undermine the entire abolitionist purpose of the colony, conspired with a local subchief, King Jimmy, who ordered the residents of Granville Town to leave. Then he burned down their houses. The initial effort to colonize Sierra Leone with free blacks had proved a disaster, but, as we will see in the next chapter, black loyalists who had initially settled in British North America after the American Revolution and a group of rebellious Jamaican Maroons who had been transported to Nova Scotia in 1796 would embark on a second voyage of exile to reinvigorate the cause.

Settlement of former slaves at Sierra Leone.

The cause—antislavery—had received impetus from the successful breaking away of the American colonies. Britain had long engaged in the slave trade and in slavery itself—indeed, as we have seen, much of its wealth derived from them—and few voices had been raised against its complicity in the unsavory practices inherent within the traffic in human beings. But in the 1770s, things changed. Abolitionist literature offered gruesome descriptions of the inhumane and brutal treatment of enslaved Africans as they huddled chained in shipholds or worked the plantations of the Caribbean and the American South. The decision of the British courts in the Somerset case of 1772 made slave-owning in Britain illegal for all practical purposes; after 1783, abolitionists and humanitarians of all stripes could now draw a clear distinction between their own country and the slave-owning United States. West Indian planters might protest, but the absence now of a huge portion of the proslave lobby diminished their clout. Public opinion did an abrupt about-face; newspapers, clergymen, politicians, and regular folks joined in an impassioned collective cry for ending the transatlantic slave trade, and their pressures created a political groundswell that could not be ignored.

Sharp, Smeathman, and a number of Quaker, Methodist, and evangelical abolitionists had worked for years to bring the iniquities of slavery and the slave trade before the British public. In 1787, under the leadership of Thomas Clarkson, a young graduate of Cambridge, the disparate forces of abolitionism came together in the Committee for Effecting the Abolition of the Slave Trade. The establishment of this association marked the moment when what had largely been a Quaker movement became transformed into a national and international political campaign. Clarkson met William Wilberforce, MP for Hull, in May 1787 and persuaded him to lead the charge in Parliament. He then traveled to Bristol and Liverpool, the two main centers of the slave trade, to gather information from merchants, sea captains, sailors, and enslaved Africans, with which he hoped to sway the public and MPs to his position. Armed with a wealth of detail, he approached the Privy Council, which agreed to establish a committee to investigate the slave trade. William Pitt, the prime minister, promised in 1788 that Parliament would debate the issue during the next session; the following year, William Wilberforce, the great parliamentary champion of abolition for the next twenty-five years, introduced the first abolition bill taken up by Westminster. It would, alas, find no traction because before it could be seriously debated, the French Revolution and a slave revolt in St. Domingue (modern-day Haiti) broke out. As we will see in the next chapter, these events would have enormous repercussions for Britain.

Women played an outsized role in the development of antislavery politics in Britain, despite increasing injunctions to keep them out of the public realm. It is important to emphasize that the ideological development of what historians call "separate spheres" for men and women—for men the rough-and-tumble life of work and politics, for women the domestic realm of home, family, and the cultivation of morality—did not necessarily reflect how men and women behaved in the course of their daily lives. Moralists, novelists, journalists, and politicians might prescribe for respectable women a highly circumscribed life of domesticity, but in many, many instances their pronouncements fell on deaf ears. In other instances, women's very nature, as eighteenth-century moralists saw it, suited them for a particular kind of politics. The conviction that women possessed a finer sensibility than men authorized many forms of public activity, especially in charity work but sometimes beyond it. The antislavery campaign of the last decades of the eighteenth century, part of a larger humanitarian movement that addressed concerns such as prison reform, protection for children, education for the poor, and the breastfeeding of infants, attracted many evangelical, Methodist, and Quaker women to its ranks.

Although some strands of antislavery thought emphasized the rights of slaves to freedom and autonomy, a position that made it more difficult for women to participate in, because they had no such rights and most could not imagine claiming them for themselves, the most successful arguments against slavery recalled Britons to the suffering and inhumane conditions imposed on slaves by their fellow countrymen and -women. The moral basis of antislavery appeals—sympathy for others, pity, compassion, the so-called "feminine" qualities associated with sensibility—dovetailed nicely with the traits purportedly possessed by women, rendering them the obvious targets of reform efforts outside of Parliament and effective propagandists with those inside Parliament. As an appeal in the Manchester *Mercury* observed in 1787,"If any public Interference will at any TIME become the Fair Sex; if Their Names are ever to be mentioned with Honour beyond the Boundaries of their Family, and the Circle of their Connections, it can only be, when a public Opportunity is given for the Exertion of those Qualities which are peculiarly expected in, and particularly possessed by that most amiable Part of Creation—the Qualities of Humanity, Benevolence, and Compassion."[11]

THE GORDON RIOTS

Antislavery advocates welcomed the material and political contributions made to their cause by respectable middle- and upper-class women. But as we saw earlier in the chapter, the participation of women in popular politics in the 1770s and 1780s often generated misogynistic responses. One such example of discrediting a political movement by equating it with "the feminine" took place during the Gordon Riots of 1780, when a large anti-Catholic crowd gathered before Parliament to protest legislation that would remove some of the legal disabilities suffered by Catholics. These had been championed by the Irish Parliament, surprisingly, in which Protestants exclusively sat. The victories achieved by the Irish in the crisis years of 1779–1782, however hedged they might have been by the continuation of keeping the executive power for Ireland in the hands of the Westminster Parliament, led to more radical questions about such issues as political representation, and this in turn inevitably raised the question of allowing Catholics to participate in politics. Some of the Volunteers who had been so instrumental in winning the reforms in Ireland had begun to call for reforms that would give religious liberty for everyone, not just Protestants. A 1778 Catholic Relief Act had removed some of the bans on Catholics owning or leasing land, and in 1782, a more ambitious measure went into effect. It removed the disabilities against Catholics owning land altogether, allowed Catholic clergy to practice, and permitted them to teach as well.

The Burning & Plundering of Newgate & Setting the Felons at Liberty by the Mob.

The Gordon Riots, 1780.

In 1779, Lord North, the prime minister, sought to extend religious rights to the small number of Catholics in Scotland, who tended to be landed gentry and aristocrats living in the Highlands. But the Protestant Association, headed by Lord George Gordon (1751–1793), vowed to foil any such reform effort. Most of the anti-Catholic sentiment in Scotland had rested on purely religious grounds, but at least some part of it derived from class- and even nationalist-based grievances against the established elite cohort of Unionists who dominated political life in Scotland and who sought to uphold British political arrangements by giving constitutional rights to Catholics. In 1780, Gordon led a march of some 20,000 to 40,000 people to the Parliament in Westminster to protest the Scottish Relief Act, as it was called, threatening MPs until they agreed to drop the bill. And then the crowd went on a rampage; anti-Catholic xenophobia reached terrible heights, culminating in some of the worst domestic violence Britain had ever seen. For five days mobs rioted through the streets of London, attacking Catholic chapels, the homes and businesses of wealthy Catholics, and those who supported the cause, like Edmund Burke, or who tried to put down the riots. They burned tollhouses and prisons, made an assault on the Bank of England, and invaded the houses of the archbishop of York, Lord North, and the lord chief justice. Observers were appalled by the frenzy of the populace, whose primitive fury and mindless destruction, as they saw it, caused even radicals like Wilkes to recoil. When he got up in the House of Commons to denounce the rioters, Edmund Burke focused his outrage on the women among the crowds, terming them degraded, ignorant "monsters." The apparent atavism and anti-Catholic fanaticism of the Gordon mobs, in conjunction with Burke's singling out of the women among them, enabled elite and middling politicians to regard the riots as an example of just what the addition of "the feminine" to the public sphere might produce.[12]

TURNING TO INDIA

The loss of the American colonies in 1783 was followed almost immediately by the more formal acquisition of a significant portion of India in 1784. As we have seen, the East India Company had been active on the subcontinent for several decades by the 1780s, having secured a number of coastal cities and then, taking advantage of conflicts between indigenous rulers, annexing large areas of territory over the course of the eighteenth century, first in Bengal, where they controlled vast resources of land, labor, and capital. EIC officials, men like Robert Clive, enriched themselves enormously by extracting huge fortunes from indigenous rulers who sought company protection and support as they vied with one another for power and created an atmosphere and expectation of plunder among adventurers and merchants that could not be reconciled with the grand rhetoric of beneficence and progress that pro-imperialists insisted characterized their relationships with North America and the West Indies. When Clive and other so-called "nabobs" (the term was a misuse of the Indian word "nawab," which means governor) returned to England and showed off their great wealth to the opinion-makers of society, the envy and anger they provoked roused Members of Parliament to take action: the abuses committed by nabobs in India looked very like those that reformers attributed to "old corruption" in Britain in a comparison that struck far too close to home.

The actions and policies of the EIC caused extraordinary destruction. In Bengal, where company officials insisted that farmers abandon food crop production to grow opium for trade with China, food shortages caused by drought in 1768 and again in 1769—in and of themselves not unusual—turned into a full-blown famine by 1770. Over the next three years as many as 10 million Bengalis, a third of the local population, died from starvation and disease. Adam Smith suggested that the disaster was caused by the behavior of the EIC and that free trade policies might well have mitigated it. In *The Wealth of Nations*, he noted that "the drought in Bengal, a few years ago, might probably have occasioned a very great dearth. Some improper regulations, some injudicious restraints imposed by the servants of the East India Company upon the rice trade, contributed, perhaps, to turn that dearth into a famine."[13]

The lack of labor resulting from the famine, combined with a European commercial slowdown, reduced company revenues significantly; by the end of 1771, bankruptcy loomed. To stave off a massive credit crisis, the government of Lord North injected nearly a million and a half pounds into the company as part of the Regulating Act of 1773. In return for stabilizing its finances, Parliament established some degree of control over the EIC by creating the position of governor-general in Bengal, which had authority over Madras and Bombay as well. A Council of Five, made up of the governor-general and four other crown appointees, but paid by the EIC, would be responsible for the company's affairs in Calcutta. This unwieldy structure lasted for eleven years, during which time Warren Hastings (1732–1818), the governor-general, increased the size and scope of the company's authority by developing systems of tax collection, administration, and civil and criminal law. He also fended off severe challenges to the company's rule in Bengal from a military alliance of three of the most powerful indigenous Indian states backed by the French, but in the process of doing so engaged in certain practices— violent and forcible extortion, seizure of treasuries, and the overthrow of princes and princesses—against his own Indian allies that raised outcries against him at home. Portrayed as the epitome of greed, corruption, and exploitation of naive and innocent native peoples, Hastings provoked outrage among a number of MPs that was all the more heated for their conviction that the British government, through its relationship with the EIC, was complicit in these sordid activities.

In 1784, the government of William Pitt passed the India Act through Parliament. By this legislation, which remained in force until 1858 when it was superseded by yet another regime of governance prompted by the Indian Rebellion of 1857 (see Chapter 7), the EIC and the British government became partners of sorts. The company preserved its jurisdiction over the commercial affairs of those parts of India over which it had control; the British government took over matters of governance and administration. The governor-general, appointed by and answerable to the crown, had the executive power necessary to carry out and enforce his initiatives; and the company, which could appoint its own officials, was

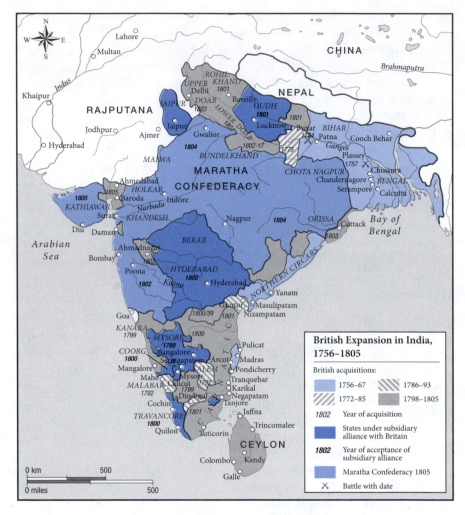

MAP 4.2
British Expansion in India, 1756–1805

free to conduct its commercial activities and control patronage. To ensure that previous abuses would not be allowed to continue, the act included a provision that the EIC clear with an oversight Board of Control in London, made up in part of cabinet ministers, any military or civil policies it wished to pursue.

In 1785, Hastings resigned his position as governor-general and returned to England. There he faced the wrath of prominent MPs like Charles James Fox and Edmund Burke for his reportedly rapacious behavior in India. In 1786, Burke brought forward a bill of impeachment against Hastings for exercising "arbitrary power" in India, which caused "cruelties unheard-of, and Devastations almost without a name!"[14] In a theatrical performance that dragged on until he was impeached by the House of Commons in 1787 and then acquitted of the charges against him by the House of Lords in 1794, the question of Britain's culpability in an imperial venture gone all wrong was displaced onto Hastings and rehearsed over and over until a solution could be found that would render Britain innocent of any wrongdoing as well.

Burke and his Whig supporters feared that the exercise of arbitrary rule over India threatened liberty at home in Britain. "I am certain," he declared, "that every means effectual to preserve India from oppression is a guard to preserve the British Constitution from its worst corruption."[15] Although he was not a proponent of independence for India, Burke castigated the behavior of EIC agents whose grabs for territory and riches shamed every freedom-loving, virtuous Briton; violated the integrity of ancient and long-civilized Indian states; and promised to stain the imperial project as a whole with their corruption and extortionate practices.

Hastings answered his critics by drawing on a kind of "when in Rome do as the Romans do" notion of government. He argued that in a land long subject to the rule of "oriental despots," he could not expect to be an effective governor-general if he did not employ the tactics and principles that his Indian counterparts used against their subjects and against one another. The concept of "oriental despotism" referred to the belief that Asians by their very nature submitted readily to absolute rule, almost as slaves submitted to their masters. It implied that Asian states possessed no system of laws and their peoples no rights. These ideas tallied well with theories about the effects of climate on civic society we saw earlier in Chapter 3: India's heat and humidity explained what to Europeans appeared to be the supineness of Indians in the face of arbitrary, despotic rulers. "The labour of being free," wrote Alexander Dow (1735–1779) in his 1770 *Dissertation on Despotism*, part of a larger history of India, required more than Indians could muster in a climate that produced overwhelming "languor" and enervation. It was much easier simply to give way "without murmuring" to the "arbitrary sway" of despotic rulers. Historian Robert Orme (1728–1801) asserted that the heat of India produced in its people an "effeminacy and resignation of spirit, not to be paralleled in the world." Noting that the fertility of the soil provided a wealth of produce, he claimed that "breathing in the softest of climates, having so few wants and receiving even the luxuries of other nations with little labour from their own soil, the Indian must become the most effeminate inhabitant of the globe."[16]

If we keep in mind that the term effeminacy referred, in the eighteenth century, not to homosexuality among men but to a weakening of men too much in the thrall of luxury, sensuality, and pleasure, that is, to the qualities ascribed to women, we can understand better the association Europeans made between despotism and sexual licentiousness. Oriental despotism conjured up images of the harem, of polygamy, of jealousy, intrigue, passion, and cunning. Like the visions produced of African societies located in the torrid zones of the globe, representations of the licentious, immoral, despotic Indians who subjected their women to the worst kind of sexual slavery offered Britons a foil against which they then imagined themselves to be. Freedom-loving, independent, industrious, manly Britons who held their women in awe and treated them with respect—these were the individuals whose imperial ventures in North America had brought wealth, acclaim, and glory to Great Britain.

Reports of the EIC's unrestrained greed and corruption and Hastings's claim to have governed of necessity in the fashion of an Asian despot threatened this image of the civilized British and caused people like Burke a great deal of anxiety about what could be easily construed as Britain's having acted no better than any other oriental despot. Burke, following a well-known rhetoric of rapine and torture attributable to peoples of "lesser" civilization, cataloged the transgressions of Hastings and his followers through an inventory of sexual sensationalism, portraying India as an innocent virgin ravished by evil-minded Britons. "The treatment of females could not be described," he thundered to the House of Commons, "dragged forth from their houses, which the religion of the country had made so many sanctuaries, they were exposed naked to public view; the virgins were carried to the Court of Justice, where they might naturally have looked for protection; but now they looked for it in vain; for in the face of the Ministers of Justice, in the face of the spectators, in the face of the sun, those tender and modest virgins were brutally violated. The only difference between their treatment and that of their mothers was, that the former were dishonoured in the face of day, the latter in the gloomy recesses of their dungeons. Other females had the nipples of their breasts put in a cleft bamboo, and torn off. What modesty in all nations most carefully conceals, this monster [Hastings] revealed to view, and consumed by slow fires."[17]

Hastings and his men were Britons, acting on behalf of the greatest commercial company in the land, whose directors enjoyed vast influence over the financial and political affairs of Britain; many of them, indeed, sat in Parliament. For Britain's grand imperial project to survive the conquest of India, Hastings and his agents would have to go down, and the EIC and Britain itself removed from any participation in arbitrary rule, with all its connotations of sexual excess. For Burke and other Whigs, this meant that Britain must not only punish the wrongdoers and impose discipline on its officials in India, but also create a colonial government that would act in the interests of Indians, which, he claimed, were "in effect, one and the same" as those of the British. In short, Burke envisaged a form of colonial rule that could be made moral through proper, just governing of Indian people.

Under the governor-generalship of Lord Cornwallis (1738–1805) from 1786 to 1793, Burke's vision of colonial rule was largely put into effect. Employees of the EIC were no longer permitted to trade as private individuals or to exact through extortion from indigenous Indian rulers vast fortunes. Rather, they were paid salaries high enough to keep them from temptation. Cornwallis's Code of Regulations made the district tax collectors accountable for every sum they received and liable to prosecution if they exceeded their authorized amounts by even a little. District judges had authority over the police and were charged with the impartial administration of a known and settled body of law, which, like its English counterpart, sought to protect property and maintain order. By establishing a colonial administration that looked much like their own in many respects, Britons could remove from themselves any taint of complicity in and displace onto Indians themselves full and exclusive responsibility for the practices of oriental despotism. While "every native of Hindustan, I verily believe, is corrupt," declared Cornwallis, Britons could congratulate themselves for what they saw as their "upright and humane intentions" for imperial power. Morally superior to the corrupt, dissembling, licentious native population, the British could go about their business of empire in India confident of their right and their duty to rule people who were fit only for subjection.

••

Prior to the Seven Years' War, Britain's colonial possessions had been few enough and the Europeans who had settled them enough like Britons to be able to fit into the picture the English liked to draw of the unique values of liberty and freedom they represented. Limited largely to the thirteen colonies of North America, populated by white, Protestant, English-speaking persons, an empire based on trade, pro-imperials could readily claim, brought significant material and moral advantages with it. The empires of France, Spain, and even the Romans, which were based on conquest and unwanted rule from the center, required constant military effort on the part of the mother country to maintain its control and had ultimately destroyed the mother country, it was believed.

Now, however, the Peace of Paris of 1763 ceded to Britain enormous tracts of territory in Canada, the West Indies, West Africa, India, Cuba, and the Philippines formerly held by France and Spain and inhabited by nonwhite, non-Christian populations. Enslaved Africans, French Catholics, Indians, Amerindians—how was rule over these "alien" peoples to be rendered compatible with the vision of empire as a beneficial product of liberty-loving commercial people? How could the British, and especially the English, who believed themselves to be uniquely free from tyranny after 1688, justify to themselves an empire that required the domination of those who inhabited it? In what ways was the British empire now any different from those of France, Spain, or Rome in its use of authoritarianism and brutal force as methods of rule? As we have seen, a body of systematized racial thought emerged that portrayed Asians, Africans, Native Americans, and, not incidentally, Irish, and Scots Highlanders as childlike, feminine, or savage peoples in need of guidance, discipline, and control. The presence of a virtuous, manly British imperial master, under whose firm but gentle tutelage these benighted people might learn the attributes of civilization, the pro-imperial line went, would benefit colony and mother country alike. This kind of thinking about race and empire took on even greater intensity when Britain lost the thirteen American colonies in 1783 and at the same time acquired control over significant portions of India.

The gendered and racialized images of legitimate and illegitimate claims to power and authority had lasting effects. In the case of gender, as we shall see in the next chapter, they served to justify a full-scale campaign to eliminate women and what was regarded as "the feminine" from the public arenas of work and politics and to restrict them to the private world of home and domesticity. In the case of race, they acted to diminish the doubts Britons had about their imperial control of millions of nonwhite subjects in Asia and to excuse their widespread, enthusiastic participation in the transport of and trade in African slaves. The intersections of racial and gender attributes appeared regularly in efforts to uphold or resist various regimes of power throughout the eighteenth, nineteenth, and twentieth centuries. The impact they had on human beings, men and women of all races, classes, and ethnicities, would be profound.

NOTES

1. Quoted in Richard B. Sheridan, "The Jamaican Slave Rebellion of 1776 and the American Revolution," *Journal of Negro History* 61.3 (July 1976): 290–308, pp. 297, 302.
2. Quoted in Sheridan, "The Jamaican Slave Rebellion of 1776 and the American Revolution," p. 302.
3. See Linda Colley, *Britons: Forging the Nation, 1707–1837* (New Haven, 2009), Ch. 3.
4. See Kathleen Wilson, *A Sense of the People: Politics, Culture and Imperialism in England, 1715–1785* (Cambridge, 1995), ch. 4.
5. Quoted in Andrew Jackson O'Shaughnessy, *An Empire Divided: The American Revolution and the British Caribbean* (Philadelphia, 2000), p. 152.
6. Quoted in Sheridan, "The Jamaican Slave Rebellion of 1776 and the American Revolution," p. 298.
7. Quoted in John Dwyer, *Virtuous Discourse: Sensibility and Community in Late Eighteenth-Century Scotland* (Edinburgh, 1987), 40.
8. Quoted in Maya Jasanoff, *Liberty's Exiles. American Loyalists in the Revolutionary World* (New York, 2011), p. 122.
9. Quoted in James Walvin, *The Zong. A Massacre, the Law, and the End of Slavery* (New Haven, 2011), p. 145.

TIMELINE

1760   George II dies; George III ascends to throne

1761   Lord Bute becomes prime minister

1763   End of Seven Years' War

1772   Somerset case makes slavery in Britain illegal

1776   Outbreak of American Revolution

Slave revolt in Jamaica

1778   France enters Revolutionary War in support of American colonists

Women banned from gallery and floor of House of Commons

1779   Irish gain "equality in trading rights" with England and Scotland

Spain enters Revolutionary War

10. Quoted in Marcus Rediker, *The Slave Ship. A Human History* (London, 2007), p. 324.

11. Quoted in Susan Kingsley Kent, *Gender and Power in Britain* (London, 1999), p. 109.

12. Iain McCalman, "Mad Lord George and Madame La Motte: Riot and Sexuality in the Genesis of Burke's *Reflections on the Revolution in France*," *Journal of British Studies* 35.3 (July 1996): 343–67.

13. Adam Smith, *The Wealth of Nations: An Inquiry into the Nature and Causes of the Wealth of Nations* (London, 1776), p. 339.

14. The discussion of Hastings's impeachment is drawn from Thomas Metcalf, *Ideologies of the Raj* (Cambridge, 1994) and Sara Suleri, *The Rhetoric of English India* (Chicago, 1992), quoted in Kent, *Gender and Power in Britain*, p. 96.

15. Ibid., quoted in Kent, *Gender and Power*, p. 96.

16. Ibid., quoted in Kent, *Gender and Power*, pp. 96, 97.

17. Ibid., quoted in Kent, *Gender and Power*, p. 97.

FURTHER READING

Moira Ferguson, *Subject to Others: British Women Writers and Colonial Slavery, 1670–1834*. New York, 1992.

Maya Jasanoff, *Liberty's Exiles. American Loyalists in the Revolutionary World*. New York, 2011.

Thomas Metcalf, *Ideologies of the Raj*. Cambridge, 1994.

Claire Midgley, *Women against Slavery. The British Campaigns, 1780–1870*. London, 1992.

Gary Nash, *Red, White, and Black. The Peoples of Early North America*. Upper Saddle River, 2009.

Sara Suleri, *The Rhetoric of English India*. Chicago, 1992.

Kathleen Wilson, *A Sense of the People: Politics, Culture and Imperialism in England, 1715–1785*. Cambridge, 1995.

1780	Gordon Riots
1781	British surrender to American forces at Yorktown
1782	Repeal of Declaratory Act of 1720
1783	William Pitt becomes prime minister
	End of Revolutionary War; British troops evacuate New York
1784	India Act
1786	Lord Cornwallis becomes governor-general of India
1787	Sierra Leone colonized, then abandoned
1788	First Fleet arrives in Australia
	Colony at New South Wales established

Massacre at Scullabogue, 1798.

CHAPTER 5

SCOTLAND

IRELAND ENGLAND

Wexford WALES

REVOLUTION, WAR, AND REACTION, 1789–1820

O n July 5, 1798, fourteen-year-old Dinah Goff smelled smoke. It had been a common occurrence over the past two weeks in County Wexford, Ireland, where rebellion against the Irish government and its British patrons had broken out. She and her family had been required to provision the rebel troops on a regular basis, offering up daily rations of salt, water, milk, cider, beer, bread, cheese, horses, sheep, and cattle. As Quakers, they held an entirely neutral position in the conflict. Their pacifism, their capacity to give the rebel troops the material resources they sought, and the affection in which they were held by the people of the area, loyalist and rebel alike, earned them noncombatant status. Although threatened occasionally by rogue elements of both armies, they remained in relative safety. They did not, however, escape the horrible sights and sounds of the battles that raged about them. Dinah watched her mother and sisters bind up the bloody, gaping wounds of fallen insurgents; she listened to rebels tell of "the fine young officers when they sickled them under the short ribs with their pikes. They curled up like wood lice and screamed like asses." Smoke and ash filled the air as soldiers on both sides of the conflict burned the houses, barns, and haystacks of their enemies. But something was different on June 5: "a strong and dreadful effluvium" mixed with the usual stench of burning wood as it "wafted . . . to our lawn."[1] It came from Scullabogue, a farmstead about two and a half miles from Dinah's house, where more than 100 loyalists were burning to death in the barn in which they had been imprisoned.

No other incident holds so vivid a place in the memory of the Irish Rebellion of 1798 as the Scullabogue massacre. Men, women, and children suffered hideously at the hands of incensed rebel soldiers who ordered that the barn holding prisoners be put to the torch. The men in charge of the prisoners had initially refused the command, but after receiving a third set of orders, they acceded to the demands of the rebels, who had just returned from a battle at New Ross. There, only a few hours earlier, loyalist militiamen had perpetrated their own incineration of some seventy wounded insurgents in a house on Mary Street.

Terrible as it was, Scullabogue constituted merely an extreme instance of the kind of warfare inflicted on the belligerent and civilian populations of Ireland in 1798. It was an event that contains within it virtually all of the elements that characterize one of the most remarkable periods in British history. Revolution, war, transportation to the penal colonies of Australia, formal union with Ireland, the expansion of empire and British state power to an unprecedented size and scope—all these emerged in the dynamic decades between 1789 and 1820.

••

THE FRENCH REVOLUTION

In the summer of 1789 revolution swept France, compelling King Louis XVI to give in to the principles of representative government and the sovereignty of the people by recognizing the existence of the National Assembly. Britons of nearly every political persuasion cheered the development. Whigs and even Tories saw in the French Revolution the epitome of their own system of balanced government, achieved exactly 100 years earlier with the ratification of the Bill of Rights; radicals seeking reform of a parliamentary system dominated by "old corruption," a broader representation of citizenship, and religious tolerance welcomed it as an indication of things to come in Britain.

In 1791, Thomas Paine (1737–1809) published *The Rights of Man*, in which he claimed that citizenship rested not on possession of property but on the capacity for individuals to reason. *The Rights of Man* landed like a bombshell, exploding Lockean notions that granted men citizenship in part on the basis of their status as heads of households. Instead, everyone, regardless of social rank—or, as people like the radical Mary Wollstonecraft (1759–1797) would soon assert, of gender—possessed the ability to reason and everyone, therefore, qualified for direct participation in the political nation. Wollstonecraft made explicit what Paine had left abstract. In 1792 she published *A Vindication of the Rights of Woman*, in which she argued for women's full admission to the political nation, with all the rights and responsibilities accorded to men, on the grounds that women, no less than men, possessed reason and contributed to public virtue through the rearing of civic-minded children. She urged that women be educated in the "manly virtues" (just as men, she asserted, should become "chaste and modest") and learn to become industrious, independent members of society rather than dependent parasites. She envisaged citizen-women taking to "the field" to "march and counter-march like soldiers, or wrangle in the senate to keep their faculties from rusting."[2]

We should recall that France had long been viewed by Britons as a "feminine" nation. Now, in the midst of a revolution in which large numbers of women participated and that became increasingly radical as months passed, Britons' anxieties about women's place in public life took on greater intensity. With the advent of the September massacres in Paris in 1792, the beheading of Louis XVI in January 1793, and Britain's declaration of war on France the following month, suggestions like Wollstonecraft's of women becoming autonomous of their husbands and fathers, of their acting openly and freely in political affairs, and of their taking to arms produced enormous disquiet. Advice manuals, conduct books, sermons from clergymen, novels, and newspaper and journal articles issued forth in a flood, asserting more forcefully than ever before that social and political order—and, indeed, women's very safety—rested on the delineation of separate spheres for men and women.

Part of the emphasis on separate spheres for men and women derived from the fear that revolutionary passions and political violence would spill over into sexual violence against women. Men who had no respect for rank, it was feared, would have even less respect for sex, and women would suffer abuse at their hands. Men and women of every political affiliation were shocked by the treatment of Marie Antoinette at the hands of the Paris crowds and her execution by the Jacobins appalled British public opinion. Accounts of her abduction from Versailles in 1789 called up images of rape, as in this description of it by Mary Wollstonecraft. "The sanctuary of repose," wrote the radical reformer, herself no fan of royalty, "the asylum of care and fatigue, the chaste temple of a woman, I consider the Queen only as one, the apartment where she consigns her senses to the bosom of sleep, folded in its arms forgetful of the world, was violated with murderous fury."[3]

The confines of the home and decidedly not the arena of political strife, conservative propagandists asserted, afforded women protection from the depredations of men. Separate sphere ideology offered women a kind of implicit quid pro quo, an unspoken bargain whereby women traded freedom and equality in the public sphere for obedience, submission, and the protection of men in the private sphere. "The whole world might be at war," Laetitia Hawkins (1759–1835) reminded her countrywomen in 1793, "and yet not the rumour of it reached the ears of an Englishwoman—empires might be lost, and states overthrown, and still she might pursue the peaceful occupations of her home; and her natural lord might change his governor at pleasure, and she feel neither change nor hardship." Women who talked of "equal rights, the abjectness of submission, the duty of every one to think for themselves," on the other hand, as Hawkins put it, endangered "the national female character" by threatening the peace of that very home that provided women with security. The rights of women, she feared, would compel women to challenge the authority of their husbands in the home, leading to revolt within the marriage and divorce to the couple, which in turn would leave women defenseless before the assaults of men who would no longer have any respect for them.[4]

Conservative women's fears for their safety at the hands of republican revolutionaries received impetus from Britain's own homegrown radical campaign, whose political demands by 1792 were being matched by social and economic demands from some quarters of the movement. The older political alignments of radicals against the aristocratic established order, of "the people" against "old corruption," now took on the appearance, in the minds of conservatives and even of most moderates, of an all-out battle of poor against rich, of the lower classes against the higher classes. In January 1792, a group of artisans and shopkeepers led by the Scottish shoemaker Thomas Hardy (1752–1832), acting on the Painite principle of the possession of reason as the sole criterion for citizenship, formed the London Corresponding Society, calling for the rights of citizenship for working men. The following month, Paine published the second part of his *Rights of Man*, in which he joined the demand for economic and social rights—minimum wages, universal education, poor relief, family allowances, old-age pensions, public works for the unemployed, all to be paid for by greater taxation of the wealthy—to those for political rights. Paine's second pamphlet appealed to great numbers of plebeians, men and women alike, whose economic situations, as we shall see below, had deteriorated in the past decade as industrialization made its way into various regions of Great Britain and contributed mightily to the momentum of the radical movement.

Within six months of its founding, the membership of the London Corresponding Society, which disseminated Paine's pamphlet far and wide in its propaganda campaign, had grown from 25 to 2,000. Following its example, provincial corresponding societies sprang up in a number of industrial cities. The followers of the radical Richard Price (1723–1791) in Wales, organized in an already existing society of patriots called the Gwyneddigion, promoted Paine's ideas through a series of hymns to liberty. In Ireland, middling and elite Protestants and Catholics established the Society of United Irishmen (UI) in 1791 to seek political reform and Catholic emancipation from legal disabilities. By the end of the eighteenth century, the second part of *The Rights of Man* had sold perhaps 500,000 copies.

Attacks on the social order seem to have posed a far greater threat to elites than the political claims of "the people." Even the moderate reformer, Christopher Wyvill, whose radical credentials dated back to the 1770s, expressed alarm at the prospect of lower-class participation. "If Mr. Paine should be able to rouze up the lower classes," he wrote, "their interference will probably be marked by wild work, and all we now possess, whether in private property or public liberty, will be at the mercy of a lawless and furious rabble."[5]

Coinciding as it did with the far more violent turn of events in France in the fall of 1792, working-class radicalism, now termed "Jacobinism" after the radical Jacobin Club in Paris, injected an element of panic into the thinking of authorities. Acting on rumors that an insurrection of London working men would break out in December, the government implemented a serious of repressive measures designed to contain popular radicalism. Scottish radicals who met in December in Edinburgh at a "National Convention" to express support for the French were arrested for reading *The Rights of Man* to the audience and charged with "Wickedly and feloniously inciting . . . a spirit of disloyalty and disaffection to the King and the Established Government." Dubbed the Scottish Martyrs, they were sentenced to transportation to Australia for fourteen years, the first political prisoners to arrive in that new penal colony. The outbreak of war with France in February 1793 and the subsequent execution of Louis XVI intensified anti-Jacobin sentiments, giving rise to the formation of private associations devoted to the protection of property and privilege among conservatives and to stamping out all evidence of popular radicalism. These, alongside the actions of the government—such as the suspension of habeas corpus in 1794, the arrest and trial for treason of Thomas Hardy and two other English radical leaders in 1795, and food shortages caused by high prices and the disruptions of war—spurred working-class "Jacobins" to even greater political activity. Waves of rioting broke out across Britain in the fall and winter of 1794–1795. At the end of October 1795, some 200,000 Londoners took to the streets and pelted the king's carriage with stones as he drove in state on his way to Westminster to open Parliament. Shouts of "Peace!," "No War!," "Down with Pitt!," "No King!" greeted him, and protesters carrying loaves of bread on staves decorated with black crepe sought to bring their grievances to his attention. By the end of 1795, radicals could organize mass meetings of 100,000 to perhaps 200,000 men and women calling for political reform and the end of war with France.

In response to such rallies and riots, the government passed the Seditious Meetings and Treasonable Practices Acts of 1795, outlawing political meetings of more than fifty persons; when members of the corresponding societies began to meet in groups of fewer than fifty, the government passed the Combination Acts of 1799 and 1800. These last proved successful in driving radical politics underground, although not before a wave of disorder and unrest, fueled by bad harvests and high prices, swept through many parts of Britain in the years 1799 to 1801.

In the Caribbean, whose involvement in the sugar trade contributed enormously to the overall economy of France, the events of 1789–1791 produced a powerful response. The French colonies' white planter elites, whose enterprises depended on the slave labor of hundreds of thousands of Africans and who had great influence with deputies of the National Assembly, ensured that any discussion of slavery and abolition would be muted. In 1790, free people of color from St. Domingue (modern-day Haiti) sent a delegation to the National Assembly seeking recognition by and membership in the National Assembly. When their request was denied, a rising of fellow mulattoes broke out in the colony, although it was readily and brutally suppressed by local authorities. In August of 1791, the slaves of St. Domingue revolted, provoking an invasion by British and Spanish troops who, already at war with France, believed they could end the rising and take the island. By springtime, the French government, besieged by enemies at

A PLACE IN TIME

Liverpool and the Wars of the French Revolution

The wars of the French Revolution, which lasted from 1793 to 1815, put great pressure on the people and prosperity of Liverpool, perhaps more than on any other population of Great Britain. Ships from the port, now the second busiest of the country after London, plied the Atlantic from east to west and north to south, exposing themselves to enemy attack and the loss of crews and cargos at the hands of the French navy and privateers. Commerce suffered dramatically from the dangers posed by enemy raids. Seamen from Liverpool were expected to help fill the needs of the British navy for sailors, a mandate that the citizens were unable to circumvent no matter how detrimental the effect on merchants and ship owners who could not obtain the labor they needed for their commercial operations. In 1795, for instance, the Admiralty demanded 1,700 sailors and forbade the departure of any ships from port until they were provided. Unable to meet the requirement through voluntary enlistments, despite handsome rewards offered by the borough for signing up, officials turned to impressment, a practice notorious for its injustice and brutality. Not only did it deplete the port of necessary resources; not only did it reduce sailors to the equivalent of slaves; but it also deprived families of material and emotional support. The impact of impressment was devastating on a number of levels.

Naval press gangs worked from shore and aboard ship, ever on the lookout for sailors returning to port or enjoying shore leave. In the town, press gangs lurked outside pubs and inns, ready to grab up seamen as they left the premises and hustle them onto navy ships. On the river, navy cutters would stop vessels as they made their way to the docks, board them, and order the crew onto warships. Often the men refused, engaging in battle with the press men. The violence reached terrible levels at times and those who fought and were overcome found themselves subject to horrific flogging as punishment. One press gang worked from the guardship *Princess*, tied up in the river just across from one of the main docks. Aware of its presence, many of the seamen entering the Mersey from the Irish Sea flung themselves into the water to swim to the Cheshire shore, where an innkeeper by the name of Mother Redcap hid them in underground cellars.

Wholly apart from impressment, thousands of seamen based in Liverpool volunteered to serve on His Majesty's warships. They included a significant number of sailors of African descent, whose presence in Liverpool dated back to the middle of the eighteenth century. Africans from Sierra Leone and freed slaves from the Caribbean and North America often settled in the port on completion of their voyages; some continued as seamen, whereas others turned to different trades. By the time of the French Revolution, a Liverpool-born black community had come into existence. One member of this small group, James Brown, may well have served on Lord (Horatio) Nelson's flagship *Victory* when it defeated the French force at Trafalgar in October 1805, the naval battle that would ultimately give Britain command of the seas for the next century.

Born around 1750 and given the name Cato or James Cato, Brown ran away to sea while still a child living in Nova Scotia. He worked on slave ships and later joined the British navy, at which time he changed his name to James Brown. At some point in his career, he earned the rank of boatswain, a position of considerable authority and significance that required him to take charge of the operations of the main deck. At 6 foot 4 inches tall and 280 pounds, he must have commanded respect. On board the *Victory*—we do not know for certain he was there but his grandson claimed he was and the ship's paybook lists a James Browne—he was one of at least ten sailors of African descent. There may have been quite a few others, but we are unable to know for sure because of the practice of blacks taking English names, just as Brown did. Paintings and friezes depicting Nelson's death at Trafalgar contain at least one black figure, testimony to the routine and commonplace presence of black seamen aboard British ships. As the port most active in the slave trade and site of a vast commerce with Africa, the West Indies, and North America, Liverpool most likely provided a significant portion of them.

The death of Nelson: note the African seaman
on the left.

The wars with France inflicted a great deal of economic distress on Liverpool, its businesses, and its citizens. A postwar depression exacerbated the situation, but by the latter part of the 1820s, with the advent of the railroad and industrialization amping up, the fortunes of the city would soon recover.

home and abroad, sought to improve its position on St. Domingue by declaring the free people of color citizens of France. It sent troops to try to hold the colony but could not gain control over the situation. Instead, the National Convention recognized the slave revolution and in 1793 offered freedom to any slave who would join the French. The next year, the Convention recognized blacks in their other colonies as free citizens of color.

The Haitian Revolution, as the events in St. Domingue came to be called, galvanized enslaved Africans in the British colonies of the West Indies and marks the beginnings of what might be called a black insurrectionary abolitionist movement. Risings and thwarted plots to revolt on the part of enslaved Aricans took place on the islands across the Caribbean throughout the 1790s and early 1800s, probably many more than have actually been recorded. Rumors of conspiracies gripped the white population and instilled massive fear among them. The wife of the governor of Jamaica, Lady Nugent (1771–1834), wrote in her December 13, 1803, diary entry of the "most frightful" anxiety created by "the rumours all day, of an understanding between the French prisoners and the free blacks, and their tampering with the negro slaves."[6] Jamaica was the site of numerous revolts on the part of enslaved Africans but also of rebellions carried out by free Maroons. As we will see later in the chapter, Trelawny Maroons would play a significant role in the consolidation of the "abolitionist" colony of Sierra Leone.

WOMEN AND WORK

Working-class "Jacobinism" and the fear evoked by it among middling and elite Britons received impetus from the economic and industrial changes taking place during this time in many parts of Great Britain. As we have seen, transformations in finance, commerce, agriculture, and demography had been proceeding throughout the eighteenth century, producing anxiety among elite and middling groups and a great deal of hardship for plebeian men and women whose livelihoods were often adversely effected by them. By the 1780s, the manufacture of cotton textiles had begun to undergo dramatic alterations in the way it was carried out, in the manner in which the work force was organized and supervised, and in the location in which all of this took place. The factory system of the nineteenth century, characterized by the large-scale organization of workers performing specialized functions on power-driven machinery according to a rhythm regulated by the clock, introduced enormous change into the lives of working people in many areas of England, Scotland, Wales, and northern Ireland. The factory became the emblem of industrialization: the symbolic locus of male workers' discontent and protest, in which the presence of working women was regarded as a threat to working men's manliness; the site of efficiency and productivity in the minds of political economists, who saw in the so-called "iron law of wages" the most effective means of controlling working-class sexuality, whose excess, they believed, brought about the poverty characteristic of this period; and the target of innumerable parliamentary and extraparliamentary campaigns aimed at removing women from the world of work.

The application of power-driven machinery to manufacturing first took place in spinning. Spinning had long been an occupation of women. For poor women, especially those in agricultural areas where labor was seasonal, it served as a source of income that often made the difference to a family's economic survival. Because they assumed that spinners operated within a family economy, where men's income provided the bulk of support for the family and women's contributions were seen to be merely supplemental, merchants paid women pitifully low wages for their work. These assumptions about women's work, and the wages paid for it, informed practices in factories as well when they came into being around 1780. The first "factories," spurred by the invention in the 1760s of a spinning jenny, which increased the number of spindles on a wheel from one to eight and later to sixteen and then to eighty, were modest affairs, often no more than a large room in a cottage or a workshop in which a number of people worked. Production of thread remained unspecialized, and because the first jennies were small, women could operate them. These early "factories" operated as domestic industry had in the past. Thus, in the first few decades of industrialization, women retained their traditional employment, as well as some degree of control over their lives within it, while increasing their output—and the wealth of their employers--dramatically. By about 1800, a new kind of entrepreneur emerged, who saw in the new technologies of cotton manufacture the means by which greater economy, efficiency, and productivity could be achieved. Interested in maximizing their profits and in establishing greater control over their labor force and cavalier about the displacement of workers that their methods might entail, these new industrialists set up large factories or mills in areas where labor, raw materials, and new steam-powered machines could be brought together and concentrated in one place. The new spinning machines, called spinning mules, were larger and heavier than the earlier jennies, requiring both skill and strength for their operation. Thus employers located their mills in towns where male artisans could be found in large numbers. All of this meant that textile production, formerly an occupation that employed all kinds of workers throughout all of Great Britain, now took place in a few specific regions, leaving plebeians in whole parts of the kingdom out of work, in poverty and distress. And spinning, which had once been the ubiquitous occupation of women, became the trade of men.

But because the costs of setting up these new mills were so great, factory owners sought the cheapest possible labor force. They turned to young women—often the wives and children of the mule spinners—to do the necessary work of piecing, carding, and reeling. Moreover, mill owners believed that women and children, considered "naturally" subordinate to their masters, were more docile, more easily controlled, and far more likely to yield to factory discipline than men. As a consequence, the number of female and child workers in factories far exceeded that of men. In one Scottish county near Glasgow in 1809, for instance, cotton mills employed some 900 men, 2,500 women, and 17,800 children. In Scotland, where single women accounted for about 20 percent of the adult female population, compared to only 10 percent in England, women comprised 61 percent of the labor force in the cotton industry. They made up 50 percent of the labor force in Lancashire, where cotton textiles were concentrated in England after 1800.

As new technologies made machines smaller and easier to operate, especially after 1815 when industrialization picked up momentum following the end of the Napoleonic wars, employers turned to lower-paid women to operate them. Men saw in women's employment an attempt to undermine their own, and, as we shall see in the next chapter, sought ways to eliminate women from factory work. They would capitalize on the rhetoric utilized by political economists and evangelical moralists to cast women as reproductive rather than productive beings, a phenomenon derived from and contributing to the intensification of the ideology of separate spheres during the era of the French Revolution.

MALTHUS AND MORE: DISCIPLINE AND DOMESTICITY

Competition in the textile industry combined with bad harvests and the economic dislocations created by the wars with France to produce a great deal of poverty and distress throughout England, Scotland, and Wales between 1790 and 1815. Food riots, machine-breaking, and demonstrations in support of political reform on the part of working men and women alarmed a great many people, especially in the context of the excitement and fear provoked by the French revolution.

Poverty, of course, was nothing new to eighteenth-century Great Britain. It had long been a staple of everyday life, acknowledged by contemporaries in theories of moral economy that understood society to be composed of mutually interdependent groups of people and that made it the obligation of the better off to attend to the economic woes of the poor through such means as poor relief, wage subsidies, and bread price supports. But in the 1790s, economists of a much more individualist stripe came to dominate understandings of the way society and the economy operated and how poverty could best be addressed. In a spate of writings produced by such classical economists as Thomas Malthus (1766–1834) and popularizers of political economy as Hannah More (1745–1833), poverty came to be regarded as the consequence of the behavior of idle men and irresponsible women for whose subsequent distress the larger society could not—indeed should not—be appealed to for amelioration. Efforts by political economists to explain poverty as a consequence of excessive births among working people rather than of unemployment and/or low wages joined with those of evangelicals who sought to defend the social order of ranks and hierarchy. In both instances, languages of gender and sexuality were mobilized to promote a social system characterized by deference to authority, morality, individualism, and separate spheres for men and women. Domesticity became the means by which revolution, whether political or economic, could be imaginatively contained and its protagonists disciplined to meet the needs of the modern, industrial state.

Malthus's *Essay on the Principles of Population* (1798) postulated two givens about human nature: "First, That food is necessary to the existence of man. Secondly, That the passion between the sexes is necessary and will remain nearly in its present state." Because, he believed, humans reproduced their numbers geometrically and agricultural output could only be increased arithmetically, population would inevitably, in the space of some two generations, outrun the food supply, producing a diseased society characterized by material want, disorder, chaos, warfare, and ultimately starvation. Malthus assumed that for the most part working people, unlike men and women of the middle and elite ranks, could not or would not control their sexual desires and that their inability to restrain themselves sexually—their vices—brought about their misery and want. He and other political economists like David Ricardo (1772–1823), whose thinking accorded with what he called "the iron law of wages," argued that if workers' wages were too high they would encourage plebeian men and women to reproduce beyond the capacity of nature to provide for them. Only a reduction in wages and the elimination of poor relief, which encouraged excessive population growth by allowing the poor to reproduce without experiencing the consequences of their acts, would enable society to avoid the disasters that were sure to follow if population growth were to continue unchecked. Their writings justified the much harsher attitudes toward poverty and the poor that had been developing throughout the 1790s as inflation and the need to finance the war against France took its toll on elite pocketbooks. In 1795, for example, Parliament had voted to eliminate minimum wage levels for workers that had been seen as a way of helping them out in times of difficulty, and in the years immediately following the Napoleonic Wars, talk of abolishing poor relief altogether ran rampant.

In his formulations about excessive sexuality, reproduction, population growth, and poverty, Malthus cast much of the responsibility for society's ills onto plebeian women, building on earlier assumptions of unreliability and immorality on the part of working women we saw being developed earlier in the century. Because they were much more visibly "idle" in times of economic downturn, because they, more often than men, sought poor relief without being able to work for it, women came to stand in for all the ills attributed to the poor by their upper- and middling-ranked critics. Their failure to limit their births and the resulting high rates of disease and mortality among their children, critics charged, were clear evidence of their irresponsibility. The problems of society, seen to be a consequence of excessive births resulting from uncontrollable sexual desire, could be laid at the feet of laboring women. Malthus transposed onto working people the assumptions about separate spheres for men and women that informed the thinking of the middling and elite ranks. His writings depicted the plebeian man as producer and provider for his wife and children and the plebeian woman as a mother who stayed at home to care for their children, a portrayal of the ideal of the male breadwinner that working people had no possibility of attaining. Working men, as we shall see in the next chapter, helped to advance this understanding of men as the sole providers, partially to boost their manly status within their homes and workplaces and partially to exclude women from competing with them for jobs and sufficient wages.

Such depictions provided middling and elite women scope for what would become their project—and through it, the source of their class and gender identities—over the next half century: the civilizing of working-class and poor women and, through them, of the working classes as a whole by inculcating the principles and practices of domesticity. Informed by the precepts of evangelical Christianity and political economy and inspired by the disorders produced by industrialization and the French Revolution, a small but influential group of male and female reformers organized in the so-called Clapham sect put forward a set of beliefs about the dual tasks of bringing spiritual renewal and social order to a nation that had, as they saw it, fallen into moral degeneracy. Under the leadership of Hannah More, the evangelical campaign to strengthen the social hierarchy and reform the "manners and morals" of the nation proceeded apace, attracting widespread support from men, and particularly women, of the mercantile and landed middling classes.

Moral regeneration, in the eyes of evangelicals, could be achieved only through individual faith in the grace of God, and the best place for such faith to be sustained, they held, was in the home. The social improvement of the poor, as well as a renewed respect for social hierarchy, it followed, required them to practice self-discipline in all aspects of their lives, whether it be refraining from alcohol consumption, gambling, or sexual activity. These were qualities that the poor would have to be taught, and it devolved on women of the middling ranks, as guardians of the domestic sphere and of morality, to serve as their instructors. Calling on middling women to "come forward with a patriotism at once firm and feminine for the general good," Hannah More urged them in 1799 to "contribute their full and fair proportion toward the saving of their country," to "raise the depressed tone of public morals, to awaken the drowsy spirit of religious principle, and to re-animate the dormant powers of active piety." But they were to do so, she insisted, in accordance with her position on women appearing in public, "without departing from the refinement of their character, without derogating from the dignity of their rank; without blemishing the delicacy of their sex." Social stability demanded that middling women eschew any claim to political or legal rights, that they sacrifice their personal aspirations to public activity or equality with men to the higher religious and social goals of deference, hierarchy, and authority. They must learn, and pass on to their working-class charges, habits of restraint. "They should, when very young, be inured to contradiction," More advised. "They should be led to distrust their own judgment; they should learn not to murmur at expostulation; but should be accustomed to expect and endure opposition. . . . It is of the last importance to their happiness in life that they should early acquire a submissive temper and a forbearing spirit."[7] Disciplining themselves and others in the ways of submissiveness, self-denial, and dependence, More assured the readers of her wildly successful *Cheap Repository of Moral and Religious Tracts* (several million of which were printed, sold, and/or disseminated among the plebeian classes between 1795 and 1810), would advance the cause of domestic purity and moral regeneration of society. The family, according to the *Cheap Repository Tracts*, offered shelter from a world of sin and temptation: within the home, men received the care and attention of diligent, industrious, sober, pious, and honest wives; children learned the lessons that would guide them throughout the rest of their lives at the feet of their parents. These virtues promised all of them a peaceable, happy, harmonious, comfortable existence. But beyond that, these were the qualities and values necessary to uphold the new industrial order of factories and disciplined work forces. One of the first lessons middling women would have to impart if morality and civility were to be attained by the working classes, More asserted, was the folly and the danger of women going out to work. They would have to be taught domestic "oeconomy," the art of keeping a home neat, orderly, and provisioned on a very small income. More was not always consistent on this point, recognizing that in many instances, working-class women had to work to help the family accumulate that small income, but she put it forward as the ideal that should be attained if at all possible.

This portrayal of working-class life in which the male breadwinner brings his hard-earned pay packet to his stay-at-home wife mirrors that drawn by Malthus in his *Essay on Population*. An arrangement of separate spheres for men and women, in which men went out to work while their wives remained at home to maintain a decent, moral, disciplined, and well-regulated domestic life—these, in the minds of evangelicals and political economists, provided the building blocks on which a stable, hierarchical, deferential social order could be constructed and sustained in the midst of industrial transformation and political revolution.

REBELLION IN IRELAND

The French Revolution produced enormous disquiet for Britain's elites, especially after 1792. But the situation in Ireland posed even greater dangers for Prime Minister William Pitt's government. War with France in February 1793 made the troubled island a potential source of real vulnerability for the United Kingdom, offering as it did the possibility of a staging ground from which the enemy could attack Britain. Impressed by this fact, Pitt did two things. He established a large Irish militia made up of both Protestant and Catholic recruits and officered by the gentry in each locality. And then he pressured the Irish Parliament to grant the vote for representatives to the Irish House of Commons to Catholics who owned the requisite amount of landed property. Designed to draw the teeth of resentful and potentially rebellious reformers, the measure stunned the Protestant Ascendancy. It did not go far enough for the reformers, however. They sought the right of Catholics to sit in Parliament and hold high office and for the power of Parliament to control the executive body—referred to as "the Castle" after the Dublin edifice in which it was housed—currently directed by the British government. Stymied by the refusal of the Castle to pursue further reform, the United Irishmen began to demand separation from Britain, a position the authorities condemned and determined to stamp out. By the spring of 1794, the UI, under the leadership of Theobald Wolfe Tone (1763–1798), had, under the impact of repressive government measures against them, moved from a position advocating constitutional reform to one embracing revolutionary republicanism. Wolfe Tone initiated talks with the French for a possible invasion, a move that found favor in Paris. The revolutionary government there dispatched an agent, William Jackson, to Ireland to gain a sense of just how ripe that country was for rebellion against Britain. When British authorities arrested Jackson, it became utterly clear to the UI and their followers—and to the British and Irish governments—that France had serious intentions of allying with the radicals.

Notice of French support galvanized a large number of potential middle- and upper-class rebels who had been watching to see which way the wind would blow. Now that a real possibility for success existed, they joined the cause, one that would require a significant fighting force if it were to prevail. The UI, largely composed of middle-class Protestants and Catholics with some urban artisans and craftsmen sprinkled in, turned to a decidedly more radical group, the secret society known as the Defenders, for support. Drawn largely from the Catholic peasantry, Defenders sought an end to the tithes they were required to pay to the established church in Ireland and relief from high rents and taxes, an agenda that necessitated that the targets of their activism were Protestants, given the character of land owning in most of the country. Through campaigns of arson, destruction of property, the maiming of cattle, assault, and even murder, they terrorized the Protestants in the countryside. But they also appealed to rural and urban people involved in manufacturing, and as the ideology of the French revolution infiltrated their ranks, they took on a kind of diffuse republican tone as well, adding a measure of political revolution to their economic demands. Their anti-Protestant actions disturbed many members of the UI, made up as it was of Protestants and Catholics, but they persuaded themselves that they could control their new allies and diminish the sectarian elements within the Defenders.

The UI–Defender alliance received impetus from the appearance of another secret society, this one made up of Protestants. Convinced that the Defenders existed only to exterminate all Protestants, they carried out attacks on Catholics, seeking to drive them off their lands and out of their counties altogether. After a particularly brutal fight in County Armagh in September 1795 known as the Battle of the Diamond, lower-class Protestants formed themselves into the Orange Order, so named for William of Orange, the king who had been victorious at the Battle of the Boyne in 1690 and forced the Treaty of Limerick on James's Catholic followers the following year. Orangemen escalated their attacks on Catholics; the Defenders responded in turn; and from that point on, sectarian hatreds could not be separated out from political demands. Religious conflict between Catholics and Protestants, however much or often condemned by the nonsectarian UI, would always inform the political differences between rebels and loyalists in Ireland. And religious hatred would make civil war, when it came, all the more vicious.

The Irish government, in concert with its British handlers, determined to stamp out the threat posed by the Defenders and the UI. It passed an Indemnity Act in 1795 that allowed local magistrates—all of them Protestants—to impose harsh punishments on offending UI and Defenders. In 1796, anxious because the militia formed in 1793 contained significant numbers of Catholics who might easily be enticed to join the UI ranks, Castle authorities established a new armed force called the Yeomanry, led by conservative Protestant landlords and manned by their mostly Protestant tenants. The Insurrection Act of that year imposed curfews and bans on assembly and gave extraordinary powers to the magistracy to ignore basic legal rights as they went about prosecuting criminal and political acts. People could be arrested and tried without juries or the presentation of conventional evidence; if found guilty, they could be sentenced to transportation to Australia for long periods. The taking of oaths—long a staple of secret society culture—could be punished by death. In October, habeas corpus was formally suspended throughout Ireland.

In December 1796, a fleet of forty-three ships carrying 15,000 French soldiers almost landed in Bantry Bay, in west Cork. Stormy weather prevented most of them from making landfall, although some 400 soldiers did so, only to be killed or captured by the local Yeomanry. The British responded with orders to General Gerard Lake (1744–1808), a member of the Protestant Ascendancy, to do whatever it took to quell revolt. Lake gave full vent to his spleen, declaring martial law in the province of Ulster and cracking down murderously on suspected rebels. He ordered the houses of UI members to be burned; he billeted his troops in the homes of civilians; he tortured prisoners in his efforts to find and disarm the opposition; and he executed men in the militia he suspected of having been converted to the revolutionary cause. His brutality alienated ever greater numbers of Irish men and women, but it had the effect of weakening the rebels in the north. Much of the Ulster leadership among the UI landed in jail.

Momentum among the radicals shifted to Dublin, where the UI set up a secret Directory, modeled after France's government. Headed by Thomas Emmet (1764–1827), a barrister, and two Protestant MPs, Arthur O'Connor (1763–1852) and Lord Edward Fitzgerald (1763–1798), the Directory began to plan for an insurrection. It enjoyed the backing of some surprising supporters—people like Margaret King (1773–1835), daughter of Lord and Lady Kingsborough, prominent members of the Protestant Ascendancy. Margaret King's aristocratic status allowed her to travel freely throughout the country, taking trips during which she passed information from one rebel group to another. She hid Fitzgerald in her various homes on a number of occasions when he was running from Castle authorities. King had, significantly, been a pupil of Mary Wollstonecraft in her adolescent years, from whom she learned not revolutionary republicanism per se as much as to think for herself. The rational approach to issues of the day that she gained from Wollstonecraft's instruction led her to tolerate Catholicism and to disdain the knee-jerk support given to British rule by most families of her stature. She became a nationalist, and a separatist nationalist at that, giving aid and resources to the UI wherever and whenever she could.

In March 1798, acting on a tip from within the ranks of the UI, Castle officials arrested a number of UI leaders who were meeting in Dublin. Lord Fitzgerald and a few others had not been present and escaped the dragnet. Their plans for insurrection continued, with local rebel commanders drilling their forces and awaiting the signal to rise. But when it became clear that the insurgents could not count on a second French invasion in aid of their rebellion—Napoleon chose instead to embark on an expedition to Egypt—the remaining members of the UI Directory decided to act, naming May 23 as the start of their rising. Once again, betrayal from within the UI ranks enabled Castle officials to arrest Lord Fitzgerald on his way to meet his troops on May 18 (wounded during his capture, he languished in prison and died of his injuries in July). But on the designated day, despite a disastrous lack of coordination from a now leaderless organization, thousands of rebels took to arms in Dublin and points south and west, the cry of "Death or Liberty" on their lips.

The chaos surrounding the situation in Dublin made it difficult for the rebels to take the capital, and Castle forces regained control there within a week. A different story, however, unfolded in County Wexford, where a local rebel army took on and handily defeated a small force of loyalists on May 27. The insurgents had been galvanized by a particularly gruesome series of atrocities committed by the North Cork militia, which, ironically, was commanded by Margaret King's brother, George, the current Earl of Kingsborough (1771–1839). From mid-May on, his charges had carried out a campaign of half-hangings, floggings, house-burning, and pitch-capping against the local population. This last entailed pouring hot tar into a paper cone placed over one's head, resulting in severe burning of the scalp and face. Kingsborough and his troops had long enjoyed a fearsome reputation for the viciousness of their repression of suspected Defenders over the past year, and now, in the midst of open rebellion, Wexford and Wicklow insurgents took their revenge at Oulart, County Wexford. Buoyed by their success, they moved on to take Enniscorthy on May 29, thence to Wexford town, whose defenders learned of the approach of the 15,000-strong rebel force and abandoned their positions. On May 31, the rebels declared a republic and established a government made up of four Protestants and four Catholics. Celebrations of victory mingled with fear of what might come. The insurgents set up camp at the base of Carrickbyrne Hill, from which they carried out "sweeps" of the surrounding countryside to round up those loyalists they deemed a threat. By June 4, they had gathered up about 124 captives: 13 of the prisoners were women, 8 were children; 15 were Catholics, and the remaining 109 were Protestants. They held them in the farmtown of Scullabogue.

But their victory was short lived. On June 5, 1798, at New Ross, the Wexford rebels engaged with units from Lord Kingsborough's North Cork militia and suffered a grievous defeat. The fighting that day proved to be particularly brutal. Once the loyalist army overwhelmed the rebels, its soldiers began killing the wounded and prisoners in the streets indiscriminately. They set on fire a house where seventy wounded rebels lay, killing them all. Insurgents retreating from New Ross brought tales of loyalist atrocities to Scullabogue and urged their fellows there to execute the prisoners they had captured earlier in the week. Rebel soldiers shot some forty prisoners on the lawn of the farmhouse and then turned their attention to those they had cooped up in the barn on the property. They set it ablaze, killing all of those inside.

Ulster had remained quiet while first the counties around Dublin and then Wexford rose. But on June 7, Ulster UI, virtually all of them Presbyterians, took up arms in County Antrim. They held the town of Antrim for a few hours, but then were ousted by volleys of artillery fire from government troops. A few days later at Ballynahinch, twelve miles outside Belfast, rebel forces gathered, where they were met by loyalist troops and decisively defeated. This marked the end of the rising in the north, which had never really ever gotten going. Able now to turn south, loyalists under General Lake laid siege to the rebel camp at Vinegar Hill in County Wexford on June 21, finally driving the insurgents out with heavy artillery bombardments. This proved to be the last real battle of the rebellion, although mop-up operations continued to generate large numbers of casualties. As they chased down the rebels of Wexford, government forces made no distinction between combatants and noncombatants, raping women en masse and sometimes killing everything that moved.

In August 1798 a French naval force landed at Killala in County Mayo, on the northwest coast of Ireland, but by that time the insurrection had been brutally put down; the forces of French general Jean Joseph Amable Humbert were captured by the British within two weeks. In October, British naval forces intercepted the French vessel carrying Wolfe Tone to Donegal in anticipation of another Irish rising. He was tried and sentenced to death but committed suicide before he could be executed. The Castle swiftly moved to punish the insurgents, executing many of the commanders of rebel forces on the spot and bringing others to trial before military tribunals. Some 300 to 600 Defenders and UI received sentences of transportation to Australia in the years between 1795 and 1806, a story we will now take up.

The Battle of Vinegar Hill, 1798.

Both sides in the conflict committed horrific atrocities and inflicted terrible losses on the country as a whole. Some 30,000 Catholic and Protestant antagonists perished in what turned out to be the bloodiest fighting in Ireland's history. Although, as we have seen, the UI consisted of both Catholics and Protestants who sought religious tolerance for all, religious hatreds at the level of the common people could never be overcome. Catholic members of the Defenders and Protestant affiliates of the Orange Order too often let their sectarian prejudices rule their actions, not surprising in an atmosphere of violence and bloodshed. The memories of atrocities on both sides would linger for decades, contaminating relationships and contributing to mistrust and misunderstanding.

Smarting from France's intrusion into the politics of Ireland, fearful of the possibility that a rebellious Ireland might again provide a staging ground for French forces to invade Great Britain, and distrusting the capability of the Anglo-Irish to control the situation, the British government moved to contain the dangers that Ireland posed. One option entailed establishing a permanent occupation force in Ireland, a possibility Pitt realized could not be sustained either politically or materially. He decided instead on a strategy that he hoped would reconcile both Catholic and Protestant factions: political association with Great Britain, proposing that Ireland be joined with England, Wales, and Scotland in the United Kingdom of Great Britain. The former lord lieutenant of Ireland, Earl Fitzwilliam (1748–1833), agreed in a formulation that equated the Irish Revolution to that in Haiti. "The whole system of the country," he declared, "the principle of conqueror and conquered, of negroes and planters, must be done away."[8]

In such a union, Ireland's Parliament would be abolished and its representation in the Parliament in Westminster determined by proportional representation. Protestants saw in the Parliament at Westminster far greater protection of their interests than the Parliament in Dublin, susceptible to Catholic pressure, could afford them. The Catholics of Ireland welcomed

MAP 5.1
United Kingdom of Great Britain, 1801

Pitt's promise of what is referred to as "Catholic emancipation," the right of Catholics to sit in the Parliament in Westminster. As had been the case almost 100 years earlier when Scotland joined with England in union, the government resorted to extraordinary acts of bribery to bring recalcitrant MPs into line with its desires. In 1801, the Act of Union brought Ireland into union with Great Britain.

To his dismay, however, Pitt's promise of emancipation could not be realized because of hostility to it from members of his cabinet and, more important, from the king. As the lord chancellor of Ireland, Baron Redesdale (1748–1830), put it, once again raising the specter of the Haitian Revolution, conceding emancipation to Irish Catholics was as foolhardy as giving freedom to St. Domginue's blacks had been. He argued that those who had advocated for equal rights for blacks and people of color had been murdered or driven off the island and insisted that "so it will be with Ireland" if Catholics were to gain emancipation.[9] Defeated on a matter of deep principle, Pitt resigned his position as prime minister rather than repudiate his oath, and a mass movement of nationalists grew up in Ireland in the 1820s surrounding the issue of Catholic emancipation.

AUSTRALIA

The Irish rebels transported to Australia joined the penal colony that had been created in 1788, when the so-called First Fleet of prisoners, under the command of Captain Arthur Phillip (1738–1814), arrived in Botany Bay in what came to be called New South Wales. Composed of eleven ships carrying 1,400 people, the First Fleet sailed from London on May 13, 1787, with 579 male convicts, 193 female convicts, and 14 children of convicts aboard; 7 other children were born during the 15,000-mile, 252-day trip. Forty-eight people died during the voyage, 3 of them children. This death rate of 3 percent, given the hardships of such a long trip undertaken by ill-prepared prisoners, was incredibly small and would not be achieved by subsequent voyages of prisoners in 1790, who died in much greater numbers.

Misled by Captain James Cook and naturalist Joseph Banks to believe they would find a landscape conducive to relatively easy settlement, the first Britons to go ashore at what would be named Sydney (after the colonial secretary who commissioned the voyage) instead discovered a land of poor soil and little fresh water. Many of them weak from the long and stressful voyage, they faced the immediate problem of building shelter and finding food in an inhospitable environment. Lacking the materials and tools necessary to build proper accommodations and suffering from malnutrition because of insufficient rations of food, the prisoners of the First Fleet barely made it through their first year. Remarkably, only 73 people had died, whereas 87 children had been born, a demographic statistic that would bode well for the struggling colony.

Entrance to Port Jackson, site of the first European settlement at Sydney, Australia, c. 1822.

From the start, Australia held a unique position among Britain's imperial possessions, which would grow dramatically in size and number by the end of the Napoleonic wars in 1815. British authorities had established New South Wales to relieve Britain of prisoners it could not handle at home, especially after the loss of the American colonies made it impossible to continue to ship convicts there. Officials determined who would settle in New South Wales through a variety of mechanisms designed to ensure a homogenous white population steeped in British traditions. Indeed, Australians came to be regarded as more British than the British. Even the first settlers, the convicts themselves, had been chosen with certain qualities in mind, characteristics that would enable the penal colony to survive and expand. They were not a random cross-section of the overall prison population. They were laborers chosen for the work they could do in agriculture or manufacturing; the Scottish and Irish political prisoners of rank would serve the colony in an administrative capacity; and women would make up the wives and mothers of the colonists. Even when free citizens sought to immigrate to Australia, their selection depended on the basis of need. Those allowed to go provided necessary experience in particular trades the colony required or possessed enough money to make the kinds of capital improvements on the land they were granted to enable their enterprises to flourish. British authorities could exercise this kind of control because ordinary people wishing to immigrate to the southern hemisphere found it too expensive to do so; they tended to go west across the Atlantic to America or Canada. This kind of selection process created a particularly pronounced social division of haves and have-nots among Australian colonists.

Australia might have begun as a penal dumping ground, but other motives for colonizing the great southern continent existed as well, not least the prospect of using it as a base from which trade with China and other Asian lands could be launched and protected. Australia offered secure ports from which Pacific whalers could conduct their lucrative hunting; settling there would also hamper French, Spanish, and Dutch efforts to expand their territorial claims. And possession of the continent served to ease somewhat the sting of defeat occasioned by the victory of the American colonists and their French allies in 1783. Above all, it was cheap. British officials expected convict labor to produce such agricultural products as wheat and maize, exports of which to the mother country would ultimately pay the costs of settlement. Australia's environment made it difficult to grow foodstuffs reliably, however, and wool turned out to be the more dependable export to Britain. Sheep proved to be the main driver of Australia's economy, promoting expansion into the interior of the country as settlers and freed convicts sought to gain the means to a prosperous life. Escaped prisoners, too, headed inland from the coast, seeking freedom in areas where the imperial state had little control. Whether as settlers granted territory by colonial authorities or as squatters who simply took what they could find and defend, British colonists wasted little time in establishing themselves on the land.

But this was land that the original inhabitants of Australia knew to be theirs. Having themselves arrived on the continent some 45,000 years earlier, the indigenous peoples of Australia numbered perhaps a million souls in 1788. Cook and Banks had reported that the country they "discovered" in 1770 enjoyed little habitation; certainly the land they observed was not cultivated by the aborigines, at least not as they understood the concept. And so the British arrived in 1788 convinced that Australia constituted *terra nullius*, a Latin legal term for "land belonging to no one." If it belonged to no one, then it was Britain's for the taking, requiring neither purchase from nor treaty with the indigenous peoples who lived on it.

Aboriginal peoples saw things differently. They did not live on or cultivate land the way Europeans did, occupying well-ordered plots carved out of the countryside, but they did observe complex rules about landownership and how the land was to be utilized and cared for. Land held a central and crucial place in their cosmologies and social and legal systems; they had grave responsibilities for tending to and protecting sacred sites that dotted the landscape. And, of course, they lived on the land, hunting, fishing, and foraging for vegetables and fruits. When Britons first arrived, indigenous peoples tolerated their presence, expecting that they would not stay long. As white people lingered, however, and began to expand their settlements and to seize as their own land that belonged to aborigines, the latter struck back, defending their homes, their food sources, and their very way of life. They attacked officers, settlers, and convicts who encroached on their lands, assaults that British authorities regarded not as acts of defense of property but as crimes that had to be punished. As violence increased across the continent, settlers and soldiers formed bands and set out on what authorities called "punitive expeditions" against indigenous peoples, carrying out horrific reprisals. The colonization of Australia, in short, required conquering the lands of the indigenous peoples there, and conquest, as one historian has written, "involved copious bloodshed."[10] When in 1803 a second colony was established on Van Dieman's Land, the island just to the southeast of New South Wales that would later be called Tasmania, the depredations against the indigenous Tasmanians reached unprecedented levels, resulting in their near extermination.

In the 1820s, white settlers and squatters moved west across the Blue Mountains into territories that would become the separate colonies of Victoria and Queensland. The presence of their livestock on the lands held by indigenous peoples changed the land dramatically, impinging on local water supplies, depleting the supply of root crops the aborigines depended on, and driving out the native animals that provided food for the local people. Unable now to hunt enough wallabies, kangaroos, and emus to feed themselves, indigenous peoples began to hunt the sheep and cattle of the settlers instead, often attacking the shepherds who tended them. Punitive expeditions against the perpetrators inevitably followed these attacks, escalating the violence on the frontier to even greater heights. As white expansion and settlement intensified in the late 1820s, resulting in the creation of yet another colony, Western Australia, in 1829, indigenous peoples lost out more and more, till it seemed that they would not survive. This possibility alarmed a number of people back in Britain, a story we will take up in the next chapter.

SIERRA LEONE

We saw in the previous chapter how the abolitionist attempt to colonize Sierra Leone on the west coast of Africa by loyalist American former slaves succumbed to British slave interests and local chiefs and failed in the late 1780s. The antislavery movement had largely fallen dormant during the years of the French Revolution and the wars against France, but Granville Sharp and William Wilberforce had continued to believe that Sierra Leone could be a powerful weapon in the antislavery struggle. In 1791, Sharp established the Sierra Leone Company and sent agents out to the West African territory to create the colony anew. Having successfully renegotiated the necessary land deals with local chiefs there, the company now needed to find people to settle the colony. This time they would come not from the freed black slaves who had emigrated to London following the American Revolution, but from those who had moved to Nova Scotia and New Brunswick following the conflict

and who had found the climate there, social and political as well as meteorological, inhospitable.

On January 15, 1792, some 1,700 free blacks set sail from Halifax, Nova
Scotia on a seven-week voyage. After a difficult and dangerous passage, the emigrants landed at what had once been Granville Town, now overgrown after five
years' abandonment. They set to work cutting down trees and raising up a
church, houses, and buildings in what they would name Freetown. But some of
the problems they had faced in Nova Scotia reemerged in West Africa, particularly the issue of allocating land to settlers. Company officials had their own
ideas about how the process would take place, putting them at odds with the
settlers. Part of the problem resided in the individual company officials charged
with carrying out company policies: one, William Dawes (1762–1836), had been
transferred to Freetown from Botany Bay, where he served as an officer; his successor, Zachary Macaulay (1768–1838), had spent five years overseeing a sugar
plantation in Jamaica. Black settlers seeking justice and respite after years of
slavery and abuse could hardly have found a more unsuitable pair of governors.
Their grievances festered as years of dissatisfaction passed with no relief. When
Macaulay left his post in 1799, a number of settlers seized the opportunity to
insist that the company give them greater freedom to determine their own governance. The company refused, and a group of settlers rebelled, declaring a new
government headed by Isaac Anderson. They took up arms and, commanding
the support of perhaps half of the black colonists, prepared to defend their liberties and their rights.

At just that moment, another group of free blacks entered the scene and,
under orders from the Sierra Leone Company, helped put down the rebellion.
These were Maroons from Jamaica, who had been transported from their lands
in the Cockpit Country of that island to Nova Scotia in 1796 following a series
of clashes with the colonial government. As we saw in Chapter 4, Maroons
lived freely in the mountains of Jamaica, enjoying autonomy and land ownership in return for their agreement to help track down and return runaway
slaves on the island. In 1795, a particular group of them living in Trelawny
Town remonstrated against the indignities they felt themselves to have suffered
at the hands of the colonial government, demanding an apology and the dismissal of a local official. In this situation of tension, heightened as it was by the
Haitian revolution and the wars with France, the new Jamaican governor, the
Earl of Balcarres (1752–1825), determined to use it to demonstrate his firm
anti-Jacobin principles. He declared the Trelawny Town Maroons to be in a
state of rebellion and sent troops against them. Fighting convulsed the island
in August and September 1795, destroying lives and property and leading ultimately to a stalemate by October. Balcarres promised that if they laid down
their arms the Trelawney Town Maroons could stay in Jamaica, an undertaking they accepted. But to the dismay of many of his officers and subordinates
in the colonial government, Balcarres reneged on his promise, exiling the
Maroons to Nova Scotia instead.

The Trelawny Maroons suffered terribly in the cold of British North America. When one of their many petitions to be relocated reached the ears of officials of the Sierra Leone Company, it found immediate approbation. Eager to continue to populate the West African colony and mindful of the services long given to Jamaican authorities in their efforts to track down escaped slaves, the company jumped at the chance to bring the Maroons to Freetown, where their numbers, officials hoped, would act to temper the rebellious nature of the colony's inhabitants. In August 1800, 550 Maroons boarded the transport ship *Asia*, arriving in Freetown just in time to help put down the revolt there. Company officials hunted down those rebels it did not kill or capture, hanged the putative governor, Isaac Anderson, and banished the other leaders of the rising, among them Harry Washington, a slave who had run away from George Washington's plantation twenty years earlier during the American Revolution.

Against the odds, Sierra Leone survived. In 1807, Great Britain outlawed the slave trade, enforcement of which required it to send the Royal Navy to intercept slave ships that defied its ban. The enslaved peoples set free by these actions were settled in Sierra Leone, augmenting the numbers of freed blacks from Nova Scotia and free blacks from Jamaica (via Nova Scotia) and contributing to the growth and development of the colony.

The settlement at Sierra Leone, c. 1820.

POSTWAR DEPRESSION

Demands for moral regeneration accelerated in the period immediately following the defeat of Napoleon at Waterloo in 1815, years that saw much social distress as efforts to return to a peacetime economy produced severe dislocation, depression, and unemployment. Workers in virtually every sector of the economy suffered hardship, and it is likely that the real earnings of average working-class families in the years 1815 to 1819 fell below what they had been in the 1780s.

Poor rates, which householders earning a certain income paid to alleviate destitution among the working poor, reached high levels, an indication that more families than usual were unable to sustain themselves economically. In 1815, too, parliament passed the Corn Law, which restricted the importation of wheat from outside Britain unless the price of domestic grain rose above a level that ensured farmers a handsome profit. The Corn Law benefitted landowners by limiting competition from abroad, but hurt working people by making the price of bread more expensive. Riots protesting the high cost of bread broke out across England in the fall of 1815, followed by a rash of machine-breaking by so-called Luddites in many of the industrial areas in 1816.

The economic dislocations caused by twenty-five years of warfare were compounded by a natural disaster on the other side of the globe that had unprecedented consequences for the western world. As the victors met in Vienna in 1815 to hammer out a postwar solution to the upheavals Napoleon had created in Europe, a volcano on the Indonesian island of Sumbawa erupted. Beginning on April 5, but seeing its most violent action on April 11 and 12, Mount Tambora's explosions of dust and ash, which could be heard up to 1,000 miles away, continued throughout April, May, June, and part of July; they proved to be the most powerful the world had seen in 10,000 years.

The volcano launched 25 cubic miles of debris into the atmosphere, depositing three feet of ash on the town of Bima, some 40 miles distant from the volcano, and reducing the height of Tambora itself by 4,200 feet. Darkness filled the sky for a distance of about 300 miles, and the cinders that fell into the sea coagulated into a solid mass some two feet thick, extending for several miles. On Sumbawa, only 26 of the 12,000 inhabitants survived the eruption; the British official resident on the island reported that "violent whirlwinds carried up men, horses, cattle, and whatever else came within their influence, into the air, tore up the largest trees by the roots, and covered the sea with floating timber. Great tracts of land were covered by lava, several streams of which, issuing from the crater of the Tambora mountain, reached the sea."[11] The eruptions and the earthquake and tsunamis that followed killed some 90,000 people. Croplands were buried, resulting in a terrible famine in which 44,000 people starved to death; the ash also caused pronounced diarrhea in horses, cattle, and people.

The amount of dust in the stratosphere triggered a massive cooling of the northern temperate zones of the earth by reducing the amount of solar radiation in the atmosphere over the next two years, which in turn caused the low temperatures of the polar and subpolar regions to move further south. The cloudy, cold spring of 1816 generated more storms than Europeans and Americans usually saw at that time of year, and the presence of ash and dust in the atmosphere produced freakish weather scenes: brownish snow fell in Hungary in January and red and yellow snow in normally mild southern Italy. Marylanders witnessed brown, bluish, and red snow land on the ground in April and May. The summer that followed in Canada, New England, and central and western Europe was no summer at all, with some of the lowest temperatures on record and heavy rains and hail that destroyed what crops did come up over the course of a growing season one-third shorter than average.

The grain shortages produced by the cold and wet weather drove prices skyward, making it almost impossible for families put out of work by the end of the Napoleonic wars to make ends meet. Thousands of demobilized soldiers and sailors joined factory and domestic workers laid off as war-related manufacturing waned; their reduced circumstances would have created hunger in any event, but the addition of weather-related harvest failures pushed them over the edge. In 1816 Britain saw the lowest wheat yield in the years 1815–1857. Not surprisingly, starvation and disease took people in greater numbers than in years past (discounting the casualties of the wars). Ill and malnourished populations succumbed to epidemics of typhus and various fevers that swept through in the aftermath of the harvest failures, and 65,000 Irish men and women died. In Glasgow, an industrial city of 130,000, about 32,000 people became ill and 3,500 of them died in 1818. Typhus raced through the working-class sections of London in 1816, placing a severe strain on the ability of relief agencies to care for the sick and the homeless. In Ireland in 1817 and 1818, typhus sickened 850,000 people.

Many thousands of Britons, made desperate by destitution, simply left. Those who could made their way across the Atlantic to the United States where they hoped to find employment and a more secure way of life: 20,000 from Ireland and many more from Yorkshire in England. Those who stayed faced increasingly difficult times, forced to seek public or private relief. Those who could not find charity were compelled to beg on the streets. Marriages and births declined in number as it became more difficult to support a family.

Hard times sparked violence in Britain. Riots protesting the high cost of bread broke out across England in the fall of 1815, followed by a campaign of machine-breaking by Luddites in many of the industrial areas in 1816. Handloom weavers most affected by the postwar depression vented their rage on the mills and machines they believed had stolen their livelihoods. British authorities dispatched 12,000 troops to the worst-hit cities of the Midlands, Lancashire, and Yorkshire and declared machine-breaking a capital offense.

The dismal economic conditions of postwar life contributed to the propensity of many working-class men and women to join with middle-class activists in demanding parliamentary reform. The Corn Law, in particular, symbolized for reformers the abuses of a parliamentary system made up of privileged, self-interested, landowning elites—aristocrats and gentry. The reform movement, a disparate group made up of Whigs sitting in Parliament, of middling people outside of Parliament seeking far-reaching reform along constitutional lines, and a number of popular radicals willing to engage in extralegal and even violent means to bring about significant political changes, sought to eliminate the old corruption of aristocratic government and to replace it with annual parliaments elected on the basis of a wider suffrage.

Only in this way, reformers believed, could cronyism, favoritism, corruption, and the influence of the House of Lords and the Anglican church be stamped out and good government designed to further the interests of the people as a whole be implemented.

Radicals could draw huge crowds in support of their demands. In Glasgow in October 1816, 40,000 men and women gathered to listen to Major John Cartwright delineate the political changes that must be implemented if working people were to obtain relief from the destitution they faced. As meetings increased in number and size and as their peaceful demands for reform seemed at times to spill over into sedition, the government grew fearful that insurrection loomed. A public meeting at Spa Fields in north London in December 1816 attracted 10,000 people hoping to hear the radical Henry Hunt (1773–1835) call for universal manhood suffrage and annual parliaments. Before he could speak, however, local authorities shut the meeting down. The government tried to suppress radical newspapers like William Cobbett's (1763–1835) *The Political Register* or the *Black Dwarf*, financed by Cartwright, but local juries proved loath to convict publishers for articulating the distress of the people. By 1819, fears of insurrection had evolved into fears of outright revolution, causing the government to panic and take ill-considered action. In August of that year, some 60,000 people crowded St. Peter's Field in Manchester to hear Henry Hunt call for parliamentary reform. The local constabulary, supplemented by regular government troops, attacked the crowd, killing at least 15 persons and wounding 500, approximately 100 of whom were women. Wits dubbed this the Peterloo Massacre, a play on the battle of Waterloo where British armed forces had just recently defeated a different enemy.

Outraged by this assault on working men and women peaceably assembled, people across England, Scotland, Wales, and Ireland decried the government that could act in such a manner, which political cartoons depicted as armed men riding down and slashing open innocent women with babes at their breasts. The public reaction to the Peterloo Massacre galvanized Parliament to act against the radical movement. It issued the Six Acts in December, among which were a prohibition on meetings larger than 50 people, a measure allowing the government to search people and property for weapons, and increased punishment for publications found to be seditious or blasphemous. These compelled radicals to go underground, in effect, and diminished the size of political meetings, but they certainly did not end radical activity. In Scotland, for example, the so-called "Radical War" broke out in April 1820, when some 60,000 workers in Glasgow and other industrializing cities went on strike in support of what was supposed to be an out-and-out insurrection. In the event, the mass rising did not materialize, although about 20–30 radicals from the weaving trades tried to capture some artillery at the Carron Iron Works in Glasgow. Their plans failed when a cavalry troop met them at what came to be called the

"Battle of Bonnymuir," where the outgunned workers fell bloodily to the soldiers. Another group of about 100 would-be rebels outside Strathaven rallied to the call, but soon abandoned their cause when it became clear that no nationwide revolt would take place. The Radical War failed to meet the expectations of its planners, but the scope and scale of the popular support it received among workers, greater than anything that took place in England, frightened the authorities grievously.

In England, what became known as the Queen Caroline affair provided radicals and reformers with an opportunity to demonstrate their defense of and claim to virtue in opposition to what they regarded as aristocratic tyranny and oppression. In 1820, George IV (1762–1830) became king after many years of ruling as prince regent on behalf of his incapacitated father, George III. His estranged and ill-treated wife, Caroline (1768–1821), who had been in self-imposed exile in Europe since 1814, when she agreed to leave England in return for an annual payment of £35,000, returned, demanding that she be recognized as queen. George responded with an action for divorce

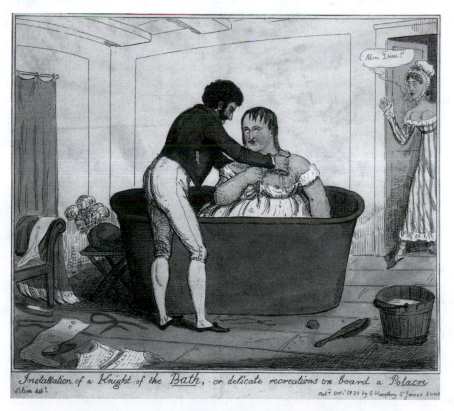

Scandalous depiction of Queen Caroline's adultery, 1820.

in the House of Lords, causing a Bill of Pains and Penalties to be brought against her that censured her for adultery and rescinded her queenly status. Coming from a man whom the radical press had denounced as a lecherous dandy, whose regency had been characterized by profligacy and debauchery, making it an irresistible magnet for charges of financial and political as well as moral corruption, the new king's charges met with an outburst of popular fury against what was perceived as the latest, most egregious manifestation of old corruption. In the melodrama that followed, Caroline, whose behavior while in Europe was hardly pristine, took on the trappings of the "poor wronged female," "a poor forlorn woman" whose virtue, sullied by an evil king and his equally evil ministers, had to be defended by the "manly," "courageous" people of Britain. The radical press exploited the scandal with ferocious and obscene satire, taking every opportunity to draw connections between old corruption and the campaign against Caroline.

The Queen Caroline affair, by linking the somewhat abstract constitutional concerns of radicalism—the role of the monarch in government, corruption and patronage, and the infringement by Parliament on the liberties of the people—with the immediately personal and moral concerns of people in their everyday lives gave radicalism a base of popular support that it had not enjoyed since the days of the civil war of the mid-seventeenth century. Anti-king feeling ran high, and the king's ministers feared for the survival of the throne. For men, the misuse of Caroline by George and his ministers resonated with the grievances plebeians and radicals experienced at the hands of "aristocratic government." By mixing the personal with the constitutional, the private with the public, working people were better able to internalize the more distant concerns of political reform and make them their own. As long-time radical Major John Cartwright observed, "the honor of the Queen is closely related with the constitutional rights of the people." Caroline exploited this sentiment regularly, telling an audience in London that "those who degrade the Queen have never manifested any repugnance in abridging the liberties of the people." "My loss of rank," she explained at another time, "would have been their loss of liberties."[12]

As it turned out, the political agenda of radicalism became subsumed under the personal, moral, and domestic concerns raised by the Queen Caroline affair. The House of Lords did indeed pass a Bill of Pains and Penalties against Caroline in October 1820, but by so narrow a margin that the government withdrew it, acknowledging its defeat at the hands of the people. But the victory of the people in this sordid episode did not translate into governmental reform. Instead, radicalism as a political force rapidly lost its vigor and its numbers, as middle-class reformers and Whigs in Parliament abandoned their alliance with the popular classes and as improving economic conditions after 1820 weakened the appeal of radical politics for masses of working people. Radicalism did not disappear, but just as its popularity had skyrocketed during the Queen Caroline affair, so too it plummeted back to earth with her "acquittal" and with her acceptance of an annual pension of £50,000 from the government in January 1821.

Although the political radicalism of the affair faded away, at least for the short term, the scandal nonetheless had a lasting impact on and consequences for governance and for all ranks of society. The debauchery, profligacy, and excesses of George IV had badly damaged the prestige of the crown. We have seen how aristocrats had become associated with effeminacy in the late eighteenth and early nineteenth centuries; George's antics confirmed contemporaries in those beliefs. The authority of the crown had been diminished relative to that of Parliament, a process that we might regard as the feminization of the monarchy that began long before the accession of Queen Victoria (1819–1901) to the throne in 1837.

••

The Queen Caroline affair also marked a historical moment when one societal model of marriage and sexuality was decisively thrown over for another. The evangelical domestic ideal, with its concomitant emphases on separate spheres for men and women; the sanctity of marriage and family; passivity, morality, and purity for women; and sobriety and respectability for men, gained a hold over British life that prevailed for the rest of the century. At the top, it would no longer be possible for royals, and by extension, aristocrats, to behave publicly in a debauched, libertine, profligate manner. Britons had made it clear that their king, if he was to be the father of the people, would be a husband to his wife as well, a true husband of devotion, fidelity, and morality. As the "Ode to George the Fourth and Caroline his wife," implored the king, "A *Father* to the *nation* prove, / A *Husband* to thy *Queen*, / And safely in thy people's Love, / Reign tranquil and serene."[13] In the persons of King William (1765–1837), who followed George IV on his death in 1830, and his consort Adelaide (1792–1849), Britain obtained a royal family that seemed to exude domesticity, even if William's ten children by his first, common-law wife gave the lie to royal morals. Victoria's accession to the throne in 1837 completed the domestication of the monarchy. Ironically, the Queen Caroline affair, which had threatened to bring down the monarchy in 1820, served instead to strengthen it in the eyes of the British people.

NOTES

1. Quoted in John D. Beatty, ed., *Protestant Women's Narratives of the Irish Rebellion of 1798.* (Dublin, 2001), p. 58.
2. Quoted in Susan Kingsley Kent, *Gender and Power in Britain, 1640–1990* (London, 1999), p. 128.
3. Quoted in Mary Poovey, *The Proper Lady and the Woman Writer* (Chicago, 1984), p. 31; and Linda Colley, *Britons: Forging the Nation, 1707–1837* (New Haven, 2009), p. 255.
4. Quoted in Colley, *Britons*, p. 256; and Poovey, *The Proper Woman*, p. 32.

5.   Quoted in Kent, *Gender and Power*, p. 135.
6.   Quoted in Carrie Gibson, *Empire's Crossroads. A History of the Caribbean from Columbus to the Present Day* (New York, 2014), p. 172.
7.   Quoted in Poovey, *The Proper Woman*, pp. 33, 34.
8.   Quoted in Kevin Whelan, *The Tree of Liberty: Radicalism, Catholicism and the Construction of Irish Identity, 1760–1830* (Cork, 1996), pp. 146–47. I am indebted to Patrick McDevitt for this information and that contained in the following endnote.
9.   Quoted in Whelan, *The Tree of Liberty*, p. 152.
10. Alan Atkinson, "Conquest," in Deryck M. Schreuder and Stuart Ward, eds., *Australia's Empire* (Oxford, 2008), p. 40.
11. Quoted in Donald R. Prothero, *Catastrophes! Earthquakes, Tsunamis, Tornadoes, and Other Earth-Shattering Disasters* (Baltimore, 2001), p. 90.
12. Quoted in Kent, *Gender and Power*, p. 160.
13. Quoted in Lee Davidoff and Catherine Hall, *Family Fortunes: Men and Women of the English Middle Class, 1780–1850* (Chicago, 1987), p. 152.

TIMELINE

1789	Outbreak of French Revolution
1791	Thomas Paine publishes *The Rights of Man*
1792	Mary Wollstonecraft publishes *A Vindication of the Rights of Woman*
	London Corresponding Society founded
	French Revolution becomes more radical
	Free blacks from Nova Scotia arrive in Sierra Leone
1793	Louis XVI executed
	War with France
1794	Suspension of habeas corpus
1795	Seditious Meetings and Treasonable Practices Acts
	Hannah More publishes *Cheap Repository of Moral and Religious Tracts*
1796	Jamaican Maroons arrive in Sierra Leone
1798	Irish Rebellion begins
	French land in Ireland in support of Irish Rebellion
	Thomas Malthus publishes *Essay on the Principles of Population*

FURTHER READING

John D. Beatty, ed., *Protestant Women's Narratives of the Irish Rebellion of 1798*. Dublin, 2001.

Anna Clark, *The Struggle for the Breeches. Gender and the Making of the British Working Class*. Berkeley, 1997.

Linda Colley, *Britons: Forging the Nation, 1707–1837*. New Haven, 2009.

Mary Poovey, *The Proper Lady and the Woman Writer*. Chicago, 1984.

Deryck M. Schreuder and Stuart Ward, eds., *Australia's Empire*. Oxford, 2008.

Deborah Valenze, *The First Industrial Woman*. New York, 1995.

1799	Combination Acts
1801	Act of Union with Ireland
1803	Van Dieman's Land colony established
1804	Pitt becomes prime minister again
1807	Slave trade abolished
1815	End of Napoleonic Wars
	Britain obtains Cape Colony in South Africa
	Corn Laws
	Mount Tambora erupts
1816	Luddite attacks on machinery
1819	Peterloo Massacre
	Six Acts
1820	Queen Caroline affair

REBECCA AND HER DAUGHTERS.

Tolltaker . . Sir R. P—l.   Irish Rebecca . . D—l O'C—l.   Rebecca's Daughters by Members of the Repeal Ass—n.

Rebecca and her daughters attacking a toll gate.

CHAPTER 6

SCOTLAND

IRELAND ENGLAND
WALES
Carmarthen

THE AGE OF REFORM, 1820–1848

On May 26, 1843, some 300 women and men dressed in women's clothes set out to destroy the Water Street tollgate in Carmarthen in western Wales. Their leader, a young farmer who styled himself "Rebecca," and his second in command, "Charlotte," set up guards to ensure that the townspeople would not interfere and ordered them to "dry fire" (no bullets, just powder) at the town constables, who stayed far enough out of the way to avoid being injured. The crowd took pains to treat the gatekeeper and his wife peacefully, but they ousted them from their cottage and took its roof off. Then they went to work on the tollgate itself, dismantling it and carting off the lumber with which it was made.

This was but one incident in the events that made up the "Rebecca riots" in 1842 and 1843. Confined to western and southern Wales, they amounted to a revolt of the peasantry against their landlords, a particularly regressive group that shared neither the language (Welsh) nor the religion (Nonconformist) of the vast bulk of the Welsh people. Governed increasingly harshly by an alien landed gentry and suffering terrible poverty in the wake of a number of depressions and crop failures that followed the end of the Napoleon wars and the intensification of industrialization, the farmers of western Wales organized themselves in protest against their abysmal conditions. They styled themselves Rebecca and her daughters—or collectively, the singular Rebecca—some say after the verse in Genesis XXIV, 60: "And they blessed Rebekah, and said unto her, Thou art our sister, be thou the mother of thousands of millions, and let thy seed possess the gates of those which hate them." Another story has it that Thomas Rees, the man tapped to perform the role of Rebecca one particular night in 1842, could not find women's clothes big enough to accommodate his muscle-bound frame (he was a

173

boxer). He borrowed and tried on many dresses, but to no avail until a tall, large woman named Rebecca stepped forward and offered up one of her gowns. With some alterations it was made to fit, and "Rebecca" came into her own.[1] Whatever the source of the name, it stuck, and various groups of protesters from large swathes of territory across western Wales adopted it.

The Rebecca riots inflicted damage on the symbols of farmers' distress across a large stretch of southern and western Wales. Tollgates, a visible sign of the increasing costs they were forced to bear as they tried to bring their products to market, proved to be the most popular target of Rebecca. But other emblems of their poverty and dispiritedness also took the force of their violence, not least the workhouses that had become the hated manifestation of the new poor law that accompanied the new liberal order in Britain. The riots constituted a kind of rearguard action on the part of those least able to adapt to the economic and political changes roiling Britain in the years following the Napoleonic wars, a last-ditch effort to restore an old way of life under siege by increased population growth, industrialization, and the social changes they were bringing about.

••

INDUSTRIALIZATION AND SOCIAL CHANGE

The process of industrialization has been called a revolution because it introduced rapid, significant, and dramatic changes into everyday life. It is important to note that its impact was uneven not only across the United Kingdom but also within England—changes that took place over the space of a few years in some areas occurred over a period of decades in others. Overall, and over time, it gave most people a better life by improving their economic condition, facilitating their control over the physical environment in which they lived, and providing a way out of their utter dependence on the vagaries of climate and nature. Changes in the means by which manufacturing took place and new techniques of production increased efficiency and productivity, which in turn increased national wealth. The profound social and political changes that emerged from the exigencies thrown up by industrialization created a society based on class. Informed by ideologies engendered by the conditions of industrialization and class society, new forms of government responsive to new constituencies appeared. Municipalities had to find ways to accommodate extraordinary population growth and the problems attending it: the need to address poverty, water, sanitation, pollution, housing, public health, lighting, transportation, fire and police protection, education—all these and more would drive the creation of new urban institutions designed to make cities manageable.

Industrialization began first in Britain for a number of reasons, among them the existence of a constitutional monarchy; a representative form of government; a legal system that applied equally to all adult white men; the absence of impediments to the free movement of goods, capital, and labor; and a social

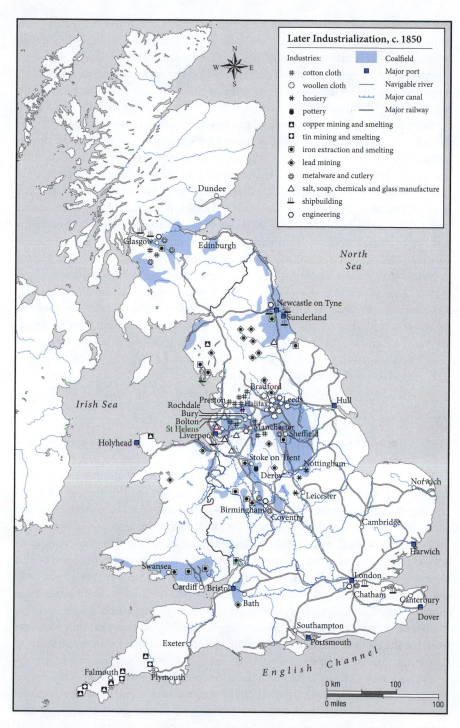

MAP 6.1

Later Industrialization, c. 1850

system that allowed for mobility across ranks. A constitution and the rule of law, in particular, gave entrepreneurs, manufacturers, and investors confidence that contracts entered into would not be abrogated by an arbitrary ruler. Reforms abolishing privileges that stood in the way of the free movement of people, goods, and capital encouraged new forms of manufacturing and facilitated the spread of industrialization.

British industrialization took place first in light industry, largely textile manufacturing, and only gradually moved into heavy industry with the development of the railroad. Lighter manufacturing required less capital, which meant that relatively small family concerns could more readily find opportunities for investment and ownership. Change was gradual for the most part, but even in England, industrialization proved shocking; in the early years, most people expressed hostility to it. "Were we required to characterise this age of ours by any single epithet," complained the celebrated writer and critic Thomas Carlyle (1795–1881), "we should be tempted to call it, not an Heroical, Devotional, Philosophical, or Moral Age, but, above all others, the Mechanical Age. It is the Age of Machinery, in every outward and inward sense of that word; the age which, with its whole undivided might, forwards, teaches and practises the great art of adapting means to ends. Nothing is now done directly, or by hand; all is by rule and calculated contrivance."[2] Change took place constantly as new machinery was invented and factories grew larger and larger, gaining efficiency and increased productivity at every turn.

The Factory System

With their division and specialization of labor, factories imposed a culture of time discipline on workers. Workers in agriculture, cottage manufacturing, and artisanal manufacturing followed what we might see as a *task*-oriented discipline; that is, they worked until the task at hand was completed. They might labor exceedingly long hours for a certain period—at harvest time, for instance, in the countryside, or to make a silver service for an impatient customer—but their work ended when their job was completed. In the factories, no job was ever completed; workers labored according to the clock, performing the same operation over and over again until the twelve- to fourteen-hour workday came to an end. The clock, not the nature of the task before them, determined their work, and before long, employers had to place a protective cage around the factory clock to keep workers from destroying it with thrown objects. The bell telling workers that they were late and that the gates of the factory would be closed against them soon became a fixture ringing throughout the industrial areas.

In the earlier phase of industrialization, production dominated economic concerns; factory owners thought little about marketing and distributing their goods. Consumption drove demand, and as population grew and prices fell, the market for goods expanded. But production began to outrun consumption, introducing overproduction and the advent of a fierce competition for markets;

without marketing and distributing infrastructures in place, the only way to compete successfully was to lower prices. This created extreme difficulty for workers, whose wages were cut to meet the price reductions. An atmosphere of anxiety and conflict grew out of these early conditions, generating a great deal of insecurity among large sectors of the population.

The factory system, *the* central institution of industrialization, served more than economic ends, however. It acted as a social and political institution as well: having been modeled on the barracks and the reformatory, factories allowed the amassing of large numbers of workers under a single roof where they could be watched, controlled, and disciplined. Strict work codes enforced conformity of behavior. Factory hands—the term "hand" offering a telling comment on the disembodied world the worker now inhabited—were prohibited from reading, eating, drinking, talking with one another, or singing. They were fined if they arrived late to work, and if their home lives displeased factory owners, they might be fired. British employers enlisted religion in their efforts to instill discipline; Methodism, so called because of its emphasis on orderliness, was regarded as an especially appropriate religion for workers because it called for subordination of its followers to authority. Supported by Sunday schools that trained children in habits of strict discipline and rote learning so that they "become reconciled to confinement," employers came to almost completely control their workers. Certainly, the factory dominated the community and influenced its day-to-day life, introducing a different set of economic and political relations between employer and employee, altering the relationship of men and women to the rhythms of nature that had determined an earlier way of life, and accelerating the pace of life generally.

We should not overstate the role played by factory work in the larger scheme of economic things, however. Even in Britain, factory work employed a minority of workers until the last third of the nineteenth century. Domestic service employed far many more men, and especially women, than did factory work. But if the factory system took some time to make its effects felt over large areas of Britain, the appearance of the railroad and its rapid extension into even the smallest towns had an immediate impact on the virtually the entire population of Great Britain.

Railroads

The same dynamics we saw at work in the early phase of industrialization in Chapter 3 applied to the development of the railroad: shortages drove innovations. In the eighteenth and early nineteenth centuries, coalmines had used railway tracks to move coal; other traders loaded barges with goods that were moved along canals. In both cases, horse power provided the motive force, pulling carts along the tracks and barges down the canals. A shortage of food for horses, resulting from the need to put more and more land under cultivation to feed a burgeoning population, made keeping horses for transportation extremely

A PLACE IN TIME

The First Passenger Railway

In 1807, Parliament outlawed the slave trade, eliminating at a stroke an important component of Liverpool's commerce and the prosperity it created. Despite the fears of merchants and others who depended on the trade, the overall wealth of the city did not suffer. What did were the myriad industries that had grown up around the African trade, the artisans who made the goods traded to Africa for slaves. Liverpool over the next few decades ceased to be a manufacturing center, a development that led to a pronounced absence of economic diversity that would plague its inhabitants in subsequent years. Its role as an entrepôt and shipping center, however, not only survived but also increased as the town's elites and those of neighboring Manchester got together to build a railroad between the two cities.

Over the course of the late eighteenth and early nineteenth centuries, Manchester's textile industry had flourished. It relied heavily on raw cotton from America and India for its manufacturing, materials that were carried to Britain by ships that came into the port of Liverpool. The products of Manchester and surrounding areas—textiles, coal, bulk foodstuffs— shipped out of Liverpool to their market destinations in the rest of the United Kingdom, the Americas, and, soon, the Far East. In the second half of the eighteenth century, newly built canals had facilitated the transportation of raw and finished materials between the two towns, but increased

Building the Liverpool and Manchester Railway, late 1820s.

production overwhelmed them by the time the Napoleonic wars ended. A new system of transportation was required.

What became the Liverpool and Manchester Railway was not the first railroad in Britain, but it was the first passenger line. The scope of the undertaking, moreover, far exceeded that of any previous railway building, and the engineering required to ensure a relatively flat and smooth progress—vast and deep tunnels, bridges, dramatic cuttings through hills and even mountains—boggled the mind. The father-and-son team of George (1781–1848) and Robert Stephenson (1803–1859) developed the locomotive that would power the remarkable new mode of conveyance. Their *Rocket* could pull a coach piled with thirty passengers along the railway at speeds up to thirty miles per hour.

George Stephenson took the young Fanny Kemble (1809–1893), famous even then for her successes on the stage, for a ride on the *Rocket* in August 1830. Her account captures the wonder inspired by the new technology and the lengths to which inventors and entrepreneurs had to go to bring it into being. "This snorting little animal which I felt rather inclined to pat," she wrote, "was harnessed to our carriage. We started at about ten miles an hour. The steam horse being ill adapted for going up and down hill, the road was kept at a certain level and sometimes appeared to sink below the surface of the earth and sometimes to rise above it. Almost at starting it was cut through solid rock, which formed a wall on either side of it, about sixty feet high. You can't imagine how strange it seemed to be journeying on thus, without any visible cause of progress other than the magical machine, with its flying white breath and rhythmical, unvarying pace, between these rocky walls. . . . When I reflected that these great masses of stone had been cut asunder to allow our passage thus far below the surface of the earth, I felt as if no fairy tale was ever half so wonderful as what I saw. Bridges were thrown from side to side across the tops of these cliffs, and people looking down upon us from them seemed like pygmies in the sky."[4]

A month later the *Rocket* embarked on its inaugural trip to Manchester. Kemble went along again, full of excitement until she discovered that her mother, who was in the same carriage, was so terrified of the machine that she was trying to jump out while the train was moving. She succeeded in calming her, and all went well until the train stopped at Parkside to replenish its water supply. A number of passengers ill-advisedly disembarked from the train, among them William Huskisson (1770–1830), an MP for Liverpool and the former president of the Board of Trade. As he crossed the tracks to try to speak to the prime minister, who was in another train, he failed to see that the *Rocket* had started up again. He fell and was run over by the locomotive. His leg crushed, he died shortly afterward in hospital.

This was an inauspicious beginning, indeed. The tragedy could not stop the progress of the railroad, however, and soon a vast network of railways traversed the island kingdom. Liverpool stood at the heart of the commerce serviced by the iron horse, cementing its position of influence and wealth and enhancing its place in what would become an increasingly global British empire.

expensive; these expenses were passed along to the shipper or passenger who depended upon it. Adam Smith estimated that feeding a single horse consumed the amount of food it would take to keep eight laborers fed. As one railway promoter argued, "the exorbitant demands now made on the public, for conveyance of goods and persons by waggons [sic] and coaches, are caused principally, if not altogether, by the enormous expense of a stock of horses, the continual renewal of the stock, and the intolerable expense of their keep."[3] Abandoning horse-drawn transport and turning to the steam railway would eliminate the need for the million horses kept for that purpose, freeing up additional food resources for 8 million laborers. That in turn would reduce the cost of food, which would make it possible to pay workers a lower wage.

Railroads transformed the landscapes and the societies they touched in almost every way—geographically, economically, socially, culturally, and psychologically. Their freedom from constraints, like the limits of animal and human power, terrain, weather, seasons, and time of day, enabled them to open up new vistas of possibility; their very attributes also closed down a way of life that existed prior to their advent and irremediably altered the relationship of humans to their natural worlds, their localities, their nations, their fellow citizens, and even to themselves.

Travel on foot, horseback, by coach, or by boat took place at the dictates of nature. Terrain determined where one might go; time of day, weather, and the condition of the motive power—whether it be human, animal, or climatological (tides, currents, or wind, for example)—influenced when one might go and how long it took to get there. Routes followed the geographical contours of the landscape on both land and water, and although they brought the traveler into an intimate relationship with the natural world, that relationship imposed limitations on the distance, speed, and comfort with which one could travel. Railroad builders certainly had to take terrain into consideration as they laid rail across topographies of steep gradients, soft or sandy soil, and watercourses, but once those obstacles had been overcome by the engineering of embankments, tunnels, and bridges, the railway, whose initial purpose was to move goods quickly and cheaply between centers of production and places that used what was produced, ran in as straight a line as possible. Liberated from geographical constraints, railroads threw off those of weather and physiology: they need not pay heed to heat, cold, rain, snow, or darkness or worry about the exhaustion of drivers, horses, or oxen. These freedoms provided obvious economic advantages. Coaches and carriages could move at about ten miles per hour under the best of conditions. Mud and rutted roads might reduce that speed considerably, and if a horse threw a shoe or could not sustain a regular pace because of fatigue, travel times might lengthen by a matter of days. Schedules had to be flexible because of the irregularity and uncertainty surrounding coach transport. Even the earliest railroads, by contrast, could reach speeds of thirty miles per hour; their rails were straight and smooth, rain and snow did not deter them, and they did not run out of steam—a railway expression, certainly—after hours in the traces.

Goods and then people could be moved at much greater speed over far greater distances than ever before, reducing the costs of transport and distribution. Farmers could get their grain, wool, meat, vegetables, and dairy products to market, and factories could obtain the raw materials they needed to fuel their machinery and send their finished products to distribution points in less than a third of the time it had taken in the past. As the speeds locomotives could attain increased over the decades after 1830, travel times became even shorter and yielded even greater economies.

The speed of railways acted to shrink space. At speeds of thirty miles per hour, trains could reach a destination in one-third the time it took by carriage, effectively shrinking the length of the space between the two points by two-thirds. The literal distance between say, London and Edinburgh, had not diminished, of course, but the perception of it had. "The annihilation of time and space" by railway travel, as Karl Marx put it, changed the way Britons related to time. When delays caused by weather conditions, the fitness of animals or humans, or the availability of food and water could be measured by days and sometimes even weeks, travelers and movers of goods had to be flexible and tolerant; they could not count on any degree of regularity and so it fostered a fairly casual approach to time. With the advent of the railroad, schedules became far more regularized and trips far more frequent; delays were not usually more than a matter of hours. Time, consequently, had to be measured more regularly to accommodate the increased transport, and people's valuation of time became more pronounced. The measurement of time moved away from the rhythms of nature—hours of daylight or time of year—toward those of the mechanical clock. Localities usually marked noon by the position of the sun in the sky; because that position varied according to location across a country or continent, times varied across country or continent: it might be 11:30 AM in Liverpool and 11:17 AM in London. These variations had no impact on earlier forms of travel, where scheduling could be haphazard and no harm would come of it. But because locomotives, unlike coaches or carriages, could not move out of the way of an approaching vehicle, scheduling had to be precise and uniform, necessitating the coordination of time across nations and continents. Railroad proprietors in England established Greenwich Mean Time as the standard measure in the 1840s, within which clocks would be set at exactly the same time. Time measured by the railroads replaced time measured by the sun, transforming people's relationship to the hours of the day.

URBANIZATION AND ITS DISCONTENTS

Industrialization was accompanied by and contributed to massive urbanization. Burgeoning population growth in the countryside caused by the agricultural revolution filled urban areas with hundreds of thousands of rural workers who could find no work. In turn, the growth of industrialization, which required huge numbers of workers, created new factory towns where virtually none had existed before. Although capital cities like London, Edinburgh, and Dublin grew rapidly as the need for commercial, financial, insurance, and administrative services increased, factory towns experienced the greatest rate of growth. Port cities, from which factory goods would be traded and exported, grew significantly as well. London's population rose from 500,000 in 1700 to 959,000 in 1800; fifty years later, it reached 2.4 million. Manchester, a sleepy town of 20,000 in 1758, grew to 400,000 by 1850 as a result of the factories that established themselves in the area. Liverpool, a port city, experienced an increase of nearly 400,000 people between 1801 and 1861. Glasgow grew from 250,000 to 500,000 between 1830 and 1871; Edinburgh from 103,000 in 1811 to 269,00 in 1891. England and Wales had become half urban by 1850, and 80 percent of its population was urban by 1895. Scotland lagged behind only slightly: it possessed the third most urban population in Europe after England and Wales. Ireland's tragic demographic history as a consequence of the potato famine, discussed below, distorts any meaningful comparisons. Dublin and Belfast could boast only small populations in 1841, 250,000 and 75,000, respectively; the massive rural mortality and emigration following the famine meant that Ireland's urban population percentages far exceeded those of the rural areas by 1851.

Overcrowding was a central aspect of urban life, and it contributed to the acute stress its inhabitants encountered as they went about trying to survive in this new—and often exciting—environment. Cities could not keep pace with the influx of so many people, a predominant proportion of whom were poor. Existing housing could not accommodate their numbers, so contractors threw up cheap, poorly constructed dwellings to rent out to families. These tenements often contained several families in a single room, a stark contrast to the homes of middle-class and wealthy residents who settled in well-built and spacious houses on the west side of town, the prevailing westerly winds ensuring that the stench of the working-class slums would be carried away from their neighborhoods. Segregation by class became a marked characteristic of cities, which had a profound impact on social relations. Formerly accustomed to meeting, interacting with, and living among all kinds of people, urban dwellers now lived and worked apart from one another depending on what they did and how much they earned. Familiarity across class gave way to unfamiliarity with the ways of people of different classes; this was soon followed by alienation that could readily turn into class antagonism.

Pollution and Disease

As populations soared and cities grew, finding a sufficient supply of safe water became increasingly difficult. In London in the mid-nineteenth century, only 17,000 of 70,000 houses got their water from wells; the remainder had to use standpipes from the street, amounting to about 1 for every 20 to 30 houses. These standpipes yielded an hour's worth of water a day for three days a week or so. Few houses possessed bathrooms and public baths were limited in number. Sanitation in the new industrial cities beggars the imagination. Lavatories existed only among the wealthy; most people had to use the streets, which ran with open sewers filled with human and animal waste. Friedrich Engels described the filth of one area of Manchester in 1844, where courtyards led down to the River Irk. "In one of these courts, just at the entrance where the covered passage ends," he noted, "there is a privy without a door. This privy is so dirty that the inhabitants of the court can only enter or leave the court if they are prepared to wade through puddles of stale urine and excrement."[5] As water closets were built, sewage from them emptied directly into rivers, turning them into sewers whose stench permeated the city. The Thames in 1858 produced so awful a stench—called "The Great Stink"—that Parliament, which sat on the banks of the river, had to be dismissed. Rivers like the Thames still provided much of the water for large numbers of inhabitants, increasing the incidence of intestinal diseases and cholera. So intimate was the relation between water pollution and disease that when the Lambeth Water Company relocated a source of water above the most polluted part of the Thames in 1853, the death rate in the part of London it served decreased from 130 per thousand to 37 per thousand!

Smoke and sulfur dioxide from coal-burning and smelting, and hydrogen chloride, a by-product of chemical manufacturing that produced such products as soaps, glass, and textiles, entered the atmosphere from thousands of unfiltered chimneys, introducing poisonous gases and fumes that corroded and infected people's lungs. Factories also dumped waste into rivers, introducing poisonous chemicals that killed most of the river dwellers and posed a significant health risk for humans. Poisoned wastelands devoid of all vegetation and animal life became familiar sights in the areas surrounding industrial areas. Acid rain, produced by sulfur dioxide, made its first recorded appearance in Manchester in the 1850s, corroding the stonework of buildings and killing off flora and fauna in local streams; as industrialization spread, acid rain ceased to be a purely local problem and took on huge dimensions.

Industrial diseases plagued the human populations residing in or near industrial areas. Potters absorbed large quantities of lead in the course of manufacturing that produced convulsive shaking, paralysis, and loss of teeth; the producers of lead itself could count on dying from the metal, but people were often desperate enough to take the chance. Glassmakers exposed to borax and antimony suffered lung and mouth ulcers; hat makers were often poisoned by the mercury they handled in the course of their production, giving rise to the expression "mad as a hatter." Makers of cutlery in places like Sheffield inhaled large quantities of dust as they ground their blades to perfection, and coal miners took in coal dust in prodigious amounts. The lint in the air in cotton mills caused a lung disease called byssinosis. The populations as a whole in the industrial areas suffered high death rates as pollutants in the air and water combined with terrible living conditions. In Manchester in the 1840s, for example, some 60 percent of working-class children did not live to the age of five; this was twice the death rate experienced by children in the rural areas of England. City populations continued to grow, but only because rural workers migrated to them; had they not, death rates would have decimated urban populations quickly.

Social Consequences

Industrialization dramatically increased the overall wealth of those countries that experienced it. Prior to industrialization, more than half of Europe's population lived below what we would consider a "poverty line." After industrialization, more than half the population lived above it. During the nineteenth century in England, for example, national income per capita quadrupled, improving the standards of living for significant numbers of people at most social levels. But the distribution of income across classes was decidedly uneven, and during some periods standards of living among various workers fell. Industrialization was thus an overall boon to societies, but its effects were felt differently across time and across social strata. The working classes enjoyed an improvement of living standards over the sixty-year period between 1790 and 1850. During that time, however, wages remained flat or actually fell while Britain was at war with France (1793–1815) and in the downturn of the 1820s and 1830s. For the well-off between 1801 and 1848, the distribution of national income turned decidedly in their favor; that is to say, the share of national income enjoyed by the wealthy in England grew relative to the rest of society. Although certain workers were somewhat better off, the well-off became rich and the rich became even richer; the gap between rich and poor widened substantially. Total national income shifted away from wages (that is, from workers) and toward profits and salaries paid out to factory owners, business concerns, bankers, insurers, financiers, and members of the professions. Not surprisingly, the upper and middle classes benefitted first from the availability of new consumer goods. Owners of factories and those merchants who sold their products followed closely behind; it took a generation or so for shopkeepers and families who owned small businesses to enjoy the fruits of industrialization. Among workers, the so-called "labor aristocracy" of skilled artisans, far less vulnerable to unemployment and economic downturns, first shared in the increase in living standards, followed by factory workers (still small in number relative to the whole working population). Those put out of work by competition from factory manufacturing—handloom weavers, knitters, and piece-workers in textiles—fared badly. Agricultural laborers did even worse: their paltry wages made their living conditions abominable and their food intake slight. Many were near starvation. For all that, however, without the agricultural revolution and industrialization, which took excess workers off the land, a far larger segment of the growing population would have died from starvation.

Divisions of rich and poor had always existed; they did not simply arise from industrialization. Industrialization, however, exacerbated the divisions, increasing the size of the income gap between rich and poor, and geographically—and then psychologically—segregating them from one another. Benjamin Disraeli

(1804–1881), who would become prime minister of Britain, described this phenomenon in his 1845 novel, *Sybil*, as the existence of "two nations, between whom there is no intercourse and no sympathy; who are ignorant of each other's habits, thoughts and feelings, as if they were dwellers in different zones, or inhabitants of different planets, who are formed by a different breeding, are fed by a different food, are ordered by different manners, and are not governed by the same laws."[6] In all the cities of Britain these "two nations," riven by class difference, would occasionally become so antagonistic to one another that violent social conflict threatened to break out. Often during those tense times—but not always, as we shall see below—elites became concerned enough about their hold on the political structures of Britain to implement significant reform.

POLITICAL REFORM

The dramatic demographic and economic changes Britain underwent over the years since 1750 or so were not accompanied by alternations in the way the country was represented politically. The discordance between the political and economic structures sparked an outpouring of protest across the country and finally compelled elites to recognize that something must be done to bring them more in line with one another. Political elites dragged their feet for some time, but agrarian violence in Ireland throughout the 1820s, machine-breaking in the industrial areas, and rural unrest in the Swing Riots in southeastern England in 1830 convinced many politicians that the time for reform had to come. The formation of hundreds of Political Unions among working and middle-class people in London and the industrial areas had combined with the revolutions of 1830 in Europe to persuade them that revolution might indeed be at hand. Whigs, who had come to power during the 1830 election following the fall of the Tory government under the Duke of Wellington (1769–1852), determined to avoid it by providing reform that would placate the middle-class elements demanding better and greater representation. But they needed the muscle that the protests of working people could provide, and they enlisted the support of the working classes in demanding parliamentary reform.

Working-class radicalism had declined significantly after the Queen Caroline affair, and popular protests demanding political reform died away for nearly a decade. Radicalism reappeared in 1830 as a result of Daniel O'Connell's (1775–1847) success in gaining Catholic emancipation for Ireland in 1829. By 1830, reformers of every stripe—radical artisans demanding universal manhood suffrage; middle-class moderates looking to enfranchise the commercial and industrial men of Britain and to gain representation for cities like Manchester, Leeds, Birmingham, Swansea, Merthyr Tydfil, which had none; evangelicals and free traders who sought to end slavery and introduce laissez-faire policies into the economy; and Whigs in Parliament seeking rational administrative reforms—followed the lead of O'Connell and exploited the potential of massive popular unrest to promote their agendas. Bowing to the arguments of Whig

MPs like Thomas Babington Macaulay (1800–1859) that some measure of reform was necessary if revolution was to be averted, the Whig government determined to bring in a reform bill.

Ireland: Catholic Emancipation

Efforts to reform the political system of Great Britain, then, appeared first in Ireland, where O'Connell, a devout Catholic of radical principles, organized thousands of people in his Catholic Association. Elected to Parliament but unable to take his seat because of his religion, he turned a network of priests into an electoral machine that was able to challenge the political monopoly of Protestant landlords. Against the backdrop of terrible depression in the agricultural sector, which produced regular famines throughout the 1820s, O'Connell rallied peasants, small landholders, larger landowners, and urban working and middling sorts into an organization that emphasized their Gaelic Catholic identity and their sense of exclusion from political life under Protestant rule. He aimed to replace Protestants as the rulers of Ireland by reforming the British Parliament, the institution that governed Ireland. In other words, O'Connell did not seek revolution or independence from Great Britain; he sought instead to make it possible for Irish Catholics to sit in Parliament so that their majority interests and concerns would be represented. Such a disparate a group of Catholics—from landless peasants to landed gentry to urban workers and artisans to shopkeepers and professionals—certainly did not share common economic interests. What welded them together, what made them a formidable interest group that could not be ignored, was their Gaelicness and their Catholicism. Cultural identity served as the adhesive, the glue, that held these different folks together. "Catholic Ireland" ranged itself against the Protestant Ascendancy in a series of "monster meetings" and, in the elections of 1826 and 1828, won a few seats in County Wexford and County Clare.

O'Connell opposed violence in all parts of his campaign, a stance that earned him the support of the Catholic clergy and its hierarchy. But he was not reluctant to use the endemic violence of the countryside to press his point about the need to reform the political structures under which Ireland was governed. Playing up both the virtues of the Irish Catholic nation and the threats of violence emanating from the countryside in the form of the Whiteboy movement, O'Connell exploited English fears of Irish civil war to wrest emancipation from the Tory government of the Duke of Wellington in 1829. Although it came some twenty-eight years after Pitt had promised it as part of the Act of Union with Great Britain in 1801, the Roman Catholic Relief Act of 1829 gave wealthy Irish Catholics the right to sit in Parliament. Protestant dissenters—Presbyterians, Congregationalists, Quakers, Baptists, and the like—also gained access to Parliament and to public office when the Test and Corporation Acts were repealed the same year. Together, these actions served to split the Tory Party and topple the government in 1830, opening the ministerial door to the Whigs.

With Catholic Emancipation, propertied Irish Catholics could now take seats in the House of Commons in Westminster, but the act did nothing to change the situation in the cities and port towns of Ireland, where the Protestant Ascendancy maintained control over the corporations that ruled and administered the urban areas. Breaking their power would require more thorough-going reform of the political system, which allowed only landed men to vote, and gave representation to old "rotten" boroughs with few to no people living there and refused it to the fast-growing cities of industrial Britain.

Nor did Catholic emancipation affect non-Christian Britons who shared the same legal disabilities. In 1830, a bill to emancipate Jews went down to defeat in the House of Commons; reintroduced in 1833, this time it passed the Commons but could not get through the Lords. Over the next twenty-four years, efforts to allow Jews to sit in Parliament met the same fate—success in the Commons, failure in the Lords. It was only in 1858, after a number of reforms eliminated virtually all other legal disabilities, that Conservatives in the Lords realized the harm their position was doing to their party and reached a compromise with the Commons. From this point on, each house would determine the nature of the oath required of their members, allowing those Jews elected as MPs to sit in the House of Commons.

The Antislavery Movement

Demands for reform came from other groups in Britain in the 1820s as well. The antislavery movement especially commanded the energies of evangelical Christians, many of whom combined their humanitarian ethos with a liberal economic rhetoric of free trade. Antislavery activity had declined considerably during the years of the French Revolution, and abolitionists directed most of their efforts in that period to improving the conditions in which slaves were held or helping to settle ex-slaves in places such as Sierra Leone, as we have seen. They achieved a stunning victory in 1807, when Parliament outlawed the slave trade, a measure that cut the continual resupply of slaves to the Caribbean. Historians have debated how it came to be that the abolition of a trade that had proved so central to Britain's wealth and power could have occurred. In 1944, the Trinidadian historian Eric Williams (1911–1981) argued in *Capitalism and Slavery* that however sincere the sentiments of the abolitionists, the men in Parliament who did away with first the slave trade and then with slavery itself acted out of economic interest. The output of the British sugar islands had grown rapidly during the Napoleonic wars, so much so that overproduction threatened profits. The abolition of the slave trade, Williams noted, would mitigate against oversupply and low prices. Other historians attacked his thesis, dismissing what they regarded as a Marxist interpretation, but the consensus today holds that although Williams might have exaggerated the extent to which the sugar islands were suffering and therefore jeopardizing the financial markets, MPs felt confident that Britain's credit-worthiness could survive ending the trade in captive Africans.

In other words, the humanitarian elements within the abolitionist movement now found parliamentary allies who no longer regarded it as economically threatening.

In 1823, the cabinet issued Orders in Council "requiring West Indian legislatures to ameliorate the conditions of slave labour," a command that fell on deaf ears. That same year, a slave revolt broke out in Demerara in British Guiana, supported by a white missionary by the name of John Smith. Following his trial and sentencing to death, Smith died in prison of consumption, an event that revivified the antislavery movement at home and turned it into a significant political force. Its leader in Parliament, Thomas Fowell Buxton (1786–1845), wanted to go slowly, bringing about emancipation gradually and by a series of remedial steps, but his caution was soon overcome by the demands of the women supporting the movement for full and immediate abolition.

Evangelical and liberal abolitionists regarded slaves as part of the human "family of man" according to a model of a universal humanity that enabled them to think in terms of equality before God and to see slavery as an abomination. Within the evangelicals' family of man rhetoric, white Britons positioned themselves as older brothers and sisters, teachers and defenders of their younger siblings who needed educating in the ways of civilization and morality, reason and domesticity, and protection from the depredations of ungodly planters. Frequently, the language of older brother and sister merged with that of father and mother, so that the hierarchies of power and inequality between whites and people of color might become even more pronounced. "Sons of Africa," "babes in Christ," as black Jamaicans were styled by white missionaries in a relationship of children to parent, "are willing to be taught," noted William Knibb (1803–1845), a Baptist missionary, "and where there is sympathy with them, they love those who instruct them."[7] Although British men saw themselves as emancipators of the poor and downtrodden in the 1830s and 1840s, they did so in a paternalistic way. Jamaican freemen and women might enjoy the potential for equality with Europeans, but by no means had they attained even a small measure of the qualities that would bring them up to the level of their white saviors. White, but especially English, superiority to people of color had never been called into question by the antislavery campaigners.

If the antislavery movement, grown now to a size and influence that political elites could not disregard, was to succeed in its aims of ending slavery, Parliament would have to be reformed. The West Indian interest in the House of Commons could count on enough support to keep the institution in place, at least for now. But when the Whigs came into office in 1830 on the fall of Wellington's government, their ranks included some of the most senior members of their faction—lords Grey (1764–1845) and Brougham (1778–1868), prime minister and lord chancellor, respectively, and the colonial secretary, Viscount Goderich (1782–1859)—all staunch abolitionists. The government reissued its 1823 Orders in Council forbidding planters to physically punish their slaves. Seeing in this action evidence that emancipation would be forthcoming and urged on by Baptist missionaries, slaves rose up in Jamaica in November 1831. The Jamaican authorities responded speedily and bloodily, introducing martial law and executing more than 300 slaves. When news of the revolt and the details of its suppression reached London, support for the antislavery movement grew even more vociferous. More important, support for the planter cause in Parliament lost ground.

The Great Reform Act

The Whig position on colonial issues called for reducing the amounts expended on colonial affairs, especially in India, ending the East India Company's monopoly on trade with China, and abolishing slavery; they knew that they could not carry their colonial agenda without parliamentary reform. Not surprisingly, MPs promoting West Indian and East Indian interests opposed the reform of Parliament, seeing in it an attack on empire. They succeeded in blocking the first Whig effort to reform Parliament in 1831 and forced the Whigs to significantly alter their legislation when Parliament resumed its business in 1832. Initially, the government had sought to reduce the number of seats in the House of Commons and to expand representation for Ireland and Scotland, thus cutting back on the number of seats apportioned to England and Wales. The colonial lobbying ensured that did not happen, although in the end it could not prevent what became known as the Great Reform Act of 1832 from becoming the law of the land.

Strictly speaking, the Great Reform Act of 1832 pertained only to England and Wales. Separate acts for Scotland and Ireland followed. Together they introduced three major changes to the British political system, whose lineaments dated back 150 years. First, they redistributed the seats in Parliament to better reflect the nature of the British economy and society. "Rotten boroughs," so-called because they contained few people yet provided numerous seats to MPs willing to pay what it cost to purchase them, yielded to new seats given to population-rich counties and the new cities thrown up by industrialization and urbanization. Manchester, Leeds, Birmingham; Dundee, Perth, and Aberdeen in Scotland; and Swansea and Merthyr Tydfill in Wales, which had not enjoyed representation in the past, now gained seats. Other cities such as Glasgow and Edinburgh and counties in Wales such as Carmarthen, Glamorgan, and Denbigh, which already possessed a seat, received an additional one to better correspond to their growth in population. As a result of these changes, Wales gained 5 new seats and Scotland 8. Had the actual size of Ireland's population been taken into account, it would have gained 100 seats. Its MPs asked for 25, but no English minister was prepared to swamp the Commons with representatives elected by a majority of Catholics; it received only 5 new seats.

Second, the criteria establishing the eligibility for voting were expanded and made uniform in the boroughs. Where before 1832 one had to *own* property worth 40 shillings to vote, largely restricting the franchise to the landed interests of the country, now any man owning £10 worth of land or buildings or paying rent of £10 a year qualified, opening up direct political representation to the middling classes of the nation. The size of the electorate skyrocketed overnight: in London, because of the high rents there, virtually every householder could vote; in England as a whole, 1 in 5 men now enjoyed voting rights, whereas Welsh voters doubled in number. Scottish voters increased by a factor of 16 from 4,500 to 65,000, whereas the Irish county electorate rose from about 37,000 to 60,000 or so. Borough voters increased, especially among Catholics, but overall Irish representation per capita fell far behind that of England and Wales. Across the United Kingdom as a whole, the electorate more than doubled.

Finally, the reform acts introduced a system of registration of voters. Only those men who had registered in the twelve months preceding an election would be allowed to vote, a condition that would ultimately help to transform the conventional factions of Whigs and Tories into more modern political parties by requiring them to attend to the organization of their constituencies. The actual emergence of modern political parties would be a while in coming, however, and the failure of reformers to either enact a secret ballot measure in 1832 or place a limit on campaign spending ensured that little changed in the makeup of Parliament in the years immediately following. In fact, the reformed Parliament returned after 1832 contained most of the same faces—noble and landed—that had dominated it previously.

Colonial Reforms

The Whig government set about implementing its colonial agenda immediately, passing legislation in 1833 that reduced the extent and power of the Anglican church in Ireland and decreased the tithes owed by Irish peasants. These carrots accompanied a particularly sharp stick, however, in the Coercion Act of 1833, which suspended habeas corpus and imposed severe penalties on those involved in the agrarian unrest that plagued the countryside. Parliament further eliminated the monopoly powers of the EIC and opened up trade with China to virtually all British merchants when it renewed the company's charter in 1833.

Momentously, Parliament abolished slavery in 1833. Given the centrality of the institution to the economies of a number of its colonies and thus to the wealth of a significant portion of the gentlemanly capitalists who governed Great Britain, the success of such a measure must count as an extraordinary achievement. Parliament abolished slavery in 1833 because it could no longer be tolerated by the vast majority of Britons—and, not incidentally, it comported with classical liberal beliefs in free trade and laissez-faire. For a brief period in the 1820s, 1830s, and 1840s, eighteenth-century notions of absolute racial difference were driven underground by liberal and humanitarian sentiments expressed through the antislavery movement. Britons found slavery incompatible with their sense of rightness, their sense of themselves. To be "British" in the 1830s and 1840s entailed holding an abolitionist position, whether for political, economic, or sentimental reasons. Britons had come to share the sentiments of Lord Grenville (1759–1834), the former prime minister, who in 1807 had demanded of his colleagues in Parliament, "What right do we derive from any human institution, or any divine ordinance, to tear the natives of Africa, to deprive them by force of the means of laboring for their own advantage, and to compel them to labour for our profit? . . . Can there be a question that the character of the country ought to be cleared from the stain impressed by the guilt of such traffic, by the effect of which we keep Africa in a state of barbarity and desolation?"[8] For British women, antislavery sentiments dovetailed precisely with their purported greater sensitivity to cruelties and injustices, their greater morality and higher spiritual natures. For British men, devotion to Christian precepts as much as to liberal principles of justice and legal equality meant that no respectable middle-class male could turn a blind eye to the brutalities of slavery. Notions of manliness contained a strong element of abolitionism, of ending the oppression of African men, women, and children at the hands of British planters and overlords.

But true to its adherence to property rights and, more crucially, cognizant of the need to placate the interests of the empire in which the country had an enormous stake, the Whigs handsomely compensated those who were financially hit by their measures. West Indian planters extorted a policy of apprenticeship and £20 million from Parliament on the manumission of their slaves in 1833, a figure that amounted to half of all the revenues Britain took in that year. Apprenticeship virtually ensured that slavery by another name would prevail: former slaves owed their masters forty hours of work each week, for which they earned no wages. If they worked beyond the forty-hour base period, they received wages for which they were able to negotiate as if they were free laborers; alternatively, they might work for themselves or for another employer. The planters won these concessions by threatening increased unrest in the West Indies that would interrupt the flow of raw materials from the islands to the industrial and commercial centers of Great Britain. The East India Company received £2 million for the loss of its monopoly; and tithe holders in Ireland who could no longer collect their payments took in £1 million.

Classical Liberalism and Domesticity

By the Reform Act of 1832, the radical vision of universal manhood suffrage and even of household suffrage was supplanted by a narrower view of political reform and citizenship that historians call classical liberalism. In its political guise, classical liberalism conferred citizenship and participation in government on independent property owners. Because married women could not own property under common law and because unmarried women were considered the dependents of men within the family, citizenship, in liberal formulations, was denied them, as it was those men who did not own property or were dependent on others, such as servants, laborers, or lodgers.

The Reform Act of 1832 explicitly barred women from the franchise by using the phrase *every Male Person* to define those eligible to vote (although the reform act for Scotland in that same year delineated merely *every Person*) and by limiting it in the boroughs to those men who occupied premises that had an annual worth of £10, effectively ensuring that the newly enfranchised voters were of the "respectable" middle classes. Working men in a number of cities lost the right to vote in 1832, although over time, as inflation rendered the £10 criterion easier to meet, the numbers of working-class voters increased. Middle class men, "the possessors of the wealth and intelligence of the country, the natural leaders of the physical force of the community," as MP Charles Buller (1774–1848) described them, men whose commercial, financial, and industrial wealth could no longer be ignored by the ruling elites of Britain, were coopted onto the side of order and conservatism to defeat working-class radical claims.[9]

The ascent of Victoria to the throne in 1837 seemed to punctuate the arrival of a new social as well as political order. Victoria has been credited or blamed for the monarchy becoming powerless in the nineteenth century, but in fact her predecessor, William IV, had had little success in impressing his political will on Parliament. He had been unable to block the reform measures championed by the Whigs, and his 1834 dismissal of the Whig government under Lord Melbourne (1779–1848) would prove to be the last such action on the part of any monarch, although no one knew it at the time. Nor could William keep the Tories he appointed to power in office for long—another indication that the crown had been significantly weakened. The arrival of Victoria on the throne rendered concrete what had earlier been symbolic—a female monarch now embodied the loss of power relative to Parliament that had been taking place for almost fifty years.

Victoria's commitment to what would come to be seen as a middle-class sensibility, in which sobriety, thrift, strict sexual restraint, responsibility, and hard work prevailed, likely saved the institution of the monarchy in Britain. The unlovely behavior of previous royals had brought the monarchy into such disrepute that its very existence was called into question. Victoria and Albert (1819–1861), whom she married in 1839, living a life of purpose, rectitude, and domesticity, provided the British people a picture of monarchy in which they could take pride. Victoria's popularity soared; she herself basked in the warmth of her people's affection, demonstrations of which she received everywhere she traveled. In contrast to monarchs on the continent, who were losing their thrones on a regular basis, it seemed, Queen Victoria only increased her hold on her subjects' loyalty.

Victoria's family life exemplified the new model of domesticity that had taken hold of the middle classes toward the end of the eighteenth century. Her marriage to Prince Albert and the birth of her nine children cemented in the minds of her subjects the image of the monarchy as middle class and domestic. The queen presented herself as the quintessential wife and mother, ensuring the survival of monarchy and even enhancing its prestige. In so doing, she inhabited a throne that by the end of her reign had lost state power but had gained extraordinary symbolic power. She effected this feat by presenting herself not as a prince presiding over her subjects but as a wife and mother ruling as a woman. Rather than appearing at state occasions in a crown and royal robes, for example, she wore a bonnet and lace. She consistently presented the royal family in imagery consonant with the values associated with domesticity. In a neat correlation between the status of monarchy in a system converting to parliamentary democracy and that of a middle-class woman inhabiting the private sphere assigned to her by separate sphere ideology, Victoria came to inhabit the personae and display the characteristics of both: passivity, duty, and moral power or influence.

The New Poor Law

When the newly reformed Parliament first met, it became clear to working-class radicals that their economic and familial concerns would not be redressed by a governing body informed by what were now deemed "middle-class" values. Instead, in keeping with those aspects of liberalism identified with utilitarianism and Malthusianism, Parliament refused to entertain measures designed to alleviate conditions of work in factories and passed legislation creating a harsh, mean-spirited, and denigrating system of poor relief. In addition to establishing principles of political rights and political liberties, classical liberalism stressed the rights of the individual to possess things. This cast on individual liberty gave activities relating to commerce and industry, like the amassing of capital, the rational utilization of labor and resources, the pursuit of self-improvement through education and training, and the cultivation of personal temperance and self-restraint a good deal of emphasis. Government's role, in the view of classical liberals, was to eliminate the barriers that hampered the exercise of these activities, to reform itself and to do away with practices, customs, laws, traditions, and ways of thinking that got in the way of the individual's right to have and benefit from his property, whether that property be material, moral, intellectual, or, indeed, in the form of a wife and children. As Harriet Martineau (1802–1876), a political economist, put it, "Laws and customs may be creative of vice; and should be therefore perpetually under process of observation and correction: but laws and customs cannot be creative of virtue: they may encourage and help to preserve it; but they cannot originate it."[10] Commercial and financial people, intellectuals, professionals, and manufacturers, but also landed gentry seeking to improve their holdings and increase their wealth, found liberalism compatible with their interests and their outlooks. Evangelicals such as Hannah More and William Wilberforce approved of liberalism's emphases on individual responsibility, self-improvement, morality, and self-restraint.

Liberal concerns about individual responsibility, self-improvement, morality, and self-restraint all came together in the New Poor Law of 1834. Informed by utilitarian fears that overpopulation would produce an overabundance of labor and by Malthusian beliefs that poverty was the consequence of promiscuous working-class sexual behavior, poor law reformers sought to drastically reduce the number of poor who would be eligible for poor relief by requiring persons seeking relief to enter workhouses to receive it. In the past, within the conceptual framework of a moral economy in which the survival of the whole society was understood to necessitate looking after the needy, the poor could expect to receive aid in the form of bread and even wage subsidies from their local communities, enabling them to remain with their families and to continue to seek out work. The Poor Law Act of 1834, by contrast, operated within the conceptual framework of political economy, in which poverty was understood to be the consequence of a refusal to work, rather than the result of low wages or of cyclical downturns in the economy. Providing wage or bread subsidies, poor law reformers and their evangelical allies asserted, only encouraged the poor in their sinful habits of indolence and promiscuity. Making them enter prisonlike, sex-segregated workhouses, on the other hand, where they would be separated from their spouses and children and compelled to perform demeaning and hard labor to obtain relief, would discourage the poor from propagating.

Cartoon depicting the practice of separating husbands and wives in the workhouse under the New Poor Law, London, 1832.

The Poor Law Act of 1834 had significant repercussions for all of society. It served to embed into liberal national consciousness the idea that the state had no responsibility for ensuring a minimum level of well-being for its people; that poverty was the fault of the individual; and that governmental attempts to ameliorate it would simply encourage the poor in their irresponsible behavior. The New Poor Law reflected and furthered the belief of political economists that the state played no role at all in the workings of the economy, although the legislation served to ensure a large supply of cheap labor to employers by making it impossible for able-bodied men and women to find material assistance except in the workhouse, where they would have to give up their dignity, their freedom, and their family life. Perceived as a concrete, visible manifestation of middle-class antipathy toward working people and the poor, its terms provoked high emotion and helped to stimulate among the working classes a movement known as Chartism to gain the vote to overturn it and to prevent further depredations against them, as we shall see later in this chapter.

The New Poor Law also served to underscore the ideology of separate spheres and to instill in the minds of working-class men and women a connection between manliness, employment, and the male breadwinner ideal. In the past, women and children had been able to obtain poor relief from parish authorities independent of their husbands and fathers. Indeed, poor women were the greatest recipients of poor relief in the eighteenth century. After 1834, women and children were considered inseparable from their husbands and fathers: should a married woman require assistance, she could only obtain it if her entire family entered the workhouse. Conversely, should a man seek material help in supporting his family, all members would have to enter the workhouse with him. In effect, the Poor Law assumed, wrongly, that working-class men supported their families single-handedly, without recourse to wages earned by their wives and children. It had the effect of placing women under economic, as well as legal, *coverture*. They were not recognized as wage earners and contributors to family survival; those functions, in ideological terms, rested exclusively with men. Those men who failed to perform them adequately placed themselves in a dependent position vis-à-vis the state's poor law guardians, a position ideologically associated with femininity. Manliness, as informed now by the New Poor Law, demanded that men demonstrate their independence through employment and their ability to maintain their families. Men who could not make enough money to support a family should not, in the minds of poor law reformers, marry at all. Until the twentieth century, however, the breadwinner ideal placed enormous strain on the relationships of working-class men and women because few men could actually command a wage that would enable them to keep their families without the assistance of their wives and children, or in dire circumstances, the poor law authorities.

The bastardy clause of the New Poor Law produced special resentment and disquiet. It allowed fathers to escape their previous responsibilities under the old poor law of helping to support their illegitimate children, leaving mothers to provide sole support. If they were unable to do so, women would have to turn to the workhouse. This alteration in the law stemmed from poor law commissioners' and moralists' conviction that "shameless and unprincipled" women who preyed on men's weakness deserved to be punished for their sins. This kind of thinking infuriated working-class activists and, along with the terrible hardships inflicted on the lower classes by the New Poor Law, contributed to the discontent that in Wales manifested itself in the Rebecca riots.

UNREST IN WALES

The demographic and economic changes of the past eighty years had rendered life in rural Wales extremely difficult for the masses of the Welsh people. As a consequence of the introduction of the potato as a staple food crop, the population of areas most closely associated with Rebecca—Pembrokeshire, Carmarthanshire, and Cardiganshire—doubled between 1750 and 1850. The excessive numbers of people on the land made it impossible for farms to yield the kinds of livelihood it would take for families to prosper or even to make ends meet; because there were so many agricultural laborers, wages were pushed down and rents up. Rural distress became acute and when harvests failed in 1838, 1839, and 1840 the depression that seized the agricultural areas increased to levels not seen before. Poverty turned into semistarvation for many, leading thousands of people to take up the call of Rebecca. They tore down toll gates and vandalized workhouses, threatening good order throughout the countryside of western Wales.

One of the most dramatic incidents of the Rebecca riots occurred in June 1843, when a peaceful crowd of 300 on horseback and 2,000 on foot confronted the magistrates of Carmarthen with a series of demands. A large number of denizens of the town, who were not so peaceful, joined them and diverted Rebecca to the workhouse, where they took the master's keys and opened the building to release the inhabitants. Chaos followed as people ransacked the workhouse, breaking furniture and tossing it out the windows. Inmates danced on tables and screamed out their rage and joy. And then someone yelled, "the soldiers are here!" Panic ensued as rioters tried desperately to escape the Fourth Light Dragoons who had been ordered to Carmarthen by the War Office days earlier and who arrived at a most auspicious moment. They took sixty rioters prisoner.

Although little known today outside Wales, the Rebecca riots constituted a serious breach of the peace and caused consternation among cabinet officials. The War Office sent an experienced soldier, Colonel James Frederick Love (1789–1866), to try to bring Rebecca to heel. Having fought alongside the Duke of Wellington against Napoleon's troops in Spain and at Waterloo and as the commander of a troop of horse during the Canadian uprisings of 1838, an event we will take up in the next chapter, Love, one would have thought, should have no trouble carrying out his charge. But despite his superior force—he enjoyed a sizeable military force and at least two pieces of field artillery—he could not track down his elusive quarry, and rioting by Rebecca persisted throughout the summer of 1843. In late August, Rebecca seemed to have changed her tactics, substituting monster meetings for the nighttime raids and drawing huge crowds of people. Sizeable numbers of coalminers, who would have had to give up a day's pay to attend these meetings, joined the farmers who massed together to hear speeches and sign petitions to Her Majesty's government. Their efforts paid off when the cabinet appointed a commission to investigate the ills faced by rural Wales in November. Its report, issued in March 1844, recommended a number of changes that were meant to alleviate the distress of farm laborers. Chief among them was the Turnpike Trusts Act of 1844, which rationalized the system of toll collection and dedicated its revenues to the maintenance of the roads so vital to the movement of farmers' produce. Certainly the passage of the act signaled a victory for Rebecca, but it took the arrival of the railroad in Wales in the 1850s to dispel the distress caused by massive population growth and pressure on the land. Once rural folk could more easily migrate to cities by rail, the problems of insufficient economic resources for excessive population on the land tended to fall off.

The Rebecca riots have been overshadowed by Chartism, a movement of working people displaced by industrialization seeking redress for their grievances, but in Wales at least, Chartism grew out of the same agrarian agonies that produced Rebecca.

CHARTISM

The grievances among working people produced by the limitations of the Reform Act, by the Coercion Act imposed on Ireland, by the New Poor Law, by Parliament's refusal to limit the hours of work in factories, by employers' determination to keep wages low and hours long, and by the persecution and transportation to Australia of factory and rural workers seeking to unionize to challenge the power of employers gave rise, by 1838, to a large and powerful movement to gain political power known as Chartism. So named because of the demand for a "People's Charter" that would establish universal suffrage, annual Parliaments, vote by secret ballot, equal electoral districts, the elimination of property qualifications for those men who would sit in Parliament, and the payment of MPs, Chartism dominated working-class politics for a decade and commanded the time, energies, and passions of working men and women across England, Scotland, Ireland, and Wales. Many Irish people in England, notably Feargus O'Connor (1794–1855) and Bronterre O'Brien (c. 1804–1864), played a prominent role in Chartism, which in its 1842 petition called for the repeal of the 1801 Act of Union between Ireland and Great Britain. The first charter petition arrived in the House of Commons in 1839 bearing 1,280,000 signatures. It was voted down handily. A second petition placed 3,300,000 signatures before the House in 1842, with the same results. In April 1848, in what would prove to be their final thrust, Chartist leaders planned a monster meeting on Kennington Common, across the Thames, from which a procession of Chartists would march to present to MPs a petition containing 2 million names.

Chartist meeting on Kennington Common, 1848.

The man in charge of planning the procession was a black tailor named William Cuffay (1788–1870). Cuffay's grandfather had been taken from Africa to the Caribbean as a captive in the eighteenth century; his father had been born into slavery on St. Kitts and, having earned his freedom as a cook on board a warship, made his way to England. William learned the tailoring craft as a teenager, worked hard and diligently as a journeyman, and joined the Chartists in 1839. Before long, he became a leader of the local movement; indeed, *The Times* referred to London's Chartists as "the Black man and his Party."[11]

Fearful of the huge numbers of demonstrators expected in London, the authorities made elaborate plans to defend the city. They sent Queen Victoria out of town to the Isle of Wight, moved the horses and royal carriages from Buckingham Palace, and packed up valuables from the palace and stored them elsewhere. Seven thousand soldiers lined the Embankment; authorities placed heavy guns along the route; and police, 4,000 strong, guarded the bridges over which the Chartists would have to cross. Feargus O'Connor, cowed by the amassed might of the state, called off the procession, delivering the petition himself to Parliament.

After the events of 1848, amid somewhat better economic conditions and a Parliament that had become more responsive to demands for improved working conditions, Chartism began to fade and its power to mobilize masses of workers to ebb. The 1848 petition, like its predecessors, also failed by a large margin. But as the first national, organized working-class movement in Britain, Chartism gave notice to middle- and upper-class elites that working men's exclusion from political power could not go on indefinitely and would have to be addressed in the future.

In the short term, authorities dealt with working-class radicals by suppressing them. In August 1848, police raided a tavern in Bloomsbury and arrested eleven men for plotting a rebellion. Cuffay had involved himself with some of the men earlier, but was not present at the pub and had not played any part in plans for a rising. Nevertheless, police arrested him at his lodgings and charged him with levying war against the queen; on the strength of evidence given by police spies, he and the others were convicted of the crime and sentenced to transportation to Van Dieman's Land "for the term of your natural lives." Long before the end of his life in 1870 at the age of eight-two, Cuffay earned a pardon, but he continued to act on his radical politics in Tasmania until he was forced into a workhouse, where he died.

THE GREAT FAMINE

In the mid to late 1840s, Chartist agitation became particularly focused on the terrible famine afflicting Ireland. In 1845, Ireland suffered a potato blight, which worsened in 1846 and again in 1847–1848. By the 1840s, the potato had become the staple crop for millions of Irish peasants, and when it failed, those peasants had little else to turn to. In the years 1845 to 1851, the country lost some 2.25 million people, perhaps half of them to death by starvation or disease and the other half to emigration to England, Australia and New Zealand, and the United States. Robert Peel (1788–1850), the Tory prime minister, responded robustly to the crisis in 1845, purchasing 20,000 tons of Indian corn and meal from the United States and exporting it to Ireland. Although initially difficult to digest and causing severe gastric problems, both because it had not been ground fine enough and because Irish stomachs were unused to it, the Indian corn soon proved sufficient to feed most of the Irish who needed it. Peel also pushed through the government the repeal of the Corn Law, which had artificially raised prices on imported grains so that English landlords could sell their crops at good prices. This step ultimately cost Peel the leadership of his party and the party its power, but he was determined to see the repeal through.

The action of Peel's government in 1845 and 1846 prevented disaster. But when the harvest failed again in 1846, the new Whig government fell far short of what was needed to relieve the hunger of so vast a population. Imbued with the ideology of laissez-faire, which preached nonintervention by the government in the workings of the economy, the Whig official in charge of the situation, Charles Trevelyan (1807–1886), refused to ban the exportation of grain from Ireland. This led to increased deprivation and then to starvation, which in turn made the population vulnerable to infectious diseases. The government tried to address the problem by putting Irish peasants to work on public works projects, by establishing soup kitchens, and then by increasing the eligibility for assistance under the poor laws by making it possible for people not entering the poor house to receive aid.

Scene outside a workhouse during the Great Irish Famine, c. 1846.

This last effort, however, included a provision put forward by a large land-holding Irish MP that no one could receive relief without surrendering their land holdings to their landlords. This meant, in effect, that Irish peasants either lost access to the land or starved because they would not give up their land. This provision proved to be the strongest evidence to later Irish nationalists that the British had intentionally starved the Irish, committing, in essence, genocide.

It was not hard to believe the charge, given the lack of information about what the government was doing and the unbelievably callous statements in the press regarding the famine. Whereas Irish liberals and nationalists attributed the disaster of the Great Famine to English land tenure policies and the existence of an absentee Anglo-Irish landowning class, English and Scottish liberals in Parliament and conservatives in and out of government believed the famine to have come about as a consequence of Irish character and morality. Some declared that God was punishing Catholics; others used the terms of classical liberalism to explain the disaster. As *The Times* asserted in 1843, before the famine broke out, "Ireland and the Irish have, in a great measure themselves to thank for their poverty and want of capital. . . . It is by industry, toil, perseverence, economy, prudence, by self-denial, and self-dependence, that a state becomes mighty and its people happy." The English and northern Irish protestants had demonstrated such national traits and the Irish Catholics, by contrast, suffered from the lack of them. They would not work, the paper added in 1845. "Of all the Celtic tribes, famous everywhere for their indolence and fickleness as the Celts everywhere are," intoned *Fraser's Magazine* in 1847, "the Irish are admitted to be the most idle and most fickle." The satiric magazine *Punch* reported them to be the laziest and dirtiest people in the world, descended from "generations of beggars. You can trace the descent in their blighted, stunted forms—in their brassy, cunning, brutalized features."[12] People like this, many Britons believed, brought on themselves the very ills they protested—poverty and famine, unemployment and landlessness, and coercive legislation from an administration firm in its resolve to bring order to an uncivilized nation. "When Ireland acts according to the principles of civilised man," announced *The Times* in 1846, "then she can be ruled by the laws of civilised man."[13] Until that time, harsh British rule would remain.

Chartists denounced the system of government that would allow the deaths of hundreds of thousands of Irish men, women, and children. The official newspaper of the organization, the *Northern Star* (which was named, not incidentally, after the United Irishmen's publication of the 1790s), declared the British policy of laissez-faire to be "MURDER." "We arraign the Legislature who can permit this as guilty of high treason to human nature. It is MURDER— and those who perpetuate it can be no better than MURDERERS—and, indeed, if the English people tamely look on they are accomplices."[14] Some Chartists, although not all, saw in Irish union with Great Britain the causes of the tragedy. Feargus O'Connor believed that the stranglehold on the countryside by wealthy Protestant landowners, propped up and enabled by their positions in Parliament and government, brought about the "oppression, tyranny and fraud" suffered by Irish peasants. He demanded repeal of the union of Ireland and Great Britain, a plank in the Chartist platform opposed by another of the movement's leaders, William Lovett (1800–1877). By the late 1840s, repeal of the union enjoyed mass support among Chartists, a position guaranteed to disturb government elites who watched as Europe erupted in a series of liberal/ nationalist revolutions in 1848.

Even with its call for the repeal of the Act of Union of 1801, the Chartist movement could not drum up broad-based support in Ireland. There, the repeal campaign, led by Daniel O'Connell, distanced itself from the policies and personnel of Chartism. O'Connell, who sat in Parliament, embraced laissez-faire, and had supported the Poor Law and other initiatives of the Whig administration, wished fervently that Ireland might reestablish its own legislature. But he was no republican and no democrat—he did not want to see Ireland separate from Great Britain, nor could he muster support for universal suffrage or for unionism. He urged his followers in the repeal campaign to remain aloof from Chartism, which they did, depriving both of greater potential.

Ultimately, O'Connell's bourgeois sensibility and adherence to Whig politics, both ideological and pragmatic, lost him control of the repeal issue. A new cadre of Irish nationalists, galvanized by the horrors of the famine and tired of O'Connell's conventional politics, would seek inspiration from revolutionaries abroad and form themselves into Young Ireland, seeking independence from Britain by any means necessary. In 1848, they engaged in a series of violent but ineffectual outbreaks across the country. They did little damage and rallied few to their cause, but their impact was felt in London just the same. In October 1848 Queen Victoria confided to her journal that the loyalty of Ireland was dubious, describing a country "quivering in our grasp, and ready to throw off her allegiance at any moment."[15]

The famine that proved so catastrophic to Ireland and the focus of much Chartist activity and pamphleteering visited Scotland as well, although the structural differences between the two countries meant that the scale of the disaster in Scotland turned out to be far less than that in Ireland. In 1846, the potato blight hit the Scottish Highlands, causing more than three-quarters of the potato crop to fail completely. Death rates in many of the Highland territories tripled as malnourished men, women, and children succumbed to typhus, dysentery, and influenza. It looked like Highland Scotland might go the way of ravaged Ireland.

It did not, fortunately, because the threat of starvation tailed off by the summer of 1847. In part this was a consequence of less dependence on the potato in Scotland and greater consumption of other foodstuffs such as grains and fish. In part, it reflected the fact that although authorities had to deal with millions of starving Irish, they had only some 200,000 or so Scots who desperately needed help. Government officials did send relief to the Scottish Highlands, but a significant amount of the distress was handled by private religious and charitable organizations, especially the Central Board of Management for Highland Relief. Local committees under the jurisdiction of the Central Board distributed food to families in return for their labor on a variety of public works projects ranging across the Highlands and the northern islands. To this day, one can still see some of the "destitution roads" built by those who received relief to avoid starvation.

But even these measures designed to ensure that recipients of relief would not fall into indolence and corruption did not satisfy some critics of the program. Stories and letters in *The Scotsman*, a liberal paper published in Edinburgh, frequently railed against the "lazy" Highlanders whose neediness drained the resources of "industrious" Lowland Scots. Charles Trevelyan, in particular, whose disdain and contempt for Irish Celts extended to the Celts of northern Scotland, believed that the famine served as a message from God that these inferior, slothful peoples must be taught the hard but moral lesson of throwing off their torpid ways and values and learning to work. Providing relief got in the way of sending that necessary message: "Next to allowing the people to die of hunger," he insisted, "the greatest evil that could happen would be their being habituated to depend upon public charity."[16] Trevelyan's influence on the Central Board proved strong enough to persuade it to implement the despised "destitution test," which required that an able-bodied adult work at least eight hours a day to receive a pound of meal. Only in this way, Trevelyan and others argued, could Highlanders be trained away from their habits of dissolution and immorality.

Relief efforts played their part in avoiding massive starvation in Highland Scotland, but by far the most effective measure proved to be the opportunities created by urban industrial centers within the country where work could be found. Ireland had few such outlets that would act as a release valve for surplus population. But Highlanders could migrate to cities and find work, and they did so in astonishing numbers. As much as one-third of the Highland population left their homes for employment elsewhere, and they did not return. In some parishes, the loss amounted to fully half of the prefamine population. Many of them migrated to Scottish and English cities, but with the help of assistance programs paid for by landlords, some 17,000 emigrated to Canada and Australia. Landlords feared that a rumored new poor law policy would require them to pay for relieving the distress of their tenants and calculated that it would be less expensive to subsidize their passages than to keep supporting them. As the 8th Duke of Argyll (1823–1900) put it in a letter, "I wish to send out those whom we would be obliged to feed if they stayed at home; to get rid of that class is *the object*."[17]

••

In the years between 1815 and 1848, Britain's social, economic, and political structures became transformed. Once a system characterized by ranks and orders, in which landed and commercial elites whose wealth derived from agriculture and commerce monopolized political power, it gave way to one in which frequently antagonistic classes vied with one another for political power within an economic system dominated by industry. After 1832, a classical liberal political system derived from a franchise restricted by property and gender qualifications came into being. It championed principles of meritocracy, individualism, free trade, and respectability. Apologists for the middle classes who gained political power with the Reform Act of 1832 explained their victory after the fact by referring to the so-called "inherent" bourgeois virtues of domesticity, drawing distinctions between the virtuous middle classes on the one hand and the purported debauched aristocracy and equally immoral working classes on the other. But working-class radicals' efforts to gain the right to vote continued long after their betrayal by former middle-class allies in 1832 in a movement known as Chartism. Their struggles extended to causes far beyond the realm of the United Kingdom itself, as we will see in the next chapter.

NOTES

1. See Henry Tobit Evans and Gwladys Tobit Evans, *Rebecca and Her Daughters: Being a History of the Agrarian Disturbances in Wales Known as "The Rebecca Riots,"* (Cardiganshire, 1910), reproduced as *Rebecca Riots!* 2010; David Williams, *The Rebecca Riots: A Study in Agrarian Discontent* (Cardiff, 1986); originally published 1955.

2. Thomas Carlyle, "A Mechanical Age" (1829), *Selections from the Edinburgh Review*, Vol. III, 1835, p. 93.
3. Quoted in Richard G. Wilkinson, "The English Industrial Revolution," in Donald Worster, ed., *The Ends of the Earth. Perspectives on Modern Environmental History* (Cambridge, 1988), pp. 91–92.
4. Quoted in Peter Aughton, *Liverpool, A People's History* (Preston, 1990), p. 129.
5. Friedrich Engels, *The Condition of the Working Class in England in 1844* (1845), p. 34.
6. Benjamin Disraeli, *Sybil, or the Two Nations* (Oxford, 1998, orig. 1845), p. 66.
7. See Catherine Hall, "Missionary Stories: Gender and Ethnicity in England in the 1830s and 1840s," in Lawrence Grossberg et al., *Cultural Studies* (New York, 1991), pp. 240–70.
8. Quoted in The Abolition Project. http://abolition.e2bn.org/people_65.html/.
9. See Dror Wahrman, *Imagining the Middle Class: The Political Representation of Class in Britain, c. 1780–1840* (Cambridge, 1995), ch. 9.
10. Quoted in Alice S. Rossi, ed., *The Feminist Papers: From Adams to de Beauvoir* (Lebanon, 1973), p. 134.
11. Quoted in Peter Fryer, *Staying Power. The History of Black People in Britain* (London, 1984), p. 239.
12. Quoted in Richard Ned Lebow, *White Britain and Black Ireland. The Influence of Stereotypes on Colonial Policy* (Philadelphia, 1976), pp. 39–40.
13. Quoted in Lebow, *White Britain and Black Ireland*, pp. 62, 63, 67.
14. Quoted in Terry Brotherstone and Liz Leicester, "Chartism, the Great Hunger and the 'Hugest Question,'" in Terry Brotherstone, Anna Clark, and Kevin Whelan, eds., *These Fissured Isles: Ireland, Scotland and British History, 1798–1848* (Edinburgh, 2005), p. 207.

TIMELINE

1823 Antislavery movement resumes

1829 Roman Catholic Relief Act

1830 Liverpool and Manchester Railway opens

Swing Riots

1832 Great Reform Act

1833 Abolition of slavery

Coercion Act in Ireland

East India Company monopoly ended

15. Quoted in Susan Kingsley Kent, *Queen Victoria: Gender and Empire* (New York, 2015), p.
16. Quoted in T. M. Devine, *The Scottish Nation, 1700–2007* (London, 2006), p. 416.
17. Quoted Devine, *The Scottish Nation*, pp. 420–21.

FURTHER READING

Terry Brotherstone, Anna Clark, and Kevin Whelan, eds., *These Fissured Isles: Ireland, Scotland and British History, 1798–1848*. Edinburgh, 2005.

T. M. Devine, *The Scottish Nation, 1700–2007*. London, 2006.

James Donnelly, *The Great Irish Potato Famine*. Stroud, 2001.

H. H. Lamb, *Climate, History and the Modern World*. London, 1982.

Richard Ned Lebow, *White Britain and Black Ireland. The Influence of Stereotypes on Colonial Policy*. Philadelphia, 1976.

Sonya Rose, *Limited Livelihoods: Gender and Class in Nineteenth-Century England*. Berkeley, 1992.

Wolfgang Schivelbusch, *The Railway Journey. The Industrialization of Time and Space in the Nineteenth-Century*. Berkeley, 1977.

Dorothy Thompson, *Outsiders: Class, Gender, and Nation*. London, 1993.

Dror Wahrman, *Imagining the Middle Class: The Political Representation of Class in Britain, c. 1780–1840*. Cambridge, 1995.

Richard G. Wilkinson, "The English Industrial Revolution," in Donald Worster, ed., *The Ends of the Earth. Perspectives on Modern Environmental History*. Cambridge, 1988.

David Williams, *The Rebecca Riots: A Study in Agrarian Discontent*. Cardiff: 1986, originally published 1955.

1834	New Poor Law Act
1838	Chartist movement begins
1843	Rebecca Riots
1845	Irish potato famine begins
1846	Corn Law repealed
1848	Chartism ends
1858	Parliament closed because of "Great Stink"

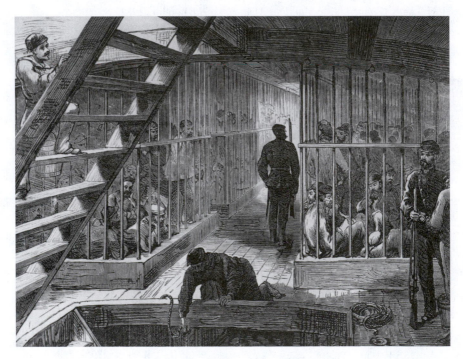
Prisoners being transported to Botany Bay, Australia.

CHAPTER 7

"LIBERAL EMPIRE," 1823–1873

Australia

Tasmania

On May 3, 1836, fifteen-year-old Agnes McMillan received a sentence of seven years' transportation to "parts beyond the seas" for the theft of a pair of stockings from a hosiery shop in Kilmarnock, a village twenty-two miles south of Glasgow. Abandoned by her father and neglected by her mother, who worked fourteen hours a day in a textile factory, Agnes had been on the streets for three years by the time of her arrest, singing for a few pennies here and there and stealing to keep herself clothed and fed. She boarded the prison ship *Westmoreland* in Woolwich and was issued a tin ticket with the number 253 impressed on it. It would serve as her identity tag on the three-and-a-half month voyage to Australia and her subsequent journey to the Cascades Female Factory on the island of Van Dieman's Land, modern-day Tasmania.

The Cascades Female Factory served as a site from which settlers selected the convicts who would labor on their holdings. Agnes was sent to the home of a Mr. Donahoo to act as a housemaid, performing endless domestic chores, chopping wood, and carrying water up and down the hills from Hobart Town. She had Sunday afternoons off, but toiled every other waking hour. Unable any longer to tolerate the drudgery and stigma of convict labor, she ran away, was caught, and returned to Cascades for a sentence of three months. Following her punishment, she was once again sent out, this time into the bush, where she encountered the most fantastic of animals and the most deadly of snakes. Frightened, repelled, and worked to the bone, Agnes again ran away and again was returned to the Cascades Female Factory for confinement. She repeated this pattern ten more times until her sentence was completed in 1843. She was twenty-three when she was released from Cascades.

Agnes teamed up with another former convict, William Roberts, who as a young man in Manchester had been caught stealing and was sentenced to fourteen years transportation. She and William ventured into the Huon Valley, where they set themselves to clearing a plot from the woods, building a cabin, and producing five children. They fared well, but by the late 1840s, as the number of convicts transported to the island increased, depression wracked Van Dieman's Land and made life more difficult. In addition to the economic problems they encountered, Agnes and William and their children found themselves the targets of resentment and hatred from settlers who despised the convicts. When gold was discovered in 1851 in the colony of Victoria on the Australian mainland, they were only too happy to pull up stakes and try their hand at gold digging. Along with hundreds of thousands of others—Australian settlers and former convicts, English, Scottish, Irish, and Welsh immigrants, and American and Chinese prospectors—the Roberts family made its way to the goldfields of Ballarat. And unlike most of their fellow miners, Agnes and William found enough gold to settle along the Richmond River of New South Wales, buy themselves a sawmill, and harvest red cedar. The rapidly developing colony ensured them a vibrant constomer base, even as it depleted the rain forests of the Australian colony.

Agnes McMillan's story incorporates elements from virtually every major economic, social, political, and imperial/colonial development of the fifty-year period between 1823 and 1873. Industrialization, population growth, social change, political upheaval, massive emigration, the establishment of settler colonies, and the resulting devastation of indigenous peoples in those lands—all these contributed to or characterize what historians describe as Britain's "liberal" empire.

••

"LIBERAL" EMPIRE

The economic and social difficulties of the years following the Napoleonic wars provided the impetus to pursue active economic expansion and settlement abroad. Lord Palmerston (1784–1865), who served as either foreign secretary or prime minister for most of the period this chapter addresses, orchestrated many of the initiatives that would ultimately make Britain one of the most powerful empires the world had ever seen. He feared that the economic depressions of the 1830s and 1840s would create a breakdown of the social order that the country simply could not withstand, and he constantly sought ways to find new markets for British goods that would help keep workers gainfully employed in factories and on the land. To that end he sanctioned the bombing of West African slave ports so as to eliminate the trade in human beings and institute "legitimate commerce" and entered a war against China to open it up to free trade—in opium. Emigration schemes seeking to ease the pressure on British society by a

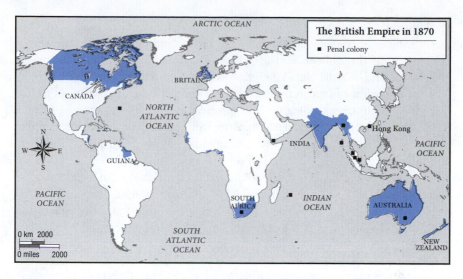

MAP 7.1

The British Empire in 1870

burgeoning population growth sent thousands of Scots, Irish, Welsh, and English to the white settlement colonies of South Africa, Canada, Australia, and New Zealand. Millions of indentured servants and convict laborers from India, China, and Southeast Asia journeyed across the oceans to work plantations in Mauritius, the Caribbean, South Africa, and Australia.

In the years following the Napoleonic wars, Britain established control over huge areas in South Africa, Asia, the West Indies, and Canada, called British North America at the time. In the decades between 1840 and 1870, it expanded its holdings by adding new colonies in Australia, New Zealand, British Columbia, Hong Kong, Lower Burma, Natal, the Transvaal, parts of what would become Nigeria and Sierra Leone, the Gold Coast, and the Punjab, Sind, Berar, and Oudh in India. Although it granted various measures of representative government to the white settlement colonies in Canada, South Africa, Australia, and New Zealand by 1860, it progressively tightened its control over millions of peoples of color.

The classical liberalism we saw being developed in the previous chapter contained within it a number of potentially incompatible elements, making it possible for individuals of different beliefs to band together under its rubric. The thinking of political economists who emphasized the individual's right to possess things readily came into conflict with notions of justice and equality stressed by others. But liberals of all stripes did share a number of tenets in common that gave the doctrine a coherence that transcended these differences. Underlying the principles of liberalism as various thinkers understood them was a fundamental belief in the universality of human nature and complete faith that the influences of law, education, and free trade could dramatically transform human beings. These liberal assumptions about human nature held true for peoples as far afield as Asia, North America, Africa, and Australasia and informed liberal approaches to British imperial rule in the period from the 1820s to the early 1850s. Reformers called on and referred to notions of domesticity and the ideology of separate spheres to explain and justify their actions, endowing the subjects of their campaigns with a humanity that differed from that of Britons only in degree. To be sure, liberal reformers and missionaries regarded Aboriginal, African, Chinese, and Indian men as children who needed to be nurtured and taught before they could grow into manhood. They utilized an ideology of similarity to themselves to make the case for inculcating what they saw as enlightened practices among Indians, North American Indians, Africans, Australian Aborigines, and New Zealand Maori.

Whereas liberalism made its entrance on Britain's home stage with the Reform Act of 1832, it appeared earlier in India, with the arrival in 1828 of Lord William Bentinck (1774–1839) as governor-general. Bentinck proceeded to implement reforms in law, education, and administration that would excite the envy of liberals at home. Employees of the East India Company such John Stuart Mill (1806–1873) and Charles Trevelyan and governmental officials like Thomas Macaulay (1800–1859) looked forward with confidence to the day when enlightened and just government, free trade, and education would uplift Indian peoples so that they would be ready for self-government. Like their eighteenth-century predecessors, they regarded Indians as indolent, sensual, wanting in "mental liberty and individuality," and in thrall to despotic rule. With British examples of firm but just government before them, and education in the ways of British law, thought, and morality, even Indians could aspire to self-rule. "Trained by us to happiness and independence," Trevelyan exclaimed, "India will remain the proudest monument of British benevolence." Macaulay echoed him in a speech in 1833 on the renewal of the EIC's charter. India, he noted, might someday, having "become instructed in European knowledge," "demand European institutions" of self-government. Such a development was only to be hoped for, he insisted, and "whenever it comes, it will be the proudest day in English history."[1]

Making self-governing Indians out of the existing population, "sunk in the lowest depths of slavery and superstition," required a wholesale reconstruction of Indian culture and society. Indians would have to be turned into Englishmen. As Macaulay's Minute on Education put it in 1835, the British must not simply educate a discrete group of Indians in English language and law so that it might help to govern the subcontinent; rather, they must create Indians who were "English in taste, in opinions, in morals and in intellect." Self-governing Indians would be those who had imbibed "our arts and our morals, our literature and our laws."[2] Indeed, in the 1830s and 1840s, the British trained a cadre of Indians, many of them Bengali Hindus, in English literature, law, history, and philosophy.

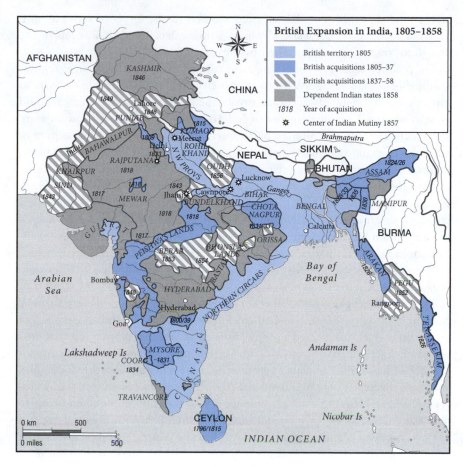

MAP 7.2
British Expansion in India, 1805–1858

Western in thought and customs, these educated Indians were often more British than the British, whose elites were educated in classical Latin and Greek rather than in English languages and literatures.

Instituting reform of legal procedure; tax collection; land ownership, usage, and tenure; education; and administrative practices proved far easier than implementing religious or cultural change, but efforts to raise Indian "morality" to a level approximating that of the British proceeded apace nonetheless. These revolved around British outrage at what they considered the "degraded" state of Indian women at the hands of Indian men, in keeping with the widespread European belief that the treatment of women in any given place provided the measure of its civilization. Closed off and confined in the *zenana*, covered by the veil, Indian women, regarded by the British as especially sexual, served as the marker by means of which Indian immorality was gauged. Since Indian men would do nothing to lift up their women to the levels of modesty and purity demanded by domestic ideology, Britons declaimed, it was left to the British to "rescue" them from their own men.

The practice of *sati*, or widow burning, offered to Britons the most egregious example of Indian savagery. It provides a clear instance of Britain's efforts to suppress crucial elements of Indian involvement in its abolition so that it could present itself as a heroic defender of Indian womanhood against Indian men. The spectacle of a living woman being burned to death on the funeral pyre of her dead husband, despite the relative infrequency with which it took place, excited condemnation among reformers and evangelicals at home and in India. Indians themselves, led by the liberal reformer Ram Mohan Roy (1772–1833), played a central role in the initiative that led Britain to outlaw *sati* in 1829, but credit for ending what Indians no less than Britons regarded as an abuse of Indian women was laid exclusively in the laps of Britons. Liberals and evangelicals could dramatically demonstrate their own "manliness" and "civilization" by stamping out such "ungodly" practices and bringing enlightened, Christian, liberal reforms in their wake.

Perhaps the single greatest liberal reform—the abolition of slavery in 1833, enacted in the empire in 1834—had an enormous impact on Indian people. The liberation of Africans created a severe shortage of labor on plantations that produced sugar, cotton, coffee, tea, rice, and other commodities. To compensate for the lack of labor, EIC officials and other British agents put together a complex and sophisticated system of indentured labor that contracted with Indian workers and shipped them to a variety of lands across the empire. Hired on three- to five-year contracts, Indian men and women without prospects at home traveled to the Caribbean islands, Ceylon, Malaya, Burma, Australia and New Zealand, and South Africa. Half a million Indians went to the Caribbean starting in 1838; 450,000 to Mauritius, 150,000 to Natal in South Africa, and thousands more to Southeast Asia. Because they often went as part of whole families, many of them never returned home, instead establishing themselves as part of the local communities and in some places, such as Trinidad, creating a distinctly Indian-inflected culture.

The system of indentured servitude was modeled after an earlier experiment carried out by EIC officials using convict labor in Mauritius. Between 1815 and 1837 the British transported some 1,500 Indian convicts to labor on plantations and build roads and bridges on the island. Mauritius was but one locale in a large network of British penal colonies in South Africa (Robben Island), the Andaman Islands, Burma, Panang, Malacca, Singapore, Australia, Bermuda, and Aden. Convict labor not only emptied the jails of India and other colonies, thus cutting down considerably on administrative costs, but also helped to establish the infrastructure necessary for empire-building. We usually think of transportation as a phenomenon in which British convicts settled Australia, but far many more prisoners from within the empire itself were shipped to other colonies to serve out their (often considerable) sentences.

Without them, Britain could not have established itself as the world's greatest imperial power by the middle of the nineteenth century.

The Opium Wars

Liberals' advocacy of free trade led them to pursue policies that to modern sensibilities look decidedly coercive. The Opium Wars of 1839–1842 and 1856–1860, during which British warships forced the Chinese government to open up the country to trade in the addictive drug, exemplify the contradictions and even hypocrisy of Britain's commitment to laissez-faire. French for "let it do" or "let it be," laissez-faire describes the policy of letting things happen as they would without interference from government or other organized entities such as chartered companies holding monopolies on trade. By the 1830s, the EIC had been engaged in commerce in opium for a number of decades, although its importation to and use in China had been banned by the Chinese emperor in 1799. Ostensibly honoring the ban by refraining from selling the drug in China outright, the company instead sold it to independent Indian and British merchants who smuggled it into Canton, the only port open to "foreign" trade, as the Chinese regarded it. Opium sales earned the company the revenues it needed to pay for the tons of Chinese tea and Chinese silks so beloved by Britons. British goods held no appeal for Chinese consumers; the only commodity they would pay for in the silver bullion required by sellers of tea and silk was opium. The British government, for its part, taxed the sale of the narcotic heavily, earning the revenues it needed to balance its budget. Indian merchants had their own motivations to ply China with opium. By the early part of the nineteenth century, they were buying large quantities of the textiles being manufactured in British factories, and to pay for the mass-produced cotton cloth, they had to sell more opium.

In 1833, as we have seen, Parliament did away with the EIC's monopoly on trade with China, opening the door to private concerns hankering to capitalize on the consumer revolution we saw unfolding in Chapter 3. The liberalizing of trade increased the amount of tea imported to Britain fourfold; the need to pay for all this tea increased the trade in opium concomitantly. In 1830, for example, merchants in association with the EIC sold 18,000 chests of opium in China. In 1833, that number had risen to a whopping 30,000 chests. The profits to be earned from trade with China—which of necessity required the buying and selling of opium—attracted large numbers of Britons. The first and most influential, two Scots named William Jardine (1784–1843) and James Matheson (1796–1878), formed Jardine Matheson & Co. in 1834 and soon dominated the commerce in the region.

The incidence of opium addiction in China alarmed the emperor, Daoquang, who sent his emissary, High Commissioner Lin Zexu, to Canton in 1836 to enforce the ban on its sale and use. When the incorruptible Lin failed to impose his will on the western traders, he amassed troops and lay siege to their factories

A PLACE IN TIME

The Opium Wars

The opening of China to the opium trade by armed force succeeded because of a technological marvel built in the shipyards of Liverpool, the iron steamship *Nemesis*. Built entirely of iron by the Birkenhead Iron Works Company, the *Nemesis* was commissioned by the Secret Committee of the East India Company. Secrecy seems to have been the point, for the vessel never appeared on the EIC's list of ships, and when it departed Liverpool in 1839 its owners put it out that is was bound for Odessa. The *Hampshire Telegraph* suspected otherwise. The *Nemesis* had been issued letters of marque by the Admiralty, licensing it to attack and seize enemy ships in time of war, and on the basis of this fact the paper concluded that it was built to "go against the Chinese."[3] Indeed it was. The vessel carried two thirty-pounder guns mounted on pivots; a number of six-pounders; and a rocket launcher. Its flat bottom enabled it to navigate the shallow waterways and rivers around Canton and Peking. It arrived in the Gulf of Canton in November 1840, having the distinction of being the first steam ship to round the Cape of Good Hope.

On January 7, 1841, the privately owned *Nemesis*, captained by officers of the Royal Navy, steamed up the Canton River to Chuanbi, where it and a number of other ships bombarded the fort occupied by Chinese troops and took out their heavy guns. An invasion force of British and Indian troops

The East India Company's steamer *Nemesis* attacking Chinese war junks during the Opium War, 1841.

went ashore and proceeded to engage in "a frightful slaughter," as one marine described it, even as their officers tried "to restrain their men."[4] Six hundred Chinese soldiers died and another 100 surrendered; not a single British or Indian fighter died in the massacre.

Three weeks later, the *Nemesis* and other ships shelled the city, reducing it to rubble and then using rockets to take out the Chinese warships that had gathered at the mouth of the river. *The Nemesis* continued upriver to Anson's Bay, where it encountered fifteen Chinese war vessels. It fired on one of them with a rocket, fortuitously hitting the junk's powder stores and blowing the ship to bits. As the captain of the *Nemesis* pointed out, "one of the most formidable engines of destruction which any vessel, particularly a steamer, can make use of is the Congreve rocket, a most terrible weapon when judiciously applied, especially where there are combustible materials to act upon. The very first rocket fired from the Nemesis was seen to enter the large junk against which it was directed, near that of the admiral, and almost the instant afterwards it blew up with a terrific explosion, launching into eternity every soul on board, and pouring forth its blaze like the mighty rush of fire from a volcano. The instantaneous destruction of the huge body seemed appalling to both sides engaged. The smoke, and flame, and thunder of the explosion, with the broken fragments falling round, and even portions of dissevered bodies scattering as they fell, were enough to strike with awe, if not with fear, the stoutest heart that looked upon it."[5] Crewmen on board the other junks, terrified by the explosive might of this unusual new ship, jumped overboard as the vessels fled.

The appearance of the iron-clad steamship with its huge guns and rocket launcher provoked dread and panic in the Chinese, who had not seen its like before. The British used the psychological impact it induced to their advantage, venturing further up the river toward Canton in February 1841. Along the way, as the *Nemesis* and its sister ships bombarded forts designed to defend the city, their inhabitants fled and spread news of the unprecedented and horrifying destruction inflicted by the steam vessel. As they approached Canton, 10,000 of its citizens ran for their lives. The terror factor of the *Nemesis* was complemented by the power of the steamship. The capacity of its engines—although at 120 horsepower relatively slight by later standards—was such that in May 1841 it was able to tow seventy British sailing ships carrying 2,000 marines upriver to a harbor north of Canton.

The *Nemesis*, Britain's "secret weapon" designed and built in Liverpool, played a crucial role in imposing the opium trade on China in one of the first examples of what would come to be called "gunboat diplomacy." British technology would make possible further encroachments on lands and peoples across the globe over the next seventy-five years.

and residences, forcing them to leave and confiscating the goods they left behind. Many merchants retreated to the safety of the harbor at Hong Kong, a sleepy village sixty-nine nautical miles to the southwest of Canton. In 1839, Lin allowed western traders to return to Canton, but only after signing a pledge that they would not engage in the opium trade. The penalty for violating their pledge would be death.

But the riches to be gained from opium finally overrode any considerations of prudence the traders might have entertained. Jardine Matheson & Co. determined to continue to traffic in the drug and announced that it had no intention of signing any pledge. At the same time, it and a number of other British concerns wrote to Parliament, demanding that the British government send troops to extract from the Chinese compensation for the goods they had lost to confiscation. Palmerston, the foreign secretary, ever on the lookout for markets for British goods, acceded to their petition, dispatching warships and troops to China in October 1839. They entered the Gulf of Canton in June 1840, blasting their way upriver to Canton and then up along the coast to Beijing. By 1842 they had reduced the emperor to signing away much of his country's sovereignty in the Treaty of Nanking, which ceded Hong Kong to Britain and opened up a number of ports to "free trade." Free trade at the point of a gun, at any rate, which *The Times* acknowledged in its reference to the British incursion as the work of "Early Victorian Vikings." Most of the British press hailed the war and the treaty it compelled; the *Illustrated London News* noted that "it secures us a few round millions of dollars and no end of very refreshing tea." Neither the treaty nor the press made any mention of the commerce in opium that stood at the heart of the invasion of China, although perhaps the *Illustrated London News* meant to allude to the ignominious *casus belli* when it called the conflict "a war which satisfies our interests more than our vanity and rather gives over glory a preponderance to gain."[6] That gain grew ever more dramatically over the next decades as Hong Kong became the main site for the transshipment of opium. At the time of the Treaty of Nanking, the taxes collected from the sale of opium made up 10 percent of the Exchequer's revenues.

Despite remaining illegal in China, the opium trade went on, largely because of its salutary effect on the balance of trade between the two nations. The Chinese still found British textiles and other manufactures inferior to the goods they produced on their own, whereas Britons continued to consume Chinese tea and silks with abandon, leaving Britain with a massive outflow of silver bullion to pay for them. Opium only partly made up for the difference, but without it, the trade imbalance would have been crippling. In 1856, increasing resentment against the British and the terms of the Treaty of Nanking spilled over into violence when Chinese officials in Canton raided and took over a ship that ostensibly belonged to a British merchant (it was actually a Chinese-owned vessel, with a British front man providing cover). In response, British naval forces bombarded Canton and, in sporadic battles with mostly ineffective Chinese troops over the next four years, gradually moved inland from Canton and from Hong Kong, reaching the capital at Peking in 1860. British and allied French troops looted and then burned the emperor's summer palaces, compelling the Chinese to accede to the terms of the Peking Convention that ended the war. By it the British compelled the Chinese government to legalize the opium trade; gained Kowloon, considerably enlarging its holdings in Hong Kong; opened up ten additional Chinese ports to foreign trade; and won the rights, along with France, Russia, and the United States, for its citizens and merchants to travel throughout interior China and navigate the Yangzi River without hindrance. China also had to pay a huge indemnity in silver bullion to pay for the costs of the war. When the court was forced to recognize Queen Victoria as the equal of the emperor, the humiliation of the divine ruler—and his subjects—was complete. The industrial might of the British empire had been impressively displayed against the ruler of "all the lands under heaven." To add insult to insult, one of the British officers stole from the emperor's palace a lap dog that had been bred to look like the lion on the Chinese imperial crest and took it home to his queen. She named the Pekinese "Lootie," a fitting sobriquet for a pet seized by marauding soldiers.

As a consequence of the second opium war of 1856–1860, the British opened up Chinese markets for their goods even further. Cotton manufactures purchased by the Chinese rose by a factor of four between 1856 and 1875 or so; opium sales nearly doubled in the twenty years following 1859. By 1870, taxes received from the sale of opium constituted 14 percent of the Exchequer's revenues, up from 10 percent in 1842. Given how much overall British output and commerce had expanded over that period, the increase is all the more impressive. The cultivation of and trade in opium stood at the heart of the colonial economies of Southeast Asia, requiring huge supplies of labor to work the fields that produced the crop. From Singapore and Hong Kong, Britain both developed networks of Chinese migrant workers—called "coolies"—and directed the commerce in the drug. Impoverished and facing a bleak future in their own land, Chinese migrant workers contracted out their labor for a specific period of time. But because they inevitably incurred debt in the course of their transport and at their destinations, they ended up paying off their obligations for many years more. Contract labor entailed on them a kind of debt slavery that was difficult to avoid and took years to pay off.

THE WHITE COLONIES OF SETTLEMENT

Many of the events we have discussed in previous chapters—population growth, industrialization, economic downturns, urbanization, and, especially, the potato famines in Ireland and Highland Scotland—contributed to a significant outmigration of Britons to its white colonies of settlement in Canada, South Africa, Australia, and New Zealand in the years following the end of the Napoleonic wars. In the five years between 1815 and 1820, 170,000 British men and women (mostly voluntarily) left their homes to travel to new and faraway lands to seek a new life. More would have gone if they could have, but did not have the funds to make the long and expensive trip. In 1820, for instance, a governmental program to establish 4,000 British settlers in South Africa received 80,000 applications. Approximately 20,000 Britons settled there by the 1840s and 180,000 emigrants voyaged to Australia and New Zealand between 1828—when the cost of the trip fell by half—and 1842. Almost 2 million Britons immigrated to Canada between 1815 and 1860. This "explosive colonization" of British and Irish settlers, as one historian has described it,[7] replicated British society in far-flung corners of the world, vastly increased the lands owned or controlled by Britons, and, not incidentally, entailed the displacement and even annihilation of the indigenous peoples who occupied those territories prior to their arrival. Moreover, although we refer to the "white colonies of settlement" as if they were made up of an ethnically homogenous population, Canada, Australia, New Zealand, and South Africa were marked by many of the same ethnic and religious tensions that characterized Great Britain.

The very existence of the white colonies of settlement provoked important philosophical and political questions. With the experience of the American colonies still strong in their minds, some Britons in the metropole believed that the white colonies should be let go before they proved to be a source of trouble. Evangelicals, on the other hand, especially those in the Aborigines' Protection Society, dedicated to "protecting the defenseless and promoting the advancement of uncivilized tribes," doubted that white colonists could be counted on to treat indigenous peoples or descendants of enslaved Africans with the respect they deserved; they insisted that rule from Britain was required to protect them from oppression. Political and military strategists saw in the white settlements the means by which to ensure their control of the oceans and feared that if they were let go, other powers would simply scoop them up to further their own ambitions. Colonial reformers such as Edward Gibbon Wakefield (1796–1862) believed further colonization of the white territories would alleviate the social problems Britain faced as industrialization displaced thousands of people and hunger stalked the land. "No pains should be spared to teach the labouring classes to regard the colonies as the land of promise" he wrote in 1839, "which it should be their highest ambition to be able to reach. Nor does this matter concern the poorer orders among us alone: in the colonies, a large proportion of the children or grandchildren of the highest families in this land must be contented to fix their abode, unless they resolve to drag on a life of dependence and indigence here. . . . If adequate encouragement be held out to enterprising young men of rank and connections; if young men and women, in the intermediate ranks of life, are accustomed to look to the colonies as the most certain means of obtaining a comfortable settlement; and if the poor could be persuaded that it would be better for them to purchase a passage, by binding themselves to serve as bondsmen a few years after their arrival in the colonies, than to wear out an abject and hopeless life at home, the country might be materially relieved of the useless population by which it is likely soon to be encumbered."[8]

For the white settlers themselves, colonial rule had begun to rankle, and sometimes vociferous demands for self-government could be heard regularly.

Canada

British North America in 1815 consisted of Newfoundland, Prince Edward Island, Nova Scotia, New Brunswick, Quebec (which in 1791 had been split into English-speaking Upper Canada and French-speaking Lower Canada), and Rupert's Land, a vast territory controlled by the Hudson's Bay Company stretching from the lands around Hudson's Bay westward to Manitoba, Saskatchewan, and Alberta. The numbers and welfare of indigenous Canadian peoples in the northeast had been reduced significantly over the past century and a half as contact with Europeans brought devastating disease, depleted hunting and farming lands, and exacerbated warfare, leaving fewer than 25,000 aborigines in the eastern lands by the middle of the nineteenth century. Most of the white population lived in the northeastern regions of the continent in what one historian has described as "various centres of ethnic settlement."[9] About one-quarter of the 2.5 million Britons living in British North America in 1850 or so hailed originally from Ireland; 16 percent of them came from Scotland and 20 percent from England and Wales. Scottish Protestants constituted by far the majority of whites living in the lands held by the Hudson's Bay Company in the far north and west of the country. Some 750,000 descendants of early French settlers lived mainly in Lower Canada, whereas people of mixed indigenous and French or Scottish background—called "Métis" by the French and "half-breeds" by the English—populated the area around what is today Manitoba in the Red River settlement. Further to the west, 100,000 or so aboriginal peoples lived mostly undisturbed by Europeans, but that situation would change dramatically after 1850. The presence of French and Irish Catholics fueled religious hatreds among Scottish and English Protestants, which only increased after the 1845 famine propelled 300,000 more Irish emigrants to settle in Canada. The same Orange Orders that sprang up in Ireland to counter what Protestants regarded as a Catholic threat appeared in the North American colonies as well in the 1830s.

In 1837 and 1838, rebellions against established political authority broke out in Lower and Upper Canada. Informed both by British liberal thought that emphasized notions of free trade and laissez-faire and by American ideas about agrarian independence and democracy, some reformers demanded that the political rights enjoyed by Britons at home be extended to the North American colonies; others sought a reform of landholding policies that benefitted the upper classes. In Lower Canada, a French Canadian nationalism played an important part in the rebellion as well. British forces easily put down the uprisings, executing some of the leaders and transporting hundreds of participants to Australia. These events reinvigorated a debate about the status of white colonies of settlement that had roiled Britons for some time now. Just how were Britons overseas to be governed? Did they—should they—possess the same rights and responsibilities as Britons at home? If so, what kind of relationship between colony and metropole should prevail? These questions became more pointed and more relevant in the aftermath of the Reform Act of 1832. The rebellions of 1837–1838 compelled British authorities to act.

The British prime minister, Lord Melbourne, turned to the man who had helped pass the Reform Act of 1832, Radical Jack Durham (1792–1840), to fashion a policy that would settle the question. The Durham Report, issued in 1839, proved to be a momentous document, although it was not accepted as official policy until 1846, when Prime Minister Lord John Russell (1792–1878), Durham's brother-in-law, finally put it into practice. The report recommended that the white colonies of settlement be regarded as extensions of British society and of the British state and, as such, urged that they be seen as polities entirely capable of governing themselves. White settlers, as merely displaced Britons, could be counted on to remain loyal to their queen and country and therefore need not be ruled by coercion from the metropole. As responsible members of the British empire, they should be permitted to form their own governments, the governor-general—formerly appointed by and answerable to the queen's government—now answerable to the elected legislatures of the white colonies.

The acceptance of the Durham Report meant that far-reaching self-government would, over the next twenty years, come to most of the white colonies of settlement. In British North America, Nova Scotia and the two Canadas—having been joined in the United Province of Canada containing Ontario and Quebec in 1841—won responsible government in 1848. Prince Edward Island followed in 1851, New Brunswick in 1854, and Newfoundland in 1855. London retained only the power to conduct foreign relations, make constitutions, carry on overseas trade, and dispose of public lands.

After years of tensions, Britain and the United States agreed in 1846 to set the 49th parallel as the boundary between the two nations running all the way to the Pacific. Britain ceded Oregon to the United States and established the island of Vancouver as a crown colony in 1849. When, eight years later, gold was found on the mainland, hundreds of miners from the United States flooded north across the border to seek their fortune. Fearful of an American effort to annex these lands, Britain in 1859 quickly, if reluctantly, declared them to be the new colony of British Columbia. Within two years, the white population had reached 50,000. In 1866, Vancouver and British Columbia joined together to form a single administrative unit.

In 1867, the four colonies of Quebec, Ontario, Nova Scotia, and New Brunswick joined together to form the Dominion of Canada, with its capital at Ottawa. This new, self-governing possession of the crown expanded dramatically in 1869 when the Hudson's Bay Company ceded its huge tracts of territory across the continental land mass to the new Canadian government; British Columbia joined it in 1871, as did Prince Edward Island in 1873, creating an enormous nation stretching from the Atlantic to the Pacific oceans. (Newfoundland remained apart from the Dominion of Canada until 1909.) The planned transcontinental

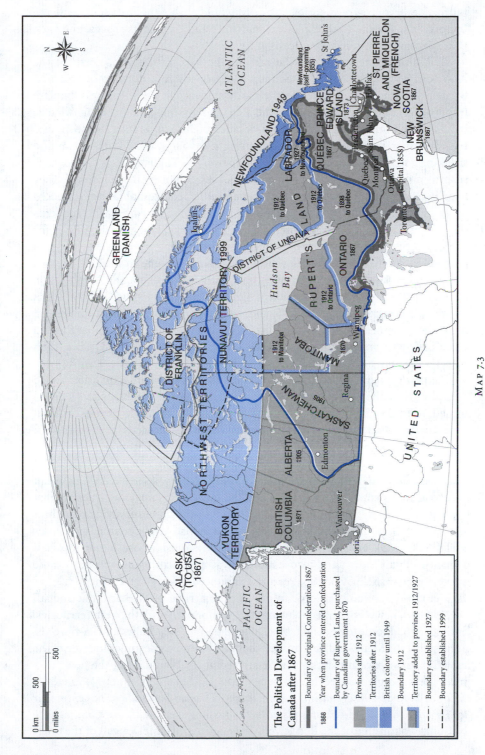

ATLANTIC
OCEAN

St John's

Newfoundland
(self-governing
1855)

ST PIERRE
AND MIQUELON
(FRENCH)

NOVA
SCOTIA
1867

Halifax

NEWFOUNDLAND 1949

PRINCE
EDWARD
ISLAND
1873

Charlottetown

NEW
BRUNSWICK
1867

Fredericton
Saint John

LABRADOR
1927
to Newfoundland

QUÉBEC
1867

Québec

1912
to Québec

RUPERT'S
LAND

1912
to Québec

1898
to Québec

Montreal
Ottawa
(capital 1858)

GREENLAND
(DANISH)

Iqaluit

DISTRICT OF UNGAVA

Hudson
Bay

ONTARIO
1867

Toronto

NEWFOUNDLAND 1949

NUNAVUT TERRITORY 1999

DISTRICT OF
FRANKLIN

NORTHWEST TERRITORIES

1912
to Québec

1912
to Ontario

Winnipeg

1912
to Manitoba

MANITOBA
1870

SASKATCHEWAN
1905

Regina

YUKON
TERRITORY

BRITISH
COLUMBIA
1871

ALBERTA
1905

Edmonton

Vancouver

Victoria

UNITED STATES

ALASKA
(TO USA
1867)

PACIFIC
OCEAN

N
W   E
S

The Political Development of
Canada after 1867

1868   Boundary of original Confederation 1867

              Year when province entered Confederation

              Boundary of Rupert's Land, purchased
              by Canadian government 1870

              Provinces after 1912

              Territories after 1912

              British colony until 1949

              Boundary 1912

              Territory added to province 1912/1927

              Boundary established 1927

              Boundary established 1999

0 km   500   500

0 miles   500

MAP 7.3

The Political Development of Canada after 1867

railroad, everyone agreed enthusiastically, would enable the British to settle the "empty" lands of the west, exploit its resources and civilize its spaces, and keep the expansionist-minded Americans at bay.

Well, almost everybody. In the area to the west of Ontario, north of the American border, the Métis, a seminomadic, racially mixed group of men and women who prided themselves on their independence in the wilderness, hunted, trapped, fished, and traded along the Red and Assiniboine rivers in what is modern-day Manitoba. Composed of decades of Indian, French, Scottish, and Irish intermarriage, most of them espousing a devout Roman Catholicism and speaking a rich patois of French, Cree, Chippewa, and English, Métis did not consider themselves "Canadian" and especially not subjects of the British empire. They lived in close proximity to the only European settlement west of Ontario, the Red River colony, a frontier outpost settled mostly by Scots. At Fort Garry (modern-day Winnipeg), traders carried out a vibrant commerce; along the Red River for some twenty miles or so, farmers homesteaded and established an Anglo-Saxon community similar to what they would have found at home in Britain. The two communities clashed with one another on a fairly regular basis, the Anglo-Saxon settlers distrusting the Métis as violent, liquor-fueled, dangerous Catholic aliens and the Métis regarding the Anglo-Saxons as agents of an expansionist empire that sought to put an end to their way of life. When they learned in 1869 that the Red River colony was now to be governed by a new authority based in Ottawa, their fears appeared to have come true.

The new Canadian government had decided that westward expansion would take place from the jumping-off point of the Red River settlement, which, it determined, needed to be reinforced by the addition of more Anglo-Saxons sent out from Ontario who would serve as a counterweight to the Métis, the Americans, and the French Canadian Catholic missions. It sent out a party of military surveyors to determine the best possible sites for the new settlers, a step the Métis seized on to make known their resentment. Fully aware that new settlement would mean an end of the openness of the prairie and the hunting, fishing, and trapping that undergirded the Métis lifestyle, a number of them accosted a surveying party outside of Fort Garry. Their leader, a feisty, buckskin-clad young man named Louis Riel (1844–1885), an ardent Catholic and fiery activist whose father was half French and half Indian and whose mother was a Frenchwoman, stepped on the surveying chain held by one soldier and announced, "You go no further."[10]

Riel mustered a militia force to prevent the arrival of William MacDougall (1822–1905), newly appointed lieutenant-governor of the North-West Territories, as the area had come to be called. MacDougall despised Catholics and half-breeds, as he styled the Métis, and determined that they would come under the rule of the new Canadian government. When he arrived at the boundary of the new province, Riel's people handed him a paper that decreed, "*Le Comité National des Métis de la Rivière Rouge intime à Monsieur McDougall l'ordre de ne pas entrer sur le Territoire du Nord-Ouest sans une permission spéciale de ce Comité*—The National Committee of the Red River Métis notifies Mr. McDougall of the order that he is not to enter the North-West Territories without special permission from the Committee."[11] In the meantime, Riel and 100 followers had made their way to Fort Garry and seized authority, assuring people there that they were not rebelling against Canadian or British rule but simply seeking to negotiate the terms by which the area would be incorporated into the new confederation of Canada. To that end, Riel called a convention made up of both English-speaking and French-speaking members; when some of the Anglo-Saxon settlers protested, he threw seventy of them in the stockade. MacDougall slunk back to Ottawa.

Depictions of Louis Riel's rebellion.

From London, colonial authorities urged restraint on Canadian officials. For the time being, the Canadian government chose a moderate course, trying to cajole the Métis into submission. If they followed the orders of the government and gave up the province, the governor-general declared, they would be allowed to go free without punishment. In the meantime, in the convention at Fort Garry, a significant portion of both Métis and Anglo-Saxons were being won over by the argument of an emissary from the Hudson's Bay Company that confederation with Canada would respect all of their civil and religious rights, confirm them in their property ownership, and confer on them the same rights that all British subjects of the dominion, no matter their race or religion, enjoyed. They were invited to send their own representatives to Ottawa to "explain the wants and wishes of the Red River people, as well as to discuss and arrange for the representation of the country in Parliament," a prospect that was met with approbation.[12] But just when it seemed that the rebellion had been forestalled, violence broke out when settlers attacked Fort Garry and freed the prisoners Riel had captured when he took over the fort. A local Scotsman and a Métis were killed in the melee; when the would-be liberators tried to return to their farms, they were stopped and thrown into the brig. One of them, Thomas Scott, an Orangeman who was known for his hatred of the Métis, was charged with taking up arms against the Red River government, found guilty in an ad hoc trial, and executed by a drunken firing squad. Public opinion in Ottawa was outraged.

Despite heightened feelings against the Métis, the delegation that had made its way to Ottawa to "arrange for the representation of the country in Parliament" received assurances that their rights would be protected. By the Manitoba Act of 1870, a new province by that name would be established, 1.4 million acres of which were to be given over to the Métis in perpetuity. The act recognized the French language, provided separate schools, and guaranteed existing land titles and occupancies. The government confided to the delegates that an imperial army would have to be sent to Fort Garry, but only to placate those who had been so outraged by Scott's murder, as they saw it; Riel would remain in control until a new governor arrived, and his militia could maintain its presence until relieved by the new force. Importantly, the act did not refer to anything like amnesty, although the delegates were told repeatedly that one was forthcoming and that all would be well. The Métis, it appeared, had won the day, preserving their heritage and way of life and claiming their rightful place in the new confederation of Canada.

But the death of Thomas Scott had not been forgotten, and the presence of a half-caste Catholic rebel at the head of the new province was never going to stand. The amnesty promised initially by the governor-general and reiterated by officials to the Red River delegates never materialized. Nor did the armed force envisioned to be a "benevolent constabulary" ever consider itself formed for that purpose. Instead, under the command of Colonel Garnet Joseph Wolseley (1833–1913), the army that rode out from Ottawa took as its charge the punishment of a rebel force. Wolseley, an Anglo-Irish Protestant with a profound dislike of Catholics, and moreover, a veteran of campaigns in Burma, the Crimea, India, and China, regarded Riel's rebellion as part of a Catholic conspiracy to block westward expansion of the empire. His mission, as he and his officers and men saw it, was to defeat these subversive Catholic elements and humiliate Riel and his followers. Many of them ardent Orangemen, they looked forward to waging "war" on the rebel Métis.

They were never given the chance. Realizing, finally, just what kind of armed force they were dealing with, Riel and his men abandoned Fort Garry, leaving open the south gate for Wolseley's charging cavalry officers. Disheartened by such a denouement, Wolseley ordered that the Union Jack be raised above the fort and a royal salute be fired from the cannons he had brought along on his misguided adventure, which marked the end of the Métis resistance in Canada. The troops headed back east, and Fort Garry grew into the bustling city of Winnipeg, from which, as expansionists had envisaged, the expansion of Canada westward went on apace.

For indigenous peoples, as for the Métis, representative and responsible government for white colonists spelled disaster, as humanitarians and abolitionists back in Britain had feared, and on which grounds they had opposed responsible government in the white colonies of settlement across the empire. White settlement and expansion necessarily took place at the expense of native peoples, as colonists and colonizers confiscated land and interrupted the migration patterns of bison and other animals that provided the food eaten by aboriginal peoples. Following the Red River debacle, the government in Ottawa sought to avoid conflict with the bands of aboriginals on the plains by signing treaties with them that created land reserves and promised the seeds, tools, and instruction that would enable them to farm the land. The treaties also guaranteed hunting and fishing rights. Facing the depletion of bison stocks, their lives and way of life endangered by encroaching white settlement, the 34 First Nations, as the native peoples called themselves, had little choice but to accede to the terms, which, in any event, proved largely illusory. White expansion continued apace. In 1872, the Dominion Lands Act provided free plots of 160 acres to settlers, further intruding on indigenous people's livelihoods; the following year, the government set up the North-West Mounted Police to police aboriginals and Métis angered and frustrated by their displacement. The Indian Act of 1876, codifying who could be defined as Indians and what rights and responsibilities they enjoyed, placed aboriginal peoples in a regime described by one historian as the equivalent of apartheid. "Its basic premise," she noted, "was that First Nations needed to be segregated until they learned to farm and govern themselves in ways acceptable to the new liberal order."[13]

South Africa

South Africa proved to be the most difficult of the colonies of settlement to handle, involving as it did numerous African peoples, British settlers, and Afrikaner farmers called Boers—descendants of seventeenth-century Dutch settlers who had worked the land of the Cape Colony for generations by the time the British gained the territory from the Dutch in 1795 during the Napoleonic wars. Fundamentalist Christians who took their direction from the tenets of the Old Testament, these latter had enslaved the local Khoikhoi people, practically exterminated the local San people, and staved off the peoples of the interior—Matabele, Sotho, and Xhosa—by force of arms. Conflict with the Xhosa in the eastern regions of the Cape occurred regularly, as Boer and Xhosa struggled over the rich pasturelands of the Zuurveld, just west of the Fish River, in a series of "Frontier Wars" in the years after 1760. The British tried to bring the ceaseless wars to an end in 1811 and 1812 by driving the Xhosa from their lands, burning their crops and settlements, and seizing thousands of cattle. In 1820, they settled 4,000 Britons on the lands confiscated from the Xhosa, an action that, in combination with further eastern expansion by British and Boer farmers and ranchers, ensured their economic collapse.

The British had little more concern for Boers than they had for Africans, regarding them as a backward, primitive people. The 1820 settlers enjoyed rights denied the Boers, who soon found it increasingly difficult to establish legal title to land. In 1826, the British made English the official language of the Cape Colony, further putting the Boers at a disadvantage and making them second-class citizens in a place they had lived for almost two centuries. But most galling to the Boers was the British insistence on telling them how they could treat their African servants and slaves. Slave-holding and abuse of Africans especially upset evangelicals, who believed it was Britain's moral obligation to ensure the welfare of indigenous peoples. In 1820, rumors of the harsh treatment of the Khoikhoi at the hands of the Boers galvanized the London Missionary Society, whose representative in South Africa, the Reverend John Philip (1775–1851), took up the cause with vigor. London newspapers soon picked up the story, and the British government felt compelled to act. In Ordinance 50 of 1828, the government declared that black and white men were, "in the most full and ample manner," equal before the law, horrifying Boer opinion.[14] This meant that Africans could possess land, travel freely, and appeal to local magistrates for redress if injured by whites. Worse still, in 1833, as we have seen, Parliament outlawed slavery and extended the ban to its colonies the following year, striking a terrible blow to the Boer way of life. They had had enough.

In the late 1830s, some 6,000 Afrikaners headed out on their Great Trek from the eastern Cape inland to the high veld of southern Africa, where they could settle where they wished and act according to their own lights. The Voortrekkers, as they called themselves, journeyed to the Orange River, which formed the boundary of the eastern Cape, settling in 1837 at the foot of the Drakensberg Mountains. They then expanded their territory, which they were beginning to think of as a state, into Natal, which the British had decided not annex to its holdings, although a small group of Britons had settled on the coast in a town they named Port Natal (present-day Durban).

The Afrikaner expansion into Natal took place with the consent of the Zulu king, Dingane (c. 1795–1840), who claimed suzerainty over the territory. He permitted the Boers to settle there in return for their promise to kill his enemies, the Sotho. They did so, in a gruesome spectacle of slaughter. Dingane, seeing the Boers now as a threat, reneged on his bargain and killed a number of them. In response, a small Boer contingent fell on the Zulus and killed 3,000 of them in what the Boers called the Battle of Blood River.

The Battle of Blood River, 1838.

Disturbed by the reports of depredations against the Sotho and the Zulu, the British government ordered the governor of the Cape Colony, Sir George Napier (1784–1855), to annex Port Natal. At the end of November 1838, a contingent of British soldiers landed in the port and took over a fort that had been built for their occupation.

The British were concerned to establish peace between the Afrikaners and the Zulus, which they did by imposing harsh terms on Dingane. The settlement required Dingane to remove himself far to the north, giving to the Boers not only the entire territory of Natal but also half of Zululand. Dominant now in what they called the Republic of Natal, the Afrikaners did not wish to see British control extended into the state. In this they were thwarted, however, when in 1842 the British claimed suzerainty over and ended the Republic of Natal. In response, the Boers embarked on another trek, this time over the Drakensberg Mountains and across the Vaal River into Matabeleland. There they set up the Republic of the Transvaal. In 1843, Britain formally annexed Natal, and in the years 1849–1852 settled 5,000 Britons to replace the Boers who had left.

At the time of annexation, the British proclaimed "that there shall not be in the eye of the law any distinction of colour, origin, race, or creed; but that the protection of the law, in letter and in substance, shall be extended impartially to all alike."[15] This declaration, so near and dear to the hearts of evangelicals and humanitarians at home and in South Africa, proved not to be effective in practice, especially as it pertained to landholding. Ninety-three percent of Natal's population of roughly 300,000 consisted of Africans; Europeans, both British and Afrikaner, comprised about 6 percent of the population; and Indians brought into the colony to provide labor made up the remainder. But a commission appointed by British officials to address the issue of land determined that of the 12.5 million acres contained within the colony, 2 million should be given over to "reservations" on which Africans were to live. The remaining 10.5 million acres fell into the hands of Europeans as private property or of the government as "crown lands." More than 90 percent of the population—Africans—in other words, obtained only 16 percent of the land; the other 84 percent of it rested in the hands of the 6 percent of the population that was white.

Following the principles of the Durham Report, the Cape Colony obtained responsible government in 1853. Three years later, Natal established its own legislature, in which a majority of the electorate was white. Not surprisingly, voters returned a white membership to the legislature. Just as evangelicals had feared, self-government in the white settlement colony of Natal proved to be a bad deal for indigenous peoples. As early as 1854, a commission reporting on "native policy" had described Africans as "savages," "superstitious," "crafty," "indolent," "bloodthirsty and cruel," and "debased and sensual;" it had declared that Africans had no right to the land of Natal and asserted that as "Natal is a white settlement," the 1843 proclamation announcing racial equality in the colony was "utterly inapplicable."[16] Over the next number of years, the rights of Africans were increasingly whittled away as Britons took

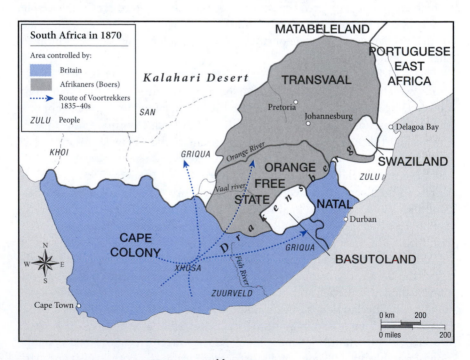

MAP 7.4
South Africa in 1870

advantage of the divisions among African chiefs to introduce policies that encroached further on their way of life and their lands. It did not always go well for the British. The Zulu people resisted British expansion with stunning success at times.

In 1860, indentured workers from India began to arrive in South Africa to work the sugar plantations in Natal. By 1866, approximately 6,500 laborers had made their way into the country, 29 percent of them women. The presence of women and the possibilities of creating a family persuaded a significant number of Indian migrants—some 60 percent—to settle down and make South Africa their home. In addition to the indentured laborers, who faced dismal working conditions for little pay, "Passenger Indians"—so called because they paid their own way to the colony—arrived and set up businesses and established themselves in professions. Over time both groups came to constitute a significant Indian presence in South Africa, not always a welcome one to many Africans, who regarded Indian businesses, in particular, as threats to their own entrepreneurial activities.

Australia

As we saw in Chapter 5, British settlers had, by 1820, established themselves on lands in New South Wales, Van Dieman's Land, Victoria, and Queensland, displacing and sometimes destroying outright the native peoples who had lived there. The numbers of whites remained relatively small up till the end of the 1820s, when, starting in 1828, a dramatic in-migration of Britons began. A total of about 180,000 people made their way to Australia and New Zealand in the years 1828–1842, establishing new settlements at Perth (1829) and Adelaide (1836) in Australia and Auckland, Wellington, New Plymouth, and Nelson in New Zealand in the years 1840–1842. The Australian governors offered large grants of free land to people of substance who could develop it, and they provided convict labor to work it. Those settlers, in turn, wrote home to extol the virtues of their new country, attracting more Britons and more capital with which to further improve the colony. All this expansion required that aboriginal peoples be removed forcibly from their ancient territories, resulting in a drawn-out and bloody "Black War" that—along with the presence of a significant number of convicts—necessitated the constant presence of British troops right up until the 1860s. Aborigines fought hard and effectively, but they could not overcome the weaponry of their European enemies, nor could they spend all of their time fighting, as professional soldiers could do.

Australia's beginnings as a penal colony and the government's grants of free land to wealthy men created a problematic social order that the descendants of convicts and new arrivals to the colony chafed against. In the 1830s, a campaign to render the colonial society more equitable and less class oriented arose; in part as a consequence of the movement, the government stopped granting land to men who would become oligarchs using unfree labor and instead put land up for sale by auction. With the revenue it earned, it sponsored more migration to Australia from Britain, dramatically changing the patterns of British emigration to that time. At the start of the 1830s, fully 98 percent of British emigrants made their new homes in the United States or Canada. By the end of the decade, 25 percent of them opted for Australia instead. During the 1840s—the Hungry '40s as they were known in Europe—80,000 settlers arrived in New South Wales.

White settlement received an even greater boost after 1851, when significant deposits of gold were found in Victoria, attracting people like Agnes and William Roberts, with whom we opened this chapter, to the territory to seek their fortune. Thousands and thousands of men and women from all over the world traveled to Australia, tripling the non-Aboriginal population in the space of ten years. Victoria's population alone grew from 77,000 in 1851 to 540,000 in 1861; the continent's population as a whole grew from 430,000 to 1.15 million in the same period. Railroads and telegraph systems began to crisscross the continent, and steamships crammed with people and commodities tramped from Europe to Australia, rapidly developing the infrastructure necessary to sustain the mining boom, which provided a third of the gold output for the entire world in the 1850s. Australia would never be the same.

In 1854, a rebellion of miners broke out at Ballarat on the Eureka goldfields. It had been brewing for some time, as corrupt local officials extorted exorbitant licensing fees, lining their pockets and harassing the golddiggers. After years of abuse, the miners had had it. Led by men who, as Irish Catholics and Chartists, had little love for officialdom, the miners formed a Reform League under the leadership of an Irish engineer, Peter Lalor (1827–1889). A thousand men rallied under a flag they made—a white cross and stars set against a blue background—built a stockade, and declared that they would put up with corruption and intimidation by officials no longer. "We swear by the Southern Cross to stand truly by each other," they vowed, "and fight to defend our rights and liberties."[17] Soldiers sent from Melbourne attacked the fort, killing twenty-two rebels, but when authorities tried the insurgents for high treason, jurors exonerated them. A royal commission formed to look into the revolt found that officials had, indeed, been engaged in dishonest practices and recommended that the miners' demands for fair dealing be granted.

The Eureka rebellion came to serve a foundational role in the creation of Australia's nationalist mythology. The Southern Cross and stars that today mark the Australian flag represent the freedom and independence demanded by the miners in 1854. And because Britain was in the process of granting responsible government to the various Australian colonies at the time of the gold rush, the rebels at Eureka won political representation as well as vindication for their demands. The year after the revolt, Peter Lalor became an MP elected on the basis of universal manhood suffrage (for whites) and ultimately would serve as a minister of the crown.

Settlers in the Australian bush.

Australian settlers moved inland from the coastal areas into the "outback" over the course of the next four decades. The climate and geography of northern Australia, in particular, offered enormous challenges to a people used to a moderate climate and a gentle topography. Families pasturing sheep and cattle on the grasslands of the continent did not require much in the way of labor, but other enterprises, such as the sugar plantations of Queensland, depended on significant numbers of laborers, far more than the population of whites could supply. The Union blockade of the Confederacy during the American Civil War sent cotton prices skyrocketing, providing opportunities in Queensland for huge profit-making for those who could cultivate the crop and secure sufficient labor. Contract workers from the Pacific Islands were brought in, some 60,000 or so over the next few decades, but when their numbers proved to be inadequate, demand for labor spurred widespread kidnapping and virtual enslavement of Pacific Islanders in a practice known as "blackbirding." Labor recruiters and ship captains used trickery and violent coercion to obtain workers. One ship owner, James Murray, admitted in 1871 that the crew of his brig, the *Carl*, had wrested about 150 Islanders from their canoes and beaten them with clubs till "the bilge water was half blood,"[18] an incident that was repeated over and over again by others trafficking in human cargo. Once on sugar and cotton plantations, laborers received harsh treatment from recruiters and planters alike, suffered high mortality rates, and earned little pay. In Western Australia, the government resumed the use of convict labor from Britain and especially from India to build roads and other infrastructure projects that would encourage pastoralism.

Grazing sheep and cattle in northern Australia offered profound challenges. First, it entailed moving aboriginal peoples off their lands, a process that involved even greater violence and death than in earlier conflicts. Aborigines fought tenaciously to protect their livelihoods, killing white men, women, and children in a number of encounters in the late 1850s and early 1860s. Bloody confrontations continued into the 1880s, as when some 600 aboriginal fighters met settlers and police in 1884 at Battle Mountain in west Queensland, and later in the decade, when some 1,000 aboriginal warriors died in fighting in Alice Springs in the Northern Territory. But ultimately they would be defeated by white force of arms and drafted into the pastoral industry as drovers, shepherds, and servants. They had not voluntarily chosen their employment in this sector of the economy, but their participation in it enabled them to fare better than Aboriginals in the southern part of the continent, where they became, essentially, wards of the state and confined to the equivalent of reserves.

New Zealand

Often lumped together with Australia, New Zealand offers a sharp contrast. The aboriginal peoples of New Zealand, the Maori, organized themselves into a number of warrior clans in fortified villages across the two islands. They managed their affairs better and for a longer period of time after coming into contact with Europeans than did the Aboriginals of Australia. They had been trading with Europeans for a number of decades in the late eighteenth century, and some had even traveled on whaling ships to Sydney, where they came to the attention of the governor of New South Wales around 1800. Maori saw opportunities in establishing links with Sydney and a brisk commerce commenced. One Maori trader, Ruatara, invited evangelicals from the Church of England to set up a mission station in the Bay of Islands in 1814, thereby securing a monopoly on supplying it with the goods and services it needed to do its work. Some of these missionaries complained to the governor about the abuse the Maori suffered at the hands of many Europeans; he responded in late 1813 by declaring that the indigenous peoples of New Zealand fell "under the protection of His Majesty." His proclamation imposed British law on those who interacted with Maori and Pacific Islanders, making them accountable for their actions and liable to punishment if they transgressed British standards of behavior.

In the years after 1815, intertribal warfare among the Maori clans increased in frequency and intensity, largely because of the pressure that population growth exerted on the resources of the two islands. In the past, warfare to settle disputes had been rule bound and even ritualistic, ensuring that few warriors died in the fighting. Now, however, with the guns made available through contact with Europeans, clashes turned more deadly and destructive. Over the next twenty-five years, the so-called "musket wars" among the Maori killed thousands of people, displaced huge numbers of others from their lands, and left some areas around what would come to be called Auckland and Wellington completely depopulated, thus opening up space where Europeans would later settle. But the wars also created a large number of Maori who were familiar with European technology, namely guns. They learned how to strategize effectively using guns, and they built forts capable of withstanding rifle fire. This knowledge would serve them well in their conflicts with Europeans in later years.

In 1833, in response to a petition from a number of chiefs in the Bay of Islands to the British king for protection against both French and British intruders, the government in Sydney sent a British "resident," James Busby (1801–1871), to New Zealand. Lacking any kind of power to enforce his pronouncements for the "maintenance of tranquility," this "watchdog without teeth," as the Maori called him, could do little to ameliorate the violence among Maori and between them and Europeans. He did, however, issue a Declaration of Independence in 1835 that proclaimed New Zealand an independent state under the protection of the British government. Thirty-five chiefs designating themselves "The United Tribes of New Zealand" signed this so-called Treaty of Waitangi, as did seventeen more chiefs a little later. The chiefs believed they were asserting their sovereignty by putting their names to the document; Busby, for his part, was seeking to ward off French intrusion in New Zealand affairs.

At home, the Colonial Office still pursued a policy of "minimum intervention" in New Zealand, a stance they would alter over the next few years as more petitions from Maori chiefs requested British protection from their enemies. By 1839, as competition with the Russians and the French heated up and Palmerston's aggressive policy toward China led to war, the British government was ready to engage more intrusively. It issued Letters of Patent that enlarged the boundaries of New South Wales to include any lands in New Zealand ceded by Maori chiefs to British settlers, gradually acceding to requests by Australian officials that Britain exert a controlling authority over British subjects there. Busby and Captain William Hobson (1792–1842), who would become lieutenant-governor of the colony, circulated a treaty to Maori chiefs that recognized British authority on the islands of New Zealand, asserted that the dissemination of land titles would be the prerogative of the British government, and guaranteed the Maori possession of their lands and property. More than 500 chiefs signed the documents, which had been translated into their language by missionaries. In the meantime, private interests in Britain that had established the New Zealand Company, a joint stock operation that sought to buy up Maori land and settle it with emigrants from Britain, moved quickly to make their purchases and claims before the government could establish its control. Their settlers arrived in Wellington in early 1840, prompting Hobson to declare in May of that year British sovereignty over the entirety of New Zealand as an offshoot of New South Wales. The following year, New Zealand became a crown colony in its own right.

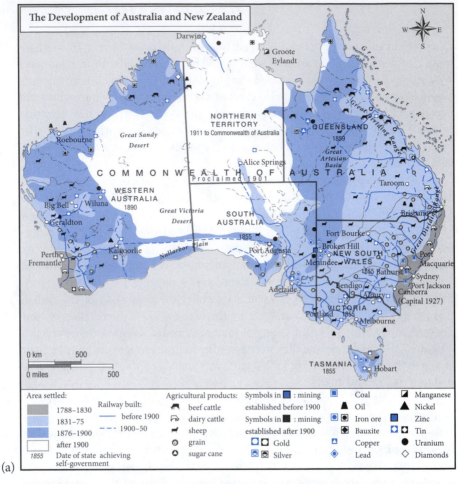

The Development of Australia and New Zealand

Darwin
Groote Eylandt

NORTHERN
TERRITORY
1911 to Commonwealth of Australia

Great Sandy Desert

Roebourne

QUEENSLAND
1859

Great Artesian Basin

C O M M O N W E A L T H   O F   A U S T R A L I A
Proclaimed 1901

Alice Springs

Taroom

WESTERN
AUSTRALIA
1890

Great Victoria Desert

SOUTH
AUSTRALIA

Big Bell Wiluna

Geraldton

Brisbane

Nullarbor Plain

1855

Fort Bourke

Broken Hill
NEW SOUTH
WALES

Port Augusta

Port Macquarie

Perth
Fremantle

Kalgoorlie

Menindee

1855 Bathurst

Sydney
Port Jackson

Adelaide

Bendigo

Albury

Canberra
(Capital 1927)

VICTORIA
1855

Portland

Melbourne

0 km   500
0 miles   500

TASMANIA
1855

Hobart

Area settled:		Railway built:	Agricultural products:	Symbols in ◼ : mining	Coal	Manganese
	1788–1830	—— before 1900	beef cattle	established before 1900	Oil	Nickel
	1831–75	---- 1900–50	dairy cattle	Symbols in ◼ : mining	Iron ore	Zinc
	1876–1900		sheep	established after 1900	Bauxite	Tin
	after 1900		grain	Gold	Copper	Uranium
1855	Date of state achieving self-government		sugar cane	Silver	Lead	Diamonds

(a)

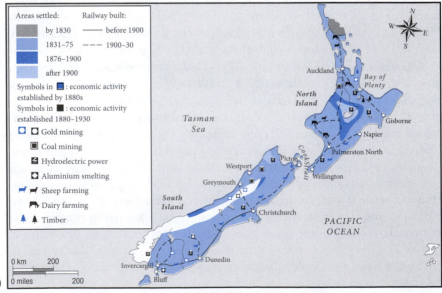

Areas settled:	Railway built:
by 1830	—— before 1900
1831–75	--- 1900–30
1876–1900	
after 1900	

Symbols in ◼ : economic activity established by 1880s
Symbols in ◼ : economic activity established 1880–1930

Gold mining
Coal mining
Hydroelectric power
Aluminium smelting
Sheep farming
Dairy farming
Timber

Tasman Sea

Auckland
Bay of Plenty

North Island

Gisborne

Napier

Palmerston North

Cook Strait

Westport

Picton

Greymouth

Wellington

South Island

Christchurch

PACIFIC OCEAN

0 km   200
0 miles   200

Invercargill

Dunedin

Bluff

(b)

MAP 7.5
The Development of (a) Australia and (b) New Zealand

At this point, Maori still enjoyed significant control over their societies, culture, lands, and livelihoods. That would change, however, over the course of the next three decades, as successive waves of British emigrants made their way to the new colony. The first, in the 1840s, saw the arrival of some 10,000 settlers sponsored by the New Zealand Company. The second occurred with the discovery of gold in Australia in the 1850s; some of those who had not found their fortune crossed the Tasman Sea to New Zealand. When gold was discovered on New Zealand's south island in 1861, a huge influx of golddiggers followed, increasing the white population by nearly 200,000 people. Not all of them stayed, but the more than 100,000 who did transformed New Zealand's social and political landscape. The vast increase in Europeans—and the relatively high infant and child death rates among the indigenous population—altered the demographic balance considerably. In the late 1850s, a roughly equal proportion of Maori to whites prevailed. By the end of the 1870s, whites outnumbered Maori by a ratio of ten to one. Maori population continued to decline, falling by 50 percent over the 1880s and into the 1890s.

The history of New Zealand from 1840 through the 1890s centered on a series of land wars fought between Maori and European settlers. Despite the terms of the Treaty of Waitangi and the intention of the colonial government to protect the interests of the Maori people, illegal land purchases and confiscations resulted in significant losses of Maori territory. Maori tried to resist land grabs by settlers and by the colonial government and succeeded in preventing some of them in the 1840s and 1850s. By 1860, the colonial government had bought two-thirds of the land in New Zealand, most of the land on the south island. The governor wished to add the north island to his territories and instigated a new round of warfare in the 1860s. Again, Maori resisted, but time and numbers were not on their side. By the 1890s, as we have seen, their population had fallen considerably, a decline matched by the loss of their lands.

••

Britain's liberal empire both reflected and contributed to its preeminent position in the world by the middle of the nineteenth century. Few other countries possessed the industrial or military power Britain enjoyed, and its dominance excited envy among a number of other European nations. By the 1870s, as we will see in Chapter 9, British success in colonizing significant areas of the globe spawned a movement among developed countries to gain their own empires, a phenomenon historians call "new imperialism." Britain's power would remain paramount, but it faced challenges and rivals that would alter the country and its imperial outposts forever.

NOTES

1. Quoted in Metcalf, *Ideologies of the Raj*, pp. 33–34.
2. Quoted in Metcalf, *Ideologies of the Raj*, p. 34.
3. Quoted in *The Times*, March 30, 1940.

4. Quoted in W. Travis Hanes III and Frank Sanello, *The Opium Wars. The Addiction of One Empire and the Corruption of Another* (Naperville, 2002), p. 118.

5. W. H. Hall and W. D. Bernard, *Narrative of the Voyages and Services of the Nemesis from 1840 to 1843* (London, 1845). http://www.gutenberg.org/files/43669/43669-h/43669-h.htm/, para. 126.

6. Quoted in Hanes and Sanello, *The Opium Wars*, p. 156.

7. James Belich, *Replenishing the Earth. The Settler Revolution and the Rise of the Anglo-World, 1783–1939* (Oxford, 2009), p. 179.

8. Edward Gibbon Wakefield, *A Letter from Sydney, the Principle Town of Australasia* (London, 1829), p. i.

9. J. M. Bumsted, "The Consolidation of British North America, 1783–1860," in Phillip Buckner, ed., *Canada and the British Empire* (Oxford, 2008), p. 43.

10. Quoted in James Morris, *Heaven's Command: An Imperial Progress* (New York, 1973), p. 342.

11. Quoted in Morris, *Heaven's Command*, p. 343.

12. Quoted in Morris, *Heaven's Command*, p. 348.

13. Margaret Conrad, *A Concise History of Canada* (Cambridge, 2012), p. 155.

14. Quoted in Morris, *Heaven's Command*, p. 54.

15. Quoted in Philip Curtin, Steven Feierman, Leonard Thompson, and Jan Vansina, *African History* (Boston, 1978), p. 323.

16. Quoted in Curtin et al, *African History*, p. 325.

TIMELINE

1820	British settlers to Cape Colony
1828	Ordinance 50 in Cape Colony
	Large-scale migration to Australia
1829	Outlawing of *sati* in India
1828	Lord Bentinck becomes governor-general of India
1833	British "resident" sent to New Zealand
1835	Macaulay's Minute on Education
	Boers' Great Trek begins
1837	Queen Victoria ascends the throne
1837–38	Rebellions in Canada
1838	British claim Natal
1839	Durham Report issued
	Opium Wars begin

17. Quoted in Stuart Macintyre, *A Concise History of Australia* (Cambridge, 1999), pp. 89–90.
18. Quoted in Matt K. Matsuda, *Pacific Worlds. A History of Seas, Peoples, and Cultures* (Cambridge, 2012), p. 221.

FURTHER READING

Clare Anderson, *Subaltern Lives. Biographies of Colonialism in the Indian Ocean World, 1790–1920*. Cambridge, 2012.

James Belich, *Replenishing the Earth. The Settler Revolution and the Rise of the Anglo-World, 1783–1939*. Oxford, 2009.

Phillip Buckner, ed., *Canada and the British Empire*. Oxford, 2008.

W. Travis Hanes III and Frank Sanello, *The Opium Wars. The Addiction of One Empire and the Corruption of Another*. Naperville, 2002.

Alan Lester, *Imperial Networks: Creating Identities in Nineteenth-Century South Africa and Britain*. London, 2001.

Matt K. Matsuda, *Pacific Worlds. A History of Seas, Peoples, and Cultures*. Cambridge, 2012.

Thomas R. Metcalf, *Imperial Connections. India in the Indian Ocean Arena, 1860–1920*. Berkeley, 2007.

Myles Osborne and Susan Kingsley Kent, *Africans and Britons in the Age of Empires, 1660–1980*. London, 2015.

Deryck Schreuder and Stuart Ward, eds., *Australia's Empire*. Oxford, 2010.

1840	Treaty of Waitangi; British claim sovereignty over New Zealand
1842	Treaty of Nanking
1843	British annex Natal
1848	Nova Scotia and United Province of Canada gains responsible government
1853	Cape Colony obtains responsible government
1851	Gold discovered in Victoria, Australia
1854	Eureka rebellion in Australia
1856	Opium Wars resume
1861	Gold discovered in New Zealand's south island
1867	Dominion of Canada formed
1869	Red River revolt in Canada
1872	Canadian Dominion Lands Act
1876	Canadian Indian Act

Anti-Catholic riots in Birmingham, 1868.

CHAPTER 8

NATION AND EMPIRE, CITIZENS AND SUBJECTS, 1848–1873

On the night of June 29, 1852, three weeks before a general election was to be held, a crowd of anti-Catholic rioters rampaged through the Irish section of Stockport, a mill town just outside of Manchester. They chased Irish men and women into their homes, "dragged them from their hiding places and beds," as the anti-Catholic *Stockport Advertiser* reported, and ransacked their homes, breaking windows and tossing furniture into the street, where they burned it. Michael Moran, a twenty-three-year-old laborer who had been staying with his sister and brother-in-law, suffered a grievous blow to the head. He died from his injuries shortly afterward. Irish rioters retaliated with an attack on the house of a prominent Protestant alderman and then turned their fury on the Anglican church and school of St. Peter's. In response, the anti-Catholic mob rushed to St. Philip and James Roman Catholic church, broke into the priest's residence, and sent him fleeing to the bell tower and then, when the crowd set fire to the church, across the rooftops to a nearby house. The rioters moved on to St. Michael's Catholic chapel, where they—the women "as eager and active in the work of destruction as males"—wrecked everything they could lay their hands on, leaving virtually nothing intact beyond the four bare walls. The local police, their insufficient numbers fortified by the addition of special constables and infantry, arrived at the various scenes of the devastation well after the fact. They arrested 113 rioters, all but 2 of them Irish. The *Manchester Guardian* decried this injustice, asserting that "the bloodshed, the violence and the rapine" were "Protestant handiwork."[1]

The anti-Catholic forces had been incited by a number of long- and short-term incidents. Two years earlier, Pope Pius IX had established twelve new bishoprics in England, and the holder of one of them, Cardinal Archbishop Nicholas Wiseman, made some unwise remarks about governing a number of English counties. Lord John Russell, head of the Whig Party in power—soon to be renamed the Liberal Party—publicly denounced the actions of the pope and the cardinal and then introduced and passed the Ecclesiastical Titles Bill in 1851, making it illegal for any Catholic bishop to hold the same title as an Anglican in any given geographical area. (This action sounds petty to us, as indeed it was; it was never enforced and the Liberal government under William Gladstone (1809–1898) repealed the legislation in 1871.) Lord John Russell's actions spurred anti-Catholic feeling, prompted demonstrations across England, Scotland, and Wales, and resurrected Protestant Associations throughout the kingdom.

When the Whig government fell at the end of 1851, the Tory government of Lord Derby (1799–1869) continued the anti-Catholic goading. Tories and the Protestant Association in Stockport, as elsewhere in the United Kingdom, exploited the religious tensions for their own political ends, preparing for the general election of July 1852 by ginning up anti-Catholic sentiment. The *Stockport Advertiser*, strongly pro-Tory and anti-Catholic, issued five editorials denouncing the Liberal candidate for his support of what it called "papal aggression" and expressing deep-seated contempt and hatred for the Irish residents in the town who, in the years following the famine, had flocked to Stockport in significant numbers until they made up more than 10 percent of its population.

In June 1852, three weeks before the general election, Derby's government issued a proclamation prohibiting the display of religious symbols during a planned procession by the Roman Catholic Sunday Schools. Public notices of the proclamation hung alongside Protestant Association placards exhorting voters not to elect a "Papist Parliament" by choosing the Liberal candidate. The nineteenth-century equivalent of "taggers" chalked messages on the stone walls alongside the formal posters, declaring "To Hell with the Pope" and "Down with the Lousy Irish." When the Catholic clergy went ahead with its annual procession—leading Catholic children through the streets of Stockport but not carrying religious symbols or even wearing their religious garb, in conformance with Derby's proclamation—their actions provoked an already fully primed reaction. Although the march itself was peaceable enough, the next night, June 28, fighting between English and Irish broke out, setting off two days of full-on religious violence and destruction.

The incidents at Stockport arose from the dramatic changes that had taken place over the first half of the nineteenth century—economic, technological, demographic, social, political, religious, environmental, and colonial. These raised an array of vital and often controversial questions about the nature of Britain and the empire in the two decades following 1850. Who and what constituted the nation? How were its constituent parts to be regarded and its peoples categorized? How were the empire and its inhabitants to be conceptualized and administered? Who should be considered citizens and who subjects? In a series of debates, legislative campaigns, challenges, protests, rebellions, and state retaliations—

usually heated and sometimes violent—the ethnic, racial, classed, and gendered contours of the British imperial state and its subjects/citizens emerged.

..

THE CELTIC "NATIONS"

The Scottish, Irish, and Welsh peoples of Britain had a complicated and often fraught relationship with the English. A significant portion of the Scottish population had reconciled themselves to integration with their southern neighbors and were largely accepted by them in turn. The English regarded the Welsh and the Catholic Irish, by contrast, less hospitably, and the feeling was mutual. During the period covered by this chapter, a reconfiguration of the relationships of the Celtic peoples of Britain to England occurred, establishing patterns that would last long into the twentieth and twenty-first centuries.

Ireland after the Famine

The famine changed everything. Socially, economically, religiously, culturally, and politically, Ireland emerged from the disaster of the 1840s and early 1850s an entirely different country. Fully 20 percent of the population had vanished, having either died or emigrated, and the numbers still have not recovered. Irish farming and the rural society it sustained—or, more accurately, failed to sustain— was transformed: tilling the land for food production gave way to grazing animals on it, and the cottagers who had done the potato farming earlier disappeared. Smallholdings and the laborers who worked them gave way to larger farms tenanted by families with fewer children. The appearance of railways in Ireland's interior made it possible to communicate with and transport products to and from formerly isolated people, and the improvement of England's economy following the "hungry 'forties" allowed wage earners there to purchase increasing volumes of Irish meat and dairy products. The standard of living among virtually all classes of Ireland rose and the amenities of life—housing, public health facilities, and the like—improved concomitantly. These benefits, it must be said, were a brutal consequence of the massive loss of population: those who were left fared better in the absence of the dead and the departed. The material "equilibrium" achieved in the postfamine years, moreover, depended on the continuing emigration of some of the most productive members of society to brighter futures in Canada, the United States, South Africa, Australia, and New Zealand. Each year some 65,000 Irish men and women left the land of their birth, only 30,000 of whom were replaced by natural increase, yielding a net loss in Ireland's population of about 35,000 annually.

Those who died in the famine had been the poorest members of this rural country, those most likely to speak the old Irish language. Their loss meant the loss of that language as well: whereas some 50 percent of the population spoke Irish in 1845, only 23 percent did in 1851. For partly the same reason, the older folk traditions of religious culture waned, exacerbated by the disillusionment with the old practices and beliefs that had so spectacularly failed to stave off disaster. As a consequence, a more formal and rigorous version of Catholicism came to predominate. It may be that the elaborate liturgical rites and rituals gave much-needed structure and sustenance to a psychologically ravaged and traumatized populace. One of the famine's most distinguished historians speaks of the "shame, resentment, and sense of loss" that characterized the self-image of the Irish people following the disaster; this collective state of mind suffered additionally from the distortions and difficulties faced by men and women who could not marry now until late in their twenties if they wished to avoid the kinds of desperation faced by famine victims.[2]

Relations between the English and the Irish worsened dramatically as a consequence of the perceived refusal on the part of England to do what was required to alleviate the suffering caused by the famine. The sense of rage, betrayal, and injustice engendered profound bitterness toward England among the vast majority of the Irish people, which in turn provoked more intense nationalist sentiment. Antipathy toward the English was not new, to be sure, but now, because of the scope, scale, and immediacy of the horrors experienced during the famine, anti-English hostility blossomed. And it exploded among a newly prosperous portion of society, mainly farmers capable of putting time, energy, and resources into a reinvigorated nationalist political agenda.

The famine had made it clear that the system of land tenure in Ireland was deeply problematic and needed to be reformed. Those who stood in the way of land reform belonged overwhelmingly to the Anglican landlord class, whose influence in the British Parliament gave them power disproportionate to their numbers and even wealth. If the land question was to be effectively addressed, it became apparent to more and more people, the national question of Ireland's relationship to England would have to be resolved in Ireland's favor. Nationalists used the famine to tie the land question to the national question and in so doing set the path of Irish politics for more than sixty years to come.

Farmers organized in a Tenant League seeking land reform joined in the early 1850s with a number of Irish MPs in the Liberal Party to establish an independent Irish Parliamentary Party. The MPs, Catholics themselves or representing Catholic constituencies, had been sickened by the anti-Catholic initiatives undertaken by their party leader, Lord John Russell, and they determined to do something about it. Styling themselves the "Irish Brigade," they began in March of 1851 to act in opposition to their own party's actions in Parliament. For the election of 1852 they fielded their own slate of candidates; in the atmosphere created by the Stockport riots and with the full-throated support of a resurgent Catholic clergy, the Irish Brigade returned some forty-eight MPs who shared their determination to act independent of the Liberals. Their success was short lived, however, and by 1859 the fledgling Irish Parliamentary Party, lacking a sustainable organization, a coherent platform, and a credible set of practices— which, after all meant supporting the Tories, the party of Irish Protestants and Irish landlords—collapsed.

In the absence of any constitutional means by which the land and national questions could be redressed, an organization pledged to the overthrow of British rule and the creation of an Irish republic emerged. The Fenians, or the Irish Republican Brotherhood as they were sometimes called, formed in Dublin in 1858 under the leadership of James Stephen (1825–1901), who enjoyed the emotional and financial support of the large Irish population in America. Within six years, the group could boast a membership of 54,000 adherents recruited largely from the farmer and artisan classes. Unable to either socially or politically advance themselves because of their status and level of income, they found in the Fenians an association of like-minded rebels. Many of them joined to partake in the comradeship the organization offered—military games, boxing, picnics, hiking, team sports. These social activities effectively served to bond the men (and some women) to one another to create a powerful and influential political movement in the 1860s.

In January 1867 a number of Fenians arrived in London and set off what was intended as a campaign of guerrilla warfare. A plan to raid Chester Castle in early February, where the British had stashed supplies of arms and ammunition, was cut short by the arrival of British police, but in September Fenians succeeded in attacking a prison van in Manchester and rescuing two of their comrades, killing an unarmed police sergeant in the process. In November 1867 the British hanged three of the Fenians for their part in the mission that led to the policeman's death. The powerful emotions generated by these executions led to the formation of the Manchester Martyrs, a patriotic movement that attracted vast numbers of previously uncommitted nationalists. Priests led their congregations in mourning across the emerald isle, performing requiem masses and conducting prayer sessions for the souls of the martyrs. They directed mock funeral processions in a number of cities; one such procession in Dublin drew 30,000 marchers. A new alliance of priests and people in support of Fenianism had come about as a consequence of British actions regarded as unjust and excessively harsh.

Fenianism lost some—but by no means all—of its appeal among Irish Catholics in December 1867 when militants blew out a wall of Clerkenwell Prison, where the Fenians' chief of arms procurement was awaiting trial. This time, twelve Londoners were killed and more than thirty others were wounded, many of them badly. These actions, as had been intended, vividly brought the Irish question and the issue of Irish grievances before the English public. They also struck terror in the hearts of many English citizens and helped to imprint the picture of wild-eyed, bloodthirsty, savage Irish rebels on the English imagination.

The Irish Fenian as monster, 1869.

In these imaginings, Catholic Irish men took on the coloration and qualities of racial "others." Like Indians and Africans, they were black. In fact, the facial and bodily features of Irish men, constantly depicted in *Punch*'s cartoons after 1860 in simian, apelike forms, testified to the fact that the Irish were "the missing link

The Liverpool Irish

Irish people have lived in Liverpool for centuries, although it was only in the eighteenth century that they migrated to the city in significant numbers. Trade between the borough and Ireland created many opportunities for immigrants to find work and prosper, and by the time of the 1841 census, the 49,639 Irish-born Liverpudlians constituted just over 17 percent of the total population of 286,656. Those numbers increased considerably during and after the famine of 1845–1848, when more than a million Irish men, women, and children left their ravaged country to seek a better life elsewhere. Most of them traveled to Liverpool, on whose ships the vast majority immigrated to the United States, Canada, and Australia, but some stayed on in the city. By 1851, Irish-born residents of Liverpool numbered some 84,000, just over 22 percent of the total population of 376,000. About a quarter of them were Protestants, but for Liverpool citizens—and for most of Great Britain—the term Irish connoted "Catholic." The Protestant Irish took care to differentiate themselves from Catholics, espousing a "British" identity they would embrace to the present day. Irish Catholics were despised and reviled as "the scum left by the tide of migration between Europe and the continent of America," as one official report stated. Their extreme poverty, high unemployment levels, and the horrific conditions in which many of them lived contributed to the negative connotations attached to Liverpool—the "black spot on the Mersey"—already blotted by its prominent role in the slave trade.[3]

In the face of bigotry and discrimination, Irish migrants to Liverpool sought to create their own version of Irish identity. By coercion and necessity rather than by choice, the poor congregated in particular parts of the city and found a solidarity and security in the streets, pubs, and parishes of their

Emigrants on the Liverpool docks, c. 1850.

neighborhoods. Many middle-class Irish families, drawn from the professions and from commerce, put their energies and resources into charitable works designed to alleviate the poverty and desperation of the poor, seeking to protect the migrant Irish from the debilitating and demoralizing influences of Liverpool life and keeping them Catholic. Some middle-class individuals undoubtedly strove to eschew their Irishness and to conduct their lives and businesses in such a way as to blend in with the Liverpool elite. But for the most part, middle-class Irish Catholics catered to the Irish community's needs and desires, playing up their own Irishness to attract custom. These people became the cultural and political leaders of what would become a large and thriving community by the late nineteenth century.

The influence of the Catholic clergy and of the Irish professional and merchant classes kept the city largely quiet during the period of the Fenian attacks in Britain in 1867. Large numbers of Liverpool Irish supported the Fenian cause, at least in principle, but despite alarms about widespread Fenian activity in the port and insurgents operating from within the 64th Liverpool Irish Rifle Volunteer Force emanating from Dublin Castle and the Home Office in London, Liverpool authorities had little trouble keeping tabs on those who would use violence on behalf of Irish independence. During the trial and execution of the Manchester Martyrs in October and November, to be sure, authorities put the city on high alert, bringing in a regiment of infantry and mooring gunboats in the river. The explosion at the Clerkenwell prison in December, likewise, led to a mobilization of force in anticipation of trouble from Irish Catholic residents in the area during a procession planned for December 15. A ban by city officials and a large police and military presence led the organizers of the march to call it off, although crowds of 3,000 to 4,000 people took to the streets to see what might happen. Nothing did, and the clergy and respectable leaders of the Irish community asserted this was a testament to the loyalty and reasonableness of the Liverpool Irish. As was the case throughout Great Britain, Irish politics in Liverpool turned to the issue of home rule.

The presence of such large numbers of Irish in Liverpool produced a distinct accent, known as Scouse, that characterizes the city to this day. The term derives from a Scandinavian dish, *Labskaus*, eaten by sailors; the equivalent of Irish stew, it became the go-to meal for seamen and dockworkers on the waterfront and migrated to Irish neighborhoods along with people. The accent gives a nasal, adenoidal quality to speech, a phenomenon some linguists attribute to the respiratory problems suffered by the poor in the nineteenth century. The sound became the norm, imitated by those who sought to identify with the Irish community, and ultimately it became associated with Liverpool as a whole. The early "Liverpool sound" of the Beatles incorporated the scouse inflections, and as the Fab Four became international icons, scouse became an even greater mark of identity. Like London Cockneys, Scousers regarded themselves—and still do—as a people apart.

between the gorilla and the Negro." Irish males were not men, not by any standard of definition put forward by the British. Rather, claimed countless English, Scottish, Welsh, and Protestant Irish observers in the new "scientific" racial language of social Darwinism, they constituted a subhuman species, located on the evolutionary chain somewhere between apes and Africans. By contrast, Britons represented themselves as chivalric defenders of a highly feminine, virtuous Ireland endangered by the Fenian menace. In an 1866 *Punch* cartoon entitled "The Fenian Pest," an innocent, chaste "Hibernia" seeks protection against the scarcely disguised sexual violence of gorillalike Fenians from a strong, resolute Britannia who, despite her female figure, exudes manly courage, confidence, and the threat of physical force. A December 1867 cartoon showed an apish Irishman sitting atop a keg of gunpowder ready to explode as a woman with a child at her bare breast and small children milled around it.

The imagery used to depict Irish Catholics as inhuman and incapable of self-government would prevail long into the 1880s and beyond, when new movements for land reform and home rule came to the fore.

Wales: "The Treachery of the Blue Books"

The English regarded the Welsh with only marginally less contempt than the Irish, although the Welsh were able to dramatically alter their place in the imagined nation in a way that Irish Catholics could not. In 1846, three young English barristers, graduates of Oxford University, traveled to Wales, charged by a royal commission with inquiring into the educational system and the "character and condition of the population" that had so recently defied the social and political order by engaging in Chartist demonstrations and following Rebecca on her path of destruction. Henry Johnson, Jelinger Symons, and Robert Lingen, all of them Anglicans, speaking no Welsh and knowing little about the country they entered or the people who inhabited it but brimming with the confidence of their class and their culture, embarked on their study of schools and school children throughout Wales, certain that they would yield an impartial and objective analysis. Unable to personally undertake investigations into the physical and moral conditions of the homes in the villages they visited, however, they relied on local agents—men like themselves, university-educated Anglican clergy—to provide the information they required.

The results, compiled in the 1847 *Report into the State of Education in Wales* and known collectively as the "Blue Books" after the color of its bindings, damned the Welsh as unwashed savages of "barbarous and immoral habits." (The term "Blue Books" generally refers to reports issued by Parliament or the government.) Women engaged regularly and promiscuously in premarital intercourse, the commissioners asserted; they were "universally unchaste." The common people revealed themselves as "thoroughly and universally depraved and brutalised."[4] Superstitious, backward, uncivilized, and intemperate, the lower classes lived in filthy hovels with their animals. "These squalid huts appear to be the deliberate choice of the people," noted Johnson, "who are not more poor than the peasantry in England."[5] The comparison to England was no idle throwaway line; it encompassed the whole point of the commissioners' findings: the inability of the Welsh to speak English and to thereby partake in the "habits and rules of conduct differing from their own"[6]—that is, the habits and rules of conduct obtaining in England—had doomed them to a dangerously backward moral and physical state. Speaking only Welsh, the people of Wales had no access to the civilizing impulses of English culture; without the intervention of education conducted exclusively in English, they were condemned to a nearly subhuman status. As the anti-Welsh *The Times* put it twenty years later, "The Welsh language is the curse of Wales, excluding the Welsh from progress and civilization." The country's "unenterprising people" would do well to jettison their ways in favor of those of England, from which any enlightened practices existing in Wales had derived.[7]

"The treachery of the Blue Books," as the maligning of their culture came to be styled, provoked a ferocious and, as it turned out, contradictory and complex response among Welsh writers, clerics, teachers, and politicians. Outraged by what they saw as a plot by English commissioners working with local Anglican elites to besmirch nonconformist Protestants, middle-class Welsh-speaking dissenters and their advocates in the press launched a spirited attack on the English government. At public meetings attended by massive crowds, local leaders decried the vicious attacks on their culture. Journalists alternated stories analyzing the data compiled by the commissioners—finding it to be wrong—with satires and cartoons lampooning the commissioners. A Welsh Anglican historian, Jane Williams (1806–1885), excoriated the commissioners for their prejudices and for producing what was intended to be "the subversion of her nationality." Another Anglican, Sir Thomas Phillips (1801–1867), the mayor of Newport, published a historical survey that showed how biased the reports were.

But the "treachery of the Blue Books" prompted an additional response as well. After venting their wrath against the English for their insults and slanders against the Welsh people, a number of opinion-makers came to accept that some of the charges leveled by the Blue Book authors could not be dismissed out of hand. Not only Anglicans like Williams or Phillips, but also nonconformists like the nationalist arts patron Lady Llanover (1802–1896) and the journalist Evan Jones (1820–1852)—"Ieuan Gwnedd"—established a new journal entitled *Y Gymres, The Welshwoman,* that aimed to teach women how "to purify the taste, enlarge the knowledge, and improve the women of our country,"[8] to present themselves, in other words, in such a way as to counter accusations of sluttishness. Other Welsh leaders founded the Society for the Diffusion of Useful Knowledge in Wales, joined, ironically, by two of the Blue Book commissioners. Festivals—*eisteddfodau*—that had earlier staged often bawdy pageants, dancing, and musical numbers turned increasingly to demonstrations of utilitarian knowledge, science, and industry. Music still dominated the *eisteddfod,* but a different kind of music now prevailed: hymns sung by respectable, disciplined, and orderly choir members replaced ballads sung by rowdy, irreverent performers. Temperance societies sprang up and gained widespread adherence.

Through such activities and the publication of such Welsh-language publications as *Baner ac Amserau Cymru*, which first appeared in 1858, a new Welsh "nation" emerged, made up of men and women possessed of deep Christian virtue and characterized by the traits of chastity, temperance, hard work, self-sacrifice, thrift, and a reverence for learning. As a "nation of nonconformists" whose majority over Anglicans was confirmed by the religious census of 1851, Welsh speakers claimed a moral superiority over the English. During the next two decades, they honed a new image of Welshness drawn from the values and virtues of the religion they practiced and articulated in opposition to the English-speaking, Anglican, Tory elite of Wales. But although the new "nation" of Wales might have presented itself in opposition to the Anglican church, it embraced, if only defensively at first, Anglicanization of its culture and its industry. The middle-class leaders and opinion-makers of Wales preached an ideology of utility, progress, and respectability that would warm the heart of any mid-Victorian bourgeois; their fostering of the attitudes and characteristics that had helped England and Lowland Scotland become economic behemoths by 1850 spurred economic growth in Wales as well, till the country became transformed from what English observers had regarded as "Wild Wales" into one of the most thriving industrialized regions of the British empire.

One of the most effective broadsides fired in the campaign to redeem Welsh culture yet articulate a wholehearted acceptance of Victorian middle-class culture came from the pen of Henry Richard (1812–1888), a Congregationalist minister and nationalist who published *Letters on the Social and Political Condition of the Principality of Wales* in 1866. He highlighted the grievances suffered by the Welsh under Anglican rule, but he also described the aspects of nonconformist culture that would become synonymous with Wales during the next decades: the puritanical constraints of the "Welsh Sunday," chapel-going, hymn-singing schools and assemblies, temperance societies, mutual improvement societies, and the literary and musical festivals known as *eisteffods*. Richard gave a copy of his book to William Gladstone, a man of Scottish parentage born in England and raised in English ways and married to a Welsh woman, Catherine Glynne. The couple spent a considerable part of each year in eastern Wales, where English speakers predominated, and Gladstone had little interest in or concern for the Welsh language. But in 1866 he became the leader of the Liberal Party, which was committed to the disestablishment of the Church of England in Ireland, a position that made him attractive to Welsh nationalists. On reading Richard's *Letters*, he gained a new appreciation for Welsh culture, telling the audience at the National *Eisteddfod* in 1873 that although he, like most Englishmen, had once thought little of the Welsh language, he had "changed my opinion." The language reflected past history of the Welsh people and constituted "a venerable relic of the past," he observed, but the fact that it was still spoken by 800,000 people was probably instrumental in Gladstone's conversion. The qualities of the Welsh as portrayed by nationalists made the Welsh natural supporters of the Liberal Party, which benefitted heavily from their votes in the years following the Reform Act of 1867. We will take up that aspect of the story later in the chapter.

The "Reinvention of Scotland"

Ironically, at just the same time that Wales sought to rid itself of its image as "wild," Scottish nationalists were lamenting the loss of that very attribute. As Sir Walter Scott (1771–1832) put it, referring to the massive transformation his country had undergone through industrialization and urbanization, "what makes Scotland Scotland is fast disappearing."[9] The elites of Scotland, moreover, had long since adopted English ways as their own, sending their sons to school at Eton and Rugby, Oxford and Cambridge, and purchasing commissions for them in the most prestigious English regiments. Scots had been contributing to the expansion and administration of the British empire for decades, and their successes in imperial affairs at all levels had provided them with a real sense of equality with the English. Economically, politically, and imperially, the Scots had made it as fully as had their English compatriots, and it gave them a great deal of pride and national esteem.

But what might be regarded as their successful assimilation into British politics and economy spurred a movement to recover what had made Scotland Scotland. In what its foremost historian calls "the reinvention of Scotland" after 1850, cultural nationalists turned to the traditions and characteristics of the Highlands, the single most impoverished and depopulated area of their country, for the symbols and memories with which to create a national identity distinct from that of England and the other nations of the United Kingdom.[10] The tartan and the kilt worn by Highlanders had been adopted decades earlier as the emblems of national dress, and as Scottish regiments performed courageously and effectively in campaigns to expand the empire, these symbols took on greater valence. Sir Walter Scott's poetry and historical novels—the best known among them being *Waverley*, *Rob Roy*, and *The Bride of Lammermore*—although written in the first two decades of the nineteenth century, celebrated the past as a heroic time when military valor and honor prevailed. They circulated widely in later years and established the myths that contemporary Scots adopted for themselves after mid-century.

The thirteenth-century Scottish lord, William Wallace (c. 1270-1305), who helped lead the Wars of Independence against England, earned cult status at this time. Statues in his memory sprang up on sites throughout the country, although none so magnificent as the one erected near Stirling. The 220-foot-high National Wallace Monument, which took ten years to build, reminded Scots that despite their union with England in 1707, they had never been conquered; it was in fact Wallace's very achievement that had made a successful and prosperous union *between equal partners* possible. The reinvention of Scotland as a Highland nation, and especially the cult of William Wallace (neither Wallace nor Rob Roy (1671-1734), ironically, was actually from the Highlands) joined national identity

The royal family at Balmoral: celebrating Scottishness, c. 1854.

and national pride with membership in the United Kingdom and the British empire.

Queen Victoria legitimated and helped to disseminate the myths and symbols of the Highlands when she bought and rebuilt Balmoral Castle in the mid-1850s. She and her family spent long summer and autumn holidays there tramping the moorlands, fishing the lochs, hunting stag, and dancing among the villagers in tartans and kilts. She commissioned leading artists of her day to paint her "paradise in the Highlands," as she called it, lending the written and oral testimonies of the Highlands' stark beauty a visual perspective. After mid-century, moreover, Britons could increasingly see for themselves the region now thoroughly thought to be "Scotland." Paddle steamers and railways enabled tourists to venture into the formerly forbidding territory, and from the comfort of their seats they could take in the magical qualities of the harsh landscape that instilled such superb qualities in the Scottish people. What most of them failed to see, however, was the tragedy unfolding among the crofters who actually lived in the Highlands, who were at that moment being dispossessed of their lands and their livings by their landlords. We will take up that part of the story in the next chapter.

As was the case in Wales, nonconformist religion played a significant role in fashioning a national identity in Scotland. Presbyterianism had long placed a premium on the qualities of thrift, independence, temperance, a strong work ethic, and education, and possession of these marked one as "respectable" throughout the United Kingdom (the text perhaps most closely associated with the early Victorian era—*Self-Help*—had been written by a Scot, Samuel Smiles (1812–1904)); but at mid-century, with the immigration of large numbers of

Catholic Irish following the famine, its function as guarantor of Scottish values took on greater urgency. Protestant Associations revived themselves in Scotland as they did elsewhere in Great Britain and devoted themselves, along with new organizations such as the Scottish Reformation Society, to defending their Protestant nation against what they regarded as an "inferior" race of people.

THE RACIAL CONTOURS OF "CITIZENSHIP" AND "SUBJECTHOOD"

Until 1948, no Briton or inhabitant of the British empire enjoyed the status of "citizen;" legally, no such category existed. Instead, Britons and the peoples of the British empire alike were "subjects" of the British crown, a condition conferred on them by virtue of the fact that they had been born in territories held by the crown, a principle called *jus soli*. As subjects, whether of the nation or the empire, they officially fell equally under the protection of the crown, no matter their ethnicity, race, class, or gender. In practice, however, the rights they held varied precisely according to these categories.

Although it was a legal fiction, citizenship was understood to be the possession of those who participated in the political life of the community through the exercise of the vote. After 1832 in Britain and in later years in the white dominions, citizenship devolved on men of a certain degree of wealth, creating an imagined political nation of white, middle-class men. British working men had been betrayed by their erstwhile middle-class allies in 1832 and women had been eliminated from consideration by the insertion of the term "Male Person" in the Reform Act. In Jamaica, free black men who held enough property qualified to vote, and the Colonial Office envisaged a time when blacks there would achieve citizenship. But the Jamaican assembly, controlled by white planters, soon raised the property requirements to levels unattainable by most black men. Various other devices such as poll taxes ensured that blacks could not vote in sufficient numbers to challenge white control of the assembly. Their path to citizenship ran up against the insistence on race as a determining factor.

By the end of the 1840s, British ideas about race had begun to change, one consequence, paradoxically, of the abolition of slavery. Where in the 1820s, 1830s, and 1840s, abolitionist and evangelical thinking about race prevailed— the belief that all human beings shared a common origin, that they were similar to one another in their capabilities, and that education could raise inferior peoples up to a level of civilization that would justify their freedom and even self-government—events in the 1840s and 1850s enabled harsher and more rigid ideas about race to first challenge and then overcome such a liberal view. During the late 1850s and 1860s, racial and ethnic differences became increasingly characterized in absolute, biological terms, so that people of non-British, and even of non-English stock in the case of the Catholic Irish, were construed as utterly different from their British overlords. Under both regimes of racial thought—of similarity before mid-century and of difference afterward—dissenting voices made themselves heard, but they were minority voices that did not express the spirit of the culture as a whole.

These ideologies of similarity and difference depended on notions of gender for their articulation. As justifications for empire moved from the mission to educate lesser peoples in the ways of civilization and self-government to assertions in the 1860s that Irish, African, and Asian peoples were inherently incapable of exercising the self-control necessary for governing themselves, colonized and nonwhite peoples became increasingly depicted as feminine. Representations of empire took on the image of masterly, manly Britons exercising control over irrational, impulsive, weak-willed, effeminate peoples. Subjecthood, like citizenship, although officially regarded as an equal status held by all people living in Britain or the British empire, in practice contained a profoundly raced and gendered component that made colonized and nonwhite peoples distinctly unequal to—indeed, entirely unlike—white, Protestant men.

The abolition of slavery led Britons to draw firmer lines between black and white peoples so that hierarchical relations of power could be sustained in the absence of legal differentiations based on race. One of the most virulent expressions of this phenomenon came from Thomas Carlyle, a celebrated intellectual and man of letters, who denounced the abolition of slavery as a ruinous failure for the economies of the West Indies and declared blacks an inferior race of peoples fit only for the yoke of compulsory labor. During the 1840s, sugar exports from the West Indies to Britain had dropped as competition from other sugar cane producers and from the production of sugar beets in Europe increased. In 1846, when Parliament repealed the Corn Law, removing protective tariffs on grain entering Britain and ushering in the era of free trade, planters in Jamaica feared for their economic livelihood. They turned to Carlyle to plead their cause before the British public. His "Occasional Discourse on the Negro Question," published in *Fraser's Magazine* in 1849 and reissued in 1853 as "Occasional Discourse on the Nigger Question," established many of the basic elements that would characterize British racial thinking in the years after 1850.

In "The Nigger Question," Carlyle railed against the "troublous condition" of Jamaica caused by the abolition of slavery and called for a version of it to be reintroduced to save black and white Jamaicans alike from destitution and degradation. Blacks would not work, he asserted, repeating the allegations of Jamaican planters who saw in blacks' preference to cultivate their own plots to sell crops at market rather than work on plantations for low wages a manifestation of their "laziness." Compel them to work, Carlyle exhorted his audience, because no man had the right to eat who would not labor on the plantations. "If Quashee," as Carlyle styled Jamaican blacks derisively, "will not honestly aid in bringing-out those sugars, cinnamons and nobler products of the West-Indian Islands, for the benefit of all mankind, then I say neither will the Powers permit Quashee to continue growing pumpkins there for his own lazy benefit; but will shear him out, . . . perhaps in a terrible manner." Compel them to work with the whip, if need be, he continued, because it was unlikely that "Quashee" would be induced to labor as white men had been by the promise of delayed gratifications.

Carlyle linked what he saw as the parlous state of Jamaica to the situation in Ireland, from which he had just returned when he first wrote "The Nigger Question." He accused liberal politicians of having produced there what he feared would occur in Jamaica if blacks were not forced to work, "a *Black Ireland*; 'free' indeed, but an Ireland, and Black!" Their free trade policies, in conjunction with Irish "laziness," he charged, referring in racial terms to the millions of people suffering from the potato famine, had given rise not to a white but to a "sallow Ireland, sluttishly starving from age to age on its act-of-parliament 'freedom.'" The Irish, like blacks in Jamaica, he declared in a letter to Ralph Waldo Emerson, would "have to learn that man does need government, and that an able-bodied starving beggar is and remains . . . a SLAVE destitute of a MASTER."[11]

The Indian Rebellion of 1857

The increasingly loud and clamorous voices of Thomas Carlyle and others began to undermine liberal understandings of racial differences and racial inequality as circumstantial and removable. Still, it was not until 1857, with the outbreak of the Indian Rebellion, that the liberal views of men like John Stuart Mill were drowned out by far more conservative assertions of the irremediable, biological nature of racial differences and inequalities.

The rebellion broke out in May 1857, when Indian sepoys of the Bengal army rose up against their British officers and marched to Delhi, where they proclaimed the descendant of the last Mogul ruler, Bahadur Shah, "emperor of Hindustan." From Delhi the rebellion spread across much of northern India, attracting alienated groups from all parts of society. For more than a year, Hindus and Muslims, merchants and landowners, princes and peasants fought against and in many cases defeated local British authorities, till it seemed that the British might be ousted altogether. They were not, but it took at least fourteen months before the army that had remained loyal to Britain, made up predominately of the "manly" warrior "race" of Sikhs, was able to reestablish control in large parts of Oudh and the Punjab and reassert their authority and rule over the subcontinent as a whole.

The mutiny, as the British regarded it, destroyed Britons' confidence in their liberal view of empire. They understood their mission in India and elsewhere to be that of educating and Christianizing the indigenous population to the point where they could expect someday, even if that day were long off, to govern themselves. They believed they were bringing progress and improvement to people who had fallen under the sway of oriental despots but who, because they were born rational men and with exposure to liberal reforms, education, free trade, and Christianity, could learn the ways of self-government. Now, the *Economist* declared in a classic statement of conservative versus liberal views of empire in September 1857, Britons had to decide "whether in future India is to be governed *as a Colony or as a Conquest*; whether we are to rule our Asiatic subjects with strict and generous justice, wisely and beneficently, as their natural and indefeasible superiors, by virtue of our higher civilisation, our purer religion, our sterner energies . . . or whether we are to regard the Hindoos and Mahomedans as our equal fellow citizens, fit to be entrusted with the functions of self-government, ripe (or to be ripened) for British institutions, likely to appreciate the blessings of our rule, and, therefore, to be gradually prepared, as our own working classes are preparing, for a full participation in the privileges of representative assemblies, trial by jury, and all the other palladia of English liberty."[12]

The answer was clear. If previously loyal sepoys, trained in the military discipline of the British army, proved so ungrateful for the tutelage of their British masters as to betray them at the first opportunity, how could other, less developed "natives" be expected to respond? In Oudh, especially, which the British annexed in 1856, dislodging the nawab and the local aristocracy and bestowing property rights upon the peasantry, the British expected the peasantry to side with them against the rebels. Instead, they followed their ruler and nobles in

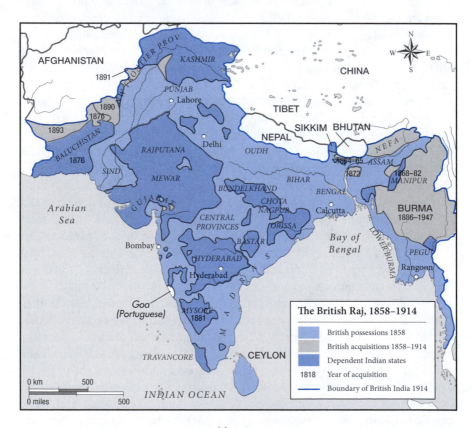

MAP 8.1
The British Raj, 1858–1914

revolt, a clear sign of their irrationality and inability to pursue their own interests. Just how possible would it be for people who demonstrated so incomplete an appreciation for their own interests that they would rise against those who sought to act for them to rule themselves? So demonstrably irrational were the actions of the Indian people that they could not be perceived any longer to be like Britons at heart and be expected to respond to efforts to educate and civilize them. From this moment on, Britons would see their role in India as one of conquest rather than civilization. They now regarded Indians not as human beings potentially like themselves but as wholly and utterly different, needing British rule if order were to be established and kept. In 1858, the government abolished the East India Company and placed the subcontinent under the direct authority of the British crown.

The rebellion led Britons to argue that Indians were not only unlike themselves, but also inhuman, cruel savages. Throughout the rebellion and long after, tales of the most horrible atrocities committed by Indian men against the British, and most especially against British women, circulated throughout India and the home country. Although these stories could not be verified and in fact were later debunked by British officials, accounts of rape, torture, mutilation, and murder of "our countrywomen" continued to circulate as truth. They electrified the British public, searing the British imagination with pictures of scalped and dismembered white women, infants cut from their mothers' wombs, children burned alive, and women crucified. In private letters home, newspapers in Bombay and London, histories of the mutiny, and subsequent novels right up through the 1960s and 1970s, the rape of English women served as the indelible sign of Indian savagery. Colonial insurrection, rebellion against imperial rule, took on not the dimensions of a political act carried out by oppressed people seeking to overthrow foreign domination but that of a sexual crime committed against an English woman, indeed, against all of British womanhood.

In story after story, British women and girls were stripped of their clothes, sexually molested, and thrown to the masses for further abuse. One clergyman claimed in a letter to *The Times* that he witnessed Indians taking "48 females, most of them girls of from 10 to 14, many delicately nurtured ladies,—violated them and kept for the base purposes of the heads of the insurrection for a whole week. At the end of that time they made them strip themselves, and gave them up to the lowest of the people to abuse in broad daylight in the street of Delhi. They then commenced the work of torturing them to death, cutting off their breasts, fingers, and noses, and leaving them to die. One lady was three days dying."[13] Reports of a massacre of British hostages at Cawnpore by a rebel leader, Nana Sahib, took on immense proportions as a myth of mass rape and torture grew up around the execution of 200 British women and children by Nana Sahib's retreating forces. The rebels threw the women's bodies into a well to conceal them. Subsequent official investigations found no evidence of rape or torture, but the site of the massacre, the Bibighar, became a shrine to desecrated womanhood for the British soldiers marching through. They passed stories of violated women along to their fellow soldiers and left messages written in blood on the walls of the Bibighar that purported to be from the "Mutiny ladies" demanding that their hideous treatment at the hands of Nana Sahib be avenged. Rebels and Nana Sahib in particular took on the persona of sexually sadistic monsters in novels about the mutiny. George Trevelyan's (1838–1928) history of the mutiny, *Cawnpore*, published in 1865, attributed its outbreak to "the ambition of the soldiery.... Chafing under restraint, they panted to indulge themselves in unbridled rapine and licence."[14]

Certainly British women and children, like those at Cawnpore, as well as British men, died at the hands of the rebels. But they died, most of them, from shots fired in battle or from diseases they contracted during long sieges of their towns and stations, where lack of clean water, food, and medical supplies made them susceptible to cholera and dysentery. Such deaths, however, could not readily be mobilized to justify a ferocious British response to the revolt, in which British soldiers retaliated against the rebels by executing whole villages, burning civilians and soldiers alive, and tying Indians to the mouths of cannon that were then fired.

Indian rebels tied to the mouths of cannon, c. 1858.

The outrages committed by British soldiers against sepoys and Indian civilians were reported at the time and in later nineteenth- and twentieth-century historical accounts to have been the consequence of uncontrollable fury provoked by the rape and torture of British women and children by the sepoys. "Remember the Ladies! Remember the Babies!" they were reported as crying as they rode into battle seeking revenge from men who had degraded their women and desecrated their homes.[15]

As a consequence of the rebellion, Indian men and men of color generally came to be regarded as defilers of innocent British women till the image of the rape and mutilation of white women by black men came to stand not only for the mutiny itself but also for the whole relationship of Britain to its colonial subjects. And Britons, having responded with fury at the outrages committed against their women, as the new imperial narrative had it, would see their mission as one of protecting innocent, chaste white women from black men and saving black women from black men as well. A new model of British manliness began to emerge from the events and accounts surrounding the Indian Rebellion. No longer exclusively the Christian man of reason, but also a man of action, passion, and romance, the postmutiny prototype of English manliness possessed a love of justice; he was slow to anger but capable when provoked of meting out a terrible, violent retribution against his foes. A man of body more than of mind now, as the notion of "muscular Christianity" promoted by Charles Kingsley (1819–1875), an Anglican priest, historian, and writer, suggests, he nevertheless continued to demonstrate his capacity to reason, one of the most important elements in distinguishing this newly aggressive Briton from the "manly" warrior tribes like the Sikhs. With the infusion of "scientific" arguments about racial superiority and inferiority drawn from the evolutionary theories of Charles Darwin (1809–1882), the story of imperialism changed from one of liberal Christian gentlemen bringing free trade, civilization, and the tools of self-government to childlike, feminized peoples of lesser development to that of an aggressive, powerful, authoritarian, racially superior British nation conquering savage, sexualized, and feminized lands and establishing order over subhuman, animal-like creatures of a biologically inferior breed.

Morant Bay, 1865

The images of dishonored white women and swift, violent retribution from manly British imperialists reverberated fiercely in the minds of Britons eight years later when Jamaican blacks rebelled at Morant Bay in October 1865 in response to high food prices, low wages, racial injustice, and the political indifference of the white-dominated legislature to their grievances. The British governor in Jamaica, Edward Eyre (1815–1901), believed that the rising would spread throughout the island and ordered a severe crackdown on the rebels. His troops killed 439 blacks and people of mixed race, whipped hundreds of men and women, and burned down some 1,000 homes. Eyre ordered the arrest of George Gordon (1820–1865), a Jamaican of mixed race and his political enemy in the House of Assembly whom he held responsible for the revolt. Eyre had Gordon tried and, on the strength of flimsy evidence, subsequently hanged for his offense.

Led by John Stuart Mill, a number of prominent liberal thinkers joined together in the Jamaica Committee to lobby the British government to prosecute Eyre for excessive force and illegal procedures. The government felt pressured enough by public opinion against Eyre to establish a royal commission to investigate the uprising and

The rising at Morant Bay, Jamaica, 1865.

Eyre's response to it. Thomas Carlyle formed a defense committee on behalf of Eyre, which included such literary lights as Charles Dickens (1812–1879) and Charles Kingsley (1819–1875). Carlyle argued that rather than be prosecuted for his actions, Eyre deserved the thanks of all of Britain for having saved Jamaica from anarchy and horrors unmentionable. As for his excesses in establishing order, they amounted to little in the scheme of things. "If Eyre had shot the whole Nigger population and flung them into the sea," he opined, no harm would have been done, because Britain "never loved anarchy; nor was wont to spend its sympathy on miserable mad seditions, especially of this inhuman and half-brutish type; but always loved order, and the prompt suppression of sedition." With the memory of the Indian Rebellion still fresh, the bulk of British opinion tended to side with Carlyle rather than with Mill.[16]

Indeed, Eyre and some who testified on his behalf explicitly raised the specter of sexual violence against women that had become synonymous with colonial rebellions. His first report back to London after the rebellion told of atrocities committed by black rebels that "could only be paralleled by the atrocities of the Indian mutiny." When news of criticism from the Jamaica Committee reached him, Eyre pointed out to the Colonial Office "that the negro is a creature of impulse and imitation, easily misled, very excitable, and a perfect fiend when under the influence of an excitement which stirs up all the evil passions of a race little removed in many respects from absolute savagery." John Tyndall (1820–1893), a prominent scientist, reminded the government and British public that Eyre, "one of the very finest types of English manhood," had provided safety for 7,000 British men and protected the honor of 7,000 British women from the "murder and lust of black savages." He recalled with approval the "conduct of those British officers in India who shot their wives before blowing themselves to pieces, rather than allow what they loved and honoured to fall into the hands of the Sepoys" and appealed to "the women of England" to make their voices heard in this matter because although British men might be able to look into the face of death, "there is nothing in the soul of woman to lift her to the level of that which I dare not do more than glance at here," a clear allusion to the atrocity stories of the rape and torture of British women at the hands of Indian men. Eyre's biographer and member of the Defense Committee, Hamilton Hume (1797–1893), made the connection to the purported rape and murder of Englishwomen in India explicit. He told readers of "those fearful and bloody acts which were scarcely paralleled by the massacre at Cawnpore." Eyre himself testified that his "proudest recollection" of his actions at Morant Bay had been that he had saved the "ladies," the white women, of Jamaica.[17]

The rising at Morant Bay convinced many colonial officials, virtually all of the white population of Jamaica, and much of the British public that what Carlyle had argued in 1849 was indeed true: blacks—whose increasing ownership of land would over time enlarge the black electorate to the point where it would outnumber that of whites—could not govern themselves and would have to be ruled by a firm but benevolent British government. Over the protests of some of the mixed-race members, Jamaica's House of Assembly and the Legislative Council abolished themselves and placed the country under the direct rule of the Colonial Office. Jamaica, like India, became a crown colony, governed from London, its white population preferring to destroy their representative government rather than see citizenship extended to its black population.

Social Darwinism

The Indian Rebellion, followed by the terror campaign of the Irish Fenians and by the revolt of black Jamaicans in 1865, led the vast majority of Britons to embrace the scientific racial views propagated by social Darwinism after 1860. This body of thought located racial difference in evolutionary stages and rendered racial inequalities a matter of evolutionary, biological development. Grounded in nature, most Britons believed, inequalities could not be redressed by social or political means. Charles Darwin's theory of the evolution of species had posited that species evolved on the basis of "natural selection," whereby random mutations in a species rendered—virtually by accident—certain members of the species more "fit" to survive its environment. Survival involved a struggle against other strains of the same species to live—nature could not accommodate all of those born, so survival rested on the capacity of certain members to eat and to reproduce, thus passing along their characteristics to subsequent generations. The failure of other members of the species to do so was not a reflection of weakness per se but of the absence of that quality that had rendered the successful strain more fit. That capacity, or fitness, for Darwin, was arrived at merely by chance. No purpose or intelligence was involved: the "survival of the fittest" in the "struggle for existence" was the survival of those most well adapted to the environment, an adaptation arrived at through random mutation. A longer beak or a different coloration meant the difference between life and death, between survival and extinction for the organisms of a particular species.

As Darwin's evolutionary theories became popularized, they were seized on by many thinkers and applied to human societies in ways that Darwin never intended. Social Darwinists, as they called themselves, extrapolated the notion of the struggle for existence and the survival of the fittest to justify and explain differences on the basis of class, race, gender, and nationality. Karl Pearson (1857–1936), one of Britain's foremost mathematicians and a deeply committed social Darwinist, insisted that "History shows me one way, and one way only, in which a high state of civilization has been produced, namely, the struggle of race with race, and the survival of the physically and mentally fitter race. If you want to know whether the lower races of man can evolve a higher type, I fear the only course is to leave them to fight it out among themselves."[18] Insidious claims that poor people, Jews, blacks, or Irish were naturally inferior to the middle and upper classes, Gentiles, whites, Nordics, or Germanic peoples circulated throughout western societies. Such assertions were not new, but now they took on the power of science and could readily be adopted to justify social inequalities. Differences of wealth and quality of life existed because one group of people—the wealthy—were naturally superior to the poor, social Darwinists asserted. Similarly, a European nation ruling over peoples of different races was justified in doing so on the basis of its natural superiority.

THE REFORM ACT OF 1867

In 1867 in England and Wales and in 1868 in Ireland and Scotland, a substantial portion of urban working-class men won the right to vote. Their victory took place amid the atmosphere of the rebellions in Jamaica, Ireland, and Canada discussed in this and the previous chapter. An economic downturn, widespread unemployment, and high prices provoked fears among elites that workers might resort to rioting just as unrest in the empire seemed to threaten Britain's control, a prophecy that appeared to be borne out by a massive and illegal demonstration of skilled and unskilled working people in Hyde Park in 1866.

Debates over granting working men the vote took place within the context of imperial problems and were framed in the language of race and empire as well as gender. Evangelicals and liberals had long seen working-class men and women as little different from the people of color they ruled over within the empire. Missionaries in particular, to justify their activities at home, frequently described the working classes in much the same and even stronger language they employed to discuss the objects of their efforts abroad. In 1829, for instance, the Newcastle Town Mission reported that the poor and outcast in their area and in other British towns were "more profligate and more perverted than Hindoos." Ten years later, a missionary observed of the poor and working-class people of Britain that "they. . . present a population as blind, corrupt, and brutish, as could be furnished from any city of the heathen world—they are seared in conscience, almost divested of moral sense, and sunk into all but hopeless degradation. They are in all respects 'earthly, sensual, devilish,' without God and without hope in the world."[19]

Opponents of the working-class franchise cast working people in decidedly racial and gendered terms. One MP asserted that granting the working-class franchise amounted to giving the "Australian savage and Hottentot of the Cape" Colony the same rights as "the educated and refined Englishman." It would lead, warned another, to "emasculation of the aristocracy." An antireform pamphlet insisted that the nation needed "independent, thoughtful voters" who could take on the problems of "cholera, cattle pest, the Nigger Pest—white murder by blacks—and Fenians," not working-class men who should themselves be governed according to the natural order of things. Thomas Carlyle castigated those who wished to enfranchise working men as "Nigger-Philanthropists," the same people who wanted to prosecute Governor Eyre, supported the North against the Southern slave states during the American Civil War, and positioned "Quashee Nigger" on the same level as Socrates or Shakespeare.[20] Class and race both, for Carlyle and others, to say nothing of gender, should determine one's position in the social and political order.

In response to this kind of characterization, advocates for political reform that would enfranchise working-class men had to reply in kind. After the demise of Chartism in 1848, for example, skilled working men built up an image of themselves as respectable, moderate, home-loving, and above all, independent and manly individuals. They employed discipline and restraint in their trade union activity, seeking to persuade employers of the rightness of their demands by adopting employers' visions of the proper patriarchal family in their demands for a sufficient wage to keep their wives and children. They turned the language of domesticity, used against them after 1832 by middle- and upper-class politicians to deny them the vote, to their own ends, embracing visions of the male breadwinner and the woman at home to demonstrate their compatibility with bourgeois notions of independence and citizenship. Their lives and values, they insisted, showed that they were no different from middle-class men. Like them, they deserved to vote on the affairs of the nation. Middle- and upper-class liberals compiled a litany of the qualities that made working men just like them. The fact that they saved money, eschewed drink, and "struggled manfully" to support their families demonstrated their virtue and guaranteed that they would be a force for stability for the state rather than one of disruption and upheaval. Prime Minister William Gladstone incorporated the language of domesticity and of empire and nation when he introduced a reform bill to grant the vote to working men in 1866 with the reminder that they were "the father of families" and "our own flesh and blood." He wished to bring them "within the pale of the constitution," a reference to the area of early English settlement in Ireland that imaginatively marked off the "civilized" English from the "barbaric" Irish. Not a race apart, as conservatives would have them, working men were "one of us," as shown by their adherence to domestic and patriarchal practices.

As it turned out, it was the Conservative government of Benjamin Disraeli that enfranchised working men in 1867 rather than the Liberal government of Glad-stone. Disraeli sought to utilize the "muscle and might" of working men to help defend Britain's imperial interests and to deflect the energies of the working classes away from potential conflict with the state toward support of the state's policies over-seas. After 1867 it was no longer possible to lump most British working-class men in with colonized subjects as unruly, barbaric, indolent, and insolent people. Disraeli's "leap in the dark" had made working-class men part of the political nation. Excep-tions to this masculine working-class citizenship certainly existed—the poor and immigrant population of London's East End, for instance, would not have qualified, nor, as we have seen, would Irish Catholics, at least in a cultural sense. In the boroughs—the cities and towns—of England and Wales, all adult men who paid rates (taxes) and all those who paid rent of at least £10 a year and had been resident in their lodgings for a year could now vote. The extension of the vote in the counties amounted to much less, but the counties did get twenty-five of the fifty-two seats in the House of Commons redistributed by the new reform act. The same terms applied to Scotland, although it only gained an additional seven seats in Parliament; Ireland received no redistribution of seats but the property qualifications for urban voters dropped by half. Because the county franchise qualifications did not change and because most Irish lived not in cities but in the rural areas, the franchise reform in Ireland had little effect. In England, Scotland, and Wales, by contrast, the number of borough voters more than doubled and the number of county voters grew by 50 per-cent. A good proportion of the new voters in English and Scottish cities were Irish, legally enfranchised if not culturally a part of the nation.

The Second Reform Act of 1867 transformed politics in ways the Great Reform Act of 1832 had not. The number of eligible voters doubled in size, and in some cities such as Glasgow, working men now made up nearly two-thirds of the elec-torate. Men seeking to challenge sitting MPs appeared in large numbers, increas-ing the number of contested seats in elections. An invigorated political culture emerged, manifested often in new political clubs seeking to address the concerns of new voters—and of the wives, daughters, and mothers of men of all political persuasions, who could not vote.

THE WOMEN'S MOVEMENT, 1850–1873

The feminist movement arose in Britain in response to the exclusion of women from participating in political and public life, especially as liberal and demo-cratic regimes obtained those rights for increasing numbers of men in the nine-teenth century. British liberalism explicitly denied women political citizenship. Women's exclusion was argued for and justified by references to their sexual differences from men, differences, it was asserted over and over again, that de-rived from nature. Moralists, physicians, scientists, and politicians defined femininity in terms completely opposite those that had warranted widespread male participation in the public sphere: men possessed the capacity for reason, action, aggression, independence, and self-interest; women, by contrast, inhabited a separate, private, domestic sphere, one suitable for the so-called inherent qualities of femininity. The qualities of emotion, passivity, submission, dependence, and selflessness—all derived, it was claimed insistently, from women's sexual and reproductive physiognomy—characterized women. On the female as a biological entity, a sexed body, nineteenth-century theorists imposed a socially and culturally constructed gender identity derived from ideas about what roles were appropriate for women. As the eminent psychiatrist, Henry Maudsley (1835–1918), put it in an 1874 article entitled "Sex in Mind and Education," women "cannot choose but to be women; cannot rebel successfully against the tyranny of their organization." He opposed education for women because it would "unsex" them. "Sex is fundamental," he insisted; it "lies deeper than culture, cannot be ignored or defined with impunity." If women persisted in trying to be like men by pursuing education or agitating for rights, they risked harming their reproductive system and rendering themselves unfit for anything. "The result," he warned, "may be a monstrosity—something which having ceased to be woman is not yet man."[21] This collapsing of sex and gender—of the physiological organism with the normative social creation—made it possible for women to be construed as at once pure and purely sexual; although paradoxical, these definitions excluded women from participation in the public sphere and rendered them subordinate to men in the private sphere as well.

Women operated under severe legal, economic, and social constraints. Under the law of coverture, for instance, married women had no rights or existence apart from their husbands. They enjoyed no legal rights to their property, earnings, freedom of movement, consciences, bodies, or children; all resided in their husbands. Throughout the nineteenth century feminists challenged these holdovers of aristocratic patriarchal society, insisting that rather than protecting women in the domestic sphere of home and family, these legal disabilities exposed them to the brutalities of the world at large. The early supporters of women's rights frequently characterized women's position in society as analogous to slavery; many of them, in fact, had come to their feminist positions after having served at length in the antislavery campaign. Without the means to become financially independent of men, women would forever be locked into the same situation of vulnerability to abuse from men as African slaves experienced at the hands of their masters. For women such as Bessie Rayner Parkes (1829–1925), Barbara Leigh Smith Bodichon (1827–1891), and Josephine Butler (1828–1906), women's inability to find respectable work by which they might support themselves rendered them vulnerable to abusive situations. As Butler put it while explaining the existence of prostitution, "so long as . . . women have no employment, this evil will go on."[22]

The most radical challenge of the women's movement to patriarchal control consisted of demands for enfranchisement on the same lines as men. The campaign for the vote was designed to eliminate the notions of separate spheres and natural differences between the sexes insisted on by domestic ideology. The women's suffrage campaign as an organized movement began in April 1866, when, in the midst of debate over what would become the Reform Act of 1867, Barbara Bodichon, Jessie Boucherett (1825–1905), Emily Davies (1830–1921), and Elizabeth Garrett (1836–1917) set out on a petition drive to demand votes for women. By June they had collected 1,499 signatures. In January 1867, Lydia Becker (1827–1890) formed the Manchester Women's Suffrage Committee. Shortly after its formation, suffrage societies in London, Edinburgh, and Bristol were organized. The four societies existed independent of one another, but participants soon recognized the need for a central body to coordinate activities and policy. The London National Society for Women's Suffrage served this purpose. In Ireland, Isabella Tod (1836–1896) established the Irish Women's Suffrage Society in Belfast in 1872; four years later, in 1876, Anna Haslam (1829–1922) founded the Irish Women's Suffrage and Local Government Association in Dublin. Wales did not see the creation of an organized suffrage association until the first decade of the twentieth century, but starting in the 1870s, women and their male allies carried out a vibrant campaign on behalf of votes for women.

When Disraeli's government introduced a bill to give the vote to a large portion of the male working classes, John Stuart Mill, who had stood for election to Parliament on a platform that had included the enfranchisement of women, seized on the opportunity to include women as well. He introduced an amendment to the bill, proposing to replace the word "man" with "person" and thereby admit women to the franchise on the same basis as men. The motion was defeated handily. Surprisingly, however, another amendment to replace the word man with "male" also went down to defeat, leading suffragists to hope that, on the basis of Lord Romilly's Act of 1850, the word man applied to women as well. Lord Romilly's Act had mandated that unless explicitly stated otherwise, the term man in parliamentary statutes was to be used generically, including women as well as men under the jurisdiction of the law. After some debate in Parliament as to the relevance of Lord Romilly's Act for the Reform Act of 1867, Disraeli ruled that it was a matter for the courts to decide. In the midst of the debate, one MP argued that "if a woman could be brought in under Lord Romilly's Act, so might a cow!!" The courts ruled that Lord Romilly's Act did not apply to the Reform Act of 1867, with one of the magistrates indicating that it could also be used to enfranchise a dog or a horse. In these rulings, judges made clear that women could not be counted as citizens; women's enfranchisement would have to wait, and far longer than any of its proponents could possibly have imagined.

Although feminists identified the contradictions contained in domestic ideology and liberalism as they pertained to power relations between women and men, they were blind to the implications they had for inequalities based on class and race. Few feminists questioned their white, bourgeois status or considered how working-class women fared under their strictures. Instead, they tended to embrace the divisions and prejudices based on class and race that informed liberalism and their societies as a whole. British feminists participated uncritically in an imperial discourse that cast subject Indian and African peoples as savage and immoral. Indeed, they furthered that discourse by positioning Indian women, in particular, as victims of a culture that degraded and humiliated them and from which they could be rescued through the good offices of British women. Suffragists claimed the right to vote on the basis of the service they provided to the nation and the empire, and they showcased the work done by British women on behalf of the dependent, pitiful, downcast Indian woman as the evidence of what women could offer as citizens.

What *white* women could offer as citizens, that is. Feminists regularly touted the work of Florence Nightingale (1820–1910) during the Crimean War as exemplary of what women could do in furtherance of Britain's imperial interests. They ignored the arguably more effective nursing done by Mary Seacole (1805–1881), a mixed-race West Indian woman of Scottish and Jamaican parentage who had practiced traditional medicine on soldiers and officers stationed in the Caribbean. When her application to serve the Crimean regiments was turned down by the War Office, the army medical department, the quarter-master-general's department, the secretary for war, and an assistant to Nightingale, Seacole made her own way to the region in the company of a distant cousin and set up a store and hotel where she offered hospitality, provisions, and medical care to soldiers. Her success in treating wounds and disease and her constant presence among the troops won her their abiding affection and respect, as a lieutenant in the 63rd West Suffolk regiment testified. "All the men swore by her," he noted, "and in case of any malady would seek her advice and use her herbal medicines in preference to reporting themselves to their own doctors." At a time when doctors could do little to stem the devastations of water- and sewage-borne diseases like dysentery and cholera and when men in war died in far greater numbers from disease than from wounds, Seacole's ministrations made a difference. "That she did effect some cures is beyond doubt," reported the West Suffolk lieutenant, "and her never failing presence among the wounded after a battle and assisting them made her beloved by the rank and file of the whole army."[23] The army later acknowledged the contributions she made to the officers and men who fought in the Crimea, but feminists, struggling to assert women's rights in the face of staunch opposition and ridicule, evidently felt they could not embrace the "coloured" Mary Seacole as they could the impeccable Florence Nightingale.

In the twenty-five years after 1848 the lineaments of the British political nation came into focus. The various constituencies involved—Welsh, Scots, Irish, Indians, Jamaicans, Africans, white working-class men, and white women—found themselves positioned in dramatically different ways relative to the imperial state, with some in, some out, and some legally in but culturally out. The winners–and especially the losers– in this struggle of defining who belonged and who did not would go on to shape the progress of Britain over the last third of the nineteenth century, as we will see in the next chapter. With the onset of depression and a new kind of imperialism in 1873, the nature of Britain and the empire would change dramatically.

NOTES

1. Quoted in Pauline Millward, "The Stockport Riots of 1852: A Study of Anti-Catholic and Anti-Irish Sentiment," in Roger Swift and Sheridan Gilley, eds., *The Irish in the Victorian City* (London, 1985), p. 208; quoted in Sarah Irving, "Stockport Riot, June 1852," Manchester's Radical History, April 8, 2010, http://radicalmanchester.wordpress.com/2010/04/08/stockport-riot/.

2. Quoted in Oliver MacDonagh, "Introduction: Ireland and the Union, 1801–70," in W. E. Vaughan, ed., *A New History of Ireland, V: Ireland under the Union, 1801–70* (Oxford, 1989), p. lviii.

3. Quoted in John Belcham, *Irish, Catholic and Scouse. The History of the Liverpool-Irish, 1800–1939* (Liverpool, 2007), pp. 5, 3.

4. Quoted in Prys Morgan, "Early Victorian Wales and Its Crisis of Identity," in Laurence Brockliss and David Eastwood, eds., *A Union of Multiple Identities: The British Isles, c. 1750–c.1850* (Manchester, 1997), p. 100; and Prys Morgan, "Wild Wales: Civilizing the Welsh from the Sixteenth to the Nineteenth Centuries," in Peter Burke, Brian Harrison, and Paul Slack, eds., *Civil Histories. Essays Presented to Sir Keith Thomas* (New York, 2000), pp. 282, 281.

5. Quoted in Gwyneth Tyson Roberts, *The Language of the Blue Books: The Perfect Instrument of Empire* (Cardiff, 1998), p. 138.

6. Quoted in H. G. Williams, "Nation State versus National Identity: State and Inspectorate in Mid-Victorian Wales," *History of Education Quarterly* 40.2 (Summer 2000): 145–168, p. 150.

7. Quoted in Quoted in Prys Morgan, "Early Victorian Wales and Its Crisis of Identity," p. 93.

8. Quoted in Prys Morgan, "From Long Knives to Blue Books," in R. R. Davies, Ralph A. Griffiths, Ieuan Gwynedd Jones, and Kenneth O. Morgan, eds., *Welsh Society and Nationhood. Historical Essays Presented to Glanmor Williams* (Cardiff, 1984), p. 210.

9. Quoted in T. M. Devine, *The Scottish Nation, 1700–2007* (London, 2006), p. 286.

10. Devine, *The Scottish Nation*, p. 287.

11. See Eugene R. August, ed., *Thomas Carlyle, "The Nigger Question." John Stuart Mill, "The Negro Question."* New York, 1971.

12. Quoted in Metcalf, *Ideologies of the Raj*, p. 58.

13. Quoted in Jenny Sharpe, *Allegories of Empire: The Figure of Woman in the Colonial Text* (Minneapolis, 1993), ch. 3.

14. George Otto Trevelyan, *Cawnpore* (New Delhi, 1992; originally published 1865), p. 18; quoted in Brantlinger, *Rule of Darkness*, p. 209.

15. Quoted in Brantlinger, *Rule of Darkness*, p. 209.

16. Quoted in Catherine Hall, *White, Male and Middle Class: Explorations in Feminism and History* (London, 1992), p. 283.

17. Catherine Hall, "Imperial Man: Edward Eyre in Australasia and the West Indies," in Bill Schwartz, ed., *The Expansion of England: Race, Ethnicity and Cultural History* (London, 1996), pp. 162, 160; Hall, *White, Male and Middle Class*, pp. 284, 285.

TIMELINE

1847	The Treachery of the Blue Books
1852	Stockport riots
	Queen Victoria purchases Balmoral Castle in Scotland
1857	Indian Rebellion
1858	Fenians form in Dublin
	First Welsh-language publication appears

18. Karl Pearson, *National Life from the Standpoint of Science* (London, 1901), pp. 19–20.
19. Quoted in Susan Thorne, "'The Conversion of Englishmen and the Conversion of the World Inseparable': Missionary Imperialism and the Language of Class in Early Industrial Britain," in Frederick Cooper and Ann Laura Stoler, eds., *Tensions of Empire: Colonial Cultures in a Bourgeois World* (Berkeley, 1997), p. 249.
20. Quoted in Kent, *Gender and Power in Britain*, p. 224. For Carlyle, see Catherine Hall, "The Nation Within and Without," in Catherine Hall, Keith Mcclelland, and Jane Rendall, *Defining the Victorian Nation. Class, Race, Gender and the Reform Act of 1867* (Cambridge, 2000).
21. Henry Maudsley, "Sex in Mind and Education," *Fortnightly Review* 15 (1874), pp. 467, 468, 477.
22. Quoted in "Report from the Royal Commission on the Administration and Operation of the Contagious Diseases Acts 1866–9 (1871), *Parliamentary Papers*, 1871 (C.408-I), XIX, p. 447.
23. Quoted in Peter Fryer, *Staying Power. The History of Black People in Britain* (London, 1984), p. 249.

FURTHER READING

Laurence Brockliss and David Eastwood, eds., *A Union of Multiple Identities: The British Isles, c. 1750–c.1850.* Manchester, 1997.

R. R. Davies, Ralph A. Griffiths, Ieuan Gwynedd Jones, and Kenneth O. Morgan, eds., *Welsh Society and Nationhood. Historical Essays Presented to Glanmor Williams.* Cardiff, 1984.

Catherine Hall, *White, Male and Middle Class: Explorations in Feminism and History.* London, 1992.

Catherine Hall, Keith McClelland, and Jane Rendall, *Defining the Victorian Nation. Class, Race, Gender and the Reform Act of 1867.* Cambridge, 2000.

Gwyneth Tyson Roberts, *The Language of the Blue Books: The Perfect Instrument of Empire.* Cardiff, 1998.

Bill Schwartz, ed., *The Expansion of England: Race, Ethnicity and Cultural History.* London, 1996.

Jenny Sharpe, *Allegories of Empire: The Figure of Woman in the Colonial Text.* Minneapolis, 1993.

1865	Morant Bay rising in Jamaica
1866	Gladstone becomes prime minister
	Women's suffrage campaign begins
1867	Fenian raid in Manchester
	Manchester Martyrs hanged
	Fenian attack on Clerkenwell Prison
	Disraeli becomes prime minister
	Second Reform Act

The Highland Clearances, 1880s.

CHAPTER 9

NEW POLITICS, NEW IMPERIALISM, 1873–1905

On April 7, 1882, a sheriff tried to serve summonses for eviction to a number of crofters in the Braes region of the Isle of Skye in Scotland; they had refused to pay their rent after their landlord denied their request to have traditional grazing rights returned to them. Some 500 men and women blocked the sheriff's way, grabbed the summonses from his pouch, and set them on fire. Ten days later, the sheriff returned, this time with 50 policemen from Glasgow in tow, to arrest the assailants. A large body of men and women armed with stones and clubs met them and in the course of what came to be called "the Battle of the Braes" inflicted injuries on 10 to 15 of the police before the constables were able to mount a baton charge against the crofters, subdue them, and arrest their quarry.

The Battle of the Braes set off a series of other actions across the western Highlands over the next number of years. Crofters instituted rent strikes, occupied sheep farms, destroyed fencing, disarmed law officers sent to arrest them, and engaged in the mutilation and killing of livestock. So great was their disruption and so potentially dangerous their disorder that the government dispatched an expeditionary force to Skye to help bring peace to the area, the first time it had done so since the Jacobite rising of 1745. Marines on board the iron-hulled gunboat *Jackal* came ashore at Glendale in early 1883 to help the local police bring some of the leaders of the agitations to heel.

More momentously, the Liberal government of William Gladstone established a royal commission under the chairmanship of Lord Napier (1819–1898) to look into the grievances of the crofters. During hearings held from the spring until the winter of 1883, commissioners heard testimony from crofters that they could not obtain the land they needed to grow crops or graze cattle and sheep; their families suffered from multiple diseases and their wives and children often had to go barefoot in winter. Landowners and their estate agents countered that the need to improve agricultural output required drastic actions to bring change to land use patterns. The commission's report, issued in 1884, made a number of recommendations, some of which resulted in the passage of the Crofters' Act of 1886. Crofters did not achieve their primary goal—the redistribution of land—but they did gain a security of tenure, the assurance of fair rents, and the right to be compensated for improvements they had made to the land and buildings they held. Landlords chafed at the restrictions on their property rights but the principles of property holding were not abridged in any substantive way.

This 1880s phase of the Crofters' War—a shorthand label given to the struggle between landlords and tenants that took place throughout much of the nineteenth century in Scotland—differed from earlier manifestations of conflicts in that it brought about significant tangible results where earlier agitations tended to simply die out. This was the result of a number of developments we will treat in the chapter below. Gladstone decided to appoint the royal commission because, he was told by his home secretary, Sir William Harcourt, "decent people" had come to the realization that the crofters' grievances were real and egregious. Political pressure, in other words, had built up sufficiently that politicians felt they had to act. That pressure derived from a number of sources. Decades-long migration from the Highlands to the cities of Scotland contributed to a broad base of support for the Liberal Party. Within and beyond Scotland, large groups of people had become aware of the difficulties in the Highlands as a consequence of new technologies that sped communications across wide geographic areas. The telegraph transmitted firsthand accounts of the Battle of the Braes overnight, and mass-produced, inexpensive newspapers broadcast them to a wide and newly enfranchised reading public. They, in turn, expressed their opinions to political organizations that could not ignore them. These innovations of the last quarter of the nineteenth century transformed Britain, and their ramifications affected both its subjects and people across the world.

..

THE SECOND INDUSTRIAL REVOLUTION

In the years following the Second Reform Act of 1867, British society changed dramatically and rapidly as a result of the development of new technologies that collectively made up what historians describe as a second industrial revolution in Britain. The first industrial revolution involved the application of steam power to manufacturing processes, raising output and productivity astronomically in already existing industries such as textiles and mining. The second industrial revolution was scientific in nature; it entailed the creation of whole new products altogether, transforming the way individuals lived their lives in the space of a single generation. Rubber for tires, minerals that made possible the cost-effective development of strong and lightweight metals like steel and aluminum, petroleum products to fuel automobiles—these and countless other discoveries and advances introduced Britons to consumer goods that we now take for granted and created an insatiable demand for raw materials.

New modes of transportation and conveyancing—bicycles, trams, trolleys, buses, refrigerator ships, automobiles, the building of the Suez Canal and tunnels through the Alps—enabled people and goods to move and be moved quickly from formerly distant parts of the world. New forms of communication—the telephone and telegraph, typewriters, mass newsprint—brought individuals, groups, and nations into almost instant contact with one another, exposing formerly isolated peoples to one another and making the long-distance governance of vast non-European populations by small numbers of Britons possible in ways it had not been before. New medicines, food stuffs, preservatives, and purification practices improved the health and longevity of the British population, vastly increasing its size despite a falling birthrate among middle- and upper-class families and a huge outflow of migration to North America and white colonies of settlement such as Australia, New Zealand, and Canada. Factories and firms became massive in scale and scope, employing thousands of workers who were situated together in huge agglomerations where they were distant from management but proximate to one another. Cities grew rapidly in terms of numbers and space, producing vast stretches of urban corridors where farm and pasturelands and forests once existed. Electricity provided lighting for homes and streets and brought recorded music into private homes by means of the gramophone, paving the way for the later twentieth-century development of consumer items like radios, washing machines, vacuum cleaners, and other household appliances.

By far the majority of the innovations characteristic of the second industrial revolution derived from the creation of new materials and the development of new sources of power. One of the most important and ubiquitous of materials produced during this period, steel, had been a semiprecious metal until mid-century. Only 80,000 tons a year were produced in Europe and America. But with new processes developed by men like Bessemer and Siemens, steel could be produced much more cost-effectively in America and Europe, reaching 28 million tons by 1900. When it was discovered that the addition of nickel would harden and toughen steel, its quality increased dramatically and it became more adaptable to a number of applications. Similarly, aluminum had been used sparingly until it was found in 1886 that applying electricity to its manufacture made it commercially possible to use the metal in all sorts of areas, not least in the aircraft industry, especially after 1900.

Automobiles increasingly made their appearance on the lanes and byways of Britain, and they required fuel. Petroleum products for lubrication, building, and lighting had been in existence since the latter part of the nineteenth century, but it was the invention of the internal combustion engine that really ratcheted up demand for oil. By 1913, Britain, France, and Germany possessed 400,000 automobiles, a figure dwarfed by the 1.25 million found in the United States. Cars necessitated the development of roads made of asphalt, another by-product of petroleum. Between 1902 and 1918, imports of fuel oil grew from 300 million gallons to 1,350 million gallons (the demands of war between 1914 and 1918 were the reason for much of that increase).

Much of the world's most accessible oil reserves could be found in the Middle East, where vast fields in what today are Iran, Iraq, Bahrain, Kuwait, and Saudi Arabia were located close to the coast, thus facilitating the transportation of petroleum to Europe. Britain obtained its first large-scale oil concession in 1908 in Persia (Iran); in 1909, it formed the Anglo-Persian Oil Company, with the British government holding a 51 percent share of ownership. Construction of a refinery at Abadan commenced; it began operation in 1913, the same year that first lord of the Admiralty Winston Churchill (1874–1965) signed an agreement with the Anglo-Persian Oil Company that would supply the royal navy with the oil it needed for its fleet, which was in the process of converting from coal to oil. As we will see in the next chapter, concerns about securing a supply of oil and protecting it from competing nationalities would play a significant role in ratcheting up the rivalries and tensions that would ultimately lead to the outbreak of world war.

Dramatic developments in chemistry transformed medicine, hygiene, and nutrition, which in turn had a huge impact on longevity and the quality of people's lives. Joseph Lister (1827–1912), a Scottish scientist after whom Listerine was branded, advocated the use of antiseptics in 1865. New dyes made it possible for scientists to stain bacteria and differentiate them from one another, enabling the development of the fields of microbiology, biochemistry, and bacteriology. Antibiotics were developed: Salvarsan, used to treat venereal disease, appeared in 1909. Vitamins and hormones were discovered in 1902, and the identification of the mosquito as the carrier of malaria occurred in 1897. Aspirin, the wonder drug, appeared on store shelves in 1899. Anesthesia and the use of antiseptic practices turned medical practice from an iffy proposition at best to a profession that could actually improve peoples' lives. Hospitals had once been places where people went to die, largely because of rampant infections coursing through them; aseptic and antiseptic methods reduced the dangers considerably.

The new fields of microbiology, biochemistry, and bacteriology provided the knowledge that enabled significant improvements in food production and preservation. Sterilization and pasteurization made preserved foods safer and tastier; they could be produced in bulk now and supplied in volume to large numbers of people at a reasonable price. Pasteurized milk could be consumed by far more people after 1890 because it could be stored for longer periods of time. The introduction of pasteurized milk had a dramatic impact on children's health in particular. Likewise, food canning, made possible by new methods of tin plating, brought vegetables into the diets of poor and working-class families who could not have consumed them otherwise. Four hundred thousand cases of canned vegetables were sold in 1879; by 1914, consumers bought 55 million

Supplying the second industrial revolution: Ceylon rubber plantation.

cases. The development of new fertilizers from the slag produced in steel manufacture expanded the wheat crop in Canada, the United States, and Russia. Transportation innovations improved food supplies as well. Steamships could carry tons and tons of goods, and when the ships became refrigerated after 1882 they could bring fresh beef to Europe from Argentina and Kansas City or fresh mutton from New Zealand. Tunnels bored through the Alps brought fresh fruits and vegetables from the Mediterranean in record time; the cutting of the Suez Canal in 1869 markedly reduced the time it took to move goods from

Europe to the east and back again. All of these inventions and innovations revolutionized the feeding of industrialized, urbanized populations throughout Britain, contributing to a vast increase in population growth there and in other parts of the world.

The development of cheap newsprint made it possible for working-class men and women and even the very poor to become aware of the world around them in ways they had never been able to in the past. Penny newspapers and mass dailies catering to a particular audience could reach virtually every home in Britain, at least in the urban areas; those who could not afford them could read the cast-off copies of their neighbors. Media barons produced papers that would appeal to readers and took advantage of the opportunity afforded them by mass circulation to express their opinions and articulate their beliefs. They played a key role in the development and mobilization of what could now truly be called "public opinion." Politicians and political parties would learn that they would need to heed the opinions of a far larger group of people than ever before, a phenomenon that would often lead them to play to the gallery in situations that required careful thought and delicate action.

MASS SOCIETY AND MASS POLITICS

Worldwide, population increased by 72 percent in the nineteenth century, growing from 957 million in 1800 to 1.65 billion in 1900. Britain's population more than doubled in that time, from just over 17 million to 41.5 million. But within the century, wide variations occurred. Between 1850 and 1870, for instance, the British population grew by 4 million (emigration from Ireland following the famine diminished what would have been a stronger growth), but because of advances in hygiene, medicine, and food supply, the death rate fell suddenly between 1870 and 1900 and the population took off, increasing by 10.5 million in that same period. That figure does not include the many thousands of Britons who emigrated from the country, let alone those Irish men and women fleeing the devastation of their country after the famine. All of this growth took place in towns and cities, placing enormous pressure on already inadequate infrastructures. Municipalities responded by installing aqueducts and pipes to bring in fresh water and to dispose of sewage; they provided gas and then electric lighting, garbage removal, and sanitation practices; they established police, fire, and health departments; and they introduced public transportation in the form of streetcars, all of which transformed urban life. Urban death rates fell as a result of improved sanitation till they lagged behind birth rates, a first for Britain. The poorest city dwellers, however, remained crammed together in slums, with substandard housing and few utilities. Their numbers increased dramatically in the years after 1881, when some 120,000 to 150,000 largely poor Jews from Eastern Europe immigrated to British cities, especially London, where they settled in large numbers in the East End to seek out a better life. After 1870, black seamen from India, the West Indies, and

Africa began to settle in port towns in England and Wales, having been stranded by tramp steamers who dumped them following a voyage or seeking casual work ashore. The vast expansion of the Welsh coalfields turned Cardiff, Newport, and Barry into vibrant port cities, and African and West Indian sailors in particular formed families and then neighborhoods there in significant numbers. Only London hosted more black families than Cardiff by the turn of the century.

As they grew, cities became segregated into industrial, commercial, and residential areas; the latter were themselves segregated by class. But no group could escape the air pollution that had become worse with the increased use of coal to fuel homes and the onset of the second industrial revolution. London's fogs—what we have come to call "smog"—increased by a factor of three after 1860 and caused death rates to rise when they were particularly bad: in December 1873 some 500 people died of complications of the fog; in a three-week period in February 1880 more than 2,000 succumbed. The air pollution in the industrialized areas of Britain took on monumental proportions, turning formerly lush habitats for flora and fauna into poisoned wastelands. A mid-nineteenth-century British observer described the area around Tyneside. "Cattle will not fatten," he wrote, "and sheep throw their lambs. Cows too . . . cast their calves; and the human animals suffer from smarting eyes, disagreeable sensations in the throat, an irritating cough, and difficulties of breathing." Queen Victoria protested in 1875 that the ammonia fumes given off by a local cement factory near her residence on the Isle of Wight had rendered habitation there impossible, although her complaints produced no improvement. Even the queen could not impose her will on the sector of the economy whose power grew with every passing year.

The new industrial technologies both enabled and necessitated the creation of huge factories, whose workers were amassed in large urban areas. Towns and cities grew so large that they ceased to be separated from one another by rural areas, a phenomenon known as conurbation. Where once the manufacture of steel, for example, could be undertaken in small family-owned workshops employing ten or twelve workmen, the introduction of the blast furnace meant that hundreds and thousands of employees could be brought on. Fewer industrial enterprises existed than in the years before 1870, but they employed fully four times as many workers as in the past. Workers became concentrated in factories, and factories became concentrated in industrial towns and cities.

New Unionism

These developments provoked changes in virtually every area of life. Among workers, broad-based industrial unions of general workers began to replace the small skilled artisan unions of mid-century. Organized according to industry—involving all transport or textile workers, for instance—rather than to skill within a craft, like engineering or weaving, these new unions could boast a membership numbering in the thousands. Moreover, they were not loath to take action on behalf of their members: where craft unions sought to demonstrate the steadiness and respectability of their workers by avoiding agitations or strike activity, the new unions embraced the strike as a weapon with which to confront industrialists on issues of wages, hours, or working conditions. In the 1880s strikes broke out in Britain with some frequency. In 1888 the women of the London match industry went out to improve working conditions; in 1889 the gas workers followed, presaging the Great London Dock Strike of the same year in which 100,000 laborers ceased work. In the 1890s, unionism spread among workers in nonindustrial trades as well, incorporating white-collar workers in shops and offices. By 1900, some 2 million Britons belonged to trade unions.

The Great London Dock Strike of 1889.

The political might of the new trade unions soon manifested itself, aided by political reforms such as the Secret Ballot Act of 1872, which reduced the power of employers or local leaders to influence the way men voted, and the 1883 Corrupt Practices Act, which limited the amount a candidate for office could spend on his campaign. Another round of reform acts in 1884 and 1885 enfranchised agricultural workers and reconfigured the system of representation in Britain.

The old distinction between two-member county and borough seats was abolished and replaced by a system in which areas of roughly equal size possessed a single seat. Voting habits among workers changed, at least in the urban areas. In the past, the old skilled craft unionists of Britain had tended to embrace liberalism and to vote for Liberal candidates, helping to create the so-called Lib–Lab alliance (for Liberal–Labour) that dominated working-class politics for almost thirty years after the Reform Act of 1867 granted working men the vote. By the 1890s, the workers organized in the new unions sought a different kind of representation, one that would express their increasingly socialist outlook. They sought not merely the amelioration of working conditions and a rise in wages but also a more collectivized system of land and industry ownership. In 1892, workers elected James Keir Hardie (1856–1915), a Scottish miner, and John Burns (1858–1943), a leader of the London dock strike, to Parliament as independents. Keir Hardie took his seat dressed in tweeds and the cloth cap worn ubiquitously by working-class men. His appearance, in contrast to that of the other members of Parliament, who wore formal dress, signaled that a new kind of working-class politics had arrived.

In 1893 Keir Hardie formed the Independent Labour Party (ILP), espousing an explicitly socialist agenda of redistribution of income from the wealthy to the poor; free secondary and university education in addition to the already available primary education; cash payments to the unemployed, disabled, and elderly; and the nationalization and therefore public ownership of land, industry, banking and financial services, and transportation systems. The Independent Labour Party gave way to the Labour Party in 1906; by that time, many workers had abandoned the program of the Liberal Party and embraced the collectivist and socialist aims put forward by Keir Hardie. They were not Marxist socialists; they eschewed any talk of revolution. Still, their demands for an eight-hour day, a minimum wage, the right to work, and municipal houses "classed a man as a fool" in the eyes of Liberals and Conservatives, but the electoral strength of the Labour Party in the decade before World War I would make it necessary for the Liberal Party to concede to some of its demands to maintain its majority after 1905. "If today there is a kindlier social atmosphere it is mainly because of twenty-one years' work of the ILP," Keir Hardie claimed in 1914.[1]

The Politics of the Celtic Nations

In Ireland, a depression that began in 1873 devastated a populace still reeling from the famine of mid-century. As prices for agricultural products dropped, so too did peasants' income, till they were no longer able to pay rent for the land they farmed. Their mostly Protestant landlords took harsh steps in response to their loss of income, evicting tenants by the thousands, many of whom then became violent. In 1879, an ex-Fenian by the name of Michael Davitt (1846–1906) formed the bitter Catholic peasantry into the Land League, an organization that sought relief for farmers in the short run and the elimination of the landlord class in the long term by nationalizing the land and giving it over to the peasants. In conjunction with a newly formed Irish Party under the leadership of the aristocratic Protestant Charles Parnell (1846–1891), whose MPs pledged themselves to obstruct the workings of Parliament until that body took up the issue of home rule for Ireland, the Land League forced politicians to pay attention to the needs and desires of the Irish people.

In 1880 Gladstone introduced a measure to assist some tenants who had been evicted. The House of Commons passed the bill, but the Lords quickly turned it down. In Ireland, a new round of agrarian violence erupted, and Parnell initiated a campaign to ostracize anyone who took over a farm from which a tenant had been evicted. These boycotts, so named after its first target, Captain Boycott, proved successful in reducing the number of tenant evictions by Protestant landlords who could no longer find tenants to work their land.

Gladstone's government, meanwhile, reacted to the violence with a coercion bill suspending habeas corpus and permitting police to arrest and detain Land Leaguers without cause. Parnell was arrested under its provisions on October 13, 1880, and the Land League was proscribed a week later. Faced with the choice of letting the Land League agitations cease upon the arrest of its leaders, Davitt persuaded his colleagues to turn the activities of the League over to women to keep the cause alive. Fearing "public ridicule," they balked at this "most dangerous experiment," but finding no alternative, they relented. In January 1881, they asked the Ladies' Land League, led by Parnell's mother Delia (1816–1898) and his sisters, Anna (1852–1911) and Fanny (1848–1882), to take over their mass movement. In London, *The Times* gloated that "when treason is reduced to fighting behind petticoats and pinafores it is not likely to do much mischief," but Davitt countered that "no better allies than women could be found for such a task. They are, in certain emergencies, more dangerous to despotism than men. They have more courage, through having less scruples, when and where their better instincts are appealed to by a militant and just cause in a fight against a mean foe."[2] Members of the Ladies' Land League like Claire Stritch, Hannah Lynch, Harriet Byrne, Hannah Reynolds, Jenny Power, and Ellen O'Leary, to name just a few, carried on the League's boycotts and campaigns of resistance against eviction and nonpayment of rent in what came to be called the Land War; they held and addressed mass meetings throughout the country. Starting in January 1882, they began to be arrested under laws targeting prostitutes. Unlike their male counterparts, who as political prisoners were isolated from the rest of the prison population and could move about and associate with one another freely, the women, having transgressed the conventions of proper womanhood, were treated as common criminals, indeed, like prostitutes.

The arrests and imprisonment of these women compelled countless others to take their place within the Ladies' League. When in early 1882 the imprisoned male leadership instructed them to drop the no-rent initiative, the

Raiding a meeting of the Ladies' Land League, 1881.

women refused, believing it impolitic to change policy mid-course. Agrarian "outrages" against Protestant landlords increased, a phenomenon credited to the Ladies' Land League. Davitt congratulated the women for producing "more anarchy, more illegality, more outrages, until it began to dawn on some of the official minds that the imprisonment of the male leaders had only rendered confusion worse confounded for Dublin Castle, and made the country more ungovernable under the sway of their lady successors." Their courage, commitment, and conviction put the male leadership to shame, as an editorial in *United Irishmen* conceded. "We only wish the men had done [their business] as stoutly, as regularly, and as fearlessly," it lamented. "Is it easier to cow a nation of men than a handful of women? Shall it be said that, while the Ladies' Land League met persecution by extending their organisation and doubling their activity and triumphing, the National Land League to which millions of men swore allegiance melted away and vanished the moment . . . policemen shook their batons at it?"[3]

From prison, Charles Parnell condemned the activities of the women, not least those of his sister, Anna. Sharing the panic of government officials over the "revolutionary end and aim" the women appeared to be creating, he began to negotiate with Gladstone for his release. By the terms of the so-called "Kilmainham Treaty"—after the prison in which he was held—of May 2, 1882, Parnell pledged to bring his influence to bear to stop the agrarian "outrages" in return for the government's promise to release the Land League prisoners and substantially address the question of rents and land tenure. While presenting the treaty as a victory for the Land League, Parnell had actually given way to the government by disavowing the agitations in the Irish countryside and clandestinely offering to cooperate with Gladstone. On his release, he expressed to Davitt his indignation over the behavior of the women and accused them of having harmed the movement. When Davitt replied that their activities—and, by implication, not Parnell's—had brought about the end of the coercion measures and the release of prisoners, he was even more incensed, declaring that if they were not eliminated from the Land League he would retire from public life. On the 6th of May, the lord lieutenant of Ireland, Lord Frederick Cavendish (1836–1882), and his undersecretary, Thomas Burke (1829–1882), were murdered in Phoenix Park in Dublin by Catholic gunmen. Parnell despaired. The English blamed him, whereas Parnell attributed the assassination, at least in part, to the Ladies' Land League. He used the incident to publicly declare his disapproval of the association and within three months brought about its dissolution. Women activists came to understand that if they were to continue to engage in political activities, they would have to do so either as subordinate to men or within their own separate organizations.

In 1886, following four years of relative calm in Parliament over the situation in Ireland, Gladstone brought forward a home rule bill, seeking to give Ireland its own legislature for consideration of most domestic Irish concerns. He had little support from his own party, and the bill failed. The Welsh Liberal MPs had supported him, both because they believed in the principle of the matter and because they were beginning to think in terms of home rule for Wales and Scotland as well. A policy known as Home Rule All Around that would grant home rule to Ireland, Scotland, and Wales found favor among a number of Liberal Unionists—so named for their desire to keep Ireland in union with Britain—but Irish nationalists rejected it for the diversion it was undoubtedly meant to be. From their perspective, the cases of Wales and Scotland simply did not equate to that of Ireland.

Gladstone's efforts to establish home rule for Ireland brought about an irreparable split in the Liberal Party that enabled the Conservatives to come to power in 1886. The Liberal Unionists joined with the Conservatives in the election that year to realize a victory over the Liberal and Irish parties. For the next twenty years, Irish politics effectively disappeared from the national political scene as a sometimes belligerently imperialist Conservative Party dominated Parliament. Liberals did return to power in 1892, dependent for a great deal of their support on Irish, Welsh, and Scottish MPs. Indeed, Liberal politicians became known in a number of circles as the party of "the Celtic Fringe" because of its advocacy of a number of issues near and dear to Irish, Welsh, and Scottish nationalists. It championed the disestablishment of the Anglican church in Wales and Scotland, something that had been achieved for Ireland in 1869. Gladstone introduced another home rule bill for Ireland that actually passed the Commons in 1893, although predictably went down to heavy defeat in the Lords. Weary and becoming ineffective, Gladstone resigned the prime ministership, yielding his position to Lord Rosebery (1847–1929). Rosebery declared his support for Home Rule All Around in 1895, an initiative picked up by the Welsh MP, David Lloyd George (1863–1945). He had, the year before, attempted to organize Welsh MPs into a disciplined bloc such as the Irish possessed. "Ireland was the only nationality which had organised the whole of her progressive forces into one compact league," he asserted. "Ireland is the college of Europe, the college of Liberty which teaches how every wronged and oppressed nationality can secure justice and redress."[4] Lloyd George and Scottish home rulers introduced a measure calling on the Commons to endorse Home Rule All Around. It did, but little came of it because the Irish Parliamentary Party opposed the gambit, refusing to accept that Scotland and Wales faced the same kind of difficulty in their relationship with Britain, as party leader John Redmond (1856–1918) pointed out on the floor of the Commons.

Lloyd George might argue that Wales had as strong or stronger a claim as Ireland, but in fact Welsh and Scottish nationalists did indeed enjoy benefits of union unavailable to Irish Catholics at least. Certainly, neither Scottish nor Welsh nationalists sought separation from Great Britain, as many Irish did. Scottish politicians had succeeded in 1885 in persuading Westminster to reestablish the office of secretary of state for Scotland as a way of addressing their particular concerns, and that seemed to take the sting out of Parliament legislating for Scotland in such areas as education or factory acts. Welsh MPs, headed by Lloyd George, might join the nationalist league, *Cymru Fydd*—Young Wales, or The Wales to Be—but they had no intention of breaking ties with the United Kingdom. At most they, like Scottish nationalists, looked to establish an elected body that would attend to issues pertaining to Welsh or Scottish issues and concerns. Such a legislature would exist only within the sovereignty of the imperial Parliament at Westminster; it would neither challenge nor replace it. In the event, Welsh nationalism petered out by the end of the nineteenth century, and Scotland sought, if anything, even stronger ties with England within the United Kingdom and the empire. Scots identified powerfully with the British empire, regarding it as a source of individual and national wealth and opportunities for occupation, status, and advancement. They had contributed heavily to its development through missionary work, commercial ventures, and colonial governance—fully one-third of all the governor-generalships throughout the empire between 1850 and 1939 were held by Scots. To leave all that the British empire offered made no sense to them.

If political nationalism held little appeal for many Welsh and most Scots, cultural nationalism did. As we saw in Chapter 8, a particular sense of Welshness had begun to emerge in the 1850s in response to "the treachery of the Blue Books." Their politics flowed from the identity they created: temperance reform through the Welsh Sunday Closing Act in 1881, which gave Wales a unique law regulating pub openings; religious equality for nonconformists (in the guise of disestablishment of the Anglican church in Wales); and, as befitting an interest group that regarded the landed elites as their enemies, land reform for the indigenous peasantry. The failure of Welsh political nationalism meant that a royal commission report calling in 1896 for a land court that would deal with questions concerning rent and land tenure was ignored by the Conservative government. That same failure, and the coopting of Lloyd George into the Liberal government when it returned in 1905, ensured that disestablishment was put off until 1914 (and then, with the outbreak of war, till 1920).

Politically ineffective, Welsh nationalists found compensation, to some extent, in their partial successes in reinvigorating the Welsh language. It made its way into the curriculum of the schools, although only as an add-on to lessons conducted in English, via the Intermediate Education Act of 1889, which established more than a hundred county schools and university colleges in Bangor, Aberystwyth, and Cardiff. Welsh literature experienced a small boom in the late nineteenth century as well, as novels by Daniel Owen (1836–1895) and the poetry of Elfed (1860–1953) and John Morris-Jones (1864–1929) made their appearance. Oxford University established a chair of Celtic in 1877; its first holder, John Rhys (1840–1915), worked hard to disseminate scholarship treating the Welsh language. He and Welsh historians such as Owen Edwards (1858–1920) disseminated their scholarship on Wales to a wide and increasingly hungry audience, especially after 1900. With David Lloyd George's elevation to the Liberal cabinet in 1905, Wales, it seemed to most Welsh people, had achieved its appropriate recognition as a central nation within the empire. Wales' "son of the cottage," as he was known to his proud compatriots, had made it, and reflected glory all over his land. But to those who felt the impact of his policies most negatively—a story we will take up in Chapter 10—Lloyd George was regarded as the "perfidious Welshman." As one historian has put it, "because of him, the entire nation was vilified in many English circles."[5] Given the way the Welsh fashioned the "nation" of Wales in opposition to England, it is hard to imagine they were anything but delighted by the criticism.

Their close economic, political, imperial, and even social association with England irked many Scots, who feared that those qualities that distinguished them from the English would be subsumed by those of their southern neighbors. "The name of my native land is not North Britain," complained the novelist Robert Louis Stevenson (1850–1894) in 1888.[6] Following the lead of Scotland's other great novelist, Sir Walter Scott, Stevenson and other Scottish romantics promoted the Scottish identity built around the figure of the Highland warrior. By far the majority of Scots resided in the Lowlands of their country, that area most identified with the union with England, with Enlightenment thought, and with industrialization; the Highlands had virtually emptied out during the clearances and the potato famine, leaving few traces behind of their distinctive culture. Yet the mighty Scot—the primitive masculine warrior in tartan and kilt, fierce and independent, wild and noble—stood as the exemplar of all things Scottish. As we have seen, the presence of Scottish regiments throughout the empire and the tales of their exploits in battles in Canton, Delhi, Red River, and Zululand gave the mighty Scot a credence and a prominence that was only enhanced by Queen Victoria's adoption of Balmoral Castle in Highland Scotland as her favored place of residence. This potent symbol of national identity, however unrepresentative of the way most people lived and unable to pay tribute to the many and profound contributions of its Lowland populations, found a special place in the hearts of Scots and English alike.

For the men and women who actually lived in the Highlands, life continued to be harsh, despite the benefits conferred by the Crofters' Act of 1886. Because it did not return land to the crofters and because it did virtually nothing for cottars—those who were landless or nearly so—the act initially engendered a good deal of hostility among them and among land reformers who had hoped for far more. The Highland Land League, formed in 1886, sought to "restore to the Highland people their inherent rights in their native soil."[7] When the Conservatives came to power following the split within the Liberal Party in 1886, crofters and cottars resumed their agitation against landlords. In the minds of Arthur Balfour (1848–1930), the new Scottish secretary, and his Conservative colleagues, the Crofters' Act had redressed the grievances held by Highlanders, thus eliminating any legitimation for illegal acts. The government sent the *HMS Ajax* and *HMS Assistance* to Tiree in July to help police deal with crofters who were resisting being evicted. The marines met with a decidedly cool reception at first, but when they began to help the crofters bring in the harvest, the locals warmed to them.

As years went by, the Crofters' Act took on a different stature in the eyes of the Highlanders. In giving them a security of land tenure that had not existed previously, the law ensured that mass evictions and clearances could no longer take place. This had a greater psychological than material impact because, for all intents and purposes, clearances had ceased by 1860 or so. But for those who had watched for decades as their neighbors and kin had been driven from their cottages and land or whose improvements to their holdings had been absorbed by their landlords, the psychological peace of mind cannot have been simply a minor victory. The fruits of this relief appeared over the next twenty years, when some 40 percent of crofters built new homes in the western Highlands.

The Rights of Women

The early suffragists had expected that their demand for the vote in 1867 would be granted without much trouble. When it was not, they had to rely on bills introduced by their parliamentary allies, but these had little chance of passing without government support. In each year from 1870 to 1879, measures to enfranchise women were introduced, and in each year they fell to defeat. Realizing just how great was the opposition to their claim to vote, suffragists turned their attention to other campaigns seeking to improve women's position in society. They succeeded in obtaining two Married Women's Property Acts in 1870 and 1882 that gave women the right to retain and own any property or earnings they might bring to their marriage; they gained admission to Girton College, Cambridge, in 1871, the University of London in 1878, and Newnham College, also at Cambridge, in 1879. In 1884 Parliament revoked the law that allowed men to have their wives jailed (!) if they refused sexual intercourse, and in 1891, a court ruling found that a man could not imprison his wife in his home to enforce restitution of conjugal rights. The idea of women as incapable of reason and as the property of their husbands or fathers slowly but surely gave way over the course of the late nineteenth century.

The feminist campaign that attracted the greatest amount of attention after 1870 was that to repeal the Contagious Diseases Acts. These laws gave police and local authorities the power to regulate prostitution in the port and garrison towns of Britain by compelling women suspected of trafficking in sex to submit to an examination by speculum for venereal disease. If found to be infected, a woman was forced to stay in a hospital until she was deemed disease free, at which time she would be given a certificate verifying her status. When efforts were made to extend the laws to other towns and cities in the country, women became aware of them and determined that not only should their jurisdiction not be enlarged but also the laws should be altogether repealed. Led by Josephine Butler (1828–1906), feminists worked tirelessly to that end, driven by the conviction that no woman, however fallen she might be, should be rendered "safe" for men by the state. Their efforts to establish what they regarded as a single standard of sexual morality for both men and women led to repeal of the acts in 1886.

With this victory in hand, Butler and her followers turned their attention to India, where contagious diseases acts had been in force since the early 1860s. (They had, in fact, provided the precedent for the acts that pertained to Britain.) They adopted much of the same rhetoric they used at home to oppose the acts, but their sense of responsibility to reclaim Indian women from immorality derived from their abiding belief in the civilizing mission of the British empire. As Butler noted of the Indian campaign, "this is natural, right and necessary because of the great responsibility England has for India."[8] Feminists drew on women's work in service to the empire to make their case for inclusion in the political nation and in so doing relied heavily on the cause of Indian women to serve as the focus of their good deeds and efforts to further the imperial interest. Turning those women into the victims of degradation and abuse in need and deserving of British women's attention, they claimed that votes for women rose to the level of a national and imperial duty. Women's suffrage in Britain would not come until the end of the Great War because, in part, those who held the power to grant it turned feminists' imperial justification on its head. A primitive country like India, antisuffragists claimed, where women enjoyed little status and were treated with disdain, would lose all respect for Britain were it to give its own women the vote. Opponents of women's suffrage argued that the very imperial interest feminists claimed in support of their movement demanded that women be denied enfranchisement.

In New Zealand, a vastly different connection between empire and women's suffrage emerged, and however rhetorical it may have been on the part of politicians, it produced a remarkable outcome. In 1893, indigenous and European women won the vote. New Zealand in the 1890s sought to assert itself as a nation rather than a colonial dependency of either Britain or Australia, which was pushing for a consolidation of the two antipodean countries. The Australasian colonists prided themselves on having left the ways and values of the old world behind; they fancied themselves to be at the forefront of progress and civilization. What better way for New Zealanders to dramatically demonstrate their advance over the rest of the world—and to distinguish themselves from Australians—than to be one of the first societies to enfranchise women? Because the country had not imposed a racial qualification at the time it wrote its constitutional provisions for male suffrage, the enfranchisement of women included Maori women in its purview. Australia did not lag far behind in adopting this new symbol of modernity; it enfranchised white, although not Aboriginal, women in 1902.

NEW IMPERIALISM

In addition to creating mass society, the second industrial revolution had the effect of integrating the world as never before. The new industrialism created enormous demand for raw materials that could not be found at home or in other parts of Europe; manufacturers had to look outside their local areas to meet the unprecedented need for basic materials that made the second industrial revolution possible. No part of the world remained unscathed as Westerners and Japanese industrialists sought to supply their factories. The acquisition of nickel from Canada; nitrates from Chile; copper and gold from Australia; zinc, tin, and rubber from Malaya; wheat and other foodstuffs from a variety of areas—all these and much, much more brought far-flung territories into the world economy to create a single economy on a global scale, creating a world market driven by world prices. Tied to one another by economies and finances, the countries of the world became interlocked in the space of a single generation. The sudden shock of this development would have profound consequences that resonated across the globe.

Technological developments in transportation and communications made possible by the second industrial revolution, and a demand for the raw materials necessary to sustain it, enabled and encouraged European countries to embark on ambitious imperial ventures. International rivalries generated by the recent appearances of a powerful Germany on the continent and a dynamic America across the Atlantic reinforced European impulses to expand in Asia and Africa and helped to instill a sharp sense of competition and conflict among the Western powers. In cultural and intellectual life, the promulgation of

Darwinist and social Darwinist theories of evolution and "racial deterioration" accompanied these developments, legitimizing some initiatives already under way and spurring others to action.

Beginning in 1873, a depression took hold of the world's capitalist economies for more than two decades. Shrinking markets and falling profits led business leaders to seek new opportunities abroad, where they hoped to find new outlets for their goods. European nations and the United States and Japan had become increasingly reliant on foodstuffs and raw materials obtained from overseas: fearful that their supplies of food and raw materials might be cut off by other powers, they determined to obtain colonies whose trade they could control. The depression compelled—and the developments in technology permitted—Britain and many of the other European powers, the United States, and Japan to embark on a path of what is called "new imperialism."

We identify the beginnings of new imperialism in Britain with Benjamin Disraeli. Although he was voted out of office by a coalition of liberals and working men newly enfranchised by the Reform Act of 1867, the former prime minister embarked on a series of ventures designed to increase Britain's empire and thereby enhance its status vis à vis the European great powers. In 1872 he delivered a speech at the Crystal Palace in which he asked Britons to decide whether they wanted to live in a "comfortable England" or in "a great country—an Imperial country," from which they would "command the respect of the world." When he came into power again in 1874, Disraeli immediately put his plans into effect.

In 1875, the ruler of Egypt, the khedive, found himself deep in debt and facing bankruptcy. When his only assets, his shares in the Suez Canal Company, came on the market, Disraeli jumped at the chance to purchase them. He told only the queen and a few of his minister of his intentions. Victoria encouraged him to act, applauding his *very large ideas*, and *very lofty views* of the position this country should hold."[9] He had to move quickly, before any other company or government could upstage him. On learning that the khedive had accepted his offer, the prime minister told Victoria, "It is settled. You have it, Madam."[10] With Parliament in recess, Disraeli turned to the Rothschilds for the funds, secretly borrowing from the banker the £4 million necessary to purchase the shares. The queen thrilled at the news that he had won the day, but he still had to explain to Parliament his unorthodox measures in purchasing the shares, essentially, behind its back. He had done so, he informed MPs, because controlling the canal was "necessary to maintain the empire." Some months later, Parliament agreed to pay the Rothschilds back.

Egypt itself did not interest the British, but its geographic position offered the possibility of shortening the route to India, about which the British cared a great deal. The canal, built by a French company, had opened in 1869, but it appears at first to have made little impression on British strategists, who believed that a railroad across the isthmus linking the Mediterranean to the Red Sea and thence to the Indian Ocean offered the best shortcut to the subcontinent. The completion of the canal, however, and its success in attracting a great deal of British maritime traffic, altered the situation completely. Egypt became the crucial link to India: whoever controlled Egypt controlled the fate of the subcontinent. The Egyptian ruler served, at least theoretically, as a viceroy to the Ottoman sultan, a ruler whose empire was constantly under pressure from Russia. Russia, moreover, posed a threat to the British in India. The prospect of this rival power potentially blocking access to the Suez Canal caused Disraeli great anxiety.

Although having purchased only a minority interest in the company that owned the Suez Canal, the British public became convinced that it owned the canal itself. Before too many years passed, this impression became more and more a reality, till finally the French company that owned and managed the canal was doing so under the protection of British authorities and the British military.

In 1876, flush with his Suez victory and in a vivid display of Britain's new imperial intentions, Disraeli's government passed the Royal Titles Bill, which conferred on Queen Victoria the title "Empress of India." This appellation signaled the culmination of a dramatic shift in Britons' understanding of empire. Where it had once connoted a relationship of white colonies of settlement, of a union between Britons and their free and loyal kin overseas, best exemplified by the colonies of Canada, Australia, and New Zealand, empire now signified possession of and despotic rule over peoples of color. "New imperialism" differed from the older imperial ventures undertaken by Spain, Holland, Portugal, France, and Britain in the sixteenth, seventeenth, and eighteenth centuries, enterprises that received their impetus from and were characterized by trade. In the years following the Napoleonic wars, Britain had established control over huge areas in South Africa, Asia, the West Indies, and Canada. In the decades between 1840 and 1870, it expanded its holdings by adding new colonies in Australia, New Zealand, British Columbia, Hong Kong, Lower Burma, Natal, the Transvaal, parts of what would become Nigeria and Sierra Leone, the Gold Coast, and the Punjab, Sind, Berar, and Oudh in India. While it granted various measures of representative government to the white settlement colonies in Canada, South Africa, Australia, and New Zealand by 1860, it progressively tightened its control over millions of peoples of color.

The Scramble for Africa

Believing that Britain's great prosperity derived from its holding of colonies, politicians and business interests in France, the United States, Italy, Belgium, Portugal, and Germany resolved to gain their own. In the early 1880s what has come to be called the "scramble for Africa" took place, whereby the various European powers carved out large areas of the continent they deemed to be their "spheres of influence." Faced with competition for imperial power they had not seen since the end of the eighteenth century, British statesmen and politicians responded in kind, formally annexing vast territories in Asia and

Africa—Egypt, the Sudan, Afghanistan, southern Africa, Uganda, Rhodesia, Kenya, and Nigeria—and placing them under the administrative control of the crown to protect British "interests" there from encroachment by other European countries. Britain faced competition from Europe and the United States in the geostrategic as well as economic realms. In 1870, the German states had unified under the leadership of the kingdom of Prussia: now a large and mighty German empire threatened to undo the balance of power that had been forged in the years following Napoleon's defeat in 1815. Under the leadership of Chancellor Otto von Bismarck, Germany contented itself with consolidating the gains it had made in central Europe and sought to calm the fears of the other European great powers of Russia, France, Austria-Hungary, and Britain by maintaining a low, peaceable profile in international affairs. With the accession of Wilhelm II to the throne in 1888, however, Germany undertook to establish itself as a world power comparable to Britain. Seeking to gain Germany's "place in the sun," the kaiser and his military and civilian officials embarked on a naval race against Britain, commenced to threaten and bully their French and British rivals unmercifully, and exploited situations where British colonial officials in South Africa and French officials in North Africa found themselves challenged by internal resistance and even revolt.

No single event set off the scramble, but two sites involving British interests contributed to the furious stampede to colonize Africa: South Africa and Egypt.

South Africa, by the early 1870s, consisted of two British colonies—the Cape Colony and Natal; two republics independent of Britain and controlled by Afrikaners, the Orange Free State and the Transvaal, the latter also known as the South African Republic; and a number of African chiefdoms: the Xhosa, the Zulu, the Pedi, the Tswana, the Sotho, the Swazi, and the Venda. In 1871, diamonds were discovered in the area that became named Kimberley in Griqualand, which the generally friendly Orange Free State and the generally antagonistic Transvaal claimed for themselves. Faced with this competition from the independent republics, the British seized the territory and annexed it, engendering the enmity of Afrikaners across the entirety of southern Africa and helping to initiate the stirrings of an Afrikaner nationalism that would have profound consequences down the road. The rivalry between the British and Afrikaners intensified as the Transvaal persisted in its efforts to expand its territory to the east and especially to secure access to the Indian Ocean with a port at Delagoa Bay. Should the republic succeed in gaining its own port, it would depend far less heavily on the Cape Colony, diminishing that entity's ascendancy in southern Africa. To prevent such a turn of events, Britain annexed Delagoa Bay for itself in 1875 and went on to formally annex the Transvaal to the Cape Colony in 1877.

Enraged Afrikaners revolted against British rule in 1880 and declared an independent republic. With an army of perhaps 7,000 mounted civilian soldiers, they prepared to defend their republic in what they called their war for independence. The British army fared badly against them, unable to lift the sieges to the garrisons that kept the troops captive inside them. A relief force suffered numerous defeats, an especially humiliating one at Majuba Hill in 1881 where six Afrikaners—"dressed in civilian corduroy trousers and floppy-brimmed hats," as one historian described the guerrilla force[11]—and 280 supposedly crack British troops were killed or wounded. The humiliation suffered by an elite force of Highlanders could not be borne by Britons at home; the army general staff and Conservative politicians demanded redress for the terrible defeat and the reestablishment of British authority. But Gladstone, having become prime minister in 1880, feared that renewed fighting would only lead Afrikaners in the Free State and the Cape to rise up. He chose instead to settle with the Transvaal rather than continue to try to fight it. In 1881, the Transvaal—the South African Republic—regained its independence. Convinced that the British would not intervene to stop them, Transvaal settlers, called "freebooters," immediately set about expanding their borders to the east and west, grabbing up the land of the African chiefdoms there. One such seizure took place in the lands just north of the Cape Colony, in what would come to be called Bechuanaland, today's Botswana.

Facing what they considered a hostile government in the Transvaal, the British moved to shore up their position, sending some 4,000 troops north in 1884 to expel the freebooters and secure Bechuanaland. Reviving its "forward policy" in response to perceived Transvaal encroachment, Britain commandeered other territory till all of the unannexed coastal and inland areas between the Cape of Good Hope and Delagoa Bay was in its hands. This aggression had the effect of pushing other Europeans to follow course, setting off the scramble to follow.

The second set of incidents that triggered the scramble for Africa took place in Egypt, and in this instance India played a crucial role in Britain's acquisitions of northern African territory. Ever since Britain had obtained shares in the Suez Canal, Egypt had taken on increasing significance in official thinking about empire. The country remained a vassal state of the Ottoman Turks, the khedive serving as the sultan's viceroy. So long as he maintained his power, British authorities were content to remain at a distance. But the finances of the Egyptian state proved to be so parlous, and the government so corrupt, that France and Britain felt they had to step in to protect their considerable financial interests. In response to this foreign intervention, an Egyptian army officer, Arabi Pasha (1841–1911), staged a revolt in 1882 designed to rid his country of outsiders. Prime Minister Gladstone determined that the time had come, regrettably, for a full-on imperial intervention.

He sent an army under General Sir Garnet Wolseley to invade Egypt. Wolseley's forces quickly defeated Arabi at the battle of Tel-el-Kebir, inflicting enormous casualties on the rebel fighters. The British then marched to Cairo, took it over, and raised the Union Jack above the city. Gladstone and his ministers insisted that their actions did not constitute annexation of the country, only a temporary occupation that would end once stability and order had been imposed. "Undoubtedly of all things in the world," the prime minister tried to reassure those who believed Britain sought to permanently seize Egypt for itself, "that is the thing which we are not going to do."[12] The khedive remained in power and the Ottoman sultan retained the title of head of state; but all power rested with the British army and the actual governing of Egypt rested in the hands of British officials. This anomalous situation gave rise to numerous confusions, not least concerning whether Britain now also had taken responsibility for ruling Sudan, the land to the south of Egypt that had been an Egyptian dependency for sixty years. British officials in Cairo and at home cared little about the desert country and would have preferred to remain aloof from it. Imperial expansionists, however, insisted that control of Suez required control not simply of Egypt, but also of Sudan because this was a territory constantly in revolt against Egyptian authority. Led by a charismatic Muslim holy man called the mahdi (leader), Sudanese rebels meant to end rule by the Egyptians, who, they believed, paid only the slightest lip service to the precepts of Islam. Before they knew it, the British had an armed insurrection on their hands, and they responded by sending an Egyptian force headed by British officers south to defend the rule of the khedive.

This adventure ended in disaster. Some 50,000 Sudanese soldiers met the 10,000-strong Egyptian army at El Obeid and destroyed it. All of the British officers fell to the opposing forces, and only a few hundred Egyptian soldiers survived. The mahdi gained control of virtually all of Sudan, leaving only a few Egyptian garrisons scattered across the countryside. Gladstone resolved, in the wake of the catastrophe, to abandon further efforts to maintain Sudan for Egypt, a position even his supporters thought unworthy of Britain, and he ordered that the Egyptian garrisons there be evacuated. To oversee the evacuation, he appointed in 1884 a popular and flamboyant—and utterly unreliable—soldier/adventurer, General Charles Gordon (1833–1885).

Gladstone may have been clear in his own mind about the necessity for evacuation, but other prominent people felt differently; indeed, there were sufficient countervailing influences that it was possible for Gordon to interpret his mission in virtually any way he wished. With encouragement from a number of imperial expansionists, he disobeyed orders from London and decided that rather than evacuating the fort at Khartoum, to which he had arrived in February, he would stand and fight to keep the Nile valley in Egyptian and British hands.

In March, forces of the mahdi laid siege to Khartoum, cutting the telegraph line to Cairo and leaving Gordon isolated. Gordon was playing a tricky, and potentially deadly, game. He would not evacuate the Egyptian forces at Khartoum or even leave the city to save himself. It gradually became apparent to Gladstone's government that the mercurial general was in effect blackmailing the government into retaking Sudan by allowing himself to be held hostage to the mahdi. The British public, for whom Gordon was a hero, a perfect Christian gentleman who had given so much of himself to the British empire, would not stand to see him abandoned in the desert by a heartless, cowardly government. Newspapers across Britain and the rest of the western world, the clergy, the army, and the queen demanded that a British force be sent to save this most selfless of men; the cabinet realized that if the government did not comply, it would be toppled from office. Against all of his principles, Gladstone knew he must act, and in the fall of 1884, he requested that Parliament grant him £300,000 "to enable operations to be undertaken for the relief of General Gordon, should they become necessary."[13]

General Wolseley assembled troops in Cairo and, after months of painstaking preparation, ventured up the Nile. Three days before the expedition force arrived in Khartoum, the mahdi's soldiers attacked the city in the middle of the night, killing the inhabitants and then Gordon himself. In the face of heated public opinion, Gladstone's government ordered a retreat from Khartoum; Wolseley and his troops returned to Egypt. The British occupation of Egypt to protect the Suez Canal and its subsequent incursions into Sudan provoked other European powers, especially France, to take steps to establish their own spheres of influence in other parts of Africa.

The scramble for Africa took place in a remarkably short period of time. In 1876, Europeans controlled perhaps one-tenth of the Africa landmass. During the 1880s, they claimed 5 million square miles containing 60 million Africans; by 1900, nine-tenths of Africa had been colonized by Europeans. But it was merely one aspect of a larger imperial impulse on the part of the industrialized powers, which by 1900 could boast that fully one-fifth of the land area of globe and one-tenth of the world's population were under their authority. The ability of Europeans to seize control of and rule over the lands of Asia, Africa, South America, and Oceania stemmed in large part from the new technologies in transportation, communications, medicine, and armaments thrown up by the second industrialization. For the first time, Europeans had the means of administering millions of people with a relatively small number of officials and soldiers. Railroads and steamships enabled explorers, entrepreneurs, and settlers to open up country that had barred their passage in earlier years. The telegraph kept colonial officials in contact with their subordinates in the "bush" and outlying regions and with their superiors in the metropolitan capitals. New medicines like quinine enabled Europeans to cope with diseases like malaria that had decimated their ranks. But above all, it was the invention of new modes of firepower that made it possible for small numbers of Europeans to impose their will over indigenous peoples armed mostly with ancient muskets, spears, and bows and arrows. The breech-loading rifle, the "repeating" machine gun invented by Sir Hiram Maxim (1840–1916), the gunboat—these weapons gave the Europeans the power to destroy those who resisted their onslaught. At the Battle of Omdurman in 1898, for example, when 40,000 Sudanese soldiers bearing muskets and spears attacked a small force of British troops traveling up the Nile, 11,000 Sudanese lost their lives at the hands of machine gunners and artillery officers. Forty-eight British, by contrast, lay

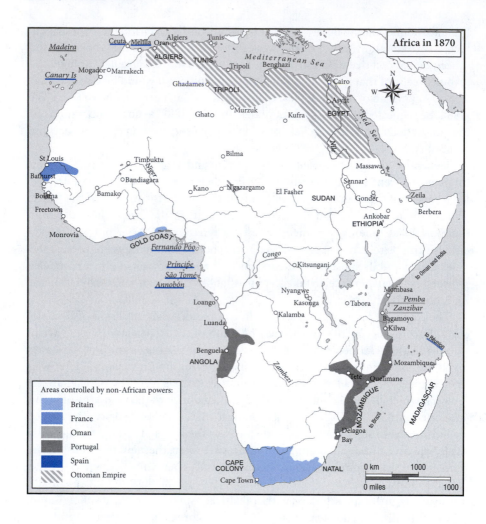

Africa in 1870

Areas controlled by non-African powers:
- Britain
- France
- Oman
- Portugal
- Spain
- Ottoman Empire

dead. The slaughter inspired British writer Hilaire Belloc (1870–1953) to pen the couplet, "Whatever happens we have got/The Maxim gun, and they have not." It evoked a different response from Winston Churchill, who was part of the expeditionary force. He decried the "inhuman slaughter" carried out by men their commander, General Horatio Herbert Kitchener (1850–1916), had trained "to regard their enemy as vermin—unfit to live."[14]

In their efforts to bring vast amounts of territory, people, and resources under their jurisdiction, the industrialized nations obliterated local economies, polities, societies, land tenure and legal systems, and cultures. Their fields left untilled so that crops attractive to Europeans might be cultivated, Africans starved to death. Forced off their lands by colonial officials who desired their labor, mine workers in South Africa were compelled to leave their families behind to fend for themselves. Farmers and pastoralists found themselves expelled from land they had

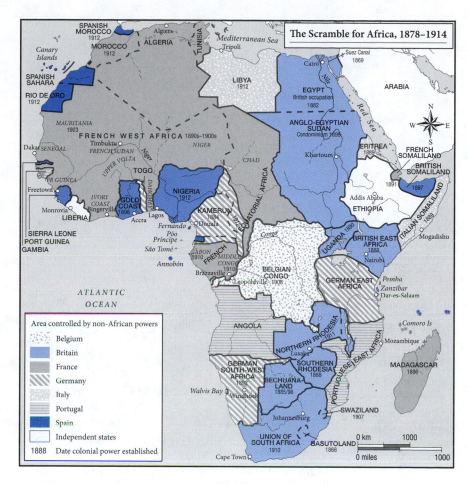

MAP 9.1
The Scramble for Africa, 1870–1914

worked for centuries, obliged to become sharecroppers or ranch hands or herded onto "reserves."

An Imperial Race

The last fifteen years of Victoria's reign saw a new, more self-consciously imperial phase of colonial acquisition that Disraeli had foreseen was England's destiny if it was to retain its status as a preeminent world power. Placed on the defensive by the rise of the new industrial powers, Britons responded with an aggressive display of imperial might designed to counter any notion of economic or military weakness. Poets and writers told of untold wealth and unparalleled adventures to be had in the frontier areas of Asia and Africa; celebrations like that of Victoria's Diamond Jubilee in 1897 made manifest the power and glory of

A PLACE IN TIME

Liverpool Blacks

Most of Liverpool's trade with West Africa during the period dominated by "new imperialism" was carried in the ships of the Elder Dempster Company, which under the leadership of Alfred Jones (1845–1909) incorporated the other steamship companies located in the city into a single, monopolistic firm between 1884 and 1891. In the process of enriching itself through commerce, Elder Dempster ensured the success of British imperializing in West Africa and brought to Liverpool the Africans who would, over the course of decades, help establish the city's black population.

Ad for the Elder Dempster shipping line to West Africa.

Following the abolition of the slave trade in 1807, Liverpool shipping merchants turned their attention to what was called "legitimate trade" in such goods as palm oil, timber, cocoa, ground nuts, and gold. Members of a West African coastal ethnic group, the Kru, had long served on the ships that transported these goods, and when the steamship came on line at mid-century, demand for their service increased all the more. Elder Dempster, like all other trading ventures in Africa, could not function without local labor, and the Kru especially enjoyed a reputation for reliability and hard work. Britons believed, moreover, that they were particularly suited for the hot labor of stoking the fires of the boilers below decks and employed them in great numbers for this kind of work. By

1900, 34 percent of the firemen and stokers aboard British steamers were foreign, usually African or Asian, doing the arduous work for which white seamen were considered unfit. One early-twentieth-century Liverpudlian described the men he saw on the docks and in adjacent neighborhoods as "poor thin creatures of all colours equally poorly clad. . . . They drove the ships through hot seas. No wonder they were walking skeletons. What a hell it must have been shoveling coal, stoking the furnaces deep in the bellies of the boat. No air conditioning then. Scarcely enough draught with the funnels extended to keep the furnaces going."[16]

As the largest single shipping company trading with West Africa, Elder Dempster transported numerous Kru seamen to Liverpool. Many caught other ships for a return to their communities on the West African coast, but some stayed on. They did so for a variety of reasons. Lack of a ship compelled some to stay in the African hostel set up by Elder Dempster to house seamen without a berth, a not incidentally useful site for a supply of reserve labor the company could call on when it needed more hands. Others went ashore to find work on land; still more settled in Liverpool because they knew they could command better wages from Elder Dempster as Liverpool-based residents rather than as African-based seamen. The numbers of Kru in Liverpool never reached more than 100 or so until the outbreak of the Great War.

Because they arrived unaccompanied by their wives or other women, the Kru seamen and laborers who settled in the city tended to marry white women. Their mixed-race children became members of the black British community in Liverpool, expanding its size and scope. They tended to live in the Toxteth area of the city, near the docks, among peoples of all colors and ethnicities. The idea of white women marrying black men infuriated a lot of Britons, but as one writer put it, "it was so prevalent that they had to keep their beliefs to themselves." He and others attributed the phenomenon purely to economics; these "fellows from the West Coast of Africa accepted by white women as equals" were, in the minds of many white women, far superior to white men. "They made better pater familiae. . . . The fact that most of the black fellows followed the sea had much to do with the local girls marrying them—much better, reasoned the girls, to put up with a negro three months of the year (while drawing his steady salary) than to marry a young dock walloper and be continually starved and beaten."[17] This kind of cynicism, although undoubtedly warranted in many instances as a consequence of the strategies pursued by working-class and poor families across Britain, belies the true love matches made between other blacks and whites in Liverpool over the course of the eighteenth, nineteenth, and twentieth centuries.

empire. Politicians, military men, and commercial adventurers extolled the virtues of imperial power for national health, seeing in empire and imperial rule the means by which Britain was to preserve its international standing. Men like Joseph Chamberlain (1836–1914), Lord Rosebery, Cecil Rhodes (1853–1902), and Lords Curzon (1859–1925) and Milner (1854–1925) regarded the empire as key to Britain's very survival, the training ground that would prepare it, Rosebery insisted, "for the keen race of nations."

The keen race of nations could get ugly, involving Britons not in war against their continental rivals but in many unsavory practices visited on subject peoples. Much of British colonization in the late 1880s took place not under the guise of the government but that of chartered companies. Men like George Goldie (1846–1925) and Cecil Rhodes (1853–1902) received charters from Queen Victoria to form companies that had the authority to raise their own armies, build cities and towns, settle territories claimed by the British in the scramble for Africa, and determine how those areas would be administered. Goldie's Royal Niger Company and Rhodes's South African Company, incorporated in 1886 and 1889, respectively, governed large portions of West Africa and South Africa without costing the British treasury a single shilling. Instead, the commercial activities these companies engaged in—initially financed by shareholders—absorbed the cost of development and rule. As one historian has put it astutely, "it was like farming out an Empire to private industry, or handing over the care of several million souls to a board of company directors."[15] Profit ruled the day, but it sat, not uncomfortably, alongside motives of advancing British civilization in the keen race of nations. Smug expressions of the British civilizing mission masked, at least at home, the profound depredations of colonial rule on African and Asian peoples.

Rhodes was perhaps the most powerful man in all of Africa by the 1890s. Having made his first fortune in the Kimberley diamond mines, he expanded the scope of his business ventures through the South African Company. His dream was to extend British rule throughout the length and breadth of Africa, from the Cape to Cairo, as he and others put it, and they nearly succeeded in their efforts. Goldie's company secured Nigeria, the Gold Coast, Gambia, and Sierra Leone in West Africa; Rhodes sent company armies and settlers north into modern-day Zimbabwe to establish the colony of Rhodesia; and Somaliland, Uganda, Kenya, and Zanzibar in the central and eastern portions of Africa fell under British rule as well. From the north, an army under General Kitchener advanced from Egypt south into Sudan in 1897 to secure the headwaters of the Nile. Only a small slice of territory in Tanganyika, held by Germany, stood in the way of a continuous British corridor running from Egypt to South Africa.

There was another formidable barrier to the consolidation of British power in Africa. The Transvaal, home to the world's principle supply of gold, remained intransigent. The Afrikaners' impertinent independence should not be tolerated, apologists for empire muttered; something must be done to bring

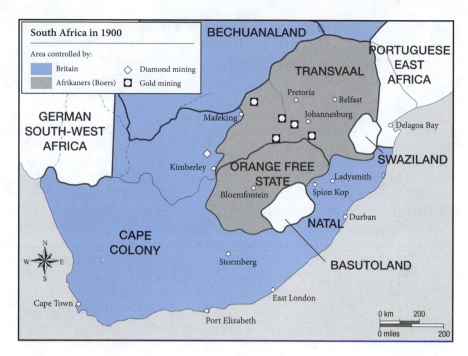

MAP 9.2
South Africa in 1900

them to heel. But however ready the British public might be to embrace the bloody conquest of African peoples, blatantly attacking European whites, officials believed, even if they were Boers, was not something it would countenance. Other methods had to be devised. Taking advantage of the discontent of British settlers in the Transvaal, people the Afrikaners called *uitlanders* ("aliens"), Joseph Chamberlain (1836–1914), the British colonial secretary, had been conniving with the British high commissioner in the Cape Colony to support the oppressed *uitlanders* should they decide to rise up against Boer rule. Rhodes, premier of the Cape Colony, went even further. He and his intimate companion, Dr. Leander Starr Jameson (1853–1917), determined to help spark an insurrection in the Transvaal by sending Jameson on a raid into the republic to overthrow the government of Paul Kruger (1825–1904) and establish a new government under British control.

The Jameson Raid started on December 29, 1895, and it failed spectacularly. The Afrikaners learned of the incursion almost immediately and sent an army to thwart it. British settlers in the republic did not rise up. On January 2, 1896, Jameson and his followers surrendered in humiliation and disgrace. The British government condemned the raid, although Chamberlain had tacitly endorsed it earlier, but the ignominious motives and behavior of the British colonists did not faze the British public in the least. Quite the contrary. People at home admired

Jameson for his reckless daring on behalf of British subjects who, they were convinced, were unjustly ruled by the Afrikaners. Kruger deserved to be overthrown, the feeling went, and the only reason Jameson and his fellows were in trouble was because they had not succeeded in their aims. Jameson, to their minds, represented exactly the kind of individual the keen race of nations required. Britain needed more of them.

Although Britain's population had grown dramatically in the late nineteenth century, it was dwarfed by those of the United States and the continental powers, and its birth rate had slowed considerably. Fears of population decline joined concerns about the quality of the British population, especially in light of a growing awareness of the depth and degree of poverty as rural migrants fled to the cities to escape the agricultural depression and of the high levels of infant mortality that existed throughout the country. Despite the improvement in real wages enjoyed by those who had regular work, poverty levels increased during the 1880s and 1890s, and urbanization made this poverty far more visible than it had been when most people lived on the land. Twenty-eight percent of York's population earned incomes insufficient to maintain a household; London's percentage was even higher. Perhaps one-third of all Britons lived below the poverty line. Moreover, infant mortality rates were on the rise. In England and Wales in the 1880s, 142 of every 1,000 infants born died within their first year of life; that figure increased to 154 during the 1890s till by 1899 it had reached 163.

The existence of so much poverty, disease, and death in the midst of such plenty demanded explanation. Physicians, scientists, politicians, churchmen, writers, and moralists believed that cities depleted the health and vigor of populations, regarding them as "the graves . . . of our race," as the dean of Canterbury put it in 1887. The *Fortnightly Review* warned its readers of the effects of urban life in its description of the "town type." "The child of the townsman is bred too fine, it is too great an exaggeration of himself, excitable and painfully precocious in its childhood, neurotic, dyspeptic, pale and undersized in its adult state, if it ever reaches it." The conditions of city life, they believed, enervated formerly healthy specimens, demoralizing them and causing physical deterioration. The solution lay in gathering up the remaining "unoccupied" territories of the world and peopling them with Britons. It was through acquisition, possession, and rule of colonies overseas that Britain's health was to be maintained. "New imperialism" gained momentum from the social Darwinist theories that saw in competition with the other European powers, the United States, and Japan the means by which to create a robust society of virile men and proper, moral women. As Lord Rosebery put it in a letter to *The Times* in 1900, "an empire such as ours requires as its first condition an Imperial Race—a race vigorous and industrious and intrepid. Health of mind and body exalt a nation in the competition of the universe. The survival of the fittest is an absolute truth in the conditions of the modern world."[18]

For others, conflict offered the most effective means of strengthening the citizens of a nation. In the eyes of many who embraced Darwin's notions of the survival of the fittest and applied them to the species of human beings as well, war constituted a positive good, an arena in which men could be hardened and those who were unfit could be selected out and prevented from procreating and thus passing on inferior or degenerate traits to a subsequent generation. Through war, the "effeminate" could be weeded out and the manly preserved. "The stimulus of a great patriotic excitement," wrote one apologist for war and empire, "the determination to endure burdens and make sacrifices, the self-abnegation which will face loss, and suffering, and even death, for the commonweal, are bracing tonics to national health, and they counteract the enervating effects of 'too much love of living,' too much ease, and luxury, and material prosperity. . . . Strength is not maintained without exercise."[19]

••

In creating a mass society, the second industrial revolution ushered in a new age of politics. No longer could political leaders focus solely on a small group of constituents as they made domestic and foreign policy decisions. Now, the existence of an enlarged electorate and a public opinion that could be mobilized in short order by mass media and new political parties required leaders to pay attention if they hoped to be elected or reelected to their positions. Sometimes, as we shall see in the following chapters, public opinion and democracy had the effect of tying politicians' hands at precisely the moment when they needed the greatest amount of flexibility.

NOTES

1. James Keir Hardie, "Sunshine of Socialism" speech. http://labourlist.org/2014/04/keir-hardies-sunshine-of-socialism-speech-full-text/.
2. Quoted in Margaret Ward, *Unmanageable Revolutionaries: Women and Irish Nationalism* (London, 1995), p. 13.
3. Quoted in Ward, *Unmanageable Revolutionaries*, pp. 30, 28–29.
4. Quoted in John Davies, "Wales, Ireland and Lloyd George," paper delivered at the National Eisteddfod in Bridgend, August 6, 1998. http://www.ballinagree.freeservers.com/walirllg.html/.
5. John Davies, *A History of Wales* (London, 1990), p. 483.
6. Quoted in Maureen M. Martin, *The Mighty Scot. Nation, Gender, and the Nineteenth-Century Mystique of Scottish Masculinity* (Albany, 2009), p. 81.
7. Quoted in T. M. Devine, *Clanship to Crofters' War. The Social Transformation of the Scottish Highlands* (Manchester, 1994), p. 231.
8. Quoted in Antoinette Burton, *Burdens of History: British Feminist, Indian Women, and Imperial Culture, 1865–1915* (Chapel Hill, 1994), p. 144.
9. Quoted in Arnstein, *Queen Victoria*, p. 140.
10. Quoted in Morris, *Heaven's Command*, p. 420.

11. Martin Meredith, *Diamonds, Gold and War. The British, the Boers, and the Making of South Africa* (New York, 2007), p. 104.
12. Quoted in David Levering Lewis, *The Race to Fashoda: European Colonialism and African Resistance in the Scramble for Africa* (New York: 1987), p. 7.
13. Quoted in Morris, *Heaven's Command*, p. 510.
14. Quoted in Brendon, *The Decline and Fall of the British Empire*, pp. 209, 210.
15. James Morris, *Heaven's Command* (London, 1973), p. 522.
16. Quoted in Ray Costello, *Black Liverpool. The Early History of Britain's Oldest Black Community, 1730–1918* (Liverpool, 2001), p. 59.
17. Quoted in Costello, *Black Liverpool*, p. 97.
18. Quoted in Richard A. Soloway, *Demography and Degeneration: Eugenics and the Declining Birth Rate in Twentieth-Century Britain* (Chapel Hill, 1990), p. 39; and Bernard Porter, *The Lion's Share: A Short History of British Imperialism, 1850–1983* (London, 1975), p. 130.
19. Quoted in Porter, *The Lion's Share*, p. 129.

TIMELINE

1869   Suez Canal opens

1870   Married Women's Property Act

       Contagious Diseases Acts repeal campaign begins

1871   Women admitted to Girton College

1872   Secret Ballot Act

1873   Depression begins

1875   Disraeli purchases shares in Suez Canal

1876   Royal Titles Act makes Queen Victoria empress of India

1878   Women admitted to University of London

1879   Land League formed in Ireland

       Women admitted to Newnham College

1882   Battle of the Braes in Scotland

       Frederick Cavendish assassinated in Dublin

FURTHER READING

Antoinette Burton, *Burdens of History: British Feminist, Indian Women, and Imperial Culture, 1865–1915*. Chapel Hill, 1994.

T. M. Devine, *Clanship to Crofters' War. The Social Transformation of the Scottish Highlands.* Manchester, 1994.

Maureen M. Martin, *The Mighty Scot. Nation, Gender, and the Nineteenth-Century Mystique of Scottish Masculinity.* Albany, 2009.

Martin Meredith, *Diamonds, Gold and War. The British, the Boers, and the Making of South Africa.* New York, 2007.

Richard A. Soloway, *Demography and Degeneration: Eugenics and the Declining Birth Rate in Twentieth-Century Britain.* Chapel Hill, 1990.

Margaret Ward, *Unmanageable Revolutionaries: Women and Irish Nationalism.* London, 1995.

1884	Third Reform Act
1884	Berlin Conference ratifies scramble for Africa
1886	Crofters' Act
	Home Rule for Ireland introduced
	Liberal Unionists split from Liberal party
	Contagious Diseases Act repealed
1888	Women's match strike
1889	Great London Dock Strike
1893	Independent Labour Party forms
	Women in New Zealand win vote
1895	Jameson Raid
1897	Mosquitos found to cause malaria
1898	Battle of Omdurman
1899	Aspirin developed
1906	Labour Party forms

Rounding up Afrikaner women during the South African War, c. 1900.

CHAPTER 10

TRANSVAAL
ORANGE
FREE
STATE
South
Cape Town *Africa*

THE CRISES OF THE *FIN DE SIÈCLE*, 1899–1914

I n 1901, Captain March Phillipps rode at the head of a small irregular cavalry unit of Rimington's Guides in the Orange Free State in South Africa with orders from his commander, General H. H. Kitchener (1850–1916), to burn down the farms of Afrikaners. "The worst moment," he recounted later, "is when you first come to the house," for the occupants usually expected that the soldiers were there for food and drink and left their chores to serve up milk or biscuits to the troops.[1] But they were not there for that, which soon became clear to the women and children, who were given ten minutes to gather up what they could of clothing and other items before the Guides set their homes ablaze. Standing dazed among the furniture, bedding, utensils, and crockery they had managed to salvage before the flames began to consume their dwellings, some Afrikaner women railed against the British troops and threatened them with the hellfire that would surely end their days; others wept as their terrified children clung to their aprons. One young girl, Phillipps recalled, vented her rage and defiance by banging out the Afrikaner national anthem on an old piano that had been dragged from a front parlor. With smoke billowing from the roofs of their houses and the sound of the fires crackling overhead, with the cries of their livestock being slaughtered in their ears, the civilian casualties of Britain's scorched-earth policy during the South African War (also known as the Anglo-Boer War) suffered depredations they would never forget.

But worse was still to come because now the burned-out Afrikaners had to be put somewhere. Kitchener established a series of concentrations camps in which to house them, because, he insisted, "every farm is to [the Afrikaners] an intelligence agency and a supply depot so that it is almost impossible to surround or catch them."[2] He ordered the inhabitants of the farms, almost exclusively women and children, into camps where he could keep them from spying and otherwise aiding the Afrikaner cause. Black South Africans were also herded into camps as their lands were cleared by British troops, so that at one point in the war, some 116,000 black and 160,000 white South Africans occupied more than 100 facilities lacking sufficient shelter, food, water, hygienic practices, and medical care. Diseases ran rampant through the camps—measles, typhoid, malaria, respiratory ailments, dysentery, and a whole host of other illnesses killed the starved and weakened inmates by the thousands. By the end of the conflict, some 25,000 Afrikaners and at least that many Africans had died in the camps.

The "methods of barbarism" employed by the British against the Afrikaners in the South African War shocked and outraged people across the globe. Britain found itself friendless in a world that was becoming increasingly more dangerous. The culmination of an approach to empire called "new imperialism," the war foreshadowed the brutalization that would characterize much of the twentieth century. More immediately, when it came to an end in 1902, British politicians and diplomats began to edge away from their long-standing policy of "splendid isolation" in favor of agreements, however vague and even toothless, with former rivals. Within two years, the country had come to a series of understandings first with France and then three years later with Russia, ultimately establishing one half of a system of alliances that would divide Europe into two armed camps.

••

THE SOUTH AFRICAN WAR

The fears of deterioration that informed the writings of imperialists and social Darwinists were confirmed and exacerbated in the last years of the nineteenth century, when Britain provoked a war against the small but determined group of Dutch Afrikaner farmers in the Transvaal in South Africa in 1899 to secure its hold on the gold mines of the Rand. Confident of their success and determined to teach the Afrikaners a lesson about the power and glory of the British empire, politicians and the public were stunned when their armies suffered a series of humiliating and embarrassing defeats in the first months of the war. By late 1900, those losses had been reversed, but the defeat of the 45,000 Afrikaner guerrilla soldiers required an additional eighteen months and 450,000 British soldiers.

Britons believed war with the Afrikaners to be inevitable. As Winston Churchill had put it, "sooner or later, in a righteous cause or a picked quarrel ... for the sake of our Empire, for the sake of our honour, for the sake of the race, we must fight the Boers." It was really for the sake of the gold mines in the Transvaal Republic, but no matter. The presence of so many Britons in the Boer republic, where they constituted a majority of the population, paid 80 percent of the taxes, and yet had no rights of citizenship, provided the "righteous cause." The picked quarrel, ironically, came from the Boers themselves, who after the Jameson raid saw the writing on the wall and felt they had to move quickly if they were to have any chance of preventing a British takeover of their country. On October 11, 1899, they launched what they regarded as a preventive invasion of the Natal province and the Cape Colony. Before a week passed, three divisions of British troops had embarked on their voyage to destroy the Boers and gain fame and glory for themselves and for their queen. Victoria had inspected the Gordon Highlanders before they left and described in her journal the "very touching" occasion. "I felt quite a lump in my throat as we drove away, and I thought of how these remarkably fine men might not all return."[3]

That was an understatement if there ever was one. For all the talk of the need to prepare for the keen race of nations, British planners had done little to modernize their army. In its attitudes and tactics, it harkened back to the days of Wellington. It might possess modern arms—machine guns and repeater rifles—but it employed them in decidedly ancient ways. Soldiers went into battle led by pipers and drummers and only recently had they shed their redcoats for a drabber olive uniform. They formed up in battle squares and advanced in close order. Moreover, they had not fought Europeans since the Crimean War in the 1850s, except for meeting the Boers in the debacle at Majuba Hill in 1881, when they had been utterly humiliated.

The Afrikaners, in many ways, looked precisely like those imperial pioneers and hunters extolled in British adventure stories. They constituted not an army per se as much as an irregular commando force made up of virtually all Afrikaner men, showing up when they felt it necessary—and departing when they had more pressing issues elsewhere—on the backs of their own horses in homespun clothing that barely resembled anything like a uniform. Their discipline was lax and they elected their own officers. But in addition to the modern weapons they brought to the battlefield, they possessed extraordinary skills of horsemanship and knew the terrain like the backs of their hands. Consummate hunters, they responded to the needs of the moment, flexible in their tactics and responsive to whatever the situation they faced might demand. They knew what they were doing in defense of their land and their way of life.

Despite being heavily outnumbered, the Afrikaners inflicted a series of losses on the British forces. The British performance in the first months of the war proved so inept that calls for an inquiry soon arose. The terrible failures started to turn around in February 1900 with the relief of two towns, Kimberley and Ladysmith. In the scheme of things, these victories should have been accepted as a matter of course, but so bad had the situation been just a month earlier that the British public erupted in wild celebration. The disproportionate response to the victory demonstrates just how bad the situation had become.

The war continued on, the fighting bitter and ugly and seemingly endless. Britain carried out a scorched-earth policy, torching farmhouses and fields. Both sides executed prisoners in the field, ignoring international rules governing warfare. Twenty-two thousand Britons died, two-thirds of them from disease.

The British threw women and children into concentration camps, among the first the world had seen, whose terrible conditions left their inmates diseased and malnourished. Twenty-five thousand Afrikaners died, 20,000 of them women and children who had suffered in the camps. When the existence of the camps became known in Britain, divisions in society over whether Britain should be involved in this conflict deepened, compelling even those who did not oppose the war outright to condemn the policy and the practice of locking up civilians. Emily Hobhouse (1860–1926), a member of a prominent Liberal family, visited the camps as part of her effort to give out clothing and blankets to inmates for the antiwar South African Women and Children's Distress Fund. Her 1901 report on the conditions she found shocked and appalled her countrymen and -women and panicked Conservative politicians who worried about its impact on their prosecution of the war.

The government commissioned its own investigation, appointing Millicent Garrett Fawcett (1847–1929), also from a prominent Liberal family and, more important, leader of the National Union of Women's Suffrage Societies, to lead a "Ladies Commission" looking into the camps. Fawcett, who supported the war effort against the Boers, traveled to thirty-three of the thirty-four concentration camps operated by the British. Her report, published as a Blue Book in 1902, attributed the terrible living conditions and the high mortality rates to the poor hygienic habits practiced by Boer women. The camps' governors, she argued, were doing their best, but were up against a primitive and backward people.

Afrikaner families in a British concentration camp during the South African War, 1900.

The concentration camps brought women into the narrative of the South African War for the first time. As was befitting a time when challenges to predominant gender ideology by British feminists had become so pronounced, the role played by women in the discourse of imperialism was not as straightforward as it had been a generation earlier. General Kitchener, who became commander in chief of the armed forces in 1900, established the camps as part of his military strategy, imprisoning women because they were acting as combatants. When the existence of the camps became known in Britain, an uproar ensued, and the war secretary, St. John Brodrick (1856–1942), faced awkward questions in Parliament. "What civilized Government ever deported women?" demanded Irish MP John Dillon (1851–1927). "Had it come to this, that this Empire was afraid of women?" Brodrick replied with the explanation Kitchener had provided him, that "women and children who have been deported are those who have either been found giving information to the enemy or are suspected of giving information to the enemy." This had the effect of spurring Dillon on to even greater rhetorical outrage: "I ask the honourable gentlemen," he sneered, "if any civilized nation in Europe ever declared war against women.... A pretty pass has the British Empire come to now![4] With no good way out of this gender morass, government officials and supporters of the war quickly changed their stories to ones that better fit the gender ideology of Victorian Britain. They insisted now that the camps had had to be built to protect Afrikaner women from the unmanly behavior of their menfolk and, more pointedly, from black Africans.

Afrikaner men had deserted their women, this new narrative asserted, leaving them alone in a dangerous land to starve. Had the men upheld their responsibilities "to provide for their women and children, many of those difficulties which are now complained of would never have occurred," declared Brodrick in 1901. And to release those women now, *The Times* insisted, would be to "expose them to outrages from the natives which would set all South Africa in flame."[5] The discourse of new imperialism, in which manly Britons had to take control over unmanly and hypersexualized indigenous peoples in defense of white women, took hold immediately. In this instance, the terms of the discourse had to be altered slightly because British women were not themselves at risk from sexually savage peoples. By including Afrikaner women among the ranks of white women, however, the ideology of vulnerable womanhood could be sustained.

Feminists who supported the conflict such as Fawcett and Josephine Butler, leader of the Contagious Diseases Acts repeal campaign discussed in Chapter 9, drew attention to the similarities between women who lacked a vote and the *uitlanders* in the Transvaal on whose behalf Britain had gone to war. Like women in Britain, Fawcett noted, the *uitlanders*' industry and productivity brought significant amounts of tax revenue to the state, but they were not accorded citizens' rights in return. "They not unnaturally raised the cry, 'No taxation without representation,'" she pointed out, and "inevitably took up and repeated the arguments and protests which for many years we had urged on behalf of the unenfranchised women of Great Britain."[6] Fawcett welcome the opportunity for women to demonstrate what they could do in support of the national and imperial interest, as did Butler, but she and Butler formed a tiny minority of feminists and suffragists who belonged to the prowar camp. Most, and especially those who would become active in the militant suffrage campaign after 1905, opposed it. These latter men and women also looked to the situation of the *uitlanders* in their fight to gain rights, but they drew an entirely different lesson from it. In going to war on behalf of men who did not have an opportunity to exercise the rights of citizenship, Dora Montefiore (1851–1933) observed, British government officials had demonstrated just how important political enfranchisement was to the national interest. By their actions, she argued, "they tell us that the unenfranchised must inevitably be the wronged," and it was encumbent on women to pay attention to the example of the *uitlanders* and "to rise in mass and claim their own rights."[7] She and others would later put forward justifications for women's suffrage that differed from those that emphasized women's contributions to the national and imperial interest, what historians have referred to as the criterion of "service" to the state. Instead, they articulated an argument that the government ruled with the consent of those it governed and those who had no say in choosing that government had not, in fact, given their consent. That being the case, they should raise questions about the obligations they had to obey laws they had no part in making. This theory of "consent," as distinct from that of "service," would mark the actions of militant suffragists in the years after 1905, as we will see later in this chapter.

As the South African War staggered toward its ignominious end in 1902, the question of the future of South Africa's black population came to the fore. African intellectuals and chiefs hoped that the peace settlement would contain at least some protections of African rights. But on this score, Britons and Afrikaners agreed. As Sir Alfred Milner, (1854–1925) the British high commissioner at the Cape, put it, "the white man must rule because he is elevated by many, many steps above the black man; steps which it will take the latter centuries to climb . . . [if] at all."[8] Milner's disinterest in African rights determined the status of Africans under the Treaty of Vereeniging, signed in May 1902 to bring the conflict to a conclusion. He and Chamberlain readily threw out any clauses protecting African rights if they stood in the way of bringing the two sides' positions closer. As Milner put it, "sacrifice 'the nigger' absolutely and the game is easy."[9]

The Peace of Vereeniging offered generous terms, designed as it was to reconcile the Afrikaners to membership in a union of the four colonies of South Africa. The treaty compensated the Transvaal for the devastation it had suffered, guaranteed full equality within the union, and formally recognized the Afrikaner language. The British hoped that their magnanimity would enable them to establish a secure Union of South Africa, dominated by British citizens who could control the gold fields and provide some degree of protection of Africans from Afrikaners. But they miscalculated voting patterns: in 1907 and 1908, Afrikaner parties won elections in the Orange Free State, Transvaal, and Cape Colony, with only Natal remaining British dominated. Ultimately, the

British left the decision of whether to grant Africans political representation and voting rights to the white populations of the Orange Free State and Transvaal, effectively guaranteeing that they would receive neither.

In 1910, the governments of each of the four colonies created a draft constitution for a union modeled on the British political system. It enacted formal color bars against voting in the Orange Free State and Transvaal, gave negligible voting rights to Africans in Natal, and maintained the nonracial franchise in the Cape Colony. The British government accepted the changes in the South African Act and on May 31, 1910, the Union of South Africa came into existence under the leadership of South African War veterans, Prime Minster Louis Botha (1862–1919) and his deputy, Jan Smuts (1870–1950). South Africa became a self-governing "dominion" of the British empire, a status it shared with Canada, Australia, and New Zealand.

The creation of the Union of South Africa paved the way for segregation in the country for virtually the rest of the twentieth century. In 1913, the South African government passed the Native Lands Act, placing 7 percent of the country's land in reserve for its African population, which in 1910 comprised two-thirds of the South African population of nearly 6 million (4 million Africans, 500,000 coloreds, 150,000 Indians, and 1,275,000 whites). Africans could only buy or rent land in these "reserve" areas, which frequently contained only poor-quality land. The Native Lands Act, the first in a long list of racialized legislation, set the tone for the segregationist impulses that would define South Africa for much of the century.

In 1912, in response to the indignities and injuries suffered by Africans at the hands of the new South African government, a number of educated, Christian African elites—Sol Plaatje (1876–1932), Saul Msane (1856–1919), Thomas Mapike (dates unknown), and Walter Rubusana (1858–1936) among them—formed the South African Native National Congress, the forerunner of what would become the African National Congress (ANC). Eleven years later, men and women organized in the South African Indian Congress joined the ANC in its campaign against segregation. Indians had been politically active in South Africa for many years by then, galvanized by Mohandas K. Gandhi's (1869–1948) civil disobedience movement in Durban in the 1890s. Gandhi cut his teeth in South Africa and would take the lessons learned there to India in the years after World War I.

RACE DEGENERATION AND A REVOLUTION IN GOVERNMENT

In the process of recruiting soldiers for the South African War, British officials discovered that fully one-third of those who sought to enlist did not meet military standards of physical health. They were too short, suffered from heart trouble or rheumatism, and had weak lungs or flat feet or bad teeth. The small-chested "new town type" could not stand up to the rigors of physical training and war, and even many of those who passed through the initial screening had to leave the army later when their health failed. Major General John Frederick Maurice (1841–1912) reckoned in 1903 that when both the first rejections and the subsequent dropouts were counted, only two of every five volunteers had proved to be competent soldiers. These figures promised disaster, he warned, because "no nation was ever yet for any long time great and free when the army it put into the field no longer represented its own virility and manhood."[10] When compared to the Germans—indeed even to the Boers and the Japanese—the British "race" of men paled. Near panic about "race degeneration," "physical degeneration," and "deterioration" ensued.

The embarrassments of the British army during the Anglo-Boer War and the hysteria surrounding "race deterioration" in the following years helped to give rise to an organization designed to prepare boys for the rigors of life in a world fraught with imperial and international competition, to prepare them, even, for war. In 1908, Robert Baden-Powell (1857–1941) published *Scouting for Boys*, a handbook that described the process of training boys in the attributes and characteristics necessary to create a race of men capable of upholding Britain's place in the world. Boys, if they were to grow into the right kind of men, would have to accept and obey the orders given them by their elders or superiors; they would have to accept that violence was a part of the natural order of things and be prepared to act violently themselves, which would require them to learn to handle firearms capably; and they would have to recognize and reinforce clear rules of separate spheres for men and women.

If scouting was to train up a new breed of men ready and able to defend Britain and the empire from international rivals and indigenous threats, the Boy Scouts, like the army, needed better raw materials from which to fashion their model citizens. "Town types" might be turned into proper soldiers but they would have to be improved physically first. Maurice and other military and civilian officials assigned responsibility for the deficiencies they found in the rejected recruits for the South African War to mothers of the working classes. "Whatever the primary cause," Maurice declared, "the young man of 16 or 18 years of age is what he is because of the training through which he has passed during his infancy and childhood. . . . Therefore it is to the condition, mental, moral, and physical, of the women and children that we must look if we have regard to the future of our land." The Inter-Departmental Committee on Physical Deterioration, reporting in 1904, stressed the "ignorance" and "fecklessness" of mothers as a factor in the physical decline of the population, blaming mothers for making their children sick. Other parliamentary committees concurred. Maurice suggested that Britons might learn from the Germans how to raise "a virile race, either of soldiers or of citizens." The one essential ingredient, he observed, was that "the attention of the mothers of a land should be mainly devoted to the three K's—Kinder, Küche, Kirche [Children, Kitchen, Church]." Others looked to practices in Japan, which was "in no danger of race-suicide." They proposed a series of reforms that would compel mothers to learn "mothercraft" to improve the health and welfare of their children and thus the health and welfare of the state.[11]

A spate of child welfare provisions followed. In this Britain lagged behind Germany and France by at least twenty years. In 1906, an education act providing for meals for poor London schoolchildren was enacted; another in 1907 required children to undergo medical inspection. The 1907 Notification of Births Act mandated that fathers or those attending deliveries register all live births with the local authorities within thirty-six hours; midwives required training. The 1908 Children Act set up a separate system of justice for youths, made it illegal for children under fourteen to enter pubs, criminalized the "overlaying" (suffocation) of children if the adult was drunk at the time he or she went to bed, and provided punishments if a child died for lack of fireguards in the home. In keeping with the often-punitive tone and substance of the infant welfare movement, much of it directed at women, the Children Act identified and penalized for the first time the neglect of children by their parents.

Contrary to liberal convictions that the individual should operate free of interference from or compulsion by the state, the infant welfare movement of the early twentieth century imposed on individuals—and in this case, particular individuals, mothers—to address and resolve national problems of public health, domestic politics, and imperial and international conflict. The raising of children now became a national obligation on the part of women rather than a moral or social duty, and if they did not perform this function adequately, the state would step in to insist that they do it better. Completely ignoring the environmental factors working-class families faced—poverty, overcrowding, unsanitary streets, water, and sewage systems, pollution, epidemic and chronic disease—the state conferred on women who had no control over them the responsibility, but not the resources, to improve the stock of the nation. And, operating according to a largely negative set of images of working-class women, state officials and voluntary agencies like the Charity Organisation Society turned to laws that coerced mothers into providing a certain kind and level of care, rather than legislation designed to help them by providing the necessary means. As working-class women saw it, reformers were requiring them to reallocate scarce resources from one part of the family to another. Given the tradition of husbands keeping a part of their pay packet for themselves to buy tobacco and drink and giving the remainder to their wives to manage as best they could, this situation demanded that women themselves go without food, clothing, rest, and good health so that the new state requirements for their children could be met. And if they were not, working-class mothers faced "countless humiliations" from officious, intrusive, arrogant, and impolite middle-class district visitors; fines; jail sentences; and even loss of their children. As Anna Martin (c. 1858–1937), a social worker and feminist, observed of the working-class mother at the time, the child welfare movement expected that she become "the unpaid nursemaid of the State."[12]

Concerns about the "deterioration of the race" and its impact on Britain's power and place in the world, as well as pressure from a restive electorate made up of many working-class voters, finally compelled the Liberal government, which had come back into power in 1905, to abdicate long-held positions about the need of the state to stay aloof from the workings of the economy and of society and to introduce measures that taxed the wealthy to provide basic (and usually inadequate) subsistence to (some of) the unemployed, the elderly, and the sick. In 1908, the chancellor of the Exchequer, Herbert Henry Asquith (1852–1928), included a plan to provide old-age pensions in the budget. The sums prescribed were small and limited to those who had earned a certain level of income before they turned seventy, but some 1 million elderly immediately benefited from them, and their provision marked an unprecedented departure from classical liberal principles. Classical liberals believed that government's proper function consisted solely in providing opportunities for the exercise of freedom and liberty; in what historians have regarded as one of the first steps on the road to creating the welfare state of the twentieth century, the government recognized that one of its major obligations was to provide some measure of material security to at least some of its citizens. In 1909, when the Welshman David Lloyd George, now chancellor of the Exchequer under the prime ministership of Asquith, presented his "People's Budget" before Parliament, he extended this obligation to the unemployed and the sick. He proposed to pay for these pensions and other social services designed to reduce poverty by levying a new "supertax" on the wealthy; the budget also raised death duties on the inheritance of large estates to 25 percent of their worth, placed a tax on gasoline and automobiles, and, worst of all, from the perspective of elites, imposed capital gains taxes on land and minerals when they changed hands. In short, the People's Budget sought to redistribute a modest portion of the wealth of the country from the very rich to the poor.

Resistance from the Conservative Party proved to be so great that the Liberal government felt compelled to cripple the power of the Lords, where Conservatives held a majority, to scuttle legislation. By the Parliament Act of 1911—which only passed the House of Lords after the king threatened to create hundreds of new Liberal peers, thus diluting both the Conservative majority and the prestige of nobility—Britain's ancient constitution was significantly altered. From here on, the House of Lords could only delay, rather than veto, legislation. If passed by the Commons in three successive years, the measures would become law. The Parliament Act ensured, as we shall see below, that legislation granting home rule to Ireland would be just a matter of time. Dependent on Irish as well as Labour votes for its majority, the Liberal Party had had to promise that it would introduce a measure for home rule the very next year.

LABOR DISPUTES AND THE MILITANT WOMEN'S SUFFRAGE MOVEMENT

The challenges to the traditional liberal order and the gender regime that upheld it became increasingly pronounced in the years after 1899. Labour disputes became harder to settle, and violence frequently accompanied workers' efforts to obtain wages with which they could support their families. The number of union members had increased to 4 million by 1914, doubling in the period since 1900. Strikes by railway workers in 1907, by shipbuilders and coal miners in 1908, by dock workers in 1911 and 1912, and by miners in 1912 testified both to the power and to the dissatisfactions of workers with their lot. Striking miners in the Welsh community of Tonypandy rioted against the policies of the Rhondda coalfield operations in 1910 and 1911; home secretary Winston Churchill sent police and then troops to quell the riot and protect the mines.

Striking coalminers in Wales, 1910.

Seamen in Liverpool went out in May of 1911, and soon workers on the docks, in the mills, and in virtually all of the transport industries followed. Mass demonstrations in support of the strikes led to riots in the late summer, resulting in the shooting deaths of a number of workers by troops dispatched by Churchill. In 1913 and 1914, miners in England, Scotland, and Wales struck again, and industrial action broke out in Dublin as well. In 1913 the "Triple Alliance" of railway workers, transport workers, and miners formed, and in 1914 they threatened a general strike designed to shut down the country. The outbreak of war in August 1914 prevented the action from taking place, a story we will address in Chapter 11.

The Parliament Act of 1911 ensured that the House of Lords could not block forever the attempts by Liberals to gain home rule for Ireland. When it became clear in 1912 that home rule would indeed prevail, northern Irish Protestants armed themselves to oppose the British government. They received support and encouragement from Conservative politicians and members of the military high command in a series of measures that came terribly close to treason. (Because this incident bore on the events leading up to Britain's decision to enter the Great War against Germany, we will deal with it more extensively later in the chapter.) Certainly it contributed mightily to the tensions and violence that characterized the years from 1911 to 1914.

Above all, a provocative mass movement in support of women's suffrage vigorously challenged the ideology of separate spheres and the understandings of masculinity and femininity and of male and female sexuality that underpinned liberal practice. By the beginning of the twentieth century, the suffrage campaign had attained the status of a mass movement. With the advent of militancy arising out of the Women's Social and Political Union (WSPU) in 1905, the whole of the feminist movement centered around suffrage as the means by which women could free themselves from servile bondage to men. As a symbol of civic and political personality, the vote would be an effective agent in eliminating the notion of women as "the Sex." As an instrument of power, feminists believed—as did their adversaries—it would transform the elevating "influence" of women into a tool with which to create a greater and truer morality among men by eliminating the distinctions between public and private spheres.

On October 13, 1905, on the eve of a general election, Sir Edward Grey (1862–1933), a prominent member of the Liberal Party, appeared on stage at Manchester's Free Trade Hall to exhort the audience to vote for his party. Annie Kenney (1879–1953), a trade unionist and member of the WSPU, rose to ask, "Will the Liberal Government give women the vote?" Grey ignored her, responding to other questions from the gallery instead. Kenney would not yield the floor and repeated her demand, prompting a number of men to drag her down into her seat and a Liberal steward to place his hat over her face. Her companion, Christabel Pankhurst (1880–1958), picked up the call as cries from audience members filled the air. "Be quiet!" railed some; others urged, "let the lady speak." Kenney climbed up on a chair to raise her question again; stewards and a plain-clothed police officer struggled with Pankhurst as she tried to keep them away from Kenney. But both were physically ejected from the hall amid protests from the audience. Grey felt compelled to answer the complaints, conceding that he may well have contributed to the "trouble" because it "arose from a desire to know my opinion on Women's Suffrage." He explained that he "would not deal with [it] here to-night, because it is not, and I do not think it is likely to be, a party question."[13]

Outside the hall, determined to bring about her arrest by committing a technical assault, Pankhurst spat at a policeman. She and Kenney were arrested and offered a choice of prison or fines. They both opted for jail, keen to obtain the press attention such a sentence was bound to generate. Assigned to the third, or lowest, division of the system, they took their place among ordinary criminals, dressed in prison garb and joining pickpockets, prostitutes, and procurers for their daily meals. As they had hoped, newspapers broadcast reports of and diatribes against their actions, creating a level of publicity for "the cause"—votes for women—that they could not possibly have secured on their own.

With the arrival of the WSPU, under the leadership of Emmeline (1858–1928) and Christabel Pankhurst, the suffrage campaign took on new life and meaning. The militant tactics of the WSPU electrified the country and galvanized the whole of the suffrage movement in England, Scotland, Ireland, and Wales. From 1897, when all suffrage societies were federated in the National Union of Women Suffrage Societies (NUWSS), to 1903, when the WSPU formed, the NUWSS encompassed only 16 societies. By 1909, 54 additional societies had come into being and joined the NUWSS. In 1911, 305 societies made up the constitutional group; that number swelled to 400 by 1913.

In marked contrast to the strategies pursued by the NUWSS, the WSPU followed a policy of spectacular protests. "Deeds Not Words" was its motto. Militancy began with Pankhurst's and Kenney's actions at the Free Trade Hall. Their treatment at the hands of men spurred many women to action. Until the summer of 1909 militancy was nonviolent: suffragists heckled cabinet ministers and obstructed political meetings, and they marched on Parliament to meet with MPs who refused to see them. When the police learned to anticipate and try to cut short militant deputations to Parliament, the suffragists responded with surprises and clever disguises to circumvent them. "Now one would appear as a messenger boy," Ray Strachey (1887–1940), a prominent member of the NUWSS, recounted, "now another as a waitress. . . . They sprang out of organ lofts, they peered through roof windows, and leapt out of innocent-looking furniture vans; they materialised on station platforms, they harangued the terrace of the House from the river, and wherever they were least expected there they were."[14]

Men often responded to nonviolent militant tactics with fury. An unprecedented display of brutality occurred on November 18, 1910, a day ever after referred to in the annals of suffrage history as "Black Friday." Three hundred suffragists marching on Parliament Square were confronted by uniformed and plain-clothed police, whose orders were to prevent the women from reaching the houses of Parliament. For six hours, the women suffered "violent and indecent treatment" at the hands of police and male bystanders, as one account described the scene. Ada Wright was "knocked down a dozen times in succession." Police "struck the women with fists and knees, knocked them down, some even kicked them, then dragged them up, carried them a few paces and flung them into the crowd of sightseers." Victims and bystanders testified to "deliberate acts of cruelty, such as twisting and wrenching of arms, wrists, and thumbs; griping the throat and forcing back the head; pinching the arms; striking the face with fists, sticks, helmets; throwing women down and kicking them; rubbing a woman's face against the railings; pinching the breasts; squeezing the ribs." Cecilia Haig died in December 1911 from injuries sustained that day. The incidents in 1912 at Llanystumdwy, in Wales, where suffragists heckled David Lloyd George, rivaled

A PLACE IN TIME

Militants in Liverpool

In 1905, Alice Morrissey, a member of the Independent Labour Party, formed the Liverpool branch of the militant Women's Social and Political Union (WSPU) after a dispute with the leadership of the Liverpool Women's Suffrage Society over its failure to appeal to working-class women. The working-class complexion of the organization throughout the period 1905 to 1914 distinguished it from the national body, which in the years following 1905 became increasingly elitist in character under the Pankhursts' leadership. The Liverpool branch, moreover, continued to enjoy the support of members and even increased in size following the embrace of violent militancy after 1912 while WSPU branches across the rest of the country lost ground. Whereas the national organization focused almost exclusively on the destruction of property during this period and demanded unquestioned loyalty and approbation of its practices, Liverpool leaders quietly went about conducting their affairs as they saw fit. Certainly they engaged in dramatic and provocative acts, including violent ones, but the working-class constituency of Liverpool found in its local society a variety of opportunities to participate in politics, and it appears not to have been put off by the kind of direct action that alienated middle- and upper-class reformers elsewhere. Liverpool suffragettes had both observed and involved themselves in similar methods carried out by the Labour and Socialist parties of the area and they regarded them as necessary to achieve their goals.

The treatment of two working-class suffragettes in 1909 caused a stir in the national press and prompted one of the most well-known incidents in suffrage history. Leslie Hall and Selina Martin were arrested for throwing an empty bottle at the car of Prime Minister Herbert Asquith during his electioneering visit to Liverpool in December. They were placed in Walton Gaol to await trial and refused to eat. Prison officials responded with brutality, clapping the women in handcuffs and, in Martin's case, dragging her down stone stairs to a room where they force fed her through a nasal tube. News of their ordeal reached the Pankhursts, who issued a pamphlet outlining the events and the suffering the two women experienced.

When Lady Constance Lytton (1869–1923), a suffragette from a prominent English family, learned of the incident, she resolved to bring attention to the injustices carried out against working-class women involved in the suffrage campaign. In October 1909, she had been jailed in Newcastle for stone-throwing, but when prison authorities realized who she was—the daughter of a viceroy of India and the sister of a member of the House of Lords—they released her. Now she disguised herself as a seamstress by the name of Jane Warton and traveled to Liverpool, where she made herself obnoxious enough outside Walton Gaol to get herself arrested and imprisoned. She refused food and over the next two weeks was force fed eight times. As she described it in her subsequent account of the event, "the pain of it was intense and at last I must have given way for [the prison doctor] got the gag between my teeth, when he proceeded to turn it much more than necessary until my jaws were fastened wide

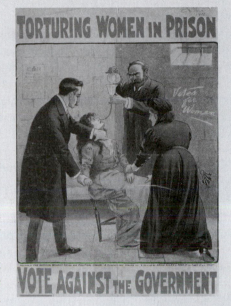

Force-feeding hunger-striking suffragettes, 1913.

apart, far more than they could go naturally. Then he put down my throat a tube which seemed to me much too wide and was something like four feet in length. The irritation of the tube was excessive. I choked the moment it touched my throat until it had got down. Then the food was poured in quickly; it made me sick a few seconds after it was down and the action of the sickness made my body and legs double up, but the wardresses instantly pressed back my head and the doctor leant on my knees. The horror of it was more than I can describe. I was sick over the doctor and wardresses, and it seemed a long time before they took the tube out."[17] The traumas of the force feeding led ultimately to a heart attack in 1910 and a stroke in 1912. Considerably weakened, Lady Lytton died in 1923 at the age of fifty-four.

Lady Lytton's subterfuge and subsequent treatment did bring attention to the disparities of class when it came to the police response to the law-breaking of the suffragettes, and her account may have helped convince authorities to give up force feeding. Within the ranks of the Liverpool WSPU, her ordeal seems to have stiffened the resolve of suffragettes, who took up violent militancy with alacrity in 1912. Their acts of arson and attempted bombings—on a school, a church, the Stock Exchange, pillar boxes, and the Liverpool Exhibition—reached nearly the level of those carried out in London and garnered a great deal of attention throughout the country.

the ferocity of Black Friday. According to Sylvia Pankhurst (1882–1960), "men and women were beaten, kicked and stripped almost naked. The hair of women was torn out in handfuls."[15]

Emmeline and Christabel Pankhurst may well have welcomed, if they did not court, these displays of sexual violence against women because they served as powerful recruiting agents for the suffrage cause. Militants and nonmilitants alike expressed appreciation that the "brute" sexuality in men had finally been exposed. Lucy Re-Bartlett, an ardent enthusiast of militancy, stated that only the militants were doing anything to eradicate from civilization the "brute consciousness" and "sexual excess" of men. Their activities had "brought to the surface the 'brute' in many men," thereby removing "the fetters of sentimentality and illusion from many thousands of women," she claimed.[16]

In the summer of 1909, militants took up stone-throwing. In a symbolic protest against the politicians who refused to meet their demands, they broke countless government windows. Stone-throwing had a more pragmatic effect as well—it cut short the struggles with the police and reduced the amount of suffering suffragists experienced before being arrested. That same summer, militant suffragists began to stage a hunger strike in prison. They demanded that their sentences be reduced to reflect more accurately the severity of their crimes—heckling, demonstrating, and stone-throwing—and that the courts regard them as political prisoners rather than common criminals. Instead, the authorities responded with forced feeding, whereby a tube was inserted through the prisoner's nostril down into the stomach and liquid nourishment poured down it. The violence of forced feeding led to a great outcry against the government's actions from sympathizers and opponents of women's suffrage alike. Like the displays of male brutality during suffrage demonstrations, it aided the suffrage societies in their recruitment efforts.

The WSPU succeeded in focusing enormous publicity on the suffrage issue, but the parliamentary response to women's demands for the vote remained cool. Suffragists enjoyed a great deal of support in Parliament, but Herbert H. Asquith, the prime minister, refused to back a women's suffrage measure. After the election of 1910, however, it appeared that a women's suffrage bill might pass. A Conciliation Committee, composed of members from all parties, formed to draft a bill that would enjoy the support of all shades of political opinion. To give the conciliation bill a chance, the WSPU called a truce in militancy. The bill passed its second reading in July 1910, but before it could go further, Asquith, with the complicity of Lloyd George, torpedoed it.

The militants immediately abandoned their truce. On November 18, 1910, suffragettes marched from Caxton Hall to Parliament, where they were attacked and sexually molested by police and male bystanders in the above-mentioned incident known as "Black Friday." The subsequent public outrage helped revive the conciliation bill in 1911, on which militants again called a truce in their activities. When the government appeared to throw over the bill for a second time by introducing a measure for manhood suffrage without an amendment including women, the WSPU erupted in acts of deliberate law-breaking. Ethel Moorhead (1869–1955) smashed the glass case holding William Wallace's sword in the Wallace Monument in Scotland. Mary Leigh (1885–1978) threw an axe into the carriage carrying Asquith and Irish leader John Redmond (1856–1918) through the streets of Dublin. On March 1, 1912, Emmeline Pankhurst and two other women broke the windows of the prime minister's residence at 10 Downing Street, while in a simultaneous attack, more than 200 other women shattered windows all over London. Police arrested 217 women. Mrs. Pankhurst was charged with inciting to riot. Court officials also issued a warrant for Christabel Pankhurst's arrest, but she evaded their grasp by fleeing to Paris. Mrs. Pankhurst received a sentence of nine months in the criminal division and immediately embarked on a hunger strike. She became so ill that officials released her from prison shortly thereafter. For the next year, under the terms of a law popularly known as the Cat and Mouse Act (1913), Mrs. Pankhurst and other militants followed a pattern of arrest and imprisonment, hunger striking, release from prison, recovery, and a resumption of activities that landed them in jail once again so that the cycle started anew.

The year 1913 saw a series of dramatic and disturbing incidents carried out by militant suffragists. Unknown perpetrators planted a bomb in the house Lloyd George was building; it exploded with no harm to human life but did £500 worth of structural damage. Others set fire to railway stations, golf clubhouses, cricket pavilions, the tea pavilion at Kew, racecourse stands, and private residences in cities across Britain. The irrepressible Mary Leigh tried to torch Dublin's Theatre Royal, and Scottish suffragettes burned down Farington Hall in Dundee. Emily Wilding Davison (1872–1913) threw herself in front of the king's horse running at the Epsom Derby and was trampled to death. Mary Richardson (c. 1882–1961) walked into the National Gallery and slashed Diego Velasquez's painting, the *Rokeby Venus*, with a meat cleaver. What seemed to much of the country to be a madness overtaking its womenfolk appeared to have no end, and it contributed markedly to the sense of chaos that characterized the years just prior to the outbreak of the Great War.

THE COMING OF THE GREAT WAR

The ignominies suffered by Britain during the South African War changed the national discourse of empire and altered the way Britain interacted with the great powers of Europe. At both the official and the popular levels of discussion and debate, the arrogant and aggressive tone of new imperialism gave way to a more sober set of calculations and less bombastic rhetoric. At the end of the war, Britain found itself the target of international condemnation and contempt. Its decision to pick on a small group of backward farmers—or so it appeared to the rest of the world—generated disdain among the European great powers and the United States. Its failure to effectively prosecute the conflict against them enabled its rivals to regard the island powerhouse as a bit of a paper tiger. So friendless was Britain and so evident its weakness that the country that had pursued a policy of "splendid isolation" vis-à-vis Europe for the past hundred years turned almost immediately to its longtime enemy, France, to improve relations. By 1904, they had put together what became called the *Entente Cordiale*, which called for both parties to settle colonial disputes, but made no provisions for assistance in the event of war. Nonetheless, it was quite an achievement: Britain and France had come perilously close to war at Fashoda in the Sudan in 1898. In 1905, provoked by the German buildup of its navy and the kaiser's increasingly bellicose posturing on the world stage, the British Admiralty began to plan for a naval war against Germany, acting in defense of France, and the War Office started to think about playing a role in continental conflicts in France and Belgium. Unofficial conversations between French and British military officials took place, establishing stronger ties between the two countries. In 1907 an Anglo-Russian understanding resembling the *Entente Cordiale* was reached.

Britain's decision to move toward France and Russia in the aftermath of the South African War had in large part been determined by the behavior of Germany under the leadership of Kaiser Wilhelm II, who came to the throne on the death of his father in 1888. Impulsive and insecure, Wilhelm and his advisors destroyed Germany's prominent role in the diplomatic arena with their blustering, bullying, and inconsistent tactics. Wilhelm often made wild gestures implying Germany's desire for foreign conquests; all subtlety was lost and the kaiser, his ministers, and even military leaders conducted policy in a boorish and bellicose manner. Their bad manners led increasingly to European distrust and fear of German intentions. At the same time, the great powers could discern no direction in German foreign policy—it was difficult to see just what Germany wanted and, in the absence of confidence, trepidation followed.

Wilhelm, the grandson of Queen Victoria, vacillated between admiration of and hatred for Great Britain, which was demonstrated in his policy of alternately courting and threatening it. In the 1890s, Britain was still committed to splendid isolation from the continent. Within ten years, largely as a result of the bullying and blackmailing tactics employed by Germany on its path to establish itself as a world power (a policy called *Weltpolitik*), Britain would end its diplomatic aloofness and takes its place in the camp of Germany's enemies. In 1897, two prominent advocates of *Weltpolitik*, Alfred von Tirpitz and Bernhard von Bülow, came to dominate military and civilian affairs. Tirpitz's naval plan was instituted in 1898 with the passage of the Naval Bill. It originally called for a ratio of one German battleship for every two of Britain's, but a supplemental bill upped the ratio to two to three. Ostensibly designed to protect Germany's newly acquired and scattered colonies, the navy in fact intended to challenge Britain's supremacy on the seas. Tirpitz was convinced that Germany was destined to become a world power and that the British were resolved to keep it from its "place in the sun." He postulated that a German navy powerful enough to threaten Britain in its home waters would force it into an alliance with Germany.

In its efforts to gain its place in the sun, Germany sought and acquired colonies in the Pacific and in Africa. It also insinuated itself into the operations of the Ottoman empire's military establishment, providing arms and training and ultimately gaining enormous influence over it. The Ottoman empire included significant territories in the Middle East and North Africa, areas that Britain increasingly regarded as crucial to its control of the routes to India, the lynchpin of the British empire. In 1903, in part as a consequence of Germany's close ties to the Ottomans, the British foreign secretary declared "a sort of Monroe Doctrine for the Persian Gulf," warning off any other great power from trying to establish a naval base or port there.[18] When Germany won the concession to build the Baghdad railway, it seriously alarmed British authorities.

German officials seem never to have considered the possibility that their provocations would act only to drive Britain into the arms of another nation. Yet that is precisely what did happen. Feeling its interests threatened, Britain turned away from Germany and began to look elsewhere for support. Tirpitz's naval program and Bulow's aggressive diplomacy so alarmed and alienated Britain over the course of ten years that Anglo-German relations became almost irretrievably ruined. The decision to embark on a course of *Weltpolitik* and to challenge Britain at sea was to prove decisive for Europe because it determined that Britain would ally with France and Russia. The discovery of the Persian oil fields in 1908 raised the stakes even higher. The Anglo-Russian agreement of the previous year had removed that power from Britain's enemies list; now only Germany presented a serious threat to British interests in the area. Gaining Britain as an ally in turn emboldened France and Russia in their dealings with Germany. Over the next seven years, European frictions would increase and hostilities intensify as a series of incidents in the Balkans and North Africa tested the strength of the British–French–Russian alliance—the Triple Entente–and progressively weakened Germany's only ally, Austria-Hungary, as it faced challenges to its hegemony in southeastern Europe. The failure of the entente to crumble under German provocations and increased challenges to Austro-Hungarian hegemony in southeastern Europe resulted in a transformation of the compact between Germany and Austria-Hungary, the Dual Alliance, turning it from a defensive to an offensive agreement. The German chief of staff of the army told his Austrian counterpart that if Austria-Hungary felt it must attack Serbia, whose military and civilian authorities supported and sometimes encouraged nationalist revolts against the empire, then Germany would assist it in doing so. He did so knowing that aggression against Serbia, a country traditionally falling under the protection of Russia, would provoke the tsar's government into taking action to defend its small ally. As soon as Russia began to mobilize, he assured Austria-Hungary, Germany would respond in kind. As one historian has put it, "adventurers in Vienna" now had the capacity to determine policy in Berlin. The stage was set. The assassination of Franz Ferdinand, the heir to the Austro-Hungarian throne, and his wife Sophie, by Serb nationalists in late June of 1914 provided the trigger that would set Europe on a course toward world war.

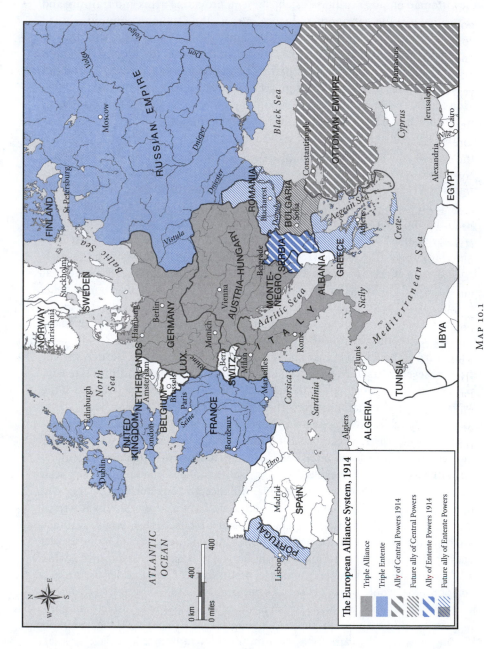

The European Alliance System, 1914

Triple Alliance

Triple Entente

Ally of Central Powers 1914

Future ally of Central Powers

Ally of Entente Powers 1914

Future ally of Entente Powers

MAP 10.1

The European Alliance System, 1914

Irish Complications

In Britain, the apparently unstoppable momentum that seemed to propel the continental powers toward the battlefield ran up against the inertia of domestic politics involving the fate of Ireland. While diplomats and politicians on the continent fumbled their way toward disaster in July 1914, British politicians and military men focused their attentions on the events unfolding in Ulster in northern Ireland. The drama taking place there, which had been at least three years in the making, preoccupied statesmen who would otherwise have been working the dispatch cases and telegraph wires between London and Paris, Berlin, Vienna, and St. Petersburg. Even Prime Minister Asquith, who with his foreign secretary, Sir Edward Grey (1862–1933), was one of the few members of the cabinet who leaned toward intervening in a war against Germany should it come to that, had set his eyes not on Europe but on northern Ireland. As late as July 24, he wrote a long letter to Venetia Stanley (1887–1948) recounting the complex ins and outs of negotiations concerning Ulster, and only at the end did he mention, almost in passing, that Austria had issued "a bullying and humiliating Ultimatum to Servia, who cannot possibly accept it."[19] What mattered most to Britons, still culturally imbued with the habits of splendid isolation, were not the goings-on of a "European quarrel," but the affairs currently convulsing the Irish.

As we saw in the previous chapter, Irish politics had ceased to occupy British politicians in the years following the failure of the last home rule campaign and the split in the Liberal Party. Irish politics returned to Westminster, however, when Liberals gained power in 1905. In 1912, acting on their bargain with the Irish Party to introduce home rule in return for the party's support for the 1911 Parliament Act, the Liberals enacted a bill that would create an Irish Parliament in Dublin through which legislation affecting local Irish concerns could be created. Although rejected by the Lords, the act, under the new constitutional terms of the Parliament Act of 1911, could not be delayed beyond 1914; home rule would come to Ireland, it was clear. Immediately, six counties of Ulster announced their intention to oppose home rule by any and all means, and under the leadership of Sir Edward Carson (1854–1935)—and with the explicit support of Conservative leader Andrew Bonar Law (1858–1923)—built up a mass movement of resistance. In 1913, Ulstermen began to arm themselves and formed the Ulster Volunteer Force, promising to defend union with the United Kingdom through violence if necessary. In April they obtained 24,000 guns from Germany.

The south of Ireland responded on November 25, 1913, with the establishment of the Irish Volunteers at a meeting in Dublin. Operating behind the scenes as much as possible, the Irish Republican Brotherhood formed a significant core of the Irish Volunteers and used the specter of the armed Protestant north to try to persuade the Irish people that independence would come not from parliamentary maneuvering but from armed conflict. The Irish Republican Brotherhood

Edward Carson and Ulster Volunteers during the Irish home rule crisis, 1914.

welcomed the provocation from the north because through armed resistance, they declared, the Irish Volunteers would make an "honest and manly stand." Through membership in the Volunteers, Irish males could "realise themselves as citizens and as men," and all those who were "manly, liberty loving and patriotic" would follow their example and join themselves.[20] In March of 1914, as home rule for Ireland was just about to be passed into law, the government ordered troops in Ireland to march north to cut off an anticipated rising by the Ulster Volunteers. In what became known as the Mutiny at the Curragh, a significant number of army officers threatened to resign their commissions rather than carry out their orders. They did so at the secret urging of Bonar Law and of Sir Henry Wilson (1864–1922), chief of military operations at the War Office. This near-treasonous act took place at a time when the situation in Europe was approaching crisis, and it may have helped to persuade the German general staff that Britain could be ignored as they went about making plans to conquer Europe.

By the end of July 1914, Ireland—and England, too, if the actions of Carson, Bonar Law, and the highest echelons of the military command are taken into account—teetered on the precipice of civil war. The Great War came just in time to prevent it, dousing the flames of insurrection with a bracing blast of cold water. Wilson and other high-ranking officers had told the government that if home rule were to be imposed and peace maintained, the entire British Expeditionary

Force would have to be to shipped to Ireland to do it, leaving no army to intervene in Europe should the need arise. Or, Wilson noted, should Britain go to war against Germany, home rule would have to be abandoned because there would be no military presence available to enforce it. Wilson's either/or formulations constituted a kind of political blackmail; certainly, given Conservatives' total opposition to home rule in Ireland, they provided strong incentive for arguing in favor of intervening on the continent.

Until the beginning of August, the cabinet and public opinion opposed going to war with Germany. But by August 1, the situation had changed dramatically, and most ministers had come round to the desirability of intervention. Their about-face had not been a result, necessarily, of compelling pro-French arguments. Rather, Asquith and Grey had threatened to resign should Britain not commit itself to the defense of its ally, and the rest of the cabinet feared that they would not be able to hold a government together without them. For the Conservatives, eager to intervene in Europe—at least in part to delay for as long as possible the imposition of home rule in Ireland—lurked in the wings, ready to establish their own government should the Liberals fall. In that case, ministers decided, why lose power to a party that would take them into war anyway? Their capitulation to political expediency would have consequences none of them could have foreseen, although Grey, the chief proponent of an interventionist policy, came nearest to comprehending the situation when he remarked, on Britain's declaration of war against Germany on August 4, 1914, "the lamps are going out all over Europe, we shall not see them lit again in our life-time."[21]

••

The years after 1911 all across Britain marked a dramatic departure from practices and policies pursued in earlier times. By the end of July 1914, striking workers, Irish rebels, Tory die-hards, and militant suffragists had brought liberal England to its knees. Virtually every principle and assumption of classical liberal thought had been called into question. Free trade, laissez-faire, constitutionalism and the rule of law, and a restricted male franchise—all came under fire from various groups ranging from union officials, Conservative and Unionist politicians, Irish Protestants and Irish Catholics, and feminists from every quarter of the kingdom. The domestic ideology of separate spheres for men and women and the notions of masculinity and femininity and of male and female sexuality that informed it had been vigorously, publicly, and spectacularly contested and masculinity was discredited.

When the war broke out in August 1914, it came as a relief to many Britons, who saw in it the opportunity to reestablish the social, economic, political, imperial, and gender orders of Britain. The civil war, the class war, and the sex war of the spring and summer of 1914, as contemporaries regarded them, would be subsumed within and extinguished by the far more seemly war of European nations.

What Britons could not know, in the first weeks before trench lines were established and a vicious war of attrition set in, was that the war would change every aspect of their lives, and forever.

NOTES

1. Quoted in Denis Judd and Keith Surridge, *The Boer War, A History* (London, 2002), p. 192.
2. Quoted in Paula M. Krebs, *Gender, Race, and the Writing of Empire. Public Discourse and the Boer War* (Cambridge, 1999), p. 59.
3. Quoted in Susan Kingsley Kent, *Queen Victoria: Gender and Empire* (New York, 2015), p. 170.
4. Quoted in Krebs, *Gender, Race and the Writing of Empire*, p. 60.
5. Quoted in Krebs, *Gender, Race and the Writing of Empire*, p. 63.
6. Quoted in Laura E. Nym Mayhall, "The South African War and the Origins of Suffrage Militancy in Britain, 1899–1902," in Laura E. Nym Mayhall, Philippa Levine, and Ian Christopher Fletcher, "Introduction," in Ian Christopher Fletcher, Laura E. Nym Mayhall, and Philippa Levine, eds., *Women's Suffrage in the British Empire. Citizenship, Nation and Race* (New York, 2000), p. 8.
7. Quoted in Mayhall, "The South African War and the Origins of Suffrage Militancy in Britain," p. 10.
8. Meredith, *Diamonds, Gold and War*, p. 495.
9. Meredith, *Diamonds, Gold and War*, p. 466.
10. Quoted in Anna Davin, "Imperialism and Motherhood," in Frederick Cooper and Ann Laura Stoler, eds., *Tensions of Empire: Colonial Cultures in a Bourgeois World* (Berkeley, 1997), pp. 93–94.

TIMELINE

1899	South Africa War begins
1902	Peace of Vereeniging ends South Africa War
1904	France and Britain form entente
1905	Women's Social and Political Union forms; suffrage militancy begins
1907	Anglo-Russian entente
1909	"People's Budget" introduced
1910	Union of South Africa forms
1911	Parliament Act

11. Quoted in Davin, Davin, "Imperialism and Motherhood," p. 94.
12. Quoted in Kent, *Gender and Power*, p. 240.
13. Quoted in Sylvia Pankhurst, *The Suffragette Movement* (London, 1931), p. 190.
14. Quoted in Kent, *Sex and Suffrage in Britain*, p. 198.
15. Quoted in Kent, *Sex and Suffrage in Britain*, pp. 173–74.
16. Quoted in Kent, *Sex and Suffrage in Britain*, p. 175.
17. Constance Lytton, *Prisons and Prisoners* (London, 1914), http://digital.library. upenn.edu/women/lytton/prisons/prisons.html/, chapter 8.
18. Kristian Coates Ulrichsen, *The First World War in the Middle East* (London, 2014), p. 23
19. Quoted in Christopher Clark, *The Sleepwalkers. How Europe Went to War in 1914* (New York, 2012), p. 490.
20. Quoted in Margaret Ward, *Unmanageable Revolutionaries: Women and Irish Nationalism* (London, 1995), pp. 90, 91.
21. Viscount Grey of Fallodon, *Twenty-Five Years, 1892–1916* (New York, 1925), p. 20.

FURTHER READING

Christopher Clark, *The Sleepwalkers. How Europe Went to War in 1914*. New York, 2012.

Ian Christopher Fletcher, Laura E. Nym Mayhall, and Philippa Levine, eds., *Women's Suffrage in the British Empire. Citizenship, Nation and Race*. New York, 2000.

Denis Judd and Keith Surridge, *The Boer War, A History*. London, 2002.

Paula M. Krebs, *Gender, Race, and the Writing of Empire. Public Discourse and the Boer War*. Cambridge, 1999.

Sylvia Pankhurst, *The Suffragette Movement*. London, 1931.

1911–1912	Dock workers strike
	Miners' strike
1912	Irish Home Rule bill introduced
1913	Triple Alliance of workers forms
	Ulster Volunteer Force forms
	Irish Volunteers form
1914	Mutiny at the Curragh
	Assassination of Franz Ferdinand
	Europe goes to war

Indian sepoys on the Western Front, 1914–1915.

CHAPTER 11

THE GREAT WAR AND THE "PEACE," 1914–1922

I n October 1914, as the exhausted British Expeditionary Force (BEF)—what was left of it—clung desperately to its position in the Ypres Salient in Belgium, German troops with far superior numbers, weaponry, and equipment threatened to break through the line that separated them from the Channel ports and possible victory. On October 22, traveling aboard a fleet of thirty-six London buses shipped over from London—still painted red and sporting advertisements for a variety of food, medicines, and whiskey—sepoys of the Indian Corps arrived a mile or so from the front and made their way to the makeshift trenches occupied by the BEF. Thus relieved, the British soldiers withdrew to the rear to replenish themselves and gain much needed rest. During the next week, the Indian troops came under sporadic but deadly assault from rifle fire and shelling, suffering serious losses, especially among their British officer corps. On March 31, nine German battalions attacked the Indian Corps at Messines, punctuating their progress with "raucous, guttural sounds" as they made their way toward the sepoys' positions. Fierce fighting during the next several hours left heavy casualties on both sides, but the Indian Corps held the line, thwarting the German offensive designed to drive the British from the continent. As one military historian has noted, their stand, which was undertaken in circumstances in which they had lost most of their officers, could not speak the language of those around them, and ended up in motley units made up of soldiers from any number of companies, was truly remarkable. They might not have saved the empire, as some have claimed, but, asserts this historian, "it was certainly true that they had saved the BEF."[1]

Five months later, on March 12, 1915, the sepoys of the Sirhind Brigade of the 1/4th Gurkhas peered through thick predawn fog as they sat huddled in their trenches in the Port Arthur portion of the British line at Neuve Chapelle. Footfalls and then loud shouting from still unseen enemy soldiers rent the air, and suddenly, just sixty yards in front of them, a large body of great-coated, spike-helmeted Germans bore down on them in dense columns. As wave after wave of seemingly unstoppable German infantrymen lurched forward toward their lines, the Gurkhas unleashed barrages of rifle- and machine-gun fire, mowing down their enemy. But still more came on. The Indian Corps artillery began to lob shells into the mass of German troops, preventing them from reaching the sepoys' trenches and allowing the Gurkhas to stand up on their parapets and fire down onto the still on-rushing ranks of enemy soldiers. As day broke, the mist—and the German assault—drifted away, leaving behind a battlefield strewn with the bodies of the dead and wounded. "Piles of wriggling, heaving bodies lay on the ground," reported one observer, "and the air resounded with shrieks, groans and curses. The wounded tried to shelter themselves behind parapets formed of bodies of their own dead comrades."[2]

The rout of the German forces was complete, and the men of the Indian Corps were fired up to continue moving forward with the objective of taking the Bois de Biez and perhaps then the Aubers Ridge, from which they could dominate the German forces and even force them to evacuate Lille. They were prevented from doing so by a combination of weather, lack of sufficient ammunition, communications failure, confusing orders, misunderstandings, and poor planning, all factors that would plague the British effort against both Germany and the Ottomans for the rest of the war. After a few more engagements with the enemy following Neuve Chapelle, the Indian Corps was withdrawn from the Western Front and transferred to Mesopotamia, where, the official thinking ran, they would be able to handle the climate and conditions better than British troops would. But as was true of most official thinking throughout the years 1914–1922, it was wrong, and the Indian Corps—battered, considerably diminished in numbers, without officers who could speak their language, and cobbled together in mixed units made up of whomever could be found to form them—soon found that it had escaped the proverbial frying pan of the Western Front to land in the fire of the Middle East.

The accounts of the Indian Corps impress on us the global and imperial nature of the Great War. This was a war of empires as well as, ultimately, a war for empire. Having mobilized its colonial subjects to preserve the power of their imperial overlords, the British empire emerged from the conflict with its territory expanded dramatically and its control—at least for the time being—extended to unprecedented reaches.

··

THE BATTLES

Europe went off to war on a gorgeous summer day in August 1914, with the sun and warm temperatures creating the illusion that it would be not only a short conflict, but also one conducted under ideal meteorological conditions. Clement weather facilitates war planning, making it easier to move troops, animals, armaments, and supplies across long distances and enabling commanders to elaborate battle plans without taking into account the realities of Europeans winters. As one observer put it, the war would be over "by the time the leaves fall," a sentiment that helped governments recruit the soldiers they initially put into the field. European men went off to a war they were sure would be won by Christmas, a war they were certain would be fought gloriously and valorously. They were sorely mistaken.

The 100,000 men who made up the BEF had only just ensconced themselves along the Western Front by the third week in August 1914 when they and the French armies were forced by German advances toward Paris to beat a hasty retreat. At the Battle of the Marne, the French forces held firm, blocking the German path and causing its planners, in frustration, to turn toward the Channel. Before the Allies could do much about it, the Germans had taken a number of Belgian ports. At the First Battle of Ypres, however, as discussed in the opening vignette, the British, whose numbers had been cut in half during the fighting, held out until the Indian Corps, the only replacement troops available, could relieve them and hold the line long enough to stall the German advance to the French ports on the Channel. By November, the war of motion undertaken by the European armies on the Western Front soon bogged down into one of near complete immobility punctuated by horrendous and futile battles, as the armies dug in in a series of trench lines running some 475 miles from the North Sea to the Swiss Alps. Although battles flared along the Eastern Front as well, and, as we shall see, in the lands held by the Ottoman empire, the trenches of the Western Front came to exemplify the fighting of the Great War, in which more than twice as many soldiers died than were killed in all of the wars between 1790 and 1914.

Britain entered the war woefully unprepared. Alone among the belligerents, it eschewed the practice of conscription, therefore ensuring that it lacked an army capable of challenging the Germans on the battlefield. Despite its nearly complete dependency on imports to feed its people, it had not made arrangements to secure a supply of food for either its armed forces or the civilian population. It relied entirely on the United States to provide the oil it needed to fuel its navy, and its industries could not produce the weaponry and ammunition necessary to prosecute what would become a total war. Efforts to recruit a "New Army" to replace the tattered BEF began in late fall of 1914, but it would be some time before these volunteers could be sufficiently trained to take up arms effectively. The spring offensive of 1915 collapsed for lack of shells, forcing a reorganization of the cabinet that brought in a number of Conservatives and Labour MPs and placed David Lloyd George in charge of a new Ministry of Munitions.

Britain's inability to mount a credible attack on the Western Front and the Ottoman empire's closing of the Dardanelles Straits to Russian shipping on October 1, thereby cutting off a major source of British foodstuffs, led Winston Churchill, first lord of the Admiralty, to begin advocating for an assault on a different front. "Are there not other alternatives than sending our armies to chew barbed wire in Flanders?" he protested to Prime Minister Asquith, and he set about planning an invasion of Turkey to force open the Dardanelles and, hopefully, compel the Ottomans to withdraw from the war.[3] Believing that the series of Balkan wars in the years just prior to 1914 had weakened the empire considerably, Churchill and others thought they saw an easy and quick victory. But poor planning and insufficient resources accompanied this complacent and shoddy thinking, producing a disaster that took more than 55,000 British, French, Australian, and New Zealander lives and should have cost Churchill his career.

The beachhead at Gallipoli: note the impossibly small size of the beach and the steep hills that overlook it.

Following two months of ineffective bombardment of Ottoman forts overlooking the Dardanelles, Allied troops landed on a series of beaches on the Gallipoli peninsula in April 1915, where they were met by machine-gun fire from Ottoman troops positioned on the bluffs above them. The soldiers kept disembarking and, like sitting ducks, they died under the barrage of bullets that poured down on them. Of the first 200 troops who came ashore, only 21 survived. British officers, now under the command of Lieutenant General Sir Frederick Stopford (1854–1929)—whose incompetence during the South African War had helped bring about the early disasters of that conflict—attempted a second invasion in August. They repeated the same mistake, sending more troops onto the beaches to meet the same fate as their earlier comrades, dying in numbers beyond comprehension as they futilely tried to establish a beachhead from which they could break through Ottoman lines.

To compound the atrocity, the British lacked the transport, the personnel, and the medical supplies to remove the wounded from their positions and treat them. Thousands died needlessly, but British officials were loath to call off their misguided and mismanaged invasion for fear that imperial prestige would be severely compromised in the eyes of their subjects, should it become known that the great power had been defeated by an "Asiatic" enemy. Instead, British authorities determined to open another theater of war against the Ottomans, in Mesopotamia and Palestine, hoping to minimize the consequences of their defeat at Gallipoli and, not incidentally, to secure the oil fields and refineries of the Anglo-Persian Oil Company. In late October 1915, a poorly planned and badly coordinated march to capture Baghdad commenced, but because Britain's army was not prepared to conduct the kind of campaign necessary to assure success, it failed badly. The Turks stopped the combined British and Indian forces at Kut, forcing them to hole up in the town for five months as a siege reduced them to starvation and death from disease in horrifying numbers. The soldiers at Kut suffered some 7,000 casualties, and another 23,000 casualties beset those troops that were sent to relieve the siege. Finally, in April 1916, the British surrendered and the Turks took over. Six thousand Indian sepoys and 3,000 British soldiers were marched 1,000 miles across the desert to Turkey as prisoners of war. In the meantime, the British had finally evacuated their forces from Gallipoli in December 1915 and January 1916. Two battles for Gaza in the spring of 1917 did not go well. Cautious leadership by British commanders enabled the Turkish forces to repel efforts to dislodge them from their positions guarding the route into Palestine.

In the summer of 1916, the British High Command embarked on one of the single most disastrous military campaigns of all time. Under pressure from France to relieve their forces from the unrelenting German assault on Verdun, the British commander of the BEF, Sir Douglas Haig (1861–1928), agreed to initiate an attack in northern France on the Somme River, despite the fact that his forces had not yet been sufficiently trained. Planners hoped that the Somme offensive would end the war in a year. Instead, it engaged British and French troops in a series of deadly and ultimately fruitless battles for nearly five months between July 1 and November 18, when Haig finally gave in to reality and called a halt to the debacle. On the first day of the Somme campaign, 20,000 British troops died, blasted apart by artillery shells and mowed down by machine-gun fire. Another 40,000 were wounded that day, and the situation never improved. Over the next number of months, continuous attacks and counterattacks brought death to more than 19,000 British and imperial soldiers; more than 57,000 suffered wounds. In September alone, Britain suffered over 100,000 casualties (killed and wounded), a figure it matched during October and November . And this was for virtually nothing—a few miles of territory had been gained, but the slaughter had no appreciable effect on the outcome of the war. The scale of these casualties shocked the British public out of its complacency; for the first time, as death roll after death roll filled the pages of the newspapers, civilians at home gained an idea of what the war on the Western Front actually entailed. Subsequent battles

A PLACE IN TIME

The Pals' Brigades

On August 24, 1914, the Earl of Derby (1865–1948), the greatest landlord in the area and former lord mayor of Liverpool, sat down with General Kitchener to discuss the creation of what would come to be called Pals' Brigades, fighting units made up of volunteers drawn from the businesses of Liverpool. Derby coined the phrase, thinking that men who worked and socialized together might want to join the armed forces together if they knew they would not be parted from each other and could be assured that they would not be asked to serve with men they did not know and to whom they could not relate. Within two weeks, Derby's call for "pals" had yielded enough volunteers from Liverpool to staff three full battalions of 1,050 soldiers each. Two additional battalions from the city formed in October and November and were placed in reserve. The notion of a social cohesion driving recruitment caught on, and Pals' Brigades were created throughout the north of England, some based on a connection of occupation and others derived from geographic proximity. No one foresaw that the slaughter of whole battalions of pals would, by the end of the war, leave entire neighborhoods and business sectors deprived of the men who had formerly lived and worked there.

The Liverpool Pals arrived in France in November 1915 and went into the line of trenches in the northern section of the Somme sector in mid-December. They found themselves in terrible cold, wet, and muddy conditions, their living standards a far cry from what they had experienced while

Liverpudlians enlisting to serve in their Pals brigade, July 1914.

in training camps in England. Private Heyes wrote to a friend in one of the reserve battalions that was still back in England to try and stay there as long as he could because he "should not think that you get a bed to lie on and lots of blankets here, you get shoved in anywhere, and nothing to lie on but the bare floor, with rats running over you the whole of the time, keeping you awake. We have been standing to, now, for over a week, expecting being shelled out day and night. . . . You don't know when one will come and lay someone out, and I can tell you we have had some fellows badly wounded."[4]

The Pals saw action on the Somme in July 1916 and again in October. In the first wave of the months-long battle, they fared reasonably well, achieving their objectives and losing relatively few men in the process compared to other Pals' Brigades, some of which lost their entire contingent. The later July and October fights proved far more destructive, however, killing sufficient numbers of men that the concept of a unit of pals who knew each other well no longer pertained. The battles over the Ypres Salient in 1917 produced even greater numbers of casualties, and by the end of the German spring offensive of 1918, 2,800 Liverpool Pals had been killed. The numbers of wounded reached astronomical proportions, upward of 75 percent of the original recruits of 1914. In early May 1918, only 27 officers and 750 "other ranks" of the Liverpool Pals' Brigade could still be considered fit for active service.

Returning Pals found it difficult to adjust to civilian life. They had gone off to war with men they had worked and socialized with; many of their friends and business associates would never again be able to join them in those activities. Moreover, the comradeship of the office or the playing field had intensified in the trenches, creating a camaraderie that could not be duplicated in the tame and callow confines of Liverpool. Those who had not fought and experienced the horrors of the Great War could not begin to understand what the Pals had gone through, leaving the veterans lost in a world they could scarcely recognize, let alone comprehend.

Demobilized Pals, like other soldiers, also had difficulty finding work; in the case of the Pals, many of the firms they had worked for before the war had lost the very personnel they needed to stay afloat and were unable to stay in business. The recession that immediately followed the war reduced employment possibilities even further. Those jobs that did exist seemed to be taken by women or by men who had been too young to go to war in 1914, and Pals' resentment against them lay only just below the surface. In Liverpool as a whole, trade dropped off dramatically, as prewar trading partners had had to find other suppliers of goods for the duration and simply did not return once hostilities ended. The economic activities of the port, in particular, slowed considerably, and the people who relied on it for their livelihoods would soon make their displeasure over the situation known in no uncertain terms.

at Passchendaele and Ypres the following year fared no better. They simply increased the death toll and drove up the casualty rates to unprecedented levels.

In the Middle East, the failed campaigns of 1916 and early 1917 at Kut and in Gaza, respectively, spurred the British army to reorganize. These reform efforts succeeded, enabling British forces to take Baghdad in March 1917 and Jerusalem the following December. But they placed an enormous burden on the civilian populations of Egypt, Mesopotamia, and Palestine, requiring quantities of food that reduced the supply available to civilians and placing them in deep economic distress. The hardships imposed on the local populations of the Middle East were felt long after the war ended and would play a part in a series of revolts against British control in the years following 1918.

In March of 1918, the Germans initiated one last campaign to break through the stalemate on the Western Front. The spring offensive, as it is called, almost succeeded, as the armies directed by Erich von Ludendorff broke through British lines near Saint-Quentin and advanced on the Marne River in May. From this vantage point, German artillery fire could reach Paris; the French government began to plan for evacuations from the capital. But when Ludendorff ordered a final push on July 15, the offensive failed. The Allies counterattacked in August at the Second Battle of the Marne, setting the stage for what would be a series of successful offensives in September and October. With American help, they began a slow but seemingly inexorable pushback of German troops, till Ludendorff, bowing to the reality of the situation, resigned his position at the end of October, making clear to German civil authorities that the country could hold out no longer. On November 11, 1918, at 11:00 AM, the Germans signed an armistice, ending the war on the Western Front.

TRENCH WARFARE

Trench warfare introduced a new dimension to the relationship of humans and landscape in wartime. Certainly, terrain had always concerned commanders and military planners in the past. But on the Western Front during the Great War, ground was more than just the space on which belligerents fought. It became their habitat, literally. Soldiers lived in and with the earth, and their very survival depended on their ability to erase any distinction between themselves and the environment in which they found themselves. Camouflage colors in browns and greens characterized military clothing, whose purpose was to disguise human beings as they moved about in their environment. Soldiers at the front lived underground, and burrowing deeper into the earth might mean getting through an artillery barrage unscathed. It was the dead who lived above ground, and they, too, soon became part of the natural landscape. One British soldier recounted that at the battle of Loos the ground was so uneven that troops could only with the greatest difficulty make their way across it. "Not uneven by nature, either," he remarked, "but by the huddled heaps of men's bodies."[5]

By November 1914 the German and Allied forces faced each other across a series of trench lines. The first line sheltered men who would be engaged in combat with their enemies. Some six to eight feet deep and four to five feet across, it contained a "fire step" from which soldiers might observe the terrain at night or shoot off a few rounds at the enemy. The second, a fallback or support line, stood behind it at a distance of several hundred yards. A third trench line stood to the rear, from which supplies were ferried to the forward lines by means of communications trenches cut perpendicularly across the three trench lines. Soldiers lived in dugouts cut into the sides of the trenches. Some of them were well-constructed, furnished, and even decorated spaces; others were put together hastily and with little care. Across a patch of territory called "no-man's land" stood the enemy's trench system, separated by as few as 5 yards or as many as 1,000. Artillery batteries, depots, and casualty clearing stations populated the rear areas of the trench systems.

A British trench on the Western Front, 1916.

The technological might unleashed in the Great War made this a war unlike any other prosecuted to date. Massive artillery barrages filled the air with cannon and mortar shells, which, when exploded, unleashed blasts of shrapnel that ripped bodies apart. Machine guns mowed soldiers down as they picked their way across no-man's land. And in 1915, poison gas made its appearance, initiated first by the Germans but quickly taken up by the Allies as well. On April 22, German forces discharged 168 tons of chlorine gas against French and Canadian troops dug in along a four-mile front on the Ypres salient. The gas paralyzed the soldiers, rendering them comatose or killing them and allowing German troops sporting gas masks to overrun their position. They took some 2,000 prisoners. In September that year, the British lobbed 5,200 gas cylinders containing 150 tons of chlorine gas against the Germans at Loos, killing 600 of them. But in one sector of the line the wind refused to cooperate, stalling a gas cloud over the British lines rather than blowing it across to the enemy; this happened many times over the course of the war. In July 1917, the Germans introduced mustard gas at Ypres; it killed many and incapacitated thousands more. In 1918, the Allies mobilized an especially effective vehicle for the dissemination of gas over enemy lines. On July 12 a railway train loaded with 5,000 gas cylinders was moved close to the front lines and detonated, creating what one witness described as "a terrific hissing noise as a huge release of gas commenced. The dense, grey cloud made an awe-inspiring sight as it rolled steadily forward, widening as it went. We watched as it poured over our own Front Lines and continued across No-Man's Land. Such a threatening cloud as this we had never before witnessed. Over the enemy Lines the gas belt spread wider and wider, engulfing them from sight."[6] Gas burned the lungs and skin and blinded those it attacked. It killed a far smaller percentage of its victims than did artillery or bullets, but it was a supremely powerful weapon in the drive to incapacitate enemy forces. Its unpredictability—blowing whichever way the wind chose to take it—made it a fearsome weapon, but its success in causing profound losses among fighting forces stimulated a huge postwar boom in the chemical industry.

Combatants frequently mentioned the severe cold they suffered while fighting the Great War. The winters of 1915/16, 1916/17, and 1917/18 were some of the coldest and snowiest on record. In Britain, weather observations show that in those years, snow fell much more frequently than usual. These were wetter years all around for Britain: June 1916 was marked by cold and clouds, with persistent rain in the north around Aberdeen. October of that year brought even more stormy weather and greater rainfall, with daily accumulation outpacing anything ever recorded to that time. The inclement weather characteristic of the areas along the Western Front, combined with the porous earth out of which the trenches were dug, made trench living miserable. Regular heavy rains brought endless mud that overran the duckboards intended to make the trenches passable; poor drainage contributed to the seemingly eternal problem. Even on clear days, men could find themselves thigh deep in mud. "Our men were never dry," wrote a wartime journalist. "They were wet in their trenches and wet in their dugouts. They slept in soaking clothes, with boots full of water, and they drank rain with their tea, and ate mud with their 'bully' [beef]." During lulls in the rain, soldiers would repair their trenches, only to have the next storm ruin them again. More rain, "and the parapets slid down, and there was less head cover against shrapnel bullets which mixed with the rain drops and high explosives which smashed through the mud." Mud clogged rifles and turned trenches into "veritable death-traps," as one soldier described it. "Men had their boots, and even their clothes, pulled off by the mud."[7] Some drowned in it. Although latrines might be available in the forward areas, these, too, lacked proper drainage systems, rendering trench living even worse. During battles—some, like the Somme battles, could last for weeks at a time—men could not access the latrines and used the trenches to relieve themselves. Lice and rats infested the men and their surroundings; the latter, often as big as cats, feasted not only on the food supplies but also on the dead bodies that populated the trenches.

The dead were everywhere. Unable to bury either their fallen comrades or their enemy dead, soldiers lived with them: they ate and slept alongside corpses and used them to mark their bearings or to rest their guns on. They might bury their comrades in the sides or floors of trenches, but persistent rainfall or shelling could readily expose corpses in varying states of decomposition. In no-man's land, thousands of decomposing corpses turned colors and bloated up with gases. The stench created by gunpowder, shit, piss, decaying flesh, and frying bacon permeated the trenches. Disease flourished in these wet, cold conditions: dysentery, respiratory ailments, and "trench foot" plagued soldiers. The latter, caused by standing in mud and slime and cold water for days on end, made feet swell up, become numb, and then burn, "as though touched by red hot pokers," as one observer reported. "Scores of men could not walk back from the trenches, but had to crawl, or to be carried pick-a-back by their comrades. So I saw hundreds of them, and as the winter dragged on, thousands."[8] Trench foot depleted battalions from the fighting lines more often than did wounds. During the winter of 1914/15 alone, 20,000 British troops were incapacitated by the malady and had to be invalided to the rear.

The numbers of deaths suffered by Britain's and the empire's soldiers and sailors beggar belief. Nearly 75,000 Indians, 336 Maori, 83 Australian Aborigines, and 5,600 indigenous South Africans died; the relatively small numbers of deaths, apart from those among Indians, reflected the fact that imperial governments did not allow most of their indigenous troops to serve in combat positions. Within the Dominion ranks, Canada lost 60,000 soldiers, Australia 60,000, New Zealand 16,000, and South Africa 11,000. Given the small size of their populations— 8 million, 4 million, 1 million, and 1.3 million, respectively—these deaths represented a significant loss of men. Among the British, Scottish deaths amounted to 147,000 (26.4% of those who served); Irish deaths reached perhaps 35,000 (17% of those who served); Welsh figures for deaths came to 40,000 (14% of recruits); and English deaths equaled well over half a million. At least a million members of the armed forces from Britain and the empire as a whole died; the figure for those wounded during the war came to more than 2.2 million people. Finally, the figure for the number of deaths does not include those Africans and other imperial subjects who were conscripted into the war effort to serve as laborers and carriers. They died in droves, mostly from disease and malnutrition, but colonial officials kept few records of their casualties.

In the final months of the Great War, influenza swept across the globe, compounding the miseries and hardships brought about by four years of war. The influenza pandemic of 1918/19 killed at least 30 million and perhaps as many as 100 million people throughout the world. Appearing in the midst of the war, it

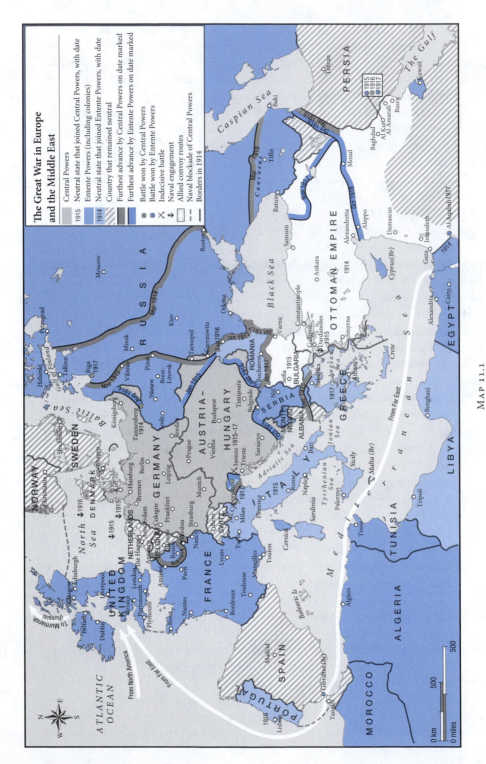

The Great War in Europe and the Middle East

- Central Powers
- Neutral state that joined Central Powers, with date — 1915
- Entente Powers (including colonies)
- Neutral state that joined Entente Powers, with date — 1914
- Country that remained neutral
- Furthest advance by Central Powers on date marked
- Furthest advance by Entente Powers on date marked
- Battle won by Central Powers
- Battle won by Entente Powers
- Indecisive battle
- Naval engagement
- Allied convoy routes
- Naval blockade of Central Powers
- Borders in 1914

MAP 11.1

The Great War in Europe and the Middle East

proved more deadly than any other disease since the visitations of the Black Death in the fourteenth century, and it killed more people than any other single event of the twentieth century except the Second World War. George Newman, chief medical officer of Great Britain's Ministry of Health in 1918, called it "one of the great historic scourges of our time, a pestilence which affected the well-being of millions of men and women and destroyed more human lives in a few months than did the European war in five years." It appeared with explosive suddenness and "simply had its way. It came like a thief in the night and stole treasure."[9] Doctors estimated that 800 of 1,000 persons who came down with the flu contracted only a mild case; but of the other 200 severely afflicted, some 80 percent of them died. Britain lost 250,000 people to the disease, one-third the number of those killed in the war. The newspaper columns listing the number of dead from flu began to rival and even outpace those listing the dead from the war. It felt like the last straw, following as it did years of deprivation, hardship, and heartache.

The mortality figures for the flu pandemic stagger the imagination. Where influenza epidemics in the past had produced death rates of about 0.1 percent of those infected, this one killed 2.5 percent of those who came down with it. Indigenous peoples in North America and in Australia and New Zealand suffered disproportionate mortality rates; some communities lost upward of 80 percent of their members. White New Zealanders had a death rate of 5.8 per 1,000; the indigenous Maori population died at a rate about seven times higher. Six times more Indians/Inuits of Canada died than whites. Africans died in greater numbers than did Europeans. Where the latter experienced mortality rates of perhaps 1–2 percent, African rates reached upward of 5 percent of the population. In Kenya, for example, 50,000 people, or 5.5 percent of the population, succumbed to the disease. South Africa lost perhaps 275,000.

THE WAR AT HOME

Keeping armies in the field in such horrendous conditions—and keeping the people at home producing for the war effort and making the sacrifices necessary to do so—required governments to continually come up with reasons to continue fighting. In Britain, which had not been invaded, the war was represented as a fight for and on behalf of Belgium, which was often depicted in the guise of an innocent woman in need of paternal protection. Such imagery became charged by and infused with sexual implications as accounts of the invasion and rumors of German atrocities reached Britain. These atrocity stories proved to be largely untrue, but they served propaganda purposes well, an increasingly important aspect of the war as the incompetence of the war effort became ever more evident to the troops in the field and even to people at home, despite censorship of news coming from the front.

The impact of war on the population at home proved to be unprecedented. This was total war, not in the sense that the battlefield came home to

Britain—although German Zeppelin raids and naval attacks in the first couple of years of the conflict did cause significant damage in a number of cities—but in the demands it made on the civilian populace to participate in the war effort. Britain was slow to gear up for the fight, as evidenced by a scandalous shortage of shells during the spring 1915 offensive, but gradually the country mobilized its human and material resources to start producing what was necessary if it was to prevail in the increasingly deadly conflict. The armed forces' recruitment efforts had succeeded spectacularly in the first months of the war, but numbers fell off by the middle of 1915 and, against the vociferous objections of Asquith, the government felt compelled to introduce conscription in early 1916, the first Britain had known. Directed at unmarried men, conscription failed to produce a sufficient number of soldiers; in May, a more stringent draft law gathered up all men between the ages of eighteen and forty-one. The upper age limit expanded to fifty-one later in the war.

Conscription placed enormous pressure on the ability of industry to hire the workers it needed to prosecute the war. The government had taken control of the munitions factories following the 1915 shell crisis, and it progressively gathered into its hands virtually all of the enterprises that fed the war effort. Coal mines,

Women manufacturing munitions for the war effort, 1917.

railways, and factories that produced aircraft, chemicals, ships, arms, and agri-cultural machinery—all these and more came under the auspices of governmen-tal management, supervision, and regulation. Unions agreed in 1915 to loosen their restrictions on employment, enabling, through a policy known as dilution, factories and enterprises to hire less skilled men and women into crucial posi-tions. They also agreed not to strike while the war continued, a promise carried out with only a few exceptions.

As millions of men marched off to war, women took their places in a variety of workplaces. They built bombs, shells, and small arms ammunition in muni-tions factories; they farmed the land; they drove buses and trams and ambu-lances at the front; they took clerical positions in offices that had only ever hired men; they nursed wounded soldiers in local hospitals and in casualty-clearing stations; and when the disasters of 1916 occurred, they served as auxiliary sol-diers. For thousands of middle-class women escaping the stifling atmosphere of domestic life, the war brought rewarding and exhilarating experiences. For laboring women who had always worked, often in dead-end and tedious posi-tions as domestic servants, the prospect of earning proper wages for the first time enhanced their lives significantly. The requirements of total war had the effect of improving the standard of living for most people in Britain because wages went up and conditions of work improved. Shortages of consumer goods caused difficulty, certainly, but a rationing system in the last year of the war at least attempted to make the deprivations somewhat equitable across class. Veterans of the fighting, however, believed that the people at home had enjoyed a cushy war, benefitting from their absence and profiting from the businesses of supplying armaments and other necessities of wartime. As we will see in Chapter 12, the attitude of returning soldiers toward the civilian population, especially women, alarmed a great many people.

THE EASTER REBELLION

In Ireland, tens of thousands of Irishmen from north and south had volun-teered their services in support of Britain's fight, and many thousands gave their lives in the effort. But some Catholic Irish refused to enlist, arguing that Britain's war had nothing to do with Ireland. On the contrary, members of the Irish Republican Brotherhood insisted, Britain's war against Germany offered the Irish an opportunity that they must not let pass. They and the leaders of the Irish Volunteers, an organization seeking to create an Irish republic through revolutionary action, determined to seize it. The government had sus-pended home rule for the duration of the war, a policy accepted by the parlia-mentary leader of the Irish Party, John Redmond, who sought to present the party in as cooperative a light as possible. Redmond, however, presided over a party and a set of parliamentary tactics that could no longer claim the alle-giance of the Irish people, losing ground to a nationalist movement led by Sinn Féin—Gaelic for "Ourselves Alone"—for which mere home rule would no longer suffice. On the day after Easter Sunday in 1916, as the war effort against Germany foundered in a morass of mud and muddle, Irish republican forces under the leadership of Patrick Pearse (1879–1916) and James Connolly (1868–1916) marched to the General Post Office building in Dublin and over-ran the unarmed guard there. Another group of rebels stormed Dublin Castle, the headquarters of British rule, while others captured City Hall, the Four Courts, and St. Stephen's Green. In a dramatic declaration from the steps of the General Post Office, Irish Republican Army commander Pearse pro-claimed Ireland a republic.

Roger Casement (1864–1916), a former British diplomat, had arranged with German officials to land arms and ammunition in support of the Irish rebels, but the ship carrying the weapons had been caught by the British navy and was scut-tled by its captain; Casement, on board a German submarine trying to put him off at Tralee Bay, was captured. The rising, without sufficient arms for its participants and, because of communications difficulties, short the 5,000 to 10,000 men ex-pected to respond to the call to arms, sputtered out after a week, but not before the rebels captured a number of significant assets in Dublin. The Irish Citizen Army, headed by Michael Mallin (1874–1916) and the Countess Constance Markiewicz (1868–1927), for example, took St. Stephen's Green and then retreated under heavy fire to the College of Surgeons, where they held out for six days, with little food or fire power. Heavy fighting took place throughout the city, with casualties amounting to 450 dead and 2,500 wounded, the vast majority of them civilians. The republican cause suffered mightily in the eyes of most Irish Catholics, who declaimed against the violence and the great losses of life.

But Pearse and Connolly had never expected to defeat the British army. Their goals had been more modest: to ignite, by means of a blood sacrifice on the part of Irish manhood, nationalist feeling throughout the country. "We die that the Irish nation may live," declared one of Pearse's lieutenants. "Our blood will rebaptise and reinvigorate the land."[10] Regarded even by its protagonists as a "rhetorical gesture," the Easter Rising, as it came to be called, could boast little support among the population. Its suppression by British forces came swiftly. The use of field artillery and naval guns on an urban population ensured that civilians would be caught in the crossfire and killed. Army officers resorted to torture and sum-mary executions in some instances.

The rising put down, British authorities took harsh action against the rebels and those they believed to be allied with them. Their punitive response, in-cluding the mass arrests of Sinn Féiners (who had not been involved in either the planning or the carrying out of the rising) and the execution by firing squad of fifteen Volunteer leaders mobilized Irish public opinion against their actions and in favor of independence where there had been none to speak of before. Irish MP John Dillon protested in Parliament the "river of blood" re-leased on the innocent people of his country. "The madness of your soldiers," as he put it, in the broader context of repressive measures put in place through martial law, served to provoke demands for self-determination among the majority of the Irish population in the south who had taken a neutral position in the past.[11]

POLITICAL REVERBERATIONS

The disasters of 1916—the evacuation of the Dardanelles, the Easter Rising and its brutal suppression, and agonies and futility of the Somme battles—took a political toll. In December Prime Minister Asquith was forced out of office, to be replaced by the energetic David Lloyd George. The "Wizard of Wales," as he was called, presided over a coalition government composed largely of Conservatives. By the time of his accession, the legislation necessary to compel Britons to go all out for the war effort had already been enacted. He used it sparingly when he could, especially as it pertained to relations with workers, preferring to persuade rather than coerce British labor into accepting such concessions as dilution and longer hours. By 1917, however, fed up with the willingness of their leaders to seemingly give away the store, trades unionists on the Clydeside in Scotland and in the coal mines of South Wales carried out a series of potentially crippling strikes. The centrality of their industries to the war effort—and the revolution in Russia that raised fears of worker revolution at home—ensured that the government would give in to their demands, setting a precedent that would raise Labour's expectations for the postwar period that would result in serious and unsuccessful disputes, as we will examine in Chapter 12.

As the war wound down in the fall of 1918, it became clear to politicians that a new election should be called to provide legitimacy for decisions about the postwar and the peace. The current electoral rolls were hopelessly out of date and would result in the disenfranchisement of a significant portion of the men who had fought in the war. Moreover, the demands of women could no longer be shunted aside, not after the contributions they had made to the war effort. Underlying this belief was a usually unspoken fear that the violence of the prewar women's suffrage campaign might resume, creating disorder and disruption that could not be tolerated in a society that had suffered such extensive stress and strain over the course of the past four years. In 1918, Parliament passed the Representation of the People Act, giving the vote to men over the age of twenty-one on the basis of occupation of premises—allowing exceptions for those nineteen and twenty year olds who had served in the armed forces—a grant of universal manhood suffrage. It enfranchised women who were householders or the wives of householders and who had reached the age of thirty. MPs introduced the age restriction so that women would not enjoy a majority over men, whose numbers had been greatly reduced in the slaughter of war. In doing so, they also ensured that those women eligible to vote were likely to be wives and mothers and not the single working-class women who had made so significant a contribution to the war effort. Those single working-class women might seek to continue their work after the war and even choose work over marriage and motherhood, a proposition that distressed those thinking about the needs and demands of the postwar period.

A WAR OF EMPIRE

Britain not only mobilized its own citizenry, but also called up virtually all of its colonial subjects. Over the course of the war, 280,000 men from Wales, 557,000 from Scotland, 206,000 Irishmen, and 4 million Englishmen either signed up to serve in or, after 1916, were drafted into the British armed forces. From the dominions, 630,000 Canadian enlistees and conscripts joined them, as did 417,000 Australians, 103,000 New Zealanders, and 146,000 white South Africans. Indigenous peoples from South Africa serving in the effort amounted to some 85,000; 4,000 Canadian Indians, 2,700 Maoris, and at least 580 Australian Aborigines joined up as well. India sent a million and a half soldiers to support the British war effort, and the West Indies contributed 15,000, 10,000 of whom hailed from Jamaica alone.

We tend to focus our lenses on the war in Europe, but the Great War involved fighting on other continents as well. In fact, the first British shots taken in the conflict occurred in West Africa, where the British were concerned to defend their shipping from German attacks originating from its colonial ports. When the German commander Paul von Lettow-Vorbeck embarked on his dash around southern and eastern Africa, British troops were forced to follow. But beyond these purely defensive aims, the conquest of additional African territory held significant attractions. Gaining German East Africa would place the Cape-to-Cairo route entirely in British hands; at the same time, in the minds of India Office officials, it would provide a destination for a great deal of Indian emigration. Not all Britons, however, shared the view that fighting the Germans in Africa was a priority. In Kenya, white settlers protested that the most important task for Europeans was not to fight one another but to secure control of Africans. Vastly outnumbered by blacks and insecure in their hold on the territory, whites feared that fighting among themselves would diminish their prestige in the eyes of Africans; moreover, enlisting Africans in the fight among Europeans would result in blacks killing whites and therefore threatening the fragile white supremacy on which their position was based. In fact, these fears did not materialize; although Europeans certainly took part in the African campaigns of the Great War, their numbers were small. By far the majority of the participants in the fighting were Africans. In the short run, the war had the effect of strengthening the cooperation of Africans with British colonial officials. In the longer term, the extraordinary impact it had on the continent, second only to that of the slave trade in its dislocations of peoples, communities, societies, and economies, contributed to the demise of colonialism some fifty to sixty years later.

More than 2 million Africans saw action in the Great War. Ten percent of them—more than 200,000—lost their lives, either killed in action or dying from disease or malnutrition in the horrific conditions under which they worked.

Some 25,000 Africans from West Africa; 30,000 from Uganda, Nyasaland, and Kenya; and 2,400 from Rhodesia served as actual soldiers under British command, but by far the majority of them worked as carriers. Carriers—or porters— were required in such large numbers because the fighting in Africa took place in areas where roads, railways, and motorized vehicles were scarce and where the presence of tsetse fly and other biting insects made it impossible for draught animals to survive. The heavy and unrelenting work of supply fell to human beings over the four-year period of the conflict. In Egypt, the British West Indies Regiment labored under terrible working conditions. Food, medical care, housing— all these fell short of the standards afforded white soldiers, a situation compounded by the racial prejudice faced by West Indians. When, for example, the regiment arrived in August 1916, hungry and tired following a thirty-five-day ship crossing in bad weather, its members tramped to a shelter inhabited by British soldiers, singing "Rule Britannia" along the way. "Who gave you niggers authority to sing that?" railed one white soldier. "Clear out of this building—only British troops admitted here."[12]

As we saw with the Indian Corps at the start of the chapter, the contributions of colonial troops made the difference between defeat and continued stalemate. Until Britain's new army could be recruited and trained, Indian, Australian, and New Zealand troops filled the breach following the collapse of the BEF in the winter of 1914–1915. The first German gas attack at Ypres in April 1915 did not result in a German breakthrough on the Western Front only because Canadian troops stood their ground and prevented it. The French and Algerian troops had fled, as had the British artillery gunners, as the gas wafted over them, leaving four miles of Allied line undefended. The Canadians stepped up to man the defenses and fought for the ground for five days against their persistent foe, gasping for air, eyes streaming, and throats burning as additional gas attacks came their way. Improbably, they held, giving up two miles of ground and losing 208 officers and 5,828 men. But they prevented the Germans from breaking through.

The courage and perseverance of the Canadian stand instilled in people at home a fierce pride in their men, even amid the grief of having lost so many in the assault. Canadians had not regarded themselves as a particularly effective, let alone martial group of British subjects and had entered the war cognizant of their lack of fighting history. Almost overnight, however, the battle at Ypres changed all that. Suddenly the respect and credence earned by the men under the prolonged gas attack gave Canadians as a people a new standing in the world. In the longer term, the actions of the Canadian troops, their "sad but sublime blood sacrifice," as one historian described it, would serve as a catalyst for the development of a Canadian nationalism.[13]

A similar process occurred among Australians and New Zealanders, only in this instance it was the tragedies of Gallipoli that sparked a new pride and sense of national worth. The bravery and determination of the ANZACs, as the Australian and New Zealand troops were known, had made possible the establishment of the first beachhead on the peninsula, and although the entire campaign—the "splendid failure"—turned into a debacle, Australians and New Zealanders at home gained from the stories of the resolution, spirit, and valor of their fighting men an appreciation of themselves as a distinct people with singular characteristics. The British effort had been ill-planned and badly executed; their Tommies had not acquitted themselves particularly well; so it was easy to contrast ANZAC resilience, independence, and insouciance to the lack of those qualities among Britons. These attributes became mythologized to all Australians and New Zealanders—the white and male ANZACs at any rate—and formed the core of a national identity that would take root over the next few decades.

The undoubted contributions of colonial troops to the British war effort, especially in light of the incompetence of British generals in the prosecution of the war effort demonstrated so clearly on the Somme, where dominion soldiers fought hard and lost dearly, put political pressure on now Prime Minister David Lloyd George to both acknowledge and take into account the concerns of the dominion civilian and military leaders. Lloyd George called an Imperial War Conference in 1917, the first of its kind, where the Canadian military in particular pushed hard for autonomous control over its armies. In the aftermath of the Somme disasters, Lloyd George could hardly refuse it, a decision that paid off handsomely in April at Vimy Ridge, when a Canadian Expeditionary Force took a German position that British forces had been trying to capture for two years. Thirty-six hundred Canadians died in the fighting, and another 7,000 had been wounded, but the battle marked the most successful effort seen on the Western Front since 1914 and it had been planned and executed by Canadians. The Australian Imperial Force gained its own autonomy of leadership in June 1918 (the New Zealand force was too small to justify a separate command). Two new "national" armies now fought alongside—not under—Britain. The experiences and events of the war set the stage for an alteration in the dominions' relationship with Britain, ultimately leading them to legal and cultural nationhood. The traumas of fighting in the Great War—the agonies, the suffering, the staggering losses of life, the courage, the resilience, and the successes—these went far in forging in the white dominion subjects of the British empire a new understanding of themselves as distinct and inherently valuable peoples.

The same could not be said for the indigenous peoples of these dominions who toiled long and hard in aid of the war effort. They had always been regarded as inferior specimens whose labor became, regrettably, more and more necessary as the casualties mounted year by year, but they were never given the consideration or respect commanded by white colonists. (To some extent, the Maoris can be regarded as an exception in this regard. After successful lobbying efforts on the part of Maori MPs, they were allowed to serve in combat positions against the Germans and not simply be used in support.) One South African officer in France summed up the prevailing attitude toward indigenous soldiers and laborers when he told a corps of Africans, "When you people get to South Africa again, don't start thinking you are Whites, just because this place has spoiled you. You are black, and you will stay black."[14] It might not be surprising to hear this come out of the mouth of a member of a society that had begun to legally institutionalize segregation, but the governments of Canada, New Zealand, and Australia demonstrated little more solicitation for their native peoples. On their return home after the peace, Indians, Inuits, Maoris, and Aboriginals earned less in the way of pay and pensions than whites; provisions for postwar employment or land settlement never reached them; they could not gain access to basic medical care for the wounds and illnesses they suffered. Gratuitous slights accompanied the material insults suffered by those whose contributions to the war effort had been so important to final victory.

WAR AIMS AND MIDDLE EAST POLICIES

Britain's objectives for fighting on the Western Front were straightforward—to remove German troops from Belgium and France and push them back onto their own territories. Its objectives in the Middle East, by contrast, involved territorial acquisition and empire building from the moment the Ottoman empire declared war on it in November 1914. Britain and France smelled blood in the water and regarded the demolition of the Ottoman empire as an opportunity to grab up real estate they had long desired to control. The viceroy of India, for instance, on learning that the British had captured Basra, in Mesopotamia (modern-day Iraq), urged his superiors in London to effect the "permanent occupation of Basra" so as to secure "our supremacy in the Persian Gulf." The prospect was just too good to pass up, he pointed out, "and this happy chance of consolidating our position there may never occur again."[15] The viceroy's advice, shared by many in the Foreign and Colonial offices, stood in marked contradiction to subsequent assurances of either a homeland or independence to a variety of interest groups in the region. One such in December 1914 promised "perfect independence" to the Arabs if they helped to expel the Turks; another, in April 1915, declared that "the Arabian Peninsula and its Mohammedan [sic] holy places should remain independent. We shall not annex one foot of land in it, nor suffer any other Power to do so."[16] British officials gave support to two rival families in the Arabian peninsula, the Hashemites on the western coastline and the Saudis in central Arabia. In the meantime, secretly, Britain and France negotiated what became called the Sykes–Picot Agreement, which, in October 1916, called for the partition of Ottoman lands between the two countries. And in December 1917, the Balfour Declaration pledged support for the establishment of a national homeland for Jews in Palestine. These various promises could not be reconciled with one another, and although they were made for strategic reasons in the heat of a conflict that had pressed Britain to the wall, they would come home to bite British officials once the war was over. Moreover, Britain had no real intention of keeping most of the promises, even if it could find a way to do so. It sought to establish its supremacy in the Middle East and now not simply to protect its "jewel in the crown," India, but to secure for itself the oil fields of Persia (modern-day Iran) and Mesopotamia. So vital had this factor become for war planners that British forces raced to occupy the city of Mosul the day before the armistice with Germany was signed—but eleven days after the armistice with the Ottoman empire had gone into effect. The Anglo-Persian Oil Company engineers strongly suspected vast reserves of oil there, and British authorities determined that they would not fall into the hands of rivals, whether French or Arab. (Their suspicions proved correct in 1927, when substantial supplies of oil were discovered.)

THE PEACE

The Great War swept away four empires—first Russia's in 1917 while the war was still going on and then the German, Austro-Hungarian, and Ottoman empires. In early 1919, the leaders of the United States, Britain, France, and Italy met in Paris to negotiate the conditions of the peace and establish a postwar settlement in the lands that had once been governed by these former empires. The peace settlements—there were five in the end—took three years to negotiate, and their terms created the conditions that would plague humanity for the remainder of the twentieth century and beyond.

The terms were harsh. Germany was forced to acknowledge its "war guilt," on the basis of which it was required to pay huge reparations for the destruction it had brought about. Alsace and Lorraine, the provinces it had won in the Franco-Prussian war in 1871, were returned to France, which also received the coal mines of the Saar Valley. Germany lost territory in the north and in Prussia, out of which was recreated a Polish state; Danzig, a largely German city, was placed under the economic control of Poland, and East Prussia was separated from the rest of the country. Germany was forced to demilitarize, forbidden to build an air force, compelled to reduce its navy to a negligible size, and permitted to hold on to an army no larger than 100,000 soldiers; the Rhine Valley, bordering France, was to be rid of all German armed forces and fortifications.

The punitive terms of the Versailles treaty generated a strong sense of humiliation among the German people. Because it had been formed to sue for peace and was then compelled to sign the hated treaty, the Weimar government—associated with socialism and liberal democracy—would be tarred with the shame of humiliation and defeat of a proud and once-mighty nation. The punitive nature of the Versailles treaty contributed to the rise of fascism in Germany, with grave consequences for all of Europe.

In January 1918, American President Woodrow Wilson had issued his Fourteen Points, principles according to which peace between the belligerent countries should be forged; it was on the basis of the Fourteen Points that Germany had signed the armistice in November 1918. French President Georges Clemenceau and British Prime Minister David Lloyd George had different ideas about peace terms, looking to impose on their defeated enemy measures that would (1) require German to pay reparations: that is, pay the Allies for the costs they had incurred in prosecuting the war; and (2) permit the Allies to occupy the Rhineland and the Saar Basin, resource-rich areas of Germany. Wilson determined to defeat such punitive measures and to ensure the creation of a just peace, but having been laid low by the flu at just the moment when momentous decisions required his attention, he could not prevail. France did not get all that it had asked for—the occupation of the Rhineland would last only fifteen years; the annexation of the Saar would be administered by the League of Nations for a period of fifteen years—but of all the concessions that had been granted, Wilson lost by far the greatest number. Virtually none of his Fourteen Points save the establishment of a League of Nations survived, which, ironically, the United States did not join because the Senate refused to ratify the terms of the agreement. The treaty that was forced on the Germans set the stage for twenty years of upheaval on the European continent.

The delegates to the peace talks in Paris had to decide what to do with the colonies and territories held by now-defeated Germany and the Ottoman empire.. The American president had declared the United States' commitment to the self-determination of nations when he entered the war, a sentiment that won significant popular support in Europe, much to the discomfiture of imperialists across the globe. Widespread acceptance of the principle meant that the victors could not simply seize Germany's colonies and the lands of the former Ottoman empire as spoils of war. To placate Wilson and bid for American friendship, Lloyd George bowed to his desire to create a mandate system under the League of Nations through which the lands of their enemies would be administered as a "sacred trust of civilization." This proved to be little more than a smoke screen behind which Britain governed the mandated territories it received just as it did its own colonies. The Union of South Africa won German South-West Africa (today Namibia), whereas Britain gained Togoland in West Africa and, more important, German East Africa, now renamed Tanganyika (today's Tanzania). This latter addition fulfilled Britain's long-held dream of an unbroken chain of territories running from the Cape to Cairo. The treaty of Sèvres, signed in 1920 to settle terms with the Ottoman empire, gave Britain and France mandates over former Ottoman lands. Britain won Palestine, Transjordan, and Mesopotamia; France controlled Syria and Lebanon. Many histories of the British empire still identify the interwar period as one when Britain's hold on its colonies began a so-called "inevitable" decline. But in fact, during the years between Worlds Wars I and II, Britain's empire increased dramatically in size, reaching its zenith from the perspective of territorial control. Certainly few official Britons envisaged any notion of relinquishing its lands within the next century or so.

The League of Nations body charged with overseeing the mandates, the Permanent Mandates Commission, sought to enforce the policy of "trusteeship" embedded in the article that established it. Mandate powers were obliged to pursue and maintain the "well-being and development" of peoples supposedly not yet able to do so in the modern world. The concept of trusteeship differed little from earlier notions of Britain's "civilizing mission" or the "white man's burden," but it differed in one important respect: it implicitly acknowledged that colonization would, at some time in the future, come to an end. Moreover, the job of the mandate powers was to prepare for that time by developing the

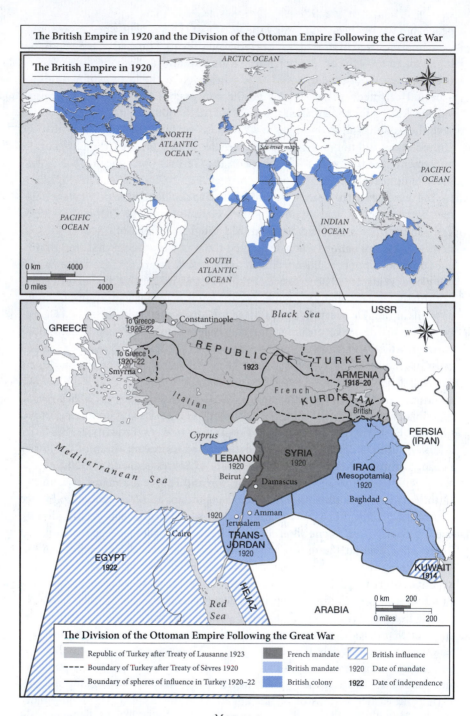

The British Empire in 1920 and the Division of the Ottoman Empire Following the Great War

The British Empire in 1920

ARCTIC OCEAN

NORTH ATLANTIC OCEAN

PACIFIC OCEAN

See inset map

PACIFIC OCEAN

INDIAN OCEAN

SOUTH ATLANTIC OCEAN

0 km 4000

0 miles 4000

GREECE

To Greece 1920–22

Constantinople

Black Sea

USSR

R E P U B L I C   O F   T U R K E Y
1923

To Greece 1920–22

Smyrna

ARMENIA
1918–20

French

KURDISTAN

British

Italian

Cyprus

Mediterranean Sea

LEBANON
1920

Beirut

SYRIA
1920

Damascus

PERSIA
(IRAN)

IRAQ
(Mesopotamia)
1920

Baghdad

Amman

1920

Jerusalem

TRANS-
JORDAN
1920

Cairo

EGYPT
1922

HEJAZ

Red
Sea

ARABIA

KUWAIT
1914

0 km 200

0 miles 200

The Division of the Ottoman Empire Following the Great War

Republic of Turkey after Treaty of Lausanne 1923		French mandate		British influence
Boundary of Turkey after Treaty of Sèvres 1920		British mandate	1920	Date of mandate
Boundary of spheres of influence in Turkey 1920–22		British colony	**1922**	Date of independence

MAP 11.2

The British Empire in 1920 and the Division of the Ottoman Empire Following the Great War

economic, political, social, and cultural institutions that would make those future former colonies viable states. The idea of trusteeship proved a useful counter to critics of colonialism at home, to whom apologists for empire could reply: "we are in (Africa, Mesopotamia, Palestine, Transjordan) not to exploit the peoples and resources of the territories but to improve them." The reality of the situation never lived up to the rhetoric of trusteeship because Britain's needs often conflicted with those of its colonies in the fraught years between the wars.

REVOLTS AGAINST BRITISH RULE

The end of the Great War resulted not only in a dramatic increase in the size and scope of the British empire; it also saw several rebellions against British rule. In the case of Ireland, previously examined in this chapter, and Egypt, the revolts produced some degree of independence, which accounts for the claims that the interwar period marked the beginning of Britain's imperial decline.

Egypt

Britain's wartime promises of Arab independence, however vaguely expressed, raised expectations among Egyptian nationalists that their calls for self-government would be heard. In early 1919, a *wafd* (delegation) of nationalists led by Sa'ad Zaghloul (1859–1927) requested that they be permitted to present their case at the Paris Peace Conference. Since British authorities allowed Faisal bin Hussein (1883–1933) of Hejaz, on the Arabian peninsula, to attend the conference, it seemed a reasonable demand, but it was refused. The *wafd* had also gotten wind of a British plan to establish a two-house legislature in Egypt that would give representation and decision-making powers to Europeans. In combination with the acute wartime distresses experienced by the Egyptian population and the impatience of members of the Egyptian army awaiting demobilization, these forceful assertions of continued British control infuriated many. In March, students in Cairo and Alexandria began to protest; transport workers, judges, civil servants, and lawyers went on strike; and soldiers joined them. Women in veils took to the streets. Unrest across the towns and cities spread into rural areas and British officials were assassinated. All this amounted to a mass rebellion involving men and women of the highest and lowest ranks of society and, most significant, the all-important Egyptian business classes. The rebellion caught the British completely unprepared, and they could do little to either stem the violence or appease the protesters.

Alfred Milner, secretary of state for the colonies, having commissioned an investigative report on the revolt, determined that Britain could no longer maintain its protectorate over Egypt. He tried to replace it with an arrangement that would give the country nominal independence, but the nationalists would not accept the conditions it contained. With unrest taking place at home and throughout much of the empire, Milner was not in a position to make many demands, so he concluded a treaty in 1919 that proclaimed Egypt "a sovereign independent state." Britain held on to some important privileges: it would guarantee

The Egyptian Revolution of 1919, which united both
Muslims and Christians in opposition to British rule..

the security of communications in Egypt; defend the country against foreign aggression or interference; protect its interests in Egypt; and protect the Sudan. Most of these conditions pertained to Britain's ability to control the Suez Canal, still regarded as crucial to the health and welfare of its empire.

India

A series of developments and events stemming from the war and the influenza epidemic in India resulted in widespread rioting across the subcontinent. In 1917, the secretary of state for India, Edwin Montagu (1879–1924), had told the House of Commons that the government sought to gradually expand self-government in India by increasing the numbers of Indians in every part of the administration. One aspect of the reforms proposed by Montagu and the viceroy of India, Lord Chelmsford (1868–1933), entailed giving greater representation to Indians in provincial assemblies, a prospect that generated a great deal of resistance among members of the Indian Civil Service and the provincial governors, chief among them Sir Michael O'Dwyer (1864–1940), governor of the Punjab. O'Dwyer and his colleagues insisted that the reforms would exacerbate the protests and rioting that had broken out in many provinces.

Conditions in the Punjab following the war made life difficult for a broad stratum of the Indian population. Wages in industries that had prospered in wartime fell dramatically, catapulting much of the population into debt. The influenza epidemic had struck the Punjab particularly hard, taking up to 25 percent of the population in some villages. Impoverished Punjabis often expressed their distress through protests, creating disorder throughout the province. The Defence of India Act of 1915, which had enabled the government to deal harshly with protestors during the war, had lapsed; colonial officials sought and received exceptional new powers to deal with disorder through the 1919 Rowlatt Acts, legislation that enabled the viceroy to suspend due process of law and to imprison Indians without trial. The Rowlatt Acts inflamed Indian public opinion. The goodwill evoked by the Montagu–Chelmsford reforms vanished, replaced by anger, disappointment, suspicion, and mistrust. Educated Indians of all political stripes submerged their differences and united against the Rowlatt Acts under the *satyagraha* movement of Mohandas Gandhi (1869–1948). Translated loosely as "truth force," *satyagraha* refers to the civil disobedience campaigns Gandhi led. Demonstrations took place in a number of cities, and rioting broke out in Ahmedabad, Delhi, and a number of Punjab provinces.

Unaccustomed to seeing Muslims and Hindus, nationalists and loyalists, conservatives and liberals working together in concert, British officials jumped to an erroneous conclusion: that a revolutionary conspiracy, probably hatched in Moscow, sought to overthrow British rule and establish Indian independence. This conspiracy did not, in fact, exist, but fear of it informed the decision making and actions of colonial and military officials, leading to severe repression against public processions and any other manifestation of protest. When on March 30 and April 6, 1919, a series of peaceful *hartals*—a kind of religious general strike—shut down much of the Punjab, rumors of mutinies and plots to end British rule swept through the Anglo-Indian population. Believing themselves to be at risk for assault and murder, British officials and civilians began to arm themselves.

In Amritsar, news that Gandhi had been arrested set off riots throughout the city on April 10. Protesters engaged in sabotage, looting, arson, and assault, beating five Europeans to death and nearly killing a European schoolteacher, who lay near death for a number of days. Authorities responded with armored cars and airplanes to restore order, and peace was eventually reestablished. April 11 and 12 passed without further violence. But on April 13, 1919, Brigadier-General Reginald Dyer (1864–1927) ordered a patrol of Indian troops under his command to fire on a crowd of some 25,000 unarmed Indian men, women, and children in the Jallianwala Bagh gardens in Amritsar. About ten minutes later, their ammunition virtually spent, he ordered them to cease shooting. Hundreds of people lay dead, and thousands more wounded littered the ground. Dyer led his troops from the Bagh, leaving the injured to fend for themselves; the curfew imposed on Amritsar kept would-be rescuers from collecting the dead and getting medical attention for the wounded until the next day. Scores died overnight.

The Amritsar massacre, as it came to be called, provoked a crisis in British and Indian affairs. For Indian nationalists, it marked the moment at which home rule within the empire would no longer suffice. Gandhi previously believed that although the British Raj might not always do the right thing, it was nevertheless just. The inquiry into the Amritsar massacre, which he dismissed as a "whitewash," changed his mind. Now, for him and for most Indian nationalists, nothing less than independence would do. Still committed to peaceable means, Gandhi and the Indian National Congress, in conjunction with a number of Muslim nationalists, called on the country to engage in acts of civil disobedience in August 1920. The response was overwhelming. Across the subcontinent, people of every caste, religion, and class joined in some form of refusal to engage with British authority, whether it be peasants ceasing to farm, laborers refusing to cultivate or harvest tea, students abandoning their classrooms, or civil servants not showing up for work. Tragically, one peaceable procession in northern India provoked troops to fire on it, inciting a number of people to chase the police involved into their station and burn it down. Twenty-three people died in the fire. Horrified, Gandhi pleaded with Congress to call a halt to the civil disobedience campaign, which it did in February 1922. But the British had been placed on notice: India would not for long accept a British Raj that failed to advance the interests of the people.

Mesopotamia

Some of the same dynamics at work in Egypt provoked revolt in Mesopotamia as well. The delineation of mandate status by the Treaty of Sèvres and its granting to Britain in 1920 flew in the face of the promises of Arab independence made throughout the war. Moreover, the promise of significant oil reserves in the land that would come to be called Iraq ratcheted up British determination to maintain control of the territory. Throughout 1919 and 1920, officials began to institutionalize many of the powers they had utilized—purportedly temporarily—during the war, making it clear to those who were watching that far from planning to relinquish their control, they were moving to shoring it up. As Gertrude Bell (1868–1926), the woman credited with "creating" Iraq, put it, "We had promised self-governing institutions and not only made no step toward them but were busily setting up something entirely different."[17] The formation of a body to collect and administer revenue, the introduction of the Indian rupee as the standard unit of currency, and the continued staffing of offices with Indians rather than Arabs (the government of India administered Mesopotamia) proved to be the catalysts that set off a rebellion across the territory. Involving local clans, Sunni intellectuals and urban elites, Shiite imams, and soldiers returning from action against Ottoman troops during the war, the revolt lasted for five months between July and November 1920. Once again, as in Egypt, the British had no idea what had been brewing among the various groups of Mesopotamian society and were caught flat-footed by the ferocity of the uprising. They had to supplement the 100,000 troops already present in the country with eighteen additional battalions from the Indian army to put down the revolt; the British air force also took to bombing Iraqi villages, in part to give its pilots some hard-to-come-by hands-on training. Finally, after losing more than 300 soldiers and spending nearly £8 million, a cost the nation could not sustain any longer, British policy makers bowed to the financial reality they faced and acknowledged that they would have to scale back their plans for the direct control of Mesopotamia. Given the turmoil they faced throughout its possessions, especially in India, the traditional provider of the troops needed to police the empire, British authorities had little choice but to find other, less expensive and intrusive, ways to protect its interests in the Middle East.

In 1921, at the Cairo Conference, Britain arranged with France to establish pro-British Arab monarchies in Transjordan and Iraq. On the throne in Iraq they set the Hashemite King Faisal bin Hussein (1833–1933), leader of the Arab fight against the Ottomans during the Great War. He enjoyed virtually no legitimacy there, having no family or clan connections in Mesopotamia; a sham "plebiscite" returned a 96 percent approval of the new king, but the rigged vote could not provide the stability the monarchy needed to survive. In 1958, military officers overthrew it and established a republic in its place. In Transjordan, Faisal's brother Abdullah (1882–1951) took the throne of the new country. He fared better; his thirty-year reign and the forty-seven-year reign of his grandson Hussein (1935–1999) provided the longevity to sustain the stability of the kingdom.

The Cairo Conference of 1921 established the postwar order of the Middle East. The new kingdoms of Iraq and Transjordan were joined by what became named Saudi Arabia after Abdul-Aziz Al-Saud (1876–1953), who was settled on the throne there in 1932. Palestine remained a British mandate, a land promised to both Arabs and Jews during the Great War. The postwar settlement of the former Ottoman empire—fraught with upheaval, broken promises, rival claims, and near-constant unrest—would haunt Britain for decades to come.

••

Victory in the Great War required the contributions of Britons of every nationality and of imperial subjects from across the empire, and in almost every instance, citizens and subjects came through. But the broken world to which belligerents returned at the end of 1918 offered little solace to societies devastated by four years of unprecedented loss and destruction. Across the United Kingdom and the empire, soldiers and civilians, men and women, elites and commoners faced disorder in every aspect of their lives. The upheavals produced by the First

World War provoked responses designed to recreate the social, political, and economic order that had prevailed prior to August of 1914. But in virtually every instance, those efforts failed, as we will see in the next chapter.

NOTES

1. Gordon Corrigan, *Sepoys in the Trenches: The Indian Corps on the Western Front, 1914–15*, loc. 1739.
2. Quoted in *Sepoys in the Trenches*, loc. 3546.
3. Quoted in Kristian Coates Ulrichsen, *The First World War in the Middle East* (London, 2014), p. 79.
4. Quoted in Graham Maddocks, *Liverpool Pals: A History of the 17th, 18th, 19th & 20th Service Battalions, The King's Liverpool Regiment 1914–1919* (South Yorkshire, 2008), ebook loc. 1535.
5. Quoted in Dorothee Brantz, "Environments of Death: Trench Warfare on the Western Front, 1914–1918," in Charles Closman, ed., *War and the Environment: Military Destruction in the Modern Age* (College Station, 2009), p. 77.
6. Quoted in Martin Gilbert, *The First World War, A Complete History* (New York, 1994) pp. 439–40.
7. Quoted in Gilbert, *The First World War*, p. 218.
8. Quoted in Martin Gilbert, *The First World War*, p. 219.
9. Great Britain, Ministry of Health, *Report on the Pandemic of Influenza, 1918–19.* (London, 1920–1921), pp. iv, xiv, 69.
10. See Sean Farrell Moran, *Patrick Pearse and the Politics of Redemption: The Mind of the Easter Rising, 1916* (Washington, 1994), especially ch. 6.
11. Quoted in Townshend, *Political Violence*, p. 308.
12. Quoted in Winston James, "The Black Experience in Twentieth-Century Britain," in Philip D. Morgan and Sean Hawkins, eds., *Black Experience and the Empire* (Oxford, 2004), p. 354.

TIMELINE

1914	Great War begins
	Battle of the Marne
1915	Gallipoli disaster
	Shell scandal
	Battle of Kut begins
1916	Battle of the Somme begins
	Conscription introduced
	Lloyd George becomes prime minister in a national government
	Easter Rising in Ireland

13. Mark David Sheftall, *Altered Memories of the Great War. Divergent Narratives of Britain, Australia, New Zealand and Canada.* (London, 2009), p. 54.
14. Quoted in Timothy C. Winegard, *Indigenous Peoples of the British Dominions and the First World War* (Cambridge, 2012), p. 252.
15. Quoted in Ulrichsen, *The First World War in the Middle East*, p. 150.
16. Quoted in Ulrichsen, *The First World War in the Middle East*, pp. 154, 155.
17. Quoted in Ulrichsen, *The First World War in the Middle East*, p. 195.

FURTHER READING

Gordon Corrigan, *Sepoys in the Trenches: The Indian Corps on the Western Front, 1914–15.* Staplehurst, 2006.

Paul Fussell, *The Great War and Modern Memory.* New York, 1975.

Samuel Hynes, *A War Imagined: The First World War and English Culture.* New York, 1991.

Winston James, "The Black Experience in Twentieth-Century Britain," in Philip D. Morgan and Sean Hawkins, eds., *Black Experience and the Empire.* Oxford, 2004.

Eric J. Leed, *No Man's Land: Combat and Identity in World War I.* Cambridge, 1979.

Sean Farrell Moran, *Patrick Pearse and the Politics of Redemption: The Mind of the Easter Rising, 1916.* Washington, 1994.

Mark David Sheftall, *Altered Memories of the Great War. Divergent Narratives of Britain, Australia, New Zealand and Canada.* London, 2009.

Kristian Coates Ulrichsen, *The First World War in the Middle East.* London, 2014.

Timothy C. Winegard, *Indigenous Peoples of the British Dominions and the First World War.* Cambridge, 2012.

1918	Woodrow Wilson issues Fourteen Points
	German spring offensive fails
	Influenza pandemic begins
	Armistice
1919	Paris peace conference
	Egyptian Revolution
	Amritsar massacre; civil disobedience campaign begins in India
1920	Treaty of Sèvres
	Revolt in Mesopotamia
1921	Cairo Conference

Striking men marching in Poplar, London, 1920.

CHAPTER 12

POLITICS AND EMPIRE IN INTERWAR BRITAIN, 1919–1935

On June 11, 1919, a carriage returning a number of black men and their white wives from an outing outside Cardiff encountered "a howling mob of young fellows and girls"—whites—who rushed the vehicle, hurling stones at its passengers. The crowd chased the holiday makers toward Bute Street, the Cardiff district where many blacks lived, and although the police stopped most of them from getting through, a number of assailants managed to avoid them and proceeded into the neighborhood. There they shattered windows and broke down doors of lodging houses, shops, and private residences, looted and ransacked them, and set upon people they found within. They then set the buildings alight. Police arrested one woman brandishing a razor and "vowing vengeance on 'niggers'"; they rescued two black men bleeding from the head and a white woman "whose mouth was bleeding," but could not prevent the white mob that had gathered from kicking and punching them as they removed them from a house on Hope Street. Whites stabbed another black man, Norman Roberts, whose abdominal injuries were severe enough that he had to be hospitalized.

Over the next few days, whites continued their attacks on the black communities of Cardiff, compelling police to cordon off and range themselves around what *The Times* called "nigger town." Still, the mobs, led by Australian soldiers awaiting demobilization, in uniform and carrying rifles, inflicted violence against blacks wherever they could find them. Using military tactics learned during the war, the whites, sometimes numbering as many as a thousand, carried out raiding parties on black premises, trashing, looting, and burning them down and attacking those inside. Somalis, Malays, West Indians, and Arabs attracted the attention of the assailants, who sent up a cry of "blacks" whenever they spotted one or blew a whistle to call other whites to the scene. "This seemed to be an expected signal," wrote a reporter, "because hundreds of persons rushed up from the neighbouring streets, including many women and girls, who had sticks and stones, and flung them at the unfortunate coloured man as they chased him along the street." Although their targets fought back with whatever they could—frying pans, pokers, table legs, knives, and even guns—they lacked the numbers and organization that would have allowed them to prevail. The white mobs severely injured dozens and killed at least three blacks. An Arab named Mahommed Abdullah was beaten so badly that he died from a fractured skull, although whether at the hands of the mob of the police it was never determined. The black areas of Cardiff sustained £3,000 of property damage.

The events in Cardiff in June 1919 concluded a series of race riots that had begun in Glasgow in 1919 and spread to Liverpool, London, and a number of towns across Britain. The government responded initially by instituting a scheme of repatriation—the removal of black seamen to their countries of origin. This action may have placated whites in Britain, but the men sent away—subjects of the empire with, supposedly, the rights guaranteed to all British subjects equally—carried the resentments engendered by the riots with them to their home countries. Several men who had been deported to Trinidad and Jamaica acted out their bitterness in a number of riots, strikes, shipboard mutinies, and street fights in the summer and early fall of 1919. In Kingston, Jamaica, fighting broke out between local seamen and sailors from *HMS Constance*. It escalated to a full-blown disturbance that had to be put down by an armed landing party from the ship. The acting governor explained the actions of the Jamaicans as a consequence of "the treatment which had been received by coloured sailors at Cardiff and Liverpool."[1]

In 1925, the Conservative government of Stanley Baldwin (1867–1947) issued the Aliens Order of 1925, legislation that delineated all black seamen, whether subjects of the British crown or not, as "aliens," making it possible for the state to deport even British subjects from its shores. This legislation effectively established a color bar in Britain.

The race riots in Cardiff were but one of several incidents that took place in Britain and the empire in the extraordinarily disturbed years following the end of the Great War. Disorder in virtually every realm of life thrown up by the war—imperial, economic, political, social, and personal—marked the decade starting in 1919, undermining the stability of the country and introducing fears and anxieties about the future of Britain and the empire.

••

IRELAND: "FLYING COLUMNS" AND BLACK AND TANS

In the spring of 1918, faced with an all-out offensive by the Germans on the Western Front, the British government revisited the question of imposing conscription on Ireland, an issue virtually guaranteed to excite massive opposition. The Irish Volunteers readied themselves to use force to prevent conscription; Sinn Féin took advantage of the threat of conscription to rally a national constituency behind it. In the general elections held in December 1918, Sinn Féin won seventy-six seats, as against the six seats held by the Irish Parliamentary Party.

Home rule was rejected by the majority of the Irish electorate in the southern counties in favor of outright independence from Britain. The newly elected MPs refused to take their seats at Westminster and instead, on January 21, 1919, met in their own assembly, the Dáil Éireann, in Dublin. There they declared themselves the elected representatives of the Irish people and established an Irish republic, pledging to "ourselves and our people to make this declaration effective by every means at our command."[2]

Sinn Féin sought to gain and maintain a peaceable independence from Britain. The Irish Volunteers, by contrast, who saw in the Dáil's Declaration of Independence an imprimatur, began to attack members of the police in Ireland, the Royal Irish Constabulary (RIC), counting them as "armed forces of the enemy." The Dáil had given the Volunteers no such charge, and most Sinn Féiners opposed their actions, but the Volunteers fashioned themselves into the Irish Republican Army (IRA); before long, it served as a legitimate force, a "National Army," of the new republic. Throughout 1919 they conducted boycotts against local RIC members, effectively alienating them from the general population; they assaulted the odd policemen unfortunate enough to find himself alone and unprotected; and they raided rural RIC outposts for arms, gradually forcing the RIC from the isolated posts of three to four men they held in the countryside into fewer but larger posts of eight to ten police. Attacks on the larger outposts commenced in January 1920; within six months, the IRA had damaged or destroyed 45 barracks, while more than 400 outposts previously abandoned were burned down as a signal to the population that the British authorities could not control the countryside. Their campaign of violence and intimidation of local populations ensured that the British legal system could no longer function. Dáil courts sprang up to take their place, so that de facto civil administration fell into the hands of the republicans. When the IRA made a failed attempt on the life of Lord French (1852–1925), the lord lieutenant of Ireland on December 19, 1919, the British responded by increasing their military presence in Ireland and trying to chase down the gunmen of the "murder gang," as they called the IRA. For its part, the IRA formed itself into more permanent units—the "flying columns," so called, that organized and carried out larger-scaled ambushes of military and police patrols.[3]

The IRA had succeeded in registering significant RIC losses through the deaths or resignations of its constables, forcing British authorities, who were unable to replenish the ranks through recruitment in Ireland, to seek replacements from among former soldiers in the British population. Right from the start, discipline loomed as a major concern. General Nevil Macready (1862–1946), commander of the British military in Ireland, had wished to recruit a special military force, in which he believed he could more easily instill the necessary discipline. But the government preferred a police force and under the authority of Major-General Henry Tudor (1871–1965) a police force was established in May 1920. It joined with the RIC, but in a move anticipating the confusion and indecision that were to characterize the government's actions throughout and to the profound dismay and frustration of military authorities, the paramilitary duties of the new force were different from those of the conventional police activities of the RIC. A second "Auxiliary Division" under the command of Brigadier-General Frank Crozier, (1879–1937) composed of ex-officers, joined the new police force in July. Blessed, in this respect, by the dearth of employment among demobilized soldiers, the government's call for police recruits yielded thousands of applicants; some 12,000 signed up between the beginning of January 1920 and the end of August 1922. These men carried out the bulk of the fighting against the IRA; it was they who conducted first unofficial and then official reprisals against the noncombatant population, garnering the hate and fear of the southern Irish that reverberates to this day at the mention of their name, the Black and Tans.

The Black and Tans and Auxiliaries killed more than 200 noncombatants in 1920 alone. Thomas MacCurtain (1884–1920), lord mayor of Cork, was shot dead in front of his wife by a group of armed men, later found to be members of the RIC, who had blackened their faces and forced their way into his home. Three other lord mayors were killed the next year in virtually the same circumstances. Between January and June 1921, when a truce between the IRA and British forces came into effect, 17 children, 5 women, and 16 unarmed men were killed in attacks carried out by Black and Tans, 30 of them in April alone. The Black and Tans and members of the armed forces meted out to the civilian population a kind and degree of violence that staggers the imagination. Weekly reports from Macready to the Situation in Ireland Committee, composed of a number of cabinet members and high government officials, testify to regular incidents of arson, beatings, shootings, molestation, rape, murder, and mutilation of the civilian population. Although they repeatedly denied that reprisals took place, government officials not only knew of them, but also excused them, justified them, often approved of them, and may well have instigated them.

From the start, officials in Ireland and members of the government like Churchill and Lloyd George regarded the reprisals inflicted on the civilian population by British forces as one of the only effective ways to deal with assaults carried out by the IRA. At home, the acts of reprisals against noncombatant Irish seemed to have elicited little response from the British public for almost a year. Ultimately, however, roused by increasing coverage in the press, especially by accounts of the sack of Balbriggan by British forces in September 1920, the burning of Cork, and the shooting down of a crowd of spectators at a soccer match in Dublin on what became called "Bloody Sunday," the public began to take notice, and it did not like what it saw.

The conservative and liberal press alike decried the reprisals that seemed to be occurring every day. Liberal and Labour politicians denounced the reprisals and the government policies that appeared to excuse them; some Conservatives joined them in their opposition, convinced that such behavior could not serve British interests. Lloyd George believed the best way to end the conflict was to revive home rule and persuaded his government to pass the Better Government of Ireland Act. The law gave a parliament to the twenty-six counties that made up what was regarded as "nationalist" Ireland and another to the six counties of Ulster, where presumably Protestant Unionists dominated. Southern Ireland never accepted the act, but the northern counties did, consenting to the mechanism that would later partition the country into two states.

Bloody Sunday, 1920, when fourteen British soldiers, fourteen Irish civilians, and three Irish Republican Army prisoners were killed.

Despite its rejection of the home rule act, the IRA could not hope to defeat British forces in Ireland. It therefore agreed to negotiations between the British government and Sinn Féin to bring the war to an end in 1921. Michael Collins (1890–1922), an IRA commander who represented the Dáil, and others representing Sinn Féin met with agents of the British government, trying in vain to impose their demands for complete independence and the establishment of a republican Ireland. The government insisted on partition for Ulster, however, and for the declaration of allegiance to the British king on the part not of a republic but of a "free state" within the British Commonwealth of Nations. The promise of the creation of a Boundary Commission to address the delineation of north from south made it possible to think that partition would be temporary. In any event, with little ability to hold out, Collins signed the treaty on December 6, 1921.

Civil war in southern Ireland ensued almost immediately. Under the leadership of Éamon de Valera (1882–1975), a number of IRA and Sinn Féin members refused to accept the terms of the treaty and took up arms against Collins and his followers. For more than a year, between April 1922 and May 1923, former comrades and colleagues fought against one another in a terrible round of assassination and execution of one another. Antitreaty forces succeeded in ambushing and killing Michael Collins himself, but that did not end the violence. Only when it became clear that de Valera's forces could not prevail did he call a halt to the fighting. In the meantime, the Better Government of Ireland Act came into effect in northern Ireland, creating a new province of Great Britain. Its borders excluded many Catholics, ensuring that Protestant Unionists outnumbered nationalist

Catholics by two to one. Catholics could play little part in the subsequent politics of what was now Northern Ireland, although few of them wished to legitimate the province by doing so. In later years, however, Catholic disabilities at the hands of Ulster Protestants would produce a series of armed conflicts that would tear the province apart. In the 1920s and 1930s, Northern Ireland found itself completely dependent on Britain for economic survival.

The events in Ireland were intricately bound up with other issues and concerns, and policies and practices there seemed, for many, to have profound

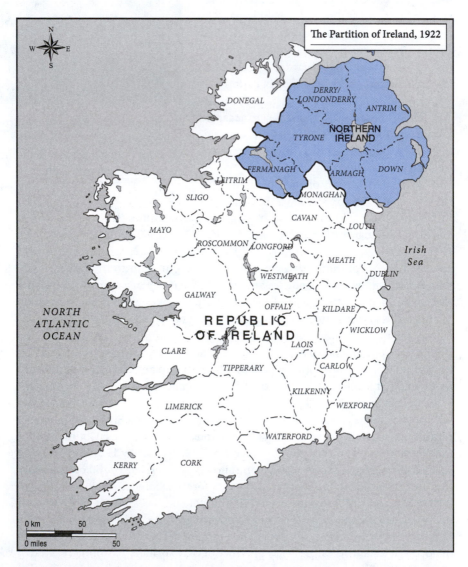

MAP 12.1
The Partition of Ireland, 1922

implications for other areas of British imperial and domestic affairs. Over and over again, for instance, Army Chief of Staff Henry Wilson despaired that he could not provide Macready with sufficient troops to get the job done. Partly that was a consequence of the need to keep troops in Europe to maintain the armistice; partly it was because of the dispersal of troops to parts of the world like Mesopotamia and Palestine that Britain now claimed an interest in. Perhaps most important, however, was the conviction on the part of politicians and military men that armed force would have to be mobilized against striking workers at home. The industrial situation, especially that in the coal mines, posed a major problem for the government, reducing it to handling the troop shortage in Ireland as best it could. Some politicians regarded the labor movement as part of "the cataract of world events" sweeping the globe, as Churchill described it, seeing in nationalist movements in India and Ireland the hand of Bolsheviks who had infiltrated unions and the Labour Party itself. Wilson repeatedly proclaimed to anyone who would listen that losing Ireland would mean losing India; losing the empire, he said, it would be only a matter of time before socialist revolution took hold.

STRIKES AND THE FEAR OF REVOLUTION

Fears and depictions of a revolutionary working class emerged immediately after the end of the war, fueled—in the context of the Russian revolution and subsequent socialist risings in Europe—by soldier and worker unrest in early 1919 that seemed to threaten revolt in Britain. Strikes occurred with disconcerting regularity throughout 1919 and 1920, culminating in the spring of 1921 with a thwarted general strike. The first of these took place on the Clydeside in Glasgow in late January and February 1919, where, in "the battle of George Square," workers—some of them carrying the red flag of revolution—were confronted and set upon by police wielding batons. When the workers fought back, troops that had been waiting outside Glasgow with tanks and machine guns moved in and established order. A strike of the railwaymen followed in September 1919; when it threatened to turn into a general strike at the hands of the Triple Alliance of railwaymen, transport workers, and coal miners, Lloyd George's government intervened to settle the strike on the side of the workers. Eight months later, in May 1920, London dock workers refused to load ships bound for Poland with arms intended to be used against Russia. In August, when the labor unions and the Labour party promised to shut down all of industry if Britain persisted in its efforts to intervene, the government capitulated. The earlier strikes, however frightening, had involved traditional wage demands; these latter actions were clearly political in nature.

A final strike threat materialized in April 1921, after a three-month period in which unemployment doubled. When the government announced that it would abdicate its wartime controls over the coal mines, mine owners declared their intention to reduce wage rates and return to the prewar system of paying wages

A PLACE IN TIME

Race Riots

Liverpool saw some of the most widespread rioting of 1919. High levels of unemployment, particularly in the shipping trade, and frustrations over the government's failure to make good on its wartime promise to create "a home fit for heroes" produced a great deal of tension. Whites tended to blame their misfortune on the black residents of the city, whom they regarded, erroneously, as newcomers who had taken advantage of the war to take jobs that by rights belonged to whites. Starting in May, mobs of whites beat blacks they encountered in the streets and vandalized and burned houses inhabited by blacks. As a police report put it, "a well organized gang consisting principally of youths and young men, soldiers and sailors, . . . commenced savagely attacking, beating and stabbing every negro they could find in the street."[5] They wrecked the hostel established by the Elder Dempster shipping company for black seamen and the David Lewis Hostel that housed black sailors of the Royal Navy. Liverpool police finally gave up trying to control the violence against the black community, estimated to be some 5,000 strong, ceding sections of the city to mob rule for three days and rounding up and placing blacks into "bridewells," local jails, for their protection. Many families regarded their imprisonment as an intimation of wrongdoing on their part and felt deep resentment that they, rather than their attackers, had been locked up.

The violence continued for a number of weeks. One black man was "beaten severely about the head with the buckle end of a belt."[6] Another, Charles Wootton (1897–1919), a ship's fireman who had served in the Royal Navy during the Great War and was discharged in March 1919, was hounded from his boarding house by a crowd of about 200–300 whites. The mob chased him to the dockside, where they beat him, wrapped an anchor chain around his body, and forced him into the water. They threw bricks at him until he drowned. The police made no arrests.

on the basis of pit production, a policy that would negatively affect those who worked inefficient or inferior mines. Miners demanded instead the continuance of equalized rates across the mines, which owners answered with a lockout. The Triple Alliance called a general strike for April 1, 1921, but before it could begin the railwaymen and transport workers chose to continue negotiations with the government, betraying, in the eyes of the miners, labor solidarity. The government had averted a general strike on "Black Friday," as embittered workers called

Sometimes whites intervened to prevent injury, as when seventeen-year-old Ernest Marke (dates unknown) and a friend were chased by a mob of about twelve white men. "Niggers, niggers, stop them niggers," the men cried, but a woman who heard them opened her door for Marke and his companion and they escaped through a back alley. A few days later, Marke "wasn't so lucky," as he put it. He and his roommate got trapped between two groups of whites and were "beat up mercilessly" outside a factory. When the lunch whistle blew, the women working inside came out, saw what was going on, and charged the mob, yelling and screaming and using their fists on them until the attackers ran off. Had it not been for their intervention, he declared, "I would not have lived to write this story." As it was, the beatings left him convalescing for three weeks.[7] In another instance, Agnes Brew (dates unknown) and her white friend, a vicar's daughter, were set upon by group of men. "We started to run," Brew recalled, "but we both had those dresses that, in those days, were tight-waisted and tight at the knee, so we couldn't. The men began to gain on us and we didn't know what to do. Well, the girl I was with . . . stopped, looked around and picked up a brick. She turned and threw it at the first of the men who were gaining on us. It hit him on the head and bounced off. When the rest saw that he'd been hurt, they stopped to see to him and we were able to get away."[8]

Other whites responded far less generously. Some suggested that blacks in Liverpool should be restricted to separate compounds in the city, just as Africans in South Africa were. The lord mayor and the head constable favored this arrangement and looked into using the camps that had held troops during the war for just such a purpose. The lord mayor also urged government authorities to repatriate all black seamen who had come to Britain to help in the war effort; soon the language used to tout the repatriation scheme came to include not only colonial blacks but also British blacks. In the event, returning colonial seamen to their lands of origin proved impracticable for the most part. Instead, British authorities implemented the Coloured Alien Seamen Order of 1925, which enabled local governments to prevent black seamen, including British black seamen, from entering their ports.

it, but could not be sanguine that another would not break out. The sense of class conflict and animosity toward workers approached dangerous levels: as war veteran Richard Aldington (1892–1962) observed, "this interminable series of strikes and lockouts looked remarkably like warfare." Indeed, battalions that might have gone to Ireland to repress the IRA could not be spared, for fear that they would be needed at home to contend with striking workers. In April 1921, Lloyd George's cabinet discussed how many troops would be necessary for "holding the

British coalfields," as Neville Chamberlain put it. Secretary of War Lamington Worthington-Evans (1868–1931) declared that "we need 18 battalions to hold London" and proposed taking two of them from Malta, four from the Rhine, and one or two from Egypt. Henry Wilson suggested that "loyal citizens could join the territorials"—the standing army—in defending London, the taking of which, Lloyd George agreed, would be "the important thing in a revolutionary movement."[4]

RACE RIOTS

The anxieties engendered by striking workers were ratcheted up by a series of race riots that rocked port towns in Britain between January and August of 1919, the likes of which, in terms of the widespread nature of the violence, were not seen again until the urban riots of 1981. First in Glasgow and then in South Shields, Salford, London, Hull, Liverpool, Cardiff, Newport, and Barry, tens of thousands of white Britons, mostly male, set upon communities of blacks who had settled there. The riots produced a number of deaths, countless injuries, hundreds of arrests, and many thousands of pounds in property damage.

Blacks had long maintained settlements in Britain, but until 1914, their numbers had been small. The need for labor occasioned by the war expanded the black population—largely male—considerably, so that by the end of the war some 20,000 blacks resided in Britain. Present in virtually all wartime industries, their numbers were concentrated in the maritime forces, leading to a dramatic increase of black sailors and seamen in the port towns. The dearth of figures makes it impossible to estimate the number of black seamen who participated in the war, but of the 15,000 merchant seamen who lost their lives during the conflict, more than 3,000 of them worked on what were called "Asiatic" contracts. When the war ended, blacks serving in nonmaritime industries tended to gravitate to port towns, where established interracial settlements of blacks and whites offered a hospitality not evident elsewhere in Britain. In the port towns themselves, employment with the shipping companies declined precipitously, and as owners chose to hire white foreign seamen rather than black British seamen, racial tensions escalated.

Violence directed against blacks by whites began first in Glasgow. In January, some thirty Sierra Leonean sailors and firemen, all British subjects, were set upon by white seamen in the yard of the Mercantile Marine offices. Chased through the streets, they were finally rescued by local police, but not before one of them, Tom Johnson, was stabbed, and two white men, Duncan Cowar and Thomas Carlin (dates for all three unknown), were shot and stabbed, respectively. In South Shields the following month, a West Indian and nine Muslim sailors from Aden—all British subjects—were confronted by a large group of white seamen at the Tyneside Shipping Office. A melee ensued, during which the crowd threw stones and bottles at the ten men. Over the next few days and sporadically into

March, British and foreign whites and black seamen fought one another. In one instance, a Muslim, Abdulia Hassan (dates unknown), was attacked by a group of British soldiers, who struck him and cut off his watch and chain with a knife. Hassan fought back, slashing one of the soldiers with a razor. As was true in Glasgow and would be evident in the subsequent rioting, the black victims of the violence were cast as instigators and were arrested in numbers far outweighing those of their white attackers.

Riots broke out in the East End of London in April 1919 and lasted through August. On April 16, white seamen besieged a restaurant on Cable Street owned by an Arab, throwing bottles and bricks at the black seamen inside. Eight Muslims, one white seaman, and two policemen were injured in the confrontation, although only Muslims were arrested for assault. In May, four days of full-scale rioting took place in the Limehouse area of the East End involving, according to some accounts, 4,000 to 5,000 people. In this instance, crowds of whites attacked blacks with fists, stone, and knives. They laid siege to a boarding house where some 100 black men resided and drove them out into the streets where "a pitched battle" ensued. In June, the Chinese community in Popular came under attack.

POLITICS

Revolutions, strikes, and race riots were not the only manifestation of the deep disruptions caused by the Great War. Political disorder, too, appeared to many to be a threatening consequence of the new franchise enacted in the 1918 Representation of the People Act, which established universal manhood suffrage and gave women over the age of thirty the vote. The age requirement ensured that women would not enjoy a majority over men, whose numbers had been greatly reduced by the war; fears of women "swamping" men at the polls loomed over the debate. Moreover, the age restriction ensured that those eligible to vote were likely to be wives and mothers; those excluded were largely single, unattached women who had made so significant a contribution to the war effort, who might seek to continue their work after the war and even to sacrifice marriage and motherhood to do so. The sexual disruption these women represented produced acute anxiety in the postwar years. The new electorate, composed of newly emancipated women and, seemingly, of frightening, angry, out-of-work demobilized soldiers, alarmed a good part of society.

Conservatives, for whom property qualifications had served as guarantors of political responsibility, recognized that their traditional strategies would not survive the postwar political world of a mass electorate, necessitating the cultivation of a more broadly based constituency. They decided to continue the wartime coalition with Liberals and Labour, not believing that they could win an election on their own, and pursued an election strategy designed to thwart the emergence of Labour as a viable party. The Coalition government of David Lloyd George, a

Liberal, and Andrew Bonar Law, a Conservative, issued letters of endorsement—derided as "coupons" by the opposition leader Herbert Asquith—to those Liberals and Conservatives deemed loyal to the government; the tactic worked, and the Coalition government was returned to power with a hefty majority. In the context of the Russian revolution of 1917 and an outbreak of strike activity at home, fear of Bolshevism obsessed many MPs and government officials and a considerable portion of the press and public. The Coalition government adopted in 1919 a series of inflationary policies designed to absorb returning soldiers into the workforce, stimulating a short-lived postwar boom.

Fears of worker revolution figured prominently in postwar politics. After the armistice, Conservatives had agreed to continue in Lloyd George's wartime coalition government because they could not be sure that the newly enfranchised working classes would not decimate their ranks at the polls. The Coalition, it seemed to them and to Liberals as well, appeared to offer the strongest bulwark against the mass of returning soldiers whose attitudes were unknown and actions unpredictable. Despite the vocal misgivings of Die-Hard Conservatives, who, at the 1920 conference of the Nation Union of Conservative and Unionist Associations castigated Lloyd George for having "hobnobbed with Bolsheviks" and charged that Labour's program of nationalization would result in "the nationalisation of women," Coalition Conservatives like Austen Chamberlain (1863–1937) persuaded the bulk of the party, which had not won a general election since 1900, that the Coalition, representing "a great middle body of opinion," was best positioned to address the political, social, and economic changes wrought by the war and, in so doing, stave off the threat of revolution. Offering increased educational opportunities, housing, unemployment payments, and, in 1921, "uncovenanted benfits" to those not making contributions to the unemployment fund seemed to Coalition members to provide, as Lloyd George put it, "a cheap insurance against Bolshevism."[9] When they grumbled about the "socialistic" nature of these expenditures, Chamberlain cautioned restive Conservatives that dissolution of the Coalition government could result in widespread disorder in the streets.

The measures instituted to absorb unemployed soldiers and fend off revolution caused inflation, alienating an increasing number of middle-class men and women with fixed incomes and a limited ability to cope with rising prices. Seeing workers making gains at their expense, these voters turned in droves to the Conservative Party. In the early 1920s, Conservatives increased their membership dramatically to some 700,000, twice the membership enjoyed by the Labour Party; much of that increase came from the middle-class suburbs. Organized in grass-roots interest groups such as the Anti-Waste League and the Middle-Class Union and given voice by newspapers such as the *Daily Express* and the *Daily Mail*, the largest mass-circulation dailies throughout the 1920s, middle-class voters made their discontent with the Coalition known, forcing the establishment, in 1922, of the Geddes Committee, which was charged with identifying areas of public expenditure that could be reduced. The committee's diligence produced deep cuts in the budget for education, housing, and the military.

Conservative successes derived from the party's ability to cast workers as a dangerous unionized force that threatened middle-class livelihoods with their unreasonable demands for higher pay, shorter hours, and better conditions. These stereotypes helped to forge a consciousness among a vast body of middle-class Britons who perceived themselves to be the "constitutional classes," the loyal bulwark standing between the country and ruin brought about by an aggressive, unionized working class.

By the summer of 1922, displeasure with Coalition Conservatives had grown sufficiently that the party could no longer hold out; it voted to secede from Lloyd George's coalition government and forced a new election. Baldwin explained that Conservatives must abandon the Coalition and return to the partisan ways of the past because the very existence of the party depended on it.

The unity of the party derived from its implacable opposition to socialism, a terrifying, if amorphous, enemy in which were lumped not only Bolsheviks and communists, but also trade unionists, the Trades Union Congress (TUC), and the Labour Party. Its effectiveness in mobilizing fears and prejudices can be seen in its polling: the Conservative Party received a majority of working-class votes in the 1920s (Scotland was the great exception to this rule). Only the presence of the Liberal candidates, who siphoned off votes that would almost certainly have gone to the Tories, gave the 1923 election to the Labour Party.

Labour's victory rocked conservatives of all stripes. Unprepared for power and unaccustomed to the responsibility of governing, Labour foundered over the issue of normalizing relations with Russia, and Prime Minister Ramsay MacDonald (1866–1937) was forced to call an election in October 1924. One of the dirtiest campaigns ever fought, the election of 1924 centered on the question of Labour's affiliation, as Conservatives and Liberals saw it, with the Bolshevik government of Russia. Labour, Conservative Party literature declared, was not above passing off communist spies as health visitors or enticing children to Sunday schools where communists would brainwash them and teach them how to carry out street fighting. In fact, only one communist stood in the election contest, Shapurji Saklatvala (1874–1936), an Indian seeking to represent Battersea, but that did not stop Conservatives from embracing demonizing language against Labour. Stanley Baldwin, leader of the Conservative Party, like William Joynson-Hicks (1865–1932) and other party campaigners, leavened his campaign speeches with healthy doses of anti-Semitic and anti-Bolshevist rhetoric. The representation of Labour as socialists, and socialists as communists, and communists as Bolsheviks operated to portray Labour Party members and union members as a non-British, alien presence.

All of this prepared the way for the "discovery," on October 25, just days before the 1924 election, of a letter to British communists, purporting to come from Grigory Zinoviev, Russian president of the Third International, characterizing

MacDonald's efforts to normalize relations with Russia as support for the revolution; he also, allegedly, commanded the British Communist Party to infiltrate the military forces with an eye to fomenting mutiny among them. The so-called Zinoviev letter, which the Conservative Party's central office made available to the *Daily Mail* for publication, virtually guaranteed Labour's defeat. Conservatives used the Zinoviev letter to cast the Labour Party—and Macdonald in particular—as the enemy of the British people.

Returning to power in 1924, many Conservatives continued to portray unionists and Labour Party members as socialists, often conflating socialists, communists, and Bolsheviks. Baldwin, having secured office for himself and his party, reverted to a conciliatory tone and tried to check some of his colleagues' excesses. Despite his efforts, Conservatives—and sometimes Baldwin himself—persisted in regarding and representing to the country the image of Labour and trade unionists as enemies of the nation.

THE GENERAL STRIKE

In the spring of 1925, coal miners threatened to strike again over the owners' efforts to cut wages and increase hours. The owners stood firm, refusing to concede any ground; a strike was averted only when the government agreed to provide a stipend to the industry that would ensure the status quo for a year, to the end of April 1926. For the next year, Conservative politicians and newspaper editors conducted a loud and incessant campaign against the purported threat of a communist rising. By the time the 1925 coal subsidy was due to expire, the government was ready. Baldwin negotiated for three days with the leadership of the Labour Party and that of the TUC to find a solution, but, pushed by members of his cabinet, he abruptly broke off talks on May 3. Strike notices that had gone out earlier in the event of a breakdown in negotiations were confirmed by telegraph, and the strike officially began at midnight on the May 3. Baldwin told the House of Commons that the government had stopped negotiations because "it found itself challenged with an alternative Government." Churchill, far more strident than Baldwin in his characterization of the strike, set the tone for the government and for much of the rest of the country as well. He declared that the unions had instigated "a conflict which, if it is fought out to a conclusion, can only end in the overthrow of Parliamentary Government or in its decisive victory," insisting that the country could demand no less than unconditional surrender of the unions.[10] The trade unions and the Labour Party regarded the General Strike as an industrial dispute, a characterization rejected by Conservative and Liberal politicians, newspapers, and interest groups who demonized unionized workers by painting the Labour Party and unions as pawns of the Bolshevik government in Russia. These groups portrayed the General Strike as a revolution, an assault on the institutions of parliamentary government, and a war against the British people.

Unrest during the General Strike, 1926.

The strike ended on May 12, when the TUC capitulated to the government's demand for an unconditional surrender. The miners, especially those in South Wales and Scotland, cried betrayal and determined to continue on their own after their erstwhile allies in the great labor action went back to work on May 13. For seven more months the miners held out, but defeat was only a matter of time. Impoverished and utterly demoralized, they returned to work in early December on terms dictated by the coal companies. The strikers got nothing but an undertaking by Baldwin that he would urge employers not to retaliate against them when they returned to work. Emergency powers that had been enacted on May 1 to meet the possibility of the strike were kept in place until the miners returned to work in December; they gave the government the continued right to use orders-in-council to set up summary courts and to take whatever actions it deemed necessary to keep essential supplies and functions up and running. The government took the opportunity presented by the strike to enact a series of policies Conservatives had long sought to impose: "vindictiveness has now seized our masters," Virginia Woolf (1882–1941) noted in her diary.[11] In the coal areas, where the miners were still out, Neville Chamberlain, as minister of health, used the newly passed Boards of Guardians (Default) Act to disband the elected boards of guardians and replace them with government-appointed commissioners. In such places as Bedwellty, in Wales, the new commissioners slashed poor relief payments to families to less than a third of that paid to feed, clothe, and house residents of workhouses in the area.

The government took advantage of labor's defeat to repeal the Eight Hours Act of 1908 and to pass the Trades Disputes Act of 1927, which rendered general strikes illegal and punishable by two years in prison; changed the system of the political levy so vital to the existence of the Labour Party so that workers had to agree to "contract in" rather than "contract out" of contributing to their unions' political funds; forbade civil servants and local government employees from new membership in unions with any TUC affiliation; and outlawed "intimidation" by strikers, which was broadly and vaguely enough defined as to mean almost anything. It certainly had the potential to make picketing employers much more difficult. As historians have pointed out, the terms of the act were rarely invoked and had little material impact on the labor movement, although Labour Party coffers certainly declined dramatically over the next few years, in some estimations by as much as a quarter. But as a symbolic measure of workers' defeat at the hands of "the nation" it held great significance, and even Churchill's wartime coalition government refused to repeal it (only when Labour came to power in 1946 was the hated act done away with). One ironic effect of Conservatives' efforts to kick their opponents when they were down, to make them "lick it," as the *Manchester Guardian* put it, was a resurgence of Labour Party votes in the 1929 election, bringing to power for a short-lived reign the second MacDonald government of the decade.[12]

Union membership declined from 5.2 million to 4.8 million between 1926 and 1928. The number of days lost to strikes fell from 162 million in 1926 to 1.2 million in 1927 and 1.4 million in 1928. Certainly, the miners lost out completely: their holdout produced no concessions. In fact, they went back to work—those of them who still had jobs to take up—at rates prevailing in 1914. Working longer hours for less pay, their union organizations in tatters, mine owners in almost complete control—for miners, the General Strike had proved a humiliating disaster.[13] Above all, the failure of the General Strike discredited it sufficiently that it would not be resorted to again as a tool in industrial disputes; workers' energies turned toward political, rather than industrial action. Their efforts had little payoff until 1929, when newly enfranchised younger women helped to sweep them to power, a topic explored later in this chapter.

CHANGES IN THE DOMINIONS

The formation of the Irish Free State in 1922, which established the country as a dominion member of the British Commonwealth, left Irish nationalists with far less than they had desired in the way of freedom and the ability to engage autonomously in external affairs. The Boundary Commission had not only failed to end partition between the Free State and Northern Ireland, but also effectively cemented the division in place as more or less permanent. The government of William Cosgrave (1880–1965) quietly but persistently pushed against the constraints of the 1922 treaty, gaining admission for Ireland to the League of Nations independent of Britain in 1923 and receiving diplomatic recognition from Washington that same year. The other white dominions, whose role in the Great War had earned them considerable stature within the British imperial structure (see Chapter 11), followed the Irish example, becoming members of the League of Nations under their own auspices and pursuing other initiatives that befit their increasing autonomy from London. At the 1926 Imperial Conference, South Africa and Canada, undoubtedly with Irish support, proposed what became known as the Balfour Declaration, so named for the former prime minister, Arthur Balfour, who presided over the meeting. It established the dominions as "autonomous Communities within the British Empire, equal in status, in no way subordinate one to another in any aspect of their domestic or external affairs, though united by a common allegiance to the Crown, and freely associated as members of the British Commonwealth of Nations." Five years later, the terms were ratified in the Statute of Westminster, by which the British Parliament gave up its powers to legislate for the dominions, except where otherwise specified by law. One observer from Australia, which did not favor the declaration, noted that it more accurately should have been called "the Statute of Dublin," given the forceful role played by the Irish delegation in inspiring and achieving sovereignty for the dominions.[14]

It might also have been called "the Statute of Pretoria," because the prime minister of South Africa, J. B. M. Hertzog (1866–1942), a general who had led Afrikaners during the South African War and went on to become head of the Afrikaner-based Nationalist Party, also worked hard to promote autonomy for the dominions. He shared Ireland's desire for a republican form of government, a possibility that was dashed by the Statute of Westminster's clause giving sovereignty to the dominions under the auspices of the British monarchy. Like many Irish Catholics, he and his nationalist followers loathed the British empire, and their political platform called for a complete severing of ties with it. They made a first step in that direction with a 1934 law, the South Africa Status Act, that asserted the divisibility of the British crown. The law made the monarch of the United Kingdom the monarch of South Africa as well, separating out the ruler's decisions and actions for Britain from those of South Africa. Practically speaking, that meant that should Britain go to war, it would not automatically follow that South Africa would as well. That would be a decision for the South African Parliament.

Following the elections of 1932 in Ireland, a new government under Éamon de Valera came to power. Its platform committed it to throwing off the ties that still bound the country to Britain, establishing a full-blown republic, and uniting northern and southern Ireland in a single nation. De Valera had to move slowly and carefully because Ireland's economic ties to Britain remained substantial and vital to the survival of the country, but he moved decisively. The Irish Citizenship Act of 1935 removed Irish men and women from the status of subjects of the British crown. The next year, de Valera took advantage of the abdication crisis (when Edward VIII (1894–1972) gave up his crown to marry Wallis Simpson (1896–1986), a divorcee, and therefore ineligible to act as queen) to remove any mention of the monarchy from the constitution. The new constitution of 1937 established the Free State as Éire and declared Catholicism the religion of the country, thus practically if not formally dissolving Ireland's ties to the British empire. It also had the effect of satisfying the desires of most Irish nationalists, dampening the sentiment for unifying the northern and southern regions of the island nation. Hardline members of the IRA continued to press for a single Irish state, resorting to violence at times to make their point, but increasingly its attempts found no support in the south, forcing the organization to look to Northern Ireland as the focus of their campaign. De Valera in fact outlawed the IRA and jailed its leadership in 1936.

The example of Ireland served to inform and even inspire many Indian nationalists in the 1920s and 1930s, even if their most visible figure, Mohandas Gandhi, dismissed it as inappropriate for India in its use of violence to achieve independence. We will pick up that story later.

WOMEN, WORK, AND EQUAL ENFRANCHISEMENT

In 1918, as we saw in the previous chapter, women over the age of thirty received the vote. Some 6 million of 11 million adult women were enfranchised. The vote was followed by the Eligibility of Women Act of 1918, which permitted women to stand for Parliament. In 1919, the passage of the Sex Disqualification Removal Act gave women access to all branches of the legal profession. By 1925, despite the ferocious opposition of entrenched bureaucrats, the civil service admitted women to its competitive examinations, although it refused to pay female civil servants the salaries given to men holding the same position, an inequity that feminists would battle against for years in their equal pay campaign of the 1930s. The Matrimonial Causes Act of 1923, a direct outcome of intense feminist lobbying, eliminated the double standard of divorce. The dissemination of contraceptive information at maternity centers and mothers' clinics, pioneered by birth control advocate Marie Stopes (1880–1958) and then established as policy by the Labour government after a long battle among feminists themselves and between men and women within the Labour Party, had an immediate impact on family size. In 1913, there were 1,102,500 births in England and Wales. That number dropped to 900,130 births in 1923; 777,520 births in 1926; and 761,963 births in 1931. The average size of the British family fell from 5.5 in the last quarter of the nineteenth century to 2.2 between 1925 and 1929. In 1928, women finally obtained the franchise on the same terms as men.

These were impressive victories by any measure. In combination with welfare benefits implemented during the war to compensate families for the loss of income as men went off to war—some never to return and others to come back too disabled to hold a job—they improved the lives of many women to a large extent. Certainly these legislative reforms, along with the gains women had made in employment and wages during the war, contributed to an impression that the war had been a boon to women, that it had enhanced their position in the workplace and in political life, and that it had done so at the expense of men. The pressures on women to leave their jobs and return to the domestic sphere were intense—and often successful. Women did leave their wartime jobs as munitions factories shut down for lack of orders. And beginning in 1921, the traditional employers of women, the great textile factories of Lancashire, began to feel the serious effects of recession, laying off both male and female workers in large numbers, as did other old industries in the north of England like shipbuilding and coal mining. By 1921, fewer women were "gainfully employed," according to the census of that year, than in 1911. Women put out of work by the end of the war and by the beginnings of economic depression refused, as they would not have in the past, to seek employment as domestic servants, an expression of self-regard that certainly helped to drive up their unemployment rates.

But this is only one part of the story. In the south of England, new industries providing household consumer goods by means of large-scale, assembly-line production began to appear, and they relied on women to make up the bulk of their semiskilled workforce. The electrical appliances and the ready-made goods that enabled middle-class women to provide even greater levels of domestic comfort in the interwar years were supplied by wage-earning women. New work opportunities for women in offices as typists, bookkeepers, or cleaning staff and in shops as assistants and cashiers cropped up, as Britain's economy underwent restructuring from heavy industry in the north to light consumer and service industries in the south.

During this period, women in the Labour Party increased their numbers and their influence. A number of women became MPs for Labour—Susan Lawrence (1871–1947), Ellen Wilkinson (1891–1947), and Margaret Bondfield (1873–1953), to name only those who became cabinet ministers—and many, many more served their communities on local governing boards and authorities. To be sure, they faced strongly antifeminist attitudes within the party and struggled, usually in vain, to gain acceptance for their demands, but their energies and their activities on behalf of poor and working women helped to improve their lives considerably.

With their enfranchisement in 1918, women joined local branches of the Labour Party to a far greater degree than did men. In 1923, 120,000 women belonged to the women's sections of the party; they increased their numbers to as many as 300,000 between 1927 and 1939, comprising at least half of the membership of the party as a whole. In some areas, like Cardiff, they made up as much as three-quarters of the membership. They made their voices heard, urging policies such as the dissemination of contraceptives or family allowances on their male colleagues. They demanded equal pay for men and women, and, because in only a few jobs could it be claimed that women and men did the same work, comparable pay for women who did work of the same value as men. They strove to endow home- and housework with the dignity of paid labor, and the majority of them believed that married women had the right to work just like their unmarried sisters. In holding this opinion, Labour women departed from the powerful cultural norm that mothers should not work.

Conservatives had attributed their electoral victory of 1924 to the votes of women. This confidence may have led the most surprising of Conservatives, Home Secretary William Joynson-Hicks, to announce almost off-handedly in 1927 the government's intention to bring in a measure to enfranchise women between the ages of twenty-one and thirty.

Feminist organizations and politicians had begun deliberating the question almost immediately after the Representation of the People Act of 1918 gave the vote to women over the age of thirty, but serious contemplation of the issue arose only after Joynson-Hicks surprised—and dismayed—a good portion of the party with his statement. At that point, the *Daily Mail* and, to a much lesser extent, the other major newspapers embarked on a crusade against the "flapper vote" that reached the point of panic. Two themes dominated the diatribes of the press: the threat of women swamping men and the prospect of the women's vote ushering in an era of socialist and—in the heated rhetoric of the period—Bolshevik government. The *Daily Mail*'s Cassandra-like warnings appeared to be borne out when the Labour Party was swept into power in the summer of 1929. It became clear in the days immediately following the election that the new women voters had gone disproportionately for the Labour Party, giving it the largest share of seats in the House of Commons, although not an outright majority. It was an inauspicious time to take control of government.

DEPRESSION, DISILLUSION, AND NATIONAL CRISIS

When Labour took office again in October 1929, it faced severe challenges in virtually every aspect of national life—unemployment, finance, international affairs, colonial policy, and political instability at home. Disruption of the international financial markets, as London ceded its supremacy to New York; dislocation of industry and trade, both at home and abroad; struggles over disarmament among the great powers; sharpening nationalist sentiments in the colonies; and the apparent failure of the three-party system to provide effective government—all of them aftershocks of the Great War—gave rise in 1930 to the conviction that Britain faced a "crisis" of grave proportions. In part a reflection of the real problems facing the country, in part a device mobilized in the hope of discrediting the Labour government and effecting a change in political power and policies, the "national crisis" transformed the political landscape in Britain.

Labour came into power as a minority government, dependent on the Liberals for their majority, just as the economy, responding to the deepening worldwide depression, took a sharp downward turn. British exports, amounting to £839 million in 1929, dropped to £666 million in 1930 and to £461 million in 1931. Figures for those who were out of work registered the declining economic fortunes of the country: the number of unemployed reached 1.520 million in January 1930, 1.761 million in April, 2,070 million in July, 2.319 million in October, and 2.5 million in December 1930. The Labour government squandered any chances it might have had to alleviate the economic distress by introducing measures no more vigorous in their vision or execution than their Conservative predecessors. Its limited commitment to public works programs did little to dent the severity of the downturn, and the government would not support more dramatic measures to stimulate the economy. It did introduce the Unemployment Insurance Bill in November 1929, increasing the numbers of those who could get relief without having made sufficient contributions to the fund and thereby placing a larger draw on the Treasury. The bill became law in 1930.

Internationally, despite truly heroic efforts by MacDonald and Foreign Secretary Arthur Henderson (1863–1935), efforts to promote peace proceeded unevenly. In 1929, the Young Plan had restructured German reparations and provided for the evacuation of the Rhineland by Allied troops in 1930. But the foreign minister, Gustav Stresemann, who had maintained good relations with France and Britain, was dead by the time Labour took office and with him the prospects of German efforts toward lasting peace. The cutoff of foreign capital to Germany in 1930 caused its artificially prosperous economy to falter; the need for budget cuts provoked unrest and led Heinrich Brüning, the new German chancellor, to invoke emergency powers. In the election in September, the National Socialist party won 107 seats in the Reichstag, an increase of 97 from its previous showing. In Italy in May, Benito Mussolini trumpeted his preference for "rifles, machine-guns, warships, aeroplanes, and cannon" over "words." And although Britain, the United States, and Japan agreed at the London Naval Conference in April 1930 to limit the size of their fleets, neither Italy nor France would sign on to the treaty, thus vitiating its effectiveness. Problems in the Mideast flared with the failure of treaty negotiations with Egypt and troubles between Arabs and Jews in Palestine. In Nigeria, Britain's second most important colony, a "women's war" protesting colonial rule elicited sufficient concern among the permanent members of the Colonial Office, if not among the politicians or the country as a whole, to bring about substantial change in the way the British ruled there. Events in India caused serious discomfort for the country. The massacre at Amritsar had inflamed nationalist opinion, sparking disorder throughout the 1920s.

Talk of a "national crisis" erupted in the fall of 1930 after months of public hand wringing about Britain's precarious state. Across all shades of political opinion, among virtually every section of public life, the idea of a national crisis approaching wartime levels took hold, fed by conviction and opportunism alike. MacDonald and Lloyd George spoke of it as the worst situation facing the country since "the darkest hours of the War."[15] The foreign and domestic difficulties facing Britain seemed beyond the ability of the political parties to manage. Labour did not by itself hold sufficient seats to govern; it depended on Liberal support to stay in office. Internally, the party faced significant dissent from its left wing. Conservatives faced their own internal strife: Baldwin came under attack by men like Churchill over issues of imperial free trade and dominion status for India. He survived those assaults and actually emerged stronger for them, but the public bloodletting did nothing to boost the confidence of the nation in the ability of its political leaders. Newspaper editors questioned the competence and capabilities of politicians; politicians themselves worried about the public's "disillusionment" with parliamentary government and noted that conditions in Britain were not dissimilar to those in other countries that had turned to dictatorship. Ordinary party politics, it appeared to more and more people, could not continue in this vein. Public momentum for a new approach to government was building rapidly.

Economic and financial conditions worsened during the spring and summer of 1931, culminating in the crisis that brought down the Labour government on August 23. Unemployment reached 2.707 million by June, leading the government to seek parliamentary approval for an increase in borrowing power for the unemployment insurance fund. The Committee on National Expenditure, formed in February 1931 under the leadership of Sir George May (1871–1946), issued its report on July 31; it predicted a deficit of £120 million by April 1932 and called for new taxes of £24 million and cuts of £96 million to meet it. Cuts totaling £66.6 million, the report recommended, should come from unemployment benefits. The May report brought home to Britain the financial crisis that had rippled through the international financial system throughout the spring and summer as skittish foreign investors, leery that a beleaguered Labour government could make such deep cuts, began to withdraw their funds; the drain on the banks continued well into August. Bankers demanded action on the part of the government to renew confidence in the pound by balancing the budget.

The draconian nature of these cuts, it became clear to many opinion makers, were beyond the capacity of any party to introduce. Cabinet officials did not dispute the need to balance the budget; they differed over the amount of cuts that would have to be made to the unemployment benefit. The cabinet's Economy Committee announced on August 13 that it would balance the budget through "equality of sacrifice," acknowledging that some of the deficit would have to be made up from the unemployment insurance fund. When it became clear to a number of cabinet ministers ten days later, however, that these cuts would be substantial, they opposed the budget plan. With a cabinet split of eleven to nine, members agreed on August 22 to resign immediately and inform the king of their decision; they recommended he convene a conference of MacDonald, Baldwin, and Herbert Samuel (1870–1963)—serving as leader of the Liberal Party in the absence of Lloyd George because of illness—to determine how power would be transferred. When he returned the next day, MacDonald informed his cabinet colleagues, to their "utter stupefaction," as one historian described it,[16] that a National government made up of Conservatives, Liberals, and Labour—with he himself as prime minister--would succeed the Labour government. It would consist of four Labourites, four Conservatives, and two Liberals.

The government was to sit for six weeks only and an election fought by the parties was to be held to replace it with a conventional party government. The response of the Labour Party and the TUC to the budget, however, forced the National government to reconsider that decision. Led by Arthur Henderson, George Lansbury (1859–1940), and TUC leaders Ernest Bevin (1881–1951) and J. R. Clynes (1869–1949), the Labour Party turned to a program far more frankly "socialist" in nature. No longer constrained by the need to be regarded as trustworthy or fit to govern through their accommodation with other parties, Labour Party members put forward ideas of state control over industry, banking, and finance, a platform, some Conservatives and Liberals feared, that would have great appeal to the public, making it impossible for any new government to continue on a course designed to sustain confidence in the financial markets and address the problems of the economy.

Labour leaders, stunned by MacDonald's decision to head a national government in August, were disgusted by his choice to lead an election against the party, a breach so grievous that they gave up any lingering loyalties they might have had to him and pursued their newly aggressive agenda with a zeal unhampered by regret or sympathy for the man who had led them for so long. At their October conference, party members and TUC delegates produced a program that made it clear that Labour would never again be, in Beatrice Webb's (1858–1943) words, "the caretaker of the existing order of society." In an election manifesto written up by Harold Laski (1893–1950), the party promised not only to restore the cuts in benefits but also to nationalize the banks and credit systems, coal mines, power, transport, iron and steel, and land, making provisions for worker participation in the management of these publicly owned industries. Philip Snowden (1864–1937), who had remained with MacDonald in the National government, denounced the Labour program as "the most fantastic and impracticable ever put before the electors." "This is not Socialism," he sputtered over the BBC airways. "It is bolshevism run mad."[17]

Proponents of the National government persuaded voters of this view: the country went overwhelmingly on October 27, 1931, for the return of the National government. Having been convinced of a "national crisis" that only a "national government" representing "national unity" could address and resolve, voters gave National government candidates 67 percent of their votes. Of the 615 MPs who would take their seats, 554 of them would be members of the National Government party, giving them a majority of more than 500. The election proved devastating for the Labour party. Of the 267 seats it had held, it lost 215 of them, leaving a party of only 46 MPs in the House of Commons. It had, to be sure, maintained and even, in some places such as Scotland, increased its popular vote, but its majorities occurred only in some locations, certainly not in enough constituencies to establish the party as any kind of electoral threat.

COLONIAL DEVELOPMENTS

The new National government pursued a colonial policy that differed little from earlier Conservative regimes, incorporating a combination of conciliatory, if poorly executed, measures of reform and harsh retaliatory actions. In 1927, Baldwin's government had established a commission headed by Sir John Simon (1873–1954) to assess the efficacy of the 1919 Montagu–Chelmsford reforms in India. Lacking any Indian representation, it aroused only disdain and rage among Indian nationalists who saw in its all-British composition a message that Indians did not possess the education or skills necessary to rule themselves. In October 1929, Lord Irwin (1881–1959), the viceroy, hoping to defuse the anger invoked by the Simon Commission, declared that "the natural issue of India's constitutional progress . . . is the attainment of Dominion status," infuriating Conservatives at home but underwhelming members of the Indian National Congress (INC), which in December of that year issued a "declaration of independence," in pursuit of which it launched a boycott of central and provincial governments and a campaign of civil disobedience, including nonpayment of taxes.[18] When the Simon Commission released its report calling for an enlarged

Gandhi and followers breaking the Salt Laws in an act of civil disobedience, 1930.

Indian electorate, more self-government in the provinces, and a conference to decide the shape of the future central government in June 1930, its measures became lost in the turmoil of Gandhi's civil disobedience campaign. The Salt March in the spring of 1930, protesting Britain's monopoly on salt production, caught the attention of the world but it had little impact on British policy.

Gandhi and a number of Congress Party leaders were jailed, along with as many as 54,000 other participants in the campaign. The Indian government hoped their arrests would curtail the disorder. MacDonald convened the first of three Round Table conferences in London in November 1930 to discuss the future of India's government, although Congress Party members refused to attend it. When the government approached the Conservative Party in January 1931 for its support for further discussions about a new constitution for India, which it received, Churchill could not contain his fury and resigned from the Conservative shadow cabinet. The second Round Table conference met in the fall of 1931, by which time the Labour government had given way to the National government, in which Churchill was conspicuous by his absence.

In India, a new viceroy, Lord Willingdon (1866–1941), vowing that he would meet any "damn nonsense" put forward by nationalists with a "blitz of *lathis*" (long clubs used by the police) and "knotted ropes," determined to answer protests against imperial rule with violence, imprisonment, and repression. He refused to negotiate with Gandhi and when the *mahatma* returned from the second

Gandhi at the Round Table Conference, 1931.

Round Table conference in London in 1931, Willingdon had him arrested, along with some 80,000 of his followers. The government of India imposed greater censorship on the press; required Indians to carry identity cards listing their religion, employment, and status; prohibited meetings of more than a few people; restricted travel; and outlawed the wearing of what were called Gandhi caps. Congress members decried the actions of the government, but could not agree on what actions to take, precisely what the government had hoped would follow its crackdown. But such measures on the part of colonial officials did not always sit well, even with themselves. Willingdon allowed that he was "becoming a sort of Mussolini of India."[19]

As part of a carrot-and-stick approach to colonial unrest, the British government passed a new measure purportedly designed to increase Indian participation in the political life of their country, but that in actuality kept power in the hands of the viceroy. The India Act of 1935 enlarged the autonomy of provincial governments, expanding the functions of legislatures and making ministers responsible to them. It also increased the size of the electorate dramatically to some 30 million Indians, including some women. But because it identified specific constituencies—women, for example, princes, and Muslims—and gave them special voting rights, Jawaharlal Nehru objected to the act, seeing it as a new mechanism for the old trick of divide and rule and thus the continuation of the British Raj. He urged the INC not to participate in the subsequent elections for provincial legislatures, but Gandhi opposed him and carried the day. In the 1937 elections, the INC won more than half of the seats contested, taking control outright in seven provinces. In the process, it turned itself into a mass political party.

But as the British had intended, the elections also served to split Indian nationalists. Muhammed Ali Jinnah (1876–1948), leader of the Muslim League and one-time proponent of Hindu–Muslim unity, regarded the victories of the INC as threats to Muslims, raising the cry of "Islam in danger" and characterizing the INC as a Hindu fascist organization. In some provinces, indeed, Congress favored Hindus over Muslims, fomenting deep resentments and making it clear, at least to Jinnah, that if Britain "really had it in mind to abandon control of this country then it was quite obvious that Muslims must bestir themselves and be ready to fight."[20] He and others began to envisage a separate country composed of the Muslim-dominated lands of Punjab, Afghanistan, Kashmir, Sind, and Baluchistan—to be called, in the event, Pakistan.

Anticolonial activities among Africans and West Indians unfolded a bit more slowly following the Great War, but picked up steam in the mid-1920s. During the interwar period, increasing numbers of mostly male students from Africa and the West Indies enrolled at Edinburgh, Oxford, Cambridge, and the colleges that made up the University of London. In 1918, activists residing there formed two new black associations to help the newcomers adjust to the environment they faced, one often marked by racism and hostility. The Union of African Descent and the African Progress Union (APU) started out with no intention of becoming political organizations, but the settings in which students found themselves made it difficult to sustain that position. By the mid-1920s, unofficial color bars and racial discrimination prompted members of the associations to take steps to change the situation. The APU in particular joined forces with the National Congress of British West Africa to lobby the colonial office for reforms. Africans in London also facilitated the interaction of various African groups. In 1920, emissaries from the National Congress of British West Africa such as Herbert Macaulay (1864–1946) traveled to London and, through the offices of the APU, met Sol Plaatje and Josiah Gumede, representatives of the South African Native National Congress, which would become the African National Congress in later years.

In 1924, the British Empire Expedition, a world's fair–type display of the products and peoples of Britain's imperial holdings, opened at Wembley. Many of the depictions of colonial peoples offered up stereotypical images of savage cannibals, backward and superstitious subhumans, and illiterate and unskilled "natives" whose future depended on continued British overlordship. They enraged many Africans, chief among them Ladipo Solanke (c. 1886–1958), a Yoruba man studying law. He railed against the Wembley representations of Africans in a series of articles published in Britain and West Africa and was moved by its racism and prejudice to establish the West African Student Union (WASU), arguably the most important African organization in Britain for the next thirty years, in 1925. In its first decade, WASU enrolled men exclusively, but in the mid-1930s, a number of African women began to join the union, including the first of the African women to seek degrees in Britain. WASU established a hostel for visiting Africans and people of African descent, insisting that its operations remain entirely independent of the Colonial Office or any other official entity so that its guests might live and work without interference. WASU's commitment to this principle made for some difficult days for the hostel, financially speaking, but the staunchness of its commitment demonstrated to all that Africans could and must attend to their own affairs.

Africans and West Indians in Britain kept in close contact with comrades at home in their efforts to improve the conditions of peoples living under British colonialism. Some of the most effective resistance to colonialism appeared in the guise of trade union formation and strike activity. These new organizations amounted to little in the way of numbers, but they served to articulate grievances and they persuaded colonial administrators at home and in Africa that a serious communist threat existed in their colonies. This latter belief was wildly exaggerated because the actual communist presence in Africa was miniscule, but it caused imperial officers to double down on their efforts to maintain order. In Gold Coast in 1933, for instance, the conditions in the mines—where workers toiled seven days a week for low wages, had to live in company housing, and purchase food sold by company agents at a jacked-up price—led miners to go on strike for the payment of wages they had earned but not received. The mine owners ordered that they be fired on. Strikes broke out in southern Nigeria in

1936 and in 1938 and 1939 in Sierra Leone. Worker revolt in the Caribbean, beginning in 1934, reached alarming levels by 1938. In Jamaica that year, strikes amounted to a rebellion of workers in which dozens of people lost their lives, hundreds were wounded, and millions of pounds of property was severely damaged. These events, in the wake of strike activity in Kenya, Tanganyika, and Northern Rhodesia, alarmed officials sufficiently to compel them to rethink imperial policies and practices. A new model of colonial rule—sometimes referred to as "development," sometimes as "partnership"—came in the late 1930s to expand the concept of "trusteeship" embodied in the League of Nations mandates charter. It emphasized Britain's obligations to establish policies and practices that would make life better for colonial subjects, but in practice, it differed little from its predecessor. Some funds were made available to colonial governments for the support of small-scale enterprises such as water projects in local communities.

The actual implementation of development policies did little to improve the standards of living for most Africans, although some privileged groups did benefit from them. They were, for all intents and purposes, too little, too late. By the late 1930s, small groups of educated, Westernized Africans, influenced by the intellectual currents of pan-Africanism emanating from the United States, the Caribbean, and London, had come to believe that social and economic reforms were simply not enough. Even reforms that would grant increased participation in the political arena and reduce segregation of Africans from Europeans—which were not, in any event, in the offing—did not go far enough for this new class of Western-educated intellectuals. Men like the editor of the *West African Pilot*, Nnamdi Azikiwe (1904–1996), and the Gold Coast teacher, Kwame Nkrumah (1909–1972), who might once have been satisfied with political reform under the auspices of British rule, began to look for self-rule and independence from Britain entirely.

Much of this shift in thinking derived from Italy's invasion of Ethiopia in 1935 and especially from Britain's failure to speak out against it (in fact, in 1938, Britain recognized Mussolini as the emperor of Ethiopia). As the last remaining African territory free from European rule, Ethiopia held a powerful symbolic place in the imaginations of educated Africans. The fall of this proud, independent state to the modern weaponry of the Italian fascist state acted to stir quiescent and diverse strands of pan-Africanism and bind them into a single stream of radical anticolonial thought. After the invasion of Ethiopia, African intellectuals insisted that Britons could not be trusted to look after their welfare. Buttressed by West Indian and African organizations in London such as WASU, this new generation of Western-educated urban Africans became anticolonialists who, in the years after the Second World War, would lead the movements for decolonization and independence in their respective lands. For now, their activities and their impact were limited to a small group of people who shared their backgrounds and beliefs.

Despite their small numbers and even smaller influence on large masses of Africans, anticolonial activists in London and Africa worried colonial officials. They sought to deal with the potential threat by resorting to the tried and true imperial tactic of divide and rule. Imperialists like Malcolm Hailey (1872–1969) urged that colonial officials identify "moderate" Africans and groom them up for participation in governance. Co-opting reasonable Africans into government, the thinking went, would preserve British rule by driving a wedge between them and more radical agitators, thus undermining the anticolonial movement. Hailey's policies went into effect during the Second World War, to which we now turn.

NOTES

1. Quoted in Peter Fryer, *Staying Power. The History of Black People in Britain* (London, 1984), pp. 304, 305, 313.
2. D. G. Boyce, *Englishmen and Irish Troubles. British Public Opinion and the Making of Irish Policy, 1918–22* (London, 1972), p. 43.
3. Quoted in Charles Townshend, *Political Violence in Ireland:Government and Resistance since 1848* (Oxford, 1983), p. 332.
4. Barbara Storm Farr, *The Development and Impact of Right-Wing Politics in Britain* (New York, 1987), p. 39;Richard Aldington, *Death of a Hero* (London, 1929), p. 206; Thomas Jones *Whitehall Diary Volume I: 1916–1925* (London, 1969), April 4, 1921, pp. 134, 135, 136.
5. Quoted in Jacqueline Jenkinson, "The 1919 Race Riots in Britain: Their Background and Consequences," unpublished thesis (University of Edinburgh, 1987), p. 172.
6. Quoted in Jacqueline Jenkinson, "The 1919 Race Riots in Britain," p. 174.
7. Ernest Marke, *Old Man Trouble. The Memoirs of a Stowaway, Mutineer, Bootlegger, Crocuser, and Soho Club Owner* (London, 1975), p. 31.
8. Quoted in Ray Costello, *Black Liverpool. The Early History of Britain's Oldest Black Community, 1730–1918* (Liverpool, 2001), p. 88.
9. E. H. H. Green, *Ideologies of Conservatism*, pp. 120, 126–27, 128; Jones *Diary*, p. 80.
10. "Industrial Crisis. Failure of Negotiations." House of Commons *Debates*, May 3, 1926, cols. 72, 73, 124–25.
11. Virginia Woolf *Diaries*, May 13, 1926, p. 85.
12. Charles Loch Mowat, *Britain between the Wars, 1918–1940* (Chicago, 1955), p. 337; quoted in *Public Opinion*, May 21, 1926, p. 451.
13. C. F. G. Masterson, "The General Strike and After," *The Contemporary Review*," CXXIX, June 1926, pp. 683, 687; Keith Laybourn, *The General Strike of 1926* (Manchester, 1993), p. 111; Renshaw, *General Strike*, pp. 242, 248.
14. Quoted in Kate O'Malley, *Ireland, India and Empire. Indo-Irish Radical Connections, 1919–64* (Manchester, 2008), p. 53.
15. Quoted in Philip Williamson, *National Crisis and National Government: British Politics, the Economy and Empire, 1926–1932* (Cambridge, 1992), pp. 1, 135.
16. Mowat, *Britain between the Wars*, p. 393.
17. Quoted in Williamson, *National Crisis*, pp. 432, 427.
18. Mowat, *Britain between the Wars*, p. 377.

19. Quoted in Piers Brendon, *The Decline and Fall of the British Empire, 1781–1997* (New York, 2007), p. 392.
20. Quoted in Brendon, *The Decline and Fall of the British Empire*, p. 394.

FURTHER READING

D. G. Boyce, *Englishmen and Irish Troubles. British Public Opinion and the Making of Irish Policy, 1918–22*. London, 1972.

Barbara Bush, *Imperialism, Race and Resistance: Africa and Britain, 1919–1945*. London, 1999.

E. H. Green, *Ideologies of Conservatism: Conservative Political Ideas in the Twentieth Century*. Oxford, 2002.

TIMELINE

1918	Women over thirty get the vote
1919	War for Irish independence begins
	Race riots throughout Britain
1921	Irish treaty with Britain; Irish civil war begins
1922	Irish Free State forms
1923	First Labour government comes to power
1924	Zinoviev letter; Labour voted out
1925	West African Student Union founded
1926	General Strike

Jacqueline Jenkinson, *Black 1919: Riots, Racism and Resistance in Imperial Britain*. Liverpool, 2009.

Susan Kingsley Kent, *Aftershocks: Politics and Trauma in Britain, 1918–1931*. Basingstoke, 2009.

Keith Laybourne, *The General Strike of 1926*. Manchester, 1993.

Marc Matera, Misty L. Bastian, and Susan Kingsley Kent, *The Women's War of 1929: Gender and Violence in Colonial Nigeria*. Basingstoke, 2012.

Kate O'Malley, *Ireland, India and Empire. Indo-Irish Radical Connections, 1919–64*. Manchester, 2008.

Philip Williamson, *National Crisis and National Government: British Politics, the Economy and Empire, 1926–1932*. Cambridge, 1992.

1928	Women obtain the franchise on the same terms as men
1929	Second Labour government forms
	Stock market crash
1930	Gandhi's Salt March in India
	Round Table talks fail
1931	National government forms
	Statute of Westminster gives dominions autonomy
1935	India Act
	Italy invades Ethiopia
1936–1939	Strikes across the empire

Children being prepared for evacuation during the Blitz, 1940.

CHAPTER 13

APPEASEMENT, WORLD WAR, AND THE ESTABLISHMENT OF THE WELFARE STATE, 1935–1962

Early in the morning of September 1, 1939, eleven-year-old Dave Pinchon left his Southampton home and walked with his parents and his friend Bobby Mills to the Taunton School. The boys carried gas masks in a cardboard box hung around their necks by a string, wore name tags on their raincoat lapels, and, along with the single small suitcase each was allowed, clutched paper bags holding biscuits, a bit of sugar, chocolate bars, and tins of corned beef. Once they reached the school, they bid Dave's parents goodbye and joined hundreds of other children lining up for what they all assumed was just another evacuation drill. It was not. Marching three abreast, they tramped to the railway station, where they would board a train bound for Bournemouth. Dave worried a little bit about the uncertainty he faced, but his apprehension could not temper the excitement he felt or quell the visions of wartime heroism and adventure he had read about in the *Boy's Own Paper*. His parents, having lived through Zeppelin raids on London during World War I and aware of the ferocious German bombings of cities like Guernica during the Spanish Civil War, had different ideas of what lay ahead.

That morning, as German tanks rolled into Poland, getting the Second World War in Europe underway, British officials implemented evacuation plans they had had in the works for years. In cities across Britain, some 1.5 million Britons—half of them children unaccompanied by their parents, who were unable to leave their jobs or homes—got on buses, trams, and trains headed for the countryside. From London, Manchester, Liverpool, Newcastle, Birmingham, Salford, Leeds, Portsmouth, Southampton, Glasgow, Edinburgh, Dundee, Clydebank, and Belfast, they journeyed to Kent, the Welsh valleys, Worcestershire, Bedfordshire, Lincolnshire, and other rural areas. When they arrived at their destinations, they were herded to schools or church halls, where prospective hosts inspected them and decided who to take home. "It was a bit like a cattle market," remembered one eleven year old. "People pulled and tugged at the children they wanted." Some faced circumstances entirely unlike those they had left behind: those who landed in Wales, for instance, could not speak the language that many of their hosts used; some of the children taken in by farmers had never seen a cow or a sheep or a pig. Some were bullied in school, and others fit right in. Many working-class children from the large urban centers had never known the luxury of a bed to themselves, a toilet, or an egg.

Some of the children lacked adequate clothing and shoes; others were sufficiently clothed for the approaching autumn but did not have what they would need to get them through the winter. The physical and hygienic state of many of the children from urban areas shocked the families taking them in. In the days immediately following the evacuation, letters appeared in *The Times* and other newspapers decrying the conditions of the women and children from the cities. "Some of the women evacuated arrived in a verminous condition," protested one local notable, "which has contaminated bedding and wallpaper in the houses where they have been billeted." Another described the children he observed as "stunted, misshapen creatures, only capable of understanding the simplest language and quite incapable of thought, moved by impulses at the best sentimental, at the worst brutal." Having never encountered children from urban slums, country families chafed at having to provide the basic necessities like clothing and shoes to their charges.

The outcry in the press and the stories told to politicians about the situations faced by host families led to debate in the House of Commons about the shortcomings of the evacuation planning. In the process, Labour MPs declaimed against the descriptions used to characterize working-class evacuees and urged their colleagues to take heed of the kind of conditions that gave rise to the problems presented by children with head lice, fleas, and undernourishment. George Buchanan (1890–1955), Labour MP for Glasgow, for instance, refused to allow the children of his constituency to be slandered by people who had no idea how they were forced to live. "They are as good as yours," he protested. He hoped that the outcry against the state of the evacuated children would result in people getting "to know something more about the slums, and that they will seek to end the slums of Glasgow and other cities." His words fell on sympathetic ears in many, many instances. One woman told Prime Minister Neville Chamberlain's daughter Dorothy that she "never knew that such conditions existed, and I feel ashamed of having been so ignorant of my neighbours."[1]

The evacuation plans of 1939 had become necessary when, after five years of provocation, fascist Germany and fascist Italy took Europe to war. Fighting the Second World War involved the participation on some level of virtually every British subject, both at home and in the empire. In return for the cooperation, time, effort, energy, resources, and sacrifices of millions upon millions of men and women, Britain had to promise that their contributions would not be in vain. For those at home, that meant a society that looked after its most vulnerable. For those in the empire, it entailed greater opportunities and rights and more participation in governance; for some, indeed, even outright independence. The degree to which Britain made good on its promises over the space of fifteen years following the end of the Second World War varied significantly.

..

THE FASCIST CHALLENGE

In October 1935, Mussolini's armies invaded Abyssinia (Ethiopia), the only independent African nation apart from Liberia. That same year, in violation of the terms of the Versailles Treaty, Hitler began to rearm Germany, reinstituting conscription and building up the armed forces, including creating an air force. Emboldened by the lack of response from the Allied powers, he embarked on the first step to incorporate all ethnic Germans living outside the borders of Germany within the Third Reich, sending troops to occupy the Rhineland in March 1936. Neither France nor Britain responded with military force; their inaction convinced Hitler that he would encounter little serious resistance to his plans to obtain *Lebensraum*—"living space"—for Germans. The groundwork for war had been laid.

Hitler tested his new armaments in the course of the Spanish Civil War, which broke out in the summer of 1936. He armed rightist forces—Nationalists—under the command of General Francisco Franco as they set out to overthrow the republican government of Spain established in 1931 although Germany had signed, along with Italy, Britain, France, and the Soviet Union, a nonintervention pact banning such action. The left wing of the Labour Party urged the British government to respond in kind in support of the republican government, as the Soviet Union had done, but cabinet ministers insisted on remaining aloof from the conflict, fearful of upsetting relations with Italy and Germany. To do otherwise, ministers believed, would be to court war, something few Britons were prepared to contemplate. Instead, private individuals such as Julian Bell (1908–1937), nephew to Virginia Woolf, and George Orwell (1903–1950) traveled to the beleaguered country along with volunteers from around the world to fight against fascism on behalf of republican Spain. A number of British MPs from across the political spectrum—Labour MP Ellen Wilkinson, Independent MP Eleanor Rathbone (1872–1946), and Conservative MP the Duchess of Atholl (1874–1960) most prominently—organized relief efforts to assist Spanish refugees, especially children. As the civil war raged on, belligerents on both sides committed terrible atrocities. German and Italian aircraft bombed the Basque town of Guernica in April 1937, killing without warning civilians gathered in the town for market day. This marked one of Germany's first forays into the campaign of terror bombing that the *Luftwaffe*, the German air force, would adopt as a doctrine of war.

In March 1938, Hitler annexed Austria to Germany in the so-called *Anschluss*, an operation that exposed the newly created and vulnerable Czechoslovakia to further German aggression. Czechoslovakia contained a large ethnic German population in its southern region; Hitler's declaration that the Sudetenland, as that region was called, constituted an integral part of the Reich compelled France and Britain to call for a conference to adjudicate the question. On September 29, 1938, prime ministers Neville Chamberlain and Edouard Daladier, along with Mussolini, met Hitler in Munich, where they negotiated away a significant portion of Czech territory while representatives of the Czech government waited outside in the hall. The new country was forced to give up not only the Sudetenland, but also military installations. Declaring that he had achieved "peace in our time," Chamberlain returned to London convinced that by giving Hitler what he wanted, he would satisfy *Der Führer's* appetite.

This policy of appeasement, whereby Britain (along with France and the United States) acceded to Germany's clearly aggressive actions flowed not from the craven nature of clueless and weak politicians, but from the clear-headed realization that the British people could not be induced to go to war, not after the devastations they had suffered during and since the Great War. The Western democratic leaders, including the American president, Franklin Roosevelt, whose people were firmly of isolationist opinion, could not simply take their countries to war; they had to respond to public opinion, which was overwhelmingly in favor of peace and disarmament. For the British government, the position of the dominions played a significant role as well: dominion leaders simply did not regard Germany as a threat to their interests, and British officials believed that if they were to go to war, they must have the unanimous backing of the dominions. At an imperial conference in 1937, South Africa declared its inclination to remain neutral in any future conflict; Canada sought to maintain an isolationist stance. From the perspective of the dominions, the decision to go to war had to been seen as one made by themselves, not by Britain, a situation that created even greater reluctance among politicians. Rearmament in preparation for war in this kind of atmosphere, then, could take place only slowly, as political leaders who understood the real threat Hitler's Germany represented positioned their nations as best they could.

They were aided immeasurably by Germany's invasion of what was left of Czechoslovakia in March 1939. The conquest of a non-German people could not be passed off by Hitler as a seemingly legitimate reunification of Germans, and it was seen for what it was: the first move in a war to dominate Europe. Britain and France began to rearm seriously and issued a guarantee of sovereignty to Poland, the country next in the path of the German war machine. The USSR, believing that the appeasing Western democracies might crack a deal with Germany that was inimical to its interests, signed a nonaggression pact with Germany, the Nazi–Soviet pact, by which they were promised parts of Poland, Finland, and the Baltic states. Having neutralized the Soviet Union, Hitler then invaded Poland on September 1, 1939, obliterating the Polish army. Britain declared war on Germany on September 3, inexorably drawn into a cataclysmic conflict that would engulf Europe for the next six years.

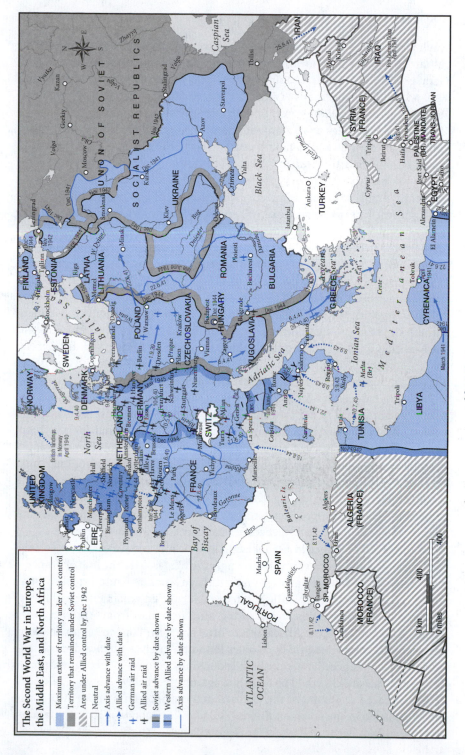

MAP 13.1

The Second World War in Europe, the Middle East, and North Africa

AN IMPERIAL WAR IN EUROPE

Having declared war in defense of Poland, neither Britain nor France had the resources to prevent or mitigate the overrunning of that unfortunate land by German and Soviet forces. Britain could do little, in fact, as Soviet troops invaded Finland and German troops invaded Denmark and Norway in April 1940. The Royal Navy had mined the waters around Norway to keep iron ore from reaching Germany, but the Germans got around the explosives and made their way inland. German submarines and bombers neutralized the threat posed by the British navy and rendered the fleet ineffective. The failure to prevent the invasion of Norway caused Chamberlain's government to fall in the spring of 1940. Winston Churchill, first lord of the Admiralty, who, ironically, had been responsible for the botched effort to defend Norway, became prime minister. For all of his past blunders and inadequacies, the man in the bowler hat with a cigar clenched in his teeth proved to be just the leader Britons needed at that time. He would rally his nation to continue to fight in what was a seemingly impossible situation, inspiring citizens and subjects with his gruff plain speaking and implacable will to defend and protect Britain and its empire.

On the very day of Churchill's accession to the post, May 10, 1940, Germany turned its *blitzkrieg*—lightning war—toward the west, attacking and occupying the Netherlands, Belgium, and then France before the antiquated British Expeditionary Force could do a thing to stop it. Ten divisions of the BEF found themselves trapped in northern France, their backs to the sea at Dunkirk. Royal Air Force (RAF) pilots battled the *Luftwaffe* in the skies above Dunkirk in the days between May 27 and June 4, 1940, as the Royal Navy and a fleet of private fishing boats, tugs, ferries, merchant ships, and pleasure craft evacuated British and French troops from the area. They rescued some 200,000 British and 140,000 French soldiers from the beaches, but left behind thousands of others, along with all of their tanks and heavy gear. The advancing German armies had created a disaster for the British at Dunkirk, but the salvaging of a significant portion of the British army by an armada of indomitable people piloting rescue craft across the English Channel gave Britons reason to believe that come what may, they would survive.

With the fall of France in 1940, Britain lost the ally and partner with which it had calculated all its strategic plans for fighting the fascists. The loss of France—and therefore its colonies as well—meant that Germany could establish bases for its U-boats along the Atlantic coast, dramatically enhancing its capability to harass and destroy the convoys carrying vital resources from America to the United Kingdom. In West Africa, where little had been done to set up defensive installations, vulnerable British colonies found themselves surrounded by those held by Vichy France; Syria and, later, Indochina could no longer provide bases from which air attacks could be launched against the enemy.

Britain faced the might of the German and Italian armies on its own now, a plight captured in the poignant *Evening Standard* cartoon of a Tommy standing atop the cliffs of Dover and gesturing defiantly toward the continent, "Very well, alone!"

"VERY WELL, ALONE"

But as yet another cartoon, this one from the satirical *Punch* magazine, pointed out, things were not quite as bleak as the *Standard* had suggested. In this drawing, two Tommies looked out across the channel, one saying to the other, "So our poor Empire is alone in the world." The other replied, "Aye, we are, the whole five hundred million of us."[2]

"So our poor old Empire is alone in the world."
"Aye, we are—the whole five hundred million of us."

Although we do not usually regard it as such, the Second World War was quintessentially an imperial war for the British, fought with imperial allies using imperial resources on imperial territory against enemies motivated by imperial ambitions of their own. As soon as Britain declared war on Germany in September 1939, the dominions followed suit. Canada, Australia, and New Zealand never hesitated, but in South Africa, where Afrikaner hatred of Britain and a positive disposition toward the Nazis created enormous resistance to aiding in the British war effort, the government won the motion to go to war by only thirteen votes. General Jan Smuts, who had orchestrated the close vote for joining the war, became a member of Churchill's imperial war cabinet in London. Ireland, which did not consider itself a dominion, despite what the British thought, declared itself officially neutral. But Éire's actual behavior during the war softened this stark assertion of separateness. It allowed British and, later, American planes to fly through its airspace, it turned over reports about German U-boat activity, it provided crucial weather reporting, it supplied equipment to help pilots navigate the area, and it participated in talks with the Allies about cooperating should Germany invade the United Kingdom. Above all, it permitted the opening and operation of a recruiting center in Dublin, through which some 2,000 people passed every week on their way to Britain to help the war effort. Most of these men and women served in essential industries and agriculture.

After the evacuation of British forces from Dunkirk in June 1940, Hitler began to plan for an invasion of the island nation—Operation Sea Lion. He knew that success depended on the ability to the *Luftwaffe* to control the skies to keep the Royal Navy from destroying his invasion forces as they made their way across the English Channel, so he dispatched his air force into action in August, setting off the so-called Battle of Britain. Throughout August and September, outnumbered RAF fighters held off the *Luftwaffe* with the aid of the new technology of radar, a fleet of cutting-edge fighter planes, and an intrepid pilot corps that would not give up. Despite suffering some devastating blows, the RAF fought on, finally compelling Hitler to halt preparations for Operation Sea Lion in October. The skill, courage, and sheer determination of the RAF saved Britain from Nazi invasion, prompting Churchill to say of his airmen, "Never in the course of human conflict was so much owed by so many to so few." Almost immediately, the German *Luftwaffe* commenced bombing British cities and towns in a campaign designed to break the morale of its inhabitants through terror. The blitz, as the British called it, lasted for nine months, wreaking indescribable damage across the strategic urban centers of the country. We will take up that story later in the chapter.

The contributions of the dominions proved crucial to Britain's survival in the terrible months before American resources started to flow into the United Kingdom in 1941. More than a million Canadian men and women—fully 10 percent of Canada's total population in 1941–signed up for military and labor service. The North American dominion sent money, food, military equipment, and armaments to Britain and permitted the United States to build a military base in

Newfoundland (U.S. President Franklin Roosevelt knew full well that America could not remain aloof from the war in Europe but was unable to convince Americans and the U.S. Congress that it should enter the conflict). New Zealand and Australia also sent food, personnel, and supplies in amounts disproportionate to their size; Australian and New Zealand forces traveled to North Africa to defend Egypt and the Suez Canal against German and Italian threats. South Africa, despite its initial resistance to supporting Britain, produced tremendous amounts of war materiel and ancillary supplies, undergoing a dramatic industrial transformation in the process. Precisely because of that early expression of Afrikaner hostility, the British government made every effort to shield the country from deprivation and other negative effects of war so as not to upset the domestic stability of the dominion. As it turned out, South African whites could only go so far in assisting the Allies. They opposed the possibility of African soldiers learning to use advanced weaponry. As a result, the segregated branches of the nonwhite military—the Cape Coloured Corps, Malay Corps, and Native Military Corps— did not carry guns until February 1944. The recruitment of Africans into the army, consequently, fell short because blacks hesitated to accept the low pay and discrimination they would encounter if they joined up. Even so, 123,000 non-white South Africans served during the war.

Whereas the dominions determined for themselves their responses to the outbreak of war, the colonies had no choice in the matter. They went to war on the command of the British government, a fact that rankled nationalists in India. The Indian viceroy, Lord Linlithgow, conferred with no one—not the INC, the Muslim League, the provincial governments, or the princes—before he declared that India was at war because Britain was at war. Responses to his unilateral assertion were mixed. The princes and the Indian army wholeheartedly supported the war effort; the Muslim League tried to stay on the fence, seeing in the conflict opportunities to further Muslim interests against those of the Congress Party; and Congress leaders held a variety of positions. Gandhi, whose influence within Congress had waned in recent years, originally urged that Indians line up behind their imperial masters to oppose fascism. (He later changed his position.) Nehru adamantly opposed assisting the British, arguing that fascism and imperialism had little to distinguish themselves from one another and that a British victory would be no better than a defeat. Subhas Chandra Bose advocated that Indians take advantage of the war to revolt against British rule.

Nehru could not go as far as Bose and he prevailed on his colleagues to let him make a deal with Linlithgow. He offered to use his influence to rally all of India to Britain's side if, in turn, the viceroy announced that India would be free after the war to determine its future. The viceroy refused to make so affirmative a statement, offering instead only tired, well-worn, and ambiguous pledges of future constitutional reform. Indian nationalists had heard all this before and withdrew their support from the Indian government. Congress members resigned their governmental offices across the continent (they held all of the provinces except Bengal, Sind, and the Punjab, where Muslim majorities held sway). Jinnah rejoiced in this expression of noncompliance, declaring December 22, 1939, Deliverance Day, when Muslims should celebrate their emancipation from the "tyranny, oppression and injustice" heaped on them by Congress.[3]

Linlithgow, who along with Churchill was furious that Congress should use Britain's wartime emergency to pursue their own ends, responded with a Revolutionary Movements Ordinance that would enable the Indian government to crush any opposition. Cooler heads in London urged a more conciliatory approach. In the summer of 1940, the secretary of state for India, Leopold Amery (1873–1955), offered to concede India's right to create a constitution after the war and to give it dominion status. He hoped that these promises would go far to generate goodwill among nationalists and secure their assistance in the war effort. But Indian nationalists refused the anemic proposal, seeing nothing new in this latest iteration of British attempts to placate Indians while maintaining their power over them. Linlithgow made the Revolutionary Movements Ordinance stronger; the INC prepared for another campaign of civil disobedience; and the British imposed direct rule over the provinces relinquished by Congress politicians. The government of India increasingly turned to Muslims for cooperation and support.

The events in India proved the exception to the rule of colonial assistance to Britain. From all over the empire subjects offered their support and their lives to Britain. Twenty thousand West Indians, for example, served as laborers, soldiers, and members of women's auxiliaries; 500 men from Honduras worked in the forestry units in the Scottish Highlands to provide timber to the war effort; members of the King's African Rifles and the West African Frontier Force fought against Mussolini's troops in northwest Africa; after the Japanese defeat of Singapore and Hong Kong and its invasion of Burma, African troops drawn from practically every British colony in Africa formed a major part of General Sir William Slim's (1891–1970) Fourteenth Army, the force ordered to advance into central Burma.

THE WAR IN THE PACIFIC

The Japanese attack on British-held Malaya and Hong Kong on December 8, 1941, came as a complete surprise. Few in government imagined tha t Japan would launch such an assault and fewer still considered Japanese people to possess the qualities and the intelligence necessary to defeat Western nations. This kind of stereotyping had bred complacency in Southeast Asia, the defense of which rested on the presence of a few antiquated battleships stationed in Singapore. Britain had followed the same strategy of appeasement of Japanese aggression in Manchuria and China in the late 1930s that characterized its responses to Germany, a policy necessitated by interwar disarmament agreements and informed by racial prejudice. The fall of Hong Kong and then Singapore marked the greatest defeat suffered by the British since they lost to the Americans at Yorktown in 1781. Britons, moreover, behaved disgracefully as the Japanese moved in. Soldiers deserted or surrendered without a fight and whole armies retreated; planters and other resident Britons ran away, looted homes and businesses, and drank themselves silly,

British troops forced to sweep streets after the fall of Malaya to the Japanese, 1941–1942.

destroying the projection of white prestige that undergirded empire. Britain never regained the respect lost during those early campaigns of the Pacific war.

New Zealanders and Australians, in particular, who depended entirely on Britain for their defense, especially after having dispatched their military forces to Europe and North Africa to fight for the British empire there, found themselves in a vulnerable position without any prospect of relief. The Japanese air assault on Darwin in northwest Australia in February 1942 and subsequent raids throughout 1942 and 1943 demonstrated just how exposed the Aussies were. Many of them never forgave Britain for its failure to provide the single most important function of an imperial power, protection. Certainly the ANZAC countries had virtually no alternative but to turn to the United States in place of Britain for support and assistance following December 1941. The United States, after all, was a Pacific power and it was not going away any time soon. The sense of betrayal felt by the Aussies and Kiwis made the transition an emotionally simple one.

Over the next four months, Japan gained control over 90 million Asians, 90 percent of the rubber produced in the world, half of its tin, and 30 percent of its rice. In January 1942 it invaded Burma, the colony abutting India's eastern border created as a separate entity by the India Act of 1935. The disasters of the Japanese campaign and the presence of the enemy so close to India prompted a government shakeup, bringing into the war cabinet as deputy prime minister the Labour leader, Clement Attlee (1883–1967) and forcing Churchill to modify his position on Indian self-government. It was clear that the defense of India would require the mobilization of the entire subcontinent for the war effort, and that meant bringing the INC on board. Churchill sent Labour politician Sir Stafford Cripps

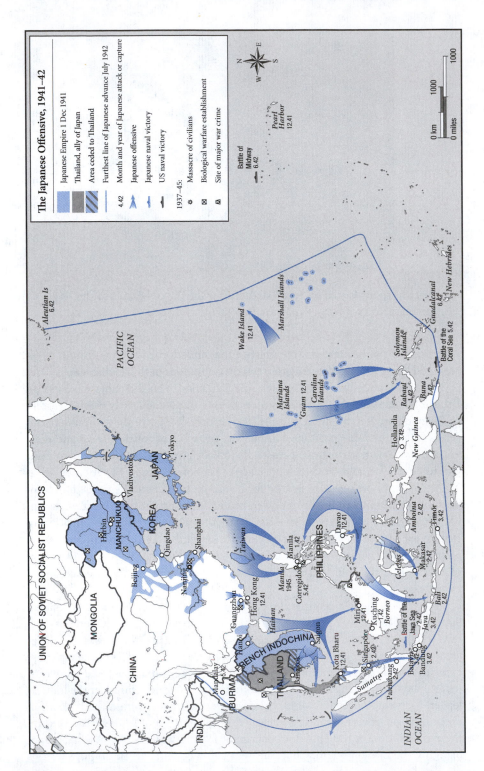

The Japanese Offensive, 1941–42

Japanese Empire 1 Dec 1941

Thailand, ally of Japan

Area ceded to Thailand

Furthest line of Japanese advance July 1942

4.42   Month and year of Japanese attack or capture

Japanese offensive

Japanese naval victory

US naval victory

1937–45:

✿   Massacre of civilians

⊠   Biological warfare establishment

⊠   Site of major war crime

0 km   1000

0 miles   1000

UNION OF SOVIET SOCIALIST REPUBLICS

MONGOLIA

CHINA

MANCHUKUO

Harbin

Beijing

Nanjing

KOREA

JAPAN

Tokyo

Vladivostok

Qingdao

Shanghai

Guangzhou

Hong Kong 12.41

Hainan

Hanoi

FRENCH INDOCHINA

Saigon

BURMA

Mandalay 5.42

THAILAND

Bangkok

INDIA

Taiwan

Manila 1.42

Manila 1945

Corregidor 5.42

PHILIPPINES

Davao 12.41

Kota Bharu 12.41

Miri 12.41

Kuching 1.42

Borneo

Singapore 2.42

Sumatra

Palembang 2.42

Batavia 3.42

Bandung 3.42

Java 3.42

Bali 3.42

Battle of the Java Sea 2.42

Makasar 2.42

Celebes

Amboina 2.42

Timor 3.42

Bandung 3.42

New Guinea

Hollandia 3.42

Rabaul 1.42

Buna 1.42

Solomon Islands

Guadalcanal 6.42

Battle of the Coral Sea 5.42

New Hebrides

Mariana Islands

Guam 12.41

Caroline Islands

Marshall Islands

Wake Island 12.41

Aleutian Is 6.42

PACIFIC OCEAN

Pearl Harbor 12.41

Battle of Midway 6.42

INDIAN OCEAN

N E S W

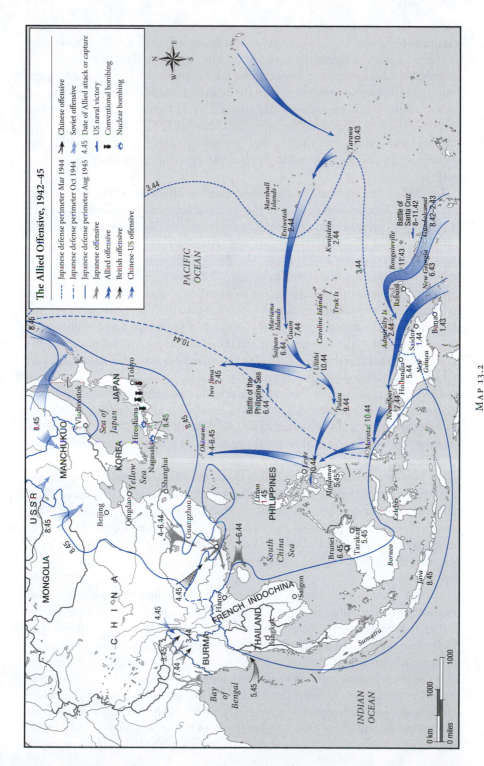

The Allied Offensive, 1942–45

Japanese defense perimeter Mar 1944
Japanese defense perimeter Oct 1944
Japanese defense perimeter Aug 1945
Japanese offensive
Allied offensive
British offensive
Chinese–US offensive

Chinese offensive
Soviet offensive
4.45 Date of Allied attack or capture
US naval victory
Conventional bombing
Nuclear bombing

MAP 13.2

The War in the Pacific, 1941–1945

PACIFIC OCEAN
INDIAN OCEAN

USSR
MONGOLIA
MANCHUKUO
Vladivostok
Sea of Japan
KOREA
JAPAN
Tokyo
Hiroshima
Nagasaki
Okinawa
Shanghai
Yellow Sea
Qingdao
Beijing
C H I N A
Guangzhou
Iwo Jima 2.45
Battle of the Philippine Sea 6.44
Saipan
Mariana Islands
Guam 7.44
Caroline Islands
Truk Is
Ulithi 10.44
Palau 9.44
Marshall Islands
Eniwetok 2.44
Kwajalein 2.44
Tarawa 10.43
Bougainville 11.43
Rabaul
Admiralty Is 2.44
New Georgia 6.43
Guadalcanal 8.42–2.43
Battle of Santa Cruz 8–11.42
Saidor 1.44
Buna 1.43
New Guinea
Hollandia 5.44
Aitape 7.44
Morotai 10.44
Leyte 10.44
Luzon 1.45
PHILIPPINES
Mindanao 5.45
Brunei 6.45
Tarakan 5.45
Borneo
Celebes
Java 8.45
Sumatra
South China Sea
FRENCH INDOCHINA
Hanoi
Saigon
THAILAND
Bangkok
BURMA
Bay of Bengal
8.45
8.45
8.45
8.45
8.45
8.45
8.45
4–6.44
4–6.44
4.45
4.45
4.45
3.44
3.44
5.45
7.44
3.44
10.44
3.44
4–6.45

0 km 1000
0 miles 1000

405

(1889–1952) to India in late March 1942 with an offer of postwar independence, a remarkable about-face on the part of the prime minister and one made only in the most dire of circumstances. In the end, the offer went too far for the viceroy, Lord Linlithgow, and not far enough for either the INC or the Muslim League, both of which rejected it. Gandhi described the offer as "a blank cheque on a crashing bank" and demanded immediate self-government.[4] When the British refused to reconsider the offer, he and other INC leaders embarked on what became called the "Quit India" movement, instituting new civil disobedience campaigns designed to hamper the government's ability to conduct business.

Linlithgow had prepared for disruption and immediately ordered a draconian response. He jailed the leadership of the INC and sent troops against the masses of people who had taken to the streets. Sixty battalions of soldiers moved on the protesters across the country, flogging and beating demonstrators, burning villages, and killing some 2,500 people. Hundreds of thousands were arrested and 66,000 spent the rest of the war in prison. The government's action ended the Quit India movement but at great cost to its prestige; many Indians who might have otherwise remained committed to the Raj gave their support instead to the INC. An Indian National Army (INA) made up of 60,000 men and women who had surrendered to the Japanese after the fall of Singapore formed under the direction of Subhas Chandra Bose. Seeking independence for India, they fought on the side of the Japanese against Britain in Burma.

The Cripps mission failed but its very existence had profound consequences. Most important, the mission had raised the possibility of independence for India in the near future, a promise that would be difficult for Britain to ignore after hostilities ended. To ensure that hostilities would be ended favorably for Britain, Raj officials had to secure the loyalty of their largely Muslim sepoys, which they did in part by establishing increasingly close ties with Muslims. In a fateful announcement, Linlithgow's administration promised Muslims that they would not have to live under an all-India government if they did not approve of it. This pronouncement gave public recognition to the possibility of a separate state for Muslims that Jinnah and the Muslim League had been advocating. Having been placed on the table by the highest authorities, it could not easily be taken off when the war ended.

In 1944 Japanese forces hoping to capitalize on Indian discontent with the British invaded northeast India. Troops from the Indian National Army led the way in battles at Imphal and Kohima, the idea being that if they broke through and made their way into the province of Assam, Indian people would join in an uprising against British rule. The Indian army withstood the onslaught and forced the Japanese back, beginning what would be a long but eventually successful retaking of Burma. Under the leadership of General Slim, 1 million Indian, Burmese, African, and British troops of the Fourteenth Army, supported by a massive infrastructure of armaments and supplies provided by the peoples of eastern India, slogged its way through the rainforests of Burma, ultimately inflicting on its enemy the most total defeat suffered by the Japanese to that point in the war. The tide was turning.

For 3 million Bengali civilians, however, it was too late. The Japanese invasion of Burma in 1942 and fears that India would be next compelled members of the war cabinet in London to adopt a "scorched-earth" policy. Resolved to remove anything that the enemy might be able to use against them if they came inland from the Bengali coast, as British officials anticipated, they seized stores of rice and other foodstuffs as well as boats, barges, and other forms of waterborne transportation and moved them away from danger. This action left little for the Japanese to confiscate but it also left Bengalis without the provisions and transport they would need to feed themselves. The absence of rice from Japanese-occupied Burma combined with weather-related harvest failures in Bengal to create a horrific famine in 1943. British authorities refused to redistribute food stockpiled for soldiers to the area, ensuring that starvation and disease would devastate the population of Bengal. Emaciated, starving Bengalis packed the villages, sitting side by side with corpses that littered the streets. Churchill rejected pleas to send supplies, regarding any such action as an appeasement of the INC. He told associates that "the starvation of anyway underfed Bengalis" could not compare to the needs of "sturdy Greeks" and asserted that Bengalis would continue to breed "like rabbits" despite the lack of food. Statements such as this led Leo Amery to tell Churchill that he possessed a "Hitler-like attitude" toward Indians.[5] It was an attitude Indians would not forget.

THE HOME FRONT

The outbreak of war had been expected for a number of years and was dreaded and feared by all those who could recall or had heard tale of the horrors and dislocations of the First World War. The men who went off to fight the Germans the second time around had none of the delusions of glory, honor, or comradeship that marked their predecessors who marched off to the trenches of the Great War. They enlisted or were conscripted fully aware of the privations and difficulties that awaited them. They knew, unlike the men of 1914, what life and death in war entailed.

People at home knew what was coming as well. Advances in industry and technology meant that civilian populations would not escape the arena of war, the consequences of which authorities had been trying to prepare the populace for for years. Air raid drills and instruction in the use of gas masks had been going on since 1937; one aspect of preparation required mothers to learn how to put gas masks on their infants and children. (Almost 4 million gas-protection apparatuses for children and infants had been manufactured by February 1941). By early 1941, under siege from constant bombardment during the blitz and facing a critical labor shortage, the British government found it necessary to impose on women aged nineteen to forty compulsory registration at employment exchanges so that the Ministry of Labour might know who was available and where for employment in the "essential" industries. At the same time, by declaring the Essential Work Order, it forced factory owners to employ and to keep women in these jobs. By this order, workers were not free to leave work in the essential industries without gaining permission from the Ministry of Labour, although the officials involved generally allowed women to leave if they could demonstrate that their absence from home caused hardship for others. The National Service Number 2 Act of December 1941 conscripted single women aged twenty to thirty into service for the state.

Resistance to the conscription of women emerged almost immediately from a variety of sources. Some women simply did not wish to leave home. Working-class women hesitated to take on what would amount to a second job. "It's all right for them young ladies with butlers and chauffeurs who don't have to worry their sweet little heads about keeping home," explained one woman from Coventry, but women without sufficient income to hire domestic help faced enormous burdens. Others warned that conscripting women to work would destroy homes and marriages as men lost the services women provided them on a day-to-day basis. A Scottish MP feared for the morality of Scottish women and for the survival of Scotland as thousands of young women deemed "mobile" by the ministry of labor were moved south to work in munitions factories. "The Scots as a nation will be wiped out if denuded of their womenfolk," he protested.[6]

But many women did want to help the war effort; some 155,000 volunteered for the auxiliary forces—the Auxiliary Territorial Service, the Women's Auxiliary Air Force, the Women's Royal Naval Service (WRNS), and the Women's Land Army—in 1941, before conscription was introduced. Most of these women hailed from middle-class families, where their income was not necessary for family survival and where the conventions of femininity chafed. "I wasn't very happy at home," recalled Joan Welch, "because my father had such a strict regime." She would have found no less strict a regime in the WRNS, however, which implemented military discipline over its charges. Despite efforts to keep meticulous order, the WRNS, along with all the other women's auxiliary services, were subject to scurrilous attack. As was the case in the First World War, rumors of promiscuity and sexual immorality followed women who enlisted. "Up with the lark and to bed with a Wren," one witty saying slurred the WRNS; another described the Women's Land Army as workers with their "backs to the land."[7]

The combination of volunteer recruitment and conscription utterly transformed the composition of the workforce and the nature of the work women did during the Second World War. Most single working-class women worked before they married in the interwar years but suspended their employment on marriage; only 16 percent of working women were married in 1931. In 1943, by contrast, 43 percent of working women were married. These figures represented only full-time wage-earning women. If volunteers and part-time workers had been counted as well, they would have shown that an impressive 80 percent of married women were working to aid the war effort. Ninety percent of the single women of Britain offered their labor.

As in the Great War, women took on work in industries formerly considered "male." Where they had worked in textile and consumer good manufacturing in the 1920s and 1930s, now they took up jobs in chemicals, munitions, transport, utilities, shipbuilding, commerce, government, agriculture, civil defense, and the armed forces. Many joined unions for the first time and involved themselves in trade union activities and politics, although their participation frequently provoked adverse comment from male leaders. Especially after 1943, women workers began to use strikes to increase their pay or to make pay scales among women more uniform, although strikes in wartime were illegal and unions refused to support them. In a Rolls Royce airplane engine plant outside Glasgow, women struck against policies that paid less experienced men more than they made for the same kinds of work. They succeeded in getting positions graded and the pay scales attached to those grades made consistent, but they did not gain equal pay for men and women. Despite the tireless efforts of feminists and women MPs, unequal wages for women and men continued to be the norm in every industry except transport.

World War II demolished the lines between civilians and soldiers, home and front, women and men. In the first three years of the war, more civilians died than did soldiers. The German air attacks on England began in 1940, as first the port towns of Plymouth, Portsmouth, Hull, and then London fell prey to endless hours of bombardment. Over the course of a few months in 1940 and 1941, Hull was bombed 70 times during the night and 101 times during daylight hours; some of the air raids went on from 9:00 PM to 4:00 AM. Beginning in September 1940, Londoners underwent 58 straight nights of bombardment.

Casualties were high and damage was severe. Of the 93,000 homes existing in Hull, only 6,000 of them did not suffer any damage. In central London and in the East End, where the bombing was the heaviest, 9 of every 10 houses were damaged. A three-day attack on Swansea in Wales in February 1941 took out half the town's center. Thirty thousand bombs fell on the city, burning nearly 600 business establishments, destroying nearly 300 homes, and damaging more than 11,000 others. More than 200 people died. Belfast took the brunt of German bombardment in April and May 1941, losing industrial and working-class residential areas to the blasts from the sky. Approximately 1,100 people died. Clydebank and Glasgow came under attack in March 1941; of Clydebank's 47,000 residents, 35,000 lost

German air raid on London during the Blitz.

A PLACE IN TIME

The Second World War in Liverpool

Liverpool played a profoundly important role in the Second World War. During the Battle of the Atlantic, which lasted for the entirety of the war, the port served as the disembarkation point for 90 percent of the food, fuel, arms, supplies, and troops shipped to Britain from Canada and the United States. These goods and resources made it possible for the country to continue to prosecute the war when its allies on the European continent had fallen to Hitler's armies. For that very reason, the city and its port became a prime target of the German *Luftwaffe* from August 1940 through December 1941. As befit its stature as the second city of empire, it had the distinction of being the second most heavily bombed area after London. It also incurred the second highest death toll after London, losing some 4,000 men, women, and children in the blitz. When placed in the context of overall population, Liverpool death rates surpassed those of any other city in Britain.

Between August 1940 and May 1941, Liverpool suffered a regular onslaught of bombing by the Germans. On November 29, in what Winston Churchill called "the worst single incident of the war," a parachute mine hit a technical school in Durning Road, where 300 Liverpudlians had gone to find shelter. The roof collapsed onto a number of people; the gas and central heating systems broke open, releasing boiling water and setting off terrible fires, which made it difficult and dangerous for rescue workers to come to the aid of the building's occupants. One hundred sixty-six people died in the bombing and many hundreds more suffered grievous injuries. Joe Lucas, whose two sisters and two brothers died in the attack, recalled that "my mother, from the trauma of that night . . . never spoke for six months."[8]

During the "Christmas blitz" of December 20–23, 365 people lost their lives, many of them in the shelters to which they had fled when the bombing began. In what residents remembered as "the May blitz" of 1941, the Germans bombed Liverpool for eight consecutive nights, wreaking incredible destruction across the city. Almost 700 *Luftwaffe* bombers knocked out nearly half of the 144 berths at the docks and demolished 6,500 homes; another 190,000 homes suffered some degree of damage. Nearly 3,000 people were killed or injured. Churchill visited the city shortly after, telling inhabitants that "I see the damage done by the enemy attacks, but I also see . . . the spirit of an unconquered people."[9]

German air raid on Liverpool, 1940.

The women of Liverpool contributed mightily to the war effort, working around the clock in factories that produced war materiel. Women comprised 8,000 of the 10,000 workers at the Kirkby munitions factory in 1941 and constituted an even more disproportionate number when the number of workers grew to 23,000. They carried out dangerous work making detonators and explosives. When explosions occurred on the premises, which they did twice in September 1944, women figured prominently in the 15 deaths and 11 injuries. But they carried on without hesitation, providing 10 percent of all the ammunition used in the course of the war. Liverpool-area women built the heavy four-engine Halifax bombers for the Royal Air Force and made the secret radar equipment that prevented Britain from enduring even greater destruction during the blitz. They also test-fired rifles and corrected their sights to ensure that British troops possessed accurate weapons.

The Germans discontinued their bombing of Liverpool after 1942, turning their attention to the invasion of the Soviet Union. But in two years their campaign had inflicted extraordinary damage on the city. Sunken ships clogged parts of the river; a good number of docks and whole neighborhoods lay in ruins; roads and railways were rendered impassable; churches were gutted; and the city center and many of the iconic buildings of the commercial hub had been smashed to bits. Residents and officials determined to rebuild their city, if only because the survival of the country depended on goods and services that came through the port. Over the next two years they undertook the necessary repairs to return the port to something resembling normal; their success would enable the preparations for the Allied invasion of Normandy to go forward.

Londoners sheltering in an underground tunnel during the Blitz, 1940.

their homes. Across Britain as a whole, 2 of every 7 houses were destroyed. Two of every 10 schools were knocked out.

Bombed out of their homes during the blitz, Britons suffered enormously. Fully one-fourth of Plymouth's population was homeless by April 1941; in London, 177,000 people slept in the underground railway stations on a nightly basis. Twelve thousand were still living there in 1945. Streets were blown apart and rendered impassable; transportation systems broke down; people lacked gas, water, and electricity; fires raged. Thousands and thousands of people died, and some 40 percent of all British children were evacuated from the cities to the countryside. Those who survived were faced with carrying on "normal" activity in the midst of devastation. Trying to keep one's house and even body clean when running water could not be readily obtained involved strenuous effort. Foodstuffs and essential commodities had to be rationed and luxuries items done away with altogether. Women walked miles and then stood in line for hours trying to obtain a bit of soap or the weekly quota of sugar due them. Charged with the responsibility of keeping their homes and families together without the proper means of doing so, women of all classes in the bombed-out cities of Britain performed heroically, but they did so at a cost. They experienced greater fatigue, strain, despair, and depression than did the men in these areas or the women in rural or less vulnerable parts of the country; mothers whose children had been evacuated suffered bouts of extreme guilt over abandoning them, compounding their sense of loss. As one Welsh woman told an inquirer who asked where her husband was after the blitz on Swansea, "He is in the army, the coward."[10]

In a bitter irony, the blitz helped women MPs achieve one major step toward equality of women with men. The Personal Injuries Act of 1939, requiring the government to compensate people injured during bombing raids, paid men seven shillings more a week than it did women. Vera Douie of the feminist Six Point Group pointed out that "there is nothing chivalrous about bombs; they do not discriminate between men and women,"[11] and women in and out of Parliament protested strongly against the presumption that women's lives were somehow worth less than men's. The government conceded the argument after months of debate in 1943 and agreed to pay out compensation equally. For the 63,000 civilian women (48% of the total number of civilians) who suffered wounds and injuries during the war, more than 25,000 of whom later died of them, this victory produced meaningful concrete results for themselves or their families.

For the most part, morale and the resilience of the British people remained remarkably high. Evidence of the high morale can be derived from the degree of compliance with rationing controls. A variety of basic goods were rationed to cut down on hoarding and profiteering, provide sufficient resources to the war effort, prevent runaway inflation, and ensure that sacrifices were distributed equally across lines of status and wealth. Strict limits were placed on the purchase of sugar, meat, eggs, tea, milk, biscuits, cereal, canned foods, chocolates and sweets, clothing, and petrol. The effect of such stringent regulation was to dramatically reduce standards of living and the quality of life for most Britons—certainly those in the middle classes and above. Steep tax rates on items such as beer and cigarettes made them prohibitively expensive for some working-class folks, and the unavailability of luxury goods cut into the lifestyle enjoyed by the wealthy. As a result of rationing and of putting industry on a war footing, total consumer spending fell off by 15 percent between 1938 and 1942; that for clothing, furniture, and petrol fell by 39 percent, 71 percent, and 87 percent, respectively. Britons seem to have understood both the need for rationing and the intention of spreading the pain equally across the social spectrum. Those who cheated the system were regarded as immoral and faced ostracism among their fellows and in the press. Public opinion frowned harshly on those who would try to get more for themselves at the expense of the rest of the citizenry. And people put their money where their mouths were: for all intents and purposes, noncompliance with rationing and other controls remained surprisingly low throughout the war years, certainly far less than economists and officials had expected. Only when the war ended but rationing did not—and in fact increased to include additional items—did greater numbers of people try to get around the constraints.

Northern Ireland proved an exception to this rule, at least for the first few years of the war. Prime Minister James Craig (1871–1940), who had been in power since the first elections following the partition of Ireland in 1922, presided over a government of Protestant Unionists whose primary goal was not necessarily the welfare of the country as much as keeping themselves in power. The depression and the collapse of industry following World War I had compounded the dire economic conditions Northern Ireland faced: the Government of Ireland Act had given all powers over trade, finance, and taxation to the government at Westminster, and Northern Irish MPs had little leverage to improve the situation. When the British government began to prepare for war by developing civil defense plans across the country, ministers at Stormont, the seat of Northern Ireland's government, hemmed and hawed, reluctant to shoulder the costs involved although it meant the protection of its citizens. The people of the region had little faith in their government, and the massive loss of life during the bombing of Belfast in 1941 only confirmed their antipathy. Far fewer men from Northern Ireland, proportionately, joined up during the war than in other parts of the kingdom; workers went out on strike far more frequently. The Unionist government had done little to inspire loyalty or sacrifice among Protestants, let alone Catholics, who made up perhaps 25 percent of the population. It was hard to avoid the conclusion that the government could not handle the job it had been elected to do.

In 1943, a kind of "Young Turk" rebellion brought about the downfall of the Unionist leadership, replacing it with a cadre of men eager to correct the mistakes and end the apathy of their older colleagues. Under Sir Basil Brooke (1888–1973) the new regime benefitted from the fact that the war had finally absorbed the legions of unemployed; Britain and its allies seemed to have turned a corner in their prosecution of the war; and Northern Ireland had begun to play a concerted role in the overall war effort. Confidence in Union leadership grew, till by 1945 it looked to be solidly in control of a bright future ahead.

THE COLOR BAR

World War II initiated a long-term process during which Britain became transformed from a largely homogeneous white society in 1939 into a multiracial, multicultural one by the 1970s. As a result of the influx of black colonial workers to alleviate the labor shortage occasioned by the war, the presence of black American soldiers between 1942 and 1945, and immigration from the colonies and commonwealth countries of Great Britain after 1948, the "whiteness" of the British nation could no longer be taken for granted. This profound change in the racial and ethnic composition of the country caused anxiety in many quarters and gave rise to calls for and ultimately legislation placing restrictions on the immigration of people of color into the kingdom. Anxiety on the part of white Britons found expression through a discourse about race steeped in the gendered and sexualized imagery that had informed Britain's dealings with its imperial subjects in the past.

Labor shortages during the war compelled the government to recruit workers from the colonies to work in a number of industries and in the armed forces. Five hundred British Hondurans, for instance, were brought to Scotland to log forests for timber; 1,000 West Indians worked in the munitions factories in Merseyside and Lancashire. Most Britons had never laid eyes on a person of color before the war; now they met them more frequently, although at first they did not know quite who they were dealing with. Lilian Barker, a West Indian worker, recounted the time a group of people evacuated from London saw her on the street and yelled out, "Nazi! Nazi!" at her, thinking that all Germans were black.[12]

When the war started, a color bar restricted recruitment into the armed forces, and the senior officers sought to maintain it, arguing that "commissions should be reserved for British subjects of British parents of *pure European descent*." They sought to register blacks living in Britain but not to call them up for training, especially not in the navy or air force. The color bar was suspended in October 1939 for as long as "the present emergency" lasted, but little really changed. Significant numbers of West Indians, Asians, and Africans did serve in the Allied armed forces, some 10,000 West Indians in the air force alone, but commissions in the armed forces were reserved for whites. Black troops were less disciplined than white troops, British officials believed. White troops would not respond to black superior officers, they argued. "British troops do not take kindly to being commanded by coloured officers and further . . . the presence of coloured officers in a unit in peacetime is apt to be a source of embarrassment," the War Office told the Colonial Office in December 1944. Because they lacked the "social" traditions of the mess, black officers would not mix well with white officers, another War Office opinion had it. They would not be able to deal with "family and personal problems" that might arise among their troops; finally, and perhaps most unsettling for military officials, there might be "incidents" in the married quarters. The unspecified nature of these incidents could not mask the fears on the part of the War Office that the sexuality of blacks, long a trope of racial thinking, could not be contained. Only one black man, Arundel Moody, obtained a commission in the army, and the color bar remained part of army and navy recruitment until 1948.[13]

The imminent arrival of American troops moved government officials to request that the black men among them not be stationed in Britain or that their numbers be limited. The Americans refused this request; when black American troops arrived in Britain in 1942, segregated from their white comrades, British officials went along with American policies. In August 1942, district commanders in Britain received copies of "notes on relations with coloured troops" instructing them to advise their charges that they should not fraternize with black American troops or comment negatively on the treatment meted out to black Americans by their white counterparts. Most of all, the instructions warned, fearing that British women and black American troops might engage in sexual relations with one another—which, indeed, they did—white women should not be permitted to socialize with black men. Fears of miscegenation seemed to permeate many layers of society. The Duke of Marlborough (1897–1972) appealed to Winston Churchill, his cousin, to do something to halt sexual activity between black troops and white Englishwomen. The Duke of Buccleuch (1894–1973) complained about the relationships between the local women and the British Honduran loggers working his estate in Scotland. And the government made it illegal for British women to marry black American soldiers, although thousands of them married white GIs.[14]

A number of British and West Indian blacks faced discrimination and insults in the course of doing their bit for the war effort. When Amelia King (c. 1917-?), for example, a third-generation black Briton, volunteered for the Women's Land Army in 1943 she was turned down because she was black. The local farmers of Essex, it seems, along with neighbors who might be expected to put her up for the duration, objected to her presence among them. Learie Constantine (1901–1971), a Trinidadian and one of the world's greatest cricket players, worked for the Ministry of Labour helping to organize, settle, and resolve disputes for the West Indians who went to work in the factories in Liverpool and other areas. While traveling in London, he was refused accommodation at a local hotel, the manager telling him and a Labour Ministry representative who intervened that his status as a civil servant and British subject had no bearing on the situation. "He is a nigger," she declared.[15] Constantine sued the hotel for breach of contract and won his case, although what might have been a blow against the color bar in hotels and restaurants did not eliminate this kind of discrimination for decades to come.

THE BEVERIDGE REPORT AND THE POSTWAR WELFARE STATE

Historians looking back on World War II have identified it as a time when an unusual degree of unity and consensus characterized the various classes of Britain. In fact, class and other divisions that had grown so acutely during the years of depression proved to be just as intransigent during the war, and the evacuation of urban dwellers had exposed the conditions in which the poor lived to people who had never imagined things were so bad. They shocked observers who had the clout to make some noise about the poverty and disease in their midst. Most important, if they were to get and keep Britons fighting on behalf of their nation, government officials had to promise that the nation for which they were sacrificing everything would, in the future, be one worth fighting for. These were not promises that could be made in a vague or unformed way, not to a population that had experienced terrible privations after the Great War under a government that would do little or nothing to remedy them. Social injustice and poverty would have to be directly and visibly addressed by the sitting government if the efforts of the nation's people were to be counted on in this war.

Accordingly, the government of Winston Churchill introduced a number of emergency welfare programs designed to sustain the population. It distributed milk and orange juice to babies and children. It rationed food fairly across social class, a policy that had a limited effect on the better-off segments of the population but actually resulted in an improved diet for most people. Churchill also appointed a commission to prepare a blueprint for social reform after the war ended. Headed by William Beveridge (1879–1963), a Liberal, the commission issued its report in late 1942. Its recommendations quickly established in the public mind the most basic of expectations for the development of welfare provisions in the postwar period; within two weeks of its appearance, nine of every ten Britons believed that its proposals should be implemented. The Labour Party immediately embraced its principles, whereas Churchill and some of his fellow Conservatives expressed reservations about the costs it would entail and the extent to which it might distract attention away from the effort of fighting the war. Labour Party leaders capitalized on their lukewarm response when elections were held at war's end in 1945. The electorate, although grateful to Churchill for having led them to victory, decisively voted the Conservatives out of office and a Labour government under Clement Attlee came to power. The upper classes knew that dramatic change was in store for them and that life as they had known it before the war would never be the same.

In formulating what he called "a scheme of social insurance against interruption and destruction of earning power and for special expenditure arising at birth, marriage or death,"[16] Beveridge articulated a number of basic assertions about the nature of the welfare state that themselves turned on assumptions about the gendered nature of home and work. His plan established some fundamental ground rules. First, social services like health care, unemployment insurance, pensions, and the like were to be paid for through a combination of contributions from employers, employees, and the state. Second, these contributions and the benefits they would pay out would be set at a standard rate across classes and not be limited to the poor. Third, all citizens could expect a minimal level of subsistence from the state, derived from a combination of full employment, social security payments, family allowances, and the provision of free or inexpensive health care through a national health service. This all added up to a view of the welfare state as the guarantor of support in the event of lost wages.

This vision of the welfare state, given the predominant thinking about who should work and who should not, shaped the way in which contributions were made and benefits paid out. Beveridge broke down the population of Britain into six categories, the largest of which consisted of employed persons. This designation encompassed both men and women working for wages, with the explicit, and large, exception of married women. The 1.4 million married women working in 1942 who would not be covered by the insurance scheme, Beveridge told the National Council of Women, constituted an "anomaly." They would not normally work, he said; they were housewives before they were wage earners. Moreover, if they became sick or unemployed, they had husbands to look after them. And most important, "she has the liability to have pregnancy, and ought to have it; that is what she is in a sense there for," he declared. Married women should not work because they had another job to do. "In the next thirty years," he stated, "housewives as mothers will have vital work to do in ensuring the adequate continuance of the British race and of British ideals in the world."[17]

A number of feminists denounced his "reactionary measure in regard to married women," as Conservative MP Mavis Tate (1893–1947) put it, but their protest fell on deaf ears. When the National Insurance Act passed in 1946, it enshrined the notion of Beveridge and others that the family unit within the welfare state consisted of a team of a husband and wife carrying out different duties. Wives bore and raised children and men worked to support them. Thus, benefits paid to the family in situations of unemployment were paid to and on the basis of the income of the husband and father. The married woman's benefit, as befitting someone dependent on her husband for material existence, was subsumed into his. Women who interrupted their waged work upon marriage and later sought to reenter the workforce found it difficult to retain their insurance rights, and when they did, they received a smaller benefit than did men. Under the provisions of the National Insurance Act, the breadwinner ideal enjoyed official sanction: unemployed, ill, or disabled men received benefits from the state to make up their lost wages; unemployed, ill, or disabled married women received (fewer) benefits from the state only when the providers of first resort—their husbands—were unable to support them.

The implementation of the Beveridge Report, along with additional provisions for secondary and university education and for housing between 1946 and 1951, dramatically transformed the ideology underpinning the British social polity. The notion that citizenship now entailed social as well as civil and political rights became part of Britons' understandings about their place within the nation. Certainly class and/or gender divisions and inequalities did not disappear, but ordinary men and women and their children now had the means of obtaining the necessities of life without inordinate struggle on a daily basis. Dental and obstetrical care, prescription drugs, and even eyeglasses that had been beyond the reach of many people now would be obtained; the state guaranteed a minimal level subsistence for all Britons; it provided secondary education for all children up to the age of fifteen and tried to increase access to university education, a lofty goal that was difficult to achieve. The government could not readily meet the need for housing, especially in London and other urban centers bombed to bits during the blitz, but it did build 1.5 million new dwellings by 1951. It would be many years before the supply of housing satisfied demand for it.

To ensure that Britons would not be hit badly again by the kind of unemployment that characterized the interwar period, the Labour government nationalized significant sectors of the economy, following the precedents established during the two world wars. The electrical and airline industries had been taken over by the government prior to 1940; coal mining, railroads, trucking, and iron and steel joined them between 1945 and 1949. Because of pronounced labor shortages following the war, Britons enjoyed a full employment economy. Nationalization did nothing to drive this scenario, and the government lacked sufficient funds to invest meaningfully in the key industries anyway.

Fighting World War II had nearly bankrupted Britain, a fact that became abundantly clear in the months immediately following the surrender of Japan in August 1945. When the government audited its books in January 1946 it found that it had a balance-of-payments deficit of £750 million. It owed the American government millions of dollars. Rationing of foodstuffs and fuel continued and in fact became more pronounced after war's end. Bread, which had not been rationed during the war itself, was now restricted. A shortage of coal and of workers to mine it left the country without heat and electricity for a number of days during the winter of 1946–1947, one of the coldest on record. The period of austerity proved massively demoralizing to a population that had endured six years of deprivation and danger, compelling the United States to provide Marshall Plan aid to the amount of $3.2 million. Despite its position on the winning side of the war, Britain received the greatest amount of U.S. assistance, a measure of just how destructive the conflict had been to its economy and financial system. Some food items had to be rationed until 1954, for example, and coal restrictions were not eased until 1958.

A deep and acute shortage of workers, especially in those industries that could earn dollars with which to pay back the Americans—coal, textiles, agriculture, steel—worsened the situation. Britain fell short of its labor needs by between 600,000 and 1.3 million workers, and a falling birth rate ensured that without a massive injection of workers from outside Britain the situation would not remedy itself with time. The chancellor of the Exchequer, Hugh Dalton (1887–1962), tried to persuade the cabinet to reduce the size of the armed forces to free up soldiers for labor, but his arguments did not sway the majority of his fellow ministers, who saw a robust military as crucial to Britain's status as a great power. Campaigns to attract men and women into essential but unpleasant work did little to alleviate the problem.

The government turned to two possible solutions to its economic difficulties. In the first it recruited some 350,000 Europeans to settle and work in Britain. Most of the emigrants from the continent came from Baltic and Balkan countries that had been devastated by the war; they lived in camps for displaced persons awaiting the day when they might begin to put their lives back together. Entreaties to come work in Britain, where they would not be British subjects or citizens but would remain aliens under the law, proved attractive to many of them. Ireland provided a second source of labor, and in this instance, the Irish gained a unique status. Under a special provision struck between Dublin and Westminster, they would not be considered either aliens or British subjects but Irish citizens with all the rights afforded to British subjects. This agreement facilitated the movement of 50,000 to 60,000 Irish men and women into Britain's labor force each year between 1946 and 1962, a massive population transfer that made British economic recovery possible. The second solution entailed passage of the British Nationality Act of 1948, by which all subjects of the British empire were recognized as possessing all the rights and privileges of British citizenship. We will take up this subject in the next chapter.

By 1951, efforts to right the British economy had begun to pay off. Exports that would earn ready cash increased steadily between 1946 and 1950; employment boomed; and supplies of essential consumer items began to be taken off the rationing list, bread in 1948 and then flour, eggs, and soap in 1950. An encouraging increase in consumer demand stimulated more manufacturing and wages rose in a number of sectors. The dismal age of austerity of the second half of the 1940s gave way to a new age of affluence that lasted until the early 1970s, driven in large part by the expansion of the American economy during the same period.

THE IMPACT OF REFORMS

The welfare state came into existence on the basis of a wartime consensus that the world for which thousands were fighting and dying would have to be rendered more fair and more just. The implementation of its policies perpetuated a belief in that consensus and contributed to the conviction that a classless society could be established. Throughout the 1950s, an ideology of "affluence" based on the postwar economic boom circulated throughout the country, giving voice to the notion that class differences and distinctions were on the wane, that poverty had been eliminated, and that anyone, regardless of the origins of their birth, could aspire to and attain the economic, educational, sartorial, and cultural attributes that signaled success. The Conservative Party rode to power on the back of this widespread set of assumptions, buoyed by the votes of women tired of years of rationing during and immediately following the war, and maintained itself in office from 1951 to 1964 on the basis of its claims that although this society might not yet be realized, it was only a matter of time until it materialized. But class distinctions, divisions, and conflicts did indeed exist, despite the real improvements in employment rates and wages. Inequalities in income had narrowed significantly, but the gap still existed. The discrepancy between an ideology that promised social equality and a reality of substandard housing, overcrowding, and dead-end jobs for a large percentage of Britons produced an angry response from an articulate literary element that castigated establishment culture and despaired of the conventional thinking that class conflict was a thing of the past.

Epitomized by playwright John Osborne's (1929–1994) *Look Back in Anger* (1956), rage over the state of things domestic and international found expression through gender. As early as 1947, critic Cyril Connolly (1903–1974) had lamented Britain's loss of power and its subsidiary relationship to the United States by comparing the "confident, affable and aggressive" Americans to the dispirited British. "Most of us are not men or women," he despaired, "but members of a vast, seedy, overworked, over-legislated, neuter class." Unmanly men, unwomanly women—these were not specimens of some sort of potentially creative androgyny but bloodless, demoralized, lifeless people, who in the 1950s contributed to the making of a stiflingly conventional society. The "dark grey undead" men attired in suits of standardized cut, color, and cloth epitomized a society touted as unified and virtually without class.[18]

The inconsistencies contained within the ideology of affluence fueled the anger and resentment of everyday people as well as that of cultural elites. Historian Carolyn Steedman (1947-) recalls, in an extraordinary account of her life and that of her mother, *Landscape for a Good Woman*, the time in 1951 when a health visitor told her mother, "this house isn't fit for a baby," reducing her mother to tears and searing Steedman's soul with "my secret and shameful defiance" against her own vulnerability to the injuries of class. "I will do everything and anything until the end of my days to stop anyone ever talking to me like that woman talked to my mother," she promises. Her class consciousness, she says, she learned at her mother's elbow as she watched her time and again being excluded and made to feel excluded from the world of opportunity, emotional security, and material possession represented by the middle-class health visitor.

The real benefits of the welfare state had the effect of cooling tensions between Catholics and Protestants in Northern Ireland, a process that undermined the ability of the IRA to stir up sentiment there for a united Ireland. We saw in the previous chapter how De Valera's adroit moves had isolated the IRA in the Republic of Ireland; lacking a constituency there, it sought a new one among Catholics in the north. In 1949 it announced that its efforts would now focus on war against the administration of Northern Ireland. In a series of incursions across the border in 1956 the organization attacked British barracks and troops, but its hopes of garnering significant Catholic support fell far short of expectations. In large part this was because of the successes of the welfare state in providing Catholics in Northern Ireland with a sense that their condition was getting better. The 1947 Education Act, in particular, by providing free secondary schooling for all, enabled a larger proportion of Catholics to go on to university. As prospects improved, Northern Ireland Catholics dropped their support for Sinn Féin and the IRA. In the south, moreover, the government in Dublin had turned to incarceration of IRA members, jailing virtually the entire IRA executive in late 1958. By 1962 the IRA had accepted that its new policy would not work, and it abandoned its campaign "to drive the British forces of occupation out of Ireland."[19]

••

The impact of World War II on Britain and its imperial holdings cannot be overestimated. Everything was different now. At home, a new society based on principles of equity and fairness and the elimination of class distinctions grew out of the sacrifices made by millions of people during the global conflict. The fact that the country did not—could not—actually institutionalize those ideals does not diminish their power or undermine the degree of change that had taken place. The war also bled Britain dry, making it impossible to sustain its imperial dominance, although it would be some time before Britons acknowledged this stark transformation of its global position. The process of decolonization came directly out of the war, leading to dramatic changes in Britain at home as well as abroad, a story we take up in the next chapter.

NOTES

1. Quoted in John Welshman, *Churchill's Children. The Evacuee Experience in Wartime Britain* (Oxford, 2010), back cover; pp. 84, 85, 87.

2. Quoted in Ashley Jackson, *The British Empire and the Second World War* (London, 2006), p. 1.
3. Quoted in Piers Brendon, *The Decline and Fall of the British Empire, 1781–1997* (New York, 2007), p. 396.
4. Quoted in Jackson, *The British Empire and the Second World War*, p. 384.
5. Quoted in Brendon, *The Decline and Fall of the British Empire*, pp. 405, 406.
6. Quoted in Gail Braybon and Penny Summerfield, *Out of the Cage: Women's Experiences in Two World Wars* (London, 1987), pp. 161–62.
7. Braybon and Summerfield, *Out of the Cage*, pp. 163, 165.
8. Quoted in "The Blitz," Merseyside Maritime Museum, http://www.liverpoolmuseums .org.uk/maritime/exhibitions/blitz/blitz.aspx/.
9. Quoted in "Liverpool Blitz 70!" http://www.liverpoolblitz70.co.uk/about/.
10. Quoted in Martin Johnes, *Wales since 1939* (Manchester, 2012), p. 17.
11. Quoted in Braybon and Summerfield, *Out of the Cage*, p. 182.
12. Bill Schwarz, "Black Metropolis, White England," in Mica Nava and Alan O'Shea, eds., *Modern Times: Reflections on a Century of English Modernity* (London, 1996), p. 196.
13. Schwarz, "Black Metropolis, White England," p. 196.
14. Zig Layton-Henry, *The Politics of Immigration* (Oxford, 1992), pp. 25, 26.
15. Quoted in Peter Fryer, *Staying Power. The History of Black People in Britain* (London, 1984), p. 366.
16. Discussion of the Beveridge report is drawn from Susan Pedersen, *Family, Dependence, and the Origins of the Welfare State: Britain and France, 1914–1945* (Cambridge, 1993), pp. 336–56.
17. Quoted in Susan Kingsley Kent, *Gender and Power in Britain, 1640–1990* (London: 1999), p. 317.

TIMELINE

1935 Hitler rearms Germany

Italy invades Ethiopia

1936 Hitler occupies the Rhineland

Spanish Civil War begins

1938 Hitler annexes Austria to Germany

Munich agreement

1939 Hitler invades Czechoslovakia

Nazi–Soviet pact

Hitler invades Poland; Second World War begins

1940 Neville Chamberlain falls; Winston Churchill becomes prime minister

18. Quoted in Robert Hewison, *In Anger: British Culture in the Cold War, 1945–1960* (New York, 1981), p. 14. See Frank Mort and Peter Thompson, "Retailing, Commercial Culture and Masculinity in 1950s Britain: the Case of Montague Burton, the 'Tailor of Taste,'" *History Workshop Journal* 38 (1994): 106–27.
19. Quoted in Caroline Kennedy-Pipe, *The Origins of the Present Troubles in Northern Ireland* (London, 1997), p. 28.

FURTHER READING

Gail Braybon and Penny Summerfield, *Out of the Cage: Women's Experiences in Two World Wars*. London, 1987.

Robert Hewison, *In Anger: British Culture in the Cold War, 1945–1960*. New York, 1981.

Ashley Jackson, *The British Empire and the Second World War*. London, 2006.

Caroline Kennedy-Pipe, *The Origins of the Present Troubles in Northern Ireland*. London, 1997.

Susan Pedersen, *Family, Dependence, and the Origins of the Welfare State: Britain and France, 1914–1945*. Cambridge, 1993.

Bill Schwarz, "Black Metropolis, White England," in Mica Nava and Alan O'Shea, eds., *Modern Times: Reflections on a Century of English Modernity*. London, 1996.

Carolyn Kay Steedman, *Landscape for a Good Woman: A Story of Two Lives*. New Brunswick, 1987.

John Welshman, *Churchill's Children. The Evacuee Experience in Wartime Britain*. Oxford, 2010.

	Fall of France
	British troops evacuate from Dunkirk
	Blitz begins
1941	Japanese attack Malaya, Hong Kong, and Pearl Harbor
	Americans enter war
1942	Subhas Bose forms Indian National Army
	Japanese invade Burma
1943	Bengal famine
	Beveridge Report issued
1944	Japanese invade northeast India
1945	World War II ends
1946–1951	Welfare state reforms implemented

West Indian immigrants sailing to Britain aboard the *Empire Windrush*, 1948.

CHAPTER 14

THE SHOCK OF THE NEW: DECOLONIZATION AND THE CREATION OF A NEW SOCIETY, 1947–1996

In 1948, a nineteen-year-old Trinidadian named Harold Phillips (1929–2000) boarded the SS *Empire Windrush* and sailed to England with the first boatload of West Indian immigrants to Britain. The former RAF member—he had lied about his age when he signed up as a fourteen year old—made his way to Liverpool, the site of a lively black cultural and social scene. Phillips took up lorry driving, became a railway engineer, built and decorated homes, ran a shop, repaired televisions, tended bar, and became the owner of a club. Most important to him, he wrote songs and performed with the All-Steel Caribbean Band, the first professional steel band in Britain. One of those songs, a calypso tune featuring characters named after cigarette brands, led to his bandmates nicknaming him Lord Woodbine. The name stuck.

Lord Woodbine loved music and he promoted it whenever and wherever he could. When two white boys started showing up at his gigs in 1958 and hanging around afterward, he befriended them, let them play the steel drums, and introduced them to blues musicians he knew. Known as "Woodbine's Boys" because they tagged along after him as he went from club to club—they "made themselves orphans, deliberately," noted Woodbine, who presumably became a father figure to them—they imbibed the rhythm and blues culture of black Liverpool. They learned the chord progressions for Chuck Berry songs from Vinnie Tow, a Somali Irish guitarist, and expanded their repertoire from three-chord songs to more sophisticated compositions of up to fifteen chords under the tutelage of a guitarist from Guyana, Zancs Logie. Woodbine hired them and two other musicians to play at his club, persuaded them to bring on a drummer, and in 1960, along with his partner, a Welsh promoter named Allan Williams (1930–), booked the

Lord Woodbine (seated left) with Paul McCartney (center) and George Harrison (close right), after their first Hamburg gig, 1960.

band into a Hamburg nightclub. The Silver Beetles, as they called themselves, did well enough to be invited back to Hamburg for another gig, but this time they went without Woodbine and Williams, not wanting to pay them their cut of the earnings. Woodbine's Boys went off on their own, found a new manager in a man named Brian Epstein (1934–1967), and renamed themselves the Beatles. "See your boys doing great, Woody," Liverpudlians would say to Woodbine in later years.

John Lennon (1940–1980), Paul McCartney (1942–), and, once he joined Woodbine's orphans, George Harrison (1943–2001) owed their start to the Trinidadian musician and his contacts in the Liverpool black music scene (Ringo Starr (1940-) came on the scene later). They learned their craft and developed their style under his influence and with his help. The explosion of pop culture with which the Beatles are most closely identified had direct connection to the dramatic transformation of British society in the years during and after decolonization. Everyone knew it. "Liverpool was a huge melting pot," McCartney recalled in 2002; "we took what we liked from it." Those from whom the Beatles took looked less kindly on the appropriation, with one women familiar with the situation describing John and Paul as "bloody white kids, trying to horn in on the black music scene."[1] As historians have noted, older and less adventurous Britons lumped together the antics of 1960s cultural rebels with the changes wrought by the wave of decolonization of the same period, alienated, frightened, and resentful of both developments. It was all so new and all so shocking and so *not* British.

••

DECOLONIZATION

The throwing off of British colonial rule by the peoples of South Asia, East Asia, Africa, and the West Indies occurred in three different phases. The first took place in 1947–1948, when India, Pakistan, Burma, and Sri Lanka—formerly called Ceylon—achieved their independence. The British hastily left Palestine as well, allowing for the creation of the state of Israel, and Ireland withdrew from the new British Commonwealth of Nations, even as India, Pakistan, and Sri Lanka, but not Burma, joined it. The second stage began in 1956, when in the context of the Suez crisis, Ghana, Malaya, and Singapore declared and won their independence. The third and largest wave of decolonization began in 1960 and swept through Africa and the Caribbean. The rapid fall of the British empire after 1956 came as a sudden and unwelcome surprise to Britons who, accepting the loss of India and Pakistan, had expected to maintain their empire for at least another fifty years. Decolonization traumatized British society, leading to the formation of a number of political movements designed to ward off the shock of the new and recreate the Britain of old.

India and Pakistan

The wartime developments treated in the previous chapter made it virtually inevitable that the British would leave India in the years immediately following the war. The people and resources of the subcontinent had been crucial to victory over the Japanese, but to secure their availability, Britain had had to resort to behaviors and practices unimaginable in peacetime. The degree of repression required to keep the country loyal and productive surpassed all previous levels, embittering Indians against the Raj and inspiring violence and disobedience that by 1945 simply could not be contained. It became clear that Indian independence— promised by the British during the war—could only be avoided by mobilizing tens of thousands of British troops, a move that Britons at home would not find acceptable and that was, in any event, impossible, given the exhausted condition of Britain. For those thinking rationally about empire, moreover—and not all people did—the economic reasons for keeping the jewel in the crown had disappeared. India no longer produced economic benefits to Britain; in fact, Britain came out of the war owing India more than a billion pounds. Now it was only a matter of when Britain would leave, not if, and the Labour government sent Lord Mountbatten (1900–1979) to hammer out the details of their unavoidable departure.

What was not inevitable was the way they did leave. Mountbatten had been given until mid-1948 to arrive at an agreement between the various Indian groups about what the newly independent subcontinent would look like and how the interests of all Indians would be protected. It was a daunting task: sectarian and communal violence had convulsed the land and mass killings of Hindus, Muslims, Sikhs, and other Indians broke out in cities, towns, and villages across India. Coming to a satisfactory accord in the midst of such carnage and revenge would require the patience and skills of all involved. Instead of using all the time he had

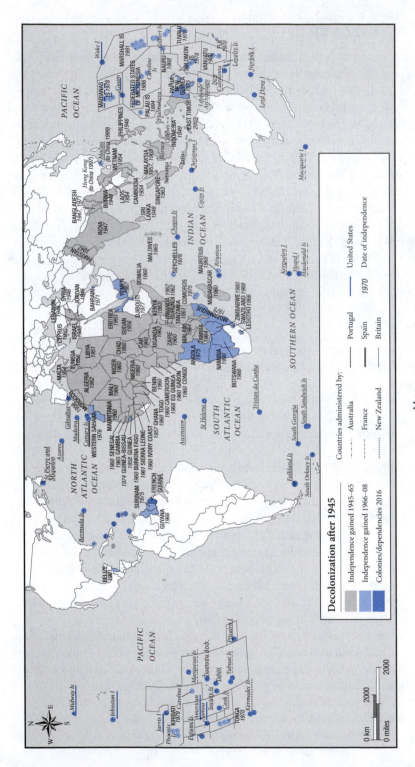

MAP 14.1

Decolonization after 1945

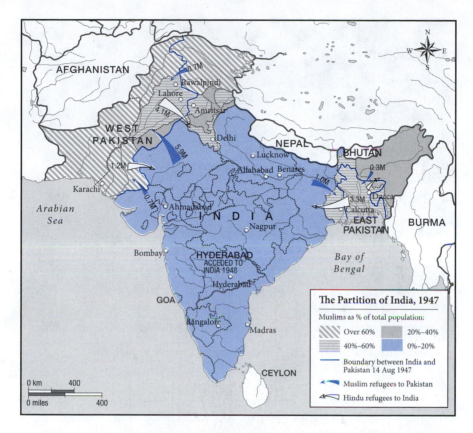

MAP 14.2
The Partition of India, 1947

been given to seek a credible solution that would safeguard the lives and livelihoods of as many Indians as possible, Mountbatten cut short the process by ten months and determined that partition of the country into India and Pakistan was the only option. His impulsive haste resulted in a two-state configuration of a Muslim Pakistan and a Hindu India—where Sikhs would fit in this new arrangement was left unaddressed. The shortcomings of the partition haunt us to this day.

Mountbatten dispatched an English lawyer, Sir Cyril Radcliffe (1899–1977), to draw the lines of partition in the huge provinces of Punjab and Bengal. Radcliffe had never been to India, and when he got there he spent all of one month dividing up territory and the people who inhabited it in a process that should have taken at least a year. On August 1, 1947, the day that British officials lowered the Union Jack in a ritual carried out across India, millions of Hindus and Sikhs found themselves living in Muslim Pakistan and millions of Muslims found themselves residing in non-Muslim India.

The division of Pakistan itself into West and East Pakistan (which would become independent Bangladesh in 1971), provinces separated by the new nation

Muslim South Asians in London calling for an independent
Pakistan, 1946.

of India, made the situation even more difficult. Facing hostile neighbors and
authorities, members of various religious groups abandoned their ancient home-
lands to make their way to the more hospitable countries of their respective co-
religionists. Some 10 million refugees traveled across the subcontinent to new
homes, facing unprecedented violence along the way. As many as 1 million died,
most of them murdered by men and women inspired by religious hatreds that the
British had played at least some part in fomenting. Churchill described Britain's
leave-taking of India as a "shameful flight."[2]

Preserving the Empire in Africa

Britons, not least the Labour government, expected the loss of India to be a one-
off event. World War II had had a profound impact on the way Britain thought
about its empire, leading officials to the conclusion that a new approach was necessary to justify British control over a continent in which its overrule was viewed
as anachronistic in the United States and Soviet Union and among intellectuals
in the colonies. As the undersecretary of state for the colonies Sir Charles Jeffries
(1896–1972) explained in 1938, it was "a matter of the highest political importance" that Britain show "unassailable justification for its claim that it acts as a
beneficial trustee for its subject peoples."[3] Gone were any mentions of "natives"
needing civilization; the way forward, as colonial officials now saw it, was through
"local government" by and for Africans in "partnership" with Britain.

These lofty aspirations informed British colonial policy in the postwar years, as the concept of the development and welfare of African states gained increasing purchase on official thinking about empire. The Colonial Development and Welfare Acts of 1940 and 1945 sought to achieve what free markets had manifestly failed to do—improve the standards of living of Africans by investing in projects that would bring better and more hygienic housing, provide education and health care, increase the yields of harvests, and establish a manufacturing sector that would enable Africans to purchase commodities unavailable to them because of the disruptions of war and inflationary pressures.

These ambitions for Africa conflicted with Britain's domestic needs, however, which, not surprisingly, given that Britons voted in elections and Africans did not, ultimately prevailed over the apparently altruistic aims of development. As we have seen, at the end of the Second World War, Britain faced a dire economic situation. Its traditional industrial strengths in shipbuilding, coal production, and textile manufacturing could not compete on the world market any longer. Shortages of the most basic commodities—food, clothing, fuel for heat and for transport—reduced Britons to standing in long queues to purchase rationed staples such as bread, milk, and lard. Meat could rarely be found. Politicians in the Exchequer and Colonial Office looked to the empire to help offset Britain's impoverishment and to provide the resources and raw materials necessary to get the country back on its feet. Moreover, when the war ended, the United States had discontinued its Lend–Lease aid to Britain, leaving the country with a crippling balance-of-payments problem. Britain looked to the foodstuffs and minerals that Africa could produce as one of the most effective ways to reduce it—by selling those commodities on the world market, Britain could earn the dollars it needed to lessen its deteriorating financial and economic situation.

This would require substantial economic development in the colonies, necessitating a level of assistance that would not be forthcoming. The sum eventually hit on by officials—£120 million to be split among the colonies over ten years—stimulated some economic growth, but not enough to meet the goals of the Welfare and Development Acts. Most of the aid went to social rather than economic development: educational initiatives, especially, received a generous portion of the amount, with health coming second. But it was not merely a shortfall in funds that rendered the program irrelevant. Administrators in the African colonies did not share the outlook of their superiors in the Colonial Office. However much the notion of economic development and welfare might have overtaken people in the metropole, colonial governors remained wedded to earlier concepts of empire.

Economic development schemes did not yield sufficient revenues to make it possible for Britain to continue to govern its colonies on the cheap. The changes in African societies wrought by two world wars and a worldwide depression confronted British authorities with a situation they lacked the personnel to control. On the most basic level, there were not enough Britons to police vast numbers of Africans who refused to act as British colonial officials insisted they must. The metropole simply could not provide sufficient numbers of Britons to police and administer the huge populations under their power. Thus, as early as the late 1940s, the Colonial Office had begun to think differently about Britain's relationship to its empire. Foreseeing a day, far down the road, when African colonies might be self-governing, imperial officials began to plan for a slow and gradual transfer of power. Of necessity, they turned their attention to the educated Africans who were yearning for self-government. Previously, British colonialism had been made possible through the cooperation of traditional chiefs, whose control over their peoples was eroding fast under the influence of world wars, urbanization, education, and upstart labor unions and political organizations. Now, if Britain was to succeed in introducing gradual political change, it would have to enlist the educated African elites. And they, it turned out, could only be brought on board if Britain agreed to the reforms they demanded. These reforms would ultimately lead not to a newly enriched relationship between Britain and its imperial possessions but to outright independence for the colonies in a second phase of decolonization.

The Nationality Act of 1948

One of Britain's most far-reaching efforts to preserve empire resulted in the passing of the 1948 Nationality Act, a law that gave full and equal rights of British nationality to all inhabitants of the dominions, colonies, and former colonies that had joined the commonwealth. As British subjects, they could enter the United Kingdom freely, take up jobs in Britain, and vote for Parliament when living in Britain. This remarkable piece of legislation emerged in response to Canada's enactment of a law of citizenship that made Canadian nationality the primary source of belonging and relegated membership in the British empire to secondary status. Fearful that other dominions would follow Canada's lead, Britain reacted to what it perceived to be a threat to its imperial supremacy by introducing its own bill, one that enabled the United Kingdom to remain at the center of empire. By refusing to privilege Britons over subjects of the empire, by making all subjects equal in the eyes of British law, the concept of a universal imperial nationality embedded in the act, officials hoped, would help stave off demands for independence in the colonies and keep the empire intact.

As opponents of the Nationality Act had predicted, equal rights of citizenship held a powerful appeal for many colonial subjects. In the ten years between 1948 and 1958 a large number of migrants from the "new commonwealth" countries of South Asia and from the Caribbean entered Britain. They came for jobs, education, for greater prosperity than they enjoyed at home, for a chance "to get the money to build a decent life," as one West Indian woman put it. Another responded to pleas from Queen Elizabeth II (1926–) to "come over and work to build up the Mother Country. Of course, that was the way Britain was seen in those days, and a lot of us really did believe that the streets were paved with gold." Once in Britain, however, having left behind spouses, parents, children, brothers and sisters, and friends, they found that all was not as they had been led to believe. One West Indian woman trained as a nurse found that hospitals "wouldn't have me. Someone had told me that they would take me on as an auxiliary nurse and that later on I could train. But when I got to the hospital, the woman there offered me a cleaning job."[4] Many other well-trained immigrants could find only the most menial of jobs because employers hesitated to employ them in skilled positions. Co-workers disparaged or shunned them, and their unions failed to protect their interests in the workplace. The first generation of commonwealth immigrants found life in Britain alienating, hostile, and difficult.

In the 1940s, no more than 1,000 people of color entered the country each year. By the mid-1950s, that figure had risen to 20,000 each year. In 1961, 100,000 black people immigrated. In 1951, the numbers of blacks in Britain totaled perhaps 74,500. By 1959, it had grown to 336,000 and reached 500,000 by 1962. These figures set off alarm bells among politicians and government officials, who saw in the flow of black migrants a threat to the identity and social stability of Great Britain. Although Britain needed workers to keep the small postwar boom going in the 1950s and although the sluggish birth rate had created fears about population decline, migrants of color from Britain's former and current colonies did not receive a warm welcome even from official sources. As the Royal Commission on Population put it in its report in 1949, "immigration on a large scale into a fully established society like ours could only be welcomed without reserve if the immigrants were of good human stock and were not prevented by their religion or race from intermarrying with the host population and becoming merged with it."[5]

As this statement and many other pronouncements, official and unofficial, infer, Britons seemed obsessed by fears of black sexuality and miscegenation. Winston Churchill opposed immigration from commonwealth countries and colonies because "we would have a magpie society: that would never do." The anthropologist Geoffrey Gorer (1905–1985) identified in 1955 the "shyness" of English people in their dealings with people who were not like them, people who might "corrupt or contaminate one, either by undermining one's moral principles and leading oneself or one's family into disapproved-of indulgences . . . or by undermining one's social position . . . through association with people 'who don't know how to behave.'" The sociologist Judith Henderson (1918–1972) asserted in 1960 that "Africans and West Indians do manifest an exuberance and lack of restraint which is the very reverse of English reserve and self control;" an official of the Conservative Party declared in 1963 that "most of them have vile habits. If only they behaved like us it would be all right." Sheila Patterson's (1918–1998) sociological study of West Indian immigrants to Brixton in the 1950s, entitled *Dark Strangers*, delineated the traits, as whites saw them, that differentiated black Britons from white Britons. "Primitiveness, savagery, violence, sexuality, general lack of control, sloth, irresponsibility—all these are part of the image." These descriptions and terms could have been lifted right out of any eighteenth- or nineteenth-century racist tract on the nature of Britain's subject peoples.[6]

Even sympathetic efforts to understand racial differences and antagonisms nevertheless reinforced through repetition the imagery of blacks as savage and sexualized. In 1955, a psychologist sought to explain "Negrophobia" as a manifestation of sexual repression on the part of white people. "There is a good deal of evidence to show that in modern Western civilization erotic or sexual impulses are subject to a great deal of repression and renunciation," he wrote. "In so far as the negro is popularly identified with the 'savage' and thought to live a life which is relatively free from the conventions and restrictions associated with 'civilization,' he is often believed to be free from sexual restraints. As a result it is suggested that the Negro comes to represent in the mind of the white man or woman that aspect of his own unconscious with which he is in a state of conflict. Hostility which the individual directs towards the part of himself that wants to break away from the sexual restraints is projected onto the Negro, who is accused of doing all the things that the white person himself would like to do, but dare not."[7] Ideas like this, even among individuals seeking to ameliorate race relations in postwar Britain, made it possible for the oft-asked question "Would you let your daughter marry a Negro?" to resonate with such force for white Britons of all classes and religious and political persuasions.[8]

By the late 1950s, white Britons in a number of communities began to act out their fears and hatreds of people of color in acts of violence against them, explaining their actions as a response to black men transgressing the boundaries that should have set them apart from white women. In August 1958, whites in Nottingham rioted after "a Jamaican" began a conversation with a white woman in a pub. Between 1,500 and 4,000 whites took to the streets and burned and looted. A month later, a four-day riot in Notting Hill in West London broke out in protest of blacks settling there.

George Rogers (1906–1983), the Labour MP for the area in which Notting Hill was located, justified the attacks by whites on blacks by calling on familiar sexualized racial stereotypes. "The government must introduce legislation quickly to end the tremendous influx of coloured people from the Commonwealth . . . overcrowding has fostered vice, drugs, prostitution and the use of knives. For years the white people have been tolerant. Now their tempers are up."[9] These riots gave the issue of immigration a national prominence it had not enjoyed before, giving rise to televised debates, editorials in the press, sermons from the pulpits, and opinion polls seeking to gauge the thinking of Britons. A Gallup poll taken just after the rioting revealed that 80 percent of the poll's respondents favored controlling immigration of people of color. In July 1962, the Conservative government obliged them, passing into law the Commonwealth Immigration Bill, which restricted the immigration of people of color, although not whites, from the commonwealth countries and the colonies of Great Britain. The act marked the first phase of the process through which people of color in Britain would be scapegoated for all the postwar problems the nation faced.

Race riots in Notting Hill, London, 1958.

The Crisis in Suez

In 1956, a crisis surrounding the Suez Canal transformed Britain's relationship to its imperial subjects. It demoralized the British, galvanized nationalists across the empire, and ushered in the era of decolonization.

In 1952, a number of young Egyptian army officers overthrew their ruler, King Farouk (1920–1965), whom they regarded as an ineffectual guardian of their nation's interests and a toady of the British government. At that time, British armed forces occupied only the canal zone of Egypt, having withdrawn from the rest of the country in 1947. But for Colonel Gamal Abdel Nasser (1918–1970) and his fellow Free Officers (as they called themselves), the very presence of the British in what they regarded as a "state within the state" served as a reminder of their nation's servile status. Its weakness had been exposed in 1948, when Israeli forces readily turned back Egypt's invading army; again in 1955, even with Nasser heading the country, the Egyptian army could not repel Israel's incursion into Gaza. To build up his country's military might and restore its dignity, Nasser approached the Western powers for arms, but was rebuffed. He turned then to the Soviet Union for support, a move that in the context of the Cold War alarmed

British ships clear the entrance to the canal during the Suez Crisis of 1956.

Britain and the United States sufficiently to lead them to offer monetary assistance for the construction of the Aswan Dam on the Nile River. When Nasser accepted Soviet aid as well, the United States and Britain backed out of the deal.

On July 26, 1956, Nasser delivered a speech to 250,000 Egyptians gathered in Liberation Square in Alexandria, which was picked up and broadcast across North Africa and the Middle East. He denounced the efforts of the Western powers to return Egypt to a position of financial subservience—"imperialism without soldiers," he called it—and then announced that Egyptian soldiers were, at that very moment, seizing control of the Suez Canal from the French and British consortium that owned and ran it. Egyptian nationalization of the canal would enable the country to collect the transport fees ships had to pay to travel through it, thus replacing the funds that the Americans and British had promised (but then revoked) to build the Aswan Dam. By this action, Nasser could also restore national dignity and pride.

This action infuriated the British and the French, who resolved to regain their property, as they saw it, and to teach Egypt a humbling—and crippling—lesson in the process. Britain's prime minister, Anthony Eden (1897–1977), had to tread carefully, however, aware that the British public would not countenance a bald act of aggression. When the French and the Israelis proposed a subterfuge that would provide cover, Eden seized the opportunity. The plan called for the Israeli army to invade across the Sinai peninsula, at which point Britain and France would mobilize their forces to "protect" the canal, as an earlier British treaty with Egypt allowed, interpose themselves between the Israelis and the Egyptians, and overthrow Nasser. They would then return the canal to British and French possession.

At the end of October, Israel crossed into Egypt and soon had the Egyptian army retreating toward the canal to defend it. France launched its military initiative, as the plan called for, forcing Britain to do the same. At the United Nations, Britain's ambassador vetoed a cease-fire that the Security Council endeavored to impose, making it clear to most of the world that Britain's intentions were not honorable at all and that it was simply looking to recapture the canal. At this stage, American distress over the situation blossomed into an all-out effort to ensure that Britain would not succeed, lest its actions send African and Asian colonies pressing for independence into the arms of the welcoming Soviets. President Eisenhower ordered the U.S. Treasury Department to call in Britain's debts, forcing the chancellor of the Exchequer, Harold Macmillan (1894–1986), to plead with his prime minister, "We must stop, we must stop, or we will have no dollars left by the end of the week."[10] Faced with financial collapse at the hand of its erstwhile ally—with whom it enjoyed a "special relationship"—Britain had to back down and call off its invasion of the canal zone.

The outcome of the Suez crisis reflected a profound and dramatic shift in the balance of power throughout the world. The Second World War had dealt a death blow to the British empire, although most did not yet know it. But the writing was on the wall: many of the Arab states that Britain had received at the end of the Great War gained their independence when Britain relinquished its "mandates" at the end of World War II. India, as we have seen, won independence in 1947 along with Pakistan, the two new countries separated along religious and sectarian lines. By the end of the Second World War, British might had diminished to the point where it could no longer claim to be a great power. Instead, it found itself in a world dominated by two superpowers, the United States and the Soviet Union, each of which espoused—at least publicly—a pronounced anticolonialism. The Cold War and decolonization were closely linked with one another, with developments in each affecting, if not determining, the other.

Publicly humiliated before much of the world by the Suez crisis, many Britons regarded this disaster as signaling the end of empire altogether. One official called the Suez fiasco the "psychological watershed, the moment when it became apparent that Britain was no longer capable of being a great imperial power."[11] For his part, Nasser gained extraordinary prestige across the colonized world. He had stood up to the once-great imperial power and won. His revolt against the British demonstrated that the teeth of the once mighty imperial behemoth had been pulled.

The Wind of Change

On March 5, 1957, the former British colony of Gold Coast, now named Ghana, won its independence, with Kwame Nkrumah at its head (after a prolonged and violent struggle, Malaya followed suit in July of that year). The arrival of this momentous day in the history of Britain's relationship with Africa galvanized colonized peoples all over the world. Nkrumah exhorted all Africans to do what Ghana had done: seize their universal right to self-government and establish sovereign rule in their own nations. His clarion call resonated across the continent. For Britons, Ghanaian independence made crystal clear that holding on to their African colonies was no longer in the cards. Colonial officers might debate matters of timing or the readiness of particular African colonies to move toward independence, but the fact that independence *would* come in the near future had been unambiguously established.

This realization found expression in the "wind of change" speech delivered by Britain's Conservative prime minister, Harold Macmillan, in February 1960. Venturing to Cape Town to celebrate the fiftieth anniversary of the Union of South Africa, he shocked his audience when he announced that a "wind of change is blowing through this continent, and whether we like it or not, this growth of national consciousness is a political fact. We must all accept it as a fact, and our national policies must take account of it." The wind of change speech acknowledged what had been evident for a few years and reflected an understanding, however reluctantly arrived at, that little could be done to preserve the British empire.

Decolonization in Africa and the West Indies occurred far more quickly than anyone could have imagined. Britain's loss of stature in the world compelled colonial authorities to be more realistic about the situation they faced, although even the most optimistic of African and West Indian anticolonialists did not envision anything like the pace at which the continent was freed. Britons, for their part, imagined that another fifty years would pass before the colonies achieved the level of modernization necessary to secure self-government. As it turned out, the process took less than fifteen years for many of Britain's African and Caribbean colonies, an acceleration that no one had anticipated. Contemporaries often described 1960 as the "Year of Africa." Seventeen nations across the continent gained independence from their colonial masters, following in the footsteps of Ghana. The next year in East Africa, Julius Nyerere's (1922–1999) Tanganyika, somewhat surprisingly, given its lack of educational facilities and economic resources, threw off colonial rule. Uganda gained independence in 1962, and Kenya followed in 1963. Finally, Zanzibar became independent the next year, before joining Tanganyika in 1964 to form the nation of Tanzania. In West Africa, as we have seen, Ghana and Nigeria had become independent in 1957 and 1960, respectively. They were followed by Sierra Leone in 1961 and Gambia in 1965.

Kenyan independence followed a decade of rebellion on the part of the Mau Mau—a revolt that looked like an anticolonial war, a clear and straightforward battle of black versus white, of dreadlocked fighters in the forests of central Kenya conducting a campaign against British troops. But in reality almost all anti-colonial struggles were never that sharply defined. The impact of colonialism over the previous half-century had been uneven and had created class distinctions among Africans. Many educated, wealthy Africans, especially among the Kikuyu, Kenya's largest ethnic group, had prospered under British rule, and they were as much the targets of anger—often even more so—as colonial officials.

Mau Mau emerged from among discontented, disenfranchised, poor Kikuyu who had no realistic means of establishing livelihoods. Members of "the movement" began meeting in secret and administering oaths to bond themselves together. They held out a vision of a renewed, ordered Kikuyu society in which the inequalities they faced no longer existed. In 1952 Mau Mau in Nairobi and central Kenya began murdering individuals they believed had betrayed their people. Their victims and their allies were known as "loyalists," Kikuyu who had been loyal to the colonial government and who often had become wealthy from years of association with it. The colony's governor, Evelyn Baring (1903–1973), declared a state of emergency on October 20, 1952. The emergency gave the government supralegal powers to clamp down on potential dissent.

Between late 1952 and early 1954, Mau Mau fighters operating from bases in the two forests of central Kenya fought a series of running engagements with British troops and their loyalist allies. Occasionally they carried out raids against isolated white settler farms, forays that led to hysterical pronouncements in the British and colonial press about blacks slaughtering whites, but settlers were rarely their targets. Only 36 settlers died during the period Mau Mau operated as opposed to the more than 20,000 Kikuyu who lost their lives at the hands of the rebels. The British hanged 1,090 "terrorists" at the gallows in the most extensive use of capital punishment in British imperial history. Unable to rapidly defeat Mau Mau, the British employed tactics utilized in the South Africa War half a century earlier. They built an extensive system of "detention and rehabilitation" camps—concentration camps—in which more than 80,000 suspected Mau Mau were held. British staff and loyalists carried out torture—including rape, castration, and murder—in the camps, actions that would later become the subject of a landmark legal case, as we will see in the next chapter.

In southern Africa, independence was inextricably linked to the demise of the Central African Federation. A union of Northern Rhodesia, Southern Rhodesia, and Nyasaland founded in 1953, the white rulers of the Central African Federation hoped to obtain dominion status for their colony and aspired to the kind of autonomy within the British empire enjoyed by South Africa, Canada, New Zealand, and Australia. African nationalist politicians feared that the federation might be replaced by informal white settler domination. They demanded constitutional change—"one man, one vote"—and spent the later years of the 1950s leading widespread campaigns of civil disobedience that resulted in their detention. But the roll toward independence was unstoppable. In 1963 the federation was wound down, with both Northern Rhodesia and Nyasaland gaining their independence in 1964 as Zambia and Malawi, respectively. Only Southern Rhodesia remained steadfast in its resistance to majority rule. In 1965, its prime minister, Ian Smith (1919–2007), issued a Unilateral Declaration of Independence (UDI) from Britain. Finally, the protectorate of Bechuanaland—where little more than half a million people lived—came into existence as Botswana in 1966. Lesotho followed the same year and Swaziland in 1968.

In the West Indies, Jamaica and Trinidad and Tobago won independence in 1962, followed by Barbados and Guyana in 1966. The 1970s saw the Bahamas, Grenada, St. Vincent, and St. Lucia gain their freedom; in the 1980s Belize, Antigua, and St. Kitts and Nevis achieved theirs. With only the tiniest of exceptions, the British empire was no more.

Racial Anxieties and National Malaise

Many people in Britain cheered Harold Macmillan's wind of change speech in Cape Town, which he intended as a signal that Britain would no longer support the Nationalist government against UN resolutions decrying its apartheid policies. A good deal of media and public opinion rallied in support of what amounted to the prime minister's denunciation of the racist regime. In South Africa, ironically, the speech helped to increase the power of the white supremacist government; whites in other settler colonies had no doubt that it meant that Britain had betrayed its obligations to its "kith and kin" who lived in places like Rhodesia and Kenya. And for precisely this reason—that the British empire was abrogating its responsibilities to sustain a white way of life, a British way of life, in Africa—an influential conservative opposition to Conservative rule in Westminster formed in the metropole in response to Macmillan's speech. A new political lobby, the Monday Club, appeared, so called for the day of the week it held its meetings. Made up of a number of prominent politicians and statesmen who saw in the decline of empire generally and the backing away of white settler communities in Africa in particular an assault on all they held dear, it formed the elite political core of what would, in the later 1960s and 1970s, emerge as the New Right in Britain.

The Monday Club championed the rights of white settlers in Africa, first those in Nyasaland, Northern Rhodesia, and Southern Rhodesia who fiercely resisted the dismantling of the Central African Federation and then, more vociferously, Rhodesians after the UDI in 1965. With the backing of powerful media and business interests, Monday Club members who sat in Parliament fought every attempt to undermine Southern Rhodesia's government; they forced the biggest split the Conservative Party had seen in more than twenty years over the issue of imposing oil sanctions on the country. Prime Minister Smith hit on precisely the fears and anxieties of large numbers of Britons at home and in settler colonies when he asserted in 1966, "If Winston Churchill were alive today, I believe he would probably emigrate to Rhodesia—because I believe that all those admirable qualities and characteristics of the British that we believed in, loved and preached to our children, no longer exist in Britain."[12]

The lament of a lost British ethos was not restricted to white settlers in Africa. At home from the late 1950s, a great many public intellectuals questioned what had happened to their country in the wake of the Second World War and especially with the loss of empire. "What's wrong with Britain?" they asked in books, articles, speeches, and interviews. A kind of national malaise emerged in response to Britons' recognition of their weakness on the world stage: where once their nation had dominated the globe, now it performed as a decidedly second fiddle to a much greater power. Imperial decline, many Britons intimated, stood at the heart of all the troubles their country faced—economic, political, social, and cultural.

For a significant portion of the British public, immigration from former colonies figured prominently among those troubles. Distress over the presence of people of color often found voice as a lament about a breakdown in "law and order," collapsing popular anxieties about postwar society into fears about crime and delinquency. By the late 1960s, these fears combined with unease about safety to produce a slightly different racial discourse. Conservatives and traditionalists decried the apparent loss of a British "way of life" consequent on the loss of empire and the immigration of former colonial subjects to their country. In 1968, Enoch Powell (1912–1998), Conservative MP for Wolverhampton, had declared the settlement of blacks in Britain to be a threat to the nation's very existence. In his so-called "River of Blood" speech, he foresaw, "like the Roman, . . . 'the River Tiber foaming with much blood,'" if immigration was not banned outright and the "re-emigration" of former colonial subjects back to their countries of origin not put into effect. He framed his images of violence around a story about an elderly white woman under siege from blacks who had "invaded" her neighborhood. "Eight years ago in a respectable street in Wolverhampton," he recounted, "a house was sold to a negro. Now only one white (a woman old-age pensioner) lives there." Powell suggested an image of "negroes" breeding like rabbits till they had overwhelmed the white population. "With growing fear, she saw one house after another taken over. The quiet street became a place of noise and confusion. Regretfully, her white tenants moved out." Without their protection, Powell intimated, the pensioner finds herself at the mercy of her new neighbors. "The day after the last [white tenant] left, she was awakened at 7:00 a.m. by two negroes who wanted to use her phone to contact their employer. When she refused, as she would have refused any stranger at such an hour, she was abused and feared she would have been attacked but for the chain on her door."

This tale utilized elements from the 1950s that emphasized the encroachment on whites' private spaces by black people and the intimations of miscegenation and hypersexuality among blacks and mixed them in with new fears about violence and personal safety. Isolated, alone, and unwilling to let rooms in her house out to immigrants, the white woman "is becoming afraid to go out. Windows are broken. She finds excreta pushed through her letterbox. When she goes to the shops, she is followed by children, charming, wide-grinning piccaninnies. They cannot speak English, but one word they know. 'Racialist,' they chant." In this account, in which the nation is represented by an elderly, frail white woman vulnerable to the sexual and physical threats of black men, Powell conveyed the ominous message that if blacks in Britain were given the same freedoms from discrimination that white Britons enjoyed, then those very freedoms and the British way of life they represented would be destroyed in a traumatic bloodletting.[13]

By the 1970s, what had once been the racist rantings of a fringe politician became core beliefs held by many Britons and manifested themselves in the ideology of the New Right. Its grassroots support would derive from Britons who saw in the immigration of large numbers of people of color from former colonies a threat to the life they had known. Crime in the forms of robbery, "mugging," and urban riots came to the fore in discourses about black settlement, race relations, and social disorder. Black people, black men in particular, came to stand in for illegality, a decidedly "unBritish" trait, conservatives told themselves, although government reports showed that "immigrant crime rates were, if anything, a little lower than those for the indigenous population." Indeed, union militancy, Ulster politics, and soccer "hooliganism" had been producing a great deal of violence among white Britons for years. For many conservatives, people of color represented the forces responsible for Britain's decline, for the social instability brought on by unemployment and recession. "The nation has been and is still being, eroded and hollowed out from within by implantation of unassimilated and unassimilable populations. . . . alien wedges in the heartland of the state," asserted Powell in 1976. By this time, his message of racial intolerance and of black people as the source of danger to British society had been embraced by a significant portion of Britons and would soon help to produce the electoral victory of the Conservative Party, with Margaret Thatcher (1925–2013) at its head. As Alfred Sherman (1919–2006), a prominent right-wing theorist, put it in September 1979, on the eve of Thatcher's election as prime minister, "the imposition of mass immigration from backward alien cultures is just one symptom of this self-destructive urge reflected in the assault on patriotism, the family—both as a conjugal and economic unit—the Christian religion in public life and schools, traditional morality, in matters of sex, honesty, public display, and respect for the law—in short, all that is English and wholesome."[14]

Many Britons had difficulty accepting the end of empire. It symbolized for them much more than the loss of colonies, or even their decline in power on the world stage. It bespoke too a loss of national values, of a "Britishness" defined by long-standing ideas about duty, loyalty, stoicism—that "stiff upper lip"—selflessness, and gentlemanly conduct. The social revolutions of the 1960s threw up new demands pertaining to sexuality, feminism, and popular culture that seemed to overthrow all that previous generations of Britons had known and esteemed. And, as we have seen, immigration from Britain's former colonies introduced what many perceived to be an alien, un-British presence. All this was too much to bear for many people. They brought Margaret Thatcher and her Conservative Party to power in 1979.

THE PERMISSIVE SOCIETY

The 1960s marked the beginning of the breakdown in what had appeared to most Britons to be a postwar consensus about the appropriate nature of government and society. Forged in the heat and tragedy of the Second World War, the belief in a common future of full employment, social justice, and a minimum level of welfare for all people informed the politics of both the Labour and the Conservative parties and served as the ideal to which their respective governments aspired while in office. As we have seen, the postwar consensus was a myth that concealed the reality for most people: inequalities remained and gave rise to protest in the late 1950s. In the 1960s, when unemployment began its dramatic climb and Britain's economic situation turned sour, a series of popular and political countercultural movements appeared, which produced throughout mainstream society a profound sense of "moral panic," as one critic has termed it, over what many people regarded as a "permissive" culture out of control.

Notions of "permissiveness" contained at least two strands of thought against which conservatives railed: in one manifestation, permissiveness connoted the sexual revolution, gay rights, and feminism; in another, it referred to a purported breakdown in respect for law and order, a situation attributed to immigrants to Britain and their children and articulated through a language of race. The advent of "Thatcherism," an economic, political, and cultural movement calling for a return to "Victorian" values, in 1979 in reaction to the "moral panics" of the late 1960s and 1970s marked a decisive end to the postwar consensus. Thatcher's call for a renewal of nineteenth-century economic, political, and even imperial philosophies and her championing of moral, social, and gender norms of an earlier time found great favor among a large segment of the population in a period when Britain's international status and economic conditions had fallen into steep decline.

The relative affluence of the 1950s and its apparent continuation in the years 1963 to 1968 among many sectors of the population spawned the creation of a dynamic and, to many, disturbing youth culture. Centered first around the mod fashions and the pop and rock offerings of the Beatles and the Rolling Stones and later gravitating toward punk groups like the Sex Pistols, youth culture marked a definitive shift of both cultural authority and resistance to mainstream society away from elite writers to a mass movement of working- and middle-class young men and women. Aware of the great pockets of poverty existing within their society of affluence and subject themselves to the dead-end jobs that offered no means of escape from a lifetime of drudgery, working- and lower-middle-class youth, followed by huge numbers of their middle-class age cohort, gave vent to their frustrations and dissatisfactions with their parents' way of life by mocking their values and traditions and celebrating their own nonconformity with them. Mod fashions, rock music, experimentation with drugs, and the flaunting of sexual conventions epitomized the generational revolt against postwar society, producing anxiety and unease among significant segments of the population.

In contrast to the mod and pop cultures, which presented an androgynous, "unisex," even feminine face to the world and were far more accessible to young women, the style and lyrics of rock groups struck observers with their sexual aggressiveness and their hostility toward women. In the songs of the Stones, for example, class antagonism frequently found expression through misogynistic diatribes against wealthy women by working-class men. "Playing with Fire" and "19th Nervous Breakdown," among others, scorned their upper-class female protagonists for their preoccupation with material possessions and their empty, superficial lives. In their live performances, the Rolling Stones sought to present themselves as sexually charged, violent, destructive, dangerous malcontents who were capable of almost any outrage. Mick Jagger (1943-), according to a contemporary rock critic, "trampled the weak, execrated the old, poured out a psychotic flood of abuse against women."[15]

Freer attitudes about sex and sexuality, although not necessarily freer practices, accompanied the flowering of youth culture in the 1960s. The so-called "sexual revolution" derived from the convergence of a number of developments. First, the consumer market for sex-related commodities burgeoned in the postwar period, as affluence and a youth-age-skewed demographic upturn increased the commercial possibilities of selling sex. Advertising firms seized on sex to sell any number and manner of products, taking their cue from the sexually explicit lyrics and erotic posturings of rock stars that so captivated youth audiences. Hugh Hefner's *Playboy* magazine capitalized on the commodification of sex with extraordinary success. London's Playboy Club opened its doors in 1966, followed by a spate of less respectable, sometimes pornographic establishments that catered to a seemingly insatiable male demand for sexual pleasure. A kind of hedonistic lifestyle emerged in the "swinging" 1960s, within which "wife swapping" and other unconventional sexual practices might take place. Censorship laws regulating the content of publications and the theater were overturned in 1959, 1964, and 1968. Savvy media types and entrepreneurs exploited the new freedom surrounding sex to improve their bottom lines and in the process extended the scope of the "sexual revolution."

Second, the material consequences of sex for both men and women changed remarkably. The availability of the "pill," a reliable contraceptive, and of legal abortion after 1967 made it possible for women to engage in sexual intercourse with a much reduced fear of pregnancy. Venereal diseases like syphilis and gonorrhea could be readily treated by antibiotics. These material improvements could help to open up whole new possibilities of physical pleasure for women, who were more free to explore and experience sexual opportunities than previous generations of women had been. But they also made it possible for men to put a great deal of pressure on women to engage with them sexually; absent the constraints of unwanted pregnancy, women were far more susceptible to accusations of prudery and other forms of verbal coercion. As Celia Haddon (1944–) put it in her 1983 *The Limits of Sex*, "in some ways, the sexual revolution had freed me from guilt and anxiety; in other ways it had enslaved me anew, with different fetters."[16] As we shall see, the negative implications of the sexual revolution for women helped to provoke a new wave of feminism in the early 1970s.

Despite what appeared to contemporaries to be a dramatic change in sexual practices, actual sexual behavior remained pretty consistent with that of earlier decades. Attitudes and styles had altered, to be sure, but little in the way of real substantive behavioral change can be detected. Young people now engaged in sexual relations at a younger age, but improved diet and health consequent on the provision of welfare benefits lowered the age of sexual maturation; physiological rather than moral shifts may well account for earlier sexual activity. In the late 1960s, a Sunday *Times* poll found that more than one-quarter of the men and almost two-thirds of the women surveyed had been virgins at the time they married. Men and women might live with one another for a considerable period of time before marriage, but the rate of marriage did not fall; in fact it went up. Divorce rates rose with a liberalization of the divorce laws in 1969, but serial monogamy in the form of second and third marriages continued to be the trend among the vast majority of men and women.

The sexual revolution may well have appeared so threatening to many traditional and conservative people because it was closely tied in with other countercultural movements that challenged the political, social, and gender orders of Britain. Antiwar protests, student demonstrations and sit-ins, racial equality and black power groups, gay rights organizations, and a powerful women's liberation movement appeared right on the heels of the sexual revolution, presenting mainstream society with a multipronged assault on its values and institutions. Union demands for higher wages and industrial unrest resulting in violence appeared endemic. The amalgamation of all these developments produced in the minds of a good portion of the population by the 1970s the sense that a general breakdown in morality had occurred during the 1960s, that "enemies within" were undermining the nation, and that something had to be done to make Britain right again.

THE "TROUBLES"

These anxieties over the perception of societal breakdown were exacerbated terribly by the situation in Northern Ireland, where the civil rights quest of Catholics in the late 1960s gave way to violence on the part of both Catholic nationalists and Protestant unionists and spilled over to the rest of the United Kingdom in the form of domestic terrorism. The civil rights movement sought to eliminate discrimination against Catholics, especially in the areas of housing and political representation at the local and provincial levels. The IRA played no part in the movement at this time, having fallen into disarray and irrelevance in 1962. In the fall of 1968, civil rights leaders led a march through Londonderry (called Derry by Catholics), an area heavily populated by Protestants, to call attention to the needs of Catholics. The Ministry of Home Affairs tried to ban it, but failed to do so. The Northern Ireland police force, the Royal Ulster Constabulary (RUC), and the Reserve Force (also known as the B-Special Constabulary, or riot squad) met the marchers and physically manhandled them, causing injuries to more than seventy-five protestors. Four constables suffered injuries as well. The Northern Irish government at Stormont tried to calm things by issuing new policies for housing, but these proved to be too little too late and in any event created anger among die-hard Protestants who refused to entertain any such concessions to Catholics. Under the leadership of the Reverend Ian Paisley (1926–2014), Protestant unionists organized and some even began to arm themselves to resist the Catholic civil rights demonstrators.

During another march by Catholics from Belfast to Derry on January 4, 1969, Protestants attacked the protestors. They included among their numbers members of the Ulster Special Constabulary. Over the next few days, RUC officers in Londonderry went into Catholic areas and assaulted people. Violence between Protestants and Catholics escalated over the next number of months, culminating in August 1969 when a Protestant march honoring the 1689 relief of Londonderry by King William's troops was pelted by stones thrown by Catholics. The B-Specials of the RUC struck back by storming through the Catholic neighborhood of "Bogside," burning and vandalizing property and assaulting people. Catholics threw up barricades to repel what they believed was a Protestant invasion till the situation devolved into the so-called "siege of the Bogside." Across Northern Ireland, riots erupted and blood spilled as Protestants and Catholics fought one another. Protestants enjoyed the support of the RUC as they burned down houses and set upon Catholics. Catholics turned to the IRA for help in obtaining arms, to no avail. At the time, the IRA possessed just ten guns.

Faced with a situation it could not handle, the Stormont government called on the British government for assistance. It arrived in August 1969 in the form of a peacekeeping force of the British army whose mission was to protect Catholic neighborhoods from attacks by Protestants. Catholics welcomed the troops with open arms, regarding them as the "cavalry" that had arrived to rescue them from the siege.

In the meantime, two government reports commissioned to investigate the August riots criticized security arrangements of Northern Ireland, generating great anger among unionists. A Protestant mob attacked British troops in mid-October, resulting in the inadvertent killing of an RUC officer by a Protestant sniper.

In the summer of 1970, the character of the Northern Irish conflict changed. By this time the so-called Provisional wing of the IRA (called Provos) had established itself as an effective organization and it determined to take over the response to the conflict. Provos regarded the British troops not as defenders of Catholics but as an occupying force that must be expelled so that Ireland might be united under the government of Éire. They embarked on a campaign to drive the British army out of Northern Ireland, using bombings and assassinations to do so. At just this moment, Harold Wilson's (1916–1995) Labour government in Westminster fell and was replaced by that of Conservative Edward Heath (1916–2005). The new prime minister, his fellow cabinet members, and the top leaders of the British army tended to see the struggles in Northern Ireland as having been caused by rebellious Catholics, a position that could only wreck relations between Catholics and the army in Northern Ireland.

Violence increased in June and July of 1970, leading the British army to declare a curfew in the Catholic neighborhoods of Belfast. Troops—led in many instances by officers who had participated in colonial counterinsurgencies in Malaya and Kenya—went on house-to-house searches looking for arms; they found a great many but also ended up killing five Catholics in the process. This action enabled the Provos to portray the army's role as a continuation of historic British incursions against Irish people; the violent and unprofessional behavior of British troops facilitated this characterization, compelling most Catholics if not to support the Provos, at least to tolerate their actions.

In response to the assassination of 13 British soldiers, 2 RUC police, and 16 civilians by the Provisional wing of the IRA (also referred to as PIRA) between January and August 1971, the British implemented a policy they had utilized in colonial Malaya and Kenya in the 1950s—internment without trial. In August the army rounded up 346 Catholics in one night, dragging them from their beds as their wives and children watched; not one Protestant was brought in. This action, intended to reduce the violence, only increased it, along with recruitment to the PIRA. By the end of 1971 the conflict had become far worse than it had been at the beginning of the year: 174 people had died, 2,375 had been injured, and 15,000 British troops occupied the province of Northern Ireland. Moreover, British measures had generated a great deal of sympathy for the IRA in Éire,

The aftermath of twenty-four bombs set off by the IRA in Belfast on July 21, 1972.

leading ultimately to a surge in the provision of arms across the border. Violence continued unabated, until on January 30, 1972, during a civil rights march in Londonderry, British troops opened fire on the unarmed crowd, killing 14 demonstrators. The action had the effect of presenting to southern Ireland and much of the world a picture of Britain's use of undisciplined troops in pursuit of an ill-formed policy toward Northern Ireland. It also led to Britain taking direct control of the government of the province in March.

In July 1972 the British increased the number of military personnel in Northern Ireland to 21,000 and embarked on a campaign to establish its presence in all the cities of the province. Their tactics included the widespread use of torture to gain "confessions" from men and women not involved in the violence, who were then locked away in prison for more than two decades. The increased British presence had the effect of lessening the ability of the IRA to act in urban areas and pushing them to the rural territories around the border with Éire. It also convinced the IRA to bring the battle to the British mainland; in 1974, it embarked on a bombing campaign in a number of British cities such as Guilford and Birmingham, bringing death and destruction to the civilian population. For the next fifteen years the conflict raged in Northern Ireland and in England, both sides committing atrocities in what appeared to be a never-ending war. In 1981, Bobby Sands (1954–1981) and other IRA members imprisoned in Belfast's Maze prison embarked on a hunger strike, demanding the status of political prisoners. Sands died after sixty-six days without food; nine others followed soon after. An international outcry followed, providing invaluable publicity to the IRA and attracting hundreds of new recruits—and a lot of money—to its ranks. Unionist followers of the Reverend Ian Paisley held a memorial service for all the victims of IRA violence on the day of Sands's funeral, further exacerbating sectarian hostilities in Belfast. On both sides, attitudes became increasingly extreme, and any prospect of peace appeared unlikely.

THATCHERISM

The 1979 election of Margaret Thatcher, the daughter of a greengrocer from Lincolnshire who became a research chemist and then a barrister, reflected deep dissatisfaction with the state of nation in the 1960s. The loss of empire, the decline in Britain's preeminent place in the world, the rise of the permissive society, a seemingly intractable economic downturn, massive unemployment, and the behavior of intransigent unions persuaded many Britons that an entirely different political regime must be instituted. For her part, Thatcher sought to return Britain to a position of global prominence; as she and other conservatives saw it, restoring Britain to greatness required above all an ideological battle against the "consensus" that had presumably marked British society since the end of World War II. "For me," she told an audience at Monash University in Australia, "consensus seems to be the process of abandoning all beliefs, principles, values and policies."[17] The problems facing the country, she insisted, required backbone; one must assert authority if economic difficulties, among others, were to be addressed. Thatcher resolved to deal with the problems facing Britain by introducing what one critic has called "authoritarian populism," a system of administration characterized by the exercise of the disciplinary powers of the state against what were regarded as disruptive elements in society that had no respect for law and order.[18] The June 1981 debate over a new nationality bill demonstrated just how readily white Britons displaced onto racial "others" the consequences of economic problems that seemed to have no solution. MP Ivor Stanbrook (1924–2004) declared, "We are in the grip of forces which, because of the large influx of immigrants into Britain, we now seem unable to control. Racial violence is occurring with increasing frequency. The British people are sick at heart about it all."[19] At a time when the number of unemployed had reached 2 million, widespread concerns about law and order enabled Thatcher's government to expand the power of the police, of the law, and of agencies of surveillance to control and suppress activities and behaviors it deemed dangerous to the state, activities and behaviors construed as "alien," "unBritish," and committed by "outsiders." One such tool was the use of mass "stop and search" powers by the police against black men and women. This provoked a major riot in Brixton in April 1981. In July of that year riots involving young people of all races and ethnicities broke out in a number of cities across the nation, prompting the *Financial Times* to declare an "Outbreak of an Alien Disease" in its headline, attributing to the presence of immigrants and their children protests produced by poverty, unemployment, and heavy-handed police measures.[20]

Thatcherism, as it came to be styled, called for an end to the policies established by the postwar Labour government and maintained by subsequent Conservative and Labour administrations. These included cradle-to-grave welfare state provisions, the nationalization of industries, government intervention to ensure full employment, and the introduction of wage and price controls to meet trade union demands. Thatcher and her ministers determined to privatize a variety of industries, limit welfare payments, and let the free market manage the economy. That meant letting unemployment rates rise to whatever levels the free market dictated. Despite the efforts of Thatcher's government to remedy them, economic difficulties and dislocations continued throughout 1981 and into 1982, creating widespread dissatisfaction. In early 1982 the Conservative Party was in danger of losing its majority in the upcoming 1983 election. Thatcher's popularity had plummeted, whereas that of the newly created alliance between the Social Democratic and Liberal parties soared.

Things looked bleak for her reelection, when, serendipitously, she and her government were rescued by an unexpected turn of events. In March 1982, the government of Argentina, acting on its claim that the Malvinas—what the British claimed as the Falklands, containing 1,800 people of British "stock" and 600,000 sheep—belonged to Argentina, invaded the islands, throwing Britons at home into a frenzy of jingoistic, neo-imperialist patriotism. It prompted the British government to send a full complement of naval, air, and land forces to the South Atlantic

A PLACE IN TIME

The Toxteth Riots

The Toxteth community of Liverpool lies just to the south of the city center. Once the site of prosperous middle-class families occupying large three- and four-story townhomes, after World War II the neighborhood increasingly became home to largely mixed-race families who had been bombed out of their homes in the streets around the docks. Developers broke the single-family townhouses into apartments to accommodate them and the hundreds of immigrants invited to the city from the Caribbean in the 1950s to help alleviate Britain's labor shortage. But Liverpool's economy did not recover robustly, and by the 1960s it faced a severe recession and massive unemployment. The people of Toxteth, largely but not exclusively black and Asian (they comprised 60 percent of the population there), suffered disproportionately in the downturn. More than 50 percent of the area's adults could not find work. They lived in decayed housing, plagued by rats and crumbling infrastructure. And in the latter part of the 1970s, they began to experience abuse on the part of the police. Ken Oxford (1924–1998), the chief constable of the Merseyside Police, had declared Toxteth "a criminal community" that his force "would police accordingly."[21] That involved the implementation of "stop and search" policies authorized by so-called SUS laws, legislation that gave police the right to act on the basis of suspicion alone. In Toxteth, police exercised their powers frequently, unreasonably, and brutally against the community, finally driving its citizens to revolt.

On July 3, 1981, police in an unmarked car stopped and arrested a black motorcyclist. A group of bystanders threw stones at the police, allowing the cyclist to get away, and when the officers called in reinforcements, a full-scale riot broke out. For six weeks, black and white people armed with baseball bats, bricks, and petrol bombs battled police, injuring more than 1,000 of them. The police responded with tear gas, but the rioters turned out in such large numbers that they lost control of large areas within Toxteth and other parts of the city. Only when the rioters ceased their violence were the police able to regain control of the situation. More than £11 million of

to defend "kith and kin" living on the Falklands. Even the *Queen Mary*, a luxury cruise liner, was pressed into service. For seventy-four days the British fought against Argentine forces till they surrendered in June, with each side suffering significant casualties. Victory in the "Falklands War" reestablished the popularity of Thatcher and the Conservative Party at record levels.

property damage had been done and more than seventy buildings had to be torn down. Liverpool appeared to be ungovernable to those from the outside, and Margaret Thatcher considered getting rid of the city council and imposing direct rule from Westminster.

But this was not simply a local problem. Riots had broken out across a number of cities in 1980 and 1981—Bristol, London, and more than thirty-five other towns and cities experienced some degree of violent protest against the police. Nor were the Toxteth riots "race riots," as much of the press asserted. Blacks and whites alike rose up against what they regarded as illegitimate, harsh, and discriminatory police policies and behaviors, demanding an end to them and reform of the law enforcement community as a whole.

The official commission charged with looking into the riots in London and Liverpool confirmed that ill-considered police practices and racial discrimination had, in the context of "complex political, social and economic factors," led to the violent outbreaks in Britain's cities. The commission's chair, Lord Scarman (1911–2004), regarded the violent protests has having "a strong racial element" to them but argued that "they were not a race riot." He warned that "urgent action" must be taken if racial disadvantage and racial discrimination were not to become "an endemic, ineradicable disease threatening the very survival of our society."[22] He urged that police forces, especially that of Toxteth, recruit ethnic minorities to their ranks so as to integrate themselves into their communities and alter the way they thought about and implemented law enforcement policies and practices.

In Liverpool authorities responded to the Scarman report with two contradictory measures. In the first, they initiated a program of community policing, a move that was defeated by the second, which entailed building up police resources so that they might better react to further disturbances. Toxteth continued to be the most heavily policed area of Liverpool until the end of the 1980s, when an inquiry into race relations in the city revealed that problems with the police remained. Since that time things have improved somewhat, although a study done in 2000 by the Home Office found that blacks in Liverpool and its surrounding areas are 7.5 times more likely to be stopped and searched than whites and 6.5 times more likely to be arrested.

"Great Britain is great again," exulted Thatcher, collapsing victory over the Argentines into that over the unions and nationalization of industry. "We have ceased to be a nation in retreat. We have instead a new-found confidence—born in the economic battles at home and tested and found true 8,000 miles away." As one perceptive critic noted of the enthusiasm surrounding the sending of the fleet to

A special relationship: The close ties that the UK has traditionally enjoyed with the US were strengthened further by US president Ronald Reagan's commitment to the same conservative principles that guided Thatcher.

retake the Falklands from the "Argies," "if the Falkland Islanders were British citizens with black or brown skins, spoke with strange accents or worshipped different Gods it is doubtful whether the Royal Navy and Marines would today be fighting for their liberation." Indeed, he pointed out, "most Britons today identify more easily with those of the same stock 8000 miles away . . . than they do with West Indian or Asian immigrants living next door."[23]

The victory over the Argentines gave white Britons something to feel good about; it seemed to mark an end to the humiliation they experienced with the loss of Britain's colonies and its preeminent position in the world. A new mood of decisiveness and strength, which Thatcher identified as the aspects of her ruling style that made her so popular with Britons at a time when economic conditions had only gotten worse, not better, reflected a nostalgia for the days when British imperialism reigned over the globe. Britain under the "Iron Lady" seemed, once again, a manly nation in control of its destiny, one that was "not prepared to be pushed around," as she put it. Its imperial incursion overseas had made it possible for Britons to "rediscover . . . ourselves" and to "recover . . . our self-respect. Britain found herself again in the South Atlantic and will not look back from the victory she has won."[24]

In the general election of 1983, Thatcher's Conservatives won a decisive victory. She capitalized on it to take dramatic steps designed to right the economy, freeing up restrictions on the financial sector, privatizing a number of industries, and introducing legislation that gutted the ability of the labor unions to impose their will on business and industry. She took especially strong action against the coal miners, insisting that the National Coal Board close down underperforming pits, no matter the loss of jobs it would entail. The National Union of Mine Workers under the leadership of Arthur Scargill (1938-) tried desperately to prevent the closures, calling out the miners in the summer of 1984. Because some mines in the Midlands, in particular, were working efficiently, the union could not count on a unified membership. The Nottinghamshire miners refused to heed the call to strike and Thatcher could reasonably claim to be protecting the rights of those miners to work. Violent battles between mounted police swinging batons and striking miners broke out in the summer and fall as trade unionists tried to preserve their jobs in the face of an adamant prime minister who had prepared for the confrontation with the miners by stockpiling supplies of coal to feed the power plants. The miners failed badly, with the labor movement suffering the worst defeat since the General Strike of 1926. Thatcher won reelection again in 1987.

Only three years later, however, she was ousted as the leader of the Conservative party by members who feared she could not take them through the next election, scheduled by law to occur in 1992. Her personal unpopularity within the party—the Iron Lady did not suffer fools gladly—combined with her insistence on levying a poll tax on the adult members of every household and her refusal to entertain British membership in the European Union led party leaders to abandon her in favor of John Major (1943–) in 1990. The poll tax proved deeply unpopular across the entire United Kingdom. It imposed a standard head tax on individuals in place of what had formerly been a levy on property, causing real hardship for poorer households who now had to pay as much as four times what they had owed in the past. For many people in Scotland and Wales its inequities cemented the conviction, growing since Thatcher had come to power in 1979, that they were ruled by an alien government. As we will see in the next chapter, this belief increased sentiment in favor of a kind of home rule for the Celtic countries—a policy called devolution that would create representative assemblies in Scotland, Wales, and Northern Ireland with significant powers for domestic government.

Far less rigid and doctrinaire than his mentor, Major led the party to another victory in 1992 but he could not prevail during the election of 1997, when the *wunderkind* of an ideologically reconfigured and newly invigorated centrist Labour Party, Tony Blair (1953-), catapulted to power with the largest majority ever enjoyed by any British political party in the twentieth century.

Thatcher might have lost power, but by no means was Thatcherism dead. It is true that the Conservatives lost all of their seats in Scotland and Wales and became an exclusively English party, but subsequent governments, both Conservative and Labour, could not simply jettison the reforms of the past two decades. Britain had indeed moved rightward, which is why the Labour Party added the modifier "New" to its branding. All the same, the party under Blair and his successor, Gordon Brown (1951-), introduced dramatic changes to the constitutional arrangement of the United Kingdom, as we will see in the next chapter. More immediately, New Labour came to power boasting 4 MPs of color and 101 women. With its victory, Britain took the first steps toward a truly multicultural society.

NOTES

1. Quoted in Yasmin Alibhai-Brown and James McGrath, "Lord Woodbine: The Forgotten Sixth Beatle," *The Independent*, July 1, 2010.

2. See Stanley Wolpert, *Shameful Flight. The Last Years of the British Empire in India* (Oxford, 2006).
3. Jeffries to Hale, December 16, 1938, cited in Joanna Lewis, *Empire State-Building: War and Welfare in Kenya, 1925–52* (Athens, 2000), p. 35.
4. See Beverley Bryan, Stella Dadzie, and Suzanne Scafe, *The Heart of the Race: Black Women's Lives in Britain* (London, 1985), pp. 22–27.
5. Quoted in Chris Waters, "'Dark Strangers' in Our Midst: Discourses of Race and Nation in Britain, 1947–1963," *Journal of British Studies* 36.2 (April 1997): 207–38.
6. Quoted in Layton-Henry, *Politics of Immigration,* p. 31; Schwarz, "Black Metropolis, White England," p. 196; Waters, "'Dark Strangers,'" pp. 207–38.
7. Quoted in Layton-Henry, *Politics of Immigration,* p. 31; Schwarz, "Black Metropolis, White England," p. 196; Waters, "'Dark Strangers,'" pp. 207–38.
8. Quoted in Layton-Henry, *Politics of Immigration,* p. 31; Schwarz, "Black Metropolis, White England," p. 196; Waters, "'Dark Strangers,'" pp. 207–38. Schwarz, "Black Metropolis, White England," p. 198.
9. Layton-Henry, *Politics of Immigration*, pp. 39, 40.
10. Quoted in Brendon, *Decline and Fall*, p. 501.
11. Quoted in Brendon, *Decline and Fall*, p. 504.
12. Quoted in Stuart Ward, "Whirlwind, Hurricane, Howling Tempest: The Wind of Change and the British World," in Sarah Stockwell and L. J. Butler, "Introduction," in Sarah Stockwell and L. J. Butlers, eds., *The Wind of Change: Harold Macmillan and British Decolonization* (Basingstoke, 2013), p. 59.

TIMELINE

1947	Independence for India and Pakistan
1948	Arrival of *Empire Windrush* carrying immigrants from West Indies
	Nationality Act
1956	Suez Crisis
1957	Independence for Ghana
	Independence for Malaya
1958	Nottingham riots
	Notting Hill riots
1960	Harold Macmillan's "Wind of Change" speech
	Independence for Nigeria
	The Beatles play Hamburg

13. J. Enoch Powell, *Freedom and Reality* (London, 1969), pp. 287–88.
14. Quoted in Gilroy, *"Ain't No Black,"* p. 43; John Solomos, Bob Findlay, Simon Jones, and Paul Gilroy, "The Organic Crisis of British Capitalism and Race: The Experience of the Seventies," in Centre for Contemporary Cultural Studies, *The Empire Strikes Back: Race and Racism in 70s Britain* (London, 1982), p. 27.
15. Quoted in Susan Kingsley Kent, *Gender and Power in Britain, 1640–1990* (London: 1999), p. 336.
16. Quoted in Weeks, *Sexuality and Its Discontents*, p. 18.
17. Speech delivered at Monash University, October 6, 1981; see http://www .margaretthatcher.org/document/104712/.
18. See Hall, *The Hard Road to Renewal*, chs. 8, 9.
19. Hansard Debates, HC Deb 04 June 1981, Vol. 5, c. 1180.
20. Solomos, Findlay, Jones, and Gilroy, "The Organic Crisis of British Capitalism and Race," pp. 29, 31.
21. Quoted in Ken Pye, *Liverpool: The Rise, Fall and Renaissance of a World-Class City* (Gloucestershire, 2014), p. 173.
22. Quoted in Diane Frost and Richard Phillips, *Liverpool '81. Remembering the Riots* (Liverpool, 2011), pp. 49, 45.
23. Quoted in Gilroy, *"Ain't No Black,"* pp. 51, 52.
24. Quoted in Susan Kingsley Kent, *Gender and Power in Britain, 1640–1990* (London, 1999), p. 349.

1961   Independence for Tanganyika

Independence for Sierra Leone

1962   Independence for Uganda

Independence for Jamaica

Independence for Trinidad and Tobago

Commonwealth Immigration Act

1963   Independence for Kenya

End of Central African Federation

1964   Independence for Zanzibar; joined with Tanganyika to become Tanzania

Independence for Northern Rhodesia, becomes Zambia

Independence for Nyasaland, becomes Malawi

FURTHER READING

Beverley Bryan, Stella Dadzie, and Suzanne Scafe, *The Heart of the Race: Black Women's Lives in Britain*. London, 1985.

Barbara Caine, *English Feminism, 1780–1980*. Oxford, 1997.

Centre for Contemporary Cultural Studies, *The Empire Strikes Back: Race and Racism in 70s Britain*. London, 1982.

Paul Gilroy, *"There Ain't No Black in the Union Jack": The Cultural Politics of Race and Nation*. Chicago, 1991.

Stuart Hall, *The Hard Road to Renewal: Thatcherism and the Crisis of the Left*. London, 1988.

1965	Independence for Gambia
	Southern Rhodesia's Unilateral Declaration of Independence
1966	Independence for Bechuanaland, becomes Botswana
	Independence for Lesotho
	Independence for Barbados
	Independence for Guyana
1968	Independence for Lesotho
	Enoch Powell's "River of Blood" speech
	Civil rights marchers in Belfast attacked by Protestants
1969	Protestant marchers in Londonderry attacked by Catholics
	British peacekeeping force arrives in Belfast
1971	British introduce internment without trial in Northern Ireland
1972	"Bloody Sunday" in Londonderry: British soldiers open fire on crowd

Joanna Lewis, *Empire State-Building: War and Welfare in Kenya, 1925–52*. Athens, 2000.

Kathleen Paul, *Whitewashing Britain. Race and Citizenship in the Postwar Era*. Ithaca, 1997.

Bill Schwarz, *Memories of Empire, Vol I: The White Man's World*. Oxford, 2013.

Sarah Stockwell and L. J. Butlers, eds., *The Wind of Change: Harold Macmillan and British Decolonization*. Basingstoke, 2013.

Stanley Wolpert, *Shameful Flight. The Last Years of the British Empire in India*. Oxford, 2006.

1973	Independence for Bahamas
1974	Independence for Grenada
	Irish Republican Army begins bombing campaign in Britain
1979	Margaret Thatcher elected prime minister
	Independence for St. Vincent
	Independence for St. Lucia
1981	Independence for Belize
	Independence for Antigua
	IRA hunger strike in Maze prison; Bobby Sands dies of starvation
	Riots in Brixton and other English cities
1982	Falklands War
1983	Independence for St. Kitts and Nevis
1984	Miners strike
1990	John Major replaces Margaret Thatcher as prime minister

Omagh Bombing Blast Site, 1998

CHAPTER 15

THE MAKEUP OF BRITAIN, 1997–2015

At 2:32 PM on August 14, 1998, Ulster Television in Omagh, County Tyrone, in Northern Ireland, received a call warning that a 500-pound bomb would go off at the courthouse on "main street" in thirty minutes. Police officers began to evacuate the area, moving people off the top of High Street down to the bottom of Market Street. At 3:10, the bomb, sitting in a maroon Vauxhall parked on Lower Market, detonated with an "unearthly bang," as one victim recalled. She searched for her missing son as screams filled the air and "bits of bodies, limbs or something" littered the ground.[1] The attack killed twenty-one people on the spot and another eight on their way to or in the hospital. Two hundred twenty people received injuries. The police, having been misled about the location of the device—there was, in fact, no Main Street in Omagh—had actually herded people in the direction of the explosion rather than away from it.

The carnage wrought by the Omagh bombing was greater than that of any other incident during the long years of "the Troubles." It killed Catholics, Protestants, six teenagers, six children, and a woman pregnant with twins. A splinter group of the IRA, the Real IRA, claimed responsibility for the murders, although it insisted that it had not intended to target civilians. Its members objected to the Good Friday Agreement reached in May that year between Sinn Féin and Ulster Protestants, and the organization sought to derail the implementation of the peace terms. Its actions had the opposite effect. International outrage joined what the BBC described as the "wave of revulsion" among Irish people on both sides of the border. Catholics and Protestants, unionists and nationalists joined together in support of the peace process and gave it the momentum it needed to move forward.[2]

Another nine years would pass before a meaningful peace can be said to have been attained, but the principles undergirding the terms of the Good Friday Agreement were themselves extraordinary. The signatories—eight Northern Irish political parties and the governments of Ireland and the United Kingdom—pledged "rigorous impartiality on behalf of all the people in the diversity of their identities and traditions" and "recognise[d] the birthright of all the people of Northern Ireland to identify themselves and be accepted as Irish or British, or both, as they may so choose."[3] The questions of identities and whether to choose to be British reverberate across the period covered by this chapter. The same kinds of questions raised in Chapter 8 for the second half of the nineteenth century pertain to the early twenty-first century as well. Who and what constitute the nation? How are its constituent parts to be regarded and its peoples categorized? Who should be considered citizens? But now additional questions posed by the end of empire and Britain's fall from dominance suggest themselves. Is the United Kingdom exclusively British or is it also European? Should it be part of Europe or should it return to its old "splendid isolation" of the nineteenth century, as so-called Eurosceptics seem to suggest? Who counts as British, anyway? Does the term mean anything more than "English?" Do the people of Scotland, Wales, and Northern Ireland think of themselves as exclusively Scottish, Welsh, and Irish or do they embrace a dual identity? Is it possible to be both (Scottish, Welsh, Irish) and British? What about the immigrants from the former colonies and their descendants? Do they consider themselves British? Do Britons consider them British? These particular questions took on greater urgency in the aftermath of the July 7, 2005, suicide bombings on the London Underground and a double-decker bus by four Islamist men, three of whom, including the apparent mastermind, had been born in Britain.

••

THE BRITAIN OF TONY BLAIR

In 1997, Tony Blair led the Labour Party out of the wilderness and into power after eighteen years of uninterrupted Tory rule. His party had been moving toward the center of the political divide for more than a decade by then, toning down its strident antibusiness rhetoric and espousing a more pragmatic politics of social democracy. Unions had lost significant power to control the destiny of the party and officials had abandoned a number of principles that had alienated middle-class voters. In 1995, for instance, the party removed from its platform the plank—Clause 4—that had since 1918 called for the public ownership of industry and finance. With his electoral majority of 177 seats, the largest ever enjoyed by any twentieth-century party, Blair continued many of the policies implemented by Margaret Thatcher, and in some cases he actually extended her agenda of privatization.

Blair differed from Thatcher in his belief in the responsibility of the state to provide a basic level of social security to its people. He shored up the embattled National Health Service, poured more money into alleviating the poverty of the elderly, and introduced preschool programs for the children of underprivileged families. He also overturned the waffling Tory position on membership in the European Union (EU), declaring Britain's intention to become a full-fledged, cooperative participant. Closer to home, Blair undermined conservatism by reforming the House of Lords. His measure, which disenfranchised 660 of the 750 hereditary peers of the realm, was in many ways more a public relations stunt than anything truly significant because the House of Lords was not able to postpone legislation passed by the House of Commons for more than one year. But the measure—along with the more substantive reforms that devolved power to Scotland and Wales and established the conditions for peace in Northern Ireland, which will be discussed later in the chapter—marked Tony Blair and New Labour as dynamic players in the creation of a new Britain.

For a decade, things went well for Blair and his government. The prime minister pursued economic and fiscal policies designed to instill confidence in the business sector: balancing the budget, keeping inflation down, and maintaining the strength of the pound on the currency markets. The economy grew, unemployment stayed relatively low, and the financial sector thrived. Britons enjoyed a comfortable standard of living, which compared favorably to that of the rest of Europe. At the same time, however, income inequality increased as people in the financial and service sectors saw a considerable rise in salary and on the returns on their investments. Labour won two more elections, in 2001 and 2005, although by far smaller majorities than in 1997.

Blair stepped down from the head of his party in 2007, transferring leadership to his chancellor of the Exchequer, Gordon Brown, whose fiscal oversight had proved so beneficial to the country. He did so after suffering a fall in his approval ratings, a consequence of his supporting the United States in its invasion of Iraq in 2003. Public opinion turned massively against him, as did members of his own party. Brown inherited the prime ministership just as the global financial system collapsed and Britain's economy, along with that of most other nations, went into a tailspin. One million Britons found themselves out of work as the greatest economic downturn since the Great Depression of the 1930s set in. Brown introduced stimulus measures that saved the economy from utter destruction, but not even the most gifted politician could have survived the fallout from the Great Recession. A gifted politician Brown was not, and in the election of 2010 the Labour Party lost its majority in the House of Commons.

The Conservative Party under the leadership of David Cameron (1966–) had increased its numbers in Parliament, but did not possess an outright majority. It was forced to enter into a coalition government with the Liberal Democratic Party, whose leader, Nick Clegg (1967–), became deputy prime minister. Prime Minister Cameron immediately acted to undo the stimulus measures put in place by Brown, using the economic crisis to return to Margaret Thatcher's agenda of shrinking the welfare state. His austerity program slashed social services and welfare benefits; raised university tuition rates by 300 percent; cut down the size of government to pre–World War II levels; and reorganized the National Health Service in favor of private health care. This latter move, regarded as an attack on the single most important symbol of the welfare state, provoked widespread dissent. Frustrations created by inequality and unemployment received a jolt from the incursions against the National Health Service, and in August 2011, rioters took to the streets in London, Liverpool, Manchester, Bristol, and Birmingham after an unarmed black man was shot by police in north London. For six days they looted and burned buildings, homes, police cars, and buses. Police responded in massive numbers, arresting some 3,000 people. Property damage estimates reached some £200 million pounds. Five men died in the violence.

Like Thatcher before him, Cameron blamed the unrest on the "moral collapse" of British society and vowed to bring the full force of the law down on those who engaged in the riots. Others saw different factors at play. A variety of commentators on the center-left side of the political spectrum cited joblessness, lack of opportunity, poverty, alienation of youth, racism, and reckless policing as contributing causes to the violence. Certainly, as was true during the Arab Spring uprisings of 2011, social media played a crucial role in getting people out into the streets in the worst rioting Britain had seen since 1995.

DEVOLUTION IN SCOTLAND AND WALES

During his 1997 election campaign, Tony Blair made devolution—the granting of significant powers to the governments of Scotland and Wales—a major element of his appeal for votes. Devolution had taken on meaningful significance for Scotland in 1973, when a popular Labour MP from Glasgow lost his seat to a member of the Scottish National Party (SNP). In the following year's general election, the SNP polled 22 percent of the vote and won seven seats in Westminster. The victorious Labour Party, having run on a platform opposing devolution for Scotland, immediately reversed its position and made it a central plank of its platform. A second election in 1974 saw an increase in SNP support to 30 percent of the electorate, displacing the Tories as the second most popular party in Scotland. Early in 1975, Labour put forward a position paper entitled *Devolution in the UK—Some Alternatives for Discussion*.

The rise of the SNP and the appearance of devolution as a substantial political issue reflected changes in Britain's place in the world. Scottish nationalism, like that of the Welsh and the Irish, was not new, as we have seen in previous chapters. But questions of national identity and the unity of the United Kingdom took on greater prominence and immediacy in the years following the end of empire. Scottish, Irish, and Welsh identity had long been formulated in contrast to that of the undisputed senior partner in the union, England, and the place of the Scots, Welsh, and Irish in the getting and running of the empire had afforded them the opportunity to carve out and articulate a distinct set of characterizations about themselves relative to England (and each other). At the same time, the empire provided the ground on which a common purpose for the four nations was established and a common set of values and norms expressed. It provided the "glue," as one historian put it, that held the peoples of the United Kingdom together.[4] With the end of empire, that glue began to dry up, fracture, and then crumble into dust, allowing the centrifugal forces of nationalism to gather steam.

The "break-up of Britain," as Tom Nairn (1932-), the most visible theorist of Scottish nationalism, terms the process of emerging challenges to the unity of the United Kingdom, has taken place gradually and in fits and starts. Britain's efforts to maintain its role as a global player in the 1960s gave impetus to Scottish dissatisfaction with its membership in the union: Harold Macmillan placed the Polaris submarine, Britain's major deterrent to a nuclear strike, in Holy Loch on the Firth of Clyde, a decision maintained by subsequent Conservative and Labour governments alike. The presence of the Polaris placed Scotland directly in the line of a nuclear attack, a fact that did not sit well with Scots of all political stripes. Political and economic developments contributed further to a sense of alienation from England. The Conservative Party—the party of unionism—increasingly lost ground in Scotland in the 1970s and 1980s as it embraced policies that devastated Scottish industries such as shipbuilding and mining. When voters grew disenchanted with Labour, now they gave their votes to the SNP rather than the Tories, virtually shutting out Conservatives from Scotland entirely.

The discovery of North Sea oil in 1970 provided increased momentum for those who would see Scotland more independent. The prospect of spectacularly profitable oil fields sitting off the coast of the nation suffering the highest unemployment rates in Western Europe grated on Scottish sensibilities; more practically, the oil revenues made it possible for nationalists to argue that Scotland could become a viable independent state. The return of numerous SNP members in the elections of 1974 indicated that significant numbers of Scots agreed, and from this point on, devolution became an agenda item that political parties ignored at their peril. Labour embraced it as a means of stopping the SNP from making any more inroads into their constituencies. In 1975 it proposed the creation of a Scottish assembly that would have jurisdiction over most domestic affairs, although it would lack the power to raise revenues. The government passed the Scotland Act in 1978, sending it to a referendum in Scotland the following year.

The referendum proved a disaster for nationalists. Only 64 percent of the electorate chose to vote, signifying little interest in the question. Of those who did go to the polls, only a slight majority favored devolution. In the final analysis, only one-third of Scots had voted for the change, delivering a death blow to the cause of Scottish independence. The election of 1979, in which Margaret Thatcher led the Tories to power, saw the SNP lose nine of its eleven seats in Westminster. Her government repealed the Scotland Act as soon as Parliament met. Devolution was dead for the time being.

But the very government that had caused its demise paved the way for its resurrection some ten years later. Thatcher introduced policies in Scotland that were deeply damaging to the country's economic prospects, especially the hated poll tax mentioned in the previous chapter. Her ideology of privatization, antiunionism, centralization, and competition flew in the face of values and institutions cherished by many Scots—community and local control. In 1987, when Conservatives won yet another government term without any support from Scotland, an organization called the Campaign for a Scottish Assembly called for a convention to hammer out the terms of Scottish home rule. The Labour Party joined with Liberal Democrats, the Scottish Trades Unions Council, the vast majority of Scotland's regional and district councils, the Scottish churches, and the SNP to develop a blueprint for the future. The document they produced proved unwieldy and impractical, but the process had committed the Labour Party to a Scottish assembly. When it came to power in 1997—the Conservatives having won not a single seat in either Scotland or Wales--devolution was high on its agenda.

The people of Wales seem to have possessed as strong a sense of identity as those of Scotland, but its expression in nationalism and a separation from England never matched that of its northern Celtic neighbor. The cultural aspects of Welshness, especially the revival of its language, gained attention throughout the 1970s and 1980s, but notions of independence or a home rule kind of assembly had little support. The government's breaking of the miners' strike in 1984 and the introduction of the poll tax in 1989 caused real anger toward the Conservatives. A strong sense of injustice prevailed and helped to reduce the number of Tories returned to Parliament in 1992 from fourteen to six, but it did not translate into a movement for devolution. The actions and ill-considered rhetoric of John Major's secretary of state for Wales, John Redwood (1951-), went further to awake a sense of nationalism. He seemed to go out of his way to offend Welsh people, not only cutting the budget for the Welsh Development Agency by almost two-thirds, but also offering gratuitous remarks about the people he administered. His behavior led the leader of the Welsh Liberal Democrats to protest that "the people of Wales are sick of being treated like a colonial outpost. The new viceroy Mr Redwood is the last straw." The reference to the position of viceroy called up images of colonial rule in India. Indeed, one pundit claimed that Redwood had brought Labour politicians around to strong national feelings of their constituents. As the party's shadow secretary of state for Wales told his colleagues at the 1994 party conference, "Like the Scots, we are a nation. We have our own country. We have our own language, our own history, traditions, ethics, values and pride."[5]

Even then, devolution in the form of a separate national assembly held little relevance for most Welsh voters. Their focus, given the state of the economy and the level of unemployment, centered much more on ousting the Conservatives from power and putting in a Labour government. When devolution did come with Tony Blair's victory in 1997, it was because of the campaign urged by the Scots, not the Welsh. Wales rode the coattails of the Scottish nationalist movement and benefitted from the pressure created by its fellow Celts. On July 1, 1999, Queen Elizabeth opened the Parliament at Holyrood in Edinburgh, the first meeting of Scottish representatives in more than 300 years. She listened respectfully as the first minister, Donald Dewar, told the gathering that the day was "about more than our politics and our laws. This is about who we are, how we carry ourselves. There is a new voice in the land, the voice of a democratic Parliament."[6] The Queen and the Prince of Wales had opened the Welsh Assembly in Cardiff earlier, in May, to much less fanfare because the Welsh had only barely voted in favor of devolution, with only 50 percent of the electorate even bothering to go to the polls.

PEACE IN NORTHERN IRELAND

Devolution for Northern Ireland was tied inextricably to the resolution of the "Troubles" and, indeed, formed one element of the terms of the Good Friday Agreement. Efforts to arrive at a meaningful peace between the 48 percent of the population that considered themselves Protestant and British and the 45 percent that identified as Irish Catholics had gone on for a number of years, without success. In the thirty years since the outbreak of the violence in 1969, nearly 3,500 people had been killed. A breakthrough occurred with the intervention of U.S. president Bill Clinton in the process during a visit to Northern Ireland in 1995. With his charm, charisma, and political ingenuity, Clinton cajoled the parties from their intransigent positions and enabled them to sit down together. He publicly recognized Gerry Adams (1948-), leader of Sinn Féin, granting him status as a credible participant in the peace talks denied him by unionists. He persuaded moderate unionists and British politicians that the United States could play a useful role—in the past, U.S. involvement in the affairs of Northern Ireland had largely consisted of contributing funds to arm the nationalist cause through the Irish Northern Aid Committee, known as NORAID. Now the Americans were regarded in a much more constructive light, providing some degree of optimism that this time, things might be different.

Clinton appointed former senator George Mitchell as special envoy to Northern Ireland to get new talks underway. The major obstacle to be overcome concerned the issue of arms. The unionists demanded that the IRA "decommission" their weapons before they would entertain any notion of talks. Sinn Féin insisted that talks begin without any preconditions, a negotiating position that only slightly disguised the fact that it had no ability to compel the IRA to disarm. Mitchell knew that and produced a set of guidelines designed to change the focus in such a way as to get around the impasse. The Mitchell Principles, as they came to be called, urged the parties to accept a commitment to nonviolence. The pledge to pursue "exclusively peaceful methods" by both unionists and republicans enabled them to circumvent the question of actual arms and allowed talks to proceed.[7]

Progress was agonizingly slow. Some important unionist leaders, such as Ian Paisley of the influential and large Democratic Unionist Party (DUP), refused to participate, whereas IRA splinter groups such as the Real IRA rejected peace outright. But by the spring of 1998, because of the herculean efforts of people like John Hume (1937-), head of the Social Democratic and Labour Party, and David

Trimble (1944-), leader of the Ulster Unionist Party, negotiators had hammered out the Belfast Agreement, an accord that became known as the Good Friday Agreement after the day on which it was signed.

The number of parties involved in the conflict made for a complicated and complex deal. In two interconnected documents, its terms included accords among the political parties of Northern Ireland itself; between Northern Ireland and the Republic of Ireland to the south; between Northern Ireland and the United Kingdom; and between the United Kingdom and the Republic of Ireland. Among themselves, the eight political parties composed of Northern Irish unionists and republicans acknowledged that a majority of the people of their country wished to remain within the United Kingdom and that a large portion of the population, along with the majority of people in the Republic of Ireland, sought a united Ireland. That said, they pledged (1) that until a majority of the Northern Irish wished to join in a united Ireland, the province would remain within the United Kingdom and (2) that should such a majority emerge, the governments of the United Kingdom and Ireland were bound to make unification happen. This provision required the Republic of Ireland to change its 1937 constitution to revise the articles that claimed all of Ireland for the republic and extended the laws of the republic to the northern counties.

The Good Friday Agreement created a legislature for Northern Ireland like those enjoyed by Scotland and Wales within the United Kingdom. The Northern Ireland Assembly, as it was called, joined with a new Northern Ireland Executive to establish a devolved government emphasizing power sharing between unionists and republicans. To ensure that no single party monopolized control, a number of "key decisions" would require cross-community consensus. The executive would be made up of a first minister, a deputy first minister, and as many as ten departmental ministers. The first and deputy first ministers would come from different sides and the ministers would be chosen so as to provide equal representation. A series of intergovernmental councils between Ireland, Northern Ireland, and the United Kingdom would work to smooth relations and help make the Good Friday Agreement work. The terms of the agreement would be put to a vote in two referenda held in May 1998 and required that both northern and southern regions ratify it.

The results of the referenda proved gratifyingly positive. Turnout in the Republic of Ireland was relatively disappointing at 56 percent—an indication, most likely, of how drained the population had been by the Troubles—but of that number, 94 percent voted to amend the constitution so as to accommodate the Good Friday Agreement. A much larger proportion of the Northern Ireland population went to the polls—81 percent—and 71 percent of voters approved of the agreement. It was this substantial consensus that the Real IRA sought to disrupt with the bombing at Omagh, but its actions served only to steel the resolve of those intent on peace.

The Good Friday Agreement went into force in December 1999, but almost immediately the devolved Northern Ireland government foundered on the questions of the decommissioning of arms and security arrangements. The British government suspended the assembly and resumed direct rule as distrust on both sides of the political divide made it impossible for the assembly and the executive to work meaningfully. In May 2000 the IRA began to disarm, allowing the devolved government to take over the reins of power again, but over the next seven years, as the paramilitaries of both unionists and republicans continued to carry out violent acts, the path of devolution became strewn with failure. In the meantime, in 2003 Ian Paisley's antiagreement DUP ousted the proagreement Ulster Unionist Party from power in the Assembly, further destabilizing the situation.

The year 2002 saw an outbreak of sectarian violence attributed to the IRA, followed by a police raid on the offices of Sinn Féin. Unionists called for the expulsion of Sinn Féin from the government, and in this atmosphere, Britain once again dissolved the Assembly and instituted direct rule. Negotiations seeking to create trust among the parties took place over the next few years. In 2005, the IRA, under pressure from Northern Ireland Catholics and Sinn Féin, declared an end to its armed struggle and ordered its units to "dump arms." Unionists continued to be skeptical, but when in early 2007 Sinn Féin agreed to accept and participate in the creation of new police and justice systems—long regarded as legitimate targets of the republican campaign of violence—the intransigence of the unionists softened. In March 2007, archenemies Paisley and Gerry Adams sat down to talks that resulted in the announcement of a historic power-sharing agreement. On May 8, Paisley and Sinn Féin's Martin McGuinness (1950-) took office as first and deputy first minister, respectively, beginning a period that, although not problem free, augured well for the future. Despite sporadic outbursts of sectarian violence, the Northern Ireland Assembly and its executive were able to hammer out a settlement in 2010 creating a ministry of justice and a new police force, replacing the notorious Royal Irish Constabulary with the Police Service of Northern Ireland.

A number of issues continued to plague Protestants and Catholics in the years following 2010. Some of them were economic and financial, but given enough money, they were not all that hard to solve. In December of 2014, the United Kingdom government agreed to grant £200 billion to Northern Ireland to address inequities of welfare payments and housing that contributed to ongoing distrust. The most contentious and intractable problems related to the cultural symbols each side mobilized as they asserted their identities—parades, marches, flags, and emblems. These may seem unimportant, even silly, to us looking in from the outside, but as reflections of deeply held convictions and reminders of centuries-old hatreds, they possess extraordinary power to disturb the peace. At the time of this writing, United Kingdom and Northern Ireland negotiators have still not been able to arrive at an accord that would put these highly charged issues to rest. Worse still, revelations that the IRA had participated in the killing of one of its former members in August 2015 has led to a crisis of conviction about the future of shared government. The first minister has stepped down, and it may well be that the government at Westminster will once again take control of Northern Ireland.

A MULTICULTURAL SOCIETY

Multicultural Britain: commuters in central London, 2015

The immigration of former colonial subjects—Indians, Pakistanis, West Indians, and Africans—that had alarmed so many in the 1960s, 1970s, and 1980s reached a critical mass by 2000, despite the restrictions placed on immigration by various acts passed in 1962, 1971, and 1981. In 2001, according to the census of that year, 1.15 million "blacks" resided in the United Kingdom, constituting some 2 percent of the total British population. The 2011 census counted 1.9 million "blacks," who made up 3 percent of the total population of 63 million Britons. When other nonwhite people are added, including those who list themselves as mixed race, the total number of people of color in Britain rises to constitute 13 percent of the population. In London the number of white residents fell for the first time to less than half of all residents, from 58 percent in 2001 to 45 percent in 2011. The trend toward a broadly diverse society across Great Britain will only continue—in 2005, 35 percent of the children born in England and Wales were nonwhite. Slightly less than 60 percent of Britons identified themselves as Christian in the 2011 census—a drop of 13 points over the past decade—whereas 25 percent claim no religion at all (an increase of 10 points) and 5 percent call themselves Muslim, up 2 percent since 2001. The total population of England and Wales (56.1 million) grew by 7 percent, an increase shared by all regions; 7.5 million of them were born outside the United Kingdom, a reflection in part of Britain's membership in the EU, which entails a commitment to allowing European migrants to freely enter the country.

The influx of people from former British colonies and the increasing number of British-born people of color has dramatically altered the complexion of British society, literally and figuratively. The large urban centers of the United Kingdom boast vibrant multicultural populations, whose economic contributions have made them a force to be reckoned with. (This is not to discount the fact that nonwhite unemployment rates in Britain surpass those of white Britons or to suggest that racial disparities and racial discrimination do not exist. They most certainly do.) Black and Asian politicians have emerged to take seats on county and borough councils and in Parliament. In 1992, six black MPs represented various London constituencies; by 1997, their numbers had grown to nine; today, twenty-eight blacks and Asians sit in the House of Commons. They hold seats in the House of Lords, occupy some of the highest positions in the labor movement, chair the boards of numerous corporations, and run some of the most vital British industries. Politicians of all stripes cannot ignore their new constituents—although, to be sure, far-right groups use them to espouse a "white Britain" policy as we will see later in the chapter—and have had to adjust their positions accordingly. In one of the more incredible instances of political accommodation to the reality of a new, multicultural British society, Foreign Minister William Hague (1961-) announced to the House of Commons in 2013 that Britain would pay reparations for the damage it had done as a colonial power in Kenya.

This remarkable development arose from a case brought by four elderly Kenyans—Wambuga wa Nyingi, Jane Muthoni Mara, Paolo Nzili, and Gitu wa Kahengeri. They sued the British government for the treatment they had suffered during the Mau Mau war of the 1950s in colonial detention camps. Nyingi had been badly beaten and disfigured during nine years of imprisonment; Mara was repeatedly raped and otherwise sexually abused; and Nzili was castrated. "I felt completely destroyed and without hope [in the camps]," the eighty-five-year-old man told reporters.[10] The government acknowledged that torture and abuse had taken place, but it declined to accept responsibility. That responsibility had passed to the Kenyan government at the time of independence, it contended.

But Britain's High Court ruled otherwise. The plaintiffs, it decided in 2011, had demonstrated that they had "arguable cases in law" and could go forward with their claims. The government appealed, arguing that far too much time had passed since the events had taken place and that it could not adequately defend itself in such circumstances, given the difficulty in obtaining the witnesses and the records it would need. In October 2012, the High Court once again found against the government and ordered that the case proceed. This time the Mau Mau veterans were not present to hear the judgment, but from Nairobi they expressed how "absolutely delighted" they were when they learned of the court's landmark decision. Their delight increased exponentially when, in June 2013, Hague announced in Parliament that the government had decided to settle the claims of some 5,000 Mau Mau fighters who, the government recognized, had been "subject to torture and other forms of ill treatment at the hands of the colonial administration" while held in detention camps. "We understand the pain and grievance felt by those who were involved in the events of the Emergency in Kenya," Hague told MPs, and "the British government sincerely regrets that these abuses took place, and that they marred Kenya's progress towards independence." Britain agreed to pay out nearly £20 million and help build a memorial in Nairobi commemorating the suffering and injustices undergone by Kenyans at the hands of imperial Britain. In settling the claims of the Mau Mau plaintiffs, the government refused to accept any legal liability, arguing that the case did not establish "a precedent in relation to any other former British colonial administration."[11] Others saw things differently, and legal commentators suggested that Britons should expect a number of similar cases to come forward. As of October 31, 2014, 41,000 Kenyans have joined in a second suit against the British government for torture and abuse suffered during Mau Mau.

The immigration of peoples from former British colonies and from the member states of the EU has provoked a political backlash from certain elements of the British population. This is not new, as we saw in the previous chapter. Extreme right-wing parties such as the British National Party (BNP) have thrived in certain constituencies since the 1970s. The BNP's frankly neo-fascist pronouncements

A PLACE IN TIME

Identities and Traditions at the Liverpool Football Club

On March 8, 2015, two solicitors, Asif Bodi and Abubakar Bhula, took advantage of the halftime break in the Liverpool Football Club's match against Blackburn to say their evening prayers in the stairwell of Anfield Stadium. As Bodi explained later, "We have a small window in which to pray, a bit like the transfer window in football. Once that closes the chance has gone. That day, the time came for prayer and the window would have closed before the game finished so we did it at half-time." Another Liverpool fan, Stephen Dodd, snapped a photo of the two men kneeling on their prayer rug with his phone and tweeted it out with the message, "Muslims praying at half time at the match yesterday #DISGRACE."

Dodd's tweet set off a heated reaction. One called him a "raging bigot." Another urged "respect to them, brother, can't believe people think this is disgusting." A third asked, "Is this a joke? What did these guys do to harm anyone?" Bodi and Buhla expressed gratitude for the support they received, but not everyone championed their choice of location. One self-identified Muslim protested that "the men should have just prayed it [sic] in a private place and not at the bottom of a stairwell midgame." Less edifying was the comment of one man who insisted that "like FGM [female genital mutilation] and the Burkha, this has little to do with religion, this is simply Political Islam exercising its power over the unbelievers, the Kafirs [sic]. YOU!"[8]

The Liverpool Football Club reported Dodd's tweet to the Merseyside police, who returned it to the club for its adjudication. While deliberating his fate, the club issued a reminder that it does not tolerate discrimination

alienated many people and have given way to more reasonable-sounding groups such as the English Defence League (EDL), Britain First, and the United Kingdom Independent Party (UKIP). These groups downplay the racial and ethnic composition of the people they wish to exclude from society and focus instead on what they call threats to "Britishness," particularly Islam. Britain First, for example, which appeared in 2011 as an offshoot of the BNP, claims on its homepage that it is "not against individual Muslims, but specifically against the doctrine and religion of Islam itself as an ideology."[12] The EDL, founded in 2009, describes itself as "a human rights organization that exists to protect the inalienable rights of all people to protest against radical Islam's encroachment into the lives of non-Muslims."[13] It explicitly denounces racism and tries to recruit blacks, Jews, and gays to its ranks. Few have taken up the invitation.

of any kind and promised that it "will take action." This prompted a fan named "Joe" to ask, "So we aren't allowed Freedom of Speech anymore?" He predicted that "Stephen Dodd will get his season ticket revoked and it will be given to thomas cook to advertise in competitions for some one from a far foreign land who'll spend £250 in the club shop."[9]

This incident, the actors involved, and the sentiments expressed by them reflect the makeup of Britain today and encapsulate virtually all of the issues facing its citizens: immigration, ethnicity, assimilation, multiculturalism, racism, anti-Islamic fears, integration with Europe, Britain's place in the world, and inequalities of wealth. Consider the two men praying. Bodi and Bhula are solicitors, beneficiaries of a presumably middle-class lifestyle afforded by their occupation, which, not incidentally, commits them to upholding and implementing British law. They are ardent fans of Liverpool football, following their beloved team along with thousands of other obsessive Scouse. And they are Muslims, practicing the requirements of their faith in a public place so as to reconcile their football fanaticism with the tenets of their religion. For many fans, Bodi and Bhula's Islamic faith poses no problems at all; they seem to be average Britons offending no one. For others, Islam constitutes more than a religion and its adherents have hidden aims: it and they brutally promote an oppressive and retrograde political agenda, especially against women. The actions of the Liverpool Football Club in first reporting Dodd's tweet to the police and then asserting that it will not tolerate discrimination of any kind are a response to a number of racial incidents involving its fans. Finally, the incident conjured up for one commentator the resentment of "foreigners" who enjoy privileges not extended to Britons. Much of the debate over membership in Europe centers on Britain providing benefits to immigrants while its own citizens struggle to maintain a decent standard of living.

The suicide bombings on the British Underground on July 7, 2005—known in shorthand as 7/7—which killed 52 people and injured 700 more, contributed significantly to the popularity of such anti-Islamic sentiments. Britain First and the EDL remain on the political margins, for the most part, limited by their excesses—"Christian patrols" and "invasions" of mosques by Britain First and attacks on Muslims and on halal restaurants during marches by the EDL—to dramatic action but having little influence on parliamentary proceedings. UKIP, by contrast, holds twenty-three seats in the European Parliament, an institution it deems destructive to Britain. Led by Nigel Farage (1964-), UKIP demands stringent restrictions on immigration, severe cutbacks of foreign aid, and the withdrawal of Britain from the EU. In the past year the Eurosceptic party has attracted defectors from the Tory, Liberal Democrat, and Labour parties to its ranks and has won a few by-elections, giving it two seats in Parliament. Its popularity reflects a high degree of anger toward immigration and dissatisfaction with EU policies, which in turn has prompted more mainstream politicians to adopt harder-line positions. Tory Prime Minister David Cameron, for example, promised to hold a referendum on membership in the EU if Conservatives won the May 2015 elections.

Cameron also took the opportunity of a speech before the Munich Security Conference in 2011 to attack multiculturalism, attributing the 7/7 attacks to a "process of radicalization" caused by the abandonment of British values and British character. "Under the doctrine of multiculturalism," he declared, "we have encouraged different cultures to live separate lives. We have even tolerated these segregated communities behaving in ways that run completely counter to our values."[14] Formerly much more moderate in tone when addressing questions of immigration, the prime minister evidently migrated to a far less tolerant position under pressure from a public deeply concerned about maintaining a British way of life.

THE BREAKUP OF BRITAIN?

Cameron's remarks raise the questions posed at the start of this chapter. What is Britishness? Who is British? Does being British entail the abandonment of other aspects of identity, especially racial, ethnic, or religious identity? And if so, what does that mean for the union itself?

For many Scots, the question of an identity separate from the English, Welsh, and Northern Irish involved greater political autonomy if not outright independence from the United Kingdom. In 2007, the SNP, campaigning only in part on a platform calling for greater powers for the Scottish Parliament, won forty-seven seats in that body, just beating out the incumbent Labour Party by a single seat. With the support of the Scottish Greens, a government under the leadership of First Minister Alex Salmond (1954) came to power. In the 2011 election, the SNP won an outright majority, an unusual and unexpected event. Almost immediately, Salmond announced an effort to gain independence for Scotland. He unveiled the "Yes Scotland" campaign in May 2012, calling for a referendum to determine the fate of Scotland within the United Kingdom and thus of the United Kingdom itself. His actions set the ball rolling for the announcement of the oppositional "Better Together"—or No—crusade in June, led by representatives of the Labour, Tory, and Liberal Democrat parties, which would fight to keep Scotland within the union. The No campaign possessed a powerful weapon in its insistence, contrary to Salmond's assertion, that an independent Scotland would not be able to form a currency union with the rest of Britain. Independence, the Nos declared over and over, would put Scotland at great economic risk. For most of 2013 and 2014, the argument seemed to be persuasive. The mainstream politicians in London had little doubt that they would prevail.

In early September 2014, two weeks prior to the day Scots would go to the polls to cast their votes, a YouGov/Times poll shattered their complacency: the No campaign had lost significant ground among likely voters. A second poll released on September 7 sent Westminster into a panic: it showed the Yes side with an out-and-out lead of 51 percent to 49 percent. In Scotland itself, businesses and financial institutions issued dire warnings about the dangers of independence; shares in a number of Scottish firms fell precipitously. All of the major Scottish banks, with the exception of the Royal Bank of Scotland, announced that they would move their headquarters south of the border into England should independence occur.

The two September polls galvanized the opposition. The mainstream parties buried their differences in the face of the prospect of the United Kingdom breaking up. The former Labour prime minister, Gordon Brown, in one of the most important actions of his political career, persuaded David Cameron and Nick Clegg to issue a joint declaration that if Scots voted against independence, Labour, the Tories, and the Liberal Democrats would initiate legislation to give "extensive new powers" to the Scottish Parliament at Holyrood. Newspapers plastered

Scottish referendum for independence, September 2015

"The Vow," as they termed it, across their front pages; the No campaign hoped that the promise would provide a kind of cover to those who might support Scottish independence in their hearts but not their heads. Brown rallied Scottish Labour to the No side in a series of appearances throughout Scotland. His passion and energy in favor of maintaining the union led one pundit to describe the last two weeks of the campaign as "Gordon's second premiership."[15]

The stakes could not have been higher for the future of the United Kingdom. The emotions and turmoil of one of the most extraordinary weeks in British political history captivated Britons and people all across the globe. In the end, the combination of fears for the economic survivability of an independent Scotland—and, most observers conclude, Gordon Brown's private and public interventions on the No side that resulted in the promise to increase Scotland's devolved power—decided the issue. The results of the September 18, 2014, gave the No campaign 55 percent of the vote. The next day, the prime minister announced the formation of a cross-party committee headed by Lord Kelvin Smith (1944-) to produce recommendations for the further devolution of powers to Scotland by the end of November.

The union might have been saved with the no vote, but the United Kingdom would be decidedly different going forward. Two hours after the referendum results came in, David Cameron went before the cameras at 10 Downing Street and proclaimed that the promised settlement for increased powers for the Scottish Parliament "must take place in tandem with and at the same pace as" what is called "English votes for English laws." "We have heard the voice of Scotland," he declared, "and now the millions of voices of England must also be heard." Amid cries of betrayal by the SNP and Labour Party leaders, the Conservatives promised to introduce reforms that would block Scottish MPs in the Westminster

Parliament from voting on issues that concerned England. Because the Conservatives have become an almost exclusively English party that can count on no electoral support in Scotland and little in Wales and Northern Ireland, the appeal to their constituents in England seemed bald, especially because Labour could hardly register a majority in the English counties. "The cross-party consensus that defeated calls for Scottish independence has been shattered immediately," lamented *The Independent*. Labour leader Ed Miliband (1969-) denounced the prime minister for putting "narrow party political advantage" above the integrity of the Vow.[16] Ex-SNP leader Alex Salmond protested that Scottish voters had been duped by a false pledge to vote against independence.

The Smith Commission began its deliberations in October 2014 and issued its recommendations on November 27. Far reaching in scope, they would give "extensive" new powers to the Scottish Parliament to set taxes, distribute welfare payments, and determine spending in a wide variety of areas. A bill containing the proposed reforms would be introduced in the Westminster Parliament following the election in May 2015. The recommendations immediately generated calls for greater devolution for Wales and Northern Ireland and for the large metropolitan areas of England as well.

Pundits in Britain and across the globe recognized that the election of 2015 would prove to be one of the country's most significant political events in decades, determining the identity and nature of the United Kingdom for the foreseeable future. The outcome, candidates declared, would resolve the issue of the place of each nation within the United Kingdom and, by doing so, potentially alter the 300-year (unwritten) constitution; it would decide whether Britain would remain in the EU or go it alone; and it would address the question of multiculturalism by restricting—or not—immigration and limiting—or not—the benefits immigrants qualified for once in Britain. Certainly other matters came before voters in the course of the campaign, but the parties tended to focus on these three concerns, seeing their emotional value for turning out the voters.

Conservatives pledged to devolve more powers to the Scottish Parliament and Welsh Assembly, but only in the context of English votes for English laws. They promised that a referendum would be held to decide the United Kingdom's future in the EU—in or out—and declared they would do away with the EU's Human Rights Act and replace it with a British bill of rights. On immigration, Conservatives vowed to keep down the numbers of those entering Britain and to impose a four-year waiting period before migrants could claim a variety of benefits. Their coalition partners, the Liberal Democrats, agreed on devolution but wished to stay in the EU, unless the organization sought to transfer significant powers from its member nations to itself; in that case, they would call for a referendum on continuing membership. Their stance on immigration called for more border control. Labour sought to give even greater powers of devolution to Scotland and Wales through a "Home Rule Bill" that would enhance their control over jobs, health, and taxation, and it called for a "people-led Constitutional Convention" to decide the governance of the United Kingdom. Like the Liberal Democrats, Labour did not support an initial referendum on the EU, preferring instead a "lock" that would ensure that no transfer of power from Britain to the EU could take place without one. Its members wished to see Britain taking a stronger leadership role within the union. They, too, wanted more border control and demanded a cap on the number of workers coming into the country from outside the EU. They sought to protect British workers by making it illegal for employers to exploit migrants and argued for a two-year waiting period before EU migrants could obtain unemployment benefits.The SNP declared that it would "always support independence," seeing devolution as falling short of its goals. It opposed a referendum on continuing membership in the EU, insisting that if there was one, all of the United Kingdom countries would have to vote in favor of exiting for it to take effect. Its immigration stance called for "sensible" policies that would meet the economic needs of Scotland. UKIP argued for greater tax powers for the devolved assemblies, but demanded that the formula for devising financial aid to Scotland and Wales be altered to give England a better deal; it also called outright for English-only votes in the Westminster Parliament. It took a vociferous stand on membership in the EU—Britain should leave it and ensure that all legislative powers remain in Westminster. It demanded a cap on skilled workers coming into the United Kingdom and an outright five-year ban on unskilled labor. For those immigrants currently in the country, they should have to wait five years before they could claim any benefits.

In the weeks leading up to the election, the polls showed a close race between the Conservative/Liberal Democrat alliance and Labour. UKIP appeared to be making gains among both constituencies with its Eurosceptic message. Everyone received a jolt when, on May 16, 2015, the returns gave a decisive victory to the Conservative Party under David Cameron. It won so many seats—holding a majority of fifteen—that it no longer needed a coalition partner. The Liberal Democrats lost badly, reducing their number in Parliament from fifty-seven to eight; Labour actually increased its overall tally of votes but lost twenty-four seats. UKIP fared well among voters, coming in third behind the Conservatives and Labour, but it only won one seat. The big winner, after Cameron, was the SNP under Nicola Sturgeon (1970-). The nationalists took fifty-six of Scotland's fifty-nine constituencies, a figure that made it the third largest party in Parliament. They did so at the expense of Labour, which lost dismally in Scotland. Nick Clegg, Ed Miliband, and Nigel Farage resigned their party leadership posts, although UKIP rejected Farage's gesture and kept him on.

What did all this mean, apart from revealing the bankruptcy of polling in the age of cell phones and social media? On the face of it, the election seemed to demonstrate a United Kingdom divided politically along national lines. Scotland had gone almost entirely for independence from Britain; Wales had voted Labour; the DUP had taken the preponderance of votes in Northern Ireland; and England had been utterly dominated by the Conservatives.

This would suggest that there is little, politically and perhaps culturally as well, to keep the United Kingdom united. England looks to have taken a harder stance on the relationship of Scotland to the Westminster Parliament, on membership in the EU, and on further immigration, at least if the votes won by Conservatives and UKIP are combined. Scotland wishes to be gone from the United Kingdom,

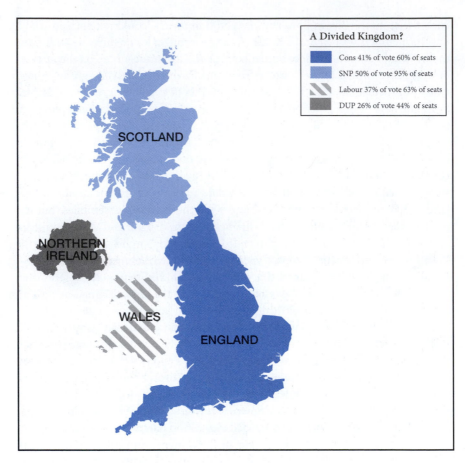

MAP 15.1
A Divided Kingdom?

according to the results. Wales retains its working-class and liberal character, and Northern Ireland appears to insist on holding on to the right to display the provocative flag and symbols of union with Britain, a main plank of the DUP's campaign platform. But if we drill down into the numbers we see a much more nuanced picture. Because of the British system of assigning votes to actual seats won, the results do not tally with the preferences expressed at the voting booth. England's Conservatives won only 41 percent of votes cast, but it earned 60 percent of the seats; Labour won only 37 percent of the vote in Wales but got 63 percent of its seats; numbers for the DUP in Northern Ireland came in at 26 percent and 44 percent, respectively; and in the most unbalanced return, the SNP won 95 percent of Scotland's seats with only 50 percent of the vote. Had a system of proportional voting been in place, the decisive Conservative victory in England and the resounding success of the SNP in Scotland would have been considerably muted.

Still, the strength of the SNP in Parliament, along with the Conservative government's plans to extend the devolution of powers to major urban areas in

England, have given rise to concern among a number of scholars and lawyers about the fate of the United Kingdom. Worried that "the piecemeal development of devolution means that the overall constitutional fabric of the UK has been weakened," they issued a report calling for constitutional reforms that would save the United Kingdom. Entitled "A Constitutional Crossroads: Ways Forward for the United Kingdom," its authors—including the historian Linda Colley (1949-), whose 1992 *Britons: Forging the Nation, 1707–1837* set off a scholarly stampede to analyze the relationship of England to Wales, Scotland, and Ireland—appeal for the creation of a "charter of the union" that would create the scaffolding for "a fair and durable settlement between the four nations." Optimally, this charter would give way to a written constitution, in which formal arrangements would be laid out delineating the powers granted to each nation and the relationship among them would be spelled out. Chief among the issues requiring attention is the manner in which finances are distributed across the four nations; resentment over the existing formula threatens the stability of the union and contributes to the widespread perception of unfairness. The authors recommend also that "English votes for English laws" be implemented in any agreement so as to reflect the disproportionate size of the English population within the union. Finally, they argue that the national government must pay concerted attention to the relationships between the four nations, suggesting that a single secretary of state for the union replace the three discrete cabinet ministers who now oversee the devolved nations. Overall, the current situation of ad hoc devolution, the prospect of more ad hoc actions, and the possibility of a showdown between the Westminster and Scottish parliaments create too much uncertainty and incoherence, the report notes, damaging Britain's ability to function effectively in the larger world outside its borders.[17]

One element of that ability will depend on the referendum to be put forward to voters by 2017 on the question of remaining within the EU. Conservatives, who campaigned on the promise to do away with the EU's Human Rights Act and replace it with a British bill of rights, appear to have accepted the reality that abolishing the EU measure will not only be difficult but also carry significant repercussions. The Northern Ireland peace agreement, to name but one instance, is predicated on the acceptance of the Human Rights Act, and doing away with it might open the door to an unraveling of other elements of the accord. Scotland, much of Wales, and Sinn Féin in Northern Ireland strongly support EU membership; should English voters choose to leave the EU, the constitutional showdown would have serious consequences for the United Kingdom. And should Britain leave the EU altogether—which a significant element within the Conservative Party, including its leader, David Cameron, opposes—it is hard to see how effective the United Kingdom would be in influencing the decisions taken in Europe or in any other part of the world. A retreat to a kind of "little Englandism" reminiscent of Gladstone would not serve British international interests well. (The recent influx of millions of refugees and migrants to Europe from the Middle East, North Africa, and Afghanistan demonstrates how crucial it is for Europe as a whole to establish policies pertaining to issues that extend beyond its borders.)

That view of a "little England" of rolling hills and quaint little villages where everyone knew their place exerts a powerful tug on the hearts and imaginations of many Britons—Scottish, Welsh, and Irish as well as English, ironically. It reflects a longing for a society devoid of ethnic, cultural, and religious conflict, a society that, as this book has tried to show, never in fact existed. Britain has always been much more than "England," and it is only by taking into account the histories of the four nations and their empire that a more complete understanding of the complex interactions of their constituent parts can be achieved.

NOTES

1. Marion Radford in *Belfast Telegraph*, August 10, 2008. http://www.belfasttelegraph.co.uk/sunday-life/they-took-away-a-lot-of-good-lives-that-day-28442738.html/.
2. Kevin Connolly, "How the Omagh Case Unravelled," *BBC News*, December 20, 2007, http://news.bbc.co.uk/2/hi/uk_news/northern_ireland/7154952.stm/.
3. The Northern Ireland Peace Agreement, p. 3. http://peacemaker.un.org/sites/peacemaker.un.org/files/IE%20GB_980410_Northern%20Ireland%20Agreement.pdf/.
4. See Krishan Kumar, "Empire, Nation, and National Identities," in Andrew Thomas, ed., *Britain's Experience of Empire in the Twentieth Century* (Oxford, 2012), p. 324.
5. Quoted in Martin Johnes, *Wales since 1939* (Manchester, 2012), pp. 335, 336.
6. Quoted in T. M. Devine, *The Scottish Nation, 1700–2007* (London, 2006), p. 632.
7. Quoted in Feargal Cochrane, *Northern Ireland. The Reluctant Peace* (New Haven, 2013), p. 167.
8. "Liverpool FC Muslim Fans Labeled 'Disgrace' for Praying at Anfield Thank Fans for Their Support," *Liverpool Echo*, March 12, 2015. http://www.liverpoolecho.co.uk/news/liverpool-news/liverpool-fc-muslim-fans-labelled-8830677/.
9. "Liverpool FC 'Will Take Action' against Fan Who Branded Two Muslim Men a 'Disgrace' for Praying at Anfield," *Liverpool Echo*, April 14, 2015. http://www.liverpoolecho.co.uk/news/liverpool-news/liverpool-fc-will-take-action-9044008/.

TIMELINE

1997	Tony Blair elected prime minister
1998	Good Friday Agreement establishing peace plan for Northern Ireland signed
	IRA bombing in Omagh, Northern Ireland
1999	Queen Elizabeth opens Welsh assembly and Scottish Parliament
2000	IRA begins to disarm; Northern Ireland assembly meets as part of peace process
2005	Islamist bombings of London Underground kill 52, injure 700
2007	Gordon Brown replaces Tony Blair as Labour prime minister

10. "Mau Mau Uprising: Kenyans Win UK Torture Ruling," *BBC News*, October 5, 2012, accessed September 17, 2014, http://www.bbc.com/news/uk-19843719/.

11. The Rt. Hon. William Hague, MP, "Statement to Parliament on Settlement of Mau Mau Claims," June 6, 2013, accessed September 17, 2014, https://www.gov.uk/government/news/statement-to-parliament-on-settlement-of-mau-mau-claims/.

12. See "Britain First Homepage—Is Britain First against All Muslims or Just Extremists?" http://www.britainfirst.org/.

13. Quoted in Lauren Collins, "England, Their England," *The New Yorker*, July 4, 2011, p. 28.

14. Quoted in Collins, "England, Their England," p. 28.

15. Quoted in Severin Carrell, Nicholas Watt, and Patrick Wintour, "The Real Story of the Scottish Referendum: The Final Days of the Fight for Independence," *The Guardian*, December 16, 2014. http://www.theguardian.com/news/2014/dec/16/-sp-real-story-scottish-referendum-final-days-fight-for-independence/.

16. Quoted in Francis Elliott, Lindsay McIntosh, Rachel Sylvester, and Alice Thoson, "Salmond Quits as Powers for Scotland Are Blocked," *The Times*, September 20, 2014, pp. 1–2; Andrew Grice and Oliver Wright, "The Disunited Kingdom," *The Independent*, September 20, 2014, pp. 1, 2.

17. See Bingham Centre for the Rule of Law, *A Constitutional Crossroads: Ways Forward for the United Kingdom* (London, 2015).

FURTHER READING

Bingham Centre for the Rule of Law, *A Constitutional Crossroads: Ways Forward for the United Kingdom* (London, 2015).

Feargal Cochrane, *Northern Ireland. The Reluctant Peace* (New Haven, 2013).

Lauren Collins, "England, Their England," *The New Yorker*, July 4, 2011.

Krishan Kumar, "Empire, Nation, and National Identities," in Andrew Thomas, ed., *Britain's Experience of Empire in the Twentieth Century*. Oxford, 2012.

2009	English Defense League founded
2010	Conservatives and Liberal Party form coalition government under David Cameron
2011	Britain First founded
2012	Scottish independence campaign launched
2012	High Court rules in favor of Mau Mau plaintiffs
2013	Britain pledges to pay reparations to Mau Mau plaintiffs, acknowledges colonial abuses
2014	Referendum on Scottish independence; "no" vote prevails
2015	Conservative Party wins national election outright; Scottish Nationalist Party sweeps Scotland

APPENDIX A

MONARCHS OF GREAT BRITAIN, 1688–2015

William III and Mary II (Stuart)	1688–1702 (Mary dies 1694)
Anne I (Stuart)	1702–1714
George I (Hanover)	1714–1727
George II (Hanover)	1727–1760
George III (Hanover)	1760–1820
George IV (Hanover)	1820–1830
William IV (Hanover)	1830–1837
Victoria I (Hanover)	1837–1901
Edward VII (Windsor)	1901–1910
George V (Windsor)	1910–1936
Edward VIII (Windsor)	1936
George VI (Windsor)	1936–1952
Elizabeth II (Windsor)	1952–

APPENDIX B

PRIME MINISTERS OF GREAT BRITAIN, 1721–2015

The role of prime minister was usually held by the first lord of the Treasury from 1721 to 1783, when the title of prime minister was conferred on William Pitt (the Younger) along with the capacity to control the selection of ministers for his cabinet. At that time, government could be said to be in the hands of a particular party.

Sir Robert Walpole	1721–1742	
John Cateret	1742–1744	
Henry Pelham	1744–1754	
Duke of Newcastle	1754–1756	
William Pitt (the Elder)	1756–1757	
Duke of Newcastle	1757–1762	
Earl of Bute	1762–1763	
George Grenville	1763–1765	
Marquess of Rockingham	1765–1766	
Duke of Grafton	1767–1770	
Lord North	1770–1782	
Earl of Shelbourne	1782–1783	
William Pitt (the Younger)	1783–1801	Tory
Henry Addington	1801–1804	Tory
William Pitt (the Younger)	1804–1806	Tory
Lord Grenville	1806–1807	Whig
Duke of Portland	1807–1809	Tory

Spencer Perceval	1809–1812	Tory
Earl of Liverpool	1812–1827	Tory
George Canning	1827	Tory
Viscount Goderich	1827	Tory
Duke of Wellington	1828–1830	Tory
Earl Grey	1830–1834	Whig
Viscount Melbourne	1834	Whig
Sir Robert Peel	1834–1835	Conservative
Viscount Melbourne	1835–1841	Whig
Sir Robert Peel	1841–1846	Conservative
Lord John Russell	1846–1852	Whig
Earl of Derby	1852	Conservative
Earl of Aberdeen	1852–1855	Whig
Viscount Palmerston	1855–1858	Whig
Earl of Derby	1858–1859	Conservative
Viscount Palmerston	1859–1865	Liberal
Lord John Russell	1865–1866	Liberal
Earl of Derby	1866–1868	Conservative
William Gladstone	1868–1874	Liberal
Benjamin Disraeli	1874–1880	Conservative
William Gladstone	1880–1885	Liberal
Marquess of Salisbury	1885–1886	Conservative
William Gladstone	1886	Liberal
Marquess of Salisbury	1886–1892	Conservative
William Gladstone	1892–1894	Liberal
Earl of Rosebery	1894–1895	Liberal
Marquess of Salisbury	1895–1902	Conservative
A. J. Balfour	1902–1905	Conservative
Sir Henry Campbell-Bannerman	1905–1908	Liberal
H. H. Asquith	1908–1915	Liberal
H. H. Asquith	1915–1916	Coalition
David Lloyd George	1916–1922	Coalition
Andrew Bonar Law	1922–1923	Conservative
Stanley Baldwin	1923–1924	Conservative
J. Ramsay MacDonald	1924	Labour
Stanley Baldwin	1924–1929	Conservative
J. Ramsay MacDonald	1929–1931	Labour
J. Ramsay MacDonald	1931–1935	National
Stanley Baldwin	1935–1937	National
Neville Chamberlain	1937–1940	Conservative
Winston Churchill	1940–1945	Coalition
Clement Attlee	1945–1951	Labour
Winston Churchill	1951–1955	Conservative
Sir Anthony Eden	1955–1957	Conservative

Harold Macmillan	1957–1963	Conservative
Sir Alex Douglas-Home	1963–1964	Conservative
Harold Wilson	1964–1970	Labour
Edward Heath	1970–1974	Conservative
Harold Wilson	1974–1976	Labour
James Callaghan	1976–1979	Labour
Margaret Thatcher	1979–1990	Conservative
John Major	1990–1997	Conservative
Tony Blair	1997–2007	Labour
Gordon Brown	2007–2010	Labour
David Cameron	2010–2015	Coalition
David Cameron	2015–	Conservative

CREDITS

Intro.1 Liverpool   The West Prospect of the Town of Liverpool, as it appeared about the year 1680, lithograph by John R. Isaac (litho), Eyes Jnr, John (fl.1730–40) (after)/Private Collection/Bridgeman Images

Photo 1.1 Liverpool   George's Dock, Liverpool, c.1830 (w/c with gouache over chalk on paper), Cox, David (1783–1859)/© Lady Lever Art Gallery, National Museums Liverpool/Bridgeman Images

Photo 1.2   James entering Dublin after the Battle of the Boyne (litho), English School, (20th century)/Private Collection/Bridgeman Images

Photo 1.3   Anne (1665–1714) Queen of Great Britain and Ireland from 1702. Second daughter of James II and sister of Mary II. Act of Union between England and Scotland read before Queen Anne in 1707. Copperplate engraving 1826/Universal History Archive/UIG/Bridgeman Images

Photo 2.1 vignette   Scene in Change Alley during the South Sea Bubble, 1853 (engraving) (b/w photo), Ward, Edward Matthew (1816–79) (after)/Private Collection/Bridgeman Images

Photo 2.2   Illustration for the 'Black Man's Lament or How to Make Sugar' by Amelia Opie (1769–1853) 1813 (coloured

Photo 4.4 Liverpool	Sailors throwing slaves overboard, from Torrey's 'American Slave Trade', 1822 (engraving) (b&w photo), American School, (19th century)/Private Collection/Bridgeman Images
Photo 4.5	The Burning and Plundering of Newgate and Setting the Felons at Liberty by the Mob, 1780 (engraving), English School, (18th century) (after)/London Metropolitan Archives, City of London/Bridgeman Images
Photo 5.1 vignette	© Mary Evans Picture Library
Photo 5.2 Liverpool	Death of Nelson (engraving), English School, (19th century)/Private Collection/© Look and Learn/Bridgeman Images
Photo 5.3	The Queen's Own Royal Dublin Militia going into action at the Battle of Vinegar Hill, Wexford, 1798 (w/c on paper), Sadler, William II (c.1782–1839)/Private Collection/Bridgeman Images
Photo 5.4	View of the Heads, at the entrance into Port Jackson, c.1822 (w/c on paper), Lycett, Joseph (c.1775–1828)/Art Gallery of New South Wales, Sydney, Australia/Bridgeman Images
Photo 5.5	Freetown, Sierra Leone (engraving), English School, (19th century)/Private Collection/Bridgeman Images
Photo 6.1 vignette	Rebecca and her Daughters (engraving) (b&w photo), Leech, John (1817–64)/Private Collection/Bridgeman Images
Photo 6.2 Liverpool	Excavation of Olive Mount, Four Miles from Liverpool, plate 3 from 'Liverpool and Manchester Railway', engraved by S.G. Hughes, pub. by Ackermann & Co., 1833 (litho), Bury, Thomas Talbot (1811–77) (after)/Private Collection/Bridgeman Images
Photo 6.3	Installation of a Knight of the Bath, or delicate recreations on board a Polacre, 1820 (hand-coloured engraving), Cruikshank, George (1792–1878)/Private Collection/The Stapleton Collection/Bridgeman Images
Photo 6.4	View of the Great Chartist Meeting on Kennington Common, 1848 (daguerreotype), Kilburn, William Edward (fl.1846–62)/Royal Collection Trust © Her Majesty Queen Elizabeth II, 2015/Bridgeman Images
Photo 6.5	The Irish Famine: Scene at the Gate of the Work-House, c.1846 (engraving) (b&w photo), English School, (19th century)/Private Collection/Bridgeman Images

Photo 7.1 vignette	Caged prisoners on route to Botany Bay (litho), English School, (19th century)/Private Collection/Bridgeman Images
Photo 7.2 Liverpool	The Hon. East India Company's steamer Nemesis and the boats of The Sulpher, Calliope,Larne and Starling destroying the Chinese war junks in Anson's Bay. January 7, 1841, illustration from 'England's Battles by Sea and Land' by Lieut. Col. Williams (engraving), Terry, G.W. (18th Century) (after)/ Private Collection/Ken Welsh/Bridgeman Images
Photo 7.3	The Rebellion of Half-Breeds in Canada under Louis Riel (engraving), English School, (19th century)/Private Collection/© Look and Learn/Illustrated Papers Collection/ Bridgeman Images
Photo 7.4	The Battle of Blood River, December 16, 1838. The Great Trek, South Africa, 19th century./De Agostini Picture Library/Bridgeman Images
Photo 7.5	Mary Evans Picture Library/Everett Collection
Photo 8.1 vignette	Scene in the 'No Popery Riots', Brimingham 1868 AD (litho), Paget, Henry Marriott (1856–1936)/Private Collection/Bridgeman Images
Photo 8.2 Liverpool	Emigrants at Liverpool Docks, c.1850s (engraving), English School, (19th century)/Private Collection/Bridgeman Images
Photo 8.3	Mary Evans Picture Library/Everett Collection
Photo 8.4	Evening at Balmoral Castle: the stags brought home, 1853–54 (w/c & bodycolour on paper), Haag, Carl (1820–1915)/Royal Collection Trust © Her Majesty Queen Elizabeth II, 2015/ Bridgeman Images
Photo 8.5	Mutineers about to be blown from guns by the Bengal Horse Artillery, c.1858 (w/c on paper), Norie, Orlando (1832–1901)/ National Army Museum, London/Bridgeman Images
Photo 8.6	© Mary Evans Picture Library
Photo 9.1 vignette	Homeless Scots (engraving), Scottish School, (19th century)/Private Collection/Bridgeman Images
Photo 9.2	Tapping rubber trees, Ceylon (b/w photo), English Photographer, (20th century)/Private Collection/© Look and Learn/Elgar Collection/Bridgeman Images

Photo 11.5	Adapting industry to the war effort: Female workers in a lathe workshop at the Cunard Shell Works in Bootle, August–September 1917 (b/w photo), Lemere, Henry Bedford (1865–1944)/Private Collection/© Historic England/ Bridgeman Images
Photo 11.6	Union of Muslim and Christian flags during the Egyptian Revolution of 1919 (b/w photo)/ Private Collection/Bridgeman Images
Photo 12.1	Bloody Sunday, 1920 (colour litho), Irish School, (20th century)/Private Collection/© Leemage/Bridgeman Images
Photo 12.2	Trouble in Hammersmith Broadway During the Passing of a Milk Lorry: An Arrested Man Between Two Constables, from 'The Illustrated London News' 15th May 1926 (b&w photo)/The Illustrated London News Picture Library, London, UK/Bridgeman Images
Photo 12.3	Gandhi breaking the Salt Laws - the civil disobedience in India, from 'The Illustrated London News', 26th April 1930 (b&w photo)/The Illustrated London News Picture Library, London, UK/Bridgeman Images
Photo 12.4	Mahatma Gandhi, Lord Sankey and Pandit Malaviya at the Round Table Conference, 1931 (b/w photo), German Photographer (20th Century)/© SZ Photo/Bridgeman Images
Photo 13.1 vignette	Evacuee's bound for Canada arrives at their assembly point for registration before going on to join their ship, August 1940 (b/w photo),/© Mirrorpix/Bridgeman Images
Photo 13.2	David Low, Evening Standard, 18 June 1940, from the British Cartoon Archive, University of Kent, www.cartoons .ac.uk © Associated Newspapers Ltd./Solo Syndication
Photo 13.3	© Punch Limited
Photo 13.4	© Imperial War Museums (HU 2769)
Photo 13.5 Liverpool	©Mirrorpix/courtesy Everett Collection
Photo 13.6	London Fire Service fighting a burning building after a bombing raid by the Luftwaffe (b/w photo),/London, UK/ © Mirrorpix/Bridgeman Images

Photo 13.7	Families take cover from the Luftwaffe bombing of London in a disused London Underground railway tunnel, September 1940 (b/w photo),/London, UK/© Mirrorpix/ Bridgeman Images
Photo 14.1 vignette	© John Lennon/Keystone Features/Getty Images
Photo 14.2	Members of the All India Muslim League during their parade in London, 15th August 1946 (b/w photo), English Photographer, (20th century)/Sean Sexton Collection/ Bridgeman Images
Photo 14.3	Scuffles and arrests, Bramley Road, 31st August 1958 (b/w photo),/© Mirrorpix/Bridgeman Images
Photo 14.4	© Hulton-Deutsch/Hulton-Deutsch Collection/Corbis
Photo 14.5	© Corbis
Photo 14.6	Courtesy of Margaret Thatcher Foundation and US Government 109617
Photo 15.1	© Reuters/CORBIS
Photo 15.2	© Matthew Chattle/Demotix/Corbis
Photo 15.3	© Gail Orenstein/NurPhoto/Corbis
Map 15.1	from the Electoral Reform Society's report 'The 2015 General Election: A Voting System in Crisis'

INDEX